INTRODUCTION TO PSYCHOLOGY AND LAW

INTRODUCTION TO PSYCHOLOGY AND LAW

Canadian Perspectives

Edited by Regina A. Schuller and James R.P. Ogloff

UNIVERSITY OF TORONTO PRESS
Toronto Buffalo London

© University of Toronto Press Incorporated 2001
Toronto Buffalo London
Printed in Canada

ISBN 0-8020-4275-9

∞

Printed on acid-free paper

Canadian Cataloguing in Publication Data

Main entry under title:

Introduction to psychology and law : Canadian perspectives

ISBN 0-8020-4275-9 (bound)

1. Law – Canada – Psychological aspects.   2. Psychology, Forensic.
I. Schuller, Regina A., 1960–   .   II. Ogloff, James R.P. (James Robert Powell).

K346.I57 2000   349.71′01′9   C00-932266-3

University of Toronto Press acknowledges the financial assistance to its
publishing program of the Canada Council for the Arts and the Ontario Arts
Council.

University of Toronto Press acknowledges the financial support for its
publishing activities of the Government of Canada through the Book
Publishing Industry Development Program (BPIDP).

Contributors

Douglas P. Boer, Ph.D., R. Psych., is a senior psychologist with the Correctional Service of Canada in British Columbia. He is employed as the senior psychologist for Mountain and Kent institutions. He is also an adjunct professor at the University of British Columbia, Simon Fraser University, and Trinity Western University. Dr Boer has conducted research and published widely in the areas of criminal offending and the prediction of risk for sexual offending. He also co-authored the Sexual Violence Risk-20 assessment instrument.

Deborah Connolly, Ph.D., LL.B. is an assistant professor in the program in law and forensic psychology at Simon Fraser University. She is the recipient of the governor general's Gold Medal for her graduate research. Dr Connolly's research interests relate to children and the law, particularly suggestibility, memory for repeated events, and perceived credibility.

Kevin S. Douglas, M.A., LL.B., is a doctoral candidate in the Program in Law and Forensic Psychology (Clinical-Forensic Stream) at Simon Fraser University. He has conducted research and published in the broad areas of forensic psychology and mental health and the law, specifically, topics relating to violence risk assessment, civil commitment, legal issues relating to risk assessment, forensic psychological assessment, and mental illness and violence.

Stephen D. Hart, Ph.D., is associate professor of psychology at Simon Fraser University. The primary focus of his research is clinical-forensic assessment, including the assessment of psychopathic personality disorder and violence risk. He has co-authored several psychological tests and manuals, including the Screening Version of the Hare Psychopathy Checklist-Revised, the Spousal Assault Risk Assessment Guide, the Sexual Violence Risk-20, and the HCR-20.

James F. Hemphill, B.A., M.A., Ph.D. He completed a 2-year Social Sciences and Humanities Research Council of Canada postdoctoral fellowship at Simon Fraser University, where he is currently a limited term assistant professor in the Department of Psychology. Dr. Hemphill has worked in a variety of correctional facilities in British Columbia, Alberta, and Saskatchewan, and his research interests include psychopathy, program evaluation, and risk assessment.

William J. Koch, Ph.D., R.Psych., ABPP, is director of psychology residency training and the Health Psychology Clinic at the University of British Columbia Hospital, and a clinical professor at the University of British Columbia. His research focuses on psychological trauma and clinical judgment, with particular emphasis on the psychological effects of motor vehicle accidents. He has a diplomate from the American Board of Professional Psychology, is a past president of the College of Psychologists of British Columbia, and current president of the Canadian Council of Professional Psychology Program Directors.

P. Randall Kropp, Ph.D., R. Psych., is a clinical and forensic psychologist specializing in the assessment and management of violent offenders. He works for the Forensic Psychiatric Services Commission of British Columbia, is a research consultant with the British Columbia Institute against Family Violence, and is adjunct professor of psychology at Simon Fraser University.

David R. Lyon received his M.A. from Simon Fraser University in 1997 and an LL.B. from the University of British Columbia in 2000. He is currently a doctoral candidate in the program in law and forensic psychology (experimental psychology and law stream) at Simon Fraser University. In his dissertation research he is investigating the utility of various risk factors and intervention strategies for the management of stalking cases.

Tonia L. Nicholls, M.A., is a doctoral candidate in the program in law and forensic psychology (experimental psychology and law stream) at

Simon Fraser University. She was awarded a Social Sciences and Humanities Research Council of Canada doctoral fellowship in 1998. Her previous publications include articles addressing domestic violence, psychopathy, and violence risk assessment.

James R.P. Ogloff, J.D., Ph.D., is the university endowed professor and director of the program in law and forensic psychology at Simon Fraser University. He is a past president of the American Psychology-Law Society and president of the Canadian Psychological Association. He has published in the areas of forensic assessment, jury decision making, professional ethics and responsibility, and training in law and psychology.

J. Don Read, Ph.D., professor of psychology at the University of Victoria, completed his undergraduate training at the University of British Columbia and his Ph.D. at Kansas State University. His research focuses on human memory in legal contexts, notably eyewitness testimony and the recovered memory debate. He is North American editor of *Applied Cognitive Psychology.*

Julian Roberts, Ph.D., is a professor of criminology at the University of Ottawa. He holds a Ph.D. in psychology from the University of Toronto. His primary area of research is sentencing. For the past 7 years he has served as editor of the *Canadian Journal of Criminology.*

V. Gordon Rose, LL.B., LL.M., M.A., P.B.D., is currently a doctoral candidate in the program in law and forensic psychology (experimental psychology and law stream) at Simon Fraser University and holds a Social Sciences and Humanities Research Council of Canada doctoral fellowship. His research interests focus on the psychology of criminal procedure and evidence, particularly in respect of juries. He was called to the bar in British Columbia in 1982.

Regina A. Schuller received her Ph.D. from the University of Western Ontario in 1990 and is now associate professor of psychology at York University. Her research interests focus on jury decision making, particularly in cases involving violence against women. In 1995 she received York University's President's Prize for Promising Scholars. She serves on the editorial boards of *Law and Human Behavior* and *Psychology, Public Policy, and Law.*

John W. Turtle received his Ph.D. in social psychology from the University of Alberta in 1988. He is now an associate professor of psychology and justice studies at Ryerson Polytechnic University in Toronto. He is involved in developing procedures and training police for obtaining eyewitness evidence, as well as laboratory and field research in the area.

Neil Vidmar is Russell M. Robinson II Professor of Law and professor of psychology at Duke University. He received his BA (1962) from MacMurray College, and MA (1965) and PhD (1967) from the University of Illinois. He taught at the University of Western Ontario from 1967 to 1990. He is author of *Judging the Jury* (with Hans, 1986), *Medical Malpractice and the American Jury* (1995), and *World Jury Systems* (2000). He has also published approximately 100 articles in law and psychology journals.

Christopher D. Webster, Ph.D., F.R.S.C., is professor of psychiatry and Criminology at the University of Toronto, professor emeritus of psychology at Simon Fraser University, and senior research consultant at the Earlscourt Child and Family Centre in Toronto. Dr Webster is a leading scholar in the field of the prediction of risk for violence and mental illness.

Karen E. Whittemore, Ph.D., R. Psych., is a clinical and forensic psychologist with the British Columbia Forensic Psychiatric Services Commission. She received her Ph.D. from the program in law and forensic psychology (clinical-forensic stream) at Simon Fraser University. She has conducted research and published in the areas of criminal competence, criminal responsibility, and jury decision making.

A. Daniel Yarmey received his Ph.D. in experimental psychology from the University of Western Ontario. He is professor of psychology at the University of Guelph and his research interests focus on eyewitness and earwitness testimony, as well as more general issues in applied social psychology. He is a fellow of the Canadian Psychological Association.

Meagan Yarmey, M.A., is currently a doctoral candidate in psychology at York University. She received her B.A. in psychology from the University of Guelph and her M.A. in community psychology from the

Contents

Acknowledgments

Over the years, a common question that we often found ourselves asking other professors teaching psychology and law classes in Canada was: "What reading materials do you assign for your class?" The answers were varied and usually ended with a note of dissatisfaction regarding the appropriateness of what was available for Canadian students. So a few years ago, we decided to do something about this perennial problem. After our initial conversation it was clear to us that the book should be a cooperative effort – many of the leading scholars in the field were in Canada and were in fact teaching psychology and law courses. Thus it was natural that the project evolved as it did and we would like to thank our contributors for their enthusiastic participation in the book. Without their contributions this book would still just be an idea.

We are also indebted to numerous individuals who shared their time and thoughts to help us prepare the final version of the book. Special thanks go to the students in our classes who read earlier versions of the manuscript; their insightful comments and suggestions were of particular benefit. We are especially grateful to three students, Sara Rzepa, Marc Klippenstine, and Vivian Koval, who devoted many hours reading, correcting, formatting, and offering suggestions for the book at its various stages; we are extremely grateful for their patience and meticulous attention to detail. The recommendations of Adelle Forth, as well as two anonymous reviewers, were also extremely helpful and did much to improve the final version of the book. We are also very grateful to Virgil Duff and the editorial staff at the University of Toronto Press for their responsive and supportive involvement in this project.

Finally, we would like to thank our respective families for their continual encouragement and support. Regina Schuller would like to thank Richard Lalonde for the guidance and assistance he offered throughout the project, and her children René and Andrée for being patient with regard to her hours away and most of all for their cheer and good humour upon her return. James Ogloff would like to thank those who matter most to him, Kathy, Aleksandra, Andrew, and Karena.

Regina Schuller and James Ogloff

University of Toronto (O.I.S.E.) in 1995. Her research interests include health psychology and legal applications.

Patricia A. Zapf, Ph.D., is an assistant professor in the clinical psychology and law program at the University of Alabama. She received her Ph.D. from the program in law and forensic psychology (clinical-forensic stream) at Simon Fraser University in 1999. Her publications in the field of psychology have focused on issues concerning the assessment and conceptualization of various types of competencies and the usefulness of various methods of competency assessment.

PART ONE

Introduction to Psychology and Law

1. An Introduction to Psychology and Law

Regina A. Schuller and James R.P. Ogloff

The law touches virtually every aspect of our daily lives. Although we don't typically think about it, much of our behaviour and daily interactions are governed and regulated by laws. For example, consider some of the things you may have done today. You may have purchased this book, for instance, which is copyrighted. You paid the GST and you may have charged the book – all of these transactions are regulated by law. You may have driven your car, presumably following the traffic laws and with a valid driver's licence. Or, you may have arrived at your destination by way of the local transit system, having paid the driver the requisite fare. Perhaps it's the end of March and you have just completed your income tax forms. We often remain unaware of the influence of the law in our lives until one of the rules (laws) has been broken or interactions or behaviour between individuals come into conflict or break down.

Should you still doubt the significance of law and legal processes in our lives, a quick perusal of your local newspaper will certainly confirm its presence. All of the excerpts described below were taken from a single week's coverage of events reported in Canadian local and national newspapers. As you read through these excerpts consider how the various events hinge upon issues and questions that are not only legal but also psychological in nature.

- In a sweeping attack on bigotry, the Supreme Court of Canada rules that, in some cases, "prospective jurors may be questioned about their racial views to root out those whose prejudices could destroy the fairness of criminal trial." The court asserts that "to suggest that all persons who possess racial prejudices will erase those prejudices from their mind when serving as jurors is to underestimate the insidious nature of racial prejudice and the stereotyping that underlies it" ("Jurors' racial views can be questioned," *Globe and Mail*, June 5, 1998).

- "A 30-nation poll of 35,000 people, co-ordinated by Canada's Environics International Ltd., shows that two-thirds of people in this country and a similar number around the world want governments to enact tougher environmental laws" ("Canadians want laws to be meaner and greener," *Toronto Star*, June 5, 1998).
- A new $32 million federal program will allow victims of crime and communities to make "decisions about crime prevention" (Minister touts community crime plan, June 5, 1998).
- "Lawsuits against Ottawa and several churches are pouring in so fast – there are 15 to 20 new ones each week – that the federal government hasn't begun to figure out its potential liability for its role in the government-sponsored, church-run schools that were set up to assimilate Indians into mainstream culture." ("Ottawa: Churches seek common front on suits," *Vancouver Sun*, June 9, 1998).
- A panel discussion at an international conference on sexually abusive youths debates the pros and cons of notifying the public about the release of high-risk sex offenders. Some members point out the dire consequences notification could have, such as "making it difficult for [offenders] to rehabilitate" and promoting vigilantism, while others on the panel argue that "people can better protect themselves when they're aware of potential dangers" ("Notification of sex offenders' release debated," *Winnipeg Free Press*, June 11, 1998).
- An innovative new court "billed as the first of its kind in Canada" is "dedicated solely to mentally ill defendants." It is expected that mentally ill accused will be diverted away from jails and swiftly steered to the psychological assessment and treatment they require ("Court for mentally ill offers new approach," *Vancouver Sun*, June 11, 1998).
- "Although Ontario prosecutors have been told to call accused people by their names and let them sit beside their lawyers, a Toronto judge says the measures are at times impossible to adhere to and can depersonalize others at trial" ("Some resist humanizing 'the accused,'" *Toronto Star*, June 10, 1998).

In addition to raising questions about law and the role of law in our lives, all of the events described above involve questions about human behaviour. Human behaviour at its most basic level lies at the heart of both psychology and law. The discipline of psychology, very broadly defined as the scientific study of behaviour and mental processes (Kassin, 1998), attempts to understand, predict, and, in some cases, control human behaviour. The legal system, comprised of a body of laws and procedures, is designed to govern, regulate, and control human behaviour (Ogloff & Finkelman, 1999). Given the similar focus of the two disciplines, the interface between law and psychology is perhaps not surprising. The subject matter of the field of law and psychology is well captured in the editorial policy of *Law and Human Behavior*, the leading journal in the area, and consists of "issues arising out of the relationship between human behavior and the law, legal system, and legal process" (Wiener, 1997). The field can thus cover a wide array of topics. Indeed, the connection and overlap between the law and psychology is both expansive and dynamic, with researchers studying both the impact of the law on individuals and the impact of individuals on the law (Small, 1993).

Consider the range of psychological issues that arise from the various news events described above. Take, for instance, the first and last bulletins, both of which deal with jury decision making. In both of these instances, assumptions about human behaviour underlie the courts' decisions: jurors' beliefs and attitudes will negatively influence their verdict decisions; racial bias exists and jurors can be assessed for it; depersonalization of the accused has a negative impact on the trial outcome. In the bulletin that outlines the proposal for greater victim involvement in crime prevention assumptions about human behaviour again abound: community involvement will have a positive impact on crime prevention; victim involvement will have a beneficial impact on the victim, the offender, and the community at large. Psychological assumptions about human behaviour likewise underlie the other news events reported.

In attempting to establish evidence in support of the various assumptions that can be identified we enter the domain of psychology. Basically, psychologists working in the field of psychology and law study empirically the assumptions about human behaviour that underlie the operation and functioning of the law. Rather than taking these claims as given, psychologists, as social scientists, attempt to assess their reasonableness and validity. What evidence is there in support of the claim that jurors' beliefs and attitudes influence their decision making? How adequately can we assess racial bias within a trial setting? Does the use of the term "the accused" actually influence jurors' beliefs and judgments of an individual on trial? What impact, if any, does it have on jury verdicts?

Given that public policies, laws, and court decisions are based on assumptions about human behaviour, the very subject matter of psychology, psychologists can play a vital and important role in this area. In the chapters that follow we introduce a variety of topics that fall within the domain of psychology and law, examining their relevance and application within the Canadian context. We have attempted as much as possible to draw on Canadian research, but of course, like any review, the material covered is illustrative and not exhaustive.

Before turning to these chapters, however, we provide a brief historical perspective of the field and various conceptualizations of the interaction between the disciplines of law and psychology. We also introduce some of the ethical issues that the psychologist working in this arena must confront and, given its importance and frequency, the role that psychologists play as expert witnesses in trial proceedings.

HISTORY OF PSYCHOLOGY AND LAW

The field of psychology and law, relatively recent in origin, can be traced back to the turn of the century when psychology was still in its infancy. Indeed, two of the earliest and most frequently cited instances of psychology's entry into the legal system occurred in the early 1900s (Ogloff & Finkelman, 1999). First, in 1906 Sigmund Freud proposed to the legal community that psychology could be of considerable assistance in the investigation and detection of truthfulness and deception (Brigham, 1999). Speaking to a group of Austrian judges, Freud paralleled the task of the therapist to that of the examining magistrate, suggesting that some of the techniques used by therapists to "uncover the hidden psychical material" could be adapted for investigative procedures (Brigham, 1999, p. 274). Two years later, Hugo Munsterberg, an experimental psychologist at the University of Harvard, published *On the Witness Stand* (1908), in which he urged the legal community to consider psychological research on such topics as eyewitness identifications and testimony. Munsterberg's call to the legal community to embrace psychology, however, was heavily criticized by legal scholars. Indeed, a satirical article, written by a renowned legal evidence expert (Wigmore, 1909), subjected Munsterberg's arguments to a scathing cross-examination and concluded that he was guilty of exaggerating what psychology had to offer the law (Brigham, 1999; Ogloff & Finkel-man, 1999).

These early attempts of psychologists to enter into the legal arena were largely ignored, and despite isolated outcroppings of legally relevant psychological research (see Ogloff, 2000; Ogloff, Tomkins, & Bersoff, 1996) it is not until the 1960s that the faint beginnings of a movement can be recognized. Psychologists' renewed interest in law at that time has been attributed primarily to two significant events (Ogloff et al., 1996): the growth of clinical psychology and the application of psychological research in a landmark Supreme Court decision in the United States. It should be noted here that the early development of the field of law and psychology began primarily in the United States. In more recent times, however, Canadians have played a significant role in its subsequent development.

The growth in clinical psychology over the first half of the twentieth century resulted in an increased demand from the legal system for clinical evaluations and diagnoses of mental disorders (e.g., in cases where insanity was raised or when the accused's mental state at the time of his or her trial was in question). The role that psychology was to play in this call was addressed directly in a U.S. appellate case in 1962 (*Jenkins v. United States*) (Fulero, 1999). In this case the American Psychiatric Association had submitted a factum or brief (referred to in American legal jargon as an "amicus curiae" brief) in which it argued that psychologists were not qualified to provide expert testimony on issues pertaining to the diagnosis of mental disorders (Fulero, 1999). Countering this position, the American Psychological Association submitted its own brief. The outcome of the court's decision in this case, that psychologists were deemed qualified to testify, helped pave the way for psychology's increased participation in the legal arena.

In Canada, the evolution of clinical psychology has been somewhat slower than in the United States. For example, the first doctoral program in clinical psychology was accredited by the American Psychological Association (APA) in 1948 (APA, 1998). In Canada the first clinical program to receive APA accreditation was that offered by McGill University in 1968 (APA, 1998) and by 1980 only three Canadian universities were APA accredited. At present, there are 13 accredited programs in Canada. Partly as a result of the relatively slow growth of clinical psychology in Canada, psychiatrists, until relatively recently, were much more likely than psychologists to provide expert evidence to the courts. But recent amendments to the Criminal Code expanded the range of experts who can testify about whether an individual meets the criteria to be found a dangerous offender from psychiatrists alone to include psychologists as well. Despite these advances, the Criminal Code provisions concerning mental disorders still limit those who can assess accused for fitness to trial and criminal responsibility to physicians. This is in marked contrast to the United States where, in many states, psychologists are routinely called upon to assess and give evidence regarding competency or fitness to stand trial and legal insanity.

The other significant event that stimulated the development of law and psychology involved the U.S. Supreme Court decision in *Brown v. Board of Education of Topeka* (1954), the now famous and celebrated case that outlawed segregated education, which was then in practice in some states. As part of the legal argument challenging the policy of segregation, a team of social scientists, lead by three social psychologists, submitted a brief to the Supreme Court. Drawing on psychological research on prejudice and discrimination, the brief outlined the detrimental impact of segregation on the self-esteem of black children. Aspects of this information found their way into a footnote of the court's momentous decision (Brigham, 1999). Although it is unclear as to whether the psychological research actually influenced the Supreme Court's decision or whether the footnote acknowledging the research served only as "window dressing" to support the decision (Brigham, 1999, p. 278; see also Cook, 1984, 1985; Gerard, 1983; Kluger, 1976), this application of research and theory highlighted the important role that social science could potentially play in the legal system. As a result, some psychologists began to channel their attention into psychological issues of legal relevance (Loh, 1981b).

Over the succeeding decades the field began to grow at an exponential rate. In 1968–69 a group of psychologists interested in pursuing psycholegal issues joined together to form the American Psychology-Law Society (Brigham, 1999; Fulero, 1999; Grisso, 1991) and interest in law and psychology as a distinct area of psychological inquiry gained incredible momentum in the 1970s, when formal scholarly organizations devoted to the field were established. By the mid-1970s, the field of psychology and law was featured in prestigious mainstream psychology books and journals (e.g., Tapp, 1976; a special issue on psychology and law was published in the *Journal of Personality and Social Psychology* in 1978; for other examples see Fulero, 1999) and in 1977 the journal *Law and Human Behavior* was established. In 1981 a separate division (Psychology and Law) of the American Psychological Association (Division 41) was established (Brigham, 1999; Fulero, 1999; Grisso, 1991). And in 1984 the two organizations merged to form the American Psychology-Law Society (Division 41 of APA). There are now over 2,100 members of this division (Brigham, 1999), with over 180 of the members residing in Canada. The role of Canadian psychologists within the organization has been quite influential: in 1998/99, when we began working on this chapter, 3 of the 13 members of the executive committee were Canadian while the president and one of the past presidents were also Canadian. The Criminal Justice section of the Canadian Psychological Association, as well as the Canadian Law and Society Association, an interdisciplinary scholarly organization that brings together law and social sciences, also represent the interests of psychologists who work within the criminal justice system.

The degree of communication and cooperation between psychology and law can now be felt at many levels. In addition to the organizations described above, there are a number of scholarly journals devoted exclusively to the field of psychology and law (e.g., *Law and Human Behavior*; *Behavioral Sciences and the Law*; *Law and Psychology Review*; *Psychology, Public Policy and Law*), with additional journals devoted to specialized topics within the field (e.g., *Expert Evidence, Criminal Justice and Behavior*). Since 1974, when the first joint law (J.D., the equivalent of a LL.B.) and psychology (Ph.D.) degree was offered at the University of Nebraska in Lincoln, undergraduate and graduate programs in psychology can now be found at a number of American universities (see Chapter 15). Within Canada, the University of British Columbia (UBC), Carleton University, Dalhousie University (DU), Queen's University, and Simon Fraser University (SFU) now offer undergraduate and graduate programs in law and psychology. Most recently, UBC and SFU cooperatively offer a joint degree in which students earn both a law degree (LL.B.) and a Ph.D. in psychology in the area of their choice (i.e., clinical-forensic or experimental psychology and law). An overview of the psycholegal training available in Canada is provided in Chapter 15.

THE INTERACTION BETWEEN PSYCHOLOGY AND LAW

Approaches in the Disciplines of Law and Psychology

The disciplines of law and psychology share a common focus on human behaviour, but, as the historical account provided above high-lights, their degree of interaction and communication has developed rather slowly. To some extent, this is due to the different way in which the disciplines approach the relationship between law and human behaviour. Indeed, in many respects, the goals, perspectives, and methods adopted within the two fields are in conflict with each other. To better understand these differences in approach and their implica-tions for the interaction between law and psychology we will review a framework first articulated by Haney (1980). Although other useful conceptualizations of the potential conflicts between law and psychol-ogy have been offered (e.g., Wrightsman, Nietzel, & Fortune, 1998), Haney's is perhaps one of the most comprehensive.

Haney enumerated eight different dimensions along which the two disciplines can be contrasted:

1 The emphasis in law is *stare decisis*, while in psychology the empha-sis is on *creativity*. In the law, past cases rather than innovation or cre-ativity are painstakingly relied upon for the development of legal arguments. The model adopted in law is one of legal precedent. In contrast, in psychology the model is one of innovation, and psychol-ogists, in both their research and theorizing, are encouraged continu-ally to explore novel ideas and methods.
2 Law is *hierarchical*, while psychology is *empirical*. Decisions within the legal system are hierarchically based and authoritative, with lower courts bound by the decisions of higher courts. In psychology, however, it is the accumulation of a body of "consistent and sup-porting data" (Haney, 1980, p. 160) that confirms the validity of a particular position or claim, not its authoritative declaration.
3 Law relies on the *adversarial* method, while psychology relies on the *experimental* method. To arrive at the "truth" in law, conflicting points of view are presented, with each side putting its best case for-ward. Bias and self-interest are not only permitted but heralded as one of the strengths of the procedure (Haney, 1980). Indeed, what is of immediate concern and the driving force for the opposing lawyers is victory. Psychology, in contrast to law, attempts to arrive at "truth" (i.e., an understanding of some phenomenon) using a variety of diverse data-gathering methods. Common to all of these methods is the systematic collection of data, using procedures that attempt to "reduce bias, error, and distortion in observation and inferences" (p. 162). Although this is not to say that bias does not enter into the

research process, the goal of the psychologist is to attain an "objective" understanding of the phenomena rather than victory over a particular viewpoint.

4 Law is *prescriptive*, while psychology is *descriptive*. The law is "primarily prescriptive," telling "people how they should behave," while psychology is "essentially a descriptive discipline, seeking to describe behaviour as it actually occurs" (Haney, 1980, p. 163). This dimension captures a difference in the values espoused in the disciplines, with law outlining how one ought to behave and psychology adopting a more nonjudgmental orientation of how people do behave.

5 Law is *idiographic*, while psychology is *nomothetic*. Law operates on a case-by-case basis, with each case decided on the basis of its specific facts. In contrast, psychology is interested in uncovering the "general principles, relationships and patterns" that govern human behaviour. The focus in psychology is not on a particular instance, but rather on what transcends the singular instance.

6 Decision making in law is based on the appearance of *certainty*, while in psychology decision making is based on *probablistic* evidence. The decisions made in the law take on an all-or-none quality – the accused in a criminal trial is deemed either guilty or not guilty, the plaintiff in a civil case is found liable or not liable. Psychologists, in contrast, operate in terms of probabilities; for example, claims are asserted on the basis of evidence associated with a probability level (i.e., level of statistical significance). As a result, conclusions drawn by psychologists are typically qualified and not categorical in nature.

7 Law is *reactive*, while psychology is *proactive*. The issues that arise in the law originate from outside the system, namely, clients' cases are brought to the attention of lawyers. In contrast, psychologists, notwithstanding the presence of various external pressures (e.g., funding availability), have considerable control over the issues they wish to study.

8 Law is *operational*, while psychology is *academic*. Law is an applied discipline and it is designed to deal with real world problems. The players within the system (e.g., lawyers, parole officers, etc.) have clearly defined roles that prescribe the issues on which they will concentrate. In contrast, similar to the distinction noted above, psychologists have considerable say over the issues they wish to pursue. The driving force tends to be more of a quest for knowledge for its

own sake (i.e., for academic reasons) rather than for purely pragmatic reasons.

These eight distinctions, admittedly overly simplistic (Haney, 1980),
help us to understand both the resistence and the receptivity of the disciplines to each other. For instance, because the orientation in law is an
ideographic one, psychologists who share this orientation are more
likely to be welcomed by the courts (Haney, 1980). Clinical psychologists and psychiatrists, who adopt more of an ideographic approach,
have a longstanding history of involvement with the legal system
(Melton, Petrila, Poythress, & Slobogin, 1997; Ogloff, Roberts, &
Roesch, 1993) while social or experimental psychologists, who are
more likely to speak in terms of general patterns of behaviour, have
met considerable resistance. As well, because of the nature of their
training, psychologists speak in terms of "statistical probabilities" or
the plausibility of their findings. The certainty sought by the law can
therefore present problems when psychologists testify in court. Most
psychologists are also uncomfortable ignoring the limitations or qualifications of research findings, yet the adversarial legal system can
sometimes limit or proscribe full disclosure. The potential for misrep-
resentation or distortion of psychological research in the courtroom
has been cited by some in the field as a reason for their reluctance to
testify (Pfeifer & Brigham, 1993).

Despite these sources of conflict, however, there is now considerable
contact between psychology and law. Within the United States the two
leading organizations in the respective fields of psychology and law,
the American Psychological Association and the American Bar Association, have co-sponsored and organized conferences on psycholegal
issues, for instance in the areas of Family Law (1997) and Criminal Law
(1998). Similarly, the Canadian Psychological Association has worked
with provincial law societies to coordinate continued educational
training in psychology for lawyers. This receptivity on the part of the
legal profession to what psychology has to offer, coupled with the
increasing application of the social sciences in the law, indicates that
the growth of the field evidenced in the last few decades will likely
continue.

The Ways in Which Law and Psychology Interact

Before turning to the myriad topics in the field of psycholegal research and practice, we will provide a conceptualization that captures the potential connections between the two disciplines. Over the years a number of conceptualizations of the relationship between law and psychology have been proposed (e.g., Haney, 1980; Monahan and Walker, 1988), but we will again draw on that offered by Haney. Haney (1980) suggests that we can conceive of the potential links between the two disciplines in terms of the particular focus taken, whether it be "psychology *in* the law," "psychology *of* the law" or "psychology *and* law."

As conveyed by the terminology itself, psychology *in* the law involves the "explicit and conventional use of psychology" in the operation of law (Haney, 1980, p. 153). The emphasis of the interaction between psychology and law is on the law, with psychology really being used by the law as it currently operates. For instance, in some legal cases information or knowledge derived from psychology may have a bearing on the questions at issue at trial (e.g., the mental state of the accused, the reliability of an eyewitness's identification, determination of a child's best interests). Psychologists may therefore be asked to provide the court with their expert opinion on the matter. Psychological research may also be explicitly used in the practice of law, for example, a lawyer may apply psychological theory and findings (e.g., in the area of attitudes and persuasion) to the development of his or her trial strategy.

In contrast to this conceptualization, the phrase psychology *and* law conveys a much more cooperative and co-equal interaction (Haney, 1980). We noted at the beginning of the chapter that the law makes numerous assumptions about human behaviour; in this conceptualization, psychology is used to evaluate *critically* the assumptions being made. For instance, researchers may assess the validity of the criteria used by the courts to determine whether a confession is likely to have been coerced or whether a police line-up was likely to have been biased (Haney, 1980). Other research captured by this phrase might involve investigations that identify biases in the system, such as investigations into the potential influence of extralegal factors (e.g., racial prejudice) in legal decision making. The research is not used in the day-to-day operation of law, but rather examines the operation of the legal system. It offers the potential to reform or change legal practices, what Haney aptly refers to as the potential to close "the gap between psychological fact and legal fiction" (p. 154).

Finally, "psychology *of* the law" represents the use of psychology to study the law itself, for example, using psychology to explain why and when people will obey the law (e.g., Tyler, 1990) or, at an even more global level, how and why law developed as it did. The "issues of psychology of law are basic and profound," and as of yet very little of this type of work has been done by psychologists (Haney, 1980, p. 156).

It should be noted that these different conceptualizations of the interaction between psychology and law are not necessarily tied to specific areas of inquiry. If we return for a moment to the news excerpts presented in the opening of the chapter, we can think of the different types of interactions psychologists might have on the same general topic of inquiry. Again, let's take the first excerpt about screening potential jurors for racial bias. A psychologist acting as a trial consultant to a lawyer in such a case – for instance, a psychologist hired by the lawyer to aid in the lawyer's selection strategy – might best be characterized as engaged in psychology *in* the law. In contrast, a psychologist involved in research that attempts to assess how adequately the practice of questioning potential jurors effectively screens out those who harbour racial bias would be engaged in psychology *and* the law. Alternatively, a psychologist might conduct a more comparative psychological investigation into jury selection practices across various Commonwealth countries (e.g., Australia, Britain, Canada, etc.) in the hopes of uncovering how and why the selection practices developed at they did (psychology *of* the law).

Areas in the Field of Law and Psychology

Although certainly a very gross distinction, one of the dichotomies in the field of psychology evident throughout its history runs along the clinical/experimental dimension, with psychologists in the former focusing on issues and practice pertaining to clinical populations and the latter focusing on nonclinical areas, such as social, cognitive, physiological, or developmental psychology. To some extent the dichotomy between clinicians and nonclinicians can also be found in the subfield of law and psychology, with the term "forensic psychology" typically reserved to refer to clinical psychologists engaged in clinical practice within the legal system.

Basically, forensic psychology involves psychological assessment, treatment, and/or research conducted within a legal context. This might encompass clinical forensic services such as psychological assessments, evaluations, and treatment of persons under court jurisdiction and determinations of child and custody evaluations, as well as evaluation and treatment of offender populations. For example, psychologists may be called upon to make clinical assessments relating to criminal responsibility (i.e., sanity), fitness to stand trial, predictions of dangerousness, or assessments about other mental health issues (Ogloff et al., 1996). Forensic psychology might also encompass what is known as criminal justice system research (Ogloff, 1990). Psychologists working within this area might focus on the impact that criminal law or legislative changes to the law might have on behaviour, for example, the impact of the new Youth Criminal Justice Act (which replaced the Young Offenders Act) on recidivism rates of young offenders (Department of Justice, 1999). Or they might focus their attention in the area of corrections and psychiatric institutionalization, studying, for example, the characteristics of offenders and institutionalized populations.

The nonclinical stream in the field of law and psychology covers a wide range of topics of relevance to the legal system. Experimental and cognitive psychologists, who study how we perceive and interpret sensory information in the world; social psychologists, who tend to focus on the factors that shape and influence our perceptions, interpretations, and behaviours; and developmental psychologists, who study the range of such processes at different developmental periods of life, have all contributed to our understanding of legally relevant phenomena. Psychologists in these various areas have studied eyewitness testimony, interrogation and investigative interviewing techniques, sentencing, and jury and judicial decision making. Although differing in orientation and particular focus, much of this research tends to involve investigations into the assumptions about human behaviour that underlie the law and, as such, provides an informative database upon which to assess and potentially alter the legal system.

THE ETHICS OF LAW AND PSYCHOLOGY AND EXPERT TESTIMONY

The Ethics of Law and Psychology

Perhaps because of the adversarial nature of the law (see Chapter 2), psychologists are sometimes drawn into the courtroom battle and almost seem to be taking sides in a case. This may lead to unethical behaviour and widespread criticism: the reputation of psychology is jeopardized if experts are seen as taking sides in cases or acting as "prostitutes in the courts." While it is perfectly permissible and appropriate for a psychologist to enter into a lawsuit as a party, when acting as an expert to the courts the psychologist must remain neutral. Indeed, regardless of their role, forensic psychologists are obligated to comply with general ethical guidelines, principles, and standards.

The Ethical Principles of Psychologists and Code of Conduct (American Psychological Association, 1992) provide that "psychologists who perform forensic functions, such as assessments, interviews, consultations, reports, or expert testimony, must comply with all other provisions of this Ethics Code to the extent that they apply to such activities" (APA Standard 7.01). In addition "psychologists base their forensic work on appropriate knowledge of and competence in the areas underlying such work, including specialized knowledge concerning special populations" (APA Standard 7.01). To emphasize that forensic psychologists, like all psychologists, must adhere to general ethical standards, the Canadian Code of Ethics for Psychologists (Canadian Psychological Association, 1991) does not differentiate among psychologists, nor does it contain specific guidelines for forensic psychologists.

Definitions of the terms "forensic psychology" and "forensic psychologist" are provided in the Specialty Guidelines for Forensic Psychologists (Committee on Ethical Guidelines for Forensic Psychologists, 1991):

> "Forensic psychology" means all forms of professional psychological conduct when acting, with definable foreknowledge, as a psychological expert on explicitly psycholegal issues, in direct assistance to courts, parties to legal proceedings, correctional and forensic mental health facilities, and administrative, judicial, and legislative agencies acting in an adjudicative capacity" (Specialty Guideline I(B)(1)(b), 657).
>
> "Forensic psychologist" means psychologists who regularly engage in the practice of forensic psychology as defined in I(B)(1)(b) (Specialty Guideline I(B)(1)(c), 657).

As these definitions show, the terms are broad and focus on the work of those people engaged in the applied areas of law and psychology.

While all psychologists must adhere to general ethical principles, psychologists who work in legal contexts, either as practitioners or researchers, often find themselves in situations where the traditional ethical and legal principles that govern their work may apply somewhat differently (Ogloff, 1999). In many jurisdictions in North America, ethics complaints against psychologists who work in forensic contexts are among the most common made to licensing boards. This is likely not because forensic psychologists are particularly evil but due rather to the heated emotions that arise in the legal system. If a parent's custody of his or her children has been jeopardized because of an assessment conducted by a psychologist, he or she may very well be inclined to make a complaint against the psychologist. The unique concerns that face forensic psychologists led the American Psychology-Law Society and the American Academy of Forensic Psychology to develop a set of specialty guidelines for forensic psychologists in 1991 (Committee on Ethical Guidelines for Forensic Psychologists, 1991). While a detailed discussion of the ethics involved in law and psychology would go beyond the scope of this book, it is important to highlight some of the ethical issues that arise in the field (see Ogloff, 1999 for further elaboration).

Who Is the Client?

In most traditional areas of psychology, the client is the person the psychologist is assessing or treating. This is not usually the case in law and psychology. Very often the psychologist will be called upon by the legal system (i.e., correctional systems, courts) to conduct an assessment or to treat a person. Concepts such as confidentiality and privilege arise out of the client's common law or statutorily guaranteed right to privacy (Reaves & Ogloff, 1996). It is consequently of utmost importance that the forensic psychologist clarify the identity of the client and ensure that the person being assessed or treated is aware of the psychologist's obligations to the client.

Examples from the private sector may be useful for making the distinction regarding the identity of the client. If a person hires a psychologist to perform psychological services for himself or herself, that person is clearly the client and he or she has a legal right to confidentiality. However, if a person applies for a job and as part of the employment screening process is required to visit a psychologist for an interview and to complete some employment testing, the employer may well be the client. In such a case, the employer "owns" the confidentiality, and the psychologist must share the results with the employer. Further, the psychologist does not have an obligation to discuss the person's test results with him or her – although the psychologist is obliged to inform the person of this fact when obtaining consent for the interview and testing, which must be done prior to beginning to work with the person.

As the above examples illustrate, determining who the client is serves as the threshold issue in establishing the nature of the psychologist's obligation to the client and to the person being assessed or treated. The psychologist must clarify these matters with both the agency contracting his or her services and the person being assessed or treated.

Limits on the Scope of Practice: Competence

The psychologist is ethically obligated to be professionally competent in any realm in which he or she works. Thus, psychologists who work in the legal arena must have professional competence in forensic psychology generally. Furthermore, if the psychologist engages in psychological services that require more specialized training, he or she must also demonstrate professional competence in that area of sub-specialty (e.g., assessment and treatment of sexual offenders, forensic neuropsychological assessment). As noted in the APA Ethics Code (1992, Standard 1.04; see also Specialty Guideline III), generally speaking, professional competence in an area of specialization may be obtained and demonstrated by a combination of the following factors: graduate-level education and training, supervised experience by a registered psychologist with expertise in the area of concern, and ongoing reading and/or research in the area of specialization. As you can imagine, partly because of the relative recency of the field, forensic psychologists may on occasion be unfamiliar with an area in which he or she is called upon to work. In such cases, psychologists must refrain from engaging in the work.

Because there is no litmus test for determining when, or if, a psychologist has professional competence in any given area, psychologists bear the burden of ensuring that their work falls within their realm of expertise, as provided for in the ethics codes. Specialty Guideline III(B) provides that "[f]orensic psychologists have an obligation to present to the court, regarding the specific matters to which they will testify, the boundaries of their competence, the factual bases (knowledge, skill, experience, training, and education) for their qualification as an expert on the specific matters at issue." Finally, forensic psychologists must be knowledgeable concerning the legal and professional standards of their work and the legal rights of the parties with whom they work.

Informed Consent

As autonomous individuals, people are usually free to decide whether to participate in psychological assessments or treatment, and forensic psychologists must normally obtain informed consent from the individuals with whom they work. To meet the requirements of informed consent, people who enter into evaluation or treatment (or research) must do so voluntarily, knowingly, and intelligently (Ogloff, 1995b; Ogloff & Otto, 1991).

The "voluntariness" requirement demands that people are not manipulated or forced (e.g., with duress or powerful incentives) to participate in the psychological evaluation or treatment process. In criminal contexts, it may seem that accused or offenders are being "coerced" to participate in assessments or treatment (e.g., they may be looked upon more favourably by the courts if they cooperate). However, the fact that they may refuse contact with the psychologist – even though the alternatives may not be attractive – means that such individuals are not, strictly speaking, being coerced to participate.

To satisfy the "knowing" requirement of the informed consent doctrine, the psychologist must make a full disclosure to the person being assessed or treated of the nature and purpose of the assessment or treatment, the procedure involved, it risks and benefits, and the alternatives available, with their risks and benefits. Consent may be handled by orally explaining the above information to the person and obtaining his or her oral consent. In some institutions, the psychologist may supplement oral consent with a written informed consent form. However, the psychologist must not rely upon a written form alone (Ogloff & Otto, 1991).

Finally, for consent to be valid, a person must have the mental capacity to understand what is being offered and to make an intelligent, informed decision of whether to participate in treatment based upon the information provided by the therapist. An intelligent decision is not necessarily equivalent to a "rational" decision. Instead, it requires that the person is able to understand the information provided by the psychologist and to balance the risks and benefits to arrive at a reasoned decision. If the person does not have the capacity to make an informed assessment or treatment decision, the psychologist must obtain consent from the legal substitute decision maker prior to beginning to work with the person.

Finally, in some circumstances, if an assessment is court-ordered or merely entails the review of an individual's file information, informed consent and consent may not be required.

Confidentiality

Confidentiality is a fundamental ethical principle (Otto, Ogloff, & Small, 1991). Under normal circumstances, psychologists would not violate a client's confidentiality. There are, however, many exceptions to this principle, some of which may arise in the forensic context. In forensic settings, as previously discussed, the person being assessed may not be the actual client or patient. If the person being assessed is not the client, the psychologist owes no duty of confidentiality to that person; the requirement of informed consent, however, means that the psychologist must inform the person being assessed that the information to be obtained is not confidential.

Given the stark differences regarding the duty of confidentiality for clients as compared to those being seen by the psychologist at the request of a third party or agency for a forensic assessment, it is important that the psychologist clarify with every person being assessed, and in every situation, who the client is, the nature of his or her contact with the person being assessed, and the limits of confidentiality.

Dual Role Conflicts

Psychologists must refrain from engaging in any activity with an examinee/client that may be construed as posing a conflict of interest and that would hamper the psychologist's objectivity in dealing with that person. One example in forensic psychology (and all other areas of psychology) worth noting here is the prohibition against "providing professional services to parties to a legal proceeding on the basis of 'contingent fees,' when those services involve the offering of expert testimony to a court or administrative body, or when they call upon the psychologist to make affirmations or representations intended to be relied upon by third parties" (Specialty Guideline IV(B)). By working on a contingent fee basis, the psychologist will develop a vested interest in the outcome of the case, which, in turn, would violate the prohibition against dual role conflicts.

The Duty to Disclose Information to Protect Third Parties

The importance of protecting third parties in the forensic context, particularly for forensic psychologists who work in criminal law areas, cannot be overemphasized. Occasions are likely to arise far more frequently in forensic settings than in traditional settings in which it will be necessary to disclose information in order to warn or protect third parties or society. Although there is no doubt that psychologists in many jurisdictions have an affirmative duty, as a result both of their employment (i.e., by correctional services or other criminal justice agencies) and relevant professional standards, to report situations where they reasonably believe that an individual will harm another person, this issue still causes confusion.

Undoubtedly, the most famous case for psychologists is *Tarasoff* (*Tarasoff v. Regents of the University of California*, 1976). In the *Tarasoff* case, a psychologist was seeing a student in therapy. The student developed a strong attachment to a female student, Tatiana Tarasoff. The attachment became lethal and in therapy the client expressed the desire to harm the young woman because she spurned his affections. Alarmed by the revelations, the psychologist attempted to take steps to prevent the harm. He consulted with his employer and called the university police. However, no steps were taken to protect the young woman, whom the client eventually murdered. The young woman's family sued the psychologist and the university where he worked. For our purposes, it is sufficient to note that in the final decision, the court found the therapist and hospital liable for failing to protect an identifiable third party (Tatiana Tarasoff) against whom the psychologist's client had made serious threats, holding that "[o]nce a therapist does in fact determine, or under applicable professional standards reasonably should have determined, that a patient poses a serious danger of violence to others, he bears a duty to exercise reasonable care to protect the foreseeable victim of that danger" (*Tarasoff v. University of California*, 1976, 345). The court further held that "the discharge of this duty may require the therapist ... to warn the intended victim or others ... to notify police, or to take whatever steps are reasonably necessary" (p. 340). Thus, the *Tarasoff* doctrine imposes on psychologists – who owe a duty of confidentiality to a client – a duty to protect third parties from foreseeable harm by therapists' clients. It was not sufficient that the psychologist telephoned the campus police; he should have called Ms Tarasoff or her parents to inform them that Ms Tarasoff may have been in danger.

Because the *Tarasoff* case was decided by the Supreme Court of California it has binding authority only in that jurisdiction (for discussions about the extent to which *Tarasoff* has and has not been followed in other jurisdictions see Birch, 1992 (Canada); Fulero, 1988 (United

States). Although no Canadian court has ever created a duty to warn or protect others for psychologists, the Alberta Court of Queen's Bench stated, in obiter dicta, that under some circumstances such a duty *might* be imposed (*Wenden v. Trikha*, 1991). In anticipation of such a possibility, and in recognition of the fact that psychologists do owe a duty to society at large, ethics codes – including those in force in Canada (see CPA, 1991, Ethical Standards II.36) – have made exceptions to the confidentiality requirement to allow for the protection of identifiable third parties at risk for harm.

To the extent that *Tarasoff* places limitations on the client's right to confidentiality, and that right is often in question in forensic settings, psychologists have a duty to warn or protect third parties and society. In fact, as stated at the outset, any information the psychologist may obtain regarding an accused's potential for jeopardizing the safety or security of others, or for creating a risk to himself or herself, must be shared if the psychologist is retained by a third party to conduct a forensic assessment. However, when the person being assessed *is* the client, the client does have a right to confidentiality. In such situations the *Tarasoff* issue needs to be more carefully considered and confidentiality should be breached only when the psychologist believes that the client will seriously harm or kill a third party.

Duty to Report Suspected Child Abuse

Like all persons in society, in virtually every jurisdiction in Canada and the United States, psychologists have an affirmative duty to report suspected cases of child abuse (see Chapter 13). Depending on the jurisdiction in which the psychologist is practising, the child abuse reporting statute may be sufficiently broad to warrant reporting past cases of child abuse, or cases in which a child may be at risk of being harmed by a known perpetrator. The psychologist may have to comply with these legal requirements.

Forensic psychologists must be well aware of the intricate rules that govern their professional behaviour. Apart from the matters noted above, the issue that is perhaps most important for psychologists working in the legal system is to ensure that they are competent to do the work in which they engage and that they are able to take a balanced approach in their reports and testimony to the court. Only when psychologists act ethically and prudently do they assist the courts and the legal system in its work.

Expert Testimony

The growth of psychological research has resulted in an exponential increase in the use of expert evidence that spans what might be more generally viewed as information falling within the domain of the behavioural sciences. Not only are psychologists called upon to provide clinical information about an accused's mental state or psychological functioning at the time of an alleged crime, they are increasingly testifying in the courtroom on a diverse range of psychological topics, such as discrimination, conformity, rape trauma syndrome, eyewitness identifications, and religious cults, to name but a few (Pfeifer & Brigham, 1993).

In general, the expert witness serves one of two functions (or very possibly both in the same court case). First, the expert may provide information that assists in the understanding of the issue facing the court. Second, the expert witness may provide the court with an opinion (Ogloff & Polvi, 1998). This is the fundamental difference between the general witness and the expert witness. "Regular" witnesses are only able to testify regarding those facts that they have directly observed. They will not be permitted to draw inferences from those facts or to state their opinions about any matter. By contrast, expert witnesses are permitted to provide their opinions pertaining to matters within their domain of expertise (for example, social workers on issues of child safety and parental discipline) in order to assist the trier of fact (judge and/or jury) in better understanding the issue or question at hand.

Due to this exception to the opinion evidence rule, courts must grapple with the issue of whether and under what circumstances expert testimony should be held admissible. That is, whenever the defence or prosecution wish to offer testimony from an expert, they must first satisfy the court that the testimony should be admitted. The Supreme Court of Canada specifically addressed the issue of the admissibility of expert evidence in *R. v. Mohan* (1994).

In *Mohan*, a pediatrician was charged with four counts of sexual assault on four female patients, who ranged in age from 13 to 16 at the time the abuse was alleged to have occurred. During the trial, the accused's lawyer indicated that he wished to call a psychiatrist to testify on his client's behalf. The nature of the psychiatrist's testimony was that the pediatrician did not fit the profile of individuals who typically committed the offences for which he was charged (e.g., sexual psychopaths, sexual deviants, or "psychosexuals" who suffer from a major mental disorder). The Crown sought a ruling from the judge regarding the admissibility of the evidence. The psychiatrist's testimony was heard by the judge alone during a voir dire (a hearing) and the judge ruled that the testimony was inadmissible. When the accused was found guilty by the jury he appealed the conviction; the Court of Appeal for Ontario allowed the appeal and ordered a new trial. The case was then appealed to the Supreme Court of Canada, which overturned the decision and ordered that the psychiatrist's testimony be excluded. The reasons the court gave in its judgment form the basis of the current rules regarding the admissibility of expert testimony – or expert opinion evidence.

As already noted, before an expert is permitted to testify in a particular case, the lawyer who wishes to call the expert must first establish that, as with any evidence, the information is legally relevant (i.e., that it bears on the issues or facts to be decided in the case). But a judge's decision that an expert's testimony will be relevant does not necessary mean that the testimony will be admitted into evidence. Courts will balance the "costs" of having the expert testify (i.e., time, the risk of having an expert's opinion carry too much weight) against its "benefit" (i.e., the extent to which the testimony will assist the judge or jury in making its decision). To help the judge balance the costs and benefits of admitting expert testimony into evidence, *R. v. Mohan* (1994) articulated the following four criteria: (1) the expert must be sufficiently skilled and qualified, either through education or experience, in the particular field of inquiry; (2) the testimony must be deemed scientifically reliable; (3) the testimony must provide unique information beyond the jurors' common understanding; and (4) the probative value of the testimony must not be outweighed by any potential prejudicial effects (e.g., concerns that the information will unduly sway the jurors, that it will be distorted or misused, or that a battle with counter experts will merely confuse the jurors).

Although there are rarely qualms about the expert's qualifications, the other three criteria are much more complex and court decisions have consequently been much more variable with respect to these criteria. With respect to scientific reliability and providing unique information the justices in *Mohan* stated that "expert evidence which advances a novel scientific theory or technique is subjected to special scrutiny to determine whether it meets a basic threshold of reliability and whether it is essential in the sense that the trier of fact will be unable to come to a satisfactory conclusion without the assistance of the expert" (p. 415). The courts recognize that expert evidence need not address a subject matter about which the jurors are completely uninformed, but rather can involve a subject matter about which the jurors may think they are knowledgeable while in fact they are not (Norris, 1998). For instance, as you will learn in Chapter 4, studies have demonstrated that people are misinformed about the factors that influence eyewitness identifications (Loftus & Doyle, 1991; Wells, 1984). Similarly, surveys have found that people adhere to misconceptions or stereotypes regarding the dynamics and impact of both woman abuse (Dodge & Greene, 1991) and sexual assault (Frazier, 1990). That popular beliefs run counter to expert opinion in these areas has also been documented via surveys of recognized experts (Greene, Raitz, & Lindblad, 1989; Kassin, Ellsworth, & Smith, 1989). Determination of whether the information provides jurors with novel information and whether it is deemed reliable, however, is ultimately left to the judge, whose decision is not always well informed by the relevant psychological literature. For instance, in a recent Canadian case, the defence attempted to proffer expert testimony (to be presented by Daniel Yarmey, the author of Chapter 3) regarding factors present at the time of the robbery "that would impair the witnesses' ability to make an accurate identification, and the problem of cross-racial identification" (p. 385). Although such expert testimony is sometimes deemed admissible in Canadian courts, the trial judge in this case refused to admit the evidence on the grounds that, in his opinion, the science of this subject matter had not "advanced that far away from the common experiences of jurors" (R. v. McIntosh, 1997, p. 117).

The courts are required to be cautious when deciding whether to admit the testimony of an expert into evidence. Although the criteria presented may appear straightforward, judges sometimes have difficulty understanding the nature of the expert evidence and whether, in fact, it should be deemed admissible.

Now that we have provided an overview of the field of law and psychology, a brief review of some of the ethical issues that arise in our field, and a discussion of the admissibility of expert testimony, we turn next to an overview of the chapters and topics covered in the remainder of this book.

AN OVERVIEW OF THE TOPICS COVERED

A fundamental distinction in law is made between criminal and civil law, a distinction that will be elaborated upon more fully in Chapter 2. Chapter 2 will familiarize the reader with the legal system in Canada and serves as a useful backdrop for the chapters that follow. Although the Canadian legal system shares many similarities with other common law countries, including the United States, there are notable differences.

It would be fair to say that much of the work in the field of law and psychology has focused almost exclusively in the area of criminal law and this is reflected in the topics subsequently covered in the book. Specifically, the material presented in Parts II and III involve applications of psychology in the criminal arena. The chapters in Part II focus on nonclinical applications, with the contributions of social, cognitive, developmental, and experimental psychology in such areas as police investigations (Chapter 3), eyewitness identifications and testimony (Chapter 4), jury decision making (Chapters 5 and 6), and criminal sentencing (Chapter 7). In Part III we return to the most familiar and longstanding research area in the field of law and psychology – clinical forensic psychology – and include assessment and treatment of offenders and inmates (Chapters 8 and 9), fitness to stand trial and criminal responsibility (Chapter 10), and violence and risk assessment (Chapter 11).

In Part IV we introduce areas of civil law in which psychological questions are particularly likely to arise, some of which have been addressed by psychologists. As the material covered in this section will show, most of the work has involved applications of clinical psychology. Chapter 12 explores civil commitment and civil competence, also known as involuntary commitment or involuntary hospitalization. It also deals with issues relating to guardianship of adults who have become incapacitated and the psychological capacity people have to make decisions about their treatment. Chapter 13 reviews the area of family law, covering the role of psychologists in child custody determinations and family interventions. Finally, Chapter 14 introduces the reader to the role that forensic psychologists can play in tort litigation, in providing psychological assessments of persons who have been injured in some manner and who have brought an action in tort against the person responsible for the injury. Psychologists have only recently become interested in the civil arena; the chapters in this section are as a result somewhat shorter and the psychological applications less well developed than in most of the other chapters. Given the breadth of areas within civil law, however, the potential range of research questions and clinical applications is far greater than those in criminal law. It is likely that experimental psychologists will soon begin to apply their knowledge to this area of law. Indeed, this has already begun in the United States on the topic of civil juries (e.g., Vidmar, 1995).

In our classes, we have noticed that students often assume that the Canadian legal system and court system are the same as those which exist in the United States. If you have never observed a trial in a Canadian court of law we encourage you to do so. If possible, attend at the Court of Queen's Bench or Supreme Court in your province. You will notice that judges in Canada are more lavishly outfitted than those in the United States. Similarly, the lawyers wear gowns and conduct themselves much more conservatively than our American counterparts, whose images are brought to mind in the weekly airings of *Law and Order*, and *The Practice* – television dramas we should note that do not necessarily reflect American legal practice either. Recently, one of the present authors (R.S.) was called for jury duty. While seated in the courtroom waiting for the jury selection proceeding to begin, the woman seated next to her leaned over and whispered, "it's sure not like this on TV." We hope that this text provides you with a more realistic and accurate picture of the legal system and its operation in Canada.

Within each of the chapters, the authors have attempted to draw as much as possible on Canadian research. As will become readily apparent, many of the leading experts on these various topics in law and psychology are working in Canada. The contributions of Canadian experimental and social psychologists – for example, on the topic of eyewitness identifications – has been explicitly recognized in the field (Wells & Turtle, 1987). As in the nonclinical domain, much of the work in the realm of clinical forensic psychology has also been conducted by Canadian psycholegal scholars (see Ogloff, 1990). In the foreword to a recent book, Professor John Monahan of the University of Virginia, who is widely regarded as a leading figure in the field, wrote: "It is hard not to notice that the cast who produced this extraordinary work is virtually all-Canadian. This is merely one more illustration, as if one were needed, of the remarkably strong international presence of Canada in forensic psychology and psychiatry, a presence out of all proportion to relative population size, not to mention relative crime rate ... the Canadian prominence in this field is clear" (Monahan, 1997, pp. x–xi).

Until now, there has not been a Canadian textbook devoted to the field of psychology and law. In the past, it has been necessary for professors in Canada to assign an American psychology and law textbook, a Canadian introduction to law, and/or packets of selected readings. Given the differences between law in Canada and the United States, however, it is critical to have a book that focuses on the Canadian experience. This is the first such book, and we hope that it will provide a useful and thought provoking introduction to the field.

2. An Introduction to Law and the Canadian Legal System

V. Gordon Rose

INTRODUCTION

Trying to "explain the law" in a couple of dozen pages is like trying to "explain psychology" in the same space – it cannot be done, and attempts to do so will vary only in the degree to which they fail. The biggest problem in trying to summarize the law is that the correct answer to a legal question is always "It depends." This is because, in a very important sense, the law is all about classification and subclassification – classification of things, behaviours, people, and so on. As well, these classifications have evolved historically, over hundreds of years, in a piecemeal fashion in response to individual cases.[1] The introduction to the law that follows is very general in nature.

Because of its categorical nature, learning about law is a constant encounter with dichotomies and organizational classifications. For example, Canada, unlike most European countries, is a common law country, as opposed to a civil law nation. Generally, this means that Canadian courts decide cases by looking at and adapting what courts have done in previous cases. In contrast, in the civil law system the courts decide cases by referring to a written list of rules or code, often based on the Napoleanic code. It should be noted that the Province of Quebec has a civil system of private law, but uses the common law approach to criminal law. Another division can be made between common law and statute law, because, while Canada is a common law country, much of the law is not purely judge made but is found in statutes or regulations passed by Parliament, the provincial legislatures, or their delegates.

To put these categorizations into perspective, it is worth briefly considering the historical source of our legal system. Gall (1995) suggests that the common law system started in England at around the time of the Norman conquest in the eleventh century and was very much a product of the feudal system. The King or Queen owned all land, and exercised power over all who lived on it. During their travels about the country it became the practice for local disputes to be brought to the monarch for resolution, as were those subjects accused of breaching "the King's peace." According to Gall, these disputes were resolved by consideration of local customs; those customs which were not peculiar to a single locale became known as common customs. As the task of travelling the kingdom dispensing justice became too onerous, the power to do so in the King's name was delegated to various courts, whose decisions according to common customs became known as the common law. As the system became more formalized, the courts came to consider themselves bound by previous decisions, resulting in a growing body of judge-made law.

Despite being a common law country, most law in Canada is passed by legislative bodies and contained in statutes. In 1215, the English nobility forced King John to sign the Magna Carta, which in part required him to accept the input of the barons on certain decisions. From time to time thereafter, the monarch would proclaim (i.e., bring into force) various pieces of legislation, containing rules governing the conduct of their subjects. Over the course of several hundred years, these law-making powers devolved to an elected legislative body, whose statutes were, as a matter of course, proclaimed to be law by the monarch. This is the system we now have in Canada. As part of the same evolution, the number of laws enacted in statute has grown, seemingly exponentially. The common law still exists, however, as the courts continue to interpret statutes according to precedent.[2] Also, the introduction of the Canadian Charter of Rights and Freedoms in 1982 granted to the courts certain powers to modify or strike down legislation, resulting in a role resembling the ability to legislate. The Charter of Rights will be discussed in more detail later in this chapter.

A body of rules and practices developed to govern how the courts apply the common law. Of these, the overarching principle is stare decisis, a Latin term meaning "to abide by decided cases." Stare decisis requires courts to adhere to settled points of law by following precedent. This prevents different courts from deciding similar cases or questions in contradictory ways, thereby ensuring a measure of certainty in the law. Of course, there must be exceptions to the general rule, to allow for the correction of errors. Thus the rule has developed to require lower courts (e.g., provincial courts) to be bound by the decisions of higher courts (e.g., courts of appeal in the same province), although not the converse. While judges are not strictly bound by decisions of other judges of the same court (e.g., one judge of the Court of Queen's Bench is not bound by a decision of another), or of the courts in other common law jurisdictions (e.g., an Alberta trial court is not bound by a decision of the Ontario Court of Appeal), those decisions are considered to be persuasive and are not lightly to be disregarded.

The courts have developed additional techniques to avoid being bound by previous decisions. First, a court may distinguish a case, finding a reason to hold that it differs in some important way and so has not really settled the question presently before the court. Similarly, it may hold that particular parts of another court's decision are not an integral part of that decision, but instead constitute obiter dicta – words which were not essential to the decision and are therefore not binding on other courts. It should be noted that the Supreme Court of Canada has ruled that lower courts are bound by its obiter dicta. The Supreme Court of Canada has also ruled that it is not bound by its own decisions and it is free to change its mind in subsequent cases.

The remainder of this chapter provides a brief introduction to and overview of specific aspects of Canadian law. Included are those areas that are either essential to an appreciation of the legal aspects of the psycholegal issues dealt with in this text or of particular interest to students of law and psychology. Discussions of the details of specific cases are avoided in favour of a broad synthesis of general principles.

LITIGATION

Litigation is the process of settling disputes in court. One of the most obvious differences between common law jurisdictions and civil law jurisdictions lies in their approaches to litigation, especially criminal litigation. Civil law countries follow an inquisitorial approach, in which the court, through its officers, conducts an investigation into allegations. The judges direct and motivate the process, with the lawyers as much assisting the court as representing their clients' interests. During trials, judges engage in extensive questioning of witnesses. The focus in an inquisitorial setting is on discovery of the truth.

Common law jurisdictions like Canada, on the other hand, employ an adversarial approach to litigation. Each party to the dispute (e.g., the Crown, the accused, the person bringing the suit, etc.) is represented by counsel, whose role is to advocate their client's position. The process is largely driven by the parties and the court plays a relatively passive role, adjudicating the matter based on what is presented to it by the parties. Although interested in truth-seeking, the adversarial system emphasizes procedural fairness.

While counsel in the adversarial system represent their clients' interests, they are also considered to be officers of the court and are therefore ethically required to refrain from misleading the court, to refer to all relevant case law in argument, even if it is contrary to their position, and so on. Further, in a criminal case, the prosecution represents the Crown, and therefore advocates for justice rather than conviction; prosecutors are supposed to be impartial and objective.

An important concept in litigation is the notion of "standing." Standing refers to possession of the legal status requisite to present one's views and arguments to the court in a given case. Normally, only the parties to a dispute have standing when that dispute comes to court. In civil cases (by which we generally mean lawsuits, in which one party is suing another), there are often more than two parties involved. In criminal cases, generally only the accused and the Crown are party to the proceedings and have standing at trial. In certain cases, most frequently on appeal (the process of asking a higher court to review the decision of a lower court), the courts may allow other interested persons or organizations to intervene in the proceedings and grant them standing to argue in a case in which they are not, strictly speaking, parties. The most common situation in which this occurs involves cases that raise important constitutional questions; in such cases, the courts will usually hear from representatives of the federal government, the governments of interested provinces, and, in some cases, the representatives of special interest groups.

CONSTITUTIONAL LAW

Distribution of Powers

Without becoming bogged down in legal history, we must remember that the independent nation of Canada was created from a British colony by an Act of the British Parliament: The Constitution Act, 1867 (formerly the British North America Act, 1867, 30–31 Vict., c. 3 (U.K.), often referred to as the B.N.A. Act). This Act detailed the form of government of the new confederation, including the distribution of legislative powers between the federal and provincial levels of government and the structure of the courts. Section 91 specifies the areas in which the federal government has exclusive jurisdiction; section 92 lists the areas of provincial jurisdiction. The federal government has jurisdiction over "The Criminal Law, except the Constitution of the Courts of Criminal Jurisdiction, but including the Procedures in Criminal Matters" (s. 91(27)) and 'The Establishment, Maintenance, and Management of Penitentiaries' (s. 91(28)). The provinces have jurisdiction over:

> The Establishment, Maintenance and Management of Public and Reformatory Prisons for the Province. (s. 92(6))
> Property and Civil Rights in the Province. (s. 92(13))
> The Administration of Justice in the Province, including the Constitution, Maintenance and Organization of Provincial Courts, both of Civil and of Criminal Jurisdiction, and including Procedure in Civil Matters in those Courts. (s. 92(14))
> The Imposition of Punishment by Fine, Penalty, or Imprisonment for enforcing any Law of the Province made in relation to any Matter coming within any of the Classes of Subjects enumerated in this Section. (s. 92(15))

Thus, the federal government has responsibility for enacting criminal law and procedure but the provinces are responsible for administering it. In other words, the federal Parliament decides what things are to be made illegal and considered to be crimes but the primary responsibility for prosecuting those crimes and enforcing the law falls on the provinces. In addition, section 96 provides that the governor general is to appoint judges of the "Superior, District, and County Courts in each Province," and section 101 allows Parliament to create a general court of appeal for Canada and to establish other courts from time to time.

Despite its independence from Britain, Canada remains a constitutional monarchy. While laws are drafted and passed by Parliament or the provincial legislatures they do not come into force until approved and proclaimed by the monarch, represented in Canada by the governor general federally and the lieutenant-governors provincially. This approval is now given as a matter of course. In name, therefore, laws are still enacted by the monarch on the advice of the legislature. In practice, however, the Crown acts in accordance with the wishes of the elected government. Constitutional law, as it deals with the distribution of powers and their exercise, is much more complex than this superficial description would suggest, but this discussion should serve as enough of an introduction to provide some perspective for students beginning their studies in law and psychology.

The Structure of the Courts

Each province has created a provincial court under subsection 92(14), which has initial jurisdiction over (i.e., right to deal with) criminal cases, and which also typically has branches to deal with family and small claims matters. Judges of these courts are appointed by the provinces. All other courts are "section 96 courts," and appointments to them are made by the governor general of Canada. In each province, these typically include one or more trial courts (known variously as the superior court, county court, district court, Court of Queen's Bench, Supreme Court, and so on), and an appeal court. The various superior courts hear criminal and civil matters arising within their province. Within each province, appeals from provincial court decisions may go to either a superior court or the provincial court of appeal, depending on the nature of the case. Decisions of superior trial courts are appealed to the courts of appeal. Appeals from decisions of the provincial courts of appeal are appealed to the Supreme Court of Canada. As well, the federal government has created several other courts, including the Federal Court – Trial Division and the Federal Court of Appeal, the Tax Court, and most notably, the Supreme Court of Canada. The various federal trial courts hear matters involving the federal government, including lawsuits against it. Appeals from federal trial courts may go to the Federal Court of Appeal, and from there to the Supreme Court of Canada. Figure 2.1 illustrates the relation between these various courts. At one time, cases could have been further appealed to the British House of Lords or the Judicial Committee of the Privy Council, but this practice ended in 1949.

The Charter of Rights

The nature of the Canadian legal system changed fundamentally on April 17th, 1982, with the proclamation of the Canadian Charter of Rights and Freedoms, being Part I of the Constitution Act, 1982, enacted by the Canada Act 1982 (U.K.), c. 11, Sched. B. (R.S.C. 1985,

Figure 2.1
The structure of the courts in Canada

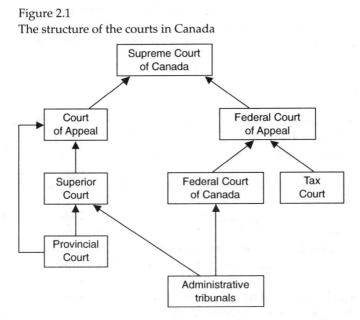

Appendix II, No. 44). The passing of this legislation was referred to as the patriation of our constitution, which could now be amended in Canada without Britain's cooperation. For the first time, Canada had a constitutionally entrenched bill of rights, meaning that it could not be amended or repealed by a simple act of Parliament, but only with substantial provincial approval. Further, subsection 52(1) of the Constitution Act states: "The Constitution of Canada is the supreme law of Canada, and any law that is inconsistent with the provisions of the Constitution is, to the extent of the inconsistency, of no force or effect." Suddenly, the courts were called upon, literally on a daily basis, to rule on the propriety of actions by governments and their officials, and on the constitutional validity of all aspects of federal and provincial legislation. Where the courts found government actions violated rights, various remedies were afforded to citizens. Where laws contradicted the Charter, the courts struck them down or read amendments into them. With the coming into force of the Charter of Rights, Canadian courts moved beyond their traditional role of interpreting legislation and approached an American position, becoming statutory lawmakers in their own right.[3] This change has greatly qualified the principle of the supremacy of Parliament, and it made the human rights aspect of

Canadian constitutional law one of the biggest growth areas in litigation, producing an area of law of almost overwhelming scope and complexity. What follows is a very brief and selective introduction to the Charter.

Section 1

While the Charter of Rights, as part of the constitution, is the supreme law of Canada, there is a major limitation to the scope of its application. Section 1 of the Charter reads: "The Canadian Charter of Rights and Freedoms guarantees the rights and freedoms set out in it subject only to such reasonable limits prescribed by law as can be demonstrably justified in a free and democratic society." Thus, when a law violates any of the rights protected by the Charter it will be struck down by the courts unless the government establishes that the violation represents a limit that is "demonstrably justified in a free and democratic society." For impugned legislation (legislation contravening a right protected under the Charter) to be saved under section 1), the law must involve an objective sufficiently important to society to justify overriding the right (*R. v. Oakes*, 1986).

Section 24

Where a law as written violates rights protected by the Charter, it will be struck down or limited by the courts unless it is saved by section 1. There may be situations, however, in which a person's rights are breached but the breach is not specified by a law that is itself unconstitutional, and section 1 is consequently not involved. For example, the sections of the Criminal Code that provide for search warrants are valid and do not contravene the Charter, but in a particular case the police may succeed in obtaining a search warrant where there are insufficient grounds to do so. In these circumstances, the search itself violates the Charter. In such cases, the aggrieved person may seek recourse under section 24, which reads:

> 24. (1) Anyone whose rights or freedoms, as guaranteed by this Charter, have been infringed or denied may apply to a court of competent jurisdiction to obtain such remedy as the court considers appropriate and just in the circumstances.
> (2) Where, in proceedings under subsection (1), a court concludes that evidence was obtained in a manner that infringed or denied any rights or

freedoms guaranteed by this Charter, the evidence shall be excluded if it is established that, having regard to all the circumstances, the admission of it in the proceedings would bring the administration of justice into disrepute.

Subsection 24(1) allows the courts to fashion a remedy appropriate to the circumstances, such as an adjournment or a judicial stay of proceedings in a criminal matter. Subsection 24(2) deals specifically with improperly obtained evidence and provides that such evidence must be excluded from court proceedings (such as a criminal trial) where allowing the evidence would bring the administration of justice into disrepute. The courts have interpreted "would" in this context as meaning "could." Thus, in the search warrant example, if the police had misled the justice who issued the warrant, or if some other impropriety had occurred, the trial court would consider whether the evidence should be excluded to protect the integrity of the justice system. On an application to exclude evidence under subsection 24(2), the court may consider such factors as whether authorities acted in good faith, whether there were exigent circumstances, whether the violation of rights was a matter of police practices, and so on.

Having looked at two general provisions of the Charter dealing with its application and remedies for its breach, let us now briefly consider some of the specific rights protected.

Section 7

Section 7 provides that "everyone has the right to life, liberty and security of the person and the right not to be deprived thereof except in accordance with the principles of fundamental justice." Although the section appears to be worded in a rather general manner, it has been applied to many specific issues. For instance, this section has been interpreted as guaranteeing an accused a right to pretrial disclosure of the Crown's evidence, as protecting an accused from the state's use of derivative evidence (evidence discovered following on information from the accused compelled during other proceedings), and as containing a right to silence.

Section 8

This section of the Charter contains the right "to be secure against unreasonable search and seizure." Perhaps no other section of the

Charter has resulted in as much litigation as this one has. Section 8 is aimed at protecting the privacy of individuals and has been used to impose on searches the standard of prior judicial authorization by way of a search warrant. Such approval must be based upon information providing some measure of credible probability that the sought-after evidence will be found in the place to be searched. Warrantless searches are now presumed to be unreasonable, although some common law powers of search without warrant, such as to search incidental to arrest, have survived.

It should be noted that the "reasonableness" of searches, under section 8, involves both whether it is reasonable to authorize or conduct a search and the manner in which the search is conducted. Thus, a lawful search that would be reasonable in the circumstances may still result in evidence that is excluded under subsection 24(2), if the search was conducted in an unreasonable fashion.

Section 10

The right to counsel is contained in section 10, which reads in part:

10. Everyone has the right on arrest or detention
    (a) to be informed promptly of the reasons therefore;
    (b) to retain and instruct counsel without delay and to be informed of that right.

This section has been interpreted as requiring the authorities not only to inform an accused of the right to counsel but to afford reasonable opportunity for the accused to exercise that right and to refrain from questioning the accused until that opportunity has been provided. Further, the right to counsel must be considered in conjunction with the informational right in section 10(a), since the decision whether to exercise one's right to counsel is made in the light of the specific offence alleged. Thus, when the nature of a police investigation changes to that of a more serious offence, an accused should be rewarned. As well, the courts have read into section 10 the right to be informed of existing provisions for free and immediate access to duty counsel, although there is no right to have such a service created or maintained by the provinces. Also, the warnings required under this section must be given in language the accused can understand. Where there are indications the accused does not understand these rights, police must take further steps to ensure comprehension.

Section 11

This section contains procedural rights and safeguards, including those listed below:

11. Any person charged with an offence has the right
    (a) to be informed without unreasonable delay of the specific offence;
    (b) to be tried within a reasonable time;
    . . . . .
    (d) to be presumed innocent until proven guilty according to law in a fair and public hearing by an independent and impartial tribunal;
    (e) not to be denied reasonable bail without just cause;
    (f) ... to the benefit of trial by jury where the maximum punishment for the offence is imprisonment for five years or a more severe punishment;

Section 11 applies only to persons charged with a criminal offence, as opposed to section 10, which applies to anyone arrested or detained for any reason. Section 11(b) guarantees the right to trial without unreasonable delay. The period of concern is the time between the laying of the charges and the completion of the trial; for instance, a lengthy investigation by authorities before laying charges is not considered. Applications for relief due to a breach of this section of the Charter will consider such factors as the complexity of the case, the reasons for the delay, prejudice to the accused, and so on.

The presumption of innocence is enshrined in section 11(d) and has been interpreted to impose the burden on the state to prove guilt beyond reasonable doubt. It also contains the requirement of procedural fairness. Section 11(e) guarantees the right to reasonable bail, and section 11(f) contains the right to a jury trial for offences with a maximum penalty of 5 or more years' imprisonment.

It is clear, then, that the Canadian Charter of Rights and Freedoms has a huge potential for impact on the law, particularly the law of criminal procedure and evidence (discussed below). The rights protected, and determining whether those rights have been breached, involve many questions of interest to legal psychologists.

TYPES OF LAW

Another way of classifying or categorizing the law is by subject matter. Accordingly, we may wish to talk about areas of substantive law (law dealing with the substance of an area) such as criminal, civil, administrative, and family law. Each of these areas of law has a distinct content and unique rules of procedure and evidence. The discussion below will concentrate primarily on criminal law, because of its relative importance in legal psychology. The criminal law will also be used as a background to introduce certain aspects of the law of evidence, which are generally common to all areas of law.

Criminal Law

Originally, our criminal law was the criminal law of England, composed of both common law and statute. In 1892, the first Criminal Code of Canada was enacted, based on draft criminal legislation that had been prepared for, though not adopted by, India. Subsection 8(2) of the current Criminal Code states that "the criminal law of England that was in force in a province immediately before April 1, 1955 continues in force in the province except as altered, varied, modified or affected by this Act or any other Act of the Parliament of Canada." Section 9 of the Code specifies, however, that no one may be convicted of a common law offence other than contempt of court, of an offence under British law, or of an offence under the legislation of any province or territory before that province or territory became part of Canada. Thus, common law offences have been abolished in Canada, although some aspects of criminal law existing at common law have survived. For instance, subsection 8(3) specifically preserves common law defences, "except in so far as they are altered by or inconsistent with" federal legislation.

Criminal law is an area of public law, in that crimes are considered to be acts against the public good. In Canada, a common law constitutional monarchy, crimes are still considered to be offences against the monarch and are prosecuted by representatives of the Crown (often referred to as Crown counsel). For this reason, in many places formal criminal charges still conclude with words claiming that the act was committed "... against the peace of our Lady the Queen, Her Crown and Dignity."

A criminal offence has two main elements: the actus reus, or evil act, and the mens rea, or evil intent. Respecting actus reus, the act must be one prohibited by law. Generally, this is a positive act of commission (such as an assault, for instance). Occasionally, a specific duty is imposed by law on a person, and in those cases the omission to act in accordance with that duty will be the criminal act. An example of a criminal omission is the failure to provide the necessities of life to one's child or spouse, contrary to section 215 of the Criminal Code.

Mens rea is a more complicated concept in law, and for psychologists, much more interesting. The general principle of criminal law in the Anglo-Canadian tradition is that no one should be punished for an act or omission unless they intended it. This, of course, assumes the accused has the capability of intending the act or omission, which is what the defences of insanity (now known as the mental disorder defence) and automatism address (see Chapter 10).

While the principle that intention is an essential element of a criminal offence is clear, what is meant by intention has been less clear from one situation to another. Although the term implies the requirement of actual, subjective intent, the law also imposes sanctions for acts involving objective intention. For instance, certain offences are crimes of negligence, where an individual is guilty if he or she knew, or reasonably ought to have known, of the probable consequences of the act. In other situations, criminal liability is imposed for recklessness – where the individual committed the act with a disregard for the consequences. Another doctrine in criminal law is wilful blindness, which prevents an accused escaping liability for lack of knowledge in a situation where he or she deliberately kept himself or herself ignorant of the facts so as to avoid the knowledge that would otherwise make the accused guilty.

The criminal law also distinguishes between specific and general intention. Thus, for a specific intent offence (e.g., murder), the offender typically has to intend the exact consequences of his or her crime, whereas an offence of general intent requires only an intention to commit the act (e.g., sexual assault), without intention of the specific consequences that follow. Additionally, the law has created the doctrine of transferred intent to prevent other attempts to avoid liability for unintended consequences. Thus, if A intended to kill B, and fired a shot at B, but instead hit and killed C, the law would transfer A's intention to kill B, holding that A had intended to kill and that that intention applies to the death of C. To further muddy the waters, motive is generally irrelevant in criminal law, although a requirement of specific intent comes close to "motive" in some contexts.

Finally, the law has traditionally classified offences into three levels: offences of intent, as we have been discussing; strict liability offences, for which an individual is liable if he or she committed the act, unless acting on a "reasonable and honest mistake of fact" that would (if true) have rendered the act innocent; and absolute liability offences, for which an individual is liable on proof of the commission of the act, with essentially no defence available and with no required mental element at all.

As if the issue of criminal intent was not already confusing enough, the Charter of Rights has been applied to the general rules of mens rea. Most particularly, the courts have held that unless an offence is merely regulatory, with penalties that are not serious enough to suggest a true "crime," there must be proof of intention. Thus, the scope of offences that may be of strict liability is quite limited, and certainly any absolute liability offence that included the possibility of a criminal penalty would violate section 7 of the Charter.

In addition to the two main elements of an offence, the Crown must also prove identification – that the accused was the one who committed the crime – and jurisdiction – that the offence was committed in a place in which the court has jurisdiction. For example, a provincial court normally only has jurisdiction over offences committed within that province.

Criminal defences must be distinguished from justifications or excuses. These two categories are conceptually different. A defence negates an essential element of the offence – for example, intoxication may mean that the accused was incapable of forming the level of intent required to make an act a crime. In contrast, a justification or excuse admits the essential elements of the offence alleged but seeks to excuse the conduct. For example, one may argue that necessity justified committing an otherwise criminal act to avoid a greater harm, such as where an individual steals the intended getaway car of someone about to commit a robbery, thereby preventing the more serious crime from occurring. A defence that negates an element of the offence need only raise a reasonable doubt, whereas a justification or excuse must be established by the accused on a balance of probabilities.

The Criminal Code classifies and groups offences by their nature: offences against public order, firearms and offensive weapons, offences against the administration of law and justice, sexual offences, invasion of privacy, offences against the person, property offences, and so on. Boyd (1995) simplifies this by arguing that there are really only three types of offences: offences against the person (such as murder or assault), offences against property (such as theft or fraud), and offences that are considered inherently evil (such as pornography or drug offences).

A final category involves so-called constructive complicity and inchoate crimes. The first term refers to parties to an offence – people who are criminally liable not because they committed the act but because they encouraged or assisted the person who did. These parties are variously known as aiders, abettors, counsellors, procurers, and accessories after the fact. The second term refers to conduct such as attempts, where the offence is not actually committed, or criminal conspiracy, where the mere act of agreeing with others to commit a crime is itself a crime. The rationale for imposing liability on parties and conspirators is that the law views groups of people combining together to commit crimes to be inherently more dangerous than individuals acting alone.

Criminal Procedure

Offences, defences, and justifications form the substantive criminal law (i.e., the law of what is or is not a crime). Also important are the rules governing how the criminal law is to be applied, before and at trial, and on sentencing and appeal. These rules are the law of criminal procedure and are generally specified in the Criminal Code, although they are interpreted in the case law. Again, this is a highly technical and involved area of the law, and the following is a very selective introduction.

In Canada, offences are either indictable or prosecuted by summary conviction. Some offences, known as hybrid offences, may be either summary or indictable, at the option of the Crown prosecutor. Indictable offences are the more serious offences whereas summary conviction offences are less serious. Only Parliament can create indictable offences, while summary conviction offences can be created by either the federal or provincial governments. Summary conviction offences, including hybrid offences that are proceeded with summarily (and a limited number of indictable offences), must be tried in provincial court. A few of the most serious indictable offences can only be tried by a superior court. All other offences can be tried in either provincial or superior court, at the election of the accused. Where an accused elects to be tried in superior court, either by judge alone or by judge and jury, a provincial court judge will normally first conduct a preliminary inquiry, at which the Crown must present sufficient evidence to justify putting the accused on trial.

"Jurisdiction" is a term with many meanings in criminal law. It involves jurisdiction over the offence – which offences a particular court is allowed to hear. It also addresses territorial jurisdiction – whether the offence occurred in a location that allows the court to hear the trial – and jurisdiction over the person – whether the accused is a person or a member of a class of persons the court may deal with. Most trial courts can hear cases arising anywhere within their province. Jurisdiction over a person is usually gained by compelling the accused to attend court in one of the ways discussed below and may be lost through certain procedural errors.

The most obvious way of compelling someone to attend court is arrest. Police officers may arrest anyone with a warrant and may arrest without a warrant anyone found committing or reasonably believed to have committed or to be about to commit an indictable offence. In the latter cases, the police officer must actually believe, and must objectively have reasonable and probable grounds to believe, that the suspect has committed or is about to commit an indictable offence. In various specified circumstances, an arrested accused must be released by the police as soon as practical. In such cases, the accused will either sign a document promising to attend court or will later be served with a summons compelling him or her to attend. In other situations, an accused will never be arrested but merely be served with a summons.

Where a person is arrested and not released by the police, he or she will be taken before a judge, where the Crown will normally be required to show cause why the accused should not be released on an undertaking (i.e., promise) to appear, without conditions. This is commonly known as a bail hearing, where the court considers judicial interim release. The court will make a decision to release or detain the accused, after considering two grounds: ensuring the accused's attendance in court and protecting the public and the administration of justice. If the court decides to release the accused a number of options are available, including conditions, cash deposits, and sureties (other people who pledge money or property to secure the accused's attendance). Normally, the court is required to release an accused on the least serious form of bail unless satisfied by the Crown that the next most stringent form is required.

No matter how a person is compelled to attend court, formal proceedings are commenced with the laying of an information, a sworn allegation of the accused's criminal conduct. This is the charging document for as long as the proceedings are before the provincial court. In the case of an indictable offence for which the accused has elected trial in superior court, at the conclusion of the preliminary inquiry (if the accused is committed to stand trial) the Crown will prefer an indictment – a formal written allegation of the specific offence – which will be the charging document for all further criminal proceedings involving that offence. In either case, an accused is arraigned when the information or indictment is read in open court and the accused is called upon to enter a plea.

A person will not be forced to stand trial unless he or she is fit to do so. Fitness to stand trial involves a determination of the accused's mental state and is discussed in Chapter 10. It is important to realize that fitness is a completely different issue from insanity. Insanity, or mental disorder, is a defence, in that it negates the element of intention at the time of the offence. Fitness involves the mental capability to follow the trial proceedings and participate in one's own defence. Being found unfit to stand trial does not absolve an accused of criminal liability, but rather merely postpones the trial until some subsequent time when he or she becomes fit again.

The purpose of the preliminary inquiry has grown beyond its original function, which was simply to ensure that sufficient evidence existed to justify putting the accused on trial. It has now become one method by which the accused can discover what evidence the Crown has against him or her. The Supreme Court of Canada has held that section 7 of the Charter guarantees an accused complete disclosure of the Crown's case, in order to make full answer and defence. There is presently no reciprocal duty on the defence to disclose its case to the Crown.

Aside from the rules governing the selection of juries (discussed in more detail in Chapter 5), the procedure at trial is much the same whether the accused is tried by a judge and jury, a superior court judge alone, or a provincial court judge alone. If there is to be a jury, the right to which is guaranteed by the Charter of Rights for every offence with a maximum penalty of imprisonment for five years or more, the Sheriff's Office will collect a group (the array) of eligible jurors. The array should be both representative and random, to some extent. In court, prospective jurors are called forward one at a time and counsel for the Crown and defence take turns indicating whether they are content with that person as a juror, in which case the person is sworn as a member of the jury, or whether they challenge that person. Challenges may be "peremptory" or "for cause". Each side has a limited number of peremptory challenges, for which no reason need be given, and an unlimited number of challenges for cause, which must be proven on specific grounds, such as partiality. As opposed to the American approach, jurors are not generally questioned, although in some circumstances very limited questioning may be permitted – for instance, where there is evidence of bias in the community against the accused. Typically, the only things counsel know about prospective jurors at jury selection are their names, addresses, and occupations. Once the twelve jurors have been selected, the trial will technically start when the accused is formally addressed and "put in the charge of the jury." During the course of the trial, jurors may be discharged (dismissed) by the judge for reasons such as illness, but no trial may proceed with fewer than ten jurors.

The actual trial starts with an opening statement by the Crown, which then leads its evidence. After the Crown questions each of its witnesses, defence counsel has an opportunity to cross-examine. Once the Crown closes its case, the defence elects whether or not to lead evidence. If the defence decides to call witnesses, defence counsel may make an opening statement to the jury, and will then present its case. Again, the Crown will have an opportunity to cross-examine each defence witness in turn. Finally, counsel will present summations to the jury. If the defence led evidence, it will go first, otherwise, the Crown will go first. Following counsels' addresses, the judge will instruct the jury on the law to be applied and the jury will retire to consider its verdict in private.

Jury verdicts must be unanimous to have any effect. If the jury cannot agree on a verdict, a mistrial will be declared and a new trial held, in front of a new jury. From time to time, during the course of the trial, it may be necessary for counsel to raise a question of law or to seek rulings on the admissibility of certain pieces of evidence, or for the judge to rule on the objections of one side or the other. In the event of such questions, the judge will declare a voir dire (a separate hearing within the trial) and excuse the jury. These issues will then be settled in the jury's absence.

In Canada, section 649 of the Criminal Code makes it illegal for a juror to discuss anything that occurred in the jury room, except in the context of an investigation or trial of charges of obstruction of justice relating to one of the members of the jury. The rationale for this prohibition, presumably, is that jurors must be free to discuss their cases fully amongst themselves without fear that they may later be accountable for some of their words taken out of context. This is arguably necessary to ensure full and frank deliberation of the issues the jury is called upon to decide. The prohibition, however, effectively prevents any direct research by social scientists of jury dynamics. While certain types of questions would seem to be technically permissible under section 649, there has been no course of research conducted in Canada involving jurors and the trials in which they have been involved.

If an accused is found guilty, he or she must be given an opportunity to address the court before sentence is imposed. The court will generally also hear from the Crown and may receive submissions or information from victims, probation officers, and so on. The accused's criminal record, if any, will also be considered. The court may also require that a psychological or psychiatric assessment be completed and the results presented. The range of sentencing options available is set by the Criminal Code (and the Act creating the offence, if it is not the Code). These options vary, in different situations, from absolute or conditional discharges through fines and suspended sentences with probation orders to conditional or actual terms of imprisonment. As well, a victim surcharge may be added to any fine, restitution may be ordered to victims, and the proceeds of crime may be confiscated. In imposing sentence, the courts are to be guided by various principles of sentencing, including punishment and the need to express society's abhorrence for the accused's conduct, general and specific deterrence (i.e., deterrence of others and deterrence of the specific offender), and rehabilitation. Sentences imposed on similar offenders for similar acts should also be in the same range (i.e., there should be parity). Sentencing is considered specifically in Chapter 7.

Finally, the Code provides certain rights of appeal, which vary depending on whether the offence was summary conviction or indictable, whether the appeal is from verdict or sentence, whether the Crown or the defence is appealing, and the nature of the issue on appeal. Summary conviction appeals are normally heard by the superior trial court of the province with further appeals to the court of appeal in some instances. Either side may appeal a verdict in an indictable matter to the court of appeal, "as of right," on a question of law alone. If the court grants leave (i.e., agrees to hear the appeal), either side may appeal a sentence or verdict on a question of mixed fact and law. The defence alone may appeal with leave on a question of fact. These terms refer to whether the issue on appeal turns on the facts, on the law or how it should be applied, or some combination of the two.

Figure 2.2
The basic procedure of a criminal trial in Canada

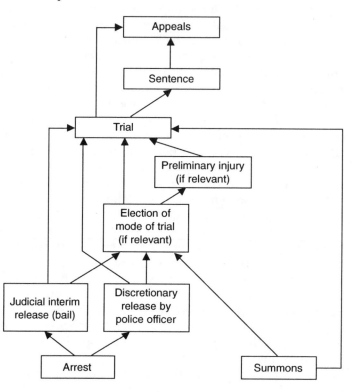

The court of appeal may dismiss or allow the appeal, and in various circumstances may either substitute the appropriate verdict or order a new trial. Further appeals to the Supreme Court of Canada may normally only be taken on questions of law, if that court grants leave, or if there was a dissent in the court of appeal. On appeal of a sentence, the appellate court will not normally substitute its own views for that of the sentencing judge but will interfere only if the original sentence fell outside of the usual range of sentences imposed on similar offenders for similar offences. The entire process discussed in this section is mapped out in Figure 2.2.

One aspect of sentencing that often confuses people involves parole. Persons convicted of a criminal offence and sentenced to imprisonment will rarely be required to serve their full sentence. Generally, the last third of their sentence will be served in the community on mandatory supervision, designed to reintegrate them into society. Further, offenders are typically eligible to apply for full parole after serving one-third of their sentence, and they may be eligible to apply for day parole or temporary absences after serving much less time than that. All offenders on parole or mandatory supervision are subject to being recommitted to their institutions if they breach the terms of their release or pose a threat to reoffend. The exception is the case of first degree murder, which carries a mandatory sentence of life imprisonment with no possibility of parole for 25 years. Parole will not automatically be granted after 25 years (or ever!), and even if released, a murderer will remain on parole for the rest of his or her life.

Evidence

As opposed to the substantive and procedural areas of criminal law, the law of evidence (both generally and as it applies specifically to criminal trials) is predominantly found in the common law, or judge-made law. There are some statutory provisions relating to evidence, however, such as those in the Canada Evidence Act. The Charter of Rights has also had a substantial impact on the law of evidence.

In a civil case, the burden of proof is on whichever side brings a claim or makes an allegation to present sufficient evidence to establish their claim on a balance of probabilities. This suggests that the evidence must leave the trier of fact (the judge or jury) convinced that the claim is more likely than not. In a criminal case, the Crown (prosecution) must prove its case "beyond reasonable doubt." While the law refuses to quantify beyond reasonable doubt, it implies a fairly high degree of certainty. Further, the Crown must prove each element of the offence beyond reasonable doubt.

Certain things will not be required to be formally proved, that is, the courts may take "judicial notice" of well-known, generally accepted facts (e.g., the high ethnic population in a particular community), and they must take judicial notice of law (e.g., decisions made by judges in other cases). In addition, in certain situations presumptions arise in which certain facts will be accepted as true unless the presumption is rebutted through the introduction of evidence to the contrary. An example would be the presumption in subsection 349(2) of the Criminal Code, which states that evidence that an accused entered a dwelling house without a lawful excuse is, in the absence of evidence to the contrary, proof of entry with the intention of committing an indictable offence.

Evidence can be considered on two different dimensions: its admissibility and its weight. Admissibility refers to whether the trier of fact is legally allowed to consider the evidence, while weight concerns how persuasive admissible evidence is. Thus, a certain piece of evidence may be admissible but of little significance. Traditionally, if evidence was relevant (if it tended to prove, disprove, or qualify some issue before the court), it was admissible. What weight a judge or jury decided to give that evidence was a different matter entirely. Also traditionally, relevant evidence was generally admissible no matter how it was obtained. This principle was qualified somewhat in later years but did not substantially change until the introduction of the Charter of Rights in 1982. As we have seen, subsection 24(2) of the Charter specifies that evidence obtained through a violation of a person's rights cannot be used against that person if its admission could bring the administration of justice into disrepute.

Formerly, the law required that only the "best evidence" be tendered at trial – copies of documents were inadmissible, for example, if the originals were available. This rule, and most of the exclusionary rules of evidence (discussed later) have been relaxed somewhat recently and the courts are now willing to consider admitting evidence so long as it is necessary and reliable.

Not surprisingly, evidence can be classified in a number of ways. For instance, evidence can be direct or circumstantial. Direct evidence tends to prove or disprove some fact in issue, whereas circumstantial evidence tends to prove some fact from which other facts can be inferred. Evidence can also be categorized by form: documentary evidence, real evidence (i.e., things, such as the murder weapon), viva voce evidence (the oral testimony of witnesses in court), demonstrative or illustrative evidence (e.g., models or diagrams of the scene of a crime), and so on.

Another category of evidence is "opinion evidence." Normally, a witness may not express an opinion on issues that the judge or jury must decide. Two main exceptions, however, are made. First, witnesses may give an opinion on issues such as speed, height or distance, or apparent age, where their opinion is really just a shorthand way of reciting a list of facts. More importantly, so-called expert opinions may be offered by anyone with special skill and knowledge, where such evidence would assist the court. Expert witnesses might include chemists, fingerprint examiners, physicians, psychologists, and psychiatrists (as discussed in Chapter 1).

In considering certain types of evidence, it is necessary to distinguish between the credibility and the character of a witness. Credibility involves whether a witness is to be believed and the weight to be attached to his or her evidence. Character deals with the type of person the witness is, and the inferences which may be drawn from that, especially if the witness is the accused in a criminal trial. Any witness who takes the stand puts his or her credibility in issue and may be examined on matters that address credibility. Character, however, is not normally in issue. Thus, an accused who testifies on his or her own behalf may not be cross-examined on character, nor may evidence be led of his or her bad character, unless the accused put his or her own character into issue. This may happen, for example, when an accused testifies that he or she is not the type of person who would commit an act such as the one charged, or where the defence calls witnesses who testify to this effect.

The distinction between character and credibility is important to the law. For instance, any witness may be cross-examined on his or her criminal record, but the judge or jury is normally only allowed to consider that record as going to the witness's credibility and not to character. Obviously, where an accused testifies in his or her own defence, there may be some question whether the jury really appreciates and applies this distinction (see Chapter 6).

Similar fact evidence is another type of evidence that is not normally admissible, as it tends to relate to character. Thus, generally, the Crown cannot introduce evidence that the accused has committed similar crimes in the past as tending to show that he or she is therefore likely to have also committed the particular offence for which he or she is on trial. The courts have developed the position that similar fact evidence may be admissible, however, where its "probative value" (i.e., its tendency to prove or disprove a fact in issue) far outweighs the prejudice to the accused of admitting it. One instance in which this may happen is where the offences all share some distinctive characteristic, and so evidence that the accused has committed some of them really does tend to suggest that he or she is responsible for the others.

Several evidentiary rules are concerned with excluding evidence from court proceedings. One very technical aspect of the law of evidence involves the rule against hearsay. Hearsay is typically defined as evidence of an out-of-court statement, made by someone other than the witness, tendered to prove the truth of what was asserted in the statement. In a very general sense, this rule is a prohibition against second-hand evidence – against letting a witness testify about what someone else said, in order to show that what that person said was true. The rationale for the rule is that the person who made the statement has not testified under oath and is not present to be cross-examined, and so there is doubt about the reliability of the evidence.

Historically a whole series of exceptions to the rule against hearsay evidence, exceptions to the exceptions, and categories of evidence that look like hearsay but are not (because they do not come within the strict confines of the definition) have developed. This is another area of the law, however, in which the courts are moving away from a rule-based categorical approach towards a case-by-case consideration based on the necessity and reliability of admitting the evidence.

Another exclusionary rule involves the notion of "privilege" – the right (and duty) not to disclose certain information, even on the witness stand. This exclusion is based not on the unreliability of the evidence, but rather on issues of public policy. Thus, it is considered more important to protect the confidentiality of discussions with one's lawyer (solicitor-client privilege), or the solidity of a marriage (spousal privilege), than to jeopardize those relationships by forcing the parties to them to divulge all possible relevant evidence. While there are several historical categories of privilege, the courts are again moving towards approaching claims of privilege on the merits of individual cases, based on the criteria of the confidentiality of the communication, the importance of that confidentiality to the relationship between the parties, the desirability of fostering that relationship, and the relative harm of forcing the disclosure versus the advantage of obtaining the evidence. There is no generally recognized privilege in Canada protecting conversations between patients and psychologists or psychiatrists.

An admission is a statement made by a person against his or her own interests, and is one of the main exceptions to the hearsay rule. Because it is against the speaker's interests, an admission is considered to be reliable. Where the admission is made to a "person in authority," such as a police officer, it is considered to be a confession. Evidence of an accused's confession is only admissible if the Crown proves beyond reasonable doubt during a voir dire that the statement was made voluntarily – without any threats or promises to induce the accused to make it. The courts have also ruled, under the Charter, that a confession is not voluntary unless it is the product of an "operating mind" capable of intending the admission and appreciating its consequences. In addition, a confession will not be admitted if there has been a breach of the right to counsel or the informational rights under section 10(b), or if the circumstances suggest a breach of the section 7 right to silence (see Chapter 3).

Administrative Law

Another area of public law is administrative law, which governs the conduct of government bodies such as tribunals, boards, and so on. The law has developed so as to impose on such bodies a duty to act fairly, in accordance with the "rules of natural justice." These principles include a duty to allow both sides to a dispute an opportunity to present their cases and a duty to be fair or unbiased. The courts will intervene to ensure that administrative bodies act in accordance with such principles. Decisions involving psychologists about parole, civil commitment and release, and so forth are frequently made by administrative tribunals (such as review panels) bound by these principles (see Chapter 12).

Civil Law

As opposed to criminal and administrative law, which are areas of public law, civil and family are areas of private law. Civil law involves the private enforcement of contracts and remedies for private wrongs (known as torts) such as trespass. In these cases, the dispute is typically between two or more individuals or companies, and is arbitrated by the courts. Thus, civil law involves private parties enforcing their own rights in their own interests, whereas criminal law has the state enforcing public rights in the public interest. In a civil lawsuit, the burden is generally on the complaining party to prove its claim on a balance of probabilities. The substantive law involved is primarily found in the common law, although the civil procedure governing the conduct of cases is typically set out in provincial legislation.

Family Law

Family law concerns marriage and divorce, custody of children, division of assets, and financial maintenance for the support of family members (or former family members). This area of the law is substantially codified by legislation. As the courts strive to make decisions on issues such as custody "in the best interests of the children," for example, psychologists become increasingly involved in family law matters (see Chapter 13).

IN CLOSING

It should be evident that there is a very broad scope of potential involvement for psychology in the legal process and system. Clinical psychologists will be directly involved in issues of insanity, fitness to stand trial, child custody decisions, sentencing recommendations, post-sentencing treatment, family interventions, civil commitment, and evaluations for parole applications, among other things. Experimental psychologists may have an even wider range of involvement, given the huge number of historical assumptions the law has made about how people operate. This cursory summary of the Canadian legal system and process should enable you to appreciate the interface between law and psychology as you consider the readings in the rest of this text.

RECOMMENDED READING

Because the law is unfamiliar to many readers and even some instructors, a bibliography of authoritative materials is provided here, followed by a bibliography of instructional and introductory materials. Readers may refer to these sources for additional information on the relevant areas and topics in law.

Authoritative Materials
Bala, N., Hornick, J., & Vogl, R. (1991). *Canadian child welfare law: Children, families and the state.* Toronto: Thompson.
Boilard, J.G. (1991, with updates). *Guide to criminal evidence.* Cowansville, PQ: Les Éditions Yvon Blais.
Brandon, S., Duncanson, I., & Samuel, G. (1979). *English legal history.* London: Sweet & Maxwell.
Driedger, E.A. (1983). *The construction of statutes* (2nd ed.). Toronto: Butterworths.
Dussault, R., & Borgeat, L. (1986). *Administrative law: A treatise* (2nd ed.). Toronto: Carswell.

Fontana, J.A. (1992). *The law of search and seizure in Canada* (3rd ed.). Markham, ON: Butterworths.

Hogg, P.W. (1996). *Constitutional law of Canada* (4th ed.). Scarborough, ON: Carswell.

Hovius, B., & Youdan, M. (1991). *The law of family property*. Scarborough, ON: Carswell.

James, P.S. (1985). *Introduction to English law* (11th ed.). London: Butterworths.

Jones, D.P., & de Villars, A.S. (1985). *Principles of administrative law*. Toronto: Carswell.

Laskin, B. (1986). *Laskin's Canadian constitutional law* (5th ed.). (Revised by N. Finkelstein). Toronto: Carswell.

Marin, R.J. (1996). *Admissibility of statements* (9th ed.). Aurora, ON: Canada Law Book.

McWilliams, P.K. (1988 with updates). *Canadian criminal evidence*. Aurora, ON: Canada Law Book.

Rose, V.G. (1982). *Parties to an offence*. Toronto: Carswell.

Ruby, C.C. (1994). *Sentencing* (4th ed.). Markham, ON: Butterworths.

Salhany, R.E. (1994, with updates). *Canadian criminal procedure* (6th ed.). Aurora, ON: Canada Law Book.

Schiff, S. (1993, with supplements). *Evidence in the litigation process* (4th ed.). Toronto: Thomson Professional Publishing.

Sharpe, R.J. (Ed.). (1987). *Charter litigation*. Toronto: Butterworths.

Sopinka, J., Lederman, S.N., and Bryant, A.W. (1992). *The law of evidence in Canada*. Markham, ON: Butterworths.

Whitely, S. (1985). *Jurisdiction in criminal law*. Toronto: Carswell.

Wright, C., & Linden, A. (1970). *The law of torts* (5th ed.). Toronto: Butterworths.

Instructional and Introductory Materials

Boyd, N. (1995). *Canadian law: An introduction*. Toronto: Harcourt Brace.

Brockman, J., & Rose, V.G. (2001). *Canadian criminal procedure and evidence for the social sciences* (2nd ed.). Scarborough, ON: Nelson Canada.

Cheffins, R., & Tucker, R. (1976). *The constitutional process in Canada* (2nd ed.). Toronto: McGraw-Hill Ryerson.

Delisle, R.J. (1996). *Evidence: Principles and problems* (4th ed.). Scarborough, ON: Carswell.

Delisle, R.J., & Stuart, D. (1996). *Learning Canadian criminal procedure* (4th ed.). Scarborough, ON: Carswell.

Friedland, M.L., & Roach, K. (1994). *Criminal law and procedure: Cases and materials* (7th ed.). Toronto: Emond Montgomery.

Gall, G.L. (1995). *The Canadian legal system* (4th ed.). Scarborough, ON: Carswell.

Griffiths, C.T., & Verdun-Jones, S.N. (1994). *Canadian criminal justice.* (2nd ed.) Toronto: Harcourt Brace.

Hovius, B. (1996). *Family law: Cases, notes, and materials* (4th ed.). Scarborough, ON: Carswell.

Mewett, A.W. (1996). *An introduction to the criminal process in Canada* (3rd ed.). Scarborough, ON: Carswell.

Mewett, A.W., & Manning, M. (1985). *Criminal law* (2nd ed). Toronto: Butterworths.

Salhany, R.E. (1994). *A basic guide to evidence in criminal cases* (3rd ed.). Toronto: Thomson Professional Publishing.

Solomon, R., Feldthusen, B., & Mills, S. (1991). *Cases and materials on the law of torts* (3rd ed.). Scarborough, ON: Carswell.

Verdun-Jones, S. (1993). *Criminal law in Canada* (2nd ed.). Toronto: Harcourt Brace.

PART TWO

Psychological Applications to
Criminal Procedure

3. Police Investigations

A. Daniel Yarmey

On 18 June 1998 nurse Gita Proudman was given a polygraph test and then interrogated by three Toronto police officers. Two weeks later Ms Proudman was charged with the murder of a severely deformed newborn who had died in her arms on 12 June 1998. Approximately a year and a half later, Ontario Court judge David Watt dismissed the murder charge. Defence lawyer Marlys Edwardh described the police interrogation as "just horrifying – the most brutal and sadistic interrogation I have ever seen." The excerpt below is taken from the police interrogation. As you read through the dialogue between the police (P) and Ms Gita Proudman (GP), and before reading further into the chapter, assess the validity of the interview and hypothesize why the police would interrogate Ms Proudman in this manner.

P: *... You know what? He didn't die by himself. You were holding him. There's a lot worse people out there, believe me. Listen. Look at me. Look me in the eye ... You knew that what you were doing was the right thing to do. You're so compassionate, so overwhelmingly compassionate that when you saw the child in so much distress ...*

GP: *He wasn't in distress.*

P: *No, listen here. If you did it because you wanted to make the child comfortable in his last moments, knowing that he was going to be with a human when he passed on, that's fine. But if you did it out of selfish reasons, or if you did it for some other diabolical reason, I want you to ...*

GP: *I don't care what your machine says.*

Author's note: Portions of this chapter, including much of the case law referred to the in the section on interviewing children, were contributed by Deborah Connolly of the University of Victoria.

P: Listen here. The issue is no longer whether or not you did it. You know the issue is why did you do it?

GP: (Cries)

P: When you pick up the child, what is going through your mind? When you're looking at the child? Is it compassion? Or is it something totally repulsive in your mind that's saying this child can't live like that?

GP: I didn't do this.

P: You hold the child in your hands. You look down at the poor infant and he's struggling.

GP: He wasn't struggling.

P: Ah, he's struggling. You knew that when your lunch break was over, he's going to go back into this incubator all by himself. You are thinking: 'My break is over. I'm going to go, and there is not going to be anyone around for Mustafa ... I bet you that when Mustafa passed on, there was a prayer. And you are the only person to say a prayer for him. He's an angel now. He's looking down, and he had the prayers given and delivered to him by you – by the only person who cares. The only person who really cares enough to hold the child, cradle the child, to comfort the child.

GP: That's all I did.

p: You're not a bad person.

GP: I don't care what your machine says. I didn't do it. I didn't smother this baby. I didn't smother this baby. I will say it with my last living breath ... Please stop trying to pretend you're my friend. Oh God, oh God, oh God.

P: He died because he was asphyxiated. That's the medical evidence, Gita. And I'm asking you to explain that. (Globe and Mail, November 10, 1999)

In 1991, in Martensville, Saskatchewan, in what has been called a modern-day witchhunt, a total of 173 charges were made against nine people, including five police officers, for allegedly operating a child sex-abuse ring. Children between the ages of 2 and 9 years of age testified that they had been physically and sexually abused, including penetration with axe handles and vibrators. No independent forensic or eyewitness evidence that could confirm the testimony of the complainants, however, was ever presented to the court. Although the children initially denied being abused, their stories changed following repeated police interviews. Two of the nine accused in the Martensville case were found guilty, but one of these convictions was reversed in 1995 by the Saskatchewan Court of Appeal, in part because of poor police interview techniques.[1] Like the excerpt that opened this chapter, these faulty techniques involved intrusive pressure tactics including leading and highly suggestive questions.

As police are not present when most crimes occur, they are dependent on victims, witnesses, fellow professionals, the general public, and even suspects for information leading to the arrest and conviction of guilty persons (Yarmey, 1990). Much of this evidence is gathered through investigative interviews conducted by police, social workers, psychologists, psychiatrists, and others. This chapter describes the psychological foundations of investigative interviews, interrogations, and confessions. As the research described demonstrates, the reliability of evidence, or lack thereof, is highly dependent upon the manner in which the information is obtained.

THE LAW PERTAINING TO INVESTIGATIVE PROCEDURES

The Canadian Charter, by guaranteeing certain rights and freedoms to individuals, has influenced how the police (and other criminal justice agencies) may operate. Following its enactment, the police became more constrained in their activities (Seagrave, 1997). As might be expected, many police officers were opposed to the Charter because they believed it would unfairly constrain their activities and give unneeded assistance to criminals (Griffiths & Verdun Jones, 1994). Others have observed that, although the Charter appears to have little impact on the rights and freedoms of individual citizens, it provides a framework of official discretion that can guide police in their routine social control tasks (Ericson, 1982).

Prior to the Charter, police did not have to inform suspects of their legal options and rights. As outlined in Chapter 2, section 10 of the Charter guarantees that everyone, upon arrest or detention, has the right to counsel and to be informed of that right without delay. Roger Salhany (1991), an Ontario Court judge, notes that the right to counsel obligates police to advise an arrested person in a meaningful manner. For example, if a suspect is told to read a sign on the wall it cannot merely be assumed that he or she can read, or can see the sign, or understands English or French. If a person is too ill or too intoxicated to comprehend his or her rights, an officer is obligated to wait until such time that that person can comprehend his or her rights before giving notice. Notice about right to counsel must, however, be given without delay, that is, as soon as is reasonably possible. Police are also obliged to offer the accused the use of a telephone and to allow as many calls as are necessary in order for counsel to be retained and instructed. An accused has the right to remain silent throughout the entire interrogation process, as well as throughout the entire trial, should one ensue. When a suspect tells the police that he or she wants to see a lawyer, the police are obliged to immediately stop all questioning and any further interrogation must be on the advisement of counsel. An accused can, however, waive his or her right to a lawyer as long as the waiver is clear and all of the consequences are fully understood.

Common law entitles police to question individuals prior to an arrest about a criminal incident and their part in it, but people are entitled to ignore these questions (other than giving their name and address) and leave. The officer is then faced with a dilemma; he or she has the choice of releasing or arresting the individual. An arrest, however, can only be made if the officer feels that there are reasonable grounds that an indictable offence has occurred. If an arrest is made, the accused must be informed about his or her right to counsel. Even without an arrest, an individual may be asked to accompany an officer to the police station in order "to clear the matter up." If the request has been made in such a manner that an individual feels he or she cannot refuse, the courts may interpret this as an arrest, even though the officer did not have that intention (Salhany, 1991).

Interrogation of a suspect may lead to a confession that he or she has "done it." A confession is defined as a written or oral statement, or even a nod of the head by an accused, which is an admission of guilt or an admission of fact that tends to prove his or her guilt. Such a statement must be voluntary, however, otherwise it may be ruled inadmissible at trial. If confessions are elicited by oppressive conditions, by questioning styles deemed to be threatening, or by an inducement for some reward, the court may rule this evidence inadmissible because it was not voluntarily given. For example, such phrases as "it would be better for you if you told us what happened" and "you will be arrested if you do not tell us where the stolen goods are," have been held to constitute a threat (Salhany, 1991, p. 150). We will return to these issues later in our review of interrogation of suspects and the use of the polygraph in obtaining confessions.

As outlined in Chapter 2, the Charter states that evidence shall be excluded if its admission "in the proceedings would bring the administration of justice into disrepute," with the onus of responsibility on the police to satisfy the court that the Charter has been followed.

INVESTIGATIVE PROCESS

The purpose of the investigative process is to obtain evidence that can substantiate an allegation. Often, because of the absence of clear physical evidence, witnesses must be interviewed in order to build a picture of what happened and to gather other evidentiary information that can be tested for its validity. In an attempt to discover historical truths of who did what, where, when, how, and why, investigative interviews, when properly conducted, elicit facts without biasing or influencing the witness. Accordingly, the interviewer is expected to be neutral and objective. Ideally, his or her approach should be to test the facts being gathered through the elimination of alternative hypotheses, rather than merely confirming predetermined assumptions.

This approach may be contrasted with therapeutic interviews, which are more concerned with the understanding of narrative truth than with historical veracity. Most, if not all, therapists attempt to be compassionate listeners in order to assess and deal with the trauma of their clients. To build a bond of trust and to uncover the meaning behind their clients' reports, therapists typically accept their clients' beliefs or subjective reality (Spence, 1994). When therapists accept narrative truth as evidence without external corroboration, however, problems can occur if the therapist acts as both the patient's advocate and the forensic investigator (Dent & Newton, 1994). It should be obvious that valid clinical opinion, particularly when it has legal consequences, should be based on scientific training and research (see Poole, Lindsay, Memon, & Bull, 1995).

If psychologists or other mental health workers accept the mantle of forensic interviewers, then the dynamics of the interview change from those present in a therapeutic context. Rather than pursuing therapeutic goals, forensic psychological interviews are structured to answer legal questions through an evaluation of relevant psychological data. Forensic interviews performed by mental health professionals, or by police, usually begin with a defining statement of legal purpose, followed by rapport building and questions that are increasingly structured and consistent with implicit legal standards. On occasion, lawyers may even be present during an investigative interview (Strasburger, Gutheil, & Brodsky, 1997).

Interviews, Information Processing, and Memory

The major purpose of an investigative interview is to obtain informa-tion that is as accurate, as detailed, and as complete as possible based upon victims' or witnesses' memory, while controlling for contextual or situational factors that can influence the validity of reports. What is astonishing to many forensic researchers are the simplistic ideas held by many legal and mental health professionals about the nature of memory (Loftus, 1986; Yapko, 1994). For example, Yapko (1994) found in a survey of more than 1,000 therapists, all of whom were qualified professionals with advanced degrees, that one-third of the respondents believed that "the mind is like a computer, accurately recording events as they actually occurred," and 41% believed that "... early memories, even from the first year of life, are accurately stored and retrievable." Both of these beliefs are incorrect (see the section on the reconstructive nature of memory in Chapter 4).

Because memory is not like a video recorder, witnesses enter an interview situation with limited memorial information about a target event. Consequently, it is understandable why interview data is usu-ally incomplete. Interviewers, no matter how well trained, cannot recover information that has not been stored in memory. Furthermore, some relevant information may be suppressed or not reported by an interviewee, either because it is too embarrassing to describe or because it is or was assumed to be unimportant (Koehnken, 1995).

Every interview is a social situation that depends upon the interper-sonal behaviour of the interviewer and interviewee. The physical set-ting, the personal and psychological state of each participant, the interviewee's comprehension of the interviewer's instructions and set of questions, verbal and nonverbal communications, and general inter-viewer behaviour in eliciting and responding to witness statements all determine the quality and quantity of interviewee reports. Interview-ers must be able to monitor and adjust their conversational styles as a function of the emotionality of the situation and changing perceptions of the interpersonal relationship (Shepherd, 1995). Moreover, not all interviewees are adults with normal ranges of intellectual capacity. When respondents have limited linguistic abilities and restricted vocabulary, as in the case of young children (Steward, Bussey, Good-man, & Saywitz, 1993; Yuille, Hunter, Joffe, & Zaparniuk, 1993) and persons with communicative disabilities or developmental handicaps (Bull, 1995; Perlman, Ericson, Esses, & Isaacs, 1994), interviewers must be knowledgeable and able to properly adjust and accommodate to these demands.

Weaknesses or inadequacies in interview data also occur because of the limited cognitive resources of the interviewer and his or her selective attention, cognitive filters, motivations, and so forth. In addition to attentional and memory overload, interviewers must adhere to general interviewing guidelines, generate specific interview strategies, construct and cover the list of topics that must be investigated, process verbal and non-verbal behaviours, and pursue follow-up questions. Finally, interviewers must at some time produce a written report, which itself is subject to general forgetting, selectivity of information, and confirmation biases.

Police Interviews

The quality of police interviews should not be taken for granted. Maxwell McLean, a police inspector with the Yorkshire Police in the United Kingdom, states that the core skill of any policing task is the ability to effectively manage conversation in a diversity of situations and with people who vary in their ability and willingness to communicate. Police are perceived to be experts (Yarmey, 1986), but how good are they, really, in this fundamental skill? Although there are few field studies to answer this question, McLean (1995) collected data that bears directly on the issue. Sixteen randomly obtained tape-recorded conversations between police officers and witnesses were compared with the quality of the police written statements of these same conversations. The analysis of this data revealed the following observations:

1 Nearly 50% of the questions asked of witnesses were leading or suggestible. A leading question is obviously problematic as it suggests by its form or content what the answer should be, leads the witness to the preferred answer, or indicates the examiner's point of view (Cahill & Mingay, 1986). Another 19% of the questions were closed ended (Yes/No). Yes/No type questions are considered unreliable because highly compliant individuals will often agree with the questioner's point of view and answer without any explanation. The danger of such questioning is that witnesses experience social pressure to live up to the expectations of the officer. Furthermore, witnesses' compliance or agreement to closed ended questions modifies their subsequent memory and recall of these events. Answers that

may have been given with uncertainty may soon become fact and held with high confidence, especially when they are seen to please the officer. When police questioned suspects, as opposed to witnesses, however, McLean found that significantly fewer counter-productive questions were used. This finding suggests that witnesses, in contrast to suspects, are much more likely to be led.

2 McLean suggested that in an effective interview 20–30% of the talking time should be taken by the officer, with 70–80% reserved for the interviewee. This study showed a 50–50 split between the officers and witness interviewees, and between officers and suspects, in shared talking time. Its findings are indicative of a highly controlled, directive style of interviewing with little listening and too much talking by police.

3 Police officers often tended to interrupt and change topics during conversation. This obstructive conversational style minimizes the depth and meaningfulness of potential responses. McLean found little evidence of probing questions.

4 McLean found that the officers' written reports of the conversation tended to be highly edited with omissions of relevant information. They also contained inclusions of contrary facts. On average, over the 16 real-life tape-recorded interviews, 14 items of relevant information provided by the witnesses were not written down. On four occasions, officers recorded facts that contradicted what the witness reported.

5 All 16 statements were signed by each of the respective witnesses as a true record of their testimony.

McLean states that his research findings "represent an accurate and true reflection of interview styles in general" (p. 121). What can be done to minimize these obvious limitations? A first step, according to McLean, is to have police audio- or videotape the entire conversation between officers and witnesses. Second, the training of police officers must be improved through the use of scientifically based interview procedures. In the next section we examine some of the investigative techniques presently employed by the police.

Memory Enhancement Techniques

The Standard Interview used by the police and other legal professionals asks witnesses to describe, in their own words, what they observed (free narration), after which they are asked specific questions to elicit additional details about the incident. Unfortunately, there is little standardization in this generic procedure. Police officers differ widely in interview procedure styles and skills. Some officers use rapid-fire questions, with frequent interruptions, whereas others use more structured interview procedures (Fisher, Geiselman, & Raymond, 1987; Memon, Wark, Holley, Bull, & Koehnken, 1997). Idiosyncratic interview techniques acquired from "practical experience," however, may do little to assist the interviewee to improve his or her memory.

Several years ago, Malpass and Devine (1981) demonstrated that eyewitness identification can be facilitated through the use of the Guided Memory Technique. In order to enhance recall, witnesses are instructed to mentally reinstate the original context of the critical event and to visualize both themselves and others present, what each of them did, where they stood, and so on. Witnesses are asked to form a mental image of the target person, to get a picture of his or her appearance, and then judge whether or not the target looks pleasant, honest, and so forth. Utilizing this procedure, the interviewee is guided through each step of an incident, noting his or her corresponding emotional reactions at the time. This technique, in contrast to a Standard Interview, has been found to significantly increase the accuracy of eyewitness identifications of the target person (Malpass & Devine, 1981).

In the mid-1980s, Ron Fisher and Ed Geiselman developed the Cognitive Interview (CI) (Geiselman, Fisher, Firstenberg, Hutton, Sullivan, Avetissian, & Prosk, 1984). Their specific goal was to provide police officers with a questioning technique based upon proven scientific principles of memory storage and retrieval. Because the CI depends upon the cooperation of the witness, the procedure is not appropriate where the interviewee is a suspect. The original CI employs four retrieval mnemonics designed to improve recall. First, interviewees are asked to mentally reconstruct the physical and personal contexts that existed at the time of the incident, to visualize the surroundings, to re-experience their emotions, and to remember what they were thinking at the time. The second mnemonic requires the interviewee to recall the event in a number of temporal orders or from different starting points, such as in reverse order, or from the middle, or from the point that was most memorable, moving forwards and backwards in time. Third, interviewees are prompted to report everything that may be related to the event, including partial or incomplete details that may not seem to be relevant. Fourth, interviewees are asked to recall the event from a variety of perspectives and locations, such as viewing and thinking about the event from the position of one of the key persons who was present. This last mnemonic, however, has recently been criticized because of the possibility that it may mislead witnesses and produce fabricated details (Boon & Noon, 1994). Empirical examination of the CI involving filmed crimes witnessed by undergraduate students, with trained and experienced police officers acting as interviewers, has revealed that the CI produces 35% more correct information than does a standard police interview, without increased errors or intrusions of false details (Geiselman, Fisher, MacKinnon, & Holland, 1985).

Over the years the original technique has been revised and developed into what is now called the Enhanced Cognitive Interview (Fisher & Geiselman, 1992). Care and attention is given to social psychological components of communication, such as rapport building and interviewer social skills. A genuine attempt is made to make the interview situation supportive, friendly, and interesting. In addition to the use of retrieval mnemonics, the role of the interviewer is to be a facilitator, assisting the witness in his or her retrieval of the information. The interviewee, not the interviewer, is in control of the interview. Thus, instead of having a list of predetermined questions, the interviewer is expected to be flexible. Questions are guided by the retrieval process of the witness and are compatible with the interviewee's train of thought. Free narration is not to be interrupted, and pauses in conversation are considered to be appropriate. Open-ended questions that allow the witness to develop and elaborate upon answers are encouraged. Interviewees are reminded of the need for detailed information and all details, regardless of their supposed triviality, are encouraged to be reported.

Table 3.1 presents a summary of the various techniques used in the Cognitive Interview, the Enhanced Cognitive Interview, and the Standard Interview (Memon, Wark, Holley, Bull, & Koehnken, 1996). Note how the interviewer using the Cognitive Interview and the Enhanced Cognitive Interview, as opposed to the Standard Interview, attempts to help the interviewee recall as much information as possible.

The original version of the CI and the Enhanced CI, in contrast to the Standard Interview, elicit significantly more accurate and complete information with no demonstrable increase in errors or plausible guesses (Appavoo & Gwynn, 1996; Memon & Bull, 1991). Of importance is the fact that tests of the Enhanced CI have been shown to generate even more information than the original CI (Fisher, 1995). No

TABLE 3.1
Components of the Cognitive Interview, Enhanced Cognitive Interview, and Standard Interview

	Cognitive Interview	Enhanced Cognitive Interview	Standard Interview
Rapport and transfer control	X	X	
Context reinstatement	X	X	
Report everything	X	X	
Free Recall (FR)	X	X	X
Ask who/what, when/how, and where			X
"Unusual technique"			X
Activate/probe images	X	X	
Change perspective	X	X	
Witness compatible questioning		X	
Reverse order	X	X	

SOURCE: Adapted from Memon et al. (1996)

significant differences in accuracy rates have been found between the original CI and the Enhanced CI, however (Koehnken, 1995).

In spite of the obvious forensic advantages of the CI and the Enhanced CI over the Standard Interview, studies show that the police officers in Britain (Boon & Noon, 1994; Longford, 1996) and Canada (Turtle, 1995) are reluctant to use the mnemonic components of the CI because they do not have the time, training, and resources to adequately incorporate these components (Clifford & Memon, in press; Croft, 1995; Kebbell, Milne, & Wagstaff, 1999). It is possible, however, that the gains made by the CI are not totally dependent on the mnemonic components. Contemporary research is focused on the theoretical question of what actually underlies the advantage of the CI (Kebbell & Wagstaff, 1996; Memon & Stevenage, 1996a, 1996b). Is it the use of the so-called cognitive retrieval mnemonic aids or the interview structure that promotes an increase in recalled information? If, as some research suggests (e.g., Kebbell & Wagstaff, 1996; Memon, 1998; Memon & Yarmey, 1999; but see also Koehnken, Thurer, & Zorberbier, 1994), the Structured Interview, which emphasizes the social psychological components of communication, yields equivalent levels of performance to the CI, then it may alleviate some of the practical problems associated with the use of the CI in forensic situations.

FORENSIC INTERVIEWS OF CHILDREN

Until very recently, courtroom testimony of children was usually ruled inadmissible. Children were, at one time, called "the most dangerous of all witnesses" (Whipple, 1911, p. 308). Another early researcher stated that "[t]hose who are in the habit of living with children do not attach the least value to their testimony because children cannot observe and because their suggestibility is inexhaustible" (Varendonck, 1911, p. 27). Young children were believed to lack credibility and were considered unreliable witnesses because it was assumed that they could not understand complex events, could not differentiate fantasy from reality, were inherently suggestible, and had limited capacity to remember what they had observed (see Ceci & Bruck, 1995; R.C.L. Lindsay, Ross, Lea, & Carr, 1995; Luus, Wells, & Turtle, 1995). These assumptions have been attacked by contemporary scientific research and our views of children's cognitive capacities have changed considerably over the last two decades.

Although children do make errors, are susceptible to suggestive questioning, lie in court, and confuse what they imagine with what they experience, so too do adults (Goodman & Bottoms, 1993). Research has demonstrated that 3-year-old and 6-year-old children's memory for salient, personally experienced events can be surprisingly good, even after a 3-week delay in testing (Ornstein, Gordon, & Larus, 1992). Children's free recall is generally correct, although it is less complete than that of adults. Whereas older children (5- and 6-year-olds) are more accurate than younger children (3- and 4-year-olds), children as young as 3 years of age can accurately recall trauma (Jones & Krugman, 1986). Since children can also report what the interviewer wants to hear, and later be certain about events that never happened (e.g., Ceci & Bruck, 1993; Lindsay, Johnson, & Kwon, 1991), however, the key issue is one of children's suggestibility.

Whether or not children are to be believed in a forensic setting is highly dependant upon the way in which they have been interviewed. Forensic interviews of children, particularly in the investigation of child sexual abuse, can contaminate a child's report and lead to a miscarriage of justice. At the present time, there are no behavioural indicators or syndromes diagnostic of sexual abuse. With the possible exception of overtly sexualized behaviour, most of the symptoms shown in sexually abused children are also present in child clinical samples in general (Beitchman, Zucker, Hood, daCosta, & Akman, 1991).

A number of researchers have made recommendations on how children are best interviewed in forensic situations (e.g., Bull, 1992, 1998; Jones & McQuiston, 1988; Lamb, Hershkowitz, Sternberg, Boat, & Everson, 1996; Yuille, Hunter, Joffe, & Zaparniuk, 1993). Because younger and older children may not spontaneously use retrieval strategies to facilitate recall, interviewers must provide the conditions that reliably support the most complete and accurate accounts of past experiences (Pipe, 1996). It is suggested that interviews be divided into separate phases: (1) rapport building, (2) free recall, (3) general questions, and (4) closure. Yuille et al. (1993), in their Step-Wise Interview method, recommend that each phase of the interview should logically lead from general to specific questions in a series of planned steps. Following the rapport building stage, a child is first asked to provide two descriptions of familiar past events, such as a school trip or a recent birthday. These preliminary questions provide some insight into how much information can be expected from the child. Next, the child is reminded about the importance of telling the truth. He or she is then encouraged to describe what happened in a totally free and open-ended narrative manner. Following this, general but non-leading questions are used to prompt recall. The child is asked to elaborate on details that he or she already recalled. And finally, for some children, it may be necessary to introduce interview aids, such as line drawings and dolls, in order to overcome language handicaps or emotional difficulties. The use of anatomically detailed dolls, however, is seen only as a last resort, and only after the child has disclosed sexual abuse (Yuille, 1988). Because of a lack of uniform standards for conducting interviews with dolls, their usefulness is very problematic. The purpose of the Step-Wise Interview is to maximize both the accuracy of recall and the integrity of the investigative interview without contaminating the evidence that has been gathered.

There are at least two other techniques available for interviewing children. Using a technique called narrative elaboration (Saywitz, 1995), children are instructed to describe the event in terms of five categories: participants, setting, actions, conversation/affect, and consequences. Another technique developed by Poole and D.S. Lindsay (1995) reported an increase in correct information without a coincident increase in errors when they prompted recall by asking children to report how things looked and what they heard (i.e., sensory cues).

Central to all of these recommended techniques for interviewing children is a strong warning to avoid leading or suggestive questions. For example, in a series of studies completed by Ceci and colleagues (described in Ceci, Crossman, Gilstrap, & Scullin, 1998), 3- to 4-year-olds and 5- to 6-year-olds were instructed to "think really hard" about four complex events (e.g., going to the hospital for stitches, getting a finger caught in a mousetrap) and to report if each event really happened (the children were told that some events had happened and that some had not). Parents confirmed that two events had not happened and that two events had happened. The children "thought hard" about the four events on nine different occasions, each separated by approximately one week. By the tenth interview about one-third of the children in each age group reported that non-events had occurred. Moreover, the children described the non-events in such a way that professionals in psychology, law enforcement, psychiatry, and social work could not discriminate reports of real events from reports of non-events. The reports of non-events contained rich detail, internal consistency, low-frequency actions, and emotional markers.

The effect of pretrial suggestive and coercive questioning was, arguably, the most important issue in the largely successful appeal in *R. v. Sterling* (1995). Sterling was convicted of eight counts of sexual offences involving six children (age 7- to 12-years at trial) who, at the time of the alleged offence, were in the care of his mother. The catalyst for this investigation was the statement of a $2\frac{1}{2}$-year-old child. She explained to her mother that the red and broken skin on her "bottom" occurred when "Ravis" (the accused's name was Travis) and "uncle" poked her with a pink rope. Consequently, several children in the care of the Sterlings were interviewed by police, professional therapists, and medical practitioners. Multiple interviews were deemed "necessary" because the children "were unwilling to disclose everything at once" (p. 516). For some children, therapy was initiated. This included play therapy, during which the Sterlings were always depicted as bad people, and disclosure sessions that presented highly suggestive questions such as "Who were you abused by?" The police investigators offered rewards (e.g., to see the police dog) to children for disclosing details of the "abuse" and the children were complimented for their bravery in disclosing details of the abuse. Eventually, reports of bizarre sexual abuse acts were "disclosed," such as having been stripped naked and placed in a cage suspended from the ceiling, having a vibrator and an axe handle thrust into the child's penis and being forced to watch the mutilation of animals and humans.

Sterling claimed that sexual abuse had not occurred and that the allegations were a consequence of aggressive and suggestive pretrial questioning. Of course, we cannot know with absolute certainty whether or not this defence is a complete and accurate explanation for the allegations. We can say that children, sometimes, will report that entire events occurred that were only suggested to have happened. It is also possible that "something" had occurred in the Sterling home and the aggressive, repeated, and suggestive pretrial questioning led children to report suggested and erroneous events that built upon some core of historical truth (see Leichtman & Ceci, 1995). Concern with pretrial suggestive and coercive questioning led the Saskatchewan Court of Appeal to quash six of the seven guilty verdicts in the Sterling case and to enter acquittals on those charges. The court of appeal's conclusion reflects the results of the above research: "... use of coercive or highly suggestive interrogation techniques can create a serious and significant risk that the interrogation will distort the child's recollection of events, thereby undermining the reliability of the statements and subsequent testimony concerning such events" (p. 555).

There are of course other factors to consider in conducting investigative interviews with children. The general tone of the interview has been shown to moderate the suggestibility effect. Goodman and Clarke-Stewart (1991) reported that, in response to suggestive questions, 3-year-olds gave twice as many incorrect answers to a neutral interviewer (distant, gave no feedback, and did not smile) than to the positive interviewer (smiled, was supportive, and provided noncontingent feedback). The tone of the interview did not effect the responses of 6-year-olds to the questions. In *R. v. Sterling* (1995), the court of appeal considered the suggestive and coercive tone of the interviews and acknowledged the testimony of expert psychologists who pointed to potential problems with the lack of rapport-building in the interviews. Unfortunately, weak interviewing procedures are not atypical. According to analyses of interviews with children by "professional" interviewers in the United States, Walker and Hunt (1998) found that there was a complete lack of rapport-building in 40% of the interviews. Similarly, often there was an appalling lack of consideration of the child's more limited linguistic abilities in the questions used by interviewers: multiple questions were often embedded within a "single" question and the level of "legalese" could easily confound an adult (Carter, Bottoms, & Levine, 1996; Walker & Hunt, 1998; Walker, 1997; see Brennan & Brennan, 1988, for instances within Australian courtrooms).

Another factor that moderates the suggestibility effect is stereotyping. When children are presented with stereotypical information consistent with prior suggestions, the impact of the misinformation increases substantially. For example, Leichtman and Ceci (1995) told some preschoolers that a man was bumbling and clumsy and later incorrectly suggested to the children that he had ripped a book and soiled a teddy bear during a recent visit. Other children were given no stereotype information, but were simply presented with suggestions that the man had done these things. During the final memory interview, 11% of the preschoolers in the suggestions-only condition insisted that the man had soiled a teddy bear and ripped a book. In contrast, about twice as many (21%) of the children in the stereotype and suggestions condition insisted that he had done these things.

In addition to eliciting incorrect information, the introduction of stereotypic information influences children's interpretation of ambiguous actions. In a study by Clarke-Stewart, Thompson, and Lepore (1989, cited in Goodman & Clarke-Stewart, 1991), 5- and 6-year-olds were visited in a waiting room by a janitor who performed several "cleaning" actions on a doll. The actions were ambiguous enough to fit either a cleaning or a playing function (e.g., splashing water on the doll's face). One hour later, an interviewer questioned the children about the janitor's actions, using either an incriminating or a neutral interviewing style. In the incriminating condition, if the child did not agree that the janitor played with the doll, the interviewer became progressively more incriminating (e.g., "I think he was really playing with the doll because he is not a very good worker"). At the end of the interview the children were asked direct questions about what the janitor was doing with the doll. Children in the neutral interviewing condition almost never reported that the janitor played with the doll. Conversely, 90% of the children in the incriminating interview condition answered at least some of the direct questions incorrectly. That is, their answers were consistent with the janitor having played with the doll. In *R. v. Sterling* (1995), the accused was described as a "bad person" during some therapy sessions. This was also noted by the court of appeal in its reasons for overturning most of the convictions.

It is evident that investigative interviews of children should be videotaped, if for no other reason than to provide a means whereby the procedures and information obtained during the interview can be exactly corroborated (Myers, 1993). Given the information derived from the scientific literature, it is obvious what procedures and techniques interviewers should follow (see, for example, Murray & Gough, 1991; White & Quinn, 1988). In contrast, as shown in Box 3.1, there are a number of common errors and faulty suggestions to be avoided. Use

Box 3.1

Faulty and Dangerous Strategies for Interviewers of Children Suspected of Sexual Abuse

1 Have your agenda set and know the answer you want before you begin the interview. The interview can then confirm your hypothesis.

2 Subtly and repeatedly influence the child with leading gestures and leading questions in order to get him or her to agree to your beliefs about what happened. If this fails, do not minimize the benefits of a threatening and suggestible atmosphere. Consistent pressure and outright coaching may be necessary to assist the child's recollections that the suspect committed these abusive acts.

3 Reinforce with praise or favours selected answers given by the child.

4 Tell the child how brave she or he is, how proud Mommy or Daddy will be, and how much better he or she will feel if the child tells about the scary secrets and bad things the suspect did.

5 Encourage the child to answer each question even if he or she does not know the answer. Do not accept "don't know" answers. Repeat your questions and give repeated examples of the abusive acts until the child agrees they occurred.

6 Ignore or disconfirm any answers that do not fit your hypotheses, especially "No" type answers that merely indicate that the child is in denial.

7 If the child does not answer your questions, read the child stories with abusive themes and introduce puppets and anatomically detailed dolls in a pretend game. Give the "bad" doll the name of the perpetrator, and encourage the child to fantasize about what happened in his or her story.

8 Don't worry about inconsistent answers. Repeat the interviews until you get agreement.

9 In order to minimize the child's trauma, on-the-spot therapy involving practices such as dream interpretation and empowerment training may be necessary.

10 Regardless of the professional obligation to keep proper records, do not videotape or audiotape the interview because such recordings can only be used against you if the case goes to court.

of one or more of these faulty applications will probably ensure that the child questioned will not provide forensically useful information.

Because it is unlikely that interviewers deliberately mislead children, why do well-intentioned examiners use such faulty procedures? According to Benedek and Schetky (1987) interviewers may simply misinterpret a child's statements. The possibility of widespread child sexual abuse may also create a state of general hysteria, which is encouraged by the media. Finally, general incompetence, if not malicious motives, may be present. The pernicious consequences of such activities, however, are that a guilty suspect may go undetected, an innocent suspect may be falsely accused, and the child (and family) may not receive appropriate therapy and resolution.

Statement Validity Assessment

A persistent concern of police and the courts is the judgment of credibility of children's statements. Research on deception demonstrates that there is no consistent, fail-safe set of behavioural signs that reflect either honesty or deceit (Ekman & O'Sullivan, 1989). A technique first developed in Europe (see Trankell, 1972; Undeutsch, 1982, 1989), however, shows some promise in allowing discrimination between truthful and fabricated statements from children allegedly involved in sexual abuse. The technique, referred to as Statement Validity Assessment (SVA), involves three major components (Raskin & Esplin, 1991). First, an open-ended investigative interview, which is either tape-recorded or videotaped, is conducted with the child as soon as possible after the abuse has been disclosed. The interview is then transcribed for the second stage, the Criteria-Based Content Analysis (CBCA). In this stage a systematic analysis is made of the child's statements judged against a set of 19 reality criteria (see Lamb, Sternberg, Esplin, Hershkowitz, Orbach, & Hovav, 1997; Stellar & Boychuk, 1992). For example, the child's statement, taken as a whole, is examined for its logical structure, for unstructured production, quantity of details, contextual embedding, descriptions of interactions, reproduction of conversation, and so on. A trained evaluator examines the statements and judges the presence or absence of each criteria using 3-point scales where 0 is allocated if the criterion is absent, 1 is assigned if the criterion is present, and 2 is awarded if the criterion is strongly present. The third stage involves a Validity Checklist (Stellar & Boychuk, 1992). The evaluator integrates the information derived from the CBCA and the investigative interview and asks further questions regarding the assessment. An analysis is made of: (1) the psychological characteristics of the child, such as whether the child's use of language and sexual knowledge was appropriate for a person of his or her age; (2) the interviewer's style or manner in conducting the interview; (3) motivations behind the disclosure and reporting of the incident; and (4) investigative questions, such as whether the described incident was unrealistic and whether responses are inconsistent with other statements or other evidence. Following this review, the evaluator draws a conclusion about the probable validity of the complainant's statements (Vrij & Akehurst, 1998).

The theoretical basis for this technique asserts that truthful accounts based on memory of sexual abuse will differ significantly and noticeably from false accounts in content and quality. Accuracy rates in experimental studies testing CBCA range between 55 and 85% (Vrij & Akehurst, 1998). Although this technique has great potential for the courts, CBCA needs more research demonstrating the adequacy of its empirical foundations (Wells & Loftus, 1991). Furthermore, SVA should be seen only as an aid to gathering evidence for criminal trials, rather than as a method to prove that a child has been truthful or not.

PSYCHOLOGICAL PROFILING

Television viewers of the program *Cracker* are probably familiar with the process of psychological assessment in crime profiling. Cracker is a criminal psychologist regularly called upon to analyse violent crimes of murder and sexual assault from a psychological perspective. The goal of Cracker and real-life profilers is to provide the police with a personality composite, behavioural tendencies, and demographic factors of the unknown offender(s).

Psychological profiles of criminal suspects have been a focus of interest of the FBI's Behavioral Science Unit and other police forces since the 1970s (McCann, 1992). Because of the extensive research base available, psychological criminal profiling is most useful for crimes in which there is evidence of offender psychopathology, such as sadistic torture, ritualistic crimes, acting out of fantasy, and so on (Pinizzotto, 1984; Pinizzotto & Finkel, 1990). The FBI has conducted extensive interviews of violent, incarcerated criminals, which reveal how victims are typically selected and approached, the criminals' reactions to their crimes, personality factors, family and demographic characteristics. Profiling has also been used to identify likely drug couriers, hijackers, and illegal aliens (Monahan & Walker, 1990). The danger of psychological profiling in such instances, however, is that it may lead to the possibility of police harassment on the basis of imprecise stereotypes of what criminals look like (*United States v. Sokolow*, 1989; Yarmey, 1993).

Psychological profiling depends, first of all, on good crime scene examination, collection of investigative information on the victim, including his or her travels prior to the crime, autopsy and forensic laboratory reports, police reports, witness statements, and photographs of the victim and crime scene. Using this assimilated data, the crime is reconstructed and a series of hypotheses about the behaviour of the victim and perpetrator, method of victim selection, modus operandi or sequence of the crime, possible motives, and typology of the crime are generated and analysed for their consistency (Holmes, 1989). Following this analysis, a hypothetical profile outlining the perpetrator's demographic, physical, and personality characteristics, as well as his or her behavioural tendencies, is constructed. The emerging profile is constantly tested against the crime scene analysis and any new evidence that is found. The final profile usually contains the following information about the suspect: demographic characteristics, including age range, sex, race, general employment, marital status, socioeconomic level, and educational background; estimates of intellectual capacity; legal and arrest history; military history; family background; habits and social interests; residence in relation to the crime scene; colour, age, and type of vehicle used by the victim; personality traits including psychopathology; degree of sexual maturity; how and when he/she is likely to act out again; and suggested interrogation techniques. The profile is then given to investigators and used to direct and limit their investigation and to interview suspects (Douglas, Ressler, Burgess, & Hartman, 1986).

Another tool recently added to the criminal profiling approach is geographic profiling which was developed by Detective Inspector Kim Rossmo Ph.D. of the Vancouver Police (Rossmo, 1995, 1996). Geographic profiling consists of a computer analysis of the spatial patterns involved in the hunting behaviour used by the serial criminal to search and attack victims, and the geographical sites connected to the crime series. Crime sites are superimposed on a grid of a city and the repeated distances between all crime sites and given grid points are analysed to determine the probability that a given grid point represents a perpetrator's home base. The combined results of psychological and geographical profiles provides the police with another investigative aid that may assist in locating suspects.

Three major criticisms have been levied against profiling. First, the descriptions generated are vague and general and fit many persons in everyday life. Profiling does not identify a specific suspect. Thus, profiles have little predictive value because too many people match the composite. Second, there is little theoretical foundation for the generated demographic and personality factors. In the absence of a sound theoretical basis, it is difficult to integrate facts from different perspectives and impossible to generate predictions about future behaviours of the offender(s). Third, profiling may lead to a narrowing of investigative perspective such that other valid information and other general hypotheses inconsistent with the profile are discounted and, of course, not tested.

In spite of its appeal, psychological profiling is more of an art, developed through experience, than a science (McCann, 1992). Laboratory research suggests that experienced criminal profilers can produce more useful and valid descriptions of possible suspects than experienced crime investigators for certain kinds of cases (Pinizzotto & Finkel, 1990). Nevertheless, the use of psychological profiles can only supplement rather than replace good investigative practices in the real world.

INTERROGATION OF SUSPECTS

When police have a suspect in custody, they have only partial or selective understanding about what took place during the commission of a crime. Physical evidence, such as fingerprints or DNA evidence, or circumstantial evidence that can tie the suspect to the crime may be lacking. In such conditions, the interrogation of a suspect is of primary importance because it may provide the inculpatory or incriminating evidence that can lead to a finding of guilt by a judge or jury (Vrij, 1998a). Also, interrogation may reveal information about accomplices, the recovery of stolen property, and clearance of other unsolved cases. The primary goal of interrogation, however, is to secure a confession. Because the police define themselves as professionals, their goal is to provide the prosecution with the strongest possible case if it goes to trial, and confessions usually lead to findings of guilt or a guilty plea (McConville & Baldwin, 1982). Police may also want to obtain a confession for more psychological reasons, that is, because it convinces them that the accused is guilty and legitimizes their, as well as society's, expectations of good police work. More than 80% of criminal cases are estimated to be solved by confessions (Zimbardo, 1967). According to legal scholars, nothing has more impact on the trier of fact (i.e., the trial judge or jurors) during the course of a trial than the revelation that the defendant had confessed earlier to the crime (Wigmore, 1970). Similarly, McCormick (1972) has stated that, "the introduction of a confession makes the other aspects of a trial in court superfluous" (p. 316).

Why would a suspect confess? Confession can lead to a number of psychological, religious, and moral benefits for the suspect, as well as legal considerations that otherwise may not be available. Confessions that are voluntarily given are readily admitted as evidence by the court. In contrast, involuntary confessions, if believed to be untrustworthy or illegally obtained, are likely to be excluded. Most lay persons have difficulty appreciating why a supposedly uncoerced suspect would confess to a crime he or she had not committed. But false confessions can and do occur and probably result from a combination of factors related to interrogative influence and psychological vulnerability (Gudjonsson, 1992). False confessions produce a high proportion of wrongful imprisonments, second only to mistaken eyewitness identification (Brandon & Davies, 1973).

It was common practice in England, up to at least the middle of the seventeenth century, to extract confessions through physical torture and intimidation. Evidence gathered in this manner was accepted by the courts, without hesitation (Wigmore, 1970). Even well into the twentieth century, the use of physical coercion, promises, threats, or what is commonly called the "third degree" was approved police practice in North America. Regular viewers of police television shows, such as *NYPD Blue*, may believe that the police still routinely use such practices. Picture the overweight, balding, anti-hero Detective Andy Sipowicz sitting at a desk in the interrogation room. Sipowicz quietly simmers, barely able to control his temper, and finally, giving in to his rage, explodes. He grabs the suspect by his jacket, picks him up out of his chair and throws him against the wall. "... Listen, dirt bag. You wanna spill now before I really lose my temper?" The suspect slowly slides to the floor, begins to sob, and confesses. Justice prevails for another week in the land of television.

Is this behaviour typical of police practice today? Hardly. Contemporary police are much more sophisticated and knowledgeable about how the courts would treat any evidence derived in such a manner. Police are trained in and can use far more superior psychologically based techniques to break down suspects' resistance to tell the truth (e.g., Inbau, Reid, & Buckley, 1986; Kalbfleisch, 1994; Macdonald &

Michaud, 1987). Psychological interrogation, however, introduces other problems for the criminal justice system. Psychological interrogation techniques such as the use of intimidation, bluff, gentle prods, silence, simulated friendship, sympathy, concern, self-disclosure, appeals to religion and God, the presentation of trickery and false evidence, and so forth can be helpful in resolving criminal cases via eliciting true confessions (Leo, 1992), but they can also induce false confessions, and, hence, false convictions.

In contemporary policing the "soft-sell"or confidence game involving "the systematic use of deception, manipulation, and the betrayal of trust in the process of eliciting a suspect's confession" is common (Leo, 1996, p. 3). Being interrogated has been compared by some observers, particularly by some defence attorneys, to brainwashing. Suspects are placed in isolated and unfamiliar surroundings. The environment is manipulated to create the impression that the police are omniscient and omnipotent (see the studies on obedience to authority by Milgram, 1963). Isolation and the experience of extreme stress can produce heightened suggestibility and loss of contact with reality, which will influence the validity of a confession (Gudjonsson, 1992). Suspects are disarmed and lulled into a false sense of security by offers of sympathy, moral justification, face-saving excuses, rationalizations, blame-the-victim accusations, and down-playing of the seriousness of the crime (Kassin, 1997). Take a moment to go back and read again the interrogation of nurse Gita Proudman by Toronto police. Most of the manipulative factors used to induce a confession addressed by Kassin (1997) and others are found in this police interrogation.

Whereas trial judges can readily understand and discount confessions obtained through obvious coercion or explicit threats and promises, false confessions given voluntarily may not be so easily recognized when they are induced by implicit threats and soft-sell procedures (Kassin, 1997). Furthermore, there is no empirical support for the hypothesis that innocent people can be differentiated from guilty suspects on the basis of their anxiety, fear, and verbal and non-verbal behaviours (Zuckerman, DePaulo, & Rosenthal, 1981). What is the worth of a confession given by someone who is intellectually handicapped, and/or extremely frightened, anxious, hyper-suggestible and overly compliant? Probably very little.

Types of False Confession

Conditions that promote a genuine confession by suspects appear to be similar to those that result in a false confession by innocent suspects (Gudjonsson & MacKeith, 1982). Three types of false confessions have been described by Kassin and Wrightsman (1985): voluntary false confessions, coerced-compliant false confessions, and coerced-internalized false confessions.

Voluntary False Confessions

People may voluntarily confess to a crime they did not commit for a number of reasons. For instance, they may offer a confession to protect someone else, in return for a reward or favour from the guilty person or his or her friends, to avoid injury from the guilty person or his or her friends, to provide an alibi for a more serious crime they actually did commit, or for pathological reasons involving attention, fame, acceptance, self-recognition, or self-punishment.

Coerced-compliant False Confessions

Confessions of this sort are the result of intense interrogation pressure. For example, an individual may comply with an interrogator and go along with the suggestion that he or she is guilty in order to avoid or escape from an extremely negative situation, or to gain a promised reward. The suspect, in this case, knowingly complies for instrumental reasons, that is, for short-term rewards and/or long-term benefits. Suspects who are predisposed to being influenced by others may be highly vulnerable to such pressures, even though they know they did nothing wrong (Gudjonsson, 1992; O'Mahony, 1992).

Coerced-internalized False Confessions

This type of confession typically is most difficult to accept and believe by lay persons. That is, people who are anxious, confused and tired, and repeatedly interrogated with highly suggestive questions may come to falsely recall and confess to a crime that they did not commit. This phenomenon involves the creation of false memories (D.S. Lindsay & Read, 1995; Read, 1996). In both laboratory and field experiments people have created false memories of being lost (Loftus, 1993), of getting fingers caught in mousetraps (Ceci & Bruck, 1995), of spilling punchbowls at wedding receptions (Hyman, Husband, & Billings, 1995), of being seriously harmed by another child, of being the victim of a serious animal attack, and of being victimized by a serious out-door accident (Porter, Yuille, & Lehman, 1999). This last experiment is particularly important because it empirically demonstrates that false memories can be created for highly emotional and potentially trau-matic incidents. Perhaps the most vivid real-life example of false memories involves the Paul Ingram case in the state of Washington (Ofshe, 1992; Ofshe & Watters, 1994). Ingram, a police officer and a highly religious man, was interviewed 23 times over a 5-month period. After being hypnotized, provided with details of his alleged rapes and satanic cult crimes (including the slaughter of newborn babies), instructed about the phenomenon of memory repression for sex crimes, and urged by the minister of his church to confess, Ingram recalled his crimes. Richard Ofshe, a social psychologist called by the prosecutor to evaluate the state's evidence, concluded that Ingram had been "brainwashed" and had constructed false memories. To support his conclusion, Ofshe concocted a phony crime, which Ingram at first denied committing. The next day, Ingram fully confessed to and dis-played confabulated memories of the cooked-up crime.

Kassin (1997) emphasizes that coerced-internalized confessions have two factors in common: (a) a vulnerable suspect, that is, a person whose memory is malleable because of "his or her youth, interpersonal trust, naivete, suggestibility, lack of intelligence, stress, fatigue, alcohol, or drug use and (b) the presentation of false evidence such as rigged polygraph or forensic tests ... statements supposedly made by an accomplice, or a staged eyewitness identification as a way to convince the beleaguered suspect that he or she is guilty" (p. 227). If a suspect confesses and a guilty plea is entered, trial judges rarely learn about the procedures employed to arrive at this decision. Furthermore, it is doubtful that professional criminals who have experienced this type of questioning would be as susceptible to such tactics as would the first-time offender or an innocent party.

Box 3.2

Police Investigation and the Wrongful Conviction of Guy Paul Morin

On October 3, 1984, 9-year-old Christine Jessop was abducted from her home in Queensville, Ontario. Her body was found three months later 50 km away in a farmer's field. Guy Paul Morin, her next-door neighbour, was arrested for the sex slaying of Christine on 22 April 1985. Morin was tried and acquitted in 1986, but the verdict was overturned on appeal. Morin was found guilty at his 1992 retrial, but, after serving several years in prison, was declared innocent in 1995 based on DNA testing of the semen found on Christine's underwear. In 1997 a public inquiry was held into the wrongful conviction of Morin. The inquiry has raised serious questions about the lengths to which both the police and Crown will go in order to obtain a conviction.

The inquiry revealed that the police bungled and probably tampered with evidence, and that the Ontario Centre of Forensic Sciences did extremely shoddy work. The former head of the Durham Regional Police force's identification bureau in charge of physical evidence was charged with perjury and obstructing justice. The charges, which involved falsifying a police notebook and planting a cigarette butt at the murder scene, were stayed in 1990 for health reasons. It is claimed that the officer disposed of a cigarette butt found at the murder scene when it was learned that Morin was a non-smoker. When the defence learned of these events, the officer apparently substituted a fresh butt for the missing one. Analysis by the Forensic Science Centre of a small number of clothing fibres found in Morin's car appeared to match six of seven fibres on Christine's sweater. This match appeared to be damming evidence of guilt. The fibres, however, somehow became contaminated with a large number of foreign fibres. Furthermore, expert evidence revealed that because the Jessops were neighbours of the Morins, it would be expected that a small number of fibres would be matched by chance alone. Finally, when the Centre learned about the contamination, they neglected to report it to the police or the Crown attorney's office.

What factors led to Morin becoming a suspect? Several of Morin's responses to an interrogation on the day of his arrest were interpreted as being highly suspicious. Morin told police that little girls started out innocent, but grow up to be corrupted. During the interrogation Morin used an odd phrase – "Otherwise, I'm innocent" – in his reports. Morin stated that Christine's body was found at the end of a road known as "The Ravenshoe." Police only later discovered that this road was a well-known route. And finally, police found it suspicious that Morin predicted that the activity at the Jessop's residence on the day of the abduction involved Christine. The police and the Crown inferred that Morin signalled his guilt when he failed to help search for the missing child, did not attend her funeral, and neglected to offer condolences to the family. Yet the prosecutor acknowledged that if Morin had assisted in the search for Christine, this could have been interpreted as the act of a guilty man.

The police and prosecutor also placed great faith in the claims of two ("unsavoury") jailhouse informants who stated that Morin had confessed to them. Ambiguous statements made by Morin to fellow inmates and an undercover police officer were interpreted as consistent with a confession.

According to Ken Jessop (brother of Christine), Janet Jessop (Christine's mother) and a former best friend of 9-year-old Christine, the police used psychological coercion to shape and bolster their testimony. Morin had an alibi that was confirmed by his parents, that is, he could not have been home from work before the time Ken and Janet Jessop discovered Christine was missing. The fact that Morin kept modifying his estimates of his arrival home after repeated police questioning, however, convinced them that he was a liar. The Jessops claimed that they felt pressured by police to falsify their evidence in order to convict Morin. The Jessops told the inquiry that detectives persistently bullied them to modify their time estimations, thereby effectively destroying Morin's alibi.

The police denied using pressure tactics and denied the accusation that they had described Morin as a sick, deviant person and a demon who had killed other young women. One officer stated that he was merely being compassionate to Janet Jessop when he suggested that a faulty clock may have misled the Jessops into giving an inaccurate original time estimation. The police felt that their suggestion about a faulty clock was merely a face-saving gesture that would nullify any assertion that Janet Jessop could be labelled a bad mother for having left Christine alone and unprotected. The police also felt that the faulty clock theory would allow the Jessops to tell the truth without being humiliated.

The former best friend of Christine, also nine years old at the time of the murder, stated that the police pressured her to inflate her testimony about Morin's behaviour. She admitted lying when she said he behaved strangely, was obsessed, and had a sinister interest in Christine prior to her abduction. She also admitted lying about a backyard chat with Morin in which she described his knuckles turning white as he gripped some hedge clippers while talking with Christine. She told the inquiry that the police embellished their notes of each account she gave in their repeated interviews, and later would confuse her with statements they composed, but claimed were her own descriptions. She testified that the police used a friendly approach to keep her on side and told her that they had further evidence that proved without doubt that Morin was the killer of Christine Jessop.

The above information suggests that the police and the Crown probably had a confirmation bias in their treatment of Morin. That is, they decided he was guilty and, on many levels, sought evidence to confirm their conclusion rather than finding evidence to test their suspicions.

On April 9, 1998 inquiry commissioner Fred Kaufman, a former judge of Quebec Court of Appeal, released his report on the Morin inquiry. Included in his observations and recommendations were the following points: tunnel vision pervaded proceedings in the most staggering proportions; although police authorities and the Crown attorney made many flagrant mistakes, they did not act out of animosity or a desire to convict an innocent man; the police drew completely unwarranted conclusions from innocuous comments made to them by Mr Morin; the police conducted improper, suggestive interviews with witnesses; the Crown attorney failed to take proper measures to preserve the integrity of the interviewing process; evidence that did not corroborate investigative theories went unrecorded by police; evidence gathered by police became a self-fulfilling prophecy in order to confirm their original hypotheses; memories of some police and civilian witnesses improved over each passing year; the police relied too heavily on polygraph evidence to clear suspects; legal authorities tailored the suspect profile to fit Morin, thus ensuring he would not get a fair trial; adults should be present during police interviews of children; and police lacked up-to-date knowledge about proper interview/investigative techniques and cognitive processes.

LIE DETECTION

In addition to judging the truth of witness and suspect statements in violent crimes and traffic accidents, legal authorities must deal with lies and deception by persons involved in a variety of non-violent crimes such as business fraud (Price, 1991), gambling scams (Ortiz, 1984), spying (Cooper & Redlinger, 1988; Girodo, 1983), and so forth. How effective are the police and non-police in detecting deception?

Polygraph

Over 70 years ago, psychologists showed that truthfulness is more dependent on situational contexts than on a general trait of honesty (Hartshorne & May, 1928). Lying has been defined by Ekman (1985) as occurring when "one person intends to mislead another, doing so deliberately, without prior notification of this purpose, and without having been explicitly asked to do so" (p. 28). When people lie, verbal and non-verbal bodily or behavioural signs may be used as cues-to-deceit (Ekman, 1985). Without a doubt the most familiar technique for judging deception is the polygraph. The fact that people may act and feel different when they are lying than when they are truthful is not a recent discovery. Indeed, the use of external devices to detect lies is quite old. For example, ancient Chinese civilizations reportedly used rice to obtain confessions. Based on the knowledge that people who are anxious experience physiological changes including dryness of the mouth and difficulty in swallowing, authorities would tell suspects that they were to swallow a handful of dry rice. They were instructed that the innocent have nothing to fear, but the guilty person would feel anxious about his or her misdeeds and would have difficulty in consuming the rice. The fact that innocent persons may be falsely accused because they feel anxious in this situation and would have difficulty swallowing apparently did not occur to the interrogators (Eysenck, 1964).

Use of the modern lie detector, or polygraph, operates in a similar theoretical fashion. The polygraph measures subtle changes in heart rate, blood pressure, respiration, and perspiration (Bradley & Rettinger, 1992). These physiological changes are predominantly associated with the autonomic nervous system. Changes in these functions typically are associated with stress. It is assumed that a guilty person, unlike an innocent person, will show involuntary alarm reactions in response to certain critical questions involving his or her participation in a crime. Responses to the questions are recorded by the polygraph through a series of channels displayed as continuous line drawings or graphs of the different measures. These graphs allow for an assessment of the individual's physiological reactions to critical questions, in contrast to control questions. It is important to note that there is no specific lie response that can be detected in these graphs. That is, lies themselves are not detected, instead, physiological responses, like changes in blood pressure, are displayed and subjected to interpretation.

A number of factors other than activation of the autonomic nervous system are involved in the final display of emotional arousal. Selective attention, stimulus quality, habituation, memory, mental associations, internal conflict, intelligence, and individual differences, to name but a few, all play some role. Thus, if these associated factors are not properly controlled, the accuracy or validity of the test is doubtful. Furthermore, the polygraph results of selected categories of individuals, such as the medically ill, the debilitated, practised liars, hardened criminals, or the highly anxious and suggestible, may be very deceiving. It is also possible that suspects who are being honest will display relevant physiological changes in their test scores that reflect their belief in what happened, rather than what actually occurred.

Contemporary lie detection primarily follows the control question technique (see, for example, Furedy & Heslegrave, 1991; Iacono, 1995; Raskin, 1989). In phase one, the polygraph examiner takes approximately 30 minutes to one hour to establish rapport with the subject, design the exact questions to be asked, convince the subject that the technique works, and check the operational aspects of the machine. In phase two, which lasts approximately 30 minutes, the individual is asked a series of questions to which he or she responds either "yes" or "no." Two or three of the questions are relevant to the focal issue under consideration (e.g., did you shoot Mr Smith on June 1st?). Control questions are also asked. These questions are designed to evoke as much emotional response to a lie as to a truthful response to a relevant question. For example, if it was learned in phase one that the subject stole some money in the past, the examiner would instruct him or her to lie by answering "no" to the control question, "Did you ever steal some money in your life?" It is assumed that an innocent person will show more emotional reactions to his or her lie on the control questions compared to his or her answers to relevant questions. In contrast, if responses to the relevant questions are greater than those to the control questions, the polygraph examiner interprets the subject to be deceptive (and probably guilty).

The use of the polygraph by the judicial process has its share of critics (e.g., Iacono, 1995; Lykken, 1981; Furedy, 1985, 1989) and advocates (e.g., Barland, 1988; Honts, Kircher, & Raskin, 1995). The major criticisms of polygraphy focus on the nature of the control questions. Do control questions truly have the same emotional impact as relevant questions? Are answers to control questions as important to the subject as his or her answers to relevant questions? Control questions change from test to test and are not standardized in the same way that an intelligence test, for example, is standardized for all examiners and test subjects. Thus, the question can be asked whether or not control questions are equivalent in meaning to the scientific sense of control conditions. Moreover, the method of scoring physiological records of trace drawings is highly subjective and dependent on particular examiners. Finally, training in psychophysiological theory and practice among polygraph examiners is highly variable, with some polygraphers having only a 6-week training course before conducting examinations (Furedy, 1989; see also Honts et al., 1995, for a reply to these criticisms).

Given the above concerns, how accurate is the lie detector? The answer to this question seems to depend on who is asked. According to proponents such as Raskin (1989), the accuracy rate is 90%, or higher. In contrast, opponents, such as Lykken (1981), argue that the accuracy rate is 70%, or lower. A mail survey of members of the Society for Psychophysiological Research (91% responded) and Fellows of the American Psychological Association's Division 1 (General Psychology, 74% responded) revealed that the majority of respondents considered the theoretical foundations of polygraphic lie detection to be unsound, that claims of high validity are suspect, and that the test can be easily beaten by learned countermeasures (Iacono & Lykken, 1997). Most survey participants also felt that the results of polygraph tests should not be admissible into evidence in courts of law. Resolution of this issue, however, is difficult and should depend on scientific investigation rather than merely sampling opinions. Until there is agreement on how data is to be interpreted, this dispute will continue. Also, it is improper to judge the accuracy of polygraphy based solely on experimental studies using undergraduate students in laboratory simulations. The alternative is to conduct field investigations based on actual criminal cases. Yet this procedure is also flawed because, unlike controlled experiments, we do not know with certainty the ground truth against which accuracy can be compared (Iacono, 1995). What is clear is that two kinds of errors can occur in deciding whether a person is truthful or deceptive. False positive errors occur when an innocent person is judged as lying and, consequently, falsely accused. False negative errors occur when a deceitful person is judged as truthful with the consequence of setting the guilty free. False positive errors are considered to be more serious by the justice system. Given that false positive errors are more likely to occur than false negative errors (Horvath, 1977), an innocent person would be ill-advised ever to agree to take a lie detector test.

According to Furedy and Heslegrave (1991), any answer to the question about the accuracy of polygraph detection of deception depends upon multiple factors, including "the skill level of the examiner, the psychological state of the subject, the scoring procedures, the questioning techniques, and the particular physiological variables measured" (p. 170). Quite clearly, the results of a polygraph examination conducted by an inexperienced, poorly trained examiner should not be accepted by law enforcement agencies. In contrast, the results of a polygraph examination from a skilled, experienced polygraph operator should be examined on a case-by-case basis, even if its purpose is simply to exclude suspects rather than to prove guilt.

In 1987, the Supreme Court of Canada concluded that the results of polygraph tests are not admissible as evidence in courts of law. However, the RCMP, provincial, and local police services use polygraph examinations as an investigative tool with the hope that the test will result in a confession. As noted earlier, however, the polygraph can have a confession-inducing function when the police indicate that the polygraph is accurate in detecting deception, that the individual has nothing to worry about if he or she is innocent, and that, while he or she does not have to take the test, participation will probably remove the individual from being seen as a suspect. The participant is usually not aware that following the test he or she may be subjected to intensive, continued questioning. Being softened up by the "good cop/bad cop" routine of interrogation, being isolated and left alone for extended periods of time prior to or following the test can heighten anxiety and suggestibility. Some individuals may feel morally responsible for what happened, although not factually or legally guilty, and this may result in physiological changes that are detected by the polygraph. If a suspect is told that the machine indicated that he or she had lied, or that the results were completely unambiguous, a confession may be induced owing to the suspect's faith in the test to distinguish lies from truth. Polygraph machines, of course, never say anything; it is the polygraph operator's interpretations that are presented as conclusive (see Furedy & Liss, 1986).

Voice Analysis

Similar to the theory of polygraphy, mechanical analysis of voice-stress has been used by police to draw causal connections between lying and emotional arousal through changes in speaking style and microtremors in the voice mechanism (Bartol & Bartol, 1994). The scientific validity of spectrogram or "voiceprint" analysis to differentiate between deception and honesty has yet to be established and has received limited acceptance by the law (Annon, 1988; Hollien, 1990).

Verbal and Non-verbal Behaviour

Another approach for detecting deception is through the analysis of verbal and non-verbal behaviour. Lying usually involves effort to conceal emotions. Detection of lying depends upon recognizing signs of emotional falsifications that "leak" through into limb movements or facial expressions (DePaulo & Kirkendol, 1989; Ekman, 1985; Ekman & Friesen, 1972). Experimental research indicates that decreases in limb movements (hand, arm, foot, and leg) are indicative of deception (Vrij, 1998b). Facial characteristics such as gaze aversion and smiling may or may not be related to deception. Ekman (1985) suggests that facial clues may indicate deception when the emotions expressed do not fit the context. Nevertheless, the presence of behavioural signs of lying does not necessarily mean a person is deceptive (Zuckerman & Driver, 1985). Research also indicates that people's beliefs, including both police officers and lay people, regarding valid non-verbal clues to deception are inconsistent with the research findings (Akehurst, Koehnken, Vrij, & Bull, 1996). This discrepancy may explain the relatively poor performance of judges in the detection of deception (Zuckerman, DePaulo, & Rosenthal, 1981; Zuckerman & Driver, 1985).

The typical experiment on the detection of deception involves participants viewing or listening to videotapes or audiotapes of speakers and then judging whether each of the presented persons is telling the truth or lying. These decisions are then correlated with the actual cues present or not present in each tape. Accuracy scores usually range between 45–60% when an accuracy score of 50% is expected by chance alone (Vrij & Graham, 1997). Individuals' confidence in their ability to detect lies has not been shown to be related to their actual skills in detecting lies (DePaulo & Pfeifer, 1986; Ekman & O'Sullivan, 1991). Judges are better on average in detecting deceit from audiotapes than from videotapes with the sound turned off (see Miller & Stiff, 1993). When speakers present verbal and non-verbal signs of emotionality that are inconsistent with each other, non-verbal behaviour is usually the more accurate indicator of the speaker's true thoughts and feelings. Non-verbal behaviour yields more accurate readings into emotional states because individuals are less able to control non-verbal leakages than verbal communication (Ekman, 1985). When speakers do not have an opportunity to fully plan their speech, deception is correlated with more speech disturbances, slower rate of speech, higher pitched voice, and longer latency periods before giving answers to questions (Goldman-Eisler, 1968; Zuckerman & Driver, 1985). Porter and Yuille (1996) have also found that deceitful reports are less detailed and coherent than true reports, and deceptive individuals are less likely than truth-sayers to admit forgetting aspects of a target event.

Given the above discussion it could be concluded that the complexity of factors involved in the detection of deception is so great that the task is more or less equivalent to guessing. Research findings reveal, however, large individual differences among observers in detecting lies (Ekman & O'Sullivan, 1991). It is possible for some people, in particular persons from certain occupational groups, such as police and psychologists with a special interest in deception, to be highly accurate in their judgments about lying and truthfulness (Ekman, O'Sullivan, & Frank, 1999). These authors caution, however, that "[i]t is unlikely that judging deception from demeanor will ever be sufficiently accurate to be admissible in the courtroom. Nevertheless, judgements based on demeanor can be quite useful in pointing to the need to develop more information" (p. 265).

SUMMARY

The purpose of the investigative process is to obtain evidence that can substantiate an allegation; this evidence must be gathered by the police in such a manner that it does not bring the administration of justice into disrepute. Investigative interviews are thus expected to be neutral and objective and facts are to be gathered and tested against alternative hypotheses. Investigation should not be used merely to confirm predetermined assumptions. One of the fundamental attributes necessary for effective policing is good communication skills, since faulty management of a police interview can lead to improper evidence.

Several memory enhancement techniques can also facilitate the investigative process.

The primary goal of any police interrogation is to obtain a confession. Confessions involuntarily given are not admitted as evidence by the court, but untrustworthy or illegally obtained confessions may not easily be detected when psychologically based interrogation techniques have been employed. In order to ascertain truth, police may also rely on the polygraph. The validity of polygraph evidence is highly controversial among forensic researchers and while the results may be used for investigative purposes, they are not admissible into evidence in Canadian courts of law.

QUESTIONS FOR DISCUSSION

1. The investigative practices of police can raise serious ethical concerns. What moral and ethical dilemmas, apart from legal issues, do police face in questioning suspects? Can deception in police interrogation ever be justified by some supposed wider benefits to society?
2. Some of the investigative techniques used by mental health practitioners and police officers interfere with, rather than facilitate, reliable fact-finding. How can forensic psychology assist the courts in determining what is reliable and what is not?
3. Should allegations of sexual abuse coming from children generally be believed? In what ways can biased and unprofessional methods of interviewing contribute to the distortion of children's reports and memory of sexual abuse ?
4. According to the Charter of Rights and Freedoms ... "Everyone has the right to life, liberty and security of the person and the right not to be deprived thereof except in accordance with the principles of fundamental justice." Some law enforcement officers feel that the Charter gives too many breaks to criminals. Why should confessions obtained through "soft-sell" psychological procedures not be admissible in court? How should the courts interpret "coercion"?

RECOMMENDED READING

Ben-Shaker, G., & Furedy, J.J. (1991). *Theories and applications in the detection of deception.* New York: Springer-Verlag.
Bottoms, B.L., & Goodman, G.S. (Eds.). (1996). *International perspectives on child*

abuse and children's testimony: Psychological research and law. Thousand Oaks, CA: Sage.

Brewer, N., & Wilson, C. (Eds.). (1995). Psychology and policing. Hillsdale, NJ: Lawrence Erlbaum Associates.

Fisher, R.P. (1995). Interviewing victims and witnesses of crime. Psychology, Public Policy, and Law, 1, 732–764.

4. Memory in Legal Contexts: Remembering Events, Circumstances, and People

J. Don Read, Deborah Connolly, and John W. Turtle

One evening in November 1995 a man was assaulted in a Fort St John, B.C. bar's well-lit entrance and, as a result of his injuries, died. A sober female escort at the bar, S.L., subsequently reported to the police that she had witnessed the brutal attack. She claimed to have observed two assailants and later identified two police suspects as the perpetrators: Randy Ballantyne and Leo McGuiness. S.L. did not, however, identify the other eventual accused, Roman Ballantyne, Randy's brother. Other patrons also reported that they had seen three young men together in and around the bar prior to the beating. Weeks later, a second woman, J.A., came forward and reported to the police that she too had seen the attack. This was after the accused had been arrested and there had been local publicity surrounding the case. J.A. indicated that she had been drinking in the bar and had seen a portion of the attack and a third assailant. She provided general descriptions of the three assailants and, based upon these descriptions, the police inserted Roman Ballantyne's photograph among seven head-and-shoulder photos of young males from the local constabulary's "mug shot" file. From this display, J. A., while under the influence of alcohol, chose two members as being one of the assailants. One of these choices was Roman Ballantyne. The police, dissatisfied with her lack of certainty, subsequently constructed a second photospread that included the identical photo of Roman Ballantyne, as well as the photos of another seven previously non-presented

Authors' note: Preparation of this chapter was supported by research funding to the first author from the National Sciences and Engineering Research Council of Canada and the Alberta Law Foundation. The authors are also grateful to the Department of Psychology and the Faculty of Law at the University of Victoria for providing an ideal environment in which to complete the research and writing of the chapter. Finally, the authors thank Charles Lugosi for his accurate recollections regarding the *R. v. McGuiness, et al.* (1997) investigation.

foils or distracters. At this test, administered 4 months later, the witness selected one person, and that person was not Roman Ballantyne. Since this witness could potentially provide strong evidence against their suspect, but the police did not have an unambiguous identification from her, J.A. was asked to undergo hypnosis, to be followed by a third identification attempt. Three months later under hypnosis she described the assault and the attacker. During the hypnotic state the hypnotist provided what is called a post-hypnotic suggestion: *an instruction that, following hypnosis, she would likely be able to see the event more clearly. Soon after hypnosis a third photospread of photos of seven new foils and the same previously presented photograph of Roman Ballantyne was presented to her. On this occasion, she chose Ballantyne with high certainty. The Crown charged Roman Ballantyne with second degree murder and proceeded to trial (R. v. McGuiness, Ballantyne and Ballantyne, 1997).*

Resolution of the *McGuiness et al.* case and others like it hinge primarily upon eyewitness testimony; that is, a recollection of the actions, circumstances, and the people involved by witnesses and/or victims of a crime. Unfortunately, in crimes involving a single witness or victim (the focus of this chapter) additional material or circumstantial corroborating evidence is often not available. As a result, during the investigation, pretrial inquiries, and the subsequent trial, considerable emphasis and reliance will be placed upon the recollections given by a victim or witness. Normally, the triers of fact (judge or jury) would be expected to weigh the quality of such testimony in the context (inter alia) of the opportunities for observation and correct identification; the trial judge, however, also evaluates the eyewitness evidence and may direct the jury to acquit if its quality is deemed to be below a threshold for conviction and there is an absence of other credible evidence (e.g., *Mezzo v. The Queen*, 1986). Concern about the reliability of eyewitness testimony, in particular eyewitness identification of a police suspect, has been expressed in many legal rulings in Canada (e.g., *R. v. Atfield*, 1983; *R. v. Sophonow*, 1986), the United States (*Neil v. Biggers*, 1972), and the United Kingdom (e.g., *R. v. Turnbull et al.*, 1976), as well as reports commissioned on the topic in both the United Kingdom (Devlin Report, 1976) and Canada (Brooks, 1983).

Scientific research on eyewitness testimony draws heavily upon the fields of cognitive psychology and social psychology. The former concerns the topics of perception, short- and long-term memory, thinking, and decision making, as reflected in both verbal and nonverbal behaviour. The latter, on the other hand, studies the influence of social variables upon human behaviour, including cognitive behaviours like decision making, as well as group pressure and conformity, self-presentation, attitudes, and beliefs. Taken together, these fields provide insight into numerous variables related to eyewitness testimony; for example, the effects of witness age, time delay between observation and report, repeated and suggestive questioning procedures, mental rehearsal, social pressure and motivation to conform, drugs and alcohol, and identification decisions, to name but a few.

A useful distinction frequently made by researchers in the area of eyewitness testimony is that between "system" and "estimator" variables (Wells, 1978, 1993). System variables are those features of the legal system that can alter the reliability of eyewitness testimony; for example, the kinds of identification procedures used. Because these features can be controlled, changes can be made to them to improve the reliability of eyewitness evidence. In contrast, estimator variables refer to the situational and personal characteristics inherent in an event, its witnesses, and its consequences, but over which we have no control and for which we must estimate the magnitude of their effects. For example, a witness's age is known to be related to identification performance, but the age of witnesses cannot be controlled. Similarly, the lighting at the scene of a crime is related to accuracy of descriptive testimony, but its effect upon a single witness can only be estimated.

To understand the impact of variables like these upon memory, data are gathered from a variety of sources, including case files from real crimes and simulations of events under the researchers' control. Such simulations have had an influential history since the turn of the century in Germany (Stern, 1904) and the United States (Munsterburg, 1908); many are scientific experiments that take place within a laboratory, while others are staged in field settings such as shopping malls and city streets. It should be obvious that researchers cannot truly mimic or simulate real crimes because of the obvious physical dangers they may present and the ethical transgressions (against the participants) they would require. As a result, researchers and triers of fact (who may learn of this research through the provision of expert testimony at trial) are often concerned with the generality of the experimental results; specifically, they ask whether we can safely apply the results of experimental simulations to real-world crimes. There has been no shortage of debate on this issue, with advocates on both sides (see, for example, Leippe, 1995; Loftus, 1986; McCloskey & Egeth, 1983; Read & Bruce, 1984; Wells, 1993; Yuille & Wells, 1991).

The information in this chapter should help you to decide the extent to which basic and applied research in this area can contribute to our understanding of the factors that influence memory for the brief observations of people and contexts that often characterize criminal events. Of course, we have time to examine only a subset of eyewitness topics; the interested reader is referred to other books, articles, and chapters listed at the end of the chapter. As Wells and Turtle (1987) point out, Canadian cases and researchers in Canada have frequently provided significant contributions to this body of knowledge.

BASICS OF MEMORY AND ITS IMPLICATIONS FOR EYEWITNESS TESTIMONY

To have confidence in the outcome of a trial we must first have confidence in the quality of the evidence presented. For this reason, most judicial systems have developed rules of evidence, whereby the admissibility of information is assessed based in part on its reliability (c.f. Paciocco & Steusser, 1996). How reliable or accurate is eyewitness testimony? Is a witness's age related to the reliability of his or her testimony? Is the confidence with which a victim asserts something a good indicator of the assertion's accuracy?

To answer these kinds of questions we need to consider some basic assumptions about memory processing. We must first assume that an event was indeed witnessed and perceived as to its meaning (called the encoding stage), and then processed in such a way (the storage stage) as to make it available later through one of several kinds of memory tests (the retrieval stage). It is important that we recognize the possibility of several stages or types of processing of event information because the greater the number of stages and cognitive activities involved, the greater the opportunities for error or low reliability.

Second, we must also recognize that memory is an active process rather than a thing or a place, like a library bookshelf, where information is located. We never actually *see* anyone's memories; instead, what we call memory, like a description or narrative of an event, is a product of a sequence of unobservable cognitive activities. This process is presumed to be reconstructive because it is impossible for anyone to have encoded and stored *all* of the details of any event. Therefore, the rememberer must necessarily reconstruct as complete a description as possible based upon less than 100% of the information. Compounding the problem of imperfect access to all of the event information is the fact that the testimony of an eyewitness, as finally offered at trial, includes information from his or her prior reports, so much so that one can ask whether trial testimony reflects memory for the event or memory for all of the prior accounts of the event.

Whether testimony reflects pure memory or something else was an important issue in *R. v. Keegstra* (1992). In this case, the Alberta Court of Queen's Bench ruled in favour of allowing written classroom notes taken by students years earlier to be admitted in place of the students' own personal memories *if* the students themselves could not remember the statements made by the accused, their teacher, Keegstra. By doing so, the court was agreeing to admit as evidence testimony known as "past recollection recorded," that is, information removed from the witness's current memory of an event and different from a currently available memory record that has merely been "refreshed" by reviewing a set of notes. This distinction is critical to legal procedure because, for evidence of the past recollection recorded variety, cross-examination can only be made on the document itself (how and where it was made, for example), not on the witness's recollective experience for the events described in the document. As we shall see what witnesses recount in court may also include information from a variety of other sources (e.g., media, investigative personnel, other witnesses) that may not easily be differentiated from their own experiences.

We also need to recognize that the use of different kinds of memory tests at the retrieval stage can influence how well something is remembered. For example, most students have experienced the different demands placed upon them by an essay (recall memory) as compared to a multiple-choice (recognition memory) examination. Discrepancies between the results of different types of memory tests can be even greater in forensic situations that involve eyewitness testimony. A witness's initial testimony is usually gained through a police interview in which the event details are described as completely as possible and specific questions are answered. We know, however, that witnesses provide different kinds of information about a detail in response to open-ended ("Tell me everything that happened") versus closed-ended ("Was he carrying a gun or a knife?") question formats (e.g., Fisher, 1995). Additionally, how the interview is conducted and the expertise of the interviewer also play important roles in the completeness and accuracy of the testimony given, particularly by young children (see Chapter 3). Another kind of retrieval test, the identification of a suspect, may occur through a single-picture "showup," a photo-spread of people's pictures from police files, or a live line-up that includes the actual suspect and several foils or distracters. The manner in which the individuals in these three kinds of tests are presented can influence the ease (and speed) with which witnesses correctly (or incorrectly) identify someone as the criminal (e.g., R.C.L. Lindsay & Wells, 1985; Sporer, 1994; Wells, 1993).

Ultimately, a selection by the triers of fact of one of the memory recollections offered (e.g., by the various witnesses and/or the accused, if any recollection is selected at all) is necessarily only an inference about historical accuracy, because these descriptions were limited to the results of memory processes on a particular day, in a particular context, and offered with a specific motivation.

WHAT THE LEGAL SYSTEM EXPECTS FROM US

The legal system's formalized procedures incorporate many implicit or tacit beliefs about the reliability of human memory. For example, eyewitness testimony is admissible as direct evidence in court, as opposed to, say, fingerprints, which are indirect or circumstantial evidence. Such status implies a high standard of reliability inherent in eyewitness testimony. Furthermore, many legal procedures are not precluded because of substantial delays between crime and legal course of action, despite research data – discussed below – suggesting that the passage of time and intervening events can lead to decrements in memory. Finally, jurors and judges are typically expected to remember the minutiae of evidence presented in complex trials without benefit of written notes or tape recordings (see Johnson, 1993; Wells, 1995; and Chapter 6 for discussion of this issue). While there are policy and practical reasons for the acceptance of such memory-based evidence, its acceptance is also based in part upon our underlying confidence in the reliability of human memory.

The amount of time a witness has to observe a perpetrator and the length of time between the witness's observations and the identification of a police suspect (called the retention interval) are two common factors to consider in crimes involving eyewitness testimony. These two temporal variables were included in a U.S. Supreme Court decision on the validity of eyewitness identifications (*Neil v. Biggers*, 1972).

That court, and many others since that time in the United States, the United Kingdom, and Canada, have consistently stated that increasing the duration of both variables has opposite effects upon reliability, such that longer observation times will increase reliability, while longer retention intervals will decrease it (e.g., Devlin, 1976; *R. v. Duhamel*, 1981; *R. v. Sophonow*, 1986; *R. v. Turnbull et al.*, 1976; Wells & Murray, 1983).

Let us focus on the retention interval for a moment and assume that equivalent opportunities for observation existed in a crime witnessed by three people. Would you predict that three separate witnesses might recall the details of a specific event equally well after 1 day, 6 months, or 15 years? Perhaps your answer is that it would likely depend upon the type and duration of the events, because some events may be well retained in memory regardless of the length of the retention interval. Indeed, many people report emotionally charged events from their lives for which this seems to be true. We say "seems to be true" because memories for the details and the meaning of most events are virtually never tested for accuracy, certainly not through rigorous direct and cross-examination in a court of law. When memories have been tested, some analyses of reports by witnesses to actual crimes have indeed found high levels of accuracy following delays of up to 6 months or more (Tollestrup, Turtle & Yuille, 1994; Yuille & Cutshall, 1986). On the other hand, so-called flashbulb memories of highly significant life events (such as hearing the news of a death of a loved one) have sometimes been shown to contain many significant errors, although held with very high confidence (Lindsay & Read, 1994, 1995; Neisser & Harsch, 1992). Similarly, lengthy observations of others do not guarantee reliable memory. For example, Adolph Beck was mistakenly identified (with high confidence) by a total of 14 witnesses as being an English scam artist who had swindled them of their jewellery and money. Beck had spent substantial periods of time with 'them (Shepherd, Ellis, & Davies, 1982; for additional examples; see Loftus, 1979a, 1986, 1993; Rattner, 1988; Sporer, Köhnken, & Malpass, 1996; Wells, 1995; Wells et al., 1998). In recent years, faulty identifications of a person by one or more eyewitnesses have only come to light because DNA testing of trace evidence has completely exonerated individuals incarcerated for crimes they did not commit (e.g., National Institute of Justice, 1996; Wells et al., 1998). In short, the anticipated general effects of these two variables are seen in research studies, but not always.

Students reading the research literature on eyewitness testimony are sometimes frustrated by a seeming lack of consensus about the effects of specific variables on memory performance. Indeed, survey research by Kassin, Ellsworth, and Smith (1989) has revealed that even the researchers often disagree among themselves. Given the multiplicity of causes for any of our behaviours, perhaps we should not be surprised by the lack of consensus about the effects of a specific variable, because those effects may often be masked by the actions of many other variables. In contrast, some variables do appear to have consistent effects upon eyewitness performance; for example, the centrality of the information to be recalled. Details that could be considered central to the perceiver's interpretation of the event (e.g., a weapon or a hold-up note) are more likely to be remembered correctly than are other, more peripheral details (e.g., the time on a wall clock). In keeping with this general finding, Read, Yuille, and Tollestrup (1992) found that research participants who viewed a simulated theft of money made more accurate identifications of an individual who interrupted the simulated crime than of another person seen just prior to it. It is also the case that, in general, the greater the emotionality of an event, the more likely it is that the witness's attention will be directed to the event's central information, although a number of factors can moderate the magnitude of this result (c.f. Christianson, 1992; Yuille & Daylen, 1998). One of the goals of eyewitness testimony research is to isolate these kinds of estimator variables so that we can better understand their consequences for the reliability of testimony – are their relationships positive or negative across some, most, or all people? A goal of understanding the effects of system variables, in turn, is to provide the impetus for changes to the legal system such that better decisions are made (Wells & Seelau, 1995).

ELICITING INFORMATION FROM VICTIMS AND WITNESSES

"Data! Data! Data!," exclaimed Sherlock Holmes, "I can't make bricks without clay!" The famous detective's declaration to his companion Watson emphasizes the importance of information to the criminal investigation process. Information is the raw material with which a case is built, and it is an investigator's ability to gather it correctly, to use it to create leads, and to admit it as evidence at trial which often determines his or her success at proving "whodunit." In this section we examine the eyewitness recall and recognition processes on which some of the police investigation procedures discussed in Chapter 3 are based.

Verbal Recall Testimony

In the initial stages of an investigation the information obtained is likely to come from the witnesses' responses to "W5" interview-type questions – "Where and when did the event occur?," "Why were you there?," "Who did you see?," and "What did the weapon look like?" – asked by a variety of professionals in the justice system, such as police investigators, social workers, lawyers, and insurance investigators, among others. We can trace the origins of the current state-of-the-art investigative interviewing procedures discussed in Chapter 3 to essentially three research areas: hypnosis, encoding specificity, and misleading post-event information.

Hypnotism (and other "altered states" such as religious trances) has fascinated humans throughout history, but scholars point to the seventeenth and eighteenth centuries as the origin of systematic study of the phenomenon (see Boring, 1950; Fancher, 1996 for complete historical reviews). Of the historical names associated with what we now call hypnosis, Franz Mesmer is the most familiar (hence, our modern use of the term "mesmerized"). Mesmer was convinced that, just as Newton's gravity explained the magnetic-like attraction between objects, *animal magnetism* explained his ability to influence other people's behaviour from a distance. It was *de rigueur* to have Mr Mesmer attend one's high-society party in 1780s Paris and perform his "animal magnetism" in the parlour for guests' amusement. He apparently cured minor ills by waving and laying on his hands to induce a sleeplike trance on those willing to participate. No one disputed the apparent effects of his procedure, but scientific investigations placed the explanation of those effects in the minds of Mesmer's subjects rather than in the hypothetical mechanism of animal magnetism. As a result of this debunking, hypnosis took an almost century-long hiatus from public and scholarly attention until Braid in England, and Charcot in France, revived interest in it in the late nineteenth century. There is still debate as to whether hypnosis represents a distinct state of consciousness, just as sleep is distinct from wakefulness, or if it merely occupies an extreme position along some continuum of suggestibility. Either way, hypnosis is a well-established technique, widely used around the world in therapeutic settings and, most relevant for our discussion, to enhance the recall of witnesses in police investigations.

"Hypnotically refreshed testimony" is the optimistic term sometimes used to describe the fact that people often recall more accurate details about an event under hypnosis than they do in a "normal" state. Its use, however, is based on some implicit and unsupported beliefs about memory: first, that hypnosis allows access to memories beyond what normal retrieval processes can provide and, second, that memories are retained permanently in the brain uncontaminated by additional experiences, thoughts, and possibly misleading information. In reality, hypnosis incorporates a combination of normal retrieval processes (e.g., relaxation instructions, increased motivation, expectancy effects, mental reinstatement of context, and cognitive focusing) that, when taken together, can assist a witness to recall additional material beyond the first police interview, some of which is incorrect (see e.g., Yuille & McEwan, 1985).

The primary arguments against the use of hypnosis in forensic settings arise from demonstrations that hypnotized witnesses more frequently recall incorrect or false (fabricated) information during hypnosis than do non-hypnotized participants, that this incorrect information can be accompanied by high confidence, and that such information can be implanted through suggestive questioning techniques – a negative triple-whammy against the use of hypnosis (see Fisher, 1995 for a review). We have special cause for concern, therefore, when testimony arises through hypnosis, because it has been demonstrated numerous times that the confidence expressed by a witness is the single best predictor of jurors' evaluations of a witness's credibility (Leippe, 1994, 1995; R.C.L. Lindsay, 1994a; Penrod & Cutler, 1995; Wells, 1993).

As a consequence of the vulnerability of reports gained through hypnosis, such testimony, or evidence gained as a result of it, is not usually admissible in Canadian courts of law. On occasion, however, it *can* be admitted, as it was from three witnesses to a shooting in *R. v. Gauld* (1994). The court in this case concluded that the hypnotic procedure followed appropriately cautious guidelines and was unlikely to have tainted the witnesses' testimony. On the other hand, in a bizarre case involving allegations of satanic abuse, the accused's testimony, amounting to a confession of sexual abuse against his daughter, served, ironically, as the basis for his acquittal (*R. v. O.(H. W.)*, 1997). This acquittal followed the court's conclusion that, because the accused's testimony arose from something akin to self-induced hypnosis, it was unlikely to be reliable. So what to do? Is there a way to incorporate the benefits that hypnosis apparently provides without paying the price of the production of erroneous information? As Yarmey points out in Chapter 3, all of these benefits are incorporated in an alternative interviewing technique called the Cognitive Interview and, according to research studies, with few, if any, of the disadvantages of hypnosis (Fisher, 1995; Fisher, McCauley, & Geiselman, 1994).

A second theoretical and empirical foundation for current interviewing techniques is Tulving and Thomson's (1973) concept of encoding specificity, which demonstrates that when the retrieval environment matches the encoding environment recall is improved. That is, to the extent that the cues or features available at encoding (interpreted broadly to mean all information in the external environment, in the materials, and in the internal physiological and/or psychological state of the witness) are present at retrieval, recall will be enhanced because the presence of the cues serves to elicit associated information. Obviously, there can never be a match on all features or cues, but the greater the overlap, the more likely it is that recall will be successful. For example, if you had completed the majority of your learning for a course in a particular home study area, its retrieval will be maximized if you recall the material in this same context or environment. To capitalize on such context effects, eyewitnesses are sometimes returned to the site of the crime and then asked to recall the details of the event. More typically, the context can be mentally reinstated when an interviewer encourages the witness to return mentally to the site, such that cues of the imagined environment serve to elicit details in memory (see Deitze & Thomson, 1993; Malpass, 1996).

Finally, many laboratory studies have demonstrated the malleability of witness memory reports through the use of misleading post-event information. In a typical post-event misinformation study the research participants are shown a target event such as a staged robbery, usually by videotape, or reenactment. This is often followed by the presentation of erroneous information about the target event in an interview, through questions that either explicitly incorporate an incorrect detail (such as "Did the man carrying the hammer run or walk out of the store?" when in fact there was no hammer) or suggest a particular event detail in a more linguistically implicit manner (such as "Did you see *the* hammer?" as compared to "Did you see *a* hammer"). Suggestibility effects occur when misled participants provide different reports than those who received no misleading information (see Weingardt, Toland, & Loftus, 1994 for a review). Misled participants may fail to report target event details, or they may report that details only suggested to have happened really had occurred. It is useful to classify explanations for the effect into three categories: memory impairment (e.g., Loftus, 1979a, 1979b), source misattributions (e.g., D.S. Lindsay, 1994), and misinformation acceptance (e.g., McCloskey & Zaragoza, 1985). Different theoretical arguments surround, respectively, the interpretation of these effects: whether the participants' memories of the event details have truly been changed (new information has displaced the original, correct information), whether the participants are simply confused as to the source of the details they report, or whether the participants have guessed an answer based upon what they heard most recently or what they think the researcher wants to hear.

Concern has been expressed recently that disclosures by clients to their therapists about sexual assaults experienced during childhood may sometimes be reflections of their acceptance of misleading information about abuse. That is, it has been argued that these clients are sometimes misled by their therapists to accept or fabricate false information about their personal histories (Loftus & Ketcham, 1994; Pendergrast, 1995). By this account, the recall of false information is seen as an attempt by the client to please or meet the expectations of the therapist. These claims have been captured in the term "false memory syndrome," a hypothetical condition characterized by the clients' strongly held but false beliefs that they were sexually abused as children and that these experiences had not been recalled by them until they entered therapy to alleviate symptoms of psychological distress, such as depression, substance abuse, and low self-esteem. More recent discussions, however, have emphasized the middle ground in this debate (e.g., D.S. Lindsay & Briere, 1998; Read, 1999). See Box 4.1 for consideration of this issue within the Canadian courts.

Box 4.1

**Recovered Memories of Childhood Sexual Abuse:
Special memory and interviewing problems?**

There is often a substantial delay between an allegation of childhood sexual abuse and the time at which the alleged event actually took place – up to 30 or 40 years in some cases (Bala, 1996; *R. v. Kliman*, 1996, 1998; Read & Connolly, 1999). It should not surprise us that children are generally reluctant to report incidents of such abuse, particularly when the perpetrator is a member of the family.

In terms of the reliability of testimony, however, these very long delays introduce a number of problems, some legal and some psychological.

Courts in the past have been reluctant to entertain allegations of decades-old abuse because of the difficulties inherent in "stale" claims; witnesses may have died, evidence has likely been lost and, as a consequence, the opportunities for the accused to provide a full defence can be limited. In Canada there is no fixed period of time during which charges may be laid for criminal acts. On the other hand, in civil matters statutes of limitations normally exist such that claims for most wrongs and damages must be filed within a limited period of time after an alleged event. Civil action arising from an allegation of childhood sexual abuse, however, can be an exception. In 1992, the Supreme Court of Canada *(M. (K.) v. M. (H)*, 1992) ruled that the period of limitation does not begin until the complainant has become aware of the abuse; that is, the clock does not start running until the point at which the victim has remembered the abuse or has come to understand the damage caused by it. In so saying, the court clearly accepted the view that temporary memory loss is a common outcome of sexual abuse. Leaving aside the court's acceptance of this highly controversial claim (see D.S. Lindsay & Read, 1995; Read & D.S. Lindsay, 1999), the court failed to address the question of whether such newly gained "awareness" is necessarily based upon historical fact.

Considering just the retention-length issue, we saw elsewhere in this chapter that the relationship between the passage of time and memory reliability has consistently been shown to be negative: the longer the interval, the less complete and reliable the recollection. Therefore, a delayed allegation may have questionable reliability simply because of the passage of time. Whether this same relationship necessarily characterizes the recollection of emotional or traumatic incidents has not yet been determined and memory researchers' views differ substantially on this question (e.g., Christianson, 1992; Pipe et al., 1997; Yuille & Daylen, 1998).

Sometimes, however, allegations are not only made some time after the alleged event, but are said to arise from "recovered" memories, with the complainant reporting being unaware of the sexually abusive incident for many years and recalling the event following an extended recollective process (D.S. Lindsay & Read, 1994, 1995; Read & D.S. Lindsay, 1997; Roe & Schwartz, 1996; van der Kolk &

Fisler, 1995). Often, the initial recollection is reported to be sudden and unexpected and may accompany a unique and salient event in one's life (e.g., birth of a baby). And not uncommonly, the initial and subsequent recollections occur within and/or following psychotherapy. For example, a school principal in British Columbia was charged with having sexually assaulted two girls when they had been in his class some 20 years earlier (*R. v. Kliman*, 1996). The two complainants reported that they had had no awareness or recollection of the abuse incidents until 15 years later. Apparently, during psychotherapy, one complainant (D) experienced memory "recovery" of incidents of sexual abuse by the accused, Kliman. The therapist reported the allegations to the authorities, who then spoke to B, a school friend of D, who subsequently also reported sexual abuse experiences by Kliman. At the first of three trials defence counsel argued that they required access to the notes recorded by D's therapist because the recollections may have been created, fabricated, or reconstructed through the therapeutic "interviews" and may have caused the complainant to honestly believe she had been sexually abused when she had not. This defence claim would have the strongest foundation if therapy had been conducted by a suggestive therapist or had employed known suggestive procedures, such as hypnosis, age regression, guided imagery, or "memory work" (for description of suggestive therapies for memory recovery, see D.S. Lindsay & Read, 1994, 1995).

The Supreme Court of Canada (*R. v. O'Connor*, No. 2) ruled in 1995 that access to therapeutic records could be gained only if the defence reasonably demonstrated that the therapy itself may have contributed to the allegations (see Bala, 1996). Normally, a judge first reviews the materials to determine their relevance to the defence. Not surprisingly, access to these records has been opposed by many groups from therapists to feminist action groups (see Brady, 1996; McEvoy, 1995–1996). In *R. v. Kliman* (1996) access to some of the therapeutic material was provided and admitted as evidence in the first trial, at which Kliman was found guilty. Defence subsequently launched a successful appeal on the grounds that an inadequate portion of the material had been provided. In the second trial there was a "hung jury" and a third trial was ordered. The outcome of the final trial (by judge only) was an acquittal for Kliman.

How critical to this judge's decision was the fact that the allegations arose through therapy? According to the judge, not at all. Was the fact that the memories were "recovered" critical to the decision? Again, not at all. Instead, the judge concluded that the complainants' testimony provided the bases for reasonable doubt because of the presence of inconsistencies and low credibility of assertions made by them (*R. v. Kliman*, 1996).

The concepts of "recovered memory," "repression," and "false memory syndrome" have been at the centre of public, legal, and scientific debates in Canada, the United States, and Europe over the past decade and discussed in numerous scientific papers, books, conference presentations, as well as the media (see Read & D.S. Lindsay, 1997). Despite such publicity, it is important to emphasize that, in fact, most cases of delayed allegations of childhood sexual abuse do not involve claims of "memory recovery." Instead, most victims of sexual abuse apparently do remember the abuse at least as well as other autobiographical events of similar age. In a case involving multiple victims of a single perpetrator (*R. v. Kenny*, 1996), there was little evidence that the abuse was ever completely forgotten. Instead, victims often reported that they did not think about the abuse for long periods of time or that they failed to interpret the events as involving sexual abuse.

Further, even in situations where complainants have indicated that they did not remember the events for long periods of time and that they subsequently "recovered" the memory, such recovery, by itself, does not mean the evidence is unreliable. To return to the initial tripartite view of memory processing at the beginning of the chapter, recovered memories are differentiated from continuous memories primarily at the retrieval stage. Given that the retrieval process is necessarily reconstructive, it is reasonable to consider the reliability of recovered memories on a case-by-case basis in terms of (a) the age of the complainant at the time of the alleged events, (b) influences available during their reconstruction, such as suggestiveness of the interviewing and therapeutic techniques, (c) consistency of reports across tellings (if adequately recorded), (d) motivation to recall, and (e) the time elapsed since the alleged events. If none of these factors suggest implausibility of the report, there seems, at this stage, little reason to believe that the previously unrecalled details of an event are necessarily unreliable (D.S. Lindsay & Read, 1995).

Recognition and Person Identification Procedures

Although eyewitness testimony includes a recounting of details of the actions, persons, objects, and environmental features of a crime, a second step is often necessary to link a particular suspect to a crime. To commit a person to trial the Crown must provide evidence of every essential ingredient of the charge, including identity. The usual method of doing so is through an identification test, wherein a suspect is presented to a witness and a decision is made as to whether the suspect is or is not the perpetrator observed by the witness. This test must provide the witness with an opportunity to fairly and unambiguously indicate whether a specific person is familiar to him or her, and whether that familiarity arises from observation of the person at the scene of the crime (Wagenaar & Loftus, 1990; Wells & Seelau, 1995). In so doing, the primary aim is to protect an innocent suspect from being identified as the culprit, while at the same time maximizing the probability of identifying the actual offender.

The preparation of an identification test usually arises from some verbally recalled information provided by a victim or witness. The verbal description can have several functions. It may provide a basis for the construction of an artist's sketch, allow investigators to narrow their search among known possible suspects, or provide the basis for the selection of foils or distracters. If an artist's sketch is developed, its fidelity depends upon several variables, most important of which is the match between a witness's verbal description and the perpetrator's features. Not surprisingly, the skills of the witness in providing a verbal translation of visual features and those of the sketch artist in eliciting useful verbal information are central to the success of this task. Unfortunately, our skills in the former have been shown to be quite limited, so much so that evaluators of the utility of police sketches in investigations have painted a pessimistic picture (e.g., Davies, 1986). With current videotaping technology in place at many potential crime locations (like banks and convenience stores) the presence of a permanent visual record may reduce error in identification decisions. On the other hand, however, new research suggests that we often overestimate our face-recognition abilities in such situations. For example, Kemp, Towell, and Pike (1997) demonstrated the surprising difficulty of matching a photo on an identity card with the live person, and Burton (1997) has shown that even the matching of good quality videotape recording with colour photographs of unfamiliar persons is subject to considerable error. Our point here is that even when courts have access to videotape recordings of a criminal act (as in *R. v. Nikolovski* (1996), where the court, rather than a witness, identified the suspect from a videotape recording) identification of the perpetrator may still be in error.

Most frequently, an identification test is heavily weighted upon facial appearance, but it may include other types of information as well, such as physique and clothing (e.g., R.C.L. Lindsay, Wallbridge, & Drennan, 1987) and voice and movement (Macleod, Frowley, & Shepherd, 1994; Yarmey, 1998). It may include even less information than this; for example, identification from "earwitnesses" by voice alone (see, e.g., Hammersley & Read, 1985; Yarmey, 1995). There is considerable research evidence, much of it related to the earlier concept of encoding specificity, to support the position that the greater the amount of encoding information available to the witness at the time of test, the more reliable the identification (Cutler, Berman, Penrod, & Fisher, 1994; Wells & Seelau, 1995). Therefore, the presentation of a suspect among a number of distracters in a well-constructed and carefully presented *live* line-up would seem to be the ideal approach to maximizing the likelihood of an accurate identification.

In practice, however, live line-ups are used infrequently in Canada and the United States. Their use is limited because of the real inconvenience of constructing an adequate live line-up with unfamiliar distracters (particularly in smaller communities), the empirical equivalence of live and photo line-ups in correct identification decisions, and the rights of the accused to have counsel present at such a line-up (Brooks, 1983; Cutler et al., 1994, R.C.L. Lindsay, 1994b; Wells, 1993, 1995; Wells & Cutler, 1990; Wells, Seelau, Rydell, & Luus, 1994; Tollestrup et al., 1994). Alternatives to live line-ups take several forms, including photospreads of several potential suspects selected from police files, "show-ups" of the suspect's photo alone, and "walk-throughs," wherein a witness is given the opportunity to observe surreptitiously a single police suspect in a natural environment like a store or café. In all cases the central question for the witness becomes, "Do you see the person who committed the crime?"

Once a decision has been made to use an identification test, many options exist as to the manner of its construction and presentation. For example, on what basis should the distracters (or foils) be chosen for inclusion in the line-up or photospread? What safeguards should be in place to prevent leakage of information from the investigating officer who oversees the line-up to the witness? How should the members of a line-up or photospread be presented, simultaneously or sequentially? To examine some of these issues, we will trace the steps in the investigation of the *R. v. McGuiness et al.* case with which we began this chapter. You may want to read over the summary of the case before proceeding further.

From both cognitive and social psychological perspectives there are a number of difficulties with the identification procedures used in the Ballantyne case, many of which may be obvious to students in psychology. First, was the fact that the witness J. A. was inebriated at the time of observation related to the accuracy of her identification? The consumption of alcohol is well known to reduce the encoding of new information (see, e.g., Steele & Josephs, 1990), but its effects may be moderated by the level of physiological arousal. For example, Read et al. (1992) found that following consumption of alcohol, identification accuracy was significantly reduced when anxiety or fear was absent, but there was no reduction when these emotions were present. It appears, at least at moderate doses, that fear served to "sober up" the research participants. Given the witness J. A.'s description of her activities on the evening of the attack, her arousal level was likely low and alcohol probably impaired her encoding abilities. On the other hand, the presentation of the first photospread while she was in an inebriated state may have capitalized on what is known as "state-dependent memory." That is, consistent with the encoding specificity concept, research has demonstrated that recollection of information encoded in one psychological and/or physiological state is best recalled in a similar rather than a dissimilar psychological (e.g., mood) state and physiological (e.g., drug) state (e.g., Eich, McCauley, & Ryan, 1994). Potentially, the similarity in states between encoding and retrieval could have benefitted J. A.'s recall somewhat.

Second, what was the basis of her final "correct" identification? The last photospread followed two observations of Roman Ballantyne's photo in the first two line-ups, but because none of the distracters was repeated across photospreads the witness could have become differentially familiar with Ballantyne's photo and appearance. Did she identify the suspect on the basis of familiarity gained from seeing that particular photograph previously, or on the basis of her recollection of the assault itself, now some 9 months in the past? Eyewitness researchers refer to this phenomenon as unconscious transference, a misidentification error in which an innocent person seen in another context (like a photo) is confused with the perpetrator from the scene of the crime (see Read, 1994; Ross, Ceci, Dunning, & Toglia, 1994). In terms of the post-event misinformation paradigm, these kinds of misidentifications are most likely to arise via memory impairment or errors in source memory (D.S. Lindsay, 1994). Thus, when asked to specify the context or source (episodic information like spatial location and time) of our memories, we do not perform particularly well (Johnson, Hashtroudi, & Lindsay, 1993). In this case, inspection of the preceding photos may well have provided the basis for an error in locating the source of J.A.'s memory because the witness may have believed that she saw the suspect at the scene of the crime when, in fact, her observation was through the photos only.

Third, what factors during the identification process may have influenced this witness's decisions? Of the cognitive factors, we know that the frequency of misidentifications is much greater when line-up photos are presented simultaneously (all at once) than when shown sequentially (one at a time). These so-called false positive errors appear to arise because the witness who views a simultaneous display of several people is more likely to choose on the basis of a relative than an absolute judgment (R.C.L. Lindsay & Wells, 1985; Wells, 1993, 1995). That is, a witness may be inclined to choose the line-up member who looks *most* like the offender, rather than relaying on a more automatic recognition process by which the appearance of a line-up member is visually matched with the information available in memory. Making a relative judgment jeopardizes the logic of a line-up because in every line-up, with or without the perpetrator present, there will always be someone who looks most like the offender to a given witness. In laboratory tests, witnesses who are presented with a perpetrator-absent or blank line-up (consisting of known-innocent foils only) falsely identify someone about 50% of the time, rather than responding with a correct "not in the line-up" response (e.g., R.C.L. Lindsay, 1994b; Read et al., 1992; Wells, 1993). These kinds of errors are made particularly frequently by children; although children are as likely as adults to be correct when shown a perpetrator-present line-up, they are much more likely to mistakenly identify someone from a perpetrator-absent line-up (Goodman, Bottoms, Schwartz-Kenney, & Rudy, 1991).

Another cognitive factor apparent in this case is the potential influence of a confirmatory bias upon the police investigation. Because the police believed their suspect, Roman Ballantyne, was guilty, decisions about the use of multiple line-ups and the manner of their construction were made that likely served to increase the chances of Ballantyne's false identification (c.f., R.C.L. Lindsay, 1994b). Confirmatory biases are well-known and ubiquitous phenomena in human cognition and may contribute to faulty convictions. For example, in the "three Ms" cases of false convictions in Canada, Donald Marshall, David Milgaard, and Guy Paul Morin (respectively, *Marshall v. Nova Scotia (A.G.)* 1989, *Milgaard v. Saskatchewan, 1994,* and *Re Ontario, 1998*), formal inquiries provided description of the confirmatory biases at work within the three police investigations (see Box 3.1 in Chapter 3).

A social factor that may be relevant to the witness's final identification decision in *R. v. McGuiness et al.* involves the feedback that was implicitly provided to J. A. about the lack of "success" of her identification efforts. Not surprisingly, when people are told that their identification choice was in "error," or that other witnesses made a different choice, they are much more likely to change their choices than if they are told that other witnesses' choices matched their own (Luus & Wells, 1994a, 1994b; Wells & Bradfield, 1998). In the recent Wells and Bradfield research, participants who received confirming feedback about their line-up choices also went on to report that, compared to other participants who received no feedback, they were more confident of their choices, they had a better view of the perpetrator for a longer time, he was easier to identify from a line-up, their image of the perpetrator was clearer, and they could, in general, more easily recognize the faces of strangers. Thus, not only may a particular decision be altered by feedback, but simply believing that the correct decision was made can greatly enhance the confidence with which it is subsequently asserted and recollection of the observation itself.

This brings us to the general issue of the relationship between the accuracy of an eyewitness's identification and the confidence with which the identification is made (for reviews, see Penrod & Cutler, 1995; Luus & Wells, 1994a; Read, D.S. Lindsay, & Nicholls, 1998). Substantial controversy has arisen regarding this issue because, despite the public's general expectation that the relationship exists, research has typically obtained evidence of very weak to nonexistent relationships (Read et al., 1998; Sporer, Penrod, Read, & Cutler, 1995). These findings are considered to be counter intuitive and have provided opportunities for expert evidence to be given in Canada and the United States by social and cognitive psychologists (Kassin et al., 1989). In our opinion, this conclusion may change in the future as more information becomes available about the so-called moderating variables that influence its magnitude. That is, certain factors inherent in naturalistic, as compared to laboratory, eyewitness situations may provide the bases for the relationship to be much stronger than earlier research has suggested. For example, when research settings and procedures provide the wide range of variability (in encoding and retrieval opportunities) seen in real-world crimes, much stronger relationships have been observed (e.g., D.S. Lindsay, Read, & Sharma, 1998; Read et al., 1998).

Another influential social factor in line-up situations is the subtle interaction between investigator and witnesses by which witnesses may be guided towards a particular choice. Because the investigator usually knows the identity of the police suspect, verbal and non-verbal cues may be relayed to the witness (perhaps unknowingly by the investigator). Unless identification tests are constructed such that the investigator is blind as to which line-up member is the police suspect, opportunities always exist for these cues to influence the readiness with which a witness selects a particular person (Wells & Bradfield, 1998; Wells & Seelau, 1995).

Finally, the use of hypnosis, in part, was credited in this case for reviving J.A.'s memory of the crime in question and thereby eliciting an accurate identification on the third attempt. We described earlier the perceived disadvantages of evidence gained through the use of hypnosis and the motivation defence counsel would normally have to ensure that such evidence is ruled inadmissible. One basis of defence objection is whether the hypnosis session followed the approved forensic hypnosis procedures deemed necessary to safeguard the testimony obtained and for it to be ruled admissible. Departures from approved procedures, such as post-hypnotic suggestions, can render the testimony inadmissible, as it was in the murder case of *R. v. Savoy* (1997), where neither audio nor video recordings were made of a hypnosis session. In *R. v. McGuiness et al.* (1997) defence counsel unsuccessfully requested a voir dire (a "trial within a trial" conducted either before or during the main trial to resolve a particular issue) on the admissibility of the hypnotic interview and the identification evidence that arose from it. As things turned out, however, J.A. was not called by the Crown as a witness and one of the co-accused, Leo McGuiness, pleaded guilty to manslaughter and received a 2-year sentence. As part of the plea bargain, he testified for the Crown and stated that Roman Ballantyne was not present at the time of the attack. This corroborated the evidence of witness S.L., who had reported seeing only two assailants. Following this disclosure by the defence and because other forensic pathology evidence established his innocence, the Crown stayed charges against Roman Ballantyne.

Our discussion of the Roman Ballantyne case highlights the kinds of procedural difficulties that can occur in investigations involving eyewitness testimony. However, over the last 4 years there has been greater recognition of these difficulties at all levels of the criminal justice system in the United States and, accordingly, greater pressure exerted for procedural change. In 1996, the U.S. National Institute of Justice (NIJ) revealed that in approximately 85% of cases in which DNA evidence had exonerated a convicted suspect the convictions in question were primarily the result of mistaken eyewitness identifications (NIJ , 1996). That is, although other evidence was also presented in many of those cases which seemed to add weight to the overall probability that the suspect was guilty, such evidence generally had low probative value (e.g., lack of alibi, matching blood type) and often would not have been collected if the eyewitness had not identified the suspect in the first place. Based primarily on these DNA exoneration cases and at the request of the U.S. Attorney General, Janet Reno, the National Institute of Justice began meeting with a group of police officers, district attorneys, defence attorneys, and eyewitness researchers. The result, a document called *Eyewitness Evidence: A Guide for Law Enforcement* (NIJ, 1999), is intended to guide the five stages of a criminal investigation specifically concerning eyewitness evidence: (1) managing witnesses at the crime scene, (2) eliciting a description of the offender by searching mug shots or creating a composite likeness, (3) follow-up investigative interviews, (4) field identifications, and (5) line-up identifications. The *Guide* recommendations show a definite preference for avoiding problems with eyewitness evidence before they occur. To accomplish this goal, training materials are being developed that will facilitate implementation of the *Guide* in future investigations.

CHILDREN'S TESTIMONY

Courts face many challenges in relation to cases involving children. The Standing Committee on Justice and the Solicitor General (1993), for example, in its 4-year review of the Act to Amend the Criminal Code and the Canadian Evidence Act, reported that child sexual abuse occurs often and that "most child sexual abuse victims are under

12 years of age, and between 15 and 22 percent are under five" (p. 4). And in *R. v. B.(G.)* (1990) identification of the accused as the perpetrator of a sexual assault against a five-year-old boy was only possible through the unsworn testimony of the child. In this case Justice Bertha Wilson of the Supreme Court of Canada stated, "In recent years we have adopted a much more benign attitude to children's evidence, lessening the strict standards of oath-taking and corroboration, and I believe that is a desirable development" (p. 219). The prevalence of young children's participation in the legal process is increasing (see Paciocco, 1996). In *R. v. B.(G.)* (1990) the Saskatchewan Court of Appeal was quoted, "... there are many more cases now coming to trial involving sexual abuse of children and requiring a very difficult evaluation of youthful testimony" (p. 207).

Where, in the preceding chapter, Daniel Yarmey detailed the police interviewing procedures used with children, in this chapter we discuss three issues involved in evaluating children's testimony after it has been obtained by police. The first is the court's inquiry into a particular child's capacity to observe, recall, and communicate, as well as the child's understanding of the need to be truthful in court. Second, we discuss the child's in-person and in-court evidence. In the final section we describe innovative changes to the legal system that facilitate children's in-court testimony.

Competency to Testify and Admissibility of Children's Testimony in Court

Section 16 of the Canada Evidence Act (CEA) states that all witnesses must (a) be able to communicate the evidence and (b) understand the difference between the truth and a lie and, in the circumstances of testifying, feel compelled to tell the truth. Any person over the age of 14 years is presumed to have the capacity to testify (CEA s. 16(5)). For persons 14 years or younger the judge is required to conduct an inquiry to satisfy himself or herself of the child's capacity to testify. An example of an inquiry of a 6-year-old's ability to communicate the evidence follows (*R. v D. (R. R.)*, 1989).

THE COURT: And how old are you?
C.D.: Six.
THE COURT: You're six. Do you know what a judge is?
C.D.: Yes.

THE COURT: What does he do?

C.D.: He works with children in court.

THE COURT: Sometimes he does, he works with children. Whereabouts do you live?

C.D.: (child reports location)

THE COURT: And do you have any brothers?

C.D.: One.

THE COURT: You have one. And what's your brother's name?

C.D.: R.

THE COURT: R. And any sisters?

C.D.: Mhmm.

THE COURT: How many sisters?

C.D.: One.

THE COURT: One. And what's your sister's name?

C.D.: K.

THE COURT: K. And do you go to school?

C.D.: Yes.

THE COURT: And what grade are you in?

C.D.: One.

THE COURT: Grade one. And what school do you go to? Do you know the name of your school?

C.D.: Yeah.

THE COURT: What's the name of your school?

C.D.: H.K.

The section 16 inquiry requires only that the child demonstrate a general ability to perceive, recollect, and communicate events (*R. v. Marquard*, 1993). It does not inquire into the child's ability to perceive, recollect, and communicate details of the specific offence, even if the alleged offence occurred at a (perhaps substantially) earlier age. An assumption implicit in this principle is that if a child demonstrates skills in one context she or he will possess those skills in other contexts. This assumption is consistent with the stage theories of cognitive development (e.g., Piagetian stages) in which cognitive development is a consequence of a progression of physiological changes that provide children with the basis for forming the cognitive structures needed to perform increasingly complex tasks in a variety of contexts.

The stage theories contrast with both contextual and information-processing views of development. According to these latter theories, cognitive development is strongly influenced by the child's social and cultural experience. Very generally, these theories assert that a child is most likely to demonstrate advanced cognitive skills in familiar contexts. Importantly, they argue that the ability to use advanced cognitive skills in one context does not establish the ability to use those same skills in other contexts. It remains to be tested whether a standard section 16 inquiry that centres on a child's ability to perceive, recollect, and communicate details of, for instance, school experience and family structure (as in the example above) generalizes to the child's ability to perceive, recollect, and communicate details of an alleged offence.

In the second branch of the inquiry, the judge must determine if the child understands the difference between the truth and a lie and, in the courtroom, would feel compelled to tell the truth. If the judge is convinced that the child satisfies this requirement, the child's evidence may be admitted in one of three ways. If the court is satisfied that the conscience of the child will be bound by making a promise to God to tell the truth then his or her evidence will be received under oath (CEA s. 16(2)). Alternatively, the child's evidence may be received if the court finds that a solemn affirmation to tell the truth will bind the child's conscience (CEA s. 16(2)). If the child does not understand the nature of an oath or a solemn affirmation but has demonstrated an ability to communicate the evidence, she or he may be permitted to testify on a promise to tell the truth (CEA s. 16(3)). An example, from *R. v. D (R.R.)* (1989), of this branch of the inquiry follows:

THE COURT: Do you know what is meant by telling the truth?
C.D.: Yes.
THE COURT: And what happens if you don't tell the truth?
C.D.: God will get upset.

Two questions form the substance of this branch of the inquiry, (a) does the child understand the difference between the truth and a lie? and (b) will the oath, solemn declaration, or promise to tell the truth optimize the truthfulness of the testimony? Generally, children as young as 4 years will identify a factually incorrect statement as a lie and a factually correct statement as the truth (Bussey, 1992; Wimer, Gruber, & Perner, 1984). Most children over the age of 4 years will probably pass this threshold test. The next question comprises the essence of the second branch of the section 16 inquiry: Is it the case that when a child takes an oath, makes a solemn declaration, or promises to tell the truth the child will not report a fact that he or she knows is false?

In suggestibility studies, commission errors occur when children report that details that had only been suggested really had occurred. The prevalence of these kinds of false reports has been reduced when (a) children were informed that anything they were told about the target event, subsequent to their experience with it, was wrong and should not be reported (D.S. Lindsay, Gonzales, & Eso, 1995), (b) suggestions were presented by a peer rather than an adult (Ceci, Ross, & Toglia, 1987), and (c) the final memory testing was done by a warm and nonjudgmental interviewer (Goodman et al., 1991). As illustrated above, circumstances can be created that reduce the incidence of false reports. The relevant question here is whether an oath, solemn declaration, or promise to tell the truth will reduce commission errors.

In-Court and In-Person Testimony

In many cases of child sexual assault, there is no physical evidence and no witnesses other than the child. Thus, these cases virtually always rest on credibility of the complainant(s) and the accused. Several factors are considered in an assessment of credibility. One particularly important factor that has been the focus of psychological research is consistency both within and across reports.

Consistency across reports refers to congruity with prior tellings of the alleged incident. Children who testify in court answer questions about the alleged offence at least twice, once during a formal pretrial proceeding and again at trial. In fact, from the investigation to the trial's end children may be questioned many, many times (Ceci & Bruck, 1995; Walker, 1997). Consistency within a report refers to the child's in-court testimony. Usually, child witnesses answer questions about the alleged event during direct examination and again during cross-examination (although the defence may choose not to cross-examine). We have dealt with the harmful effect of suggestive questioning previously; here the concern is with the effect of repeated nonsuggestive questioning.

Repetition of open-ended questions across interviews may inoculate children's memory against later forgetting. This effect depends, in part, on the initial interview being reasonably close in time to the target event, and on children recalling an adequate amount of information in the initial interview. Open-ended questions repeated in the same interview may provide additional accurate information without a coincident increase in new inaccurate information. Repetition of closed-ended questions within an interview is not recommended, particularly with preschoolers, because there is convincing evidence that young children will change their response on the second presentation. For excellent reviews of the literature and elaboration of these effects see Poole and White (1995) and Ceci & Bruck (1995).

Legal Innovations in Taking Children's Testimony

Testifying in court can be a terrifying experience for young children (for a comprehensive study see Goodman, Taub, Jones, England, Port, Rudy, & Prado, 1992). Recently, important statutory changes have made Canadian courtrooms more accessible to young children while maintaining judicial integrity by continuing to protect the rights of accused persons. For example, devices such as screens that allow children to testify without seeing the accused are sometimes allowed (Criminal Code, s. 486(2.1); *R. v. Levogiannis*, 1993), although the accused and the trier(s) of fact must be able to see the child. Also, if a child's evidence was recorded on videotape shortly after the alleged event, the child adopts the contents of the videotape in court, and the child is available to be cross-examined, the videotape may be admitted in lieu of the child repeating his or her evidence (Criminal Code, s. 715.1; *R. v. L. (D.O.)*, 1993).

IN-COURT PRESENTATION OF INFORMATION CONCERNING EYEWITNESS TESTIMONY

Surveys of the lay public in North America have shown that some information about eyewitness testimony and memory functioning gained from scientific studies runs counter to popular belief and common sense (Kassin et al., 1989; Loftus, 1986). For example, the weak relationships often obtained between confidence and accuracy in laboratory studies are frequently received with scepticism; the fallibility of identification evidence in general is often seen as distressing and compromising of the justice system; and the range and variety of perceptual and memorial variables that contribute to good and bad eyewitness evidence is seen as confusing. Because rules of evidence prevent defence and prosecution counsel from simply expounding on the topic of witness fallibility to the triers of fact, they sometimes seek to admit what is called expert evidence as a way of bolstering their side of a case (see Chapter 1).

From the Experts

First, if defence or prosecution counsel seek to have expert evidence admitted, the court must rule whether the proffered opinion evidence would be relevant and of assistance to the trier of fact and, if so, whether the expert advocated is indeed an expert. As described in Chapter 1, to decide whether expert evidence will be heard in any trial, the Supreme Court of Canada decision in *R. v. Mohan* (1994) is consulted. This decision provides the guidelines or tests of the admissibility of opinion evidence and lower courts are bound by it. With respect to eyewitness testimony and memory, opinion evidence has been provided in Canadian cases (e.g., *R. v. Marinelli*, 1988), including many instances of recovered memory (Bala, 1996). However, if the court believes that the admission of experts on behalf of both Crown and defence will degenerate into a contest of experts their evidence may not be admitted, on the ground that such a contest may confuse rather than assist the triers of fact. In the eyewitness area there is good reason to fear such an outcome because the experts on the topic themselves do not always agree (Loftus, 1993; Kassin et al., 1989) and the bases of disagreement are often well known to courts (e.g., Paciocco, 1996; Paciocco & Steusser, 1996, pp. 125–130; D.S. Lindsay & Read, 1995).

In the past, eyewitness experts who spoke to the courts usually did so in regard to the perceptual variables that influence interpretation and encoding of an event and the nature of identification processes from photospreads and line-ups (see *R. v. Marinelli*, 1988). In recent years, however, the use of experts on these topics in Canada has declined, largely because, as a matter of course, the court provides instructions (see below) to the triers of fact regarding the fallibility of eyewitness perception and memory (see Ferguson & Bouck, 1997), and because it is expected that jurors can understand and appreciate the inherent risks of eyewitness testimony evidence (e.g., *R. v. Carter*, 1994; *R. v. McIntosh*, 1997). Even relatively rare eyewitness phenomena, such as unconscious transference errors (as was suggested in the *McGuiness et al.* case described earlier) has also been considered well within the jurors' understanding and, therefore, not in need of expert opinion (e.g., *R. v. Peter To Kan Tsang*, 1987). These developments suggest that general public awareness of eyewitness fallibility now exists and that the results of scientific research on the topic have reached a broad audience, from the public to the judiciary. However, empirical research has not yet demonstrated such changes in knowledge. None-theless, a few exceptional topics remain for which Canadian courts have concluded that the public is still not sufficiently informed. The topic of recovered memories, for example, has been discussed by experts on many occasions in Canada (see Bala, 1996; *R. v. Norman*, 1993; *R. v. O.(H.W.)*, 1997; *R. v. Kliman*, 1996, 1998).

From the Court: Judges' Instructions about Memory

Judges provide instructions to juries about many matters throughout a trial, including the assessment of expert evidence and eyewitness evidence – for example, how much weight, including none at all, jurors should assign to expert evidence about eyewitness testimony. Ultimately, what matters is whether the inclusion of expert opinion allows the triers of fact to make better decisions. How would we know whether decisions have been affected and on what basis could we say that they are "better" decisions? If, for example, we believe that triers of fact are overly impressed by the level of witness confidence, perhaps expert testimony that has modestly increased their scepticism about confidence judgments may be seen as better. To date, there has been little work on this issue in Canada, but in the United States the role of expert evidence in eyewitness testimony cases has been studied carefully (see Cutler & Penrod, 1995; Leippe, 1995).

On the topics of memory and eyewitness evidence, judges' instructions usually emphasize the frailty of such evidence, particularly in matters of identification and especially when identification evidence is the primary evidence against the accused. Jurors are instructed to consider a wide variety of facts, including many of those discussed in this chapter, from the witness's opportunity to observe the perpetrator, time since observation, the initial description given by the witness, witness confidence, and prior opportunities to see the accused to the potential suggestiveness of the identification procedure. The relevant Canadian cases in which the dangers of conviction upon eyewitness testimony alone are emphasized are *R. v. Duhamel* (1990), *R. v. Atfield* (1983). These in turn have relied heavily upon *R. v. Turnbull et al.* (1976) in the United Kingdom.

SUMMARY

Because eyewitness testimony evidence implicates every cognitive activity in which we engage, including perception, reasoning, decision making, and memory, many variables can affect, either directly or in interaction with other variables, each of these activities. Understanding those effects, making available such understanding to others, and applying that knowledge within the legal system will ultimately provide the most solid foundation on which the triers of fact may interpret and reach just decisions about persons accused of criminal acts.

QUESTIONS FOR DISCUSSION

1. Television leads us to believe that a witness to a crime will be asked to review a collection of mugshots at the local police station with the goal of recognizing and identifying the perpetrator of the witnessed crime. Imagine that a witness to a crime does so but identifies none as the perpetrator. Two weeks later a physical line-up is constructed that includes one of the men shown in the mugshot collection along with another suspect and three known foils (volunteers selected from the community). The witness is asked to study the line-up and indicate whether the perpetrator is present. Describe the possible decisions a witness may make in this line-up task. In what ways would the interests of police and defence differ for each type of decision? What difficulties do you see with the identification procedure used throughout?

2. Imagine that you are the judge in a jury trial involving eyewitness testimony from a witness who has testified that she saw the accused strike the victim with a gun. The observation was made at night in a well-lit parking lot from a distance of 10 m. The line-up identification was made one week later. Both the Crown and defence counsel wish to call upon expert testimony from psychologists knowledgeable in the subjects of perception and memory. As judge, of course, you may allow testimony by none, one, or two of the experts proffered. What factors would be weighed in your decision? If the experts were allowed to provide an opinion, what issues relevant to the reliability of eyewitness testimony will likely be discussed by them?

3. Describe the ways in which eyewitness memory is similar to traditional types of "trace evidence," such as hair, fibre, blood, and semen samples. Are the accepted standards for treating such evidence applicable to the case of eyewitness memory? Can "science" be used in an equally effective manner in both cases? Why or why not?

4. It has been suggested that the section 16 inquiry be eliminated. That is, children should testify in court without undergoing a section 16 inquiry; the

trier of fact will evaluate the credibility of the evidence and decide how much weight to give to it. Do you agree with this recommendation? What are some of the implications of accepting it? Are there alternative measures that should be considered (e.g., change the age at which a section 16 inquiry is mandatory, change the section 16 inquiry to explore the child's memory for the alleged offence)? Are there any problems associated with your alternative measures?

RECOMMENDED READING

Doris, J. (Ed.). (1991). *The suggestibility of children's recollections: Implications for eyewitness testimony.* Washington, DC: American Psychological Association.

Ross, D.F., Read, J.D., & Toglia, M.P. (Eds.). (1994). *Adult eyewitness testimony: Current trends and developments.* New York: Cambridge University Press.

Sporer, S.L., Malpass, R.S., & Koehnken, G. (Eds.). (1996). *Psychological issues in eyewitness identification.* Mahwah, NJ: Lawrence Erlbaum Associates.

Thompson, C.P., Herrmann, D., Read, J.D., Bruce, D., Payne, D., & Toglia, M.P. (1998). *Eyewitness testimony: Theoretical and applied perspectives.* Mahwah, NJ: Lawrence Erlbaum Associates.

Zaragoza, M.S., Graham, J.R., Hall, G.C.N., Hirschman, R., & Ben-Porath, Y.S. (Eds.). (1995). *Memory and testimony in the child witness.* Thousand Oaks, CA: Sage Publications.

5. The Jury: Selecting Twelve Impartial Peers

Neil Vidmar and Regina A. Schuller

In May 1995, 980 individuals appeared for jury duty at the ballroom of the Royal York Hotel in downtown Toronto. Jury selection for what was undoubtedly one of Canada's most gruesome and heinous murder trials was about to begin.[1] The accused, Paul Bernardo, was charged with two counts of first degree murder, kidnapping, unlawful confinement, and aggravated sexual assault, and one count of causing an indignity to a corpse. The horrific events that lead to this trial are familiar to most Canadians.

The police investigation of the sexually abused and mutilated bodies of two teenage girls, Kristen French and Leslie Mahaffy, who went missing in 1991 and 1992, was stymied until January 1993 when an attractive 23-year-old St Catharines woman, Karla Homolka, was severely beaten by her 29-year-old husband. In a most bizarre and unlikely turn of events the police investigation that ensued eventually resulted in Homolka confessing that she had participated with Bernardo in the kidnapping, sexual enslavement, and degradation of the two teenagers (she nevertheless insisted that Bernardo alone had committed the murders). As well, she implicated both herself and Bernardo in a series of other sexual crimes, including the death of her younger sister, who died after being drugged and raped by the couple (a death that until then had been treated as natural but unexplained). Further, Homolka indicated that these acts, some of which occurred over several days, had been videotaped by Bernardo. Over the next couple of months, extensive searches of the couple's home failed to uncover the videotapes. With Karla Homolka as the Crown's key evidence against Bernardo, a controversial plea bargain was struck. In return for her full cooperation and testimony Homolka would receive two 12-year sentences for manslaughter (to be served concurrently). The media, although present at her plea and sentencing hearing in June 1993, was forbidden from publishing any details until the conclusion of Bernardo's trial.

Despite the publication ban, public rumours about the Homolka and Ber-

nardo crimes were rampant. *Intense media and print coverage in American cities such as Buffalo and New York reported some of the banned information, with these accounts easily finding their way back into Canada via facsimile or Internet communications. One of the rumours that had surfaced, that the missing videotapes had been found, turned out to be true. Widespread dissemination of anonymous flyers reported erroneous and gruesome details about the crimes. The media coverage and public interest in the case was extremely intense. Thus, in May 1995, the 980 individuals who filed into the makeshift courtroom in the Royal York had been exposed to such extensive information, misinformation, and speculation about the case that Bernardo's right to a trial of impartial jurors was in jeopardy.*

In an effort to curb the potential negative effects caused by the pretrial publicity, the prospective jurors, in a procedure referred to as a "challenge for cause," were randomly called one by one from the ballroom, taken to a nearby courtroom, placed under oath, and asked up to eight of the following questions:

1 *Have you read, heard or seen anything about this case in the media (i.e., newspapers, radio or television)?*
2 *Have you obtained information about it from anywhere else?*
3 *Have you read, heard or seen anything about the accused's, Paul Bernardo's, background, character or lifestyle?*
4 *Have you read, heard or seen anything about Karla Homolka or about her trial?*
5 *As a result of this case some groups and organizations have circulated petitions or have sought support concerning issues which relate to this case, the victims or their families. Have you supported any of these groups or associations, for ex.: by signing a petition, writing a letter of support or by making a donation?*
6 *As a result of any knowledge, discussion and/or contact with any group or organization, have you formed any opinion about the guilt or innocence of the accused, Paul Berndardo?*
7 *If you have formed an opinion about the guilt or innocence of the accused, are you able to set aside that opinion and decide this case only on the evidence you hear in the court room and the judge's directions on the law?*
8 *Answer the following question with a yes or a no: Is there anything we have not asked you about why you could not judge this case fairly and impartially according to the evidence heard at trial and the judge's directions on the law?*

Other than the responses to these questions, the only other information available to the Crown prosecutors and defence lawyers was each prospective juror's name, address, occupation, demeanour, and physical appearance. Over a 5-day period 225 jurors were called. Many were excused for hardship, others for lack of impartiality, and others because the prosecution or defence exercised peremptory challenges. Finally, eight men and four women were selected as the jury. They were admonished (i.e., ordered) by the judge not to discuss the case with anyone and ordered to return in 2½ weeks for the commencement of the trial. During the trial itself the jurors returned to their respective homes each evening. They were sequestered – that is, kept together in isolation from the rest of the world – only when they began deliberations.

As we will see in this chapter, the Holmolka-Bernardo trials were unusual in many respects. Many of the procedures involved – the publication ban surrounding Homolka's sentencing hearing; the relocation of the trial from St Catharines to Toronto; the length and intensity of the selection process; the questioning of the jurors – were exceptions to the rule rather than the norm of Canadian jury practice and procedure. Compare this exceptional trial with a trial in the United States that occurred at approximately the same time: the trial of football and television star O.J. Simpson, who was charged with the gruesome knife slaying of his ex-wife and her friend. The preliminary hearing and the trial proceedings were televised across the United States, and indeed across the world, through the CNN television network. The process of jury selection took many weeks and jurors were asked extensive and intrusive questions about their personal lives. Even after the jury and alternate jurors were chosen, some jurors were dismissed under suspicion that they planned to sell the inside story of the jury deliberations to tabloid newspapers and book publishers. The jury was sequestered for the whole duration of the trial, which lasted more than six months. Prosecution and defence lawyers held news conferences throughout the trial in an attempt to influence public opinion. The Simpson trial was extraordinary for an American trial too, but you can easily see some marked differences between the two systems.

This chapter, as well as the chapter that follows, focuses on the jury, with particular emphasis on the unique aspects of the Canadian jury. Not surprisingly, jury behaviour is an area in which psychology has much to offer, and considerable research on the topic exists. We will first address issues relating to the selection of the jury, reserving questions of jury behaviour and other matters for the following chapter.

THE ROLE AND CHARACTERISTICS OF THE JURY

The Role and Function of the Jury

The right to trial by jury in criminal cases was first transported to the

Canadian colonies from England in the mid-1700s. It is now enshrined in the Canadian Charter (ss. 11(d) and 11(f)) and is integral to the Canadian system of criminal law. Juries are used in some civil cases as well, but not nearly as frequently as in the United States. The right to civil jury trial is a common law right that is not specifically enshrined in the Charter, and its use has slowly eroded over the last two centuries (see Bogart, 1999). There are still over a thousand civil jury trials in Ontario each year (Bogart, 1999; Ontario Law Reform Commission, 1994), but they occur much less frequently in some of the other English provinces and not at all in Quebec's civil law system. They have also not received the research attention devoted to criminal juries. Thus, this chapter will focus on matters pertaining to criminal juries.

In contrast to the United States, where the right to a criminal jury is more extensive, Canadian law provides for jury trials in only the more serious classes of offences (recall the three classes of offences outlined in Chapter 2). Indeed, in the case of the most serious crimes, such as murder and treason, which are referred to as indictable offences, a jury trial is mandatory. The least serious class of offences, summary offences (which involve punishment of less than two years in jail and a fine of less than $5,000) are tried by judge alone, and the accused does not have the right to a jury trial. For all other types of offences (i.e., those for which the maximum punishment is imprisonment for five years or more), which are referred to as hybrid offences, the Crown can decide to proceed by either an indictable offence or a summary offence. Once the Crown has decided to proceed by indictment, however, the accused has the right to decide whether to be tried by judge and jury or by judge alone. If the Crown decides to proceed by summary offence, the accused does not have the right to a jury trial and will be tried by a judge alone.

If we consider that all summary convictions are tried by judge alone, and that only a portion of accused charged with indictable offences will elect to be tried by a jury, we can see that the vast majority of criminal cases in Canada are tried by judge alone. Canada-wide statistics on the absolute numbers of jury trials or the percentage of accused persons who elect trial by jury when they have the option of doing so are difficult to obtain. In 1997 in Ontario, however, a province with about 11 million persons (approximately one-third of Canada's population), trial proceedings were initiated for 4,672 criminal cases (i.e., the case was added to the trial list).[2] Of these, 34% were disposed (i.e., resolved) by trial. Of the 1,585 cases dealt with at trial, 834 (53%) involved jury trials and 751 (47%) involved non-jury trials. These data suggest comparable rates for jury and non-jury trials, but we must keep in mind that some of the jury cases involved murder or other indictable offences that are required to be tried by a jury. This makes it difficult to determine whether accused individuals are more or less likely to elect trial by jury if given the choice.

Although jury trials represent only a fraction of the cases that proceed through the criminal justice system, by their very nature the types of cases that come before a jury are the most serious. The significance and impact of jury decisions can also extend far beyond the specific trials to which they pertain (Hans, 1992). Let us briefly consider some of the roles and functions of the jury that have been outlined in the literature and case law (Hans & Vidmar, 1986; Kassin & Wrightsman, 1988; *R. v. Sherrat*, 1991; Saks & Hastie, 1978).

The specific legal function of the jury, like that of a judge acting alone, is to decide the facts from the trial evidence presented and to apply the law (provided by the judge) to those facts to render a verdict. Its strength as a fact finder, in comparison to, say, a single judge, is that a jury combines the wisdom and perspective of 12 ordinary persons chosen from the community who must unanimously agree in order to reach a verdict. It is contended that, because jury verdicts are rendered by members of the community their legal decisions about guilt or innocence are assumed to have greater legitimacy and public acceptance than decisions of a single judge. The jury also serves as the conscience of the community because it is drawn precisely from the community in which the crime was committed. In addition, because the jurors can apply their own sense of fairness in reaching a verdict, never having to justify that decision, it can serve as a guardian against oppressive or rigid laws. Indeed, cases of symbolic significance (e.g., abortion, euthanasia) are typically tried by juries. Jury decisions in such cases can signal a message from the community to the government, as was the case when juries continually returned verdicts of not guilty in the prosecution of Dr Henry Morgentaler for providing abortions (see Box 6.1, in Chapter 6). Finally, it has also been noted that jury service performs an important educative function in that it teaches citizens about the laws of their country.

Sentencing the accused person is *not* a function of the jury in Canada. Determination of appropriate punishment is the responsibility of the trial judge alone and is determined after the jury finds the accused guilty. There is a partial exception to this rule. In cases where a person is found guilty of second degree murder, the judge must inform the jury that the convicted person would ordinarily be eligible for parole after serving ten years in prison and then ask the jurors if they wish to make a recommendation as to the number of years (between 10 and 25 years) that the convicted person should serve before being eligible for parole. The judge is not bound by the recommendation, but the provision allows the jury to provide community input into the punishment process. Sometimes this recommendation has interesting consequences. Many of you will recall the case of Robert Latimer, who was found guilty of second degree murder for the killing of his severely disabled daughter. Ignoring the law, the jury recommended a 1-year parole eligibility date. Considerable public debate on the issue of mercy killing surrounded the case. Ultimately, the trial judge granted Mr Latimer a constitutional exemption to the mandatory minimum sentence and sentenced him to a 1-year period of incarceration, followed by a 1-year period of probation. The Crown appealed both the conviction and the sentence to the Saskatchewan Court of Appeal. The court, ruling that Latimer had received a fair trial and that the judge erred in granting him a constitutional exception to the mandatory sentence, imposed a life sentence with no chance of parole for ten years. The defence immediately appealed this decision to the Supreme Court of Canada, which has now heard but has yet to decide on the case (*Latimer v. The Queen*, June 2000).

Characteristics of the Jury

What does it mean to be judged by a jury? In a number of decisions, the Supreme Court of Canada has articulated the important characteristics that the jury should possess (see Granger, 1996; Tanovich, Paciocco, & Skurka, 1997). Foremost among these are representativeness and impartiality. Let us consider the issue of representativeness first. We are all familiar with the notion of a jury of "one's peers," but what does this really mean in practice? It may surprise many students to learn that as little as 25 years ago, most jury pools in Canada were composed overwhelmingly of males and that members of minority groups were seldom called for jury duty. Today, however, jury lists are drawn from a broad cross-section of the community in which the trial is being held. Although there is some variation across the provinces and territories in terms of the procedure used, basically, individuals from the local community are randomly selected by voter registration or enumeration lists and summoned to appear for jury duty. These individuals form the panel, or array, from which the actual jurors for any given trial will be selected. This procedure does not in itself guarantee that the panel will contain individuals from all groups in the community or even that it will be composed of the accused's peers, but rather that the pool from which the panel is selected is representative of the wider community and that the selection was conducted randomly. Statutory exemptions, found in the provincial jury acts, prohibit some individuals from serving on a jury (e.g., legislators, police officers, lawyers, and in some provinces doctors, veterinarians, and firefighters), which does restrict representativeness to some extent.

In some cases, courts have ruled that the jury panel was assembled in a way that violates the Charter (Granger, 1996; Tanovich et al., 1997). For instance, in *R. v. Nepoose* (1991) the jury array was successfully challenged because it had too few women and in *R. v. Nahdee* (1993) the jury array was successfully challenged for improper exclusion of inhabitants of Native reserves. In *R. v. Born with a Tooth* (1993), an Alberta case, the Crown successfully challenged a panel in which a list of 200 randomly selected persons was supplemented by adding 50 Aboriginal persons who were not randomly selected.

It is worth reflecting on the social psychological issues raised by these cases. Is a jury panel that has too few women or too few Aboriginal persons likely to result in a less competent or less impartial jury? What number would constitute too few? Would too few female or Aboriginal perspectives affect the accuracy of verdicts in some cases? Or might unrepresentative panels create a public perception of unfairness, thereby lowering public respect for the justice system? Of relevance to this latter question is the body of research on procedural justice (Lind & Tyler, 1988; Tyler, 1990), which suggests that public belief about the fairness of legal systems is largely determined by perceptions of the fairness of the procedures used.

Representativeness only partially defines the notion of a "jury of one's peers." In *R. v. Sherratt* (1991) the Supreme Court asserted that the jury must be composed of impartial peers: "[The] perceived importance of the jury and the Charter right to jury trial is meaningless without some guarantee that it will perform its duties *impartially* and represent, as far as possible and appropriate in the circumstances, the larger community" (p. 525) (emphasis added). There are instances, however, as we saw in the Bernardo case, in which some of the prospective jurors on the panel from which the jury will be drawn may not be impartial, or, as the courts refer to it in their formal language, "not indifferent between Her Majesty the Queen and the accused at bar."

The issue of partiality or bias was specifically addressed in *R. v. Parks* (1993). As you read through this description, think about how comfortably this definition would fit into any modern social psychology textbook (e.g., Alcock, Carment, & Sadava, 1998; Myers, 1999) addressing the subject of prejudice: "Partiality has both an attitudinal and a behavioural component. It refers to one who has certain preconceived biases and who will allow those biases to affect his or her verdict despite the trial safeguards designed to prevent reliance on those biases. A partial juror is one who is biased and who will discriminate against one of the parties to the litigation based on that bias" (*R. v. Parks*, 1993, p. 336). Like social psychologists, the courts recognize the important distinction between the attitude (prejudice) and the expression of that attitude in terms of behaviour (discrimination). Prejudice, which researchers have defined as "a negative prejudgment of a group and its individual members" (Myers, 1999, p. 336), is a combination of affect (feelings and emotions), behaviour (actions), and cognitions (beliefs, and in some cases stereotypes). These three components have been referred to as the ABCs of attitudes (Myers, 1999). What is of particular concern for the courts is expression of the behaviour. Thus, there are two essential issues nestled in the *Parks* statement about juror partiality, or, if you prefer to think in standard psychological terminology, "prejudice," that we need to consider. First, what forms can juror prejudice take in the context of a trial and how does it arise? That is, where might various sources of partiality stem from? Second, what was *Parks* referring to by the phrase "trial safeguards"? That is, what precautions are there in place to prevent the behavioural expression of these potential biases in jurors' decisions? Let us begin by considering the potential sources of bias.

Sources of Potential Juror Bias

Four types of prejudice, which are implicit in Canadian cases dealing with the issue of juror impartiality, have been delineated by Vidmar (1997). The first type, referred to as *interest* prejudice, involves biases that jurors may harbour as a result of their direct interest or stake in the outcome of the case (e.g., their relation to the accused or to a witness who might testify). A second type, referred to as *specific* prejudice, involves attitudes or beliefs about the specific case that may interfere with the juror's ability to decide the case fairly. These attitudes and beliefs may exist because of publicity through mass media, such as newspaper and television coverage, and/or discussion and rumour about the case arising through social networks within the community. Another category of prejudice, referred to as *generic* prejudice, concerns general attitudes and beliefs about certain groups of people or even certain types of crimes that may prevent a juror from deciding a case without bias. Racial or ethnic prejudices would be instances of this form of prejudice. The concern here is that a person who holds prejudicial beliefs or stereotypes about a particular group (e.g., blacks, Natives, homosexuals) may judge an accused who is a member of that group on the basis of his or her identity as a group member rather than on the facts of the case at trial. Finally, *normative* prejudice refers to biases that occur when a juror perceives that there is such strong community interest in a particular outcome of a trial that he or she is influenced in reaching a verdict that is consistent with community sentiment rather than one based on an impartial evaluation of the trial evidence. In an important 1998 case (*R. v. William*, 1998), the Supreme Court of Canada explicitly acknowledged these four sources of potential juror bias.

How might these various forms of bias influence the partiality of jurors? The task of jurors involves encoding information, combining it together and forming a judgment. Thus we can turn to the body of theory and research on social cognition and information processing for answers to this question. Indeed, over the last few decades, research in the area of social cognition has uncovered a range of cognitive processes that help us to understand how we make sense of people and their actions, which is essentially what the jurors are trying to do. Basically, this body of work demonstrates that the expectations and beliefs that we hold about others, as well as our expectations about how the world operates, influences the way in which we view and integrate information. In other words our expectancies, or what psychologists refer to as schemas, guide our attention (e.g., the type of information we will notice and pay attention to), our recall (e.g., what aspects of the information we will remember or misremember), our interpretation (e.g., the meaning we will ascribe to the information), and our integration (e.g., how that information fits together) of information. Ultimately, these schemas help to determine the inferences and conclusions we draw from the information presented to us (see Fiske & Taylor, 1991).

A model of juror decision making, referred to as the Story Model (Pennington & Hastie, 1986, 1993), which outlines this process more fully, is presented in Chapter 6. For the moment, however, let us just consider some of the implications of this work for concerns about juror impartiality. In a trial the Crown prosecutor and the defence present conflicting stories about what occurred and place different interpretations on the meaning of trial evidence. Jurors are legally required to base their decisions only on the evidence presented at trial. In attempting to decide which story to believe, however, they will invariably draw upon their common knowledge of the world, their beliefs, and their attitudes to make sense of the often contradictory testimony and evidence before them (Pennington & Hastie, 1986). Thus, if a juror harbours negative attitudes, erroneous beliefs, or misconceptions about the participants in the trial, his or her evaluation of the trial evidence and how that evidence is put together to make sense of what occurred (i.e., the story constructed of the events) can be negatively coloured by these pre-existing attitudes and beliefs. For instance, if a juror holds negative attitudes or beliefs about members of a particular ethnic or racial group (e.g., that they are likely to be violent), the juror's initial assumption about an accused from that group may be one of guilt. Alternatively, the impact on the juror's decisions might be more subtle. For example, since people are more likely to notice and recall information that confirms their prior expectations, often ignoring or minimizing the significance of disconfirming information, evidence that otherwise might be viewed as ambiguous (e.g., reaching into one's coat pocket) may be more likely to be interpreted as threatening behaviour (e.g., suggestive of reaching for a weapon) if committed by a member of that group.

THE PRESUMPTION OF IMPARTIALITY

We need to back up a little in our discussion of juror prejudice or partiality because we have gotten a bit ahead of the story. Questioning of jurors about their potential biases, as occurred in the Bernardo case, is the exception rather than the rule in Canadian trials. In most cases jurors are chosen without any questioning at all. Their names are randomly selected from the assembled panel and they are called to the front of the courtroom. Without any information other than the juror's name, address, occupation, physical appearance, and demeanour the Crown prosecutor or the accused's lawyer may reject the juror by using one of a limited number of peremptory challenges allotted to each side (20 each in murder trials and 12 each for most other crimes).

If neither side exercises a peremptory challenge, the person becomes a member of the jury. This procedure is in striking contrast to the selection procedure used in the United States, which, as in the O.J. Simpson trial, often involves detailed and personally intrusive examination of aspects of prospective jurors' private lives.

In the important case of *R. v. Hubbert* (1975), an appeal court stated that Canadian law begins with a presumption that jurors will follow their oath to listen to the evidence with an open mind and decide the case fairly and impartially. One reason for this presumption is that, unlike the United States, where the First Amendment to the constitution has been interpreted to mean that the news media should almost always be given access to all phases of the trial process, Canada imposes some limits on what the press may report before the start of trial. In the preliminary inquiry held to determine if there is enough evidence against the accused to warrant the trial the judge almost routinely enters an order forbidding media to report any details of the hearing until the end of the trial. This is done to prevent the potential jury pool from being tainted by emotions about the case or about evidence that may not be admitted at trial (e.g., a confession that the judge decides was improperly obtained by the police). Additionally, section 649 of the Criminal Code forbids persons who serve on a jury in Canada from discussing anything about the deliberations that led to their verdict. To do so would be a summary offence, punishable by a fine of up to $5,000 and/or imprisonment for up to 6 months. Thus, the jurors in the Bernardo case did not attempt to be selected for jury service in order to sell their stories to a tabloid newspaper or to sign a lucrative book contract, a problem that may have compromised some of the jurors in the Simpson murder trial.

The *Hubbert* court provided two other reasons for the presumption of impartiality. It noted that the trial judge admonishes jurors to be impartial and reminds them that they have sworn an oath to be impartial. Additionally, the fact that the verdict is decided by 12 persons means that any individual biases will be cancelled out during jury deliberations. Although not extensively studied, social psychologists have conducted some research that bears on both of these assumptions and we can assess how they stand up empirically.

In an experimentally sophisticated study of pretrial publicity, Kramer, Kerr & Carroll (1990) had groups of college students and jury-eligible non-students from the community watch a videotaped trial of an armed robbery. Prior to participating in the study, participants viewed (either immediately before or about 12 days before the experiment) a videotape of ostensibly real media (television and newspaper) reports of the alleged robbery. For a third of the participants, the media coverage conveyed *factually* biasing information. That is, prior to the trial component of the study, these participants learned that the accused had a prior criminal record and that incriminating evidence (which, due to a faulty police search, was inadmissible at trial) had been found. Neither of these pieces of evidence was presented at trial. Another third of the participants learned that a car involving a hit-and-run accident that seriously injured a 7-year-old girl matched the description of the robbery get-away car and that the accused was a prime suspect in the hit-and-run. This type of biasing information was referred to as *emotionally* biasing; it conveyed information that had no evidentiary bearing on the case but that could potentially arouse negative feelings towards the accused. As in the factually biasing condition, the emotionally biasing information was not mentioned at trial. The remainder of participants, those in the control condition, were exposed to media accounts that merely conveyed basic facts of the case (e.g., the arrest, the charge) that would be presented at the subsequent trial. After viewing the trial, the participants rendered an individual verdict and then were asked to deliberate in small groups of 4–6 to reach a unanimous verdict.

Some of the most interesting results in the study were found by comparing the verdicts decided by the jurors as individuals to those produced after deliberation. Although the researchers found that neither the factual nor the emotional form of the biasing information influenced the participants' predeliberation verdicts, effects did occur for judgments collected after the deliberations. That is, following the deliberations, those who had been exposed to the biasing pretrial information rendered more negative evaluations and verdicts compared to those in the control group. For the factually biasing information, however, the negative impact occurred only when the publicity had been presented immediately prior to the trial (we will return to the significance of this finding in a later section of the chapter). In contrast, the negative impact of the emotionally biasing publicity occurred regardless of when participants had been exposed to it. That is, those who had been exposed to emotionally arousing publicity, regardless of when they heard it, were more prone to evaluate the defendant negatively; and the verdicts of these juries were more likely to be guilty, compared to those not exposed to such publicity.

Also interesting was the finding that when the initial verdict preferences of the jury were evenly split between guilty and not guilty, the jurors were more likely to emerge from their deliberations with a guilty verdict if they had been exposed to the emotionally biasing information. This finding is in contrast to what occurred in the other conditions in the study, as well as what has consistently been found in other jury research. Typically, researchers find what has been referred to as a leniency effect; when initial verdict preferences are evenly split, the jury tends to vote not guilty (MacCoun & Kerr, 1988; see Chapter 6). Thus, contrary to the court's assumption in *Hubbert* that juror biases will be cancelled out during deliberation, the deliberation enhanced, rather than diminished, the impact of the biasing information. These findings suggest that in circumstances where jurors hold strong feelings about a case, the assumption that deliberation will ameliorate these biases may not hold.

The Kramer et al. study also investigated whether the presence of judicial cautionary instructions to ignore pretrial publicity might ameliorate the impact of the two different forms of publicity. To this end, half of the participants in the study had been instructed by the judge at the end of the trial to "not ... use pretrial publicity or their reactions to it as a basis for judgment in the case" (p. 419). The other half heard instructions in which no reference was made to the pretrial publicity. Consistent with other research investigating the effectiveness of cautionary instructions (see Chapter 6), the presence of the admonition to ignore the publicity had no impact on either individual jurors' verdicts or the jury verdicts decided by deliberation. In terms of the courts' reliance on judicial admonishments to deal with the problems raised by prejudicial publicity, the researchers found no support for the contention that the negative impact of pretrial publicity can effectively be curbed by the use of judicial cautionary instructions.

Another study (Study 1, Freedman, Martin, & Mota, 1998) that investigated the impact of judicial admonishments pertaining to pretrial publicity similarly found no evidence for their effectiveness. Like the Kramer et al. study, the negative prejudicial information used in this study failed to have an impact on participants' judgments. Only individual judgments were collected, however, and it is unclear whether the pretrial information would have exerted an impact if deliberations had been included (as in the Kramer et al. study). In any event, since the publicity had no impact, the study does not provide an adequate test of the effectiveness of judicial instructions to ignore its influence.

REMEDIES: WHEN THE IMPARTIALITY PRESUMPTION IS OVERCOME

Although there is a presumption that jurors will be impartial, the Criminal Code and case law recognize that in some circumstances jurors may not be impartial. There are three solutions, or remedies, under these exceptional conditions: an adjournment, a change of venue, and a challenge for cause.

An Adjournment

The most rarely used solution to deal with pretrial prejudicial information involves an adjournment, which involves a delay of the trial. This remedy is premised on the assumption that the passage of time will reduce the salience and potential impact of the prejudicial information as people's memory of the information fades over time. Because the availability and memory of witnesses also fades over time, the courts, not surprisingly, are very reluctant to resort to this solution. Other than the Kramer et al. (1990) study described above, which utilized a relatively short time delay, very little research exists on the extent to which the passage of time reduces the effects of pretrial prejudicial information. The results of the Kramer et al. study certainly raise some very interesting questions. The time delay between exposure to the publicity and the trial reduced the negative impact of the factually biasing information but not that of the emotionally arousing information. These findings suggest that if the information conveyed in the pretrial publicity is of such a nature that it is unlikely to be forgotten or that it evokes such strong emotions (as in the case of Bernardo), a delay is unlikely to have much impact.

Change of Venue

Following the tradition set in English law, the accused is ordinarily expected to be tried in the community where the crime occurred. However, as the Criminal Code states, if "it appears expedient to the ends of justice," either the Crown or the accused can ask that a trial be moved to a new location. In practice, this happens infrequently and the burden for getting the trial moved is on the party who wishes to have it moved. The standard for relocating a trial is that there is a "fair and reasonable probability of partiality or prejudice" in the community.

Bernardo was moved from St Catharines to Toronto on the grounds that a fair trial might not be held in the St Catharines community.

Mass Media Effects

Most often the reason for requesting a change of venue is prejudice against the accused person on the grounds that many members of the potential jury pool have been tainted by mass media coverage of the case. A number of researchers (e.g., Bronson, 1989; Freedman & Burke, 1996; Moran & Cutler, 1991, 1997; Nietzel & Dillehay, 1982; Vidmar & Judson, 1981) have conducted surveys involving media coverage of notorious crimes that were coming to trial. The surveys ask questions about the amount of knowledge the public has about the crime, the attitudes held about the accused person, and the extent to which people indicate that they believe the accused person is or is not guilty. Such studies have found that the more media exposure a potential juror has had regarding a particular case, the greater the likelihood that the juror will believe the accused person is guilty. Although these correlational findings are indicative of the negative impact of the publicity, there is of course another possible interpretation. Perhaps individuals who are inclined to believe that people charged with a crime are guilty are the same people who are likely to read or watch stories about crime events.

To study causation more clearly, social psychologists also conduct controlled experiments (see also Chapter 6). For instance, Ogloff and Vidmar (1994) conducted an experiment arising out of the trials resulting from the Mt Cashel Orphanage cases in Newfoundland. In 1989 17 members and former members of the Congregation of Irish Christian Brothers of Canada, who ran the orphanage, were charged with sexually abusing the boys under their care during the 1970s. Before the men came to trial, the government of Newfoundland set up a Royal Commission of Inquiry to determine if there had been an obstruction of justice regarding a police inquiry about irregularities at the orphanage (i.e., an investigation that started in the early part of that decade had suddenly been called to a halt and there were allegations that government officials had ordered it stopped). Lawyers for the accused brothers argued that publicity from the inquiry into these allegations would prejudice their clients' rights to a fair trial. They asked that the public inquiry be postponed until after the trials. When the government replied that the inquiry was to proceed as scheduled, the lawyers requested that television cameras be barred from the hearing because of the negative impact television coverage would have on viewers. They argued that newspaper coverage would be less prejudicial. In fact, the hearings were televised for 150 days in the St John's metropolitan area and indeed much of the time throughout the rest of Canada. The testimony of the boys, now young men in their twenties, was very graphic and disturbing, as they told about specific sexual acts and about being beaten severely by leather straps.

To test the hypothesis that television coverage of the Mt Cashel case was more prejudicial than newspaper coverage, Ogloff and Vidmar (1994) exposed some research participants to televised excerpts of the testimony while other participants read near identical testimony in printed form. Still other participants in control groups saw or read some neutral material. Consistent with the concerns of the lawyers for the accused brothers, compared to the print version, the televised material had a greater negative impact on the participants and on their beliefs that the accused were guilty. Exposure to the combination of both print and television had the most biasing impact on the participants' evaluations.

The study also raised important questions about whether, under such conditions, people's assertions that they can be impartial should be trusted. Even though exposure to the prejudicial material produced clear bias in the experimental groups, when participants were asked at the end of the experiment if they could be unbiased in judging the guilt of the brothers they were as likely to claim impartiality as those persons in the control conditions. These findings are consistent with other studies showing the effects of mass media coverage (Kerr, Kramer, Carroll, & Alfini, 1991; Nietzel & Dillehay, 1982; Simon & Eimerman, 1971; Vidmar & Melnitzer, 1984). It is possible, as Ogloff and Vidmar proposed, that the participants were unaware of the connection between their attitudes and the potential impact of media coverage (e.g., Nisbett & Wilson, 1977), or they may have been aware of the connection but for socially desirable reasons misreported their feelings (e.g., Bronson, 1989; Crowne & Marlowe, 1964). Alternatively, participants may have been correctly reporting on their ability to set these prejudices aside and judge the case fairly. Because the study did not involve a trial component, the question still remains as to whether these individuals would in fact have evaluated the case differently than participants who had not been exposed to the pretrial information.

Using a different setting, Wilson and Bornstein (1998) exposed research participants to either emotional or factual publicity presented via videotape or written format. Both factual and emotional publicity produced bias, but there was no difference in effect between the video and print formats. These results are not consistent with the findings of Ogloff and Vidmar (1994) or the finding of Kramer et al. (1990), which indicated that the video and emotional publicity had a greater negative impact than the print and factual publicity, respectively. Various methodological differences across the studies may account for these discrepancies and future research is necessary to unravel precisely what variables are responsible. For instance, in the Wilson and Bornstein study the video and print conditions presented participants with exactly the same information, conveyed in the video condition via a clip of a news reporter reading it and in the print condition via a written news article. In contrast, in the Ogloff and Vidmar study actual video and newspaper reports were used. Thus, the video condition included actual segments of testimony from the victims. This may account for the greater impact of the information.

Also at issue in this research is the question of whether the presentation of the trial evidence weakens the impact of the pretrial publicity (Freedman et al., 1998; Otto, Penrod, & Dexter, 1994). Of relevance to this question are the results of an experiment conducted by Freedman et al. (Study 2, 1998). Two weeks prior to being exposed to a trial, participants in this study were provided with either prejudicial or neutral publicity about the case. Half of the participants were asked to form an opinion about the guilt of the accused immediately after reading the publicity. The researchers found evidence for the negative impact of the pretrial information, but only for those participants asked to rate the accused's guilt immediately after reading the publicity. It is possible, as the researchers conclude, that by asking participants to form an initial judgment about the accused's guilt, these individuals may have given the material greater attention than those not asked to form a judgment. This greater attention and thought may have resulted in greater commitment to a decision, which subsequently affected post-trial verdicts. If such attention is unrepresentative of what occurs in real-life cases involving heavy pretrial publicity, this suggests that studies that do not include trial presentations may overestimate the impact of pretrial publicity. If, on the other hand, the attention is more akin to what occurs in real-life cases involving heavy publicity, the findings would provide support for the negative impact of the publicity.

Recently, a group of researchers conducted a meta-analysis of the hypothesis that exposure to negative pretrial publicity increases people's perceptions of an accused's guilt (Steblay, Besirevic, Fulero, & Jimenez-Lorente, 1999). This statistical procedure, which is designed to uncover patterns across studies that have addressed the same question, included 44 tests of the pretrial publicity hypothesis that were performed across 26 different investigations on the topic. The results of this analysis were clear: participants exposed to negative pretrial publicity were more likely to judge the accused guilty compared to those exposed to less or no negative pretrial publicity. The analyses also revealed that the effects of negative pretrial publicity were strongest in the studies that were "parallel in ... features to the experience of real jurors" (p. 229); that is, effects were strongest for those that included "a pretrial verdict assessment, use of the potential juror pool as subjects, multiple points of negative information included in the PTP [pretrial publicity], real PTP, crimes of murder, or drugs, and greater length of time between PTP exposure and judgment" (p. 219).

Rumour and Gossip

Sometimes strong prejudice against an accused person arises among members of a community even when prejudicial mass media coverage is absent. Canadian and American social psychologists have studied the psychology and sociology of rumour transmission since the First World War (Allport & Postman, 1947; Irving, 1943; Logan, 1918; Rosnow & Fine, 1976). A basic finding of this research is that when events are of high relevance and concern to the community, both factually accurate and inaccurate information are likely to be spread by word of mouth through informal social networks, particularly when the community is less urbanized.

These basic insights have been applied to help understand an additional source of pretrial prejudice. Vidmar and Melnitzer (1984) demonstrated these processes in a case involving the death of a small child in a rural Ontario community (*R. v. Iutzi*, reported in Vidmar & Melnitzer, 1984). Both the father and mother were charged with the crime and each denied it. The lawyers for the accused obtained an order preventing the media from reporting about the preliminary hearing and, indeed, media coverage of all aspects of the case was minimal. Nevertheless, a telephone survey of the community plus follow-up interviews with a sample of residents uncovered the fact that there was a great deal of informal discussion of the event at home, between friends, and at work. Moreover, the discussions were prejudicial against the accused parents. Some people had heard that the parents had killed the child for insurance money, others that the parents had killed the child by putting him in a washing machine, and still others that the mother had a previous child taken away by Child Services. None of these rumours were factually correct. Additionally, many people were ashamed that the event had occurred in their community because, in their view, such things were only supposed to happen in big cities like Toronto. Although the judge did not grant a change of venue in this case, he did consent, on the basis of the survey evidence presented by the defence, to a request for a "challenge for cause," the most frequently employed remedy for dealing with pretrial prejudice, to which we now turn. For another example of the use of survey research in jury selection, see Box 5.1.

Box 5.1

Providing Social Science Evidence

When arguing for a change of venue, the accused person has to convince a judge that there is a "fair and reasonable probability" that an impartial jury cannot be obtained in the community. And judges frequently question whether any prejudice that existed around the time of the crime has dissipated as the case comes to trial months later, on the grounds that emotions cool and people forget details. In the past, the primary evidence used to argue that prejudice still existed in the community involved documentation of newspaper articles about the case. This evidence, however, was often rejected on the grounds that it was unsystematic and unreliable (Vidmar & Judson, 1981). Thus, it has now become increasingly common for lawyers to seek evidence that directly assesses public opinion on the case, and social psychologists or sociologists are sometimes hired to conduct scientific surveys of the community close to the time of trial. Typically carried out by telephone on a sample of persons screened to establish if they would be eligible to serve on a jury, such surveys attempt to determine what people in the community know about the crime and what they think about the guilt or innocence of the accused person (see Bronson, 1989; Nietzel & Dillehay, 1982; *R. v. MacGregor*, 1993; Vidmar & Judson, 1981).

Good surveys attempt to follow methodological guidelines that meet scientific criteria for any survey research (see Diamond, 1994) in order to withstand scrutiny by the judge. The respondents should be chosen by some random method. Initial questions should be open-ended to allow respondents to relate what they know and how they feel about the crime in their own words. Attempts should be made to avoid socially desirable responses. The questions should speak directly to the court's concern, as expressed in *R. v. Parks* (1993), about partiality being an expressed inability to judge the case fairly under the instructions of the judge, as opposed to merely having negative feelings about the accused person or the crime.

R. v. Theberge (1995) involved the stabbing death of the daughter of a local doctor in a northern Ontario city. Due to psychiatric examinations of the accused and some legal technicalities, the case was not ready for trial until almost 4 years had passed. The defence in this case was seeking a change of venue application and the first author (N.V.) of this chapter was called by the defence to conduct a scientific survey of the community that would assess public knowledge about the accused and his crime. The results of the survey demonstrated that prejudice against Theberge was still high and that many people had heard that Theberge was going to plead not guilty by reason of mental illness and were opposed to the plea. In addition, many members of the community were patients of the victim's father or had social ties to her family. Among other questions, the respondents were asked the following question near the end of the interview: "Assume that you were called as a potential juror in the Theberge case and assume you were told by the judge that it was your duty to keep an open mind about the insanity defense. Do you honestly think that you could do so or do you think that your existing attitudes about Mr. Theberge might make you biased against the insanity defense in this case?" Thirty-three per cent of respondents said that they would be biased and most explained that they had too much information about the case and had already formed an opinion that Mr Theberge was guilty of murder. The survey also showed that another 18% of the persons who stated that they could be fair had, in response to earlier questions in the interview, volunteered opinions that Mr Theberge was "definitely guilty," "it was a horrible crime and the insanity defense should not be allowed," or that if a judge and jury found Mr Theberge "not guilty by reason of insanity" they would personally find the verdict "very unacceptable." Thus, about 51% of respondents reflected an inability to be impartial.

After hearing testimony about the survey and after the social scientists who carried out the research were extensively cross-examined by the Crown attorney, the judge granted a change of venue.

Challenge for Cause

A challenge for cause is considered a less extreme remedy than a change of venue. It assumes that a smaller proportion of potential jurors in the population may be biased. The burden of proof to overcome the presumption of impartiality is a realistic potential, a standard lower than the reasonable probability test for a change of venue. The *Hubbert* case laid out the rule that the trial judge has discretion to decide whether jurors should be questioned about bias. It also ruled that the judge should ensure that the questioning is limited to the potential juror's state of mind. Exploration of the juror's personality or background was not to be permitted. In effect the *Hubbert* court stated that the juror was not on trial and that wide-ranging questioning, such as that which takes place in some American trials, was contrary to Canadian law and tradition. Consequently, when Canadian jurors are challenged the questions judges allow are similar to those asked in *Bernardo*, though ordinarily even fewer questions are asked.

Once the judge agrees that a challenge for cause will be allowed, the process of jury selection begins. In contrast to American practice, in which it is the judge who determines whether or not bias has been demonstrated, the jurors themselves are responsible for this decision. This occurs because the question of whether prospective jurors are impartial is a factual question. The procedure is quite unique to Canada and we need briefly to review it. To begin the process, two individuals are randomly chosen from the jury panel and sworn to serve as "triers." In effect the challenge involves a mini-trial on the impartiality of the prospective juror. The two triers listen to the prospective juror's responses to the questions and, under instructions from the judge, render a unanimous decision on whether or not the individual is "impartial between the Queen and the accused." Although the triers may retire to consider their decision, they typically conduct their deliberation (in hushed voices) in open court. If they find that the individual is "not impartial," another juror is called. This process continues until an unbiased juror is found. If neither lawyer exercises a peremptory challenge to this individual the unbiased juror then replaces one of the initial triers and becomes a trier for the selection of the second juror. The first two jurors then serve as jurors for the third juror, jurors two and three are triers for juror four, jurors three and four are triers for juror five, and so the process continues until twelve jurors are seated.

The utility of the challenge obviously depends on the ability to elicit and detect partiality, and this process raises some very interesting psychological questions. To what extent is a juror's self-assessment an accurate indicator of partiality? Are the lay triers competent assessors of partiality? From a psychological perspective, are some questioning methods better than others at identifying partiality? Are some methods better at eliciting disclosure? To answer these questions, let us consider the social psychological dynamics that underlie the challenge process.

Accurate self-assessment is premised on both the individual's awareness of the bias, including its potential to interfere with his or her decision, and honest disclosure of that bias. As a number of psychological studies indicate (e.g., Nisbett & Wilson, 1977), awareness of one's biases and their potential impact, even at the best of times, is no simple matter. To this we must add the novel and unique features of the courtroom setting. Not surprisingly, most prospective jurors enter the courtroom with some trepidation. To be questioned about one's ability to serve as a juror only adds to this already intimidating environment. In this context the demand characteristics of the situation are fairly salient to the potential jurors and the pressures to provide socially desirable responses are heightened (Nickerson, Mayo, & Smith, 1986). Although there is little empirical research that directly examines the effectiveness of the challenge process, social psychological research does suggest some conditions under which disclosure is more likely to occur. For instance, within Canada, the challenge or questioning is conducted by the lawyers. Within the United States, however, where the right to question each prospective juror on the panel is available in virtually all criminal and civil cases, the questioning (referred to as the voir dire) can be conducted by either the judge or the lawyers. Although one might hypothesize that prospective jurors might be more honest in their responses to a judge, as opposed to an attorney, research suggests that greater candour is elicited by an attorney-conducted voir dire because the evaluative pressures of the situation are less salient (Jones, 1987).

Another factor related to the potential effectiveness of the challenge concerns whether or not the questioning of the prospective juror is conducted in the absence of the other potential jurors. Although it seems that the preferred position of the Canadian courts is that the prospective jurors (with the exception of the two triers) remain outside the courtroom during the challenge process (*R. v. English*, 1993), this is not required (see Tanovich, Paciocco, and Skurka, 1997). Some legal commentators have also argued that the prospective jurors should remain in the courtroom during the challenge (Cooper, 1994). The research, although not extensive, tends to support the preferred practice of the trial courts. Because it is more difficult for people to admit socially unacceptable or negative information about themselves, especially in public or group settings (Suggs & Sales, 1978), the presence of others is more likely to inhibit honest disclosure of prejudice and bias. As well, if prospective jurors are present during the questioning of others, the demand characteristics of the situation become abundantly clear. The potential juror may learn the types of responses that result in getting on or off the jury and may tailor his or her responses accordingly (*R. v. English*, 1993). Honest responses are more likely if they have been elicited spontaneously.

Let us return for the moment to the *Iutzi* case described above. While the entire jury panel was still seated in the courtroom, the presiding judge asked any "persons to come forward who had a relationship with any of the parties to the case or who could not, on other grounds, be impartial" (Vidmar & Melnitzer, 1984, p. 497). Four of the 123 persons on the panel did so. The challenge for cause process then began. Each prospective juror was asked up to 15 questions (far more than would be permitted today). Fifty of the 75 prospective jurors called were challenged for cause.

Finally, it is also possible that the challenge process itself may enhance the ability of the jurors to be impartial since they are asked themselves and hear other jurors being asked if they can be impartial. The Ontario Court of Appeal asserted in the recent case of *R. v. Koh et al.* (1998) that the process not only removes jurors who are forthright about their prejudices, it sensitizes the remaining jurors about their duty to be impartial. This is an interesting and testable hypothesis for some social psychologist to investigate.

We now turn our attention to a more recent and controversial applications of the challenge for cause: challenges for cause on the basis of generic prejudice.

Generic Prejudice: Race

While the challenge for cause procedure is sometimes used to screen jurors for the effects of media or community publicity, as in *Bernardo* and *Iutzi*, its most recent and controversial use has been to screen for generic prejudices. The *Parks* case, discussed above in the context of its articulation of a definition of partiality, was about racial generic prejudice. Parks, a Jamaican immigrant and an alleged drug dealer, was charged with second degree murder following the death of a white person, a cocaine user, in Toronto. The trial judge refused a defence request to challenge the jurors about whether they could be fair and impartial considering that the accused was involved with cocaine and other drugs and considering that he was a black Jamaican accused of killing a white person. The Ontario Court of Appeal agreed with the trial judge on the issue of drugs in this case, but ordered a new trial for Parks because, the court asserted, Parks should have been allowed to question jurors about potential racism.

In considering the propriety of Parks's request, the appellate court posed two questions. Was there a realistic possibility that a potential juror would be biased against a black accused charged with murdering a white person? And was there a realistic possibility that the juror would be influenced in the performance of his or her judicial duties, that is, he or she might be unable to follow instructions to decide the case impartially? With respect to the first question, the court noted "an ever growing body of studies and reports documenting the extent and intensity of racist beliefs in contemporary Canadian society" (p. 338). When it turned to the second question it referred to social psychological research that challenged the presumption that traditional trial safeguards would suffice to overcome such prejudice. For instance, reviews of experimental studies by Johnson (1985) and Pfeifer (1990) showing juries are more inclined to convict defendants who are not of the same race as the juror were cited. The court observed that these effects tended to occur "where the evidence against the accused is not strong or where the victim of the offence is of the same race as the juror" (*R. v. Parks*, 1993, p. 345). Thus, social psychological research played an important part in helping the court to articulate why racial prejudice might be translated into a juror's behaviour, resulting in a verdict based on stereotypes or hostility.

A year later in British Columbia, however, the courts differed with the reasoning articulated in *Parks* with respect to racial prejudice against Native Canadians (*R. v. Williams*, 1994). Victor Williams, a Native Canadian, was charged with robbing a Victoria pizza parlour. Using *Parks* as a partial basis for the motion asking for a challenge for cause, defence counsel wanted to ask the jurors if they held any biases about Native Canadians that would prevent them from being fair and impartial, particularly since the main witness against the accused was white. Williams submitted some social psychological and sociological studies, as well as experts to support his claim about potential prejudice. The trial court rejected his motion. Interestingly, the judge conceded that there was widespread prejudice against Native Canadians, stating: "Natives historically have been and continue to be the object of bias and prejudice which, in some respects, has become more overt and widespread in recent years as the result of tensions created by developments in such areas as land claims and fishing rights" (*R. v. Williams*, 1994, p. 198). The judge also acknowledged that there was a realistic possibility of prejudice because the accused was Native and the victim was white. But he asserted that there was no reasonable possibility that the prejudice would affect the jurors' verdicts, since the jury system provides effective safeguards against such bias.

Williams was convicted but appealed his conviction, citing the failure of the trial judge to allow the challenge for cause. The British Columbia Court of Appeal upheld the conviction, citing the same basic reasons as the trial judge (*R. v. Williams*, 1996). Williams then appealed to the Supreme Court of Canada. In a unanimous decision (*R. v. Williams*, 1998) the nine Supreme Court justices reversed the British Columbia court's decision, ruling that Williams should have been allowed to ask jurors about whether they could be impartial. Williams was entitled to a new trial.

The Supreme Court's decision in *Williams* seems to be consistent with a number of studies involving attitudes towards Native Canadians. Haddock, Zanna, and Esses (1994), conducted three studies in which they assessed a range of stereotypic beliefs among Canadians. Among their findings they found that many persons characterized Natives as "alcoholics, lazy and uneducated." Moreover, the studies also found that emotions of anger and uneasiness were associated with the stereotypes. Donakowski and Esses (1996) found a relationship between stereotypes of Native persons and beliefs that Natives were less likely to "promote [Canadian] traditions and culture, more likely to threaten the work ethic, and perhaps more likely to threaten national unity" (p. 89). These findings are consistent with other studies by Mackie (1974), Berry and Kalin (1995), Berry and Wells (1994), and Bibby (1987) showing that, among a substantial portion of Canadians, Native Canadians are held in low regard compared to other ethnic groups that make up the Canadian mosaic.

It is still too early to determine the full impact of the *Williams* decision, but its potential implications may be quite far reaching. For instance, are there other ethnic or racial groups that evoke strong negative stereotypes? Berry and Kalin (1995), for example, analysed a nationwide survey that showed that for some Canadians "Arabs," "Moslems," "Indo-Pakistanis," and "Sikhs" were rated more negatively than "Native Indians" and "West Indian Blacks." Does this suggest that some jurors may be impartial in judging accused who belong to one of these racial or religious groups? Does the issue of partiality relate to the victims and witnesses as well? What if the victim is of the same race as the accused person? And, finally, how might the race of the accused interact with the type of crime he or she is accused of committing? For instance, some research has documented the existence of crime-related racial stereotypes, with "blue collar" crimes (e.g., robbery, assault) associated with black accused and "white collar" crimes (e.g., fraud, embezzlement) associated with white accused (Gordon, Michels, & Nelson, 1996; Sunnafrank & Fontes, 1983). Drawing on this research, Gordon and his colleagues (Gordon, 1990, 1993; Gordon, Bindrim, McNicholas, & Walden, 1988) varied both the race of the accused (black vs. white) and the type of crime committed (burglary vs. embezzlement). Findings from these studies suggest that people judge the accused more harshly if he or she is accused of committing a race-stereotypic crime (e.g., white-embezzlement, black-burglary). In *R. v. Koh et al.* (1998) the Ontario Court of Appeal seemed to agree with the *Parks* reasoning and extended the right to challenge on the grounds of racial or ethnic prejudice to persons of Chinese heritage, as well as other visible minorities.

In a number of cases Canadian courts have emphasized that not only must trials be fair, they must also be seen to be fair (*R. v. Parks*, 1993; *R. v. Sherratt*, 1991). Even the British Columbia courts, while rejecting a challenge for cause, conceded that Aboriginal peoples have little trust in the fairness of the criminal justice system (*R. v. Williams*, 1994; *R. v. Williams*, 1996). A body of social psychological research on procedural justice (Lind & Tyler, 1988) has shown that when people perceive a process to be fair they are more likely to accord the process legitimacy, even when the outcome is not in their favour. This would suggest that accused persons who are members of racial minority groups and other members of their community may accord greater legitimacy to the trial process when challenges for cause are allowed than when they are not.

Generic Prejudice: Sexual Preference

There is a substantial body of social psychological and sociological research indicating that some persons hold deeply hostile feelings about homosexual behaviour. Herek (1986, 1988, 1989) has shown that among substantial segments of North American society strong negative emotions are attached to homosexuality. Because of these attitudes, homosexuals are frequent victims of hate crimes. As Herek (1986) observed, "what a person *does* sexually defines who the person *is* ..." and, "[n]ot being what one is supposed to be receives many labels including criminal wicked and sick" (p. 568). A study by Bibby (1987) reported that 70% of Canadians believed two adults of the same gender having sexual relations was wrong. Another nationwide survey of Canadians (*Reid Report*, 1994) found that 46% of Canadians believed that anyone who openly admitted homosexuality would face job discrimination. A Canadian Gallup survey in 1994 (*Gallup Report*, 1994) found that 20% of Canadians indicated that homosexuals should not be employed as doctors, 31% said that they should not be employed as junior school teachers, and 31% thought that they should not be members of the clergy. The extent to which individuals harbour negative attitudes towards homosexuals has also been confirmed in correlational studies (Haddock, Zanna, & Esses, 1993). Might these attitudes also affect the ability of some jurors to be impartial?

In *R. v. Alli* (1996) the accused was convicted of sexual assault on another male prisoner while both were confined in the "drunk tank" of a local lock-up and sentenced to ten months in jail. Alli had sought to challenge jurors on the grounds of potential prejudice against homosexuals, but his motion was denied by the trial judge. The Ontario Court of Appeal upheld the trial judge's ruling, but it did not deny that such prejudice could exist. The problem was that Alli had produced no evidence to substantiate his claim regarding homosexual prejudices. You will recall that the accused person has the burden of providing some evidence to back up a claim of potential prejudice, though a judge has discretion to allow a challenge if there appears to be an air of reality to a claim of potential prejudice.

In *R. v. Welch* (1996) the trial judge did allow a challenge for cause in a case involving a first degree murder charge in which both the accused and the victim were homosexuals. Thirteen jurors, constituting 21% of those challenged, admitted prejudice and were found to be partial. In *R. v. Musson* (1996) the accused was charged with a sexual offence against another adult male. Musson denied not only that the assault had taken place but that he was homosexual. He introduced a substantial body of research findings to back his claim about prejudice against homosexual acts. The trial judge concluded that homophobia and attitudes about sexual assault were often linked and allowed a challenge for cause. Of 21 jurors challenged, 4 admitted to prejudice and were excused from jury service for the case.

Generic prejudice: Offence based: Various judges, primarily in the Province of Ontario, have occasionally recognized another form of generic prejudice, "offence based," and allowed challenges for cause. Such cases have involved offences related to drugs, domestic violence against a spouse or partner, and violence involving vulnerable persons such as children or the elderly (see Tanovich et al., 1997). Although such challenges have been infrequent, the judge has typically noted that the particular crime in these instances was likely to evoke strong negative emotions or revulsion in some members of the community; thus there was "a reasonable prospect that some members of the jury panel may be unable or unwilling to adjudicate impartially" (Tanovich et al., 1997, pp. 119–120). For instance, some judges in Ontario have allowed challenges for cause in cases involving charges of sexual assault, particularly when the alleged victim was a child. Vidmar (1997) reviewed 25 trials in which such challenges had been allowed. Across these cases, substantial percentages of challenged jurors stated that they could not be fair and impartial in deciding the guilt or innocence of the accused and were excused from serving on the jury (see Table 5.1). In *R. v. Betker* (1997), however, the Ontario Court of Appeal reviewed a case involving an accused charged of sexual assault and concluded that such offence-based challenges should not be allowed. The judges' reasoning was complicated, but asserted that the issues in sexual assault differed from racial prejudice and did not fall under the permissible grounds for challenges set out in the Criminal Code. While this case appeared to have closed the doors to offence-based challenges, in light of the Supreme Court's decision in *R. v. Williams* (1998), some judges in Ontario began to allow challenges in sexual assault trials again, but these lower court decisions are now being challenged in higher courts. The future of offence-based challenges is unclear but

TABLE 5.1
Challenge for cause by case, city, and date, sex/age of complainant, relation of complainant to defendant, number of jurors questioned, number rejected as partial, and percent of jurors found "Not Impartial"

Case	City/date	Sex/age complainant(s)	Relationship to defendant	Jurors questioned	Jurors found partial —	%
1. Jackson	Ottawa, 1991	Female: 14 yrs	Daughter	27	13	48
2. Boardman	Ottawa, 1992	2 Females: unknown age	Nieces	36	13	36
3. Thomas	Toronto, 1993	Female: 5 yrs	Unrelated	36	4	11
4. Higson	Hamilton, 1993	Female: 10 yrs	Unrelated	31	13	42
5. McGuire	Hamilton, 1993	Female: 8 yrs	Granddaughter	32	14	44
6. R.G.	Hamilton, 1994	Females: 7 yrs	Daughter	22	4	18
7. Talbot	Toronto, 1994	Males: 3 teenagers	Unrelated	47	16	34
8. Greenwood	Barrie, 1994	Female: 5 yrs	Foster child of his parents	30	7	23
9. Lewis	Barrie, 1994	Male: 16 yrs	Unrelated	35	9	26
10. McBirnie	London, 1994	Female: 9–11 yrs	Stepdaughter	35	14	40
11. Rosler	Toronto, 1994	Male: 7 yrs	Unrelated	35	11	31
12. Pascoe	Whitby, 1994	Males: 8 and 12 yrs	Unrelated	37	17	46
13. Chaimovitz	Hamilton, 1994	Males: Many; 13–17 yrs	Unrelated	34	20	59
14. Llorenz	Toronto, 1994	Female: at 10–16 yrs	Unrelated	34	10	29
15. Kerr	Toronto, 1994	Males: 3, "children"	Unrelated	37	7	19
16. M. and M.	Toronto, 1994	Females: unknown	Daughters	36	17	47
17. Lawrence	Downsview, 1995	Female: 6 yrs	Daughter's girlfriend	32	13	41
18. Pihlberg	Toronto, 1995	Female: 23 yrs	Stranger	43	13	30
19. Gallager	Toronto, 1995	Female: 8 yrs	Unrelated	28	14	50
20. Webb	Niagara Falls, 1995	Female: at 15 yrs; at 21 yrs	Unrelated	56	31	55
21. M.H.	Whitby, 1995	Female: 7–14 yrs	Daughter	26	10	38
22. Chisolm	Milton, 1995	Female: 14 yrs	Babysitter	21	3	14
23. Henderson	Kitchener, 1995	6 Females: 9–14 yrs	Daughter, friends	41	20	49
24. Jones	Hamilton, 1994	Female under 14 yrs, at 29 yrs	Daughters	26	8	31
25. Mattingly	Whitby, 1994	Females: 4 children, 8–17 yrs, multiple times	Sister-in-law and foster child of parents	32	14	44

SOURCE: Vidmar (1997)

social psychologists can contribute by further researching the issues raised in these cases.

SUMMARY

The jury system is an important and highly visible part of Canadian legal culture and the right to trial by jury for serious crimes is enshrined in the Canadian Charter. While the idea of being judged by a "jury of one's peers" is part of popular knowledge about the legal system, this chapter has introduced the idea that a jury of peers is limited to persons who are "impartial." We live in an age when mass media and other technologies can quickly disseminate potentially damaging information about a trial. As well, Canada has evolved into a country containing highly visible minority groups and, unfortunately, prejudices held by some against those minorities. Canadian courts are engaged in a continuing process of attempting to ensure that the jurors who are called upon to judge their fellow Canadians at trial are fair and are also seen to be fair. The courts have sometimes relied upon social science findings to help formulate rules and remedies for prejudice and to implement those rules. The approach they have taken makes the Canadian jury distinctly different from the system in the United States, particularly in the procedures used to select the jury. Social psychological research, both laboratory studies and field studies, has taught us a great deal about jury behaviour as it pertains to issues of prejudice and the chances of obtaining a fair trial. Nevertheless, as this chapter demonstrates, many questions of a social psychological nature remain to be investigated.

QUESTIONS FOR DISCUSSION

1. In both the *Williams* (1998) and *Parks* (1993) decisions discussed in the chapter, the court took note of the fact that not only must trials be fair, they must also be seen to be fair by the accused, and by the whole community, particularly any members who belong to racial minorities. Discuss the importance of the emphasis on this issue. What types of studies could be undertaken to test the hypothesis of "perceived procedural fairness" in the specific context of the *Williams* and *Parks* decisions?
2. In light of the research documenting crime-related racial stereotypes, discuss whether homophobia and type of crime may be intertwined to pro-

duce juror bias. For example, are homophobic attitudes more likely to be linked to lack of impartiality if a homosexual is charged with sexual assault on a minor than if the same person were charged with bank robbery or burglary?

3. What types of social psychological research do you think might be relevant to assess potential juror bias in cases involving pretrial publicity? What type of information might be relevant to the court's decision about whether or not to allow a change of venue or a challenge for cause?

4. Might the process of being questioned about personal prejudices have an impact on jurors' deliberations? Might the challenge process sensitize even those jurors who are found impartial to the need to be more careful to avoid any prejudicial attitudes? Discuss some of the broader implications of the challenge process.

RECOMMENDED READING

Hans, V., and Vidmar, N. (1986). *Judging the jury.* New York: Plenum Press.

Kramer, G.P. Kerr, N.L., & Carroll, J.S. (1990). Pretrial publicity, judicial remedies and jury bias. *Law & Human Behavior, 14,* 409–438.

Peterson, C. (1993). Institutionalized racism: The need for reform of the criminal justice system. *McGill Law Journal, 38,* 147–179.

R. v. Williams (1998), 124 C.C.C. (3d) 481.

Tanovich, D.M., Paciocco, D.M., & Skurka, S. (1997). *Jury selection in criminal trials: Skills, science, and the law.* Concord, ON: Irwin Law.

6. The Jury: Deciding Guilt and Innocence

Regina A. Schuller and Meagan Yarmey

On 31 August 1986, Angelique Lavallee killed her common law husband, shooting him in the back of the head. This fatal shot, which culminated a 3-year relationship in which she had been repeatedly brutalized by her husband, resulted in a charge of second degree murder. At trial, the defence did not dispute that Ms Lavallee had shot her husband, but claimed that she committed the act in self-defence, that is, out of fear for her life. The fact that her husband was shot as he was leaving the room clearly presented difficulty to her claim. In support of her defence, two expert witnesses testified regarding the battered woman syndrome. One of these experts also provided the following opinion evidence: "I think ... she felt in the final tragic moment that her life was on the line, that unless she defended herself, unless she reacted in a violent way, that [sic] she would die. I mean, he made it very explicit to her, from what she told me and from the information I have from the material that you forwarded to me, that she had, I think, to defend herself against his violence" (R. v. Lavalle, 1988, p. 393). Evidence presented at trial indicated that Ms Lavallee's lethal actions had been preceded by years of physical abuse at the hands of her husband. The aim of the expert testimony, which described the dynamics and impact of physical abuse on a woman, was to provide the jurors with a framework for understanding her perceptions and actions at the time of the killing. As the court stated, "Why would a woman put up with this kind of treatment? Why would she continue to live with such a man? How could she love a partner who beat her to the point of requiring hospitalization? We would expect the woman to pack her bags and go? Where is her self respect?" (Lavallee v. R. 1990, p. 112)

Authors' note: Preparation of this chapter was supported by a research grant from the Sciences and Humanities Research Council to the first author.

The jury acquitted Ms Lavallee, but a subsequent appeal by the Crown on evidentiary issues involving the expert testimony was affirmed by the Manitoba Court of Appeal and a new trial was ordered (R. v. Lavallee, 1988). Before this trial took place, however, the defence appealed the decision, ultimately forcing the Supreme Court of Canada to consider the general issue of the admissibility of battered woman syndrome evidence. Writing on behalf of a near unanimous court, Madam Justice Bertha Wilson overturned the lower court ruling, arguing that the testimony was both "relevant" and "necessary" to the jurors' understanding of a battered woman's actions. In May 1990, Ms Lavallee's acquittal was restored.

Once jurors are selected, their official adjudicative task begins. We can think of the trial as a forum for presenting contested versions of some "reality" or set of events that has occurred in the past. It is the jury's task to determine that reality. What events and psychological states account for Ms Lavallee's behaviour? What events might have precipitated her actions? Do these actions constitute murder or a self-defensive response? The necessity of expert testimony in the case described above clearly illustrates the profound impact that psychological research can play at the trial level. In addition to the direct participation of psychologists in the courtroom, psychological theory and research has also greatly informed our understanding – and to some extent the functioning – of the jury trial. In this chapter we examine a well-researched area within the field of law and psychology – juror/jury decision making. As we will see, the seemingly straightforward task of determining guilt and innocence involves a range of complex decision processes.

THE JURY AND THE LEGAL SYSTEM'S EXPECTATIONS

Unlike the American jury system, which has undergone some structural changes (see below), the institution of the Canadian jury has remained structurally unaltered since the mid-1700s (Hans & Vidmar, 1986). With some minor deviations, the old adage that twelve heads are better than one is well enshrined in Canadian criminal jury trials. And although jurors have the right to disagree about various aspects of the case, they must all be in agreement with the final verdict. The law also clearly articulates what information the jurors are to use in arriving at their verdict. The laws governing the case at hand are the sole domain of the judge. The facts of the case are the sole domain of the jurors. The trial judge determines and instructs the jury on the relevant laws and how they relate to the specific case (additionally, the judge may provide an overview of the evidence or the respective theories of the prosecution and defence), but the jury ultimately determines what events actually transpired. Jurors are expected to apply the laws they are given by the judge to the facts of the case as they see them. For an illustration of the potential conflict that can occur between the jurors' sense of justice and the letter of the law see Box 6.1

Box 6.1

Conflicts between the Jurors' Sense of Justice and the Law

The name of Dr Henry Morgentaler is a familiar one to most Canadians. Openly disobeying the then-existent abortion provisions of the Canadian Criminal Code, Dr Morgentaler opened a private clinic in Montreal in 1970 and, contrary to the Code provisions, began providing abortions in a non-accredited or approved hospital without the approval of a hospital "therapeutic abortion committee" (Wardhaugh, 1989). He was charged and subsequently acquitted by a jury. The Crown appealed the decision. The Quebec Court of Appeal reversed the jury's acquittal, substituting a guilty verdict. This decision was subsequently upheld by the Supreme Court of Canada. Throughout the trial and following his sentence (an 18-month jail term), Dr Morgentaler, in open defiance of the law, continued to operate his Quebec clinic. Again, charges were laid, and again, in two separate trials, the jury found Dr Morgentaler not guilty. Similar events unfolded when Dr Morgentaler opened a clinic in Ontario. In his final trial, in 1984, he was once again tried before a jury and once again found not guilty. Dr Morgentaler's actions were clearly in contravention of the Criminal Code, yet in four separate trials the jury failed to find guilt. How is this possible?

Although there was certainly some variation in the defence offered in each of these trials, basically the jury was invited to acquit Morgentaler on the grounds that "the law under which he was being tried was bad/immoral" (for a detailed account see Wardhaugh, 1989). In essence, the jury in each of these trials was being asked to "nullify" – that is, to ignore – the law. This invitation was most blatant in Dr Morgentaler's final trial in 1984, in which his attorney explicitedly urged the jurors to ignore the law and not apply it to Dr Morgentaler's case, notwithstanding the direction of the trial judge's instructions (Wardhaugh, 1989).

This defence raised a controversial issue that lies at the very heart of the role of the jury. Is the jury bound to follow the law as instructed by the trial judge, or might the jury, as representatives of the community, act as the "conscience of the community" and disobey the law when its application leads to what jury members view as an injustice. The Canadian Supreme Court (*R. v. Morgentaler*, 1988) clearly rejected the former position, strongly arguing against its legitimacy: "A jury ... encouraged to ignore a law it does not like, could lead to gross inequities. One accused could be convicted by a jury who supported the existing law, while another person indicted for the same offence could be acquitted by a jury, with reformist zeal, which wished to express disapproval of the same law. Moreover, a jury could decide that although the law pointed to a conviction, the jury would simply refuse to apply the law to an accused for whom it had sympathy. Alternatively, a jury who feels antipathy towards an accused might convict despite a law which points to acquittal" (pp. 77–78). Some empirical research conducted in the United States bears directly on these hypotheses.

In contrast to the situation in Canada, within the United States nullification is a power rightfully possessed by the jury (Wiener, Habert, Shkodriani, & Staebler, 1991). However, there is no obligation on the part of the court to inform the jury of its nullification powers. At present, only a handful of states (Maryland, Indiana, Georgia) provide jurors with judicial instructions informing them that they have the power to nullify the law (Wiener et al., 1991). For instance, in criminal trials in Maryland, jurors are informed that, while the law "is intended to be helpful to you in reaching a just and proper verdict in the case, it is not binding upon you as members of the jury and you may accept or reject it." To examine some of the issues raised by the nullification controversy, Horowitz (1985) conducted a study in which mock jurors presented with a criminal case were provided with either one of two forms of nullification instructions (the original Maryland instructions or a more radical (i.e., explicit) form of instructions) or no nullification instructions at all. Decisions for three different types of trials were examined: (1) a murder case within the context of a robbery, (2) a drunk driving case involving vehicular homicide, and (3) a euthanasia case involving a "mercy" killing of a terminally ill patient. In all cases, an individual had been killed and the facts were not in dispute.

Although all of the juries exposed to the murder case rendered a guilty verdict, clear differences emerged across the other two trial conditions as a function of the nullification instructions. For the euthanasia case, those jurors presented with the radical instructions were more likely to render a not guilty verdict compared to the jurors provided with the Maryland or no instructions. The reverse pattern of results occurred for the drunk driving case; in this situation, the presence of the radical instructions led the jurors to render harsher verdicts compared to the other two conditions. When the content of the jurors' deliberations were examined Horowitz found that the jurors spent less time discussing the evidence and more time discussing defendant characteristics and personal experiences, leading him to conclude that their presence tended "to 'liberate' the jurors from the evidence of the case" (p. 35). The question of whether nullification instructions would lead to "gross inequities," as suggested by the Canadian justices, was also addressed in series of studies conducted by Horowitz and his colleagues. In one study, Horowitz (1988) found that mock jurors' nullification tendencies were triggered by jurors' interpretations of the accused's motives – when the nullification defence was present, jurors were "more likely to acquit a sympathetic defendant and more likely to deal harshly with an unsympathetic defendant" (p. 451). Another series of studies (Niedermeier, Horowitz, & Kerr, 1999) examined whether the presence of nullification instructions would amplify the impact of "commonplace" biases (e.g., gender, race, national origin). No support for the notion that their presence would heighten the impact of these extralegal factors was found. Rather, the presence of nullification instructions merely encouraged the jurors to nullify when the application of the letter of the law was contrary to their sense of justice.

In determining exactly what occurred (e.g., did the accused actually do it? what provoked her actions?), the law requires jurors to base their decisions solely on the admissible evidence presented at trial. Thus, some of the information jurors are exposed to at trial and, in some cases outside of the courthouse (e.g., media accounts), is not to be

relied upon in reaching a decision. For instance, the opening and closing statements made by lawyers are the opinions of the lawyers only
and do not constitute evidence. As well, remarks or questions ruled
inadmissible do not constitute evidence and cannot be used by the
jurors. For example, the favourite trial tactic of television's leading
legal dramas – the attorney's inflammatory remark followed by the
opposing attorney's vociferous objection and the judge's admonishment to the jury to "disregard that statement" – presents jurors with
information that the law expects them to erase from their minds. The
accused is to be tried, according to the law, solely on the basis of the
admissible evidence presented at trial.

Underlying the basic principles that govern the practice of the jury
are assumptions about human behaviour that are psychological and
testable in nature. How accurate and competent are jurors as information processors? Can their focus remain solely on the evidence alone or
might extralegal factors creep into their decision? How does the individual juror, and, more importantly, the jury as a group, assimilate the
evidence to arrive at a final verdict? Might other factors, such as normative pressure, influence the verdict? Given that these questions lie at
the very heart of much of psychology (involving as they do social cognition, attitudes, persuasion, and small groups research), psychologists, not surprisingly, have quite a bit to say on the subject of how, and
how well, jurors perform their duties.

METHODS USED TO STUDY THE JURY

In Canada, jury deliberations are completely shrouded in secrecy as
Canadian jurors are forbidden by law from disclosing the contents of
their deliberations (s. 649 of the Criminal Code). Gaining access to the
jury is thus impossible for social scientists in Canada and a variety of
unique methods – post-trial interviews with non-Canadian (primarily
American) jurors, examination of archival records, and jury simulations – each with their own strengths and weaknesses, have been
developed to study jury decision making.

Post-trial interviews with jurors are one of the most straightforward
strategies utilized by researchers within the United States. American
jurors, unlike their Canadian counterparts, are permitted, as we have
seen in recent notorious cases (e.g., the trials of O.J. Simpson or the
Menendez brothers), to engage in post-deliberation discussions. Taking advantage of this opportunity, researchers have interviewed jurors

following their jury service. For example, LaFree, Reskin, and Visher (1985) conducted in-depth interviews with 331 jurors who had served in forcible sexual assault trials, asking them about their attitudes towards rape as well as their reactions to the victim and defendant on trial. On the basis of this information, the researchers were able to identify a number of extralegal factors underlying the jurors' decisions. For instance, in those trials in which consent was at issue, jurors were less likely to believe that the defendant was guilty if the victim "had reportedly engaged in sex outside marriage, drank or used drugs, or had been acquainted with the defendant" (p. 397). Post-trial interviews can provide a rich and valuable data source, but their limitations must be kept in mind. Primary among these limitations is the reliability problem associated with the retrospective nature of the jurors' accounts: jurors may be inaccurate in their recall, they may distort their responses to present themselves in a favourable light, or they may be unaware of the factors that influence their behaviour and thus unable to accurately report on the impact of these factors (Nisbett & Wilson, 1977).

Researchers studying jury behaviour can also turn to archival records to uncover patterns in jury decision making. For example, to identify the types of factors jurors consider when making their decisions Myers (1979) examined prosecution files, police records, and criminal report records. She coded 201 jury trials by a range of legally relevant (e.g., eyewitness identification, recovered weapon) and legally irrelevant (e.g., victim conduct, racial composition) factors. Overall, she found that the jury verdicts were primarily related to variables legally relevant to the accused's guilt and credibility, while the extralegal factors had limited impact.

Although archival records are not subject to the same types of limitations associated with post-trial interviews, typically the data have not been collected with a research purpose in mind. The types of questions researchers can ask are thus limited by the nature of the information collected, which is often demographic. As well, with no control over the collection of the data, the information may suffer from other sources of unreliability and bias – such as inconsistencies within the collection itself or changes in the way in which the cases were treated over time (Vidmar, Beale, Rose, & Donnelly, 1997). The strength of post-trial interview and archival studies, however, is their high external validity; significant patterns among the variables assessed are identified using real jurors deciding real cases. The drawback, as with all correlational research, is that, given the many plausible alternative hypotheses to explain the relationship between the variables, the studies cannot tell us why the particular variables are related.

The most commonly employed and perhaps the most powerful research method used to study jury decision making involves simulation techniques. This procedure involves presenting mock jurors with a simulated trial (via written, audio, or video format) and then asking them to render a verdict and answer various questions about the case. Within the trial presented, the variable(s) of interest (e.g., the presence of expert testimony, defendant attractiveness) is or are then varied so that different individuals are exposed to alternative forms of the case. Participants' responses to the different versions of the case can be elicited individually; alternatively, the research participants may form a jury group and be asked to deliberate to a unanimous verdict. Comparisons of the participants' responses and/or jury verdicts across the various versions of the trial are then conducted to assess the impact of the variable under investigation. For example, utilizing juror simulation techniques, Douglas, Lyon, and Ogloff (1997) assessed whether or not jurors' decisions might be prejudicially affected by graphic photographic crime evidence. Some of the mock jurors in their study were exposed to graphic autopsy photographs while others did not receive them. The researchers found that the jurors who were exposed to the photographs, regardless of whether they were colour or black and white, were twice as likely to render a guilty verdict compared to the jurors in the control condition (i.e., those who were not exposed to the photos).

In jury simulations, because the researcher systematically varies the variable of interest within the simulation, he or she is able to isolate and directly assess its impact on the decision process. This ensures that the independent variable is responsible for any differences between the conditions. Internal validity, however, is attained at a cost. In contrast to a real trial, the simulation is brief and less complex, and the decisions the mock jurors are asked to render are hypothetical with little at stake. Although not necessitated by the method itself, the focus is often on individual mock jurors (usually psychology undergraduates) as opposed to juries (Weiten & Diamond, 1979; Vidmar, 1979). The external validity – the extent to which the findings generalize to actual trial situations – of such artificial studies can be called into question.

Ideally, the ultimate goal of the researcher is to obtain converging evidence that capitalizes on the strength of these different research methodologies – the advantages and disadvantages of each can complement each other. A recent examination of the research pertaining to juror/jury behaviour conducted between 1977 and 1994 reveals that the majority of the scholarship pertaining to juries has been based on juror simulations (Nietzel, McCarthy, & Kern, 1999). As well, it has been primarily conducted using undergraduate students as research participants: Neitzel et al. found that only 11% of the research spanning this time period involved real jurors or juries. Although simulations with undergraduates as participants are still the norm in jury research, we are increasingly seeing research that utilizes more representative samples as research participants and that involves more realistic and complex trials, incorporating group deliberations and verdicts (e.g., Diamond & Casper, 1992; Ellsworth, 1989; Hastie, Penrod, & Pennington, 1983; see Diamond, 1997). This trend was evident in Neitzel et al.'s review. When evidence from a variety of studies utilizing different methodologies and diverse populations leads us to the same conclusion, our confidence in the findings are strengthened. Such evidence is particularly important, since findings that converge on the same conclusion are more likely to be persuasive and convincing to policy makers and the courts (Diamond, 1997).

JURORS AS INFORMATION PROCESSORS

Models of Jury Decision Making

Since the 1970s, various models of juror decision making have been proposed and, with varying success, empirically tested. These models tend to fall into one of two camps, utilizing the mathematical or the explanation-based approach. Basically, within the mathematical type models (e.g., algebraic, Anderson, 1981; stochastic, Kerr, 1993), jurors are conceptualized as performing a series of "mental" calculations that represent the perceived importance and strength of the various sources of information. The outcome of this calculation is then compared to a decision criterion for a determination of guilt. In contrast to the mathematical modelling approaches, recent conceptualizations of the jurors' task have emphasized the jurors' cognitive organization or representation of the evidence (Bennett & Feldman, 1981; Pennington & Hastie, 1986). The most theoretically advanced of these explanation-based approaches is the Story Model developed by Pennington and Hastie (1986). Within this model, the juror, in his or her attempt to understand the meaning of the evidence, is engaged in an "active, constructive comprehensive process in which evidence is organized elaborated and interpreted" (Pennington & Hastie, 1993, p. 194). By establishing the causal and intentional relations between the various pieces of evidence presented at trial, the juror organizes the information into a coherent whole or narrative story structure (Pennington & Hastie, 1986, 1988). Once the judge provides the jurors with the legal instructions explaining the relevant law (e.g., what the Crown must prove for the accused to be found guilty) and the verdict options (e.g., second degree murder, manslaughter, self-defence), the decision process then involves the jurors' attempts to find the best fit or match between the story constructed and one of the verdict categories provided by the judge (e.g., murder, manslaughter, not guilty).

The Story Model has strong intuitive appeal. It also provides a useful theoretical context for both understanding and generating hypotheses about jury decision making. Why, and how, might different story interpretations be derived from trial evidence? One of the obvious sources underlying story construction is the trial evidence, which is by far one of the most important factors influencing jurors' decisions (Myers, 1979). Perhaps less obvious, however, is the manner in which evidence is presented. Along these lines, Pennington and Hastie (1988) conducted an experiment in which they manipulated the ease with which a particular story could be abstracted from the trial testimony. When the prosecution's evidence was presented in a story order (closely following the chronological order of the alleged events) and the defence's evidence was given in witness-by-witness order, verdicts were more likely to be guilty, whereas the reverse pattern occurred when the defence adopted a story order presentation and the prosecution adopted a witness-by-witness order presentation. Thus, the easier it was for an individual to construct a particular story from the trial evidence, the more likely it was that a verdict consistent with that story was rendered.

Since jurors, despite hearing the same trial evidence, are not all in agreement when they enter their deliberations, individual differences can clearly play a role as well. Why does one juror see a story consistent with guilt, while another sees a story consistent with innocence? Story interpretations are derived not only from the trial evidence, but also from the jurors' factual or social knowledge of the world – the beliefs, attitudes, and experiences that they bring with them into the courtroom. Jurors may draw different interpretations from the same evidence because of their different knowledge and experiences. This is not to say that we can reliably predict jurors' decisions from mere knowledge about their characteristics. Researchers have not found stable and consistent relationships between demographic or personality variables and jurors' verdicts (Kassin & Wrightsman, 1988); indeed, the effects that have been found are often not strong and, more problematic, the relationships between these variables and verdicts often vary from study to study (Ellsworth & Mauro, 1998).

In contrast to demographic and personality variables, researchers have had somewhat greater success at identifying relationships between jurors' attitudes and verdict decisions. This statement, however, must be qualified. Individual differences in attitudes and beliefs (which in some instances may be related to demographic variables) may be predictive of verdicts and decision processes, but only if the attitudes and beliefs are specifically relevant to the particular case at hand (e.g., attitudes towards the death penalty in capital murder trials (Ellsworth, 1991); beliefs about woman abuse in trials of battered women who have killed (Schuller, Smith, & Olson, 1994); see Kassin & Wrightsman, 1988). The difficulty, of course, lies in identifying which attitudes are of relevance for a particular case. In the next section, we examine juror decision making in sexual assault trials, a context that illustrates the way in which people's prior knowledge and beliefs may colour their interpretations of the evidence, which in turn, may influence their verdict decisions.

Juror Decision Making within the Context of a Sexual Assault Trial

The crime of sexual assault evokes both strong and ambivalent emotions in people. Apart from the horror and outrage generated by the crime, many people also blame the victim, holding her responsible for what occurred. For example, in 1980, Martha Burt identified a series of rape-supportive beliefs (e.g., "a woman who goes to the home or apartment of a man on the first date implies that she is willing to have sex") held by a large portion of the population. More recent studies investigating the prevalence of rape-tolerant attitudes in samples of college students have similarly found that just over half of the respondents surveyed typically report that "you can tell a girl's character by how she dresses," that if a woman says "no," she really means "maybe" or even "yes," and that rape is often provoked by the victim (e.g., Dull & Giacopassi, 1987; Gilmartin-Zena, 1987; Holcomb,

Holcomb, Sondag, & Williams, 1991). Since Burt's original Rape Myth Acceptance scale, a variety of scales have been developed to assess attitudes and beliefs about sexual assault "that are generally false but widely and persistently held" (Lonsway & Fitzgerald, 1994, p. 134). Although studies have utilized different scales, rendering comparisons difficult, taken in their entirety they demonstrate that a significant portion of the population adheres to myths surrounding sexual assault, with males more accepting of these myths than females (see generally, Lonsway & Fitzgerald, 1994; Muir, Lonsway, & Payne, 1996).

How might rape myths affect jurors' perceptions and jury verdicts in a case of sexual assault? Before reading on, consider the Story Model for a moment and try to generate some hypotheses about how jurors' rape-related beliefs might influence their interpretations and perceptions (perhaps misperceptions) of an alleged sexual assault and, ultimately, the jury's verdict. Once you have given the issue some thought, compare your hypotheses against some of the findings from juror simulation studies that have attempted to assess empirically the impact of these beliefs on jurors' decisions.

In one of the earliest of these studies, Burt and Albin (1981), using Burt's original rape myth acceptance scale, found that the more supportive individuals were of rape myths, the more likely they were to hold the victim responsible for the assault, and the less likely they were to convict the man accused of the rape. Coming to similar conclusions, several other juror simulation studies have demonstrated that the stronger an individual's support for these myths, the narrower his or her definition of what constitutes a "real rape" and the less likely he or she is to find the accused guilty of rape (Borgida, 1981; Burt & Albin, 1981).

The impact of rape myths on the adjudication of sexual assault is perhaps most readily apparent in the case of date or acquaintance rape. Contrary to the common belief that most sexual assaults are committed by strangers, perpetrators of sexual assault are typically known to the victim (Harney & Muehlenhard, 1990; Koss, 1992). Several studies have demonstrated that mock jurors' perceptions about an acquaintance rape as opposed to a rape committed by a stranger are markedly different. For instance, Szymanski, Devlin, Christer, & Vyse (1993) found that people attributed greater responsibility to the victim of an acquaintance rape, viewed her more negatively, and viewed the perpetrator less negatively. Not surprisingly, the mock jurors were less certain of the defendant's guilt when he was an acquaintance as opposed to a stranger. Harsher judgments for the victims of date or acquaintance sexual assault have now been demonstrated across a number of simulation studies (Bell, Kuriloff, & Lottes, 1994; Bridges, 1991; Johnson, 1994; Johnson & Russ, 1989).

In the case of date rape, various contextual factors surrounding the alleged assault may also play a role in the jurors' decisions. For instance, one variable just beginning to receive empirical attention is the role of alcohol intoxication. Numerous surveys have documented the high co-occurrence of alcohol consumption (on the part of either the perpetrator and/or victim) in instances of sexual assault (Koss, Gidyez, & Wisniewski, 1987; Muehlenhard & Linton, 1987), with estimates ranging from one-third to three-quarters of all sexual assaults involving alcohol (see Testa & Parks, 1996). Although drunkenness is not a defence to a charge of sexual assault nor is intoxication on the part of the complainant indicative of consent (see 1992 amendments to the Criminal Code, ss. 273.1 and 273.2), several lines of research suggest that alcohol consumption on the part of the parties involved may influence jurors' evaluations of the alleged assault.

In a series of studies (George, Cue, Lopez, Crowe, & Norris, 1995; George, Gournic, & McAfee (Study 2), 1988) research participants were presented with a brief vignette depicting a heterosexual dating couple, in which the beverage consumption of the woman varied (the man was always portrayed as drinking). In half of the cases the woman was drinking alcohol (beer) and in the other half she was drinking a non-alcoholic beverage (Coke). After reading the vignette, the participants were asked to make a number of judgments about the individuals involved. When the woman was portrayed as drinking, she was viewed by the participants as more sexually responsive, easier to seduce, and more likely to engage in foreplay and intercourse compared to her non-drinking counterpart. In two similar studies (Abbey & Harnish, 1995; Corcoran & Thomas, 1991), which also varied the beverage consumption of the male target portrayed in the vignette, it was found that respondents viewed the couple as most sexual and the possibility of sexual intercourse most likely when both parties had consumed alcohol. Such findings have led researchers to suggest that shared alcohol consumption may be interpreted by people as a "sign of sexual interest" (p. 299).

Findings such as these would suggest that a woman's claim of sexual assault may be less likely to be believed by jurors if she had been drinking at the time of the alleged assault, especially if her male companion was also drinking at the time. A handful of studies have investigated this hypothesis. For example, Richardson and Campbell (1982) found that, in response to a scenario describing a date rape situation, respondents assigned an intoxicated victim more responsibility for the sexual assault and viewed her more negatively compared to her non-drinking counterpart. In contrast, they ascribed less relative blame to the perpetrator and more to the situation, if the assailant was intoxicated as opposed to sober. Results from a similar study found that, when both the man and woman were drinking, people were more likely to question the validity of the sexual assault allegation, to view the victim negatively, and to judge the assailant as more likeable (Norris & Cubbins, 1992). Consistent with these findings, the interview study conducted by LaFree et al. (1985), discussed above, identified the complainant's alcohol consumption as one of the factors that jurors reported as influencing their verdict decisions.

To examine what role, if any, alcohol intoxication on the part of the accused and complainant might play in the adjudication of a sexual assault trial, Schuller and Wall (1998) conducted a jury simulation in which the beverage consumption of both the accused and complainant was systematically varied, such that the targets were portrayed as either drinking cola or beer prior to the alleged assault. Consistent with the prior research, when the complainant had consumed alcohol she was viewed as less credible and the accused was viewed as less likely to be guilty. Contrary to the prior research in the area, however, when the accused had consumed alcohol he too was perceived as less credible and more likely to be guilty. Thus, rather than operating as an exculpatory factor as has been found in other research, the defendant's alcohol consumption was associated with increased perceptions of guilt. As well, in contrast to the notion that shared alcohol consumption serves as a cue for mutually intended sexual behaviour, the mock jurors were more likely to render a guilty verdict when both the defendant and complainant had consumed alcohol. One of the potential explanations offered by Schuller and Wall for this finding involves the inclusion of Canadian judicial instructions that informed the mock jurors that self-induced intoxication on the part of the accused is not a defence for the accused's belief that the complainant consented. It is possible that these instructions may have sensitized the mock jurors to the legally impermissible link that alcohol may play in the decision process. Given the recent attention to alcohol intoxication in the Canadian courts (e.g., the brief history of the "drunkenness defence," *R. v. Daviault*, 1994; 1992 amendments to the Criminal Code provisions, see s. 273), additional empirical inquiry examining jury decision making in this area is clearly warranted.

When Juror Knowledge Is Deemed Faulty

In the *Lavallee* (1990) case described in the opening of this chapter, the Supreme Court of Canada expressed the view that the jurors required the aid of expert testimony. Because the jury members were likely to harbour a range of myths and stereotypes about battered women and the battering context (e.g., battered women are masochistic, they are in some way responsible for the abuse), the jury's ability to perform its function had been challenged on the grounds that its members lacked the requisite knowledge to evaluate the case (see Schuller, 1990). In terms of the Story Model, what the jurors lacked was an adequate framework for evaluating the trial evidence. As outlined in Chapter 1, one approach that the courts have taken for dealing with this problem involves the introduction of expert testimony at trial. The expert presumably informs the jury members about the particular phenomena in question, thereby providing them with an alternative framework for evaluating the evidence. This form of expert testimony has been aptly labelled "social framework" testimony (Monahan & Walker, 1988), as it provides the fact finders with a context or novel framework for evaluating particular trial evidence. For instance, the testimony proffered by the expert in Ms Lavallee's trial addressed the issue of why she might have perceived herself to be in danger at the time of the shooting, even though she was not under immediate attack by her husband, and also the question, typically asked by jurors (Gillespie, 1989), why, if things were as bad as she claims, "didn't she just leave the relationship earlier?"

What impact does such evidence have on jurors and their subsequent decision? Were the jurors more lenient in Ms Lavallee's case because of the presence of the expert evidence? Although one can never be certain at an individual case level, as we never know what would have occurred had the evidence not been present, jury simulations, which systematically examine the impact of expert evidence pertaining to battered women, provide us with some insights. In a series of studies Schuller and her colleagues (Schuller 1992; Schuller & Hastings, 1996; Schuller, Smith, & Olson, 1994) presented mock jurors with simulated trials involving battered women who had killed their abusers. Some of the mock jurors across these studies were provided with expert testimony regarding the dynamics and impact of woman abuse, while others were not. In one study (Schuller, 1992, Study 1), two different forms of the testimony were examined: a general form of the testimony in which the expert presented only the general theory and research in the area of wife abuse (e.g., battered woman syndrome), and another form in which this basic research was supplemented with the expert's opinion that the accused fit the battered woman syndrome. It was predicted that the expert testimony would lead the mock jurors to interpret the evidence in a manner that was more consistent with the woman's account of what occurred, and further, that because people find it hard to utilize aggregate information unless it is specifically linked to an individual, that this effect would be stronger when the expert provided an opinion about the woman on trial. As the results displayed in Figure 6.1 convey, the prediction was confirmed. The mock jurors provided with the specific expert testimony were more likely than those not provided with the testimony, or those who had been provided with only the general form of the testimony, to view the woman's perceptions and actions – her fear and her inability to leave – as consistent with a self-defensive response. Moreover, these jurors, in contrast to those who did not receive the expert testimony, rendered more lenient verdicts. In another study conducted by Schuller (1992, Study 2) in which these same three conditions were contrasted, participants were required to deliberate in small groups to a unanimous verdict. It was found that the presence of the expert testimony, in either form, led the mock jurors to raise more favourable interpretations of the woman's claim of self-defence in their deliberations.

The beneficial impact of expert testimony has been noted in other domains of expertise as well (e.g., rape trauma syndrome, Brekke & Borgida, 1988; child abuse, Kovera, Levy, Borgida, & Penrod, 1994; eyewitness testimony, Cutler, Penrod, & Dexter, 1989). Given the exponential growth of expert testimony in the courtroom, researchers in this area are now beginning to examine the myriad factors that influence the impact of expert testimony on jurors' decisions. For instance, expert testimony has been found to be more persuasive when presented early as opposed to late in the trial (Brekke & Borgida, 1988; Schuller & Cripps, 1998) and when it is specifically tied to the individual rather than consisting solely of a general presentation of the

Figure 6.1
Verdict rendered by condition

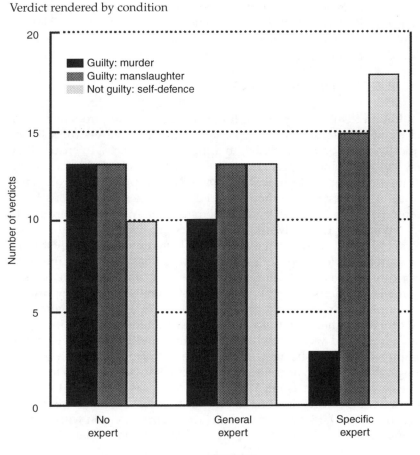

findings in the area (Brekke & Borgida, 1988; Gabora, Spanos, & Joab, 1993; Schuller, 1992, Study 1; see Nietzel et al., 1999), although this latter finding appears to be qualified by the degree of fit between the behaviour of the individual and the testimony provided (Kovera, Gresham, Borgida, Gray, & Regan, 1997). The impact of expert testimony may also vary depending on the gender of the expert (Memon & Shuman, 1998; Schuller & Cripps, 1998), the expert's credentials and the complexity of the testimony (Cooper, Bennett, & Sukel, 1996), whether the expert testimony is countered by an opposing expert (Brekke & Borgida, 1988; Kovera, Levy, Borgida, & Penrod, 1994), or whether the expert is court appointed (Brekke, Enko, Clavet, & Seelau, 1991; Cutler, Dexter, & Penrod, 1990).

THE JUDGE'S INSTRUCTIONS

In addition to mastering a complex array of case facts, jurors must also master and integrate the body of law that the judge instructs them, typically at the end of the trial, to apply to those facts. To ensure that they can withstand appeal (Hans, 1991), judicial instructions are written in very complex technical language. Not surprisingly, jurors have difficulty understanding them. Indeed, the judges' instructions have been referred to by some legal scholars as merely a "meaningless ritual" (Winslow, 1962; Elwork, Alfini, & Sales, 1982; see English and Sales, 1997) and laboratory assessments have demonstrated just how incomprehensible jurors find judicial instructions. Efforts to improve juror comprehension have lead several researchers to advocate rewriting the instructions. Such proposals are strongly supported by principles of psycholinguistic theory. For instance, by employing common and concrete rather than unfamiliar or abstract terms, by avoiding negatively modified words, and by eliminating multiple negatives, juror comprehension can be improved. By rewriting judicial instructions along these lines, Elwork, Alfini, and Sales (1982) were able to increase juror comprehension from 51% to 80%, as measured on a test that assessed their understanding of the instructions. Other researchers have found similar improvements in juror comprehension with rewritten instructions (Charrow & Charrow, 1979; Elwork, Sales, & Alfini, 1977; Severance & Loftus, 1982). In light of findings such as these, pattern jury instructions that attempt to simplify the language and structure of the instructions have been developed within Canada (see Ferguson, 1989). The extent to which jurors find these instructions comprehensible or whether they are in fact utilized by Canadian judges, however, has not been assessed and awaits future research.

In some instances, the problem of juror incomprehension may have more to do with what jurors are being asked to do than how they are being instructed to do it. Because of its relevancy, we will focus again on the area of sexual assault to illustrate this point.

Judicial Instructions Pertaining to Specific Use of Evidence

Prior to 1983, evidence regarding a woman's prior sexual behaviour was deemed admissible evidence in a rape trial and could be used to infer the woman's credibility as a witness, as well the likelihood that she consented to the sexual encounter. Recognizing the negative impact that people's rape-related beliefs could have on their decisions, and in an effort to protect the victim, the rape shield provisions were implemented. These provisions prohibited the Crown from introducing evidence pertaining to the complainant's prior sexual history. Since the 1990s, however, the rape shield provisions have become the centre of several constitutional challenges, with court decisions concluding that, in certain cases, the provisions violate the accused's right to a fair trial (e.g., *R. v. Seaboyer*, 1991; *R. v. Gayme*, 1991; see Delisle, 1993). In 1992 the rape shield provisions were amended to allow discretionary inquiry into the complainant's prior sexual history, with the judge determining whether the information should be admitted or not. For example, the defence may argue that inclusion of this information is necessary to present the accused's defence of an "honest but mistaken belief in consent." Cognizant of the potential prejudicial impact this information may have, however, the Supreme Court of Canada (*R. v. Seaboyer*, 1991) recommended that the trial judge give cautionary instructions to the jury regarding the purpose for which the sexual history evidence can be used. That is, the jurors must be cautioned that the information cannot be used to prove that the woman is less worthy of belief or that she is more likely to have consented to the sexual intercourse, but rather is only relevant to the accused's claim of an "honest but mistaken belief in consent."

Whether jurors are capable of making such a fine-grained distinction is an empirical question. Will the woman's credibility be impeached if jurors learn that she has had consensual sex with the accused on a prior occasion? Will this information influence jurors' perceptions of the accused's belief or alternatively, might it erroneously influence the likelihood that she consented? The results of a recent juror simulation study (Schuller & Hastings, 2000) suggest that the latter scenario is a likely possibility. That is, when evidence in a simulated sexual assault trial that involved a date rape indicated that the complainant and accused had engaged in consensual sexual intercourse prior to the alleged assault, mock jurors were more likely to find the accused inno-

find the accused innocent. This finding alone, however, is not necessarily indicative of improper use of the evidence. Had the reduction in guilt occurred because the mock jurors were more likely to believe the accused's claim of a reasonable but mistaken belief in consent, it would suggest that the mock jurors were using the evidence as the courts intended. Results of the study indicated, however, that the information did not influence the mock jurors' perceptions of the accused's mistaken belief. Rather it decreased their perceptions of the woman's credibility and increased their perceptions of the likelihood of consent.

A similar task is required of jurors when an accused's criminal record is introduced at trial. Section 12 of the Canada Evidence Act permits the introduction of this evidence for the sole purpose of evaluating the accused's credibility as a witness. Canadian researchers (Doob & Kirshenbaum, 1972; Hans & Doob, 1976) have questioned whether jurors are able to use this information for assessing credibility only, or if they might use the information inappropriately for evaluating the defendant's guilt. To test this hypothesis, they presented research participants with a case in which information about the prior criminal record of the accused was either absent or present. Both this research, as well as an American study that examined the issue (Wissler & Saks, 1985), demonstrate that prior conviction evidence, while having little impact on mock jurors' assessments of credibility, influenced (albeit improperly) their perceptions of guilt. Further, the presence of judicial limiting instructions regarding the proper use of the testimony did little to ameliorate the negative impact of the evidence.

Other research has similarly demonstrated the ineffectiveness of judicial instructions to disregard evidence later ruled to be inadmissible (Carretta & Moreland, 1983; Saunders, Vidmar, & Hewitt, 1982; Sue, Smith, & Caldwell, 1973; Thompson, Fong, & Rosenhan, 1981; Wolf and Montgomery, 1977). As the Story Model would suggest, interdependencies in the trial evidence render it difficult to erase the impact of a particular piece of evidence. Once a juror has heard the information, ignoring it may be difficult. Sometimes highlighting the information can backfire and render it more prejudicial, a result researchers have referred to as a "boomerang effect" (Tanford & Cox, 1987). As well, the information may already have coloured the jurors' perceptions of the entire case, a situation which may be difficult to alter at the conclusion of the trial evidence (Paglia & Schuller, 1998). For example, Saunders et al. (1982) presented mock jurors with a case in which some of the jurors were informed that the eyewitness identification by one of the defence's witnesses was discredited, while the identification was not discredited for other participants. Their examination of the mock jurors' deliberations revealed that, although the mock jurors in the eyewitness condition indicated that they were less impressed with the identification when it was discredited, their verdicts, as well as their discussion of the other trial evidence, were similar to that found for the juries exposed to the reliable eyewitness. Moreover, compared to a control condition in which the eyewitness account was omitted, discussion of the other trial evidence was viewed as more persuasive when the eyewitness account was present. It seems that the impact the eyewitness information had on the other evidence could not be disentangled retrospectively by the jurors. It had already exerted its impact.

Courtroom Innovations to Aid Comprehension

A structural characteristic of the trial that may impede juror comprehension of judicial instructions concerns the timing of their presentation. Although tradition dictates that the judges' instructions follow the presentation of legal evidence, there is evidence to suggest that juror comprehension improves when jurors are provided with pretrial instructions (FosterLee, Horowitz, & Bourgeois, 1993; Smith, 1991). In terms of the Story Model, this finding certainly makes intuitive sense. As Heuer and Penrod (1989) point out, pretrial instructions provide a framework or causal schema for organizing the subsequent trial evidence into a narrative structure. Kassin & Wrightsman (1979) investigated the effects of the timing of instructions on jurors' verdict decisions and found that mock jurors who received general procedural pretrial instructions (e.g., requirements of proof, reasonable doubt) were more likely to render not guilty verdicts than participants who received either no legal instructions or post-trial instructions. Pretrial instructions provided the jurors with a presumption of innocence framework that guided their evaluations of the evidence and thus, their subsequent verdict decisions.

The beneficial effects of pretrial instructions were also identified in a study conducted by Smith (1991). The pretrial instructions in this instance included information about the jury's duties, how to evaluate evidence, the requirements of proof, and the definitions of the particular crime charged in the case. The researcher found that the mock jurors who received the judicial instructions both before and after the trial evidence presentation were better able to integrate the facts and law in the case at hand. Smith also found that mid-trial verdict judgments of the pre-instructed mock jurors, in comparison to those instructed only at the end of the trial, were more likely to contain responses of "I don't know." This latter finding addresses a concern about pretrial instruction often raised by the courts: that pretrial instruction would encourage jurors to settle on a verdict early on in the case. Contrary to the fears of the critics, these results suggest that pretrial instruction may in fact encourage jurors to maintain an open mind throughout the evidence presentation.

Findings from other studies that have varied the timing of judicial instructions, in particular those pertaining to jurors' specific use of evidence (e.g., hearsay, past criminal record, as described in the previous section), however, indicate that presenting such instructions early does little to improve their use (Greene & Loftus, 1985; Paglia & Schuller, 1998; Tanford & Cox, 1988). Such results suggest that the psychological demands required of jurors in some instances – for example, using information for one purpose but not another – may render these instructions difficult to follow. It should be noted, however, that there is little reason to suspect that other decision makers, such as judges, would not be subject to these same cognitive limitations. Studies have not assessed this issue with judges.

Other attempts to increase juror comprehension involve the use of comprehension aids within the courtroom. Along these lines, two courtroom innovations, juror note-taking and question asking, have been advocated. For instance, it has been argued that allowing jurors to take notes would enhance their comprehension and memory of the evidence (see Heuer and Penrod, 1994). A number of potential disadvantages associated with note-taking, however, have been articulated by the Canadian courts (R. v. Andrade, 1985): (1) jurors who have taken notes may exert undue influence over those who have refrained from note-taking during the deliberation process. If disputes occur regarding the evidence, jurors who took notes will be relied upon to clarify the situation; (2) note-taking may be incomplete and/or may result in an inappropriate emphasis upon immaterial matters; and (3) the act of keeping notes may distract other members of the jury, and/or may place unnecessary pressure on jurors, thereby limiting their ability to concentrate on the court proceedings. The appellate court, in this instance, however, noted that the Law Reform Commission of Canada reviewed and discredited the arguments against note-taking (see LRCC, 1980), thus concluding that it is up to the presiding trial judge to determine, based upon the circumstances of the particular case, whether the jurors should be permitted to take notes. In terms of the status of juror note-taking in Canada, the decision is left to the trial judge, with no uniform regulations governing the procedure (Granger, 1996).

The issue of enabling jurors to ask questions of witnesses at trial has received some legal discussion in the United States, with various advantages and disadvantages noted by the courts. On the plus side are such advantages as the following: it would promote greater juror understanding, help to get to the truth, alert lawyers to any issues that need more attention, and would generally increase satisfaction with the trial process (Heuer & Penrod, 1994). Because jurors are not versed in the law, however, the following concerns have been voiced: jurors will ask impermissible questions; so as not to offend the jurors, lawyers may be reluctant to object to an inappropriate question; or, if the question is objected to by one of the lawyers and the objection is sustained, jurors may draw an inappropriate inference from the lack of response; and that jurors will view their role as advocates, as opposed to neutral triers of fact. In Canada, there does not appear to be any laws or authority that would prevent jurors from asking questions of witnesses. In 1980 the Law Reform Commission of Canada recommended that jurors who wished to ask a question of a witness be permitted to submit the questions in writing to the judge, but only after the lawyers had completed their questioning of the witness. The judge would then determine whether the question was appropriate and permissible. Thus, like juror note-taking, the decision of whether to permit jurors to ask questions during the trial appears to be at the discretion of the judge. While some judges have allowed jurors to ask some questions, Canadian courts have devoted very little attention to this practice.

Discussion of the merits of either juror note-taking or question-asking, until quite recently, had been based largely on speculation and unfounded assumptions. In an effort to bring some data to bear on the issue, Heuer and Penrod (1988, 1989, 1994) conducted a series of sophisticated field studies. In the most elaborate of these studies, they randomly assigned 160 actual jury trials, both criminal and civil, to conditions in which jurors were either permitted or prohibited from taking notes and asking questions. At the end of each trial, the jurors received a questionnaire designed to assess a range of concerns regarding the impact of the procedures. With respect to jury question-asking, the results were quite favourable. The jurors reported that question-asking increased juror understanding of the legal facts and issues and did not negatively affect court proceedings. They found no evidence to suggest that note-taking served as a memory aid or that it increased juror satisfaction with the trial process or verdict. On the other hand, however, there was also no evidence supporting the negative claims associated with note-taking; the noted evidence was not overemphasized, it did not lead to distorted perceptions of the case, it did not distract other jurors, and non-note-takers were not unduly influenced by note-takers. In contrast to these findings, other researchers (e.g., FosterLee, Horowitz, & Bourgeois, 1994; Rosenhan, Eisner, & Robinson, 1994) have found that in jury simulation experiments, note-takers in contrast to non-note-takers performed more competently, had superior recall, and became more involved in the trial proceedings.

JURY DELIBERATIONS

The jurors' deliberations take place in privacy with the jury members sequestered until a final verdict is rendered. Communication with anyone outside of the jury, with the exception of the appointed officer of the court, is not permitted until the verdict has been reached and the jury has been discharged by the judge (Granger, 1996). This custom was established to ensure that outside influences, such as media portrayals of the trial or public pressure, do not sway the jury's decision.

In their private chambers, the jury is expected to review the evidence, assess its importance, and determine the best match between the verdict options available and the facts of the case. In the case of criminal juries, results of numerous jury simulations have found that most final group verdicts follow from the majority of the jury members' initial verdict opinions (see Davis, 1980; Stasser, Kerr, & Bray, 1982; Zeisel & Diamond, 1978). On the basis of post-trial interviews with jurors from 225 actual criminal cases, Kalven and Zeisel (1966) found that in roughly nine out of ten cases, the final verdict could be predicted by the verdict distribution of the jury's initial poll, with the majority's position prevailing. It should be noted, however, that the preferences expressed by the jurors in their first ballot are not necessarily equivalent to the jurors' predeliberation opinions. By interviewing actual jurors, Sandys and Dillehay (1995) found that in the majority of cases, considerable discussion had occurred among the jurors before their first verdict poll was ever taken. Indeed, experimental studies have demonstrated that such discussion can alter the actual outcome of the initial verdict distribution (e.g., Davis, Kameda, Parks, Stasson, & Zimmerman, 1989). In short, there is some evidence to believe that – contrary to what one might expect – considerable group impact has already occurred before the first poll is ever taken.

Juries are decision-making groups, and as such, are subject to myriad social psychological group processes. Their decisions are perhaps best captured by the process of "group polarization," a phenomenon first identified by social psychologists in the 1970s. This refers to the tendency of individuals to become more extreme in their initial positions following group discussion (Baron & Bryrne, 1991). An interesting twist to this simple "majority rules" decision, referred to as the leniency bias, however, occurs in the case of criminal jury decisions. MacCoun and Kerr (1988) investigated both pre -and post-deliberation verdict preferences and found that jurors moved towards greater leniency following deliberations. They also found that a proaquittal faction was more influential than a proconviction faction, and that when a clear majority did not prevail, verdicts were more likely to result in acquittals than in convictions. This asymmetry was attributed to the standard of proof required in the trial. Although the majority tends to prevail, the standard of guilt beyond reasonable doubt results in a bias that favours the accused.

Although initial verdict preferences are highly predictive of jury verdicts, the quality of the deliberations also plays a significant role in the outcome of the decision. As with small groups research more generally, the study of jury behaviour has primarily focused on two group processes: normative and informational influence. Normative influence refers to the desire for individuals to be liked, accepted, and approved of by others, whereas informational influence refers to the desire to be correct (Deutsch & Gerard, 1955). Research has found that both of these social processes are evident in jurors' deliberations (Kaplan & Scherching, 1981; Stasser & Davis, 1981; Tanford & Penrod, 1986). When jurors are persuaded by discussions regarding trial evidence, testimony, or the judge's instructions, they are responding to informational influence. In contrast, when jurors are persuaded by judicial and/or societal expectations or the desire for a unified decision, they are heeding normative influence (Hansen, Schaefer, & Lawless, 1993; Smith & Kassin, 1993).

Although both forms of influence are used to reach unanimity, they produce different outcomes. Informational influence produces private acceptance (i.e., conversion) whereas normative influence elicits public agreement (i.e., compliance) (Smith & Kassin, 1993). Researchers have found that the amount of time jurors devote to discussions of an informational versus normative type corresponds to a temporal pattern, reflecting the goals of the jury as they progress through the different segments of deliberations. According to Hansen et al. (1993), mock jurors tend to focus discussions around informational content, turning to normative and procedural-legal issues only as the jury nears a final verdict. Studies that have closely examined the content of jurors' deliberations (Ellsworth, 1989; Hastie et al., 1983) have found that jurors approach their task quite seriously, with close to 80% of the deliberations devoted to discussion of the case facts and important contested issues, while just over 20% of the deliberation is devoted to discussions concerning the law and the judicial instructions.

Does Size Matter?

Not surprisingly, the size of a jury can affect the deliberation process. In Canada, the legal system requires a 12-member jury for criminal cases (Granger, 1996).[1] This differs from the American system, in which some states permit six-person juries in some cases that do not involve the death penalty. During the 1970s, the U.S. Supreme Court (*Williams v. Florida*, 1970) addressed the issue of jury size, ruling that a reduction in size would not adversely affect the judicial process. In what has been viewed as a cost-saving measure, the court reasoned that juries, regardless of their size, were functionally equivalent, and thus, 6-member juries were not unconstitutional. Following this ruling, a flurry of studies, as well as critiques of the ruling (Zeisel, 1971), were conducted by social psychologists to address this issue empirically. Taken in their entirety (Saks & Marti, 1997), these studies demonstrate that the size of the jury can indeed affect the deliberation process in a number of important ways. In contrast to 12-member juries, 6-member juries tend to be less representative of the community, recall fewer aspects of the evidence, spend less time deliberating, and are less likely to declare themselves hung (Kerr & MacCoun, 1985; Nemeth, 1981; Saks, 1977; Zeisel, 1971; for a review see Saks & Marti, 1997). Thus, although smaller juries may arrive at quicker decisions, they are less likely to represent minority positions than 12-member juries. In addition to the decreased variability in the perspectives, the smaller the group, the greater the pressure on a dissenting member to conform (Asch, 1951, 1956; see Saks & Marti, 1997).

Does Decision Rule Make a Difference?

Around the same time that they were examining the issue of jury size, another structural condition of the jury was examined by the American courts. Prior to the 1970s, juries within the United States, like Canadian criminal juries, were required to render unanimous verdict decisions. In 1972, however, the U.S. Supreme Court permitted non-unanimous verdicts of 11 to 1, 10 to 2, and 9 to 3 in specified cases (*Apodaca v. Oregon*, 1972; *Johnson v. Louisiana*, 1972). A significant number of states continue to permit non-unanimous verdicts in criminal trials. Similarly, within the United Kingdom juries who have deliberated for a minimum of two hours are permitted to return non-unanimous verdicts of 10 to 2 and 11 to 1 in criminal cases (Granger, 1996).

In favour of non-unanimous verdicts, the U.S. Supreme Court argued that since most final verdicts follow from the majority of the jury members' initial verdict votes, the final verdict would remain unchanged. But how might a non-unanimous decision rule alter the dynamics of the jurors' deliberations? As with the question of jury size, there is some empirical research that bears directly on the issue, and hence on the validity of the court's rationale. In a rather sophisticated study, Hastie et al. (1983) had 69 12-member mock juries (totalling over 800 participants who were on actual jury duty) view a videotape of a murder trial and deliberate to a final jury verdict The jurors were informed that they were required to arrive at either a unanimous verdict (i.e., 12–0) or a majority verdict (either 10–2 or 8–4). A number of differences were found as a function of the decision rule assigned to the juries. Specifically, those juries assigned to a majority, as opposed to a unanimous, decision rule, discussed both the evidence and the law less thoroughly, took less time to arrive at a decision, and were less likely to result in a hung verdict. Moreover, members of small factions in the majority decision rule juries were less likely to express themselves and were less satisfied with the jury verdict compared to members of small factions in the unanimous juries. Thus, like 6-member juries, majority decision rules result in quicker decisions but this efficiency may come at a cost. The quality of the decisions may be compromised.

Within Canada, the courts have resisted any movement towards structural changes in the size or unanimity requirement of the jury in criminal cases (Law Reform Commission of Canada, 1980). As one can imagine, however, a unanimous verdict may not always be attained by a group of 12 individuals. When a jury becomes deadlocked (i.e., consensus among the jury members is unattainable), a mistrial must be declared. Given the costs and time involved in retrying the accused, this outcome is highly undesirable. Thus, before declaring them hung, the judge will typically recharge the jurors in an attempt to encourage the continuation of deliberations, urging them to reach a verdict (Granger, 1996). Although a unanimous verdict is the goal, a judge must be careful not to pressure or coerce the jury to reach agreement. There appears to be some judicial discretion both with respect to the way in which judges exhort the jury to reach unanimity and the determination of whether or not the judges' exhortation unduly (and hence improperly) pressured the jurors into their decision. For instance, in a sexual assault case (*R. v. Halliday*, 1992) in which the jury informed the judge after 10 hours that they were evenly divided, the trial judge told the jurors that if no verdict could be reached the accused would have "the charge hanging over him for another four or five months ... and it will mean that [the complainant] will have to come back to court and testify and be subject to cross examination again" (p. 484). On appeal, this exhortation was deemed to be proper. In contrast, in another case (*R. v. Alkerton, 1992*) in which the jury declared it was deadlocked, this time after 6½ hours of deliberations, the judge addressed the jurors by highlighting the "enormous amount of effort put into presenting the case at considerable expense to the state" and the importance of attaining a resolution for the accused and his wife that day (p. 186). Within 14 minutes, the jury returned with an acquittal. In this instance, the judge's instruction was deemed improper. Granger (1996) notes that the following judicial comments have been relied on for guidance on the issue: "He (sic) reminds them that it is most important that they should agree if it is possible to do so; that, with a view to agreeing, they must inevitably take differing views into account; that if any member should find himself in a small minority and disposed to differ from the rest, he should consider the matter carefully and weigh the reasons for and against his view, and remember that he may be wrong; that if, on so doing, he can honestly bring himself to come to a different view and thus to concur in the view of the majority, he should do so ... but if he cannot do so ... then it is his duty to differ ..." (*Shoukatallie v. R.*, 1962, p. 90).

Might such a charge to the jury be viewed as coercive? A similar but more extreme form of judicial instruction, coined the "dynamite charge" and characterized as "blasting deadlocked juries into a verdict" (Kassin, Smith, & Tulloch, 1990), has been approved in many American courts. Although the merits and potential problems of these instructions have been debated within the legal community, their impact on deadlocked juries, until just recently, has received little research attention. To examine the potential impact of the charge on the deliberations of deadlocked juries, Smith and Kassin (1993) conducted a study in which some of the mock juries were recharged after 20 minutes of deliberation with the following instructions: "a dissenting juror should consider whether his or her doubt is a reasonable one, considering that it made no impression upon the minds of so many other equally honest and intelligent jurors ... the minority ought to ask themselves whether they might not reasonably doubt the correctness of a judgment which is not concurred by the majority" (p. 629). On the basis of their predeliberation preferences, the juries were rigged 4–2 in favour of either conviction or acquittal. Compared to juries in which the jurors were not recharged, those juries provided with the charge were more likely to shift towards unanimity, with the minority group members of the jury changing their vote. If the shift occurred as a result of the jurors' careful reconsideration of the evidence (i.e., informational influence), this would suggest that the charge serves a very useful function. The researchers, however, found that it was best explained by the decreased pressure felt by the majority members and the increased coercion and social pressure (i.e., normative influence) felt by the minority members.

SUMMARY

The institution of the Canadian jury is an important and fundamental component of our legal system. Because of its importance and perhaps because of the nature of the jury's task itself, the topic has attracted considerable interest from psychologists. In this chapter, we covered a range of psychological factors and processes underlying jury behaviour. As the research indicates, the determination of guilt and innocence involves a complex array of individual and group-level decision processes. In addition to the content of the trial evidence, the format and structure of its presentation can influence the way in which jurors process the information. As well, jurors do not enter the courtroom as "blank slates," but rather with a host of attitudes and beliefs that, in some cases, may be of relevance to the case at hand.

Since the jury verdict is a product of the collective interpretation and recollection of twelve members, a variety of perspectives will be represented in the decision. Research examining the processes involved in arriving at this decision has revealed that the jurors devote most of their time to the case facts and contested issues. Although the majority predeliberation opinion of the group tends to prevail, in criminal trials there is a greater shift towards verdict leniency. Finally, structural characteristics of the jury, such as its size and decision rule (which have not been altered in the Canadian jury), can alter the quality of the jury's deliberations, and ultimately, its verdict.

QUESTIONS FOR DISCUSSION

1. Section 649 of the Criminal Code prevents jurors from disclosing any information pertaining to the jury's deliberations. Discuss both the merits and problems associated with the shroud of secrecy surrounding the verdict. What impact might allowing juror disclosure have on jurors' deliberations? On jurors' decisions? And on the public's perceptions of justice?
2. Assume you have been asked to participate on a Task Force formed to examine and potentially reform judicial jury instructions. What factors would you consider in your discussions? Are there particular areas you think are in need of reform?
3. In *R. v. McIntosh* (1997), the judge makes the argument that expert testimony pertaining to eyewitness identifications is unnecessary and a waste of court time. The judge further notes that introduction of information such as this could perhaps best be handled by conveying the information via judicial instructions. Discuss and assess the implications of such a procedure.
4. You have been contacted by a defence lawyer for advice on how she should present her case to the jurors. Knowing what you know about jury decision making, what general factors would you recommend she consider in her decision about how to present the case? (You may want to frame your advice in terms of the Story Model.)

RECOMMENDED READING

Granger, C. (1996). *The criminal jury trial in Canada* (2nd ed.). Scarborough, ON: Carswell.

Hans, V.P., & Vidmar, N. (1986). *Judging the jury.* New York: Plenum.

Kalven, H., & Zeisel, H. (1966). *The American jury.* Toronto: Little, Brown and Company.

Kassin, S.M., & Wrightsman, L.S. (1988). *The American jury on trial.* New York: Hemisphere Publishing Corporation.

Nietzel, M.T., McCarthy, D.M. & Kern, M.J. (1999). Juries: The current state of the empirical literature. In R. Roesch, S.D. Hart, & J.R.P. Ogloff (Eds.), *Psychology and the law: The state of the discipline* (pp. 23–52). New York: Kluwer Academic/Plenum Publishers.

7. Sentencing, Parole, and Psychology

Julian V. Roberts

Sentencing: You Be the Judge

In British Columbia, five young men pleaded guilty to manslaughter in a case that attracted national attention. They had beaten and kicked an Indo-Canadian man to death. Evidence heard at the sentencing hearing revealed that the young men hated racial minorities and had often discussed committing crimes against this category of individuals. On one occasion they had talked about bombing a school attended by children of the Sikh community. The Crown was able to establish at the sentencing hearing that the crime had been racially motivated. According to section 718.2(a)(i) of the Criminal Code, crimes motivated by hate or bias should result in the imposition of a harsher than average penalty. But how much harsher? What sentence is appropriate in a case like this? No minimum penalty applies. When sentencing an offender convicted of manslaughter, a judge can choose any sentence between a suspended sentence and life imprisonment. The average sentence imposed is 5 years. At the end of the chapter we shall discuss the sentences imposed on the five men.

Parole Eligibility: Should offenders serving life and who are applying for a jury review of their parole eligibility date be allowed to question jurors about their attitudes to parole?

Fifteen years ago Antonio Norona was convicted of the murder of his wife and sentenced to life imprisonment without parole until he had served 25 years in prison. However, there is a provision in the Criminal Code (s. 745.6), known as the 'faint hope' clause, which permits most lifers to apply for parole before they have served 25 years. According to this provision Norona has the right to apply for a jury review of his parole eligibility date.

The jury has the power to bring forward that date (from 25 years to some year between 15 and 25).

Opinion polls suggest that most Canadians are strongly opposed to granting parole to murderers at any point in a life sentence. This means that most potential jurors will already have a position on applications under this section of the Code. Although jurors are supposed to be neutral with respect to the case, favouring neither the Crown nor the applicant, the likelihood is that they will oppose an application for early parole from someone convicted of murder, no matter what evidence is introduced during the course of the hearing. This is the equivalent of a murder trial in which most jurors intend to vote for the Crown before they have heard a single witness.

As we saw in Chapter 5, the Criminal Code has a mechanism to permit counsel for the defence to "challenge for cause," that is, to ask certain questions of potential jurors in order to determine whether they are biased against an accused from the outset. Should Norona have the right to ask potential jurors whether they could evaluate his application for early parole fairly, if they think that no inmate serving life for murder should ever get parole? The Norona parole review raises the issue of public attitudes towards sentencing and parole, one of the areas in which psychologists have conducted a great deal of research. Psychologists have documented the nature of public opinion on these issues and alerted the criminal justice system to its likely consequences. This chapter explores the contributions psychologists have made to the sentencing process in Canada.

Psychologists have actively contributed to knowledge in the area of sentencing for many years now. Areas of research in Canada include evaluations of rehabilitation programs (e.g., Gendreau & Ross, 1987); the factors predicting recidivism (Gendreau, Little, & Goggin, 1996); the effects of imprisonment (Zamble & Porporino, 1988); predictions of dangerousness (Webster, Dickens, & Addario, 1985); sentencing disparity (Doob & Beaulieu, 1992; Palys & Divorski, 1986); judicial decision making (Andrews, Robblee, & Saunders, 1984); sentencing options (Tremblay, Gravel, & Cusson, 1987); sentencing information systems (Doob & Park, 1987); attitudes towards sentencing and parole (Doob & Roberts, 1984; Cumberland & Zamble, 1992; Douglas & Ogloff, 1997; Roberts & Stalans, 2000; Zamble & Kalm, 1990); sentencing policy (Roberts, 1999; Roberts & von Hirsch, 1999); and sentencing patterns (Roberts, 1995; 1999). In addition, recent contributions have focused on the effectiveness of different sanctions (e.g., Andrews &

Bonta, 1998; Gendreau, Goggin, & Cullen, 1999). In terms of research, psychology has contributed more than any other social science to our understanding of this component of the criminal justice system.

As discussed in the introduction to this book, psychologists are concerned with changing human behaviour. We study the conditions under which behavioural change occurs, whether from the perspective of learning theories (e.g., behaviour modification) or from a radically different orientation such as personality theories (e.g., psychoanalysis). In this respect, the aims of psychology (understanding and changing human behaviour) coincide with those of the sentencing process. Sentencing also attempts to affect behaviour, through the threat of punishment (the maximum penalties contained in the Criminal Code) or the actual imposition of punishments on convicted offenders. The utilitarian aims of sentencing (i.e., those sentencing goals that attempt to achieve some measurable objective, namely, the prevention of crime) reflect this attempt to prevent crime through changing human behaviour. Utilitarian goals include the inhibition of criminal behaviour through fear of punishment (general deterrence), actual punishment (specific deterrence), or the reform of the individual (rehabilitation). Given these common goals, it should come as no surprise that psychology has made a significant contribution to the sentencing process.

INTRODUCTION TO SENTENCING STRUCTURE IN CANADA

Sentencing can be defined as the imposition of a legal sanction on persons convicted of a criminal offence. One of the obvious characteristics of the sentencing process is that it has several different (and sometimes conflicting goals). There is no single purpose or objective of sentencing offenders. Some sentencing purposes (such as punishment or deterrence) have been around for centuries. Other goals, such as incapacitation, are relatively new. The challenge to judges, and to reformers in this area, is to decide what the purpose(s) of sentencing should be and how they should be applied to different cases. A number of primary purposes have been ascribed to the sentencing process over the years, and continue to be important today. The following objectives are identified by section 718 of the Criminal Code:

(A) Denunciation: the attempt to censure an individual for culpable criminal conduct. The court imposes a sentence to denounce the crime of which the offender has been convicted.

(B) Specific deterrence: the attempt to prevent crime by arousing fear of punishment in the individual being sentenced. Individual offenders are inhibited from further offending by fear of what will happen to them if they are re-convicted.

(C) General Deterrence: the attempt to prevent crime by creating fear of punishment among the general public. Potential offenders are said to be deterred by being made aware of the punishments imposed on convicted offenders.

(D) Incapacitation: the prevention of crime by the incapacitation of the individual offender for a specified period of time. This usually means incarceration.

(E) Rehabilitation: the attempt to change an individual by promoting law-abiding behaviour. This usually involves sentencing the offender to some alternative to custody, such as probation with conditions.

(F) Reparation: the court may order the offender to make reparations to individual victims or the community.

(G) Promote a sense of responsibility in offenders.

When sentencing an offender, a judge has to consider all of these objectives and decide which is most appropriate in each specific case. As well, judges will be guided by the "Fundamental Principle" of sentencing, namely: "A sentence must be proportionate to the gravity of the offence and the degree of responsibility of the offender." This principle is also contained in the Criminal Code (s. 718.1).

Let us return to the case described at the beginning of this chapter to illustrate the difficulties of selecting a sentencing purpose. In your view, which sentencing goal should be most important in determining the sentence that should be imposed on the five men who killed the Indo-Canadian? Some purposes are clearly not appropriate. Reparation is not possible, given the loss of life. What about rehabilitation? The offenders are all under 24 years of age, one was only 17 when the crime was committed. Generally speaking, rehabilitation is more important in cases involving younger offenders, but this crime is simply too serious to allow the judge to give much consideration to the rehabilitation of the offender when sentencing. Should the court pursue the purpose of general deterrence, with the aim of sending a message to other people who might be considering attacking minorities? The resolution of the question of sentencing purposes is clearly not easy. The application of psychology in Box 7.1 is an illustration of one way in which psychologists might have an influence over the sentencing process.

Box 7.1

Would Longer Prison Terms Lower the Incidence of Domestic Violence?

The testimony of psychologists is sometimes used by the courts of appeal who play a large role in guiding judges at the trial court level. In this case, *R. v. Edwards*, 1996, the Ontario Court of Appeal used the testimony of Professor Anthony Doob, a professor of psychology and criminology from the University of Toronto, to help resolve a sentencing appeal.

The Offence

The offender, now 40 years old, shot his former common law wife four times: three times to the head and once to the chest. Fortunately, she survived. Her assailant pleaded guilty and was convicted of attempted murder, contrary to s. 239 of the Criminal Code. He was sentenced to nine years' imprisonment in addition to the approximately one year that he had already spent in jail awaiting trial.

The Appeal

The Crown appealed the sentence to the Ontario Court of Appeal. The Crown argued that sentences should be significantly harsher for cases involving domestic violence. Their justification for this view was that there is a greater need for deterrence in such cases. The Crown introduced survey evidence to show that domestic violence is a widespread phenomenon in Canadian society. Accordingly, it is necessary to "send a message" to men contemplating the assault of their partners. The Crown argued that harsher penalties – in this case a term of imprisonment longer than nine years – would lead to greater deterrence and lower the crime rate of this form of criminality.

Dr Doob, an expert in the area of sentencing research, testified that there were several reasons to reject the Crown's position. First, deterrence theory assumes that people consider the nature of the penalty when they contemplate committing a crime. While this may be true for some economic crimes, like fraud, it is farfetched to argue that an offender about to kill his wife would be deterred if the likely penalty were 12 years, but not if it was only 9 years. Doob testified that research on general deterrence has shown that the magnitude of the penalty has little impact on potential offenders, since they assume that they will not be caught. As for individual deterrence, Doob concluded that "there is no evidence that suggests that more severe sentences would make offenders such [as this one] less likely to commit further offences." Thus, while there may be other valid justifications for increasing the severity of the sentence from 9 years to 12, doing so would not result in more effective deterrence.

The Decision of the Court of Appeal

The Ontario Court of Appeal concluded: "While I acknowledge that the principle of general deterrence is of paramount importance in ... cases of domestic violence ... it is simplistic to assume that the problems of domestic violence can be successfully attacked by increasing the sentencing tariffs." The appeal was dismissed, leaving the sentence at 9 years.

In addition to deciding which purpose is most important, judges have to select a specific sentence that will fulfil the sentencing objective. Canadian judges have a wide range of sentencing options available to them, including the following: imprisonment, suspended sentence with probation, probation, a fine, conditional and absolute discharge, restitution, and various prohibitions (such as possessing a firearm). Imprisonment alone can be ordered in several ways. The term may be continuous (such as 6 months' "straight time"), conditional (meaning that it may be served in the community), intermittent (served on weekends) or indeterminate (no fixed period specified). As well, a court may impose a term of life imprisonment, which usually means that the offender will serve a number of years in prison before becoming eligible to apply for parole. The imposition of these sentencing options is regulated by a number of rules (for further information on sentencing options in Canada, see Edgar, 1999).

As for the case of the five young men guilty of manslaughter, the choice of sentence is fairly straightforward: nothing but imprison-

ment will acknowledge the seriousness of the crime. But imprisonment for how long? The most recent statistics reveal that the median
sentence for manslaughter is 5 years (see Table 7.1), but this case is
more serious than the average manslaughter. The challenge to a
judge is to decide how many years these offenders should spend in
prison.

Sentencing Reform in Canada

This is an important time to study the sentencing process in Canada.
After many years of discussion and consultation, the federal government passed significant reform legislation in 1996 (see Roberts & Cole,
1999a). That reform will be described in due course in this chapter, but
first, it is important to understand some basic facts about the sentencing system in this country.

Judges in Canada, like their counterparts in the United Kingdom
and other common law countries, have a great deal of discretion with
respect to the type and severity of sentences they can impose. A small
number of offences carry minimum penalties, and an even smaller
number carry a mandatory penalty. One such offence is first degree
murder; all offenders convicted of this crime are sentenced to life
imprisonment without the possibility of parole until they have served
at least 25 years in prison. For most offences, though, the Canadian
Criminal Code prescribes a maximum penalty and the rest is left to the
individual judge. For example, the maximum penalty for breaking and
entering a private residence is life imprisonment, and there is no minimum penalty. There are in fact over 70 crimes in the Code that can be
punished by a term of imprisonment of 14 years or life. This reality
gives rise to an area of research to which psychologists have made a
significant contribution: sentencing disparity. There are several possible definitions of sentencing disparity. In essence this term refers to
variation in sentencing patterns due to the influence of factors that are
not legally relevant to the case. The personality of the judge, for example, is a variable that, in an ideal world, should not influence the
nature of the sentence imposed.

The degree of discretion afforded judges in sentencing offenders
does not mean that judges may impose any sentence they choose.
Judges are guided by precedents in the case law, that is, by sentences
imposed in similar cases in the past. Nevertheless, judges in Canada
have more discretion than the judiciary in the United States, where

most states employ sentencing guideline systems that mandate a fairly narrow range of sentence lengths for most offences.[1] The issue of guidance has become critical to the debate on sentencing reform. In fact, the central question at the heart of discussions about sentencing reform is how to constrain or guide judges to a greater degree than at present. If judges have a great deal of freedom when sentencing, the result will inevitably be disparity of treatment. On the other hand, if judicial decision making is overly constrained, with very rigid rules for sentencing, then the process will become unjust as offenders of differential culpability are given the same sentence.[2]

There are many different ways in which more guidance could be provided to judges. One possibility is to provide a typical or "benchmark" sentence for each offence in the Code. Judges in America have a system of this kind. Each offence carries a recommended sentence, and in the cases of imprisonment, a range. Robbery, for example, might carry a benchmark sentence of 2 to 4 years. Unless exceptional circumstances existed, the judge would be required to sentence the offender to a period of imprisonment within this range.

The sentencing process in Canada has many problems, including too much variation in sentencing patterns; an over-use of incarceration; a lack of "truth in sentencing" (as a result of the parole process, the time served in prison can bear little relation to the sentence imposed in court); an out-dated maximum penalty structure; and a lack of public confidence in the system (see Canadian Sentencing Commission, 1987, for a discussion of these and other problems).

Table 7.1 provides the median sentence length and the maximum penalty for selected offences. This table shows the weakness of the current maximum penalties contained in the Criminal Code: most maximum penalties are so high that they are never imposed and thus provide little practical guidance to judges regarding the relative seriousness of different crimes. As well, the unrealistically high maximum penalties can create false expectations among members of the public. Sometimes media reports state that an offender received a 6-month sentence for sexual assault, when the maximum penalty for this crime is 10 years' imprisonment. This creates the impression that judges are too lenient. However, the reality is that almost all sentences for sexual assault are less than 2 years; the maximum is almost never imposed.

Awareness of the many problems associated with sentencing led to the creation, in 1984, of a royal commission to study the sentencing

TABLE 7.1
Maximum penalties and median sentences (selected offences)

Offence	Maximum penalty	Median sentence length
Sexual assault with a weapon & aggravated sexual assault (ss. 272–273)[1]	Life	2 years
Manslaughter (s. 234)	Life	5 years
Robbery (s. 343)	Life	1.5 years
Break and enter (ss. 348, 349)	Life	3 months
Aggravated assault (s. 268)	14 years	10 months
Procuring (s. 212)	14 years	1 year
Use of a firearm to commit an offence (s. 85)	14 years	1 year
Forgery (s. 366)	14 years	2 months
Sexual assault (s. 271)	10 years	4 months
Possession of burglary tools (s. 351(1))	10 years	2 months
Forcible confinement (s. 279)	10 years	6 months
Assault with weapon (s. 267)	10 years	3 months
Assault peace officer (s. 270)	5 years	1 month
Obstruct police (s.129)	5 years	1 month
Assault (s. 265)	5 years	1 month
Drive while disqualified (s. 259(4))	2 years	1 month
Unlawfully at large (s. 145(1b))	2 years	1 month
Mischief under (s. 430)	2 years	1 month
Gaming and betting (ss. 201–209)	2 years	14 days
Theft under (s. 334 (b))	2 years	1 month

[1]Offences were combined due to small numbers of cases.
SOURCE: Roberts and Birkenmayer (1997)

process in Canada. Following 3 years of study and consultation, the Canadian Sentencing Commission released its report in 1987. That commission recommended the creation of an information system for judges that would provide them with guidelines as to when imprisonment was necessary, and, if so, for how long. As well, the commission's proposed guideline system provided information relating to case law and relevant mitigating and aggravating factors for all offences in the Code. This guideline system was rejected by the federal government, which was not convinced that the amount of disparity was sufficient to justify its creation. It was also felt that judges would oppose such a system on the grounds that it would unduly limit their ability to impose a just sentence.

Sentencing Reforms of 1996

After many years of study and consultation, sentencing reform legislation was finally passed by Parliament in 1996. The two most important reforms introduced by Bill C-41 involved the creation of a statutory statement of the purposes and principles of sentencing and the creation of a new sanction (a conditional sentence).

Statement of Purpose and Principles of Sentencing

Prior to Bill C-41, judges were free to choose from among a diversity of purposes. There was some limited guidance from the courts of appeal. For example, a court of appeal decision might state that the primary purpose of sentencing offenders convicted of tax evasion was general deterrence. Otherwise, judges were free to follow their own sentencing theories about which purposes were appropriate for which kinds of cases. That has now changed. Judges still have considerable freedom, but they are constrained by the statement of purpose and principle, which is now contained in section 718 of the Code. Section 718.1 states: "A sentence must be proportionate to the gravity of the offence and the degree of responsibility of the offender." This means that the severity of sentences must be proportionate to the seriousness of the crimes for which they are imposed. In theory, the presence of this clear principle in the Code should prevent judges from handing down a harsh sentence in order to "send a message to others" (the purpose of general deterrence) (see Roberts & von Hirsch, 1999, for further discussion).

Conditional Sentence

Almost all commissions of inquiry (including the Law Reform Commission of Canada and the Canadian Sentencing Commission), as well as the federal government, have noted that Canada has a high rate of incarceration. The most recent analysis of international imprisonment rates found that Canada's rate of 115 inmates per 100,000 population was higher than many other Western nations[3] (see Walmsley, 1999).

The sentencing reforms introduced in 1996 contained a provision designed to reduce the use of incarceration as a sanction. This provision created a new disposition called a conditional sentence. Here's how it works. At sentencing, a judge determines whether the offender must be incarcerated. This determination reflects the purposes and principles of sentencing as outlined in section 718 of the Code (see above). Once the judge has decided to incarcerate the offender, he or she may consider allowing the offender to serve the sentence in the community, provided certain conditions are followed. This means that the offender will have to abide by the conditions of the conditional sentence order (which are similar to the conditions of a probation order). Violation of these conditions may result in the imprisonment of the offender.

Not all offenders are eligible for a conditional sentence. First, the sentence originally imposed must have been for less than 2 years. Second, the offence must not be punishable by a minimum sentence. Third, the court must be satisfied that "serving the sentence in the community would not endanger the safety of the community and would be consistent with the purpose and principles of sentencing as set out in sections 718 to 718.2" of the Code. The idea then, is that some of the offenders who in the past would have received a term of imprisonment will now serve their sentence in the community, under supervision. It is too soon to tell how effective this reform has been, but early indications are that judges are frequently using the new disposition. Thousands of conditional sentences were imposed in the first 6 months after the disposition was created (for further information on conditional sentencing, see Healy, 1999; Roberts, 1999). Psychological research that explores how judges react to and interpret the sentence itself in light of the purpose and principles contained in section 718 of the Criminal Code should be of use to reformers in this area in the future.

The conditional sentence itself will also raise issues that have been explored by psychologists. In other jurisdictions, such as the United Kingdom, when a judge makes a sentence of imprisonment conditional, he or she may add a number of other sanctions, such as community service, a fine, and so on. Although the offender does not have to go to prison (so long as conditions are followed), he or she has to pay some penalty. The offender sentenced to a term of imprisonment that is then made conditional avoids prison, but not punishment. This maintains some equity in the sentencing process. It also raises complex issues, however, relating to the equivalence of sanctions. What kind of fine is the equivalent of 30 days in prison? What length of probation is the equivalent of 90 days' imprisonment? These questions can only be resolved by developing scales of equivalence. If such scales were available, it would be possible to impose a non-custodial sentence that would be as punitive as a period of custody. Equity in sentencing would be preserved and public confidence would be maintained in the sentencing process. Psychologists have been working on this problem for some time (see Tremblay, 1989).

The sentencing reform bill also contained a number of other elements, including sections enabling jurisdictions to establish diversion programs, a code of procedure and evidence for sentencing hearings, and a new regime for fines (for further information about Bill C-41, see Daubney & Parry, 1999).

JUDICIAL DECISION MAKING AND SENTENCING

Research Methods in the Area of Sentencing

The most powerful research design is an experiment. In the classic experiment, research participants are assigned, at random, to some treatment or condition. For example, in a study designed to evaluate the effects of television violence upon aggression, half the participants will be randomly assigned to watch violent television, half will watch non-violent programs. Then the researcher will measure the amount of aggression displayed by the participants in the two groups. Since participants were randomly assigned to either the experimental or control condition, any differences between the groups in terms of the amount of aggression observed must be due to the experimental manipulation (violence or the absence of violence) and not as a result of other factors. But we cannot randomly assign offenders to judges to see if the same offender receives a different sentence from different judges. There are two solutions to the problem. Neither is perfect, but taken together they give us a good answer to the question of whether unwarranted disparity in sentencing exists in Canada.

One method used to study judicial sentencing decisions involves the use of simulated cases. A group of judges are given a description of a crime to read and afterwards asked to impose a sentence on the convicted offender. The extent of variation among judges constitutes the measure of disparity. The weakness of this approach is that the "sentencing" lacks reality. There is no actual offender, no Crown attorney, no defence counsel and, above all, no consequences for the judge. This research design lacks external validity, because it does not necessarily reflect the "real world," or the phenomenon that the simulation is trying to capture (Lovegrove, 1989). It might be unwise to generalize from the results of a study such as this to actual sentencing practices. On the other hand, experimental simulations are strong in terms of internal validity. This means that there are no ambiguities of interpretation. If disparity in sentencing occurs when the same case is used, it is clear that the judge is responsible, rather than some legally relevant characteristic relating to the offence.

The alternative approach consists of examining actual sentencing statistics. For example, a study of sentencing trends showed that the incarceration rate for manslaughter was much higher in Quebec than Ontario. Almost all (94%) offenders convicted of this crime were imprisoned in Quebec, whereas only half of those convicted in Ontario were incarcerated (Roberts, 1995). This is suggestive of unwarranted disparity. But can we conclude that disparity exists as a result of a simple discrepancy between two provinces? There may be legally relevant explanations for the difference in incarceration rates. Research that uses sentencing statistics is high in terms of external validity (since we are dealing with real sentencing decisions, not simulations). On the other hand, making comparisons between jurisdictions and drawing the conclusion that unwarranted disparity exists lacks internal validity, since there may be other, legally relevant explanations for variation in sentencing patterns from court to court. The best research strategy would employ both simulations and comparisons using actual statistics. In this way, the researcher gains the advantages of both research approaches. No single study has attempted to combine the strategies, but, since a great deal of research has now accumulated on this issue, we can evaluate whether sentencing disparity exists by examining studies from both traditions.

Sentencing Disparity

A certain degree of sentencing variation is both inevitable and essential. Sentencing without any variation would be sentencing without justice. But what about unwarranted disparity? Is it a problem in Canada? After reading the following summary of research conducted on this question, you be the judge. Sentencing variation is arguably the most important issue in terms of sentencing reform. All major reforms that have been proposed or implemented in the United States or Canada over the past 20 years have attempted to address the problem of disparity. Psychologists have approached the issue in a number of different ways. In fact, the first scientific demonstration of disparity in sentencing appeared in the *Journal of Applied Psychology* over 60 years ago (Gaudet, Harris, & St John, 1932). As it turns out, whichever research approach is adopted (the experimental or the "natural variation" approach) the result is the same. Let's look at a couple of actual research examples.

Sentencing Simulations

Palys and Divorski (1986) gave a number of case descriptions to over 200 provincial court judges, who were asked to state what sentence they would impose. If sentencing disparity does not exist, sentences should not vary much from judge to judge (since all judges read exactly the same case). However, these researchers found a high degree of variation. For example, one case involved an armed robbery. Sentences imposed ranged in severity from a suspended sentence to 13 years in prison. Another case, this time of a less serious crime (theft), generated sentences that ranged from a fine to three years in prison (see Palys & Divorski, 1986; Table 7.1). Some offences generated less variation. For a case of break and enter, for example, the most lenient sentence imposed was a suspended sentence, while the most severe was a year in prison. This suggests that the nature of the offence may determine how much variability exists. Other researchers have used the same approach to explore sentencing disparity at the youth court level. Doob and Beaulieu summarize their simulation study results by noting that there was "substantial variation both in the dispositions these judges indicated they would hand down and the priority of goals that they were trying to achieve" (1992, p. 47). Similar research from the United States, which has used the simulation approach, has also uncovered a high degree of variation in judicial sentencing decisions (e.g., Austin & Williams, 1977).

Court Statistics

A study conducted in 1971 (Hogarth, 1971) attempted to determine how much variation in predicting the sentences assigned could be accounted for by the case and how much by the judge. This researcher examined a number of sentencing decisions in considerable depth, measuring variables associated with the case (such as the seriousness of the offence, whether the accused pleaded guilty, etc.), characteristics relating to the offender (such as age, employment status, criminal record, etc.), and characteristics of the judge. If sentencing disparity did not exist, then the characteristics of the judge would have no impact on the sentence imposed. This, however, was not the case. Hogarth's conclusion was clear: "it appears from the analysis that one can explain more about sentencing by knowing ... about the judge than by knowing a great deal about the facts of the case" (p. 350). In statistical terms, Hogarth found that only about 9% of the variation in sentencing could be explained by objectively defined facts of the case, while over 50% of such variation could be accounted for simply by knowing certain facts about the judge. Hogarth's finding was consistent with earlier research (e.g., Jaffary, 1963) and confirmed by later work.

The most recent analysis of actual sentencing patterns also finds considerable variation that is suggestive of unjustified disparity. This study consisted of an analysis of the imprisonment rates in a number of provincial courts across the country (see Roberts, 1999). Results indicated that the incarceration rate varied considerably, from 14% in one location (Calgary) to 41% in another (College Park, in Toronto). Of course, it is possible that legally relevant factors can account for this discrepancy. For instance, perhaps cases in Toronto are more serious. Or perhaps Toronto courts sentence a higher proportion of crimes involving violence. Since these are generally more serious than crimes involving property, a higher overall incarceration rate would be expected.

The same phenomenon is observed, however, when comparisons are made between different jurisdictions after having first controlled, statistically, for the seriousness of the offence. Table 7.2 provides the incarceration rates across nine jurisdictions for a limited number of offences. As can be seen, they vary considerably. For break and enter, the imprisonment rate varied from 33% in Quebec to 78% in Prince Edward Island. Similarly, the imprisonment rate for impaired driving ranged from 4% (in Nova Scotia) to 75% in Prince Edward Island (see Birkenmayer & Besserer, 1997; Birkenmayer & Roberts, 1997). Viewed in conjunction with the results of the sentencing simulations, these "real life" statistics suggest that a considerable degree of the variation in sentencing patterns is accounted for by the judge rather than the legal characteristics of the case (the seriousness of the crime, the criminal history of the offender, etc.). This conclusion was reached by the Canadian Sentencing Commission when it conducted a major review in 1987 (see Canadian Sentencing Commission, 1987).

Explaining sentence disparity: In addition to providing the documen-

TABLE 7.2
Incarceration rates, nine jurisdictions

Offence	Percentage of offenders sentenced to prison								
	Nfld.	P.E.I.	N.S.	Que.	Ont.	Sask.	Alta.	Yuk.	N.W.T.
Assault Level 2	50	43	32	19	59	32	45	61	77
Assault Level 1	10	39	8	5	25	11	16	23	26
Break and enter	55	78	46	33	72	47	56	33	37
Theft under $1,000	4	9	7	20	26	9	11	27	24
Impaired driving	20	75	4	8	23	12	12	29	20
Drive disqualified	42	14	16	36	78	20	41	65	30
Fail to appear	51	38	22	24	62	22	16	47	37
Narcotics Control Act: possession	5	3	3	9	20	6	5	6	2

SOURCE: Birkenmayer and Roberts (1997)

tary evidence for the existence of disparity, theories in social and perceptual psychology have taught us why we should expect disparity to exist (see also Chapter 6). A single stimulus will be perceived very differently by different observers; the same set of facts in a criminal case will provoke different reactions from judges, which will, in turn, give rise to different dispositions. And, when the law permits a wide latitude of action to the decision maker (the judge), as is currently the case in Canada, the result will inevitably be unwarranted disparity in sentencing.

PUBLIC ATTITUDES TOWARDS SENTENCING AND PAROLE

Another area in which psychologists have made a contribution to our understanding of the sentencing process involves public attitudes towards sentencing and parole. Although neither judges nor parole boards directly take public opinion into account, public reaction to sentencing plays an important role in determining sentencing policy and practice. Public opinion has also influenced the reform process with respect to sentencing and parole. One example of this concerns the issue of early parole for inmates serving life sentences.

As noted earlier, offenders convicted of first degree murder are automatically sentenced to life imprisonment; the judge has no discretion. In the case of such offenders, this means that they must spend at least 25 years in prison before they become eligible to apply for parole.[4] When capital punishment was abolished in Canada (in 1976), legislation gave life prisoners the right to make an application for a review of their parole eligibility after having served only 15 years. This provision became known as the "faint hope" clause.

The provision allows most inmates to apply for a jury review of their parole eligibility date. Before the jury hears the evidence, a judge will decide if the applicant has a reasonable chance of convincing the jury to grant him the right to make an early parole application. Only if the judge believes the inmate has a good chance of convincing the jury will the applicant proceed. If the jury does review the case, they will hear evidence relating to the original offence, the inmate's progress towards rehabilitation, his plans for life on the outside (if released), and many other issues. The jury may grant the applicant the right to make an early parole application, or it may refuse the request. If the applicant is successful, he or she will then make an application to the National Parole Board, who will conduct their own review to determine whether the individual would pose a threat to the community if he were released on parole.

Once applications under this provision began to be heard, there was a great deal of public opposition to the faint hope provision. This opposition grew particularly widespread when convicted mass murderer Clifford Olson made an application in 1997 and the public outcry was instrumental in having the section of the Code amended in 1997. Under the new, tighter rules, it will be much harder for such inmates to get early parole (see Roberts and Cole, 1999b for discussion). Thus, for a number of reasons, the importance of the views of the public with respect to sentencing and parole must be acknowledged.

Research Methods in the Area of Public Attitudes

As with the issue of sentencing disparity, psychologists use diverse approaches to gain an understanding of public attitudes towards sentencing and parole. These include representative surveys of the public, focus groups, and experimental research. Representative polls employ a large sample of respondents who are asked a limited number of multiple choice questions. For example, people might be asked, "In your opinion, are sentences too harsh, too lenient, or about right?" Respondents have little time to reflect prior to responding, and usually give their "top of the head" reaction. The results of such a question also lack precision and provoke more questions: sentences for what kinds of crimes, what kinds of offenders? The advantage of a Gallup-type poll, however, is that the researcher can generalize the results to the population. The margin of error is low. This means that if a standard Gallup sample finds that 33% of respondents favour the abolition of parole, the actual percentage, if the entire population had been questioned, would fall between 29% to 37%, the known limits of error in this case. The researcher can, therefore, generalize from the views of the sample to the opinions of the population from which the sample was drawn.

No such generalization is possible for findings from small-scale, qualitative methods such as focus groups. These involve a small number of people (15–20) who are asked to discuss issues in considerable depth. They may have several hours in which to do so, and they may be provided with additional information as the discussion proceeds. A moderator takes notes or records the comments of group members.

This procedure permits researchers to get beyond a simple "yes–no" question, but the results cannot be generalized to the population since the sample is not large enough to be representative (examples of focus group studies in the area of sentencing can be found in Environics Research Group, 1989 and Hough, 1996).

The final category of research, the experimental approach, has been most widely used by university-based psychologists and relies heavily on university students, usually drawn from the subject pool of a psychology department. Such a research participant population, of course, may not be representative of the general population, but the advantage is that in some cases the participants are available for several sessions. This permits researchers to employ experimental manipulations, which would not be possible with the preceding methods (examples of research using this approach can be found in Vidmar & Dittenhoffer, 1981).

In the final analysis, a comprehensive and accurate portrait of public attitudes to sentencing and parole can only be obtained by drawing upon all three research methods: representative polls provide an idea of the broad trends in public opinion; focus groups are needed to evaluate the depth of public sentiment on a particular issue, and to find out what specific issues people are talking about in the area of sentencing; and laboratory-based research is essential for hypothesis testing (see Roberts & Stalans, 2000, chap. 1).

Public Attitudes towards Sentencing

Polls constantly demonstrate that public interest in, and opposition to, sentencing practices is considerable. For this reason, one of the goals of the sentencing reform was to promote public confidence in the sentencing process. What then have we learned about public attitudes as a result of empirical research by psychologists? A number of important findings stand out. Whenever a poll is conducted on sentencing trends, the result is generally the same. Over 80% of respondents in Canada, the United States and the United Kingdom respond that sentences are not harsh enough (Roberts & Stalans, 2000; Hough & Roberts, 1997). A wealth of evidence in all three countries, however, shows that when confronted with a specific case, or when given more information about the facts of the case, the public are less punitive than many politicians believe.

Effects of the Media on Public Views

To explore the effects of the media on public views, one study compared two groups of research participants. One group was asked to read news media reports of a sentencing decision in a case of assault, while the other group was given a summary of all the court documents to read. Afterwards, members of both groups were asked whether the sentence imposed was too lenient, about right, or too harsh. Participants who had read the newspaper account had the typical reaction: almost two-thirds said that the sentence was too lenient. Over half of the other group, however, felt that the sentence was too harsh (Doob & Roberts, 1988). The sentence was of course the same in both conditions (21 months' imprisonment for the crime of assault causing bodily harm); what was different was the context. The point of this study was to demonstrate that surveys of public opinion generate an oversimplified portrait of public attitudes towards sentencing.

It is also important to note the results of surveys that explore public *knowledge*, rather than opinion regarding sentencing. The gap between the public and the courts (manifested in public disapproval of sentencing trends) is in part explained by misperceptions about the system. For example, most members of the public in Canada (and other Western nations) underestimate the severity of sentencing patterns. This was demonstrated in research conducted for the federal Department of Justice. For example, although sentencing statistics reveal that approximately 90% of offenders convicted of robbery are imprisoned (Birkenmayer & Besserer, 1997), when asked to estimate the incarceration rate for this crime, three-quarters of the public estimated the figure to be under 60%. The same is true for other crimes and other countries (Hough & Roberts, 1997). In general, findings from several countries indicate that the public systematically underestimates the severity of sentencing. No wonder then, that most people want harsher sentences. This finding suggests that if the public had a more accurate idea of sentencing trends, they would be less critical about the sentencing process and less likely to demand harsher punishments for convicted offenders. (For a review of public misperceptions regarding sentencing and parole, see Canadian Sentencing Commission, 1987, chap. 4.)

As with the issue of sentencing disparity, researchers in the field of psychology have also provided explanations for how negative attitudes to sentencing and parole arise. Indeed, the field of social cognition has shown that the average member of the public has difficulty in drawing the appropriate conclusions when provided with case-relevant information. For example, in a classic study from social psychology, Hamill, Wilson, and Nisbett (1980) demonstrated that people are insensitive to the notion of representativeness. Research participants in this study watched a videotaped interview of a prison guard who acted in one of two ways, either as a kind and humane person or as someone who was cruel and inhumane. After watching the videotape, half of the participants were told that this particular guard was typical of correctional officers, whereas the remaining participants were told that he was highly atypical. The participants' task in the experiment was to describe the characteristics of the average prison guard. The study specifically assessed the extent to which the representativeness information (whether the interviewee was typical or atypical) affected the judgments. Those participants who had been told that the guard they had seen interviewed was atypical should not have used his behaviour as a guide to determine the way that prison guards behave in general. In contrast, those who were informed that his behaviour was typical should have used that information to guide their judgments of prison guards. The representativeness information, however, had no effect on participants' responses. In short, people do not seem to reason in a scientific manner when making everyday judgments.

Translated to the issue of sentencing, it is clear that people fail to appreciate that the sentences reported in the news media are unrepresentative of sentencing patterns. When people read a newspaper headline that reports what appears to be a very lenient sentence for a serious crime of violence, they assume that most sentences are lenient. They fail to consider that this sentence may be unusual or unrepresentative of most sentences imposed for the crime in question.

Once the perception of judicial leniency has taken hold in the public mind, it is unlikely to change quickly. Research in social psychology has shown that people are selective in the information they acquire, and that important social attitudes change very slowly. As noted, the vast majority of the public in Canada, the United States, and Great Britain believe that sentences are too lenient. Two domains of research shed light on the origin and maintenance of this attitude.

Sentencing in the Media

Public knowledge of sentencing is based on an unsystematic and highly selective database, namely, sentences reported in the news media. Lenient sentences are particularly likely to be reported by the news media, especially when the crime involved violence (Roberts, 1995). When judges impose a sentence that they believe may attract public criticism, they frequently take pains to explain why the particular sentence was imposed. However, a content analysis of newspaper reports found that the reasons for a sentence are almost never provided to the reader (Roberts, 1995). In fact, in three-quarters of the news media accounts of a sentencing decision, there was no mention of any reason for the sentence! It is hardly surprising that surveys of the public show widespread dissatisfaction with sentencing trends. However, the public appear to be reacting to what they read in the news media, rather than what actually goes on in court.

The second area of research that shows how the widespread perception of leniency is maintained comes from social psychology. Research in social cognition has indicated that the public are susceptible to a number of cognitive biases. These include failing to take the representativeness of a case into account, generalizing from one case to a whole population, failing to appreciate the statistical weakness of small samples, and allowing existing attitudes to affect the processing of new information (see Fiske & Taylor, 1991).

Public Attitudes towards Parole

There are clear parallels between attitudes to sentencing and attitudes towards parole. Once again, polls reveal widespread public opposition to parole, but, as with sentencing, public misperceptions of the parole process abound. A national survey conducted in 1998 found that over half the sample overestimated the parole grant rate (Roberts, Nuffield, & Hann, 1999). The general public perception is that parole boards are too lenient and release too many inmates into the community. The public are also misinformed about the risk that parolees represent to the community. Misperceptions include the issue of reoffending by parolees. Only a small percentage (8%) of offenders released on parole have their parole status revoked as a result of fresh criminal charges (Solicitor General Canada, 1998). This, however, is not the way the public sees it. A representative survey of Canadians recently found that fully 85% of the public overestimated the recidivism rate of parolees (Roberts, Nuffield, & Hann, 1999). Members of the public oppose parole because they are afraid that parolees will reoffend before their parole expires, when in fact this is a very rare occurrence. Once again, the argument can be made that if the public had a more realistic perception of the parole system, there would be less opposition to releasing inmates on parole.

At this point, we return to the case of Mr Norona, which is being reviewed by a jury that has to decide the date at which he may make an application to the parole board. In light of the fact that many people have negative views of the parole process (and are fearful of parolees), it is reasonable to assume that the public would be particularly opposed to letting someone convicted of murder be eligible for parole before reaching the 25-year mark. The consequence for Mr Norona is that his jury will begin their review of his application for "early parole" with a negative opinion of his case. In light of this, it seems reasonable for Norona's defence counsel to have the right to ask certain questions of potential jurors, in an attempt to eliminate those who cannot be impartial. Otherwise, the process is simply not fair. Some jurors may well have prejudged the issue.

General versus Specific Measures of Public Opinion

We conclude this section by pointing out an element of public opinion that has important consequences for our understanding of attitudes to sentencing and parole. People tend to be fairly punitive when responding to a general question such as "Are sentences too harsh, too lenient, or about right" or "Should the parole board release more or fewer inmates on parole?" One reason for this is that people, when making this decision, must first *interpret* the question, and when they do so, most think of the worst-case scenario. That is, respondents think of violent offenders with long criminal records. If the researcher provides the participants with a specific case, however, people tend to be less punitive.

This can be illustrated in the area of parole by a study conducted by psychologists at Queen's University. Cumberland and Zamble (1992) gave participants a description of an inmate who was applying for parole. Before the study began, participants were asked whether they were satisfied with the parole system. Consistent with global surveys, approximately four out of five participants said that they were dissatisfied with the parole system. They were then given a description of an individual applying for parole. Interestingly, a substantial majority favoured releasing the individual, even in the case of a violent offender with several previous convictions. The researchers summarized their results in the following way: "As in the case of sentencing, the specific case method indicates that people are more liberal and flexible than is suggested by responses to global questions" (Cumberland & Zamble, 1992, pp. 452–453).

Sentencing Outcome in the Manslaughter Motivated by Hate

Finally, let's return to the case of the five individuals who pleaded guilty to the crime of manslaughter, described at the opening of this chapter. The judge found the crime to have been racially motivated, and according to subparagraph 718.2(a)(i) of the Criminal Code, the sentence should be significantly harsher in such cases. The judge in the case sentenced two of the offenders to 18 years in prison and the other three offenders to 15 years' imprisonment. The sentences would be reduced somewhat to take into account the time that the individuals had already served in custody. In his reasons for sentence, the judge wrote: "What can be achieved by what I am doing today is to send a loud, clear and unequivocal message, not only to these five accused, but to others who share their views, that if they commit acts of violence against persons or property out of hatred they will be condemned and punished severely" (the full reasons for sentence can be found in *R. v. Miloszewski, Synderek, Nikkel, Leblanc and Kluch*, 1996).

SUMMARY

Research by psychologists has demonstrated the significant degree of variability that is inevitable when a large, diverse group of individuals (judges) respond to complex stimuli (criminal cases). In the absence of a formal sentencing guideline system, sentencing disparity is a problem in Canada. The sentence imposed in a criminal case will be affected by an individual judge's perceptions (and personal sentencing goals), as well as the legal characteristics of the case. This conclusion is supported by a number of studies on the sentencing process, which have utilized various research methods.

Psychologists have contributed to our understanding of the sentencing process in a number of ways. These contributions are not merely theoretical; they carry practical implications for sentencing reform as well as specific lessons for judges. In terms of sentencing reform, research on sentencing patterns and judicial decision making suggests that sentencing disparity is an important problem that needs to be addressed. The sentencing reform of 1996 stopped short of introducing sentencing guidelines. In fact, it can be argued that with the introduction of a new disposition (the conditional sentence), without any guidance on how to use this new sentencing tool (i.e., what kinds of cases, what types of offenders), matters have deteriorated. Judges may interpret the new sanction in their own way, and the result will be that offenders in one province or court will receive a conditional sentence while comparable offenders elsewhere will be imprisoned.[5] The lesson of psychological research has yet to reach politicians and policy makers.

With respect to public opinion, research in social psychology has shown that the conventional way of gauging public opinion – a simple survey – is inadequate. In the United States, politicians have been guided by a shallow interpretation of public opinion and the consequences for the sentencing process have been negative, to say the least. A good example of this is the "three strikes" laws. These exist in several states and at the federal level. They mandate very severe penalties for offenders convicted of a felony for the third time. The result has been that offenders have been sentenced to life imprisonment for a fairly trivial offence because it happened to be their third conviction. Moreover, the three strikes policy will have little or no impact on the crime rate, and it will cost millions of dollars (for further information see Schichor & Sechrest, 1996).

The growth in research into public opinion and sentencing/parole means that we are likely to see public attitudes to sentencing being increasingly utilized by the courts. At present there are over 2,000 inmates serving life terms for murder in Canada's penitentiaries (Department of Justice Canada, 1996). According to section 745.6, many of these inmates will have the right to apply for a jury review of their parole eligibility dates. As noted in the Norona application that opened this chapter, public attitudes are likely to be critical to jurors' reactions to section 745.6 applications. It seems probable that, at some future date, counsel for inmates applying for a review will be allowed to ask a range of questions to potential jurors. When that occurs, it will have been as a direct result of the wealth of research in this area by psychologists.

QUESTIONS FOR DISCUSSION

1. Should judges in Canada be given fairly rigid sentencing guidelines (as they

have in the United States) or should they be free to impose any sentence so long as it remains within the very broad range provided by the Criminal Code?

2. Should judges take the victim's recommendation of sentence into account? After all, the crime was committed against a specific individual, not the state. Can you see any dangers in giving the individual victim more influence over the nature and severity of the sentence imposed on the offender?

3. Should the views of the public be incorporated into the sentencing process? For example, panels of laypersons (selected like juries) could be asked to rank crimes in terms of their relative seriousness and then to assign penalties. These could then be used by judges to determine sentences in specific cases. Would this make the sentencing process more democratic? Would it decrease the widespread public criticism of sentencing? Are there any disadvantages to this approach?

4. Offenders convicted of murder (first and second degree) are sentenced to life imprisonment. However, almost all are eventually released on parole. Should life imprisonment mean natural life, or should these inmates be given the opportunity to apply for parole? If parole were abolished for lifers, what problems would this create for penitentiaries? Would public safety be increased?

RECOMMENDED READING

Birkenmayer, A., & Besserer, S. (1997). *Sentencing in adult provincial courts.* Ottawa: Statistics Canada (Catalogue no. 85–513–XPE).

Canadian Sentencing Commission. (1987). *Sentencing reform: A Canadian approach.* Ottawa: Supply and Services Canada.

Fitzmaurice, C., & Pease, K. (1987). *The psychology of sentencing.* Manchester: University of Manchester Press.

Roberts, J.V., & Cole, D.P. (1999). *Making sense of sentencing.* Toronto: University of Toronto Press.

Roberts, J.V., & Stalans, L. (2000). Sentencing and parole. In J.V. Roberts & L. Stalans (Eds.), *Public opinion, crime, and criminal justice.* Boulder, CO: Westview Press.

PART THREE

Introduction to Forensic Clinical Psychology

8. The Assessment and Treatment of Offenders and Inmates: General Considerations

James F. Hemphill and Stephen D. Hart

Bill, a 58-year-old man, was arrested for killing his next-door neighbour and taken to a provincial remand facility. As was standard for every admission to the correctional facility, Bill showered and was then seen by a nurse for a brief medical evaluation and by a graduate student in clinical psychology for a 25-minute mental health screening. The primary purpose of the mental health screening was to identify possible psychological concerns that might put Bill at risk of harming himself or others in the facility. The student discussed a broad range of topics with Bill, including marital and interpersonal adjustment, family relationships, employment status, substance use and abuse, and previous mental health contacts. In addition to administering the semi-structured interview, the student paid attention to Bill's personal hygiene and dress, demeanour, and cognitive and emotional functioning. No significant mental health concerns were apparent until the student asked Bill to state the charges for which he was being detained. Bill said he was charged with murder after he shot and killed a next-door neighbour who had been trying for months to poison him. After obtaining more details from institutional files concerning the alleged offence, the student referred Bill to the institutional psychologist and recommended that Bill be carefully monitored during his stay in the facility. The institutional psychologist conducted a more detailed follow-up assessment and provided supportive therapy throughout Bill's stay. Bill's lawyer, who conferred with his client in the remand centre, arranged to have his client transferred to a provincial forensic psychiatric facility to examine Bill's fitness to stand trial and his mental status at the time of the shooting.

An institutional psychiatrist interviewed Bill shortly after admission to the forensic psychiatric facility and placed him on antipsychotic medications. Bill was interviewed by other psychiatrists and psychologists during his stay and received several comprehensive evaluations. His description of his life circumstances and events surrounding the current charge remained consistent across time and across interviewers. He stated that he was currently retired and lived with his wife in a rural area. Bill's wife had apparently hired the neighbour to do general maintenance and repairs around their house. Bill believed that his neighbour had used this access to their house to try and poison him. To illustrate his point, Bill described the time when the neighbour had sprayed Bill and his wife's garden with poisonous "pesticides" and when the neighbour had offered Bill "something" to drink when Bill was working outside on a hot day. On the day of the alleged offence, Bill's wife was at work and the neighbour was repairing their roof. Bill reported that his neighbour was trying to poison him via the chimney and that he now no longer felt safe from his neighbour even while inside his own house. Bill retrieved his gun, went outside, and shot and killed his neighbour. Bill then phoned police and told them that he had just killed his neighbour who had been trying to poison him. Bill's wife, visibly distraught, confirmed many of these details and indicated that her husband "did not get along" with their neighbour.

The judge reviewed the psychological and psychiatric assessments prepared by staff at the forensic psychiatric facility. Bill was found fit to stand trial because his mental functioning was sufficient that he could confer with and assist counsel, follow courtroom proceedings, and participate in the trial process. At trial, however, Bill was found not criminally responsible on account of mental disorder. The judge found that Bill suffered from a mental illness that caused him to believe sincerely (but incorrectly) that the neighbour was trying to poison him. In short, the judge found that Bill was incapable of understanding that the shooting was not an act of self-defence. After being found not criminally responsible, Bill was detained in a psychiatric hospital and continued to receive psychotropic medications. Psychologists in the hospital participated in the development and administration of interventions (e.g., anger management, social skills training, substance abuse treatments) designed to address factors that placed Bill at risk for committing future violence. Bill is currently institutionalized in the psychiatric hospital and receives periodic review board hearings. He will be detained until the review board is convinced that he no longer has active symptoms of mental illness and that he does not pose a significant risk of committing future harm. A multidisciplinary team, which includes a psychologist, decides what treatments Bill receives in the hospital and assists Bill in the development of release plans.

The assessment and treatment of inmates and offenders are considered in both this chapter and the next. We explore a diverse set of topics associated with the involvement of psychologists in the criminal justice system. In particular, we examine reasons for that involvement, the progression of individuals through the criminal justice system and the psychological services they receive, the characteristics of formally processed inmates and offenders, and general principles for assessing and treating inmates and offenders. More detailed information about the assessment and treatment of specific offender populations – adolescent offenders, spousal assaulters, sexual offenders, mentally disordered offenders, and female offenders – is provided in Chapter 9.

REASONS FOR INVOLVING PSYCHOLOGISTS IN THE CRIMINAL JUSTICE SYSTEM

Psychologists provide assessment and treatment services at virtually every juncture of the criminal justice system, and there are four main reasons for their involvement. First, psychologists help correctional agencies further their primary goal of protecting society. By identifying and treating inmates and offenders with psychological problems, psychologists help maintain a safe environment for inmates and offenders, correctional staff, and other members of the community (Ogloff, Roesch, & Hart, 1994). Second, psychologists help the courts to determine legal culpability. This is important because a basic premise of Canadian criminal law is that individuals must have the requisite states of mind to be culpable for their actions (see Chapter 10). Third, psychologists provide psychological assessments to assist the courts with judicial decisions. The clinical involvement of psychologists is diverse and broader in focus than simply assessing legal culpability. For example, in addition to influencing fitness to stand trial and insanity determinations, psychological assessments influence sentencing or disposition decisions, dangerous offender determinations, and decisions to transfer youths to adult court (see Chapters 9 and 11). Fourth, psychologists assess and treat factors that they believe have contributed to psychological distress or to antisocial and criminal behaviours. The goals of these intervention services are to ameliorate suffering and to reduce the risk that inmates and offenders will commit future crimes (Andrews, Bonta, & Hoge, 1990; Justice, 1994). The latter two reasons for involving psychologists in the criminal justice system are discussed throughout this book, so below we elaborate on only the first two reasons.

Protecting Society

Ogloff et al. (1994) state that "there is little question that the primary and explicit goal of correctional systems ... is protection of the public through safe and efficient management of offenders/clients" (p. 118). It is therefore incumbent upon those who work in correctional institutions or in the community to identify and manage mentally disordered inmates and offenders who compromise the safety and well-being of themselves and others. Within institutions, mentally disordered inmates may compromise the safety of correctional staff, visitors, and other inmates. Mentally disordered inmates and offenders can contribute to unstable correctional or community environments, and they can jeopardize the safety of others. Their involvement in disruptive behaviours put themselves and others at risk. Mentally disordered inmates and offenders, for example, can traumatize others by attempting or committing suicide (Bland, Newman, Thompson, & Dyck, 1998; Rosine, 1995), and they can become targets for physical and/or sexual abuse (Ogloff et al., 1994). Mentally disordered inmates and offenders who are poorly treated or managed may have an adverse impact on public safety and the continuity of operations in correctional facilities.

Serious mental disorders are prevalent among correctional inmates and offenders. Hodgins (1995) summarizes the research on this topic by noting that "the rates of mental disorder among inmates in correctional facilities in North America far exceed the rates for these disorders in the general population ... individuals with major mental disorders are far more prevalent within correctional facilities than had previously been assumed" (pp. 15–16). In order to achieve the correctional goal of protecting the public, inmates and offenders with serious mental disorders must be effectively identified and managed.

Determining Culpability

Canadian criminal law and influential theories of crime are predicated on the assumption that crimes are the result of rational decision-making processes; that is, offenders commit crimes because they choose to do so. Classical theory, for example, emphasizes the importance of free will and its contributions to criminal behaviour (see Andrews & Bonta, 1998; Jackson, 1995; Jackson & Griffiths, 1995).

Evaluations of psychological functioning help the courts to establish the mental element of culpability. The subjective nature of mens rea determinations (Osborne, 1995) is a key reason why psychologists are involved in criminal proceedings. Defendants who do not display criminal states of mind at the time of their actions are not held criminally responsible. In order to be exculpated, however, it is not enough simply to establish that inmates satisfy formal psychiatric criteria such as those outlined in the fourth edition of the *Diagnostic and Statistical Manual of Mental Disorders* (American Psychiatric Association, 1994). Rather, specific legal criteria must be satisfied (Ogloff, Roberts, & Roesch, 1993; see also Chapter 10).

The courts use psychological assessments not only to help determine culpability but also in the selection of appropriate dispositions and disposition lengths. Psychological assessments often provide information relevant to the consideration of mitigating and/or exacerbating circumstances. Although legally culpable for their actions, offenders with mitigating circumstances may obtain reduced penalties for their crimes, whereas those with exacerbating circumstances may obtain increased penalties.

THE CANADIAN CRIMINAL JUSTICE SYSTEM

The Canadian criminal justice system consists of many sectors: the policing/law enforcement sector, the legal prosecution (i.e., Crown counsel) sector, the court services sector, and the correctional services sector (see Chapter 2). The correctional services sector includes correctional institutions and community supervision services. Individuals who have contravened the Criminal Code or other relevant provincial/territorial or federal statutes and who are seriously mentally ill may be diverted from the criminal justice system to the provincial/territorial mental health system. The progression of inmates and offenders through the criminal justice system is depicted in Figure 8.1. To be exculpated from criminal responsibility, individuals must be diverted before they are convicted. Sometimes the police or prosecutors divert mentally disordered individuals early in the process; at other times they are diverted at a later stage. Diversion to involuntary civil commitment occurs under respective provincial/territorial Mental Health Acts.

Correctional facilities under provincial/territorial jurisdiction include remand/detention centres, probation facilities, and correctional institutions that house offenders who have received sentences of less than two years or young offenders. Correctional facilities under

Figure 8.1

Progression of inmates and offenders through the Canadian criminal justice system from criminal offences to correctional sanctions

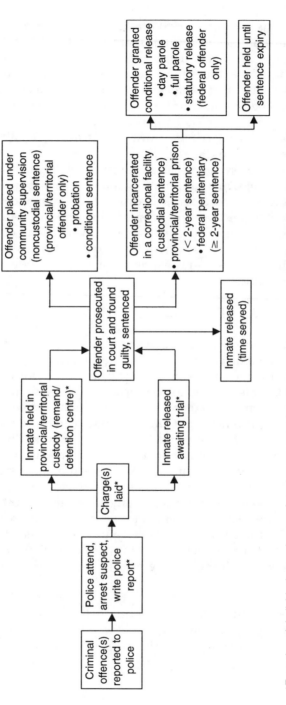

*Even though individuals may be transferred at any point from the criminal justice system to the mental health system for mental health concerns, diversion must occur *before* individuals are found guilty to be exculpated because of mental health concerns.

SOURCE: Adapted from Statistics Canada (1998), p. 13

federal jurisdiction include institutions that house or supervise offenders who have received sentences of two or more years. Mental health
or psychiatric facilities, including forensic psychiatric facilities, are
under provincial/territorial jurisdiction. Of the 199 adult correctional
facilities in Canada, 151 are provincial/territorial institutions and 48
are federal institutions. Most inmates and offenders (63%, or 23,679)
are registered in provincial/territorial institutions; the remaining inmates and offenders (37%, or 13,862) are registered in federal institutions (Robinson, Porporino, Millson, Trevethan, & MacKillop, 1998).

A progressive sequence of events and decisions within the criminal
justice system occurs for individuals to be convicted of offences.
Victims, perpetrators, witnesses, or others decide whether or not to
report crimes to the police; if accusations are made, the police must
decide whether or not they will attend to the events, write formal
police reports, arrest the individuals, and lay charges; if formal charges
are laid, lawyers must decide whether or not to prosecute; if cases are
prosecuted in court, the triers of fact (i.e., judges or juries) must decide
whether or not accused individuals are guilty or not guilty; and if the
verdict is guilty, a variety of dispositions or sentences can be imposed.
Indeed, only a minority of convicted offenders will be sent to custodial
facilities. Decisions must be affirmative at each step in this complex
sequence of events for criminal behaviours to culminate in convictions.
The reduction in the probability of being convicted at each step in this
process is referred to as the "winnowing effect." Socio-political factors,
as well as characteristics of individuals and the crimes they commit,
influence the probability that offenders will proceed to the next step in
the sequence of events and eventually be convicted.

For example, Dutton (1987) reviewed the empirical literature
pertaining to the response to wife assault at each step of the criminal
justice system. He found that "for every 100 wife assaults, about 14
are reported, 7 detected, 1 arrest is made, 0.75 men are convicted, and
0.38 men are punished with a fine or jail" (p. 200). Dutton further concluded "that the winnowing effect of the criminal justice system for
wife assault cases is not appreciably different than for other crimes"
(p. 202). In recent years police departments have changed their policies
and practices so that more individuals who assault their partners are
arrested (see the section on the assessment and treatment of spousal
assaulters in Chapter 9). Nonetheless, Dutton's findings suggest that,
relative to individuals who initially commit criminal acts, offenders
who are formally processed through the criminal justice system and

convicted represent a biased group. This is true even for individuals convicted of serious offences such as murder (e.g., see Daly & Wilson, 1988, p. 15).

PSYCHOLOGICAL SERVICES

The brief description of the Canadian criminal justice system provided above illustrates the involvement of many people: victims, police, lawyers, triers of fact, and correctional personnel, among others. Psychologists contribute to this system by providing clinical and consultation services in four broad areas: assessment; treatment, and intervention; crisis intervention; and program development, delivery, and evaluation (e.g., see the Commissioner's Directive regarding psychological services in Leis, Motiuk, & Ogloff, 1995). Although some psychologists provide services to criminal justice personnel and to victims of crime, in this section we focus on assessment and treatment services they provide to inmates and offenders. Although important in many forensic settings and facilities, most psychologists spend proportionately little time providing crisis intervention and management services; readers interested in crisis intervention services provided in Canadian correctional settings are referred to Rosine (1995).

Assessing Risk and Providing Support in Remand/Detention Centres

Remand/detention centres, also referred to as pretrial centres and jails, are provincial/territorial facilities designed to detain individuals awaiting trial or sentencing by the courts, those who are serving shorter sentences, or those awaiting transfers to other facilities. They comprise one-third of all provincial/territorial facilities and house one-quarter of all inmates and offenders (Robinson et al., 1998). Persons accused of crimes are presumed innocent until they have been formally convicted; many accused are therefore released into the community on judicial interim releases rather than being detained (Statistics Canada, 1998a).

There are four main reasons why people may be held in remand/detention centres. First, accused persons may be detained if the courts are concerned with their behaviour. This includes those who are considered at risk to reoffend, destroy evidence, harm themselves or others, or fail to attend scheduled court dates (see also Statistics Canada,

1998a). Second, offenders convicted of federal sentences (i.e., 2 or more years) are held in detention centres until their 15-day appeal periods have expired (Statistics Canada, 1998a). Third, sentenced offenders are held in remand/detention centres if they have outstanding charges or are awaiting placement in other institutions. Finally, inmates and offenders are held in remand/detention centres for a variety of administrative or legal reasons, including immigration holds and temporary detentions.

Psychologists provide assessment services and short-term interventions in remand/detention centres. A large proportion of individuals in remand/detention centres have significant psychological problems, and thus these services have important implications for the psychological well-being of inmates and offenders. Some inmates experience psychological problems in response to the stresses of incarceration, including the abrupt loss of freedom and other liberties, unfamiliar surroundings, overcrowding, restricted contacts with families and other sources of social support, withdrawal from substances, involvement in criminal trials, and the prospect of serving custodial sentences (Ogloff, Finkelman, Otto, & Bulling, 1990; Ogloff & Otto, 1989). Others may experience acute psychological distress as a result of the crime(s) that they have committed. For example, a significant percentage (approximately 25%) of male perpetrators commit suicide shortly after they kill their intimate partners (Daly & Wilson, 1988, pp. 217–218). A large majority of offenders, however, present major mental disorders even before they are incarcerated for their most recent offences (Hodgins & Côté, 1990).

The percentage of mentally disordered inmates in remand/detention centres is difficult to estimate across correctional facilities because estimates are greatly influenced by differences in jurisdictional processing of inmates and by methodological factors such as the selection of samples, the diagnostic criteria used to assess mental disorders, and guarantees of confidentiality (Teplin, 1983; see also Hodgins, 1995). Despite these considerations, the best estimates of psychiatric disorders come from studies that include large numbers of randomly sampled inmates assessed using standardized instruments. One such study was conducted by Roesch (1995) using a sample of remand/detention inmates admitted over a 12-month period to the Vancouver Pretrial Services Centre in British Columbia (see also Hart & Hemphill, 1989; Hart, Roesch, Corrado, & Cox, 1993). Most inmates were young, white, unemployed, English-speaking males with previous criminal histories. Estimated rates of mental disorders in this remand/detention centre were 15.6% for major mental disorders – primarily major affective and schizophrenic disorders – 85.9% for substance use disorders, and 64.3% for antisocial personality disorder (Roesch, 1995). Clinical pictures of mentally disordered inmates are further complicated by high rates of co-occurring disorders.

Psychological assessments in remand/detention centres typically involve a brief (e.g., 25-minute) screening of the inmate shortly after his or her admission to the facility (e.g., Roesch, Ogloff, Zapf, Hart, & Otto, 1998; Teplin & Swartz, 1989; see also Chapter 9). The main goal of these assessments is to identify inmates with mental health needs requiring immediate clinical attention (e.g., Ogloff et al., 1994). Correctional staff may have difficulty identifying inmates who satisfy diagnostic criteria for some disorders (e.g., depression) unless they systematically evaluate the mental functioning of *all* inmates (Roesch et al., 1998). The lack of extensive collateral information in remand/detention centres means that clinicians must often rely heavily on their own observations and on inmates' self-reports to identify those who are mentally disordered or at risk of harming themselves or others. Inmates identified during this screening process as having marked psychological concerns are carefully monitored and receive psychological interventions, provided either on an ongoing or an as-needed basis. Contact with psychologists may be initiated by staff members or by inmates who request psychological assistance.

Psychologists who work in remand/detention centres typically provide supportive or acute crisis interventions (e.g., for disruptive or suicidal behaviours). They are not likely to provide lengthy or involved interventions because stays at remand/detention centres are relatively short. Hart and Hemphill (1989) found, for example, that the modal stay at the Vancouver Pretrial Services Centre at that time was one night and the median stay was nine nights.

Mentally disordered inmates detained in remand/detention centres pose unique management concerns and require more intensive psychological, medical, and security interventions than do other inmates (Hart & Hemphill, 1989). Ogloff et al. (1994) have emphasized, however, that "correctional institutions are not mental health facilities" (p. 134). Correctional facilities must, therefore, have formal or informal mechanisms for diverting seriously mentally ill inmates to secure mental health facilities.

Assisting the Courts with Judicial Decisions

The main purpose of many psychological assessments is to assist the courts with judicial decisions. Psychological assessments are most useful to the courts if they address the relevant legal or psychological issues for which the referrals were made (Roesch et al., 1998). It is important to recognize that psychologists act as consultants to help decision-makers evaluate options and that judges and juries – not psychologists – make legal decisions (see s. 11 of the Commissioner's Directive for psychological services in Leis et al., 1995). Even though courts are not bound by the recommendations provided in psychological assessments, they frequently implement recommendations considered reasonable and feasible for referral questions (Jaffe, Leschied, Sas, & Austin, 1985).

Disposition assessments are conducted on inpatient or outpatient bases after findings of guilt but before sentencing, and their purpose is to help the courts arrive at appropriate dispositions or sentences. Psychologists can provide the courts with information concerning the offences, the degree of harm committed against victims, the risks posed to the public, and the characteristics of the offenders, all of which are considered during sentencing (Statistics Canada, 1998a). Disposition assessments, particularly when accompanied by formal psychiatric diagnoses, can play an important role in providing access to treatment (Jack & Ogloff, 1997). Disposition assessments are common in some clinical settings. For example, in approximately 90% of cases, the legal reason that courts offer for referring young offenders under section 13 of the Young Offenders Act is "to make or review a disposition" (Jack & Ogloff, 1997; Jaffe et al., 1985).

After having been found guilty of crimes, offenders are sentenced by judges to one of three options: release, imprisonment, or alternatives to imprisonment. Releases include absolute discharges and conditional discharges; imprisonment includes sentences to provincial/territorial prisons or to federal penitentiaries; and alternatives to imprisonment include suspended sentences, probation, fines, compensation or restitution, suspension of privileges (e.g., driving), community service orders, and treatment orders. For offenders convicted of multiple offences, judges impose sentences that are served either concurrently or consecutively. Concurrent sentences are served at the same time, whereas consecutive sentences are served one after the other.

Intermittent custodial sentences of 90 days or less may be granted to first-time offenders or to those who have committed minor offences (Robinson et al., 1998; Statistics Canada, 1998a). Offenders serving intermittent sentences comprise 10% of the custodial population (Robinson et al., 1998). Intermittent sentences are typically served on weekends for two or three days at a time and allow offenders to serve their sentences with less disruption to their employment and family responsibilities than would be the case with regular custodial sentences.

Assessing Risk and Treatment Needs in Prisons and Penitentiaries

Offenders who receive custodial sentences serve time either in provincial/territorial prisons or in federal penitentiaries. Canada has 45 penitentiaries and over one hundred prisons and alternative correctional facilities such as camps, day detention centres, and treatment centres (Robinson et al., 1998). Each offender receives a security classification, and psychological assessments may be used to help classify offenders into minimum, medium, or maximum security institutions (see Chapter 11). Offenders' freedom of movement and the physical structures of institutions define the security level of correctional facilities. Most federal offenders (63%) are housed in medium security facilities, whereas most provincial/territorial inmates and offenders are housed either in maximum security facilities (39%) or facilities that combine features of two or more security levels (40%). The higher security level among provincial/territorial inmates and offenders is likely due to the number of remanded inmates housed in maximum or multilevel institutions (Robinson et al., 1998).

Just as mental disorders are more prevalent among remand/detention inmates than among the general population, so too are they more prevalent among prison and penitentiary offenders. Indeed, Hodgins and Côté (1990) found that the lifetime prevalence rate of mental disorders among male offenders housed in a Quebec penitentiary exceeded 95%, and Bland et al. (1998) found that the rate among male prisoners from Edmonton, Alberta, exceeded 90%. The comparable rate for a random sample of male community residents from Edmonton stratified on age and marital status was less than 45% (Bland et al., 1998). Hodgins and Côté (1990) reported lifetime prevalence rates of 7.5% for schizophrenia, 4.8% for bipolar affective disorder, 16.9% for major depression, 66.9% for severe alcohol abuse/dependence, and 49.4% for severe drug abuse/dependence. These rates represent risks that are, respectively, approximately seven, four, two, three, and five times greater than the nonincarcerated male rates (Hodgins & Côté, 1990). Bland et al. (1998) and Motiuk and Porporino (1991) reported similar prevalence rates. Between one-half and three-quarters of all offenders satisfy the diagnostic criteria for antisocial personality disorder (Bland et al., 1998; Hodgins & Côté, 1990b; Motiuk & Porporino, 1991), which largely reflects persistently antisocial and/or criminal conduct.

Despite high rates of major mental disorders among inmates and offenders, many receive no treatment (Teplin, 1990b). For example, Hodgins and Côté (1990) found that few offenders (36%, or 40 of 112) with major mental disorders discussed their serious symptoms with professionals and that even fewer (21%, or 24 of 112) offenders with psychological problems were transferred to psychiatric care while in the penitentiary. It is unclear whether offenders did not report their symptoms to others because they were not asked the relevant questions or because they feared these disclosures might be used against them (see also Hodgins, 1995). The former concern can be reduced by conducting systematic screenings of all new admissions using structured or semi-structured psychological instruments that measure a broad range of psychological functioning.

Psychological intake assessments that identify intervention needs and criminogenic factors are provided at admission to many correctional institutions. The term criminogenic needs refers to variables that, when influenced, are associated with changes in the likelihood of recidivism. Antisocial attitudes and abuse of substances are examples of criminogenic needs because these factors place offenders at risk to commit future criminal and antisocial acts. Psychological assessments are mandated for offenders with adjustment problems, mental health problems, suicide potential, histories of violence, histories of sexual offences, or offenders who have "high needs" (National Parole Board, 1999a). Moreover, some problems common among offenders should routinely be assessed (see Ferris et al., 1997; Webster, Douglas, Eaves, & Hart, 1997a). Dutton and Hart (1992b), for example, found that approximately 30% of offenders in a British Columbia penitentiary had histories of spousal assaults that were documented in their institutional files (see also Hart, Kropp, Roesch, Ogloff, & Whittemore, 1994). Interviews conducted with these offenders and with their partners indicated that the percentage of offenders involved in spousal assaults was even higher than that estimated from institutional files.

As in remand/detention centres, identifying and managing mentally disordered offenders in prisons and penitentiaries is an important clinical task, the goal of which is improving safety among offenders, correctional staff, and institutional visitors. Ogloff et al. (1994) emphasize that the psychological status of offenders, particularly those serving long sentences, can change across time. It is therefore important to monitor psychological functioning in prisons and penitentiaries on an ongoing basis; early identification and treatment can address mental health concerns before they develop further and become more difficult to treat.

Providing Treatment in Prisons and Penitentiaries

The provision of psychological interventions is consistent with one of the primary goals outlined in the mission statement of the Correctional Service of Canada: "The Correctional Service of Canada contributes to the protection of society by actively encouraging and assisting offenders to become law-abiding citizens, while exercising reasonable, safe, secure and humane control" (Correctional Service of Canada, 1991, p. 4). Psychological assessments and treatments designed to reduce criminal recidivism can be administered to offenders in inpatient or outpatient settings.

Offenders incarcerated in prisons or penitentiaries, sometimes for long periods of time, must adjust to institutionalization, decide how to apportion their time, establish work or employment routines, and develop socialization patterns with individuals both inside and outside of the institution (Zamble, 1992; Zamble & Porporino, 1990). Many of the challenges offenders face in prisons and penitentiaries clearly differ from those faced by inmates in remand/detention facilities, and these differences have important treatment implications. In remand/detention centres, psychologists provide brief supportive therapy to help inmates adjust to institutionalization; in prisons and penitentiaries, however, psychologists have greater opportunities to develop and implement treatment programs designed to target criminogenic needs (see Chapter 9). Put another way, interventions in remand/detention centres are focused on immediate needs, whereas interventions in prisons and penitentiaries are focused on both immediate and long-term needs.

Treating correctional offenders is challenging because many exhibit long-standing problems across multiple domains of functioning (see, e.g., Andrews & Bonta, 1998; Motiuk & Porporino, 1991; Zamble & Quinsey, 1997). From their prospective study of male offenders incarcerated in the Ontario region of the Correctional Service of Canada, Zamble and Porporino (1990) concluded that offenders "showed deficits that were much more serious and widespread than our expectations. Indeed, these results can justify the view that coping difficulties are a central cause of the maintenance and repetition of criminal acts, if not their origin ... It was abundantly clear that inmates' coping efforts did not accomplish the function of remediating problems. Even worse, their efforts made difficult situations worse" (pp. 56–57). Offenders admitted to prisons or penitentiaries report experiencing marked emotional distress and anxiety early in their correctional terms. Many investigators (e.g., Prochaska, DiClemente, & Norcross, 1992; Rosenbaum & Horowitz, 1983) argue that clinicians should capitalize on the motivating aspects of these affective states to mobilize change. Zamble and Porporino (1990), for example, contend that correctional treatment will be maximally effective if offered at the beginning of correctional terms when emotional distress is high and offenders are motivated to reduce their distress. Clinicians who offer treatments later in correctional sentences may be unable to capitalize on these initial dysphoric emotional states, because they subside with time (MacKenzie & Goodstein, 1985; Zamble, 1992; Zamble & Porporino, 1990). Indeed, among offenders sentenced to federal terms, psychological and institutional functioning improves across time; compared to functioning shortly after incarceration, long periods of incarceration are associated with large decreases in emotional dysphoria, improved adaptation to institutionalization, greater involvement in work and structured activities, stable social involvements, decreases in stress-related medical problems, and fewer disciplinary incidents (MacKenzie & Goodstein, 1985; Zamble, 1992; Zamble & Porporino, 1990).

Unless concerns that contribute to offenders' problems are also addressed, incarceration alone is expected to have little long-term impact on behavioural change or on reducing reoffending. Zamble and Porporino (1990) summarize the issue as follows: "While prisons constrain behavior considerably, they provide very little in the way of contingencies that would lead to progressive changes in behavior. Thus we were led to summarize what happens during imprisonment as a 'behavioral deep freeze' in which a person's set of outside-world behaviors are stored until his release" (p. 62).

The most effective contemporary correctional treatment programs are those that target the criminogenic needs of offenders that research has shown to be related to recidivism (e.g., Andrews & Bonta, 1998;

Andrews, Zinger, et al., 1990; Bonta, 1996; Palmer, 1996). Regardless of whether or not offenders have diagnosable mental disorders, interventions that are appropriately identified and administered can have beneficial effects for both offenders and the community. Clinicians may select treatment programs for particular offenders by conducting detailed assessments, identifying their criminogenic needs, and referring them to appropriate intervention programs (e.g., anger management, social skills training). Alternatively, clinicians may create programs that address needs common to one subgroup (e.g., sexual offenders) and treat them together. Cognitive-behavioural interventions are among the most popular and effective interventions for treating correctional populations (e.g., Andrews, Zinger, et al., 1990).

Conducting Assessments to Release or Detain Offenders

The Corrections and Conditional Release Act and respective provincial/territorial legislation indicates that all adult offenders who have been imprisoned must be considered for some form of early conditional release.[1] Escorted and unescorted temporary absences from custodial institutions are typically the first types of conditional releases granted to offenders. Offenders who successfully complete these temporary absences are then given progressively more access to the community via day parole and full parole. Offenders who fail to satisfy the conditions of their release may be reincarcerated. Most offenders serving federal terms who have not been released on parole are released on statutory release (see Correctional Service of Canada, 1997; National Parole Board, 1999a; Statistics Canada, 1998a). In contrast to parole, statutory release is granted automatically to eligible federal offenders who have served two-thirds of their imposed sentences in custodial institutions; the remaining one-third of sentences are served in the community. Offenders serving life sentences are not eligible for statutory release.

Appropriate release planning and preparation are fundamental to the successful reintegration of offenders into the community (Correctional Service of Canada, 1997; National Parole Board, 1999a). Supervising and assisting offenders on conditional releases during the latter portions of their sentences is referred to as "community corrections" and is designed to facilitate the "timely reintegration of offenders as law-abiding citizens" (National Parole Board, 1986, p. 1). Community correctional measures are considered important because offenders are at high risk to reoffend shortly after their release from prisons or penitentiaries (Hemphill, 1992; Leschied, Austin, & Jaffe, 1988; Visher, Lattimore, & Linster, 1991; Zamble & Quinsey, 1997; see also Correctional Service of Canada, 1997).

The National Parole Board has the jurisdiction to grant, deny, or revoke parole for offenders serving sentences of 2 or more years in all provinces/territories and for offenders serving sentences of less than two years in all but three provinces: British Columbia, Ontario, and Quebec. These three provinces operate their own parole boards and provincial legislation governs the process of parole (Correctional Service of Canada, 1997). While parole boards are independent of corrections, they rely on information provided by correctional employees in making release decisions and they consider psychological assessments. Note, however, that provincial/territorial offenders typically are not required to undergo formal psychological assessments to evaluate their suitability for conditional release (National Parole Board, 1999a).

Parole boards engage in a two-step process when making release decisions (see National Parole Board, 1999a). First, they consider criminal history and criminogenic needs associated with risk to the community. Second, they consider factors present during incarceration or on conditional release that might modify this risk. Psychological assessments are often considered at both steps. For example, comprehensive psychological assessments conducted during admissions to correctional facilities might identify substance abuse and anger problems as criminogenic needs for particular offenders. The parole board then determines whether or not offenders have participated in programs designed to modify these criminogenic needs. If relevant programs have been completed, the parole board examines psychological assessments concerning treatment progress and the perceived impact of the programs on risk.

Federal offenders may be detained beyond their statutory release dates up until their warrant expiry dates if parole board members at detention hearings believe that offenders will cause death or serious physical or psychological harm to other people, commit sexual offences against children, or commit serious drug offences (National Parole Board, 1999a). Again, parole members consider psychological assessments when deciding whether or not to detain offenders.

Providing Treatment in the Community

Probation and parole are similar to each other in many respects, but also differ in other respects. Both involve supervision of convicted offenders in the community who are required to comply with conditions of their release, both have standard conditions to which all offenders must adhere, and both have optional conditions that can be mandated. In terms of their differences, probation is a sentence imposed by a judge – often instead of imprisonment – whereas parole is granted by parole boards after offenders have served part of their sentences in institutions. In other words, probation is a noncustodial disposition, whereas parole and statutory release follow custodial dispositions. Probation is a provincial/territorial correctional measure, whereas parole is both a provincial/territorial and a federal correctional measure (Statistics Canada, 1998a).

Whether offenders are released into the community on probation, parole, or statutory release, their release conditions may require that they participate in psychological treatment. Offenders who fail to comply with their release conditions might receive new charges (e.g., failing to comply with probation orders) and/or might be required to serve custodial sentences. Programs similar to those available in custodial institutions (e.g., anger management, substance abuse treatment) are also offered in the community.

The goal of providing treatment in the community following treatment in custodial institutions is to maintain a continuity of care that facilitates the successful reintegration of offenders into the community (Correctional Service of Canada, 1997; Hodgins, 1995; Ogloff et al., 1994; Ogloff, Tien, Roesch, & Eaves, 1991). Moreover, treatment offered during probation permits offenders to benefit from treatment programs without serving custodial sentences. After offenders have completed the terms of their dispositions or sentences and are no longer under the jurisdiction of the criminal justice system few assessment or treatment services are typically available and further participation in treatment programs is voluntary. This means that only the most motivated offenders remain in treatment beyond the expiration of their sentences.

Conducting Program Evaluations

One role of psychologists is to develop, monitor, and evaluate the efficacy of treatment programs. Formal and informal program evaluations are important because they can influence the manner in which future assessments and treatments are delivered. Program delivery and evaluation is an ongoing and constantly evolving process that involves feedback opportunities to modify service delivery. Psychologists conduct program evaluations to determine the success of programs in achieving their intended goals and to improve the efficiency and effectiveness of the delivery of programs.

Program evaluation is a complex topic, and detailed discussion of it is beyond the scope of this chapter. However, there are four points worth mentioning. First, program evaluations can proceed along a number of different paths. Successful treatment outcome, for example, can be defined by the acquisition of skills that the program was designed to target or by a reduction in the reoffending rate following treatment (see Andrews & Bonta, 1998). Second, outcome can be measured using different procedures: criminal records, self-report measures, behavioural ratings, or physiological measures (Hinshaw & Zupan, 1997). Third, outcome can be measured from different perspectives: that of offenders, therapists, or family members (Achenbach, McConaughy, & Howell, 1987; McCord, 1982; Watson, Henggeler, & Borduin, 1985). Fourth, prospective studies vary considerably in their lengths of follow-up, which might restrict the types of outcomes (e.g., violent, sexual) researchers can evaluate (Hemphill, 1998; Hemphill, Hare, & Wong, 1998; Quinsey, Harris, Rice, & Cormier, 1998). All of these factors greatly influence the results of program evaluations and the conclusions that investigators can reach regarding program implementation and effectiveness (see also Hart, 1998b).

CHARACTERISTICS OF INMATES AND OFFENDERS

In large part the public has a generally poor understanding of offenders, their crimes, and the criminal justice system – because of its heavy reliance on the media for information (Surette, 1998). Often the media selectively organizes and presents information that does not accurately reflect either the criminal justice system or crimes that occur (Fishman, 1978; Hans, 1990; Hans & Dee, 1991; Johnson, 1996; Roberts & Doob, 1990). An example of the media's selective focus on particular crimes involves offences that result in deaths. Even though murders and attempted murders combined represent approximately 0.05% of crimes reported to the police in Canada (e.g., 1,442 of 2,685,681 incidents in 1997, Kong, 1998), murder accounts for one-quarter of all newspaper stories on crime (Graber, 1980). To the extent that members of the public are influenced by media portrayals of the criminal justice system and form impressions consistent with these portrayals, they are likely to harbour views inconsistent with statistical information concerning crime (e.g., see Chapter 7; Surette, 1998), to be overly fearful of crime, and to take precautions to prevent criminal victimization (e.g., Besserer, 1998; Sacco, 1995). We believe that it is important to have an accurate understanding of the characteristics of inmates and offenders formally involved with the criminal justice system, and of their patterns of crimes, because these characteristics influence the delivery of psychological services.

The most common cases that appear in adult criminal court (see Brookbank & Kingsley, 1998) involve impaired driving (15%), common assault (12%), theft (11%), and failure to appear in court (9%). Males and young adults are overrepresented in adult criminal court statistics relative to their representation in the population. Most cases (62%) tried in adult provincial/territorial criminal courts result in convictions, whereas few (3%) result in acquittals. Probation, a noncustodial disposition, is granted in 43% of cases and is the most serious disposition in 30% of cases. Prison and penitentiary sentences are custodial dispositions and are granted in 33% of cases. Half of the custodial sentences (49%) involve sentences of 1 month or less; few (3%) involve sentences of 2 years or more. The longest sentences are imposed for violent crimes and for cases involving multiple charges. The majority of convictions for violent crimes are for categories that result in the least victim injury and that do not involve weapons (Johnson, 1996; Kong, 1998). Many Canadians have official criminal records. Approximately 10% of Canadians have been criminally convicted (Correctional Service of Canada, 1997, p. 6), and 0.17% of Canadians are incarcerated on a single day (Robinson et al., 1998). Among 11 Western industrialized countries, Canada incarcerates individuals at a rate second only to that of the United States.[2]

Almost all offenders granted temporary absences successfully complete them; the success rates are 99.7% for escorted temporary absences and 98.8% for unescorted temporary absences (Correctional Service of Canada, 1997). The National Parole Board grants day parole to 66% of federal offenders and to 46% of provincial/territorial offenders. In contrast, it grants full parole to 40% of federal offenders and to 52% of provincial/territorial offenders. The percentage of offenders granted parole, of course, varies according to the types of crimes committed; of the cases involving violent and/or sexual offences, eight out of ten are denied parole (National Parole Board, 1999b). Most (97%) offenders successfully complete day parole and most (89%) successfully complete full parole. These rates are similar to the 88% who successfully complete their statutory releases. Only 1.4% of offenders serving time on conditional release (i.e., day parole, full parole, statutory release) are charged with serious offences (Correctional Service of Canada, 1997, p. 52).

To summarize, many Canadians have criminal records; most offenders are charged with nonviolent offences and with offences that result in little physical injuries to victims; two-thirds of offenders are convicted and serve either short custodial sentences or noncustodial sentences in the community; and almost all offenders released into the community successfully complete their early releases. We should emphasize that this summary involves information reported in official documents; researchers who have obtained this information have used particular definitions, measures, and methodologies to define their research variables. Results would be expected to differ if researchers' definitions, measures, and methodologies varied, or if they studied behaviours that did not come to the attention of the authorities. Indeed, failure rates on conditional releases reported above (i.e., between 3% and 12%) are lower than those typically found by other researchers. Hart, Kropp, and Hare (1988), for example, found that failure rates on conditional releases were 25.3% for parole and 56.4% for statutory releases; "failures" were defined by Hart et al. (1988) as conditional release revocations or convictions for new offences. It is also important to recognize that, because of plea bargaining to lesser offences, in some cases official conviction titles may appear more minor than the crimes to which they refer.

The high prevalence of charges and convictions for impaired driving, common assaults, and sexual assaults (see also Robinson et al., 1998), coupled with the high prevalence of unstable relationship histories found in inmate and offender populations, suggest that treatment programs should address inmates' and offenders' problems with substance abuse, anger management, assertiveness training, and interpersonal skills. Clinical interventions are challenging because inmates and offenders often have multiple and long-standing problems (e.g., Motiuk & Porporino, 1991; Robinson et al., 1998; Roesch, 1995; Zamble & Porporino, 1990). Vocational training and educational upgrading can provide skills that target high rates of unemployment among offenders. The delivery of treatment programs should reflect the particular abilities, learning styles, and social and family environments of each offender (Andrews, Bonta, & Hoge, 1990; Bonta, 1996). Complex programs that require advanced reading, comprehension, and abstraction skills, for example, are perhaps less appropriate for inmates or offenders with little formal education than are practical programs with hands-on experiences.

GENERAL PRINCIPLES FOR ASSESSING AND TREATING OFFENDERS

Now that we have considered characteristics of inmates and offenders, we turn to the general principles that guide psychological assessments and the provision of treatments in correctional facilities.

Assessing Offenders

Assessment is a term that refers to the process of evaluating the cognitive, emotional, and behavioural functioning of individuals. The assessment process is guided by the particular assessment question, or questions, and by the legal context. For example, in fitness to stand trial decisions, courts may request assessments to help determine if individuals are able to participate in their own defence. In the current context, we will use the term assessment to refer primarily to the process of evaluating offenders to help make intervention or treatment recommendations (see Chapter 9). The main goal of an assessment is to obtain information that provides a better understanding of an individual and that helps guide subsequent decision making, intervention plans, or management strategies.

Before conducting psychological assessments or treatments, clinicians should obtain informed consent from offenders. In accordance with the *Canadian Code of Ethics for Psychologists* (Canadian Psychological Association, 1992), information must be provided in language that each person can understand. For consent to be "informed" it must satisfy three components: consent must be made voluntarily, knowingly, and intelligently (Ogloff, 1995). "Voluntarily" means that offenders must not be forced, coerced, or manipulated into participating in assessments or interventions. "Knowingly" means that clinicians must fully disclose to offenders "the purpose, procedure, risks and benefits, and alternative[s]" (Ogloff, 1995, p. 18) of the assessments or treatments. For example, before assessments or interventions are conducted, offenders should be clearly informed of whether the information will be shared with others (e.g., correctional personnel) and of the limits to confidentiality. "Intelligently" means that offenders must have the intellectual capacity to understand information presented to them and to weigh the risks and benefits so that they can arrive at reasoned decisions. In the case of offenders who do not have the intellectual capacities to make reasoned decisions, clinicians must obtain consent from substitute decision makers.

To facilitate the assessment and treatment process clinicians must establish rapport with the offender, as personally sensitive topics (e.g., relationships, experiences of abuse, criminal histories) are discussed. Once rapport is established, many offenders openly reveal personal information and admit to their participation in socially undesirable behaviours. Nonetheless, clinicians working in forensic settings routinely evaluate the honesty and self-disclosure of offenders (Pope, Butcher, & Seelen, 1993; Rogers, 1988). Depending on the assessment context and characteristics of the offender, some offenders either deny or exaggerate psychological symptoms (Rogers, 1988; Rogers, Salekin, Sewell, Goldstein, & Leonard, 1998; Rogers, Sewell, & Goldstein, 1994). In addition to self-reports by offenders, forensic clinicians rely heavily on information obtained from collateral informants and from agencies or facilities that have had past involvement with the offenders. This use of collateral information and informants is important because different people and different sources of information often provide varying or unique perspectives.

Classification, which refers to the process of placing individuals into one or more discrete categories (Hinshaw & Zupan, 1997), is often one goal of assessments. Clinicians may use explicit diagnostic criteria, such as those outlined in the *Diagnostic and Statistical Manual of Mental Disorders*, fourth edition (American Psychiatric Association, 1994), to classify, categorize, or diagnose individuals. It is not uncommon in both prisons and the general population for a single individual to display characteristics that meet the diagnostic criteria for two or more disorders. Having many co-occurring disorders complicates the clinical picture and is often associated with poor treatment outcomes (e.g., Lahey & Loeber, 1997). Clinicians consider the identification of comorbid (or co-occurring) disorders to be important because their presence may influence the expected course, prognosis, and treatment recommendations offered.

Clinicians engage in a two-step assessment process, with reducing crime as the primary goal. During the first step, broad-based and comprehensive assessments using a variety of methods and procedures permit clinicians to identify individual criminogenic needs. Assessment measures include clinical interviews, self-report measures, rating scales or behavioural checklists, peer ratings, direct observations, actuarial instruments, physical examinations, laboratory tests, and psychological instruments (Hinshaw & Zupan, 1997). During the second step, assessment findings are used to plan interventions and treatments that address identified criminogenic needs. The rationale of this two-step process is that reoffending will be reduced if factors thought to have contributed to antisocial or criminal behaviours are specifically targeted (Andrews, Bonta, & Hoge, 1990).

Using this model of assessment, the intervention process is guided by the individual criminogenic needs the clinician believes have contributed to the antisocial behaviour. General assessment guidelines that are empirically and theoretically derived (e.g., Webster, Douglas, Eaves, & Hart, 1997a) may help clinicians decide which areas are most appropriate to assess. Many clinicians routinely administer semi-structured interviews and core sets of psychological instruments that measure a broad range of functions and abilities. Then, depending on the assessment results, the particular referral question, and the client population, clinicians may administer additional interview questions and standardized instruments. Areas frequently assessed include general cognitive abilities and intelligence; specific aptitudes such as reading, comprehension, and arithmetic; academic achievement; vocational aptitudes and interests; personality and self-concept; adaptive functioning; social and emotional understanding and competence; peer group associations and school adjustment (particularly among adolescents); family functioning; antisocial or criminal attitudes, values, and beliefs; problems abusing alcohol or other substances; and delinquent and self-destructive behaviours (Hoge & Andrews, 1996).

Hoge and Andrews (1996) maintain that standardized psychological assessments provide a number of advantages over other assessment procedures. They argue that these advantages can improve the quality of inferences and judgments made about offenders and thus the management of offenders within the criminal justice system. The term standardized psychological assessment refers to the process of evaluating the cognitive, emotional, and behavioural functioning of individuals using a fixed set of stimulus, response, and scoring formats for which statistical information is available. Standardized psychological assessments often provide important information that is not readily obtained by other means (Sattler, 1988).

Despite the advantages of conducting standardized psychological assessments, the assessment process and the interpretation of assessment findings remains a clinically based skill and not a science. There is no single, generally agreed upon way of how best to weigh and combine assessment findings from a variety of domains and a variety of information sources (Hinshaw & Zupan, 1997). Clinicians examine information on a case-by-case basis, evaluate consistency between and within each information source, and subjectively weigh the importance of the information in order to arrive at particular treatment or management recommendations.

Courts generally accept intervention and treatment recommendations provided that they seem appropriate for the identified problems and that the interventions are feasible. Jaffe et al. (1985) found that the courts accepted and implemented their intervention recommendations in more than 80% of cases. It is therefore useful for clinicians to be familiar with community resources available to address the social, emotional, and educational needs of offenders and their families.

Treating Offenders

After identifying particular criminogenic needs for each offender, clinicians plan treatment strategies and make intervention recommendations that target these needs. Many interventions – which can be incorporated into relapse prevention programs (see below) – have been developed to target specific criminogenic needs: anger management, social skills training, assertiveness training, stress management, life skills training, recreation therapy, substance abuse groups, alcoholics anonymous, educational upgrading, occupational therapy, pharmacotherapy, and psychological (individual, family, group) therapy, among others. Treatment programs are frequently provided to offenders in groups because group treatment is an economical way to deliver services. To be effective, treatment requires a commitment by offenders to actively participate. Poor motivation can hinder treatment efforts; consequently, many clinicians assess the offenders' motivation and willingness to change before they accept them into treatment. Offenders who display little motivation to participate in treatment may benefit more from interventions aimed at enhancing readiness to change than from action-oriented interventions (Prochaska et al., 1992). The level of treatment and management provided to offenders should match their level of risk (Andrews, Bonta, et al., 1990; Gendreau, 1981, 1996). Treatment interventions should primarily target offenders who are at moderate risk or high risk to reoffend and who would likely benefit from participating in interventions designed to manage or reduce their risk. However, not all high-risk groups will respond well to treatment. Psychopaths, for example, are considered among the most difficult to treat successfully (see Lösel, 1998, for a literature review). Low-risk cases may not benefit from intensive interventions and, if provided with these interventions, there is some suggestion that they may become at even higher risk to reoffend (e.g., Andrews and Kiessling, 1980).

Many offenders selected for treatment display not only antisocial behaviours but also a lack of prosocial behaviours. Consequently, there are often two important goals for treatment: to reduce antisocial behaviours and to increase prosocial behaviours. One currently popular and promising form of treatment for offenders is relapse prevention (Howell & Enns, 1995; Marlatt & Gordon, 1980, 1985; Pithers, Marques, Gibat, & Marlatt, 1983). This treatment attempts to reduce reoffending among offenders by increasing self-awareness of factors that place them at high risk to reoffend and by providing skills to manage these factors. Offenders are taught to identify thoughts, feelings, behaviours, and situations associated with their unique pattern of crimes. Offenders who recognize their high-risk patterns in the future presumably are better equipped to interrupt or stop the sequence of events before it progresses to criminal behaviour. Many participants find this approach empowering because it emphasizes self-efficacy, personal control in the involvement of one's own criminal behaviours, and improving self-management.

Relapse prevention is based on several key assumptions that have generally received support from both clinicians' experiences and empirical research. Relapse prevention approaches assume that antisocial and criminal behaviours do not simply occur without warning, but instead represent the end product of a somewhat predictable sequence of events specific to each offender; that offenders are not fully aware of the complex series of factors that precede, contribute to, and culminate in their criminal behaviours; that offenders can learn to identify the sequence of thoughts, feelings, behaviours, and situations that place them at risk to reoffend; that future crimes will be committed under similar situations or experiences; that offenders can develop effective coping strategies; and that offenders who implement these coping strategies when they are confronted with high-risk cues will be less likely to reoffend than those who do not implement them.

There are several reasons to believe that relapse prevention will reduce reoffending (Howell & Enns, 1995). First, relapse prevention targets personal and environmental variables associated with individual patterns of criminal behaviour. Interventions that directly address these variables are more likely to reduce reoffending than are interventions that address variables of unknown relevance to offending (Andrews, Bonta, et al., 1990). Second, relapse prevention is based on a cognitive-behavioural approach, and these interventions have been effective in reducing reoffending (Andrews, Zinger, et al., 1990; Gendreau, 1996; Lipsey, 1992; Palmer, 1996). Third, relapse prevention is designed to maintain prosocial behaviour in the long term rather than simply to stop antisocial behaviour in the short term. Fourth, relapse prevention interventions have shown promise for treating individuals who have substance abuse problems (Somers & Marlatt, 1992) or who have offended sexually (Marshall, Hudson, & Ward, 1992). An example of a relapse prevention treatment program is presented in Box 8.1.

Box 8.1

Example of a Relapse Prevention Treatment Program

The amount of group structure and specific interventions vary from one relapse prevention program to another. Here we briefly describe the High Risk Recognition Group, a relapse prevention program designed to treat adolescent offenders (see Howell & Enns, 1995, for more details). Between four and eight adolescents and several staff members participate in the High Risk Recognition Group. During early treatment sessions staff describe the interventions in general terms and explain the rationale underlying relapse prevention training. This helps adolescent offenders understand the interventions and reasons for participating in treatment. Recidivism rates among adolescent offenders are presented to highlight their risks to reoffend and to illustrate the importance of active involvement in treatment.

Each adolescent in the High Risk Recognition Group describes in detail both his or her current offence(s), and the events preceding the offence(s). The participant initially focuses on concrete and easily identified behaviours and later explores intrapersonal thoughts and feelings, which are often more difficult to identify. The individual is taught that many of these thoughts, feelings, and behaviours serve as warnings or cues to indicate that he or she is at risk to reoffend. Adolescents and treatment staff provide support, assistance, and feedback to each participant. They help identify additional risk factors and ensure the identified risk factors are accurate and complete. Adolescent offenders share their relevant experiences with the group, and clinical staff review collateral file information to further elaborate and refine the risk factors identified for each offender. Despite the collaborative nature among participants of the High Risk Recognition Group, assessments and interventions are ultimately tailored to the experiences of each offender.

After identifying a number of risk factors and associated experiences, each individual in the High Risk Recognition Group seeks to identify common experiences across several of his or her criminal or antisocial behaviours. Commonalities concerning thoughts, feelings, behaviours, and situational contexts are explored, and the individual creates a list of high-risk factors that have contributed to his or her criminal behaviours. It is important to fully and separately explore each offence, because different antecedents are often associated with different offences. Adolescent offenders, for example, report that aggressive thoughts and retaliation are associated with their violent offences, but that curiosity and involvement with delinquent peers are associated with their non-violent offences (Agnew, 1990; Howell, Reddon, & Enns, 1997).

Each adolescent offender takes his or her list of high-risk thoughts, feelings, behaviours, and situations and rearranges them to form a progressive sequence that ends in antisocial or criminal behaviours. More than one set of high-risk sequences may be identified for a single individual. The purpose of rearranging high-risk factors into a progressive sequence or set of sequences is to help each offender recognize factors that signal to him or her that he or she is at risk to reoffend. The individual is encouraged to consider the degree of risk posed by each factor in the sequence.

After high-risk factors and their sequence(s) are identified, each individual is taught to develop coping strategies to address these high-risk factors. Clinicians assume that antisocial behaviours are easier to prevent if coping strategies are implemented earlier rather than later in the sequence of events and if the adolescent avoids or leaves situations that put him or her at risk to reoffend. Each individual is presented with hypothetical scenarios and is taught to identify the high-risk factors, to think of several coping responses, to select a response from the alternatives, to effectively implement the response, and to reinforce himself or herself for coping effectively. The adolescent repeatedly practises solving hypothetical scenarios so that he or she can quickly generate effective coping strategies. All factors that contribute to risk, including distorted thoughts and feelings, may be addressed in treatment. A fair amount of treatment time is spent emphasizing personal control and considering how to respond effectively to peer pressure. Modelling effective coping strategies and role-playing with peers are important to prepare the adolescent for dealing with real-life situations.

Follow-Up Sessions

Offenders are most at risk to reoffend shortly after their release into the community (Leschied, Austin, & Jaffe, 1988; Visher, Lattimore, & Linster, 1991; Zamble & Quinsey, 1997). This finding suggests that ongoing treatment and follow-up sessions in the community are important for reducing the likelihood that high-risk offenders will reoffend. During the follow-up period offenders can discuss real-life difficulties that they have encountered, explore why coping strategies did or did not work for them in particular situations, practise and refine their coping strategies, and obtain additional support and guidance from other group members. The support and contributions from peers during this high-risk period may be particularly important for adolescent offenders.

SUMMARY

Psychologists are involved at virtually every juncture of the criminal justice system and provide services that fall into four broad areas: assessment, treatment, crisis intervention/management, and program evaluation research. The high rates of mental disorders and psychological difficulties among inmates and offenders mean that correctional settings offer important opportunities for the provision of psychological services.

Clinicians assess offenders to identify appropriate intervention and treatment strategies. Assessment is a complex process and requires the evaluation and integration of material obtained from a variety of sources and informants. Clinicians assess a broad range of domains and abilities to help them identify criminogenic needs of offenders and to help plan interventions designed to address these needs. Relapse prevention is a promising form of treatment that attempts to reduce crime among offenders by increasing their self-awareness of factors that place them at high risk to reoffend and by providing skills to manage these high-risk factors. Continuity in the delivery of services between institutional programs and community programs is important because half of all offenders are considered to be "high" or "very high" risks to commit future crimes (Robinson et al., 1998, p. 12).

QUESTIONS FOR DISCUSSION

1. Describe clinical services (assessment, treatment, crisis intervention, program evaluation) that psychologists perform at the various junctures of the Canadian criminal justice system. Consider the different clinical services provided to individuals in jails and in prisons.
2. Describe the processes used to assess and treat inmates and offenders and consider how these processes differ from those used to assess and treat nonforensic patients.
3. Given the characteristics of offenders and their patterns of crimes, what types of concerns should clinicians routinely consider when they develop assessment and treatment protocols? Why might forensic clinicians focus on treating criminogenic factors rather than other factors?
4. Consider why it is difficult to determine the effectiveness of correctional interventions. In particular, consider the variety of ways that program evaluators might conceptualize and measure "success" in treatment programs and the difficulties they might have in identifying appropriate control or comparison groups.

RECOMMENDED READING

Andrews, D.A., & Bonta, J. (1998). *The psychology of criminal conduct* (2nd ed.). Cincinnati, OH: Anderson Publishing.

Gendreau, P. (1996). The principles of effective intervention with offenders. In A.T. Harland (Ed.), *Choosing correctional options that work: Defining the demand and evaluating the supply* (pp. 117–130). Thousand Oaks, CA: Sage.

Leis, T.A., Motiuk, L.L., & Ogloff, J.R.P. (Eds.). (1995). *Forensic psychology: Policy and practice in corrections*. Ottawa, Canada: Correctional Service of Canada.

Stoff, D.M., Breiling, J., & Maser, J.D. (Eds.). (1997). *Handbook of antisocial behavior*. New York: Wiley.

Zamble, E., & Quinsey, V.L. (1997). *The criminal recidivism process*. Cambridge: Cambridge University Press.

9. The Assessment and Treatment of Offenders and Inmates: Specific Populations

Tonia L. Nicholls, James F. Hemphill, Douglas P. Boer,
P. Randall Kropp, and Patricia A. Zapf

Mr Williams is a 42-year-old Caucasian male sentenced to 2 years for sexual interference of a female minor. He was transferred from a medium security institution to a regional health centre (RHC) to undergo a comprehensive risk assessment, including phallometric testing. At the start of the interview Mr Williams indicated that he was aware of the purpose of the assessment and understood the limits of confidentiality.

Upbringing and Relationship History: *Mr Williams described his parents as hard-working and stated that he enjoyed an average, middle-class upbringing. He recalled fighting with peers and having a history of truancy that resulted in trouble at school. His first sexual experience was at the age of 12 with a 14-year-old female schoolmate. He claims that he had little knowledge of sex prior to this experience and that sex was a taboo topic at home. He completed high school and has some post-secondary education. In addition to his current common law relationship of 1 year, Mr Williams reported two previous common law relationships each lasting less than 2 years.*

Criminal History: *According to court records, Mr Williams's current offence resulted from repeated sexual contacts over a 2-month period with his common law wife's 7-year-old daughter. Mr Williams has no official criminal history, although he indicated that his first common law relationship ended when the woman's daughters made allegations similar to the current convictions. Mr Williams denied any sexual involvement with the daughter. Results from the phallometric testing (see below), and from the current offence and the previous allegation against him, indicate that Mr Williams is sexually interested in female children.*

Offender's Account of the Current Offences: *Mr Williams reported that a friend died 6 months prior to the index offence. He claimed that, shortly after this event, he started drinking heavily, hanging out in bars, and neglecting his responsibilities and family. Mr Williams reported that after having a "few" drinks his common law wife's daughter crawled onto his lap while he was watching television. He denied any sexual involvement with the daughter.*

Clinical Observations: *Mr Williams presented with above average intelligence, excellent abstract thinking, and an extensive vocabulary, all of which are consistent with his post-secondary education. He showed no signs of thought disorder or perceptual difficulties and was oriented to time, person, and place. Mr Williams displayed little affect while discussing his current offence. When he described feeling guilty or remorseful, he focused on the trouble his actions had caused him (e.g., disruption of his life, a long penitentiary sentence). He appeared to have little appreciation of the impact his actions have had on his victim.*

Assessment Measures: *Mr Williams's responses to the Millon Clinical Multiaxial Inventory-II and the Minnesota Multiphasic Personality Inventory-2 suggest that he attempted to portray himself as an individual with few psychological problems. Individuals with similar responses are typically described as charming, manipulative, and unconcerned with social rules. His responses to the Multiphasic Sex Inventory are consistent with those obtained by individuals who downplay their deviant sexual interests. Mr Williams obtained an overall score on the Hare Psychopathy Checklist-Revised (PCL-R) that placed him in the average range for male offenders. However, there were substantial differences on the two factors of the PCL-R: Mr Williams received a high score on PCL-R Factor 1, but a low score on PCL-R Factor 2. These results suggest that, even though Mr Williams does not present with a chronically unstable and antisocial lifestyle relative to other male offenders, he does present with characteristics that are described as superficial, manipulative, and callous. The phallometric assessment indicated that Mr Williams is physiologically aroused by females between the ages of 5 and 15, but not to adult females or to males.*

Treatment Recommendations: *Given his denial of the current offence, his denial of sexual arousal to female children, his poor understanding of the factors that contribute to his criminal offending, and his scores on the psychological instruments, it is recommended that Mr Williams be encouraged to apply for the intensive sex offender program. To his credit he has indicated that he is willing to take part in the program; however, treatment will likely be challenging because he minimizes responsibility for his actions and demonstrates little remorse or empathy for his victim. If he participates in treatment, Mr Williams should be reassessed following completion of the program. Given that the offence occurred while Mr Williams was intoxicated, it is recommended that he take part in a substance abuse treatment program. Without treatment,*

Mr Williams would seem to pose a moderately high risk of committing similar offences under similar conditions in the future.

The previous chapter considered features common to the assessment and treatment of all inmates and offenders. In this chapter we consider features unique to the assessment and treatment needs of five specific offender populations: adolescent offenders, spousal assaulters, sexual offenders, mentally disordered offenders, and female offenders. Each section begins with an overview of the characteristics of the offender group, followed by a review of the legislation pertinent to that group and a discussion of the assessment and treatment factors unique to it. Particular attention is paid to the research contributions made by Canadian scholars.

ASSESSMENT AND TREATMENT OF ADOLESCENT OFFENDERS

Most adolescents engage in some antisocial and illegal behaviour. Indeed, approximately 85% to 95% of adolescents report having participated in at least one criminal act in the previous year (LeBlanc, 1983; LeBlanc & Fréchette, 1989). Similarly, relative to their representation in the population, a disproportionately high percentage of youths are charged with crimes; even though adolescents aged 12 to 17 represent 10% of the population, they are charged with approximately 30% of property offences and with 15% of violent offences (Statistics Canada, 1996c). It is important to understand the legal context and characteristics of adolescent offenders because these factors affect the way in which adolescents are assessed and treated.

Relevant Law

Adolescents between the ages of 12 and 17 who are accused of committing offences are typically afforded limited legal accountability (see Bala, 1997) under the Young Offenders Act (YOA). Children younger than age 12 are exempt from criminal prosecution under section 13 of the Criminal Code but may still be governed by provincial child welfare legislation and by mental health legislation. The YOA has been described as "[w]ithout a doubt ... one of the most significant pieces of social policy legislation enacted in Canada during this generation, perhaps this century" (Hylton, 1994, p. 229). Passed in 1984, the YOA legislation replaced the Juvenile Delinquents Act (1908) legislation and represents a significant shift from a paternalistic child welfare approach to a more legalistic due process and accountability approach (Corrado, Bala, Linden, & LeBlanc, 1992; Hak, 1996).

As expressed in its Declaration of Principles, the YOA attempts to strike a balance between the protection of adolescents' civil rights and the protection of the community. The YOA acknowledges that youths, although responsible and accountable for their behaviour, may be less accountable than are adults. Youths are considered to have special needs and to require guidance and assistance "because of their state of dependency and level of development and maturity" (s. 3(1)(c)).

Section 13 of the YOA outlines factors that can initiate medical or psychological assessments of young offenders. These include helping the courts to decide to transfer cases from youth court to "ordinary" (i.e., adult) court and to arrive at dispositions or sentences. The latter factor is by far the most common reason that youths typically receive psychological assessments (Jack & Ogloff, 1997; Jaffe, Leschied, Sas, & Austin, 1985). A provision in the originally enacted YOA, which has since been repealed, concerned the detention of adolescents in treatment facilities rather than in custodial facilities (see Bala, 1997, pp. 238–240). This section was among the most controversial of the YOA because it required adolescents to consent to treatment; some writers contended that many youths would refuse treatment because they did not appreciate their need to receive it (Leschied & Gendreau, 1994; Leschied & Hyatt, 1986). Under the current legislation, adolescents have access to treatment in custodial facilities without court orders provided they consent to treatment. Further, even without their consent, adolescents may be required to receive treatment because of involuntary commitment or to satisfy conditions of their probation.

In March 1999, the Honourable Anne McLellan, Minister of Justice and Attorney General of Canada, introduced the Youth Criminal Justice Act in the House of Commons; this new Act is to replace the existing Young Offenders Act.

Salient Characteristics

According to official statistics (see Statistics Canada, 1995c, 1996d, 1997b, 1997c), half of adolescents who appear in court are 16- or 17-year-olds, approximately 80% are males, and half are charged with property offences. Approximately one-fifth of the most serious offences involve violence. In general, antisocial behaviours are more normative if they involve the theft of less expensive property or the use of more socially acceptable substances, or if they result in less victim injury or in less damage to property (e.g., LeBlanc, 1983). This is reflected in sentencing patterns: One-third of convictions result in custodial sentences, and three-quarters of custodial sentences result in sentences for three months or less. Unlike adult offenders, who are governed by legislation and who typically receive early releases from custodial sentences (see the section on statutory release and parole in Chapter 8), adolescent offenders are regulated by the court review process and receive early releases only if youth court judges decide to reduce their originally imposed dispositions (see Bala, 1997, pp. 248–249).

Adolescents are part of a larger social context; peers and parents are two important sources of influence that shape the social development of adolescents. By the time adolescents are involved with the criminal justice system, they often have strained family relationships. Moreover, when it comes to resolving family problems, adolescents and other family members often have conflicting goals. Parents may want mental health providers to simply "fix" their defiant adolescent, whereas adolescents may want their parents to become more accepting and less punitive, to treat them with more respect, and to grant them more autonomy. Conflicting treatment goals, strained family relationships, strong peer alliances, and – in many cases – adolescent offenders' distrust of authority figures make working with adolescent offenders and their families particularly challenging.

Adolescents vary greatly in terms of their cognitive, emotional, and behavioural development. Adolescents often have less developed verbal skills and psychological insight than do adults. This means that clinicians must make a concerted effort to establish rapport, to be patient, and to encourage adolescents to explore their problems from psychological perspectives. Problems with peers, schoolwork, and family may reflect broader psychological problems because adolescents may indirectly communicate their concerns by acting out and by misbehaving.

Clinicians who assess or treat adolescent offenders must carefully consider antisocial behaviours within a developmental context. Often the only factor that distinguishes a particular behaviour as deviant or nondeviant is the age at which it occurs. For example, engaging in minor vandalism may be normative among adolescents, but the occurrence of this behaviour earlier – or later – in life may signal potential problems to investigate further. Other aspects of antisocial behaviours that should be considered within a developmental context are their frequencies, severities, and durations.

Adolescent offenders form a heterogeneous group. Various typologies of adolescent offenders have been proposed to better understand the etiology, developmental course, appropriate interventions, and prognosis of each offender type. One influential typology emphasizes the stability of the antisocial behaviour across the lifespan and the age at which it occurs (e.g., see Moffitt, 1993, and the diagnosis of Conduct Disorder in the *Diagnostic and Statistical Manual of Mental Disorders*, fourth edition, American Psychiatric Association, 1994). Moffitt (1993) has termed antisocial behaviour that begins at an early age and persists across time "life-course-persistent," whereas she describes antisocial behaviour that begins in adolescence and desists in late adolescence as "adolescence-limited." Moffitt (1993) argues that each type can be distinguished by its etiology and developmental trajectory (see also Bartusch, Lynam, Moffitt, & Silva, 1997). In particular, she argues that life-course-persistent antisocial behaviour is pathological and is produced by a combination of neuropsychological dysfunction and an adverse rearing environment. In contrast, antisocial behaviour of adolescence-limited individuals is normative and plays an important social developmental role. Moffitt further argues that antisocial behaviour committed by adolescence-limited offenders helps them to adopt an adult role and to assert their personal independence and autonomy until they enter adulthood. The number of adolescents who satisfy characteristics of the life-course-persistent type is thought to be much smaller than those who satisfy characteristics of the adolescence-limited type.

Moffitt's typology has important implications for the assessment and treatment of adolescent offenders. Because life-course-persistent offenders are expected to have long-standing biopsychosocial problems in multiple domains (Moffitt, 1993), assessments and interventions for life-course-persistent offenders are often more complex and multifaceted than are those for adolescence-limited offenders.

Assessment of Adolescent Offenders

Consent of minor children or adolescents is often accepted as legally valid if minors understand the purpose and nature of the proposed activities, if they can properly weigh the risks and benefits, if they understand alternative courses of action, and if they are not prohibited by legislation from consenting (Hesson, Bakal, & Dobson, 1993). Clinicians should obtain consent from parents or guardians of adolescents who are not legally capable of giving consent as well as consent from the adolescents themselves.

Several reliable and independent sources of information are necessary to adequately assess antisocial behaviour among adolescents (McMahon, 1994). This is particularly important because descriptions of adolescents' antisocial behaviours are often not consistent across sources (e.g., parents, teachers, peers; see Achenbach, McConaughy, & Howell, 1987; Moffitt, 1993). For example, individuals who display the adolescence-limited pattern may engage in antisocial behaviours with peers but in prosocial behaviours with parents, other adults, and teachers.

Three psychiatric diagnoses are particularly common among adolescents who come into conflict with the law: Attention-Deficit/Hyperactivity Disorder (ADHD), Oppositional Defiant Disorder (ODD), and Conduct Disorder (CD) (American Psychiatric Association, 1994). ADHD is defined by a persistent pattern of inattention and/or hyperactivity-impulsivity; ODD is defined by a recurrent pattern of negativistic, defiant, and hostile behaviour directed towards authority figures; and CD is defined by a repetitive and persistent pattern of behaviour that violates basic rights of others or age-appropriate societal norms. It may be important to identify which psychiatric disorder or disorders are present among adolescents because these can influence treatment recommendations and approaches.

Appropriate and contemporary norms are essential for interpreting adolescents' responses to standardized psychological assessments (Butcher et al., 1992; Wechsler, 1996). Adolescents will often appear more psychologically disturbed if adult norms, rather than age-appropriate norms, are used to interpret assessment findings (Archer, 1984). The appearance of psychological disturbance among adolescents is due in part to the greater participation in social deviance reported by adolescents than by adults. For example, Hemphill and Howell (1999) found that adolescent offenders reported engaging in more socially undesirable behaviours such as lying, swearing, disobeying laws, littering, and stealing than did adult male offenders serving sentences of two or more years in a federal penitentiary.

Treatment of Adolescent Offenders

Many adolescent offenders are not motivated to participate in therapy because they want to obtain greater autonomy and independence from parents and authority figures. Moreover, adolescents often lack self-reflection, which is important for many psychologically based therapies. Successful interventions typically involve the cooperation of the adolescents' families. If either the adolescents or their families are unwilling or unable to fully participate with intervention plans, successful outcomes may be difficult to achieve. Peer influences, which are particularly strong in adolescence, may also hamper the success of treatment. Clearly, it would be desirable to include in treatment programs only the most motivated adolescents.

To the extent that adolescents commit different types of offences and for different reasons than do adults, we might expect particular antecedents, sequences of events, and coping strategies to differ between adolescents and adults who participate in relapse prevention treatment (see Chapter 8). In addition, adolescents – particularly older adolescents – embark on many new sets of experiences and responsibilities; they obtain paid jobs, start dating, or begin considering career options. Problems in these areas, and concerns distinct to adolescents – such as the perceived importance of "fitting in" with peers – should be incorporated into treatment plans for adolescents.

Among the most effective interventions for adolescents are those that incorporate the larger social context (Henggeler, Schoenwald, & Pickrel, 1995). Multisystemic therapy, for example, views social networks as interconnected systems that influence, and are influenced by, adolescent offenders and their families. Multisystemic therapy brings about change by mobilizing social networks: families, schools, work, peers, the community, and cultural systems. Henggeler et al. (1995) have concluded that recent studies of multisystemic therapy "represent the first randomized trials to demonstrate long-term reductions in violent and criminal offences with samples of serious juvenile offenders" (p. 709).

ASSESSMENT AND TREATMENT OF SPOUSAL ASSAULTERS

Spousal violence is widespread in North America and the physical and psychological damage resulting from such violence has been well documented in recent years (Gelles & Straus, 1988; Island & Letellier, 1991; Kurz, 1993; Renzetti, 1992; Straus, 1993). Evidence suggests that approximately 20% of people have experienced moderate violence (e.g., throwing things, pushing, shoving) and 6% to 8% have experienced severe violence (e.g., biting, punching, beating, weapon use) at least once in an intimate relationship (Dutton, 1995). As discussed in Chapter 8, few spousal assaulters are formally identified by the criminal justice system and even fewer are sanctioned. Incidence rates of spousal assault are comparable for men and women; however, women are far more likely than men to be seriously injured. Women are also predominantly the victims of sexual aggression and of extreme violence following separation. Given that most patients admitted to hospitals following domestic disputes are women, this section will focus on male assaulters. Most definitions of spousal assault include any actual, attempted, or threatened physical harm perpetrated by a man or woman against someone with whom he or she has, or has had, an intimate sexual relationship (Canadian Centre for Justice Statistics, 1994; Canadian Panel on Violence Against Women, 1993; Gelles & Straus 1988; Straus, Gelles, & Steinmetz, 1980).

Relevant Law

Over the past decade, increased awareness of spousal assault has led to changes in criminal justice policy. Many jurisdictions in the United States now have domestic violence laws that provide special penalties for spousal assault and family violence (Ford & Regoli, 1992). Similarly, Canadian and American jurisdictions have developed policing and prosecutorial policies that encourage or mandate the arrest of spousal assaulters (Canadian Centre for Justice Statistics, 1994; Sherman, 1992). One apparent consequence of these changes has been a marked increase in the number of men charged with assaulting female partners (Canadian Centre for Justice Statistics, 1993). The Correctional Service of Canada (CSC) started a Family Violence Initiative (1993) based in part on research indicating that at least 25% of incarcerated male offenders have a documented history of physical or sexual assault against family members (e.g., Dutton & Hart, 1992a, 1992b). Indeed, research shows that many spousal assaulters are not identified by the criminal justice system (Hart, Kropp, Roesch, Ogloff, & Whittemore, 1994).

Salient Characteristics

Several risk markers are significantly related to husband-to-wife violence. Hotaling and Sugarman (1986) reported that witnessing violence as a child or adolescent, alcohol use/abuse, lack of assertiveness, low income, low educational level, and sexual aggressiveness were significantly associated with wife assault. A history of abuse as a child/adolescent, unemployment, a criminal record, low self-esteem, and a need for power or dominance were found to have an inconsistent relationship with spousal violence. The profile of a wife abuser also includes generalized violent behaviour and personality disorders (Dutton & Hart, 1992a, 1992b). In particular, Dutton (1995) proposes that borderline personality disorder may be positively associated with wife abuse.

Assessment of Spousal Assaulters

The increased awareness of spousal assault and the increase in arrests and prosecutions for this offence has placed pressure on correctional and community organizations to assess, manage, and treat spousal assaulters. As a result, there has been a recent trend to conduct risk assessments of spousal assaulters. Properly done, risk assessments can help determine strategies for managing risk and reducing recidivism.

Although a number of risk assessment/management instruments have been developed in recent years (Roehl & Guertin, 1999), few have been published with validity data. Two exceptions are the Danger Assessment (DA) by Campbell (1995), and the Spousal Assault Risk Assessment Guide (SARA) by Kropp, Hart, Webster, and Eaves (1995, 1999). Campbell's instrument is designed primarily for assessing risk for spousal homicide, but has shown some promise in predicting future spousal assaults (Campbell, 1999). Drawing on a careful review of the clinical and empirical literatures on risk for violence, with particular emphasis on spousal assault (Cooper, 1993), the SARA consists of twenty items grouped into five content areas: criminal history, psychosocial adjustment, spousal assault history, current/most recent offence, and other considerations (see Table 9.1). Research on the SARA has demonstrated good interrater reliability and promising validity (Borum, 1996; Kropp & Hart, 2000).

Any assessment of a spousal assaulter, whether to specifically address risk or simply to better understand the individual, should

TABLE 9.1
Spousal Assault Risk Assessment Guide

	Rating (0-1-2)	Critical item (Check box)
Criminal history		
1. Past assault of family members	☐	☐
2. Past assault of strangers or acquaintances	☐	☐
3. Past violation of conditional release or community supervision	☐	☐
Psychosocial adjustment		
4. Recent relationship problems	☐	☐
5. Recent employment problems	☐	☐
6. Victim of and/or witness to family violence as a child or adolescent	☐	☐
7. Recent substance abuse/dependence	☐	☐
8. Recent suicidal or homicidal ideation/intent	☐	☐
9. Recent psychotic and/or manic symptoms	☐	☐
10. Personality disorder with anger, impulsivity, or behavioural instability	☐	☐
Spousal assault history		
11. Past physical assault	☐	☐
12. Past sexual assault/sexual jealousy	☐	☐
13. Past use of weapons and/or credible threats of death	☐	☐
14. Recent escalation in frequency or severity of assault	☐	☐
15. Past violation of "no contact" orders	☐	☐
16. Extreme minimization or denial of spousal assault history	☐	☐
17. Attitudes that support or condone spousal assault	☐	☐
Alleged (current) offence		
18. Severe and/or sexual assault	☐	☐
19. Use of weapons and/or credible threats of death	☐	☐
20. Violation of 'no contact' order	☐	☐
Other considerations		
• _____	☐	☐
• _____		
• _____		

Summary Risk Ratings

	Low	Moderate	High
1. Imminent risk towards partner	☐	☐	☐
2. Imminent risk towards others	☐	☐	☐
Specify: _____			

SOURCE: British Columbia Institute on Family Violence; Spousal Assault Risk Assessment Guide. Kropp et al. (1995).

include information obtained from the perspective of the accused and from perspectives independent of the accused. Obtaining information from collateral sources is important because often the spousal assaulter is mandated for treatment by the court, is reluctant to report current and/or past violence, and may fail to comply with the assessment altogether. Collateral sources include interviews with the victim(s) and information obtained from police reports, criminal records, and victim impact statements. Clinicians can often obtain much of this collateral information through the prosecution or probation offices involved with the case. Criminal records are helpful in determining past arrests or convictions for assault and breaches of conditions of bail, probation, parole, and so forth. Victim impact statements provide a measure of the physical and emotional effects on the victim(s).

Standardized measures have been developed to assess both physical and emotional abuse (e.g., Gelles & Straus, 1988; Marshall, 1992; Tolman, 1989) and common ancillary problems such as substance abuse (e.g., Selzer, 1971; Skinner, 1982). It is useful for both the accused and the victim to rate the accused's behaviour; discrepancies between these sources can be clinically useful. Other procedures to gather additional information include standardized personality inventories that assess psychological symptoms and disorders, psychopathy, jealousy, dependency, intrusiveness, anger, and so forth.

Treatment of Spousal Assaulters

In the past 15 years there has been a proliferation of treatment programs for spousal assaulters, but the program objectives – apart from ending violence – tend to vary according to the theoretical principles adopted (Dutton, Bodnarchuk, Kropp, Hart & Ogloff, 1997). Even though the content and focus of treatment also varies according to the theoretical perspectives of treatment providers and the types of clients (e.g., court mandated vs. self-referred; couples vs. individuals), Dutton (1998) emphasizes that the objective of treating wife assaulters remains constant: to "demonstrate to the clients how their use of violence is a learned behavior sustained by their own perceptions" (p. 251). Dutton proposes that treatment groups for wife assaulters should attempt "(1) to alter unrealistic male expectations about their wives, (2) to improve assertive communications as a means of non-violent conflict resolution, and (3) to improve the male's empathy for his victim and to instil in him processes of self punishment for aggression" (p. 87). Empathy with victims can be achieved by having spousal assaulters examine their own victimization experiences (e.g., abuse as children). Spousal assaulters frequently minimize or externalize their behaviours, and it is therefore recommended that court-mandated treatment providers use highly structured, confrontational techniques (Dutton, 1998). Treatment with court-mandated men is typically short (e.g., 16 weeks), so treatment goals that can be realistically addressed within that time frame should form the focus of treatment.

Most programs for spousal assaulters are diverse "hybrid" programs that capitalize on the valuable aspects of several approaches (Bell, Browning, & Hamilton, 1992). Gondolf (1993) identified three common types of treatment programs for spousal assaulters: anger management programs, profeminist resocialization programs, and skills-building programs. A central goal of each approach is to have spousal assaulters accept personal responsibility for their behaviours. Anger management programs focus on helping offenders to identify the sequence of events associated with their physiological, cognitive, and behavioural precursors to violence (Gondolf, 1993). The objective is to increase the appreciation among spousal assaulters that their perceptions and behavioural responses are learned and amenable to change (Dutton, 1998). Anger management programs use strategies such as anger diaries (e.g., to record incidents of anger), relaxation exercises, and group discussions covering topics such as empathy building and improved communication skills. The goal of feminist approaches to treating wife assaulters is to help males identify power imbalances in their relationships and to understand that sharing power with partners can be mutually enhancing. The goal of cognitive-behavioural therapy is to have spousal assaulters learn to reinterpret others' motivations and their own emotions. For example, assaultive males tend to misinterpret a variety of their own emotions (e.g., embarrassment, anxiety, sadness) as anger. Therapists repeatedly challenge offenders' explanations for their behaviour, which include the beliefs that their behaviours are caused by external sources (e.g., the victim's behaviour), by situational factors (e.g., having a bad day at work), or by uncontrollable dispositions (e.g., having a bad temper or substance abuse problems).

Due in part to methodological problems, the program evaluation research that has assessed treatment programs for spousal assaulters has resulted in inconsistent conclusions regarding the efficacy of treatment for spousal assaulters (see reviews by Burns & Meredith, 1993;

Cooper, 1995; Edelson & Syers, 1990; Hamberger & Hastings, 1993; Rosenfeld, 1992). Despite the variable results, it is reasonable to conclude that even though treatment does not reliably effect change for all spousal assaulters, it probably works for certain individuals. This conclusion is rooted in a commonly held assumption that wife assaulters are not a homogeneous group and distinctions can be made regarding treatability (Hamberger & Hastings, 1988; Saunders, 1992). Thus, a relatively recent trend has been to tailor treatment modalities to different "types" of spousal assaulters (Healey, Smith, & O'Sullivan, 1998). Probably the most cited typology was described by Holtzworth-Munroe and Stuart (1994), who reviewed the literature and proposed three primary types of batterers: family-only, dysphoric/borderline, and antisocial. This approach holds promise, as it is possible that programs targeting the specific needs of offender types will lead to more demonstrable treatment success.

ASSESSMENT AND TREATMENT OF SEXUAL OFFENDERS

Sexual violence is a pervasive problem. Definitions of sexual aggression include "actual, attempted, or threatened sexual contact with a person who is nonconsenting or unable to give consent" (Boer, Wilson, Gauthier, & Hart, 1997, p. 9). Official sources may underestimate the actual rates of sexual offending (Dempster, 1998). Victims are often reluctant to report their sexual victimization experiences and individuals who have committed sexual offences are not always charged with sexual offences. For example, many individuals who have committed sexual assaults may instead be convicted of general (i.e., nonsexual), assaults either because evidence is lacking to establish the sexual components of the offence(s) or because they have successfully plea-bargained their sexual offences to nonsexual offences (Finkelhor, 1994; Quinsey, Harris, Rice, & Cormier, 1998). Hudson and Ward (1997) contend that, because of low reporting rates and conviction rates for sex offenders, most of our knowledge of sexual crimes comes from research with university and college samples and from a small minority of sexual offenders convicted of sexual offences; information obtained from these groups may not be representative of sexual crimes in general. Estimates of sexual victimization derived from self-report data range from 1 in 10 to 1 in 2 adolescent and adult women (e.g., Furby, Weinrott, & Blackshaw, 1989; Koss, 1992, 1993). The prevalence of sexual violence against children is no less alarming. Finkelhor (1994) found that 7% to 36% of women and 3% to 29% of men in large non-clinical populations of adults across countries report a history of childhood sexual abuse (see also Finkelhor, 1984; Finkelhor, Hotaling, Lewis, & Smith, 1989).

Relevant Law

Sex offenders have long been the targets of controversial commitment and detainment legislation (Bonta, Zinger, Harris, & Carriere, 1998). As early as 1948, statutes designed to control the threat posed by violent sex offenders – termed "criminal sexual psychopaths" – were in place (Bonta et al., 1998). Under the "Dangerous Offender" (DO) legislation of the Criminal Code (R.S.C. 1985; Part XXIV, s. 752 (b)), sex offenders who present ongoing risks to other persons and have been convicted of "serious personal injury offences" can be sentenced to indeterminate terms as DOs. Part XXIV was expanded in 1997 to include legislation for Long-Term Offenders (LTOs), which applies to sexual offenders who pose substantial risk of reoffending and whose risk can be controlled in the community. Upon release, a LTO designation mandates offenders to receive community supervision for up to 10 years (para. 753.1(3)(b)).

Salient Characteristics

According to the fourth edition of the *Diagnostic and Statistical Manual of Mental Disorders* (American Psychiatric Association, 1994), sexual assault – unlike sadism or masochism – is not considered a "paraphilia" or a mental disorder. One of the defining features of paraphilias is that "[t]he behavior, sexual urges, or fantasies cause clinically significant distress or impairment in social, occupational, or other important areas of functioning" (p. 523). Clearly, many sex offenders experience little personal distress or deficits in social functioning related to their offending and, as such, do not meet the diagnostic criteria for paraphilias.

Sex offenders are a heterogenous population (Hudson & Ward, 1997). Different groups of sex offenders are found to be unique in terms of their psychiatric histories, familial and environmental experiences, personalities, criminal offending, and sexual offending (Ward, McCormack, Hudson, & Polaschek, 1997). Attempts to categorize subtypes of sexual offenders have been conducted, but there is currently no generally recognized classification system that adequately informs psychologists about the treatment needs of sex offenders. These conceptual difficulties have handicapped our pursuit of coherent assessment and treatment theories and models for use with sexual offenders (Grubin & Kennedy, 1991; Hudson & Ward, 1997).

Despite the lack of a generally recognized classification system, researchers have found that categorizing sex offenders into "rapist" and "child molester" groups has important clinical utility; rapists and child molesters form two distinct groups. Rapists sexually assault men or women and they comprise the majority of incarcerated sex offender samples; child molesters sexually assault boys or girls and they comprise a smaller percentage of sex offender samples (Quinsey et al., 1998). Ward and colleagues (1997) found that men who sexually assault children are distinct in many ways from rapists, and that rapists are similar in many ways to the general prison population. Researchers have found that personality disorders are more common among rapists than among child molesters (Quinsey et al., 1998). For example, rapists receive higher scores on the Hare Psychopathy Checklist-Revised (PCL-R; Hare, 1991) than do men who sexually assault children (e.g., Serin, Malcolm, Khanna, & Barbaree, 1994). Quinsey and colleagues (Quinsey et al., 1998) describe the finding of differential recidivism rates among subgroups of offenders as one of the most important discoveries in the sex offender literature. Father-daughter incest offenders, for example, have among the lowest rates of recidivism, whereas offenders who molest young boys have among the highest rates of recidivism.

Assessment of Sexual Offenders

Clinicians must critically evaluate the reliability and validity of information offered by sexual offenders and should always supplement it with collateral information. Ward and colleagues (1997) propose a balanced use of open-ended and closed-ended questions and advise against using an aggressive confrontational approach with sexual offenders, who have generally become skilled at maintaining their secrecy. Many sex offenders have never spoken to anyone about their offences and are reluctant to discuss the details with clinicians assigned by the courts to conduct forensic assessments. See Box 9.1 for a discussion of general principles for assessing sexually violent behaviour.

Box 9.1

Principles for Assessing Sexually Violent Behaviour

Regardless of the specific techniques or measures used, risk assessments of sexual violence should be guided by the following principles. Risk assessments should:

- gather information concerning an individual's sexual, intra-personal, interpersonal, and biological functioning. Examples include, respectively, sexual preferences and deviations; antisocial attitudes; relationships with family, friends, and sexual partners; and neurological disease;
- gather information using multiple methods (e.g., interviews; behavioural observations; reviews of case records and medical, psychological, and correctional reports; psychological tests; medical examinations). The use of physiological assessments (e.g., phallometric measures) may also be warranted;
- gather information from multiple sources (e.g., the offender; the victim(s); the offender's family, friends, and coworkers; police; mental health professionals familiar with the offender);
- gather information concerning both static and dynamic aspects of risk. While static predictors may be the best long-term predictors of sexual violence, dynamic factors are reliably associated with short-term fluctuations in risk and are, therefore, important in developing intervention programs (Kropp & Hart, 1997a);
- explicitly evaluate the accuracy of the information gathered (Kropp & Hart, 1997a);
- recognize that dynamic and static risk factors change over time and that risk assessments should be repeated at regular intervals (e.g., every 6 to 12 months or whenever there is an important change in the status of the case).

The above guidelines and information should be considered together to answer the following questions: (1) What is the likelihood that the individual will engage in sexual violence? (2) Who are the likely victims of any future sexual violence? (4) What steps can be taken to manage the individual's risk for sexual violence? (5) What factors or warning signs might markedly increase the individual's risk for sexual violence?

Psychological assessments of sexual offenders focus on a broad range of factors that include developmental and environmental factors, psychological characteristics, and offence characteristics (e.g., Ward et al., 1997). Clinicians rely heavily on interviews and on standardized psychological tests to assess sexual offenders. Although there is no standard battery of psychological tests or structured interview administered to sex offenders, many clinicians assess the degree of denial and social desirability; sexual knowledge, sexual history, and sexual attitudes and beliefs; family upbringing, educational achievement, and occupational and social functioning; emotional functioning, attachment, empathy, and anger; intelligence, cognitive processes, and problem-solving skills; social skills, social competence, and history of interpersonal violence; personality and psychopathology; factors leading up to the offence, cognitive distortions, victim characteristics, and acceptance of responsibility (Ward et al., 1997; Williams, 1995).

Phallometric testing of sexual arousal involves placing rubber strain gauges filled with mercury halfway up the shafts of offenders' penises. Offenders are then exposed to slides, audio recordings, or video recordings depicting deviant and appropriate sexual stimuli. As offenders watch and/or listen to the stimuli, the circumferences of their penises change with fluctuations in sexual arousal and the fluctuations are monitored. Marshall (1996) has criticized sexual arousal testing because of the lack of standardized or widely accepted phallometric testing techniques, because of ethical concerns regarding the use of stimuli that depict sexual aggression against women and children, and because data indicate that the technique may lack reliability and validity. Despite these limitations, researchers have shown that phallometric testing is able to discriminate between sexual and nonsexual offenders (Lalumière & Quinsey, 1994) and that phallometric measures are associated with sexual recidivism and with violent recidivism for both rapists (Rice, Harris, & Quinsey, 1990) and for child molesters (Lalumière & Quinsey, 1993). Indeed, Rice and Harris (1997) found that psychopaths who exhibited phallometric arousal to deviant sexual stimuli had a much higher risk of committing sexual offences than did psychopaths and nonpsychopaths who did not exhibit this pattern of phallometric arousal. Hanson and Bussière (1996) provide additional validity for phallometric measures; they reviewed the literature and found that phallometric measures were among the single best predictors of sexual recidivism. Sexual arousal testing is currently used inconsistently within the Correctional Service of Canada (CSC). Some regions (e.g., Ontario) use it routinely for all intake assessments of sexual offenders (Williams, 1995), whereas other regions (e.g., British Columbia) only use it only when requested. Quinsey and colleagues (1998) summarize the literature by stating that under "limited circumstances" (p. 121) phallometric testing yields reliable and valid measures, but they caution that phallometric measures should not be used to identify or establish guilt.

Clinicians use assessment instruments designed to identify offenders who are at risk for committing future sexual offences. Four measures will be briefly discussed here: the Sexual Violence Risk-20 (SVR-20), the Psychopathy Checklist-Revised (PCL-R), the Sexual Offender Risk Assessment Guide (SORAG), and the Rapid Risk Assessment for Sexual Offence Recidivism (RRASOR). Boer and colleagues (1997) reviewed the clinical and empirical literature on sexual offenders and developed the SVR-20, identifying variables that were empirically and/or conceptually related to sexual recidivism. This 20-item scale is divided into three major areas (psychosocial adjustment, sexual offending, future plans) and serves as a guide to ensure that assessors conduct systematic and reasonably comprehensive risk assessments. Research examining the reliability and validity of the SVR-20 is currently under way. Hare (1991) developed the PCL-R to measure the concept of psychopathy. As mentioned above and in Chapter 11, the PCL-R has been a useful tool for assessing risk among sex offenders (Hemphill, Hare, & Wong, 1998; Quinsey, Lalumière, Rice, & Harris, 1995; Quinsey, Rice, & Harris, 1995; Rice & Harris, 1997; Rice et al., 1990). Although the strength of the relationship between the PCL-R and sexual recidivism is modest (see Hanson & Bussière, 1998), researchers have found that sex offenders who have high scores on both the PCL-R and sexual deviance are at very high risk for being convicted of sexual offences in the future (Quinsey et al., 1998). Quinsey, Rice, et al. (1995) developed the SORAG by selecting 14 variables that were found to be associated with sexual recidivism among samples of previously incarcerated sex offenders (see also Quinsey et al., 1998; Quinsey, Lalumière, et al., 1995; Rice & Harris, 1997; Rice et al., 1990; Rice, Quinsey, & Harris, 1991). The SORAG has lower predictive accuracy than other measures designed to predict violent recidivism, and it requires further testing to clarify the strength of its predictive validity (Hanson, 1997; Quinsey et al., 1998; Rice & Harris, 1997). Hanson (1997) developed the RRASOR after identifying a small set of sociodemographic and criminal history variables that predicted sexual violence (Hanson & Bussière, 1998). This 4-variable measure (prior sex offence, age at release, victim gender, relationship to victim) correlated .25 with sexual recidivism. Although the above risk assessment instruments show promise, few prospective and cross-validated studies examining their predictive validity have been published. It is therefore difficult to evaluate their utility for identifying individuals who are at risk to commit future sexual offences.

Treatment of Sexual Offenders

The primary objective of programs designed to treat sex offenders is the reduction of their inappropriate sexual behaviour; a secondary objective is to promote a healthy lifestyle that encourages prosocial behaviour and positive relationships. As noted in the previous chapter, the main philosophy of many contemporary treatment programs for offenders is relapse prevention, an approach that focuses on "enabling the person to prevent relapse and thereby to maintain the newly adopted behaviour pattern" (George & Marlatt, 1990, p. 2). Different treatment programs for sex offenders are based on this relapse prevention philosophy and have many characteristics in common. The "Standards and Guidelines for the Provision of Services to Sex Offenders" (Correctional Service of Canada, 1996) and the Vermont Network of Sex Offender Therapists (1995), for example, have identified several treatment goals for sex offenders. Offenders are to learn to accept full responsibility for their behaviour and its consequences; learn to identify connections among attitudes, cognitions, and violent behaviour and to modify their attitudes and distorted cognitions; improve their social skills and learn prosocial coping responses; increase their knowledge concerning sexuality and intimacy, control deviant sexual arousal, and increase appropriate sexual arousal; become aware of the effects that sexual assaults have on victims and develop empathy towards them; develop awareness of the patterns of their violent behaviour so that they can interrupt these patterns before additional offences occur; and maintain a network of treatment specialists involved in their treatment and supervision on an ongoing basis. Anger management and impulse control are two areas of psychological functioning that should also routinely be included in treatment programs of sex offenders (Correctional Service of Canada, 1996).

Similar to findings with other offender groups, research among sex offenders that evaluates the efficacy of treatments in terms of their ability to reduce recidivism or the severity of subsequent offences remains equivocal. Some reviews (e.g., Furby et al., 1989; Quinsey, Harris, Rice, & Lalumière, 1993) and well-designed treatment studies (e.g., Marques, Day, Nelson, & West, 1993) provide little support for the contention that treatment programs designed to treat sexual offenders reduce rates of sexual recidivism. In contrast, other researchers (e.g., Marshall & Pithers, 1994) argue that treatment effects may be observed if researchers focus on variables other than recidivism; these include improvements in measures of prosocial responses or variables presumed to contribute to sexual recidivism. Quinsey and colleagues (1998) contend that cognitive-behavioural programs are ineffective in reducing the rates of criminal recidivism among serious adult offenders and argue that "to the extent that treatment is ineffective, supervision must be emphasized" (p. 194).

ASSESSMENT AND TREATMENT OF MENTALLY DISORDERED OFFENDERS

Mentally disordered offenders (MDOs) are those individuals who have come into contact with the criminal justice system and who also have a mental disorder. The term MDO can refer to individuals who satisfy either legal or psychological criteria. MDOs include individuals found unfit to stand trial, offenders found not criminally responsible on account of mental disorder (i.e., insanity acquittees), offenders who are seriously mentally ill, mentally disordered sex offenders (most commonly paedophiles or sexual sadists), sexual predators, and offenders transferred to secure mental health facilities. Mentally ill individuals are more likely to be arrested than are individuals in the general population (Hylton, 1995; Teplin, 1984). As mentioned in the previous chapter, the rate of mental disorder in correctional populations is significantly higher than the rate among the general population from comparable socio-economic backgrounds (Ogloff, Roesch, & Hart, 1994; Teplin, 1990b). Between 6.5% and 10% of incarcerated individuals suffer from "serious" mental illnesses, and between 15% and 40% of incarcerated individuals suffer from "moderate" mental illnesses (Hodgins, 1995; Ogloff, et al., 1994). However, Ogloff and colleagues (1994) caution that these statistics should not be interpreted to suggest that the majority of incarcerated individuals are in good mental health. Indeed, up to 90% of inmates have a diagnosable mental disorder – most commonly antisocial personality disorder or substance use disorders – and many of these offenders are generally chronic and "difficult or even impossible to treat" (Ogloff et al., 1994, p. 116).

MDOs have needs that can be addressed under two separate systems: the mental health system and/or the criminal justice system. Often, at the initial stages in the criminal justice system (i.e., apprehension and arrest), police have the discretion either to process MDOs through the criminal justice system or to divert them into the mental health system (see also Chapter 8 and Figure 8.1). In recent decades there has been a move towards deinstitutionalization in the mental health system. Some researchers have speculated that the decrease in the number of available beds in mental health hospitals has lead to an increase in the number of MDOs processed through the criminal justice system (Allodi, Kedward, & Robertson, 1977; Maier & Miller, 1989; Pogrebin & Poole, 1987; Teplin, 1983, 1984, 1990b).

In chapter 10 Ogloff and Whittemore outline the process of pretrial assessments of MDOs. Here we will focus on post-dispositional assessments and treatments of MDOs within the criminal justice system. Mentally disordered individuals who do not meet the criteria to be found unfit to stand trial or not criminally responsible on account of mental disorder (see Chapter 10) proceed through the criminal justice system as would offenders without mental disorders. The criminal justice system, however, must still deal with the special needs of MDOs. The process of post-dispositional assessments and treatments of MDOs incarcerated within the provincial and federal domains of the Canadian criminal justice system is described below.

Relevant Law

As discussed in the subsequent chapter, the law makes allowances for individuals charged with criminal offences who are also believed to be mentally ill. In the vast majority of cases, the mental illnesses of these individuals are not formally recognized by the criminal justice system until these persons have been convicted, sentenced, and incarcerated (Hylton, 1995). Ogloff (1991b) concluded that proceedings to determine fitness and sanity at the time of the alleged offences are generally reserved for offenders charged with the most serious offences.

Salient Characteristics

As with most offender populations, the majority of MDOs are male, although research indicates that female offenders have higher rates of mental disorders than do male offenders (see the section below on female offenders). Mentally ill offenders are described as a "heterogeneous and poorly defined group" (Quinsey et al., 1998, p. 75) who commit offences across the continuum of seriousness. They come from all ethnic backgrounds and age groups. As discussed in Chapter 8, the disruptive behaviour of MDOs must be managed and treated to control their potentially negative impact on the functioning of correctional institutions.

Assessment of Mentally Disordered Offenders

Ogloff (1998) and colleagues (Ogloff & Nicholls, 1997; Ogloff et al., 1994) have developed a comprehensive model for the provision of mental health services in jails and prisons (see Figure 9.1 and Chapter 8). This model consists of intake screening, ongoing monitoring/screening of inmates and offenders, comprehensive psychodiagnostic assessments of MDOs, mental health treatments, gradual post-release monitoring/supervision, and maintaining continuity of services. This model is relevant for use with all offender populations discussed within this chapter but is particularly useful for MDOs.

Given the high rate of mental illnesses among inmates and offenders, all offenders are screened for mental disorders soon after admission to correctional facilities (Ogloff, 1998). Since the majority of offenders do not suffer from serious mental disorders, however, it would not be efficient or cost effective to complete comprehensive assessments on all incoming individuals – hence the use of brief (e.g., 20- to 30-minute) screening interviews. The primary goal of screening interviews is to identify individuals who require mental health services and to refer them for further assessments and/or treatments; individuals who do not require mental health care are screened out. This process maximizes the number of MDOs who are provided with necessary treatments. Several evaluations of intake screenings have been conducted, and results have been positive (Ogloff, 1996; Roesch, 1995; Tien et al., 1993). Ogloff (1998) recommended that, under certain circumstances, additional measures should be used to complement routine screening. For example, individuals who appear to be at risk for self-harm or suicide should be more carefully assessed (see for example Polvi, 1997). The suicide rate among inmate and offender populations is estimated to be between three and nine times that of the

Figure 9.1
Multi-stage mental health services program for MIOs

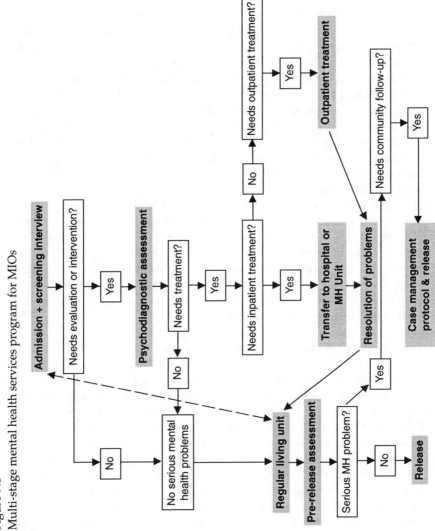

general population (Arboleda-Florez & Holley, 1988; Hayes, 1983, 1994). Mental illness is a risk factor for suicide (Roy, 1985) and, as noted above, mental illnesses are disproportionately present in correctional samples.

Ogloff's (1998) model emphasizes "prevention and early intervention" (p. 43). With that in mind, Ogloff recommends both ongoing formal monitoring (e.g., by psychological assessors) and informal monitoring (e.g., by correctional officers, nurses, teachers, chaplains, and offenders themselves). Formal and informal monitoring of the mental health of inmates is essential throughout the entire period of incarceration, because they can experience deteriorations in mental health across time (Hodgins, 1995).

Inmates and offenders with mental health concerns identified by screenings or monitoring undergo more comprehensive assessments to identify the "existence and severity of psychopathology" (Ogloff et al., 1994, p. 126). Comprehensive assessments cannot always be completed for those who serve short sentences. Mental health assessments, however, can be informative for classification and treatment decisions (Ogloff, 1998). Offenders determined to be acutely mentally ill (i.e., certifiable under the provincial Mental Health Act; see Chapter 12) during incarceration may be transferred to a psychiatric facility that is more equipped to intervene. Once offenders are through the acute stages of their disorders and have been stabilized, they are usually returned to their original correctional institutions.

Treatment of Mentally Disordered Offenders

There is substantial variation in the availability of treatments offered in jails and prisons. As mentioned in Chapter 8, the opportunity for providing treatment in jails as opposed to prisons is more limited because inmates in jails are typically detained for short periods of time. The federal correctional system allows for more intensive and longer-term interventions with offenders (Webster, Hucker, & Grossman, 1993). This is particularly important for MDOs, who generally require long-term care. Assessments of offenders incarcerated in the federal system are used to identify MDOs who would benefit from mental health interventions. The CSC has implemented a number of treatment programs designed to focus specifically on the needs of MDOs.

Ogloff's model (1998; Ogloff et al., 1994) places great emphasis on post-release follow-ups and treatments. The CSC has implemented programs that serve to facilitate the reintegration of MDOs into the community. These programs generally occur in the context of community correctional centres after offenders have been granted day parole from the National Parole Board. Offenders on day parole are expected to become involved in work, school, treatment, and social programs while they reside in community correctional centres. These programs allow MDOs to learn important skills required for successful integration into the community while both the programs and living arrangements provide structure and supervision.

There is a dearth of research investigating the effectiveness of treatment programs for MDOs. Recently, however, administrators have begun to recognize that program evaluation is required to justify the continuance or elimination of programs. The CSC has a mandate to rehabilitate offenders; to receive funding for programs that would serve to fulfil this mandate, program evaluation is necessary. Current research is underway to evaluate the effectiveness of various treatment programs. Evaluating the efficacy of interventions for MDOs is a complex process because of the diversity of presenting problems and interventions (e.g., psychopharmacotherapy and psychological interventions).

ASSESSMENT AND TREATMENT OF FEMALE OFFENDERS

Historically, female offenders have been described as an "invisible" minority because of their small numbers (Adelberg & Currie, 1987; Arbour, 1996) and the lack of research investigating their experiences and needs (Kendall, 1993a; Shaw, 1994). An important and controversial area relevant to the assessment and treatment of female offenders is whether or not the causes and explanations of crime for female offenders are similar to or different from those for male offenders (Kendall, 1997). If the former perspective – a "nongendered perspective" – provides a good explanation of female criminality, then assessment and treatment protocols and procedures developed on male offenders can be directly applied to female offenders (e.g., Simourd & Andrews, 1994). In contrast, if the latter perspective – a "gendered" perspective – provides a good explanation for female criminality, then assessment and treatment protocols and procedures developed on male offenders will either be inappropriate for use with female offenders or they will require substantial modification (Correctional Service of Canada, 1994a). Traditionally, mental health professionals and corrections have implicitly adopted a nongendered perspective and applied male-based models of assessment, treatment, and program development and evaluation to women (Blanchette, 1997; Correctional Service of Canada, 1994a, 1994b; Shaw, 1994). In recent years, however, there has been a growing interest in the unique features of female offenders and an accompanying surge in research and literature on this population (see for example Kendall, 1993a; O'Shea & Fletcher, 1997). Despite the increasing interest in female criminal behaviour, the research is still in its infancy and the conclusions drawn from the literature often depend on the sources cited (Morris, 1990).

Recent Canadian cases involving women such as Marlene Moore, Karla Homolka, Lisa Neve, and Krystal Hendricks have raised awareness of the risk to the public posed by some female offenders. Despite the publicity of these cases, females are far less likely than are males to be charged with criminal offences (Arbour, 1996; Joel, 1985). Women comprise 23% of youths and 18% of adults charged with Criminal Code offences, 7% to 9% of the provincial offender population, and 2% of the federal offender population (Scarth & McLean, 1994; Shaw, 1994; Statistics Canada, 1999). This lower rate for female offenders than for male offenders is true for both property offences and violent offences, although the results are more pronounced for violent offences. For example, women are charged with 29% of property offences and 18% of violent offences (Statistics Canada, 1999); the latter category is composed of charges for homicide, sexual assault, assault, and robbery. In total, crimes against persons accounted for 50% of convictions against men and 33% of convictions against women (Statistics Canada, 1998b). Over the last several decades, there have been decreases in the ratios of males to females convicted of various categories of crimes (Joel, 1985). Women who receive sentences of 2 or more years have most frequently been charged with importing and trafficking drugs, whereas their male counterparts have been charged with property offences and offences against persons. The gender gap is generally smaller among young offenders than among adult offenders (Boritch, 1997).

Relevant Law

The Corrections and Conditional Release Act (CCRA) requires that "correctional policies, programs and practices respect gender ... differences and be responsive to the special needs of women ..." (s. 4(h)). As recently as the early 1990s, the CSC was found to be negligent in providing female offenders with comparable – or even adequate – facilities, services, programs, and training to those available for male offenders. In *Attorney General of Canada v. Daniels* (1991; for a brief discussion see Vachon, 1994), the Saskatchewan Court of Queen's Bench held that, contrary to sections 15 and 28 of the Canadian Charter of Rights and Freedoms, Daniels was being discriminated against on the basis of her gender. The decision was based on the recognition that programs available to male federal offenders were superior to those available to female federal offenders. Furthermore, the Saskatchewan court found that Ms Daniels's right to life and security (s. 7) and her right not to be subjected to cruel and unusual punishment (s. 12) would be violated if she were to be incarcerated in the only institution at the time for federally sentenced women, the Kingston Prison for Women (P4W). It was argued that incarceration at P4W would take her far from her support system of family and friends and place her at increased risk of suicide. Although the *Daniels* decision was eventually overturned on technical grounds, the case demonstrates the inequalities in the delivery of services between male and female offenders.

In a similar case in British Columbia, Gayle Horii was successful in her application to prevent her transfer from Matsqui (a medium security federal institution for male offenders) to the newly opened Burnaby Correctional Centre for Women (BCCW) (Law Society of British Columbia, 1992). Horii had been pursuing post-secondary education at Matsqui and would have been required to discontinue university-level courses if she was transferred to BCCW. Horii successfully argued that the transfer would result in cruel and unusual punishment and would violate her right to equal protection and equal benefit of the law without discrimination based on sex.

Salient Characteristics

A large percentage of women sentenced to two years or more have no prior convictions (36%), have never served a prison term (50%), and the vast majority are serving their first federal sentence (87%) (Shaw et al., 1990). Shaw (1994) concluded that incarcerated women are generally less of a threat to public safety than are incarcerated men because fewer women are incarcerated – and they received shorter sentences – than men (see also Statistics Canada, 1990). It is unclear, however, the extent to which these factors reflect differences in the severity of female and male criminality, differences in processing and sentencing practices of the criminal justice system between men and women, or a combination of these factors. The fact that women are less likely than men to reoffend or to breach their parole (Arbour, 1996; Shaw, 1994) and the finding that female offenders have less extensive criminal histories than do male offenders (Hemphill, Templeman, Wong, & Hare, 1998), suggest that female offenders do indeed pose a less serious risk to public safety than do male offenders. Female offenders may therefore be good candidates for community supervision, alternative measures, and low security classification. As is always the case, however, thorough assessments have to be conducted on case-by-case bases to evaluate the appropriateness of various interventions. Indeed, as noted above, some female offenders pose high risks to public safety and have committed serious violent crimes. The Correctional Service of Canada (1994a) recognizes that many women are "active agents rather than passive victims" (p. 6). The criminal justice system accordingly holds female offenders accountable for their actions while at the same time it recognizes that women's status in society, poverty, and abuse may influence their behaviour and patterns of offending.

First Nations individuals are disproportionately represented in the prison population relative to their representation in the general population, and the difference is even greater for female First Nations offenders (Arbour, 1996; La Prairie, 1984a, 1987a, 1987b; Shaw, 1994; Sugar & Fox, 1990). For example, First Nations individuals comprise 2% to 3% of the Canadian population but 33% of female admissions – and 17% of male admissions – to provincial facilities (Sugar & Fox, 1990). Research suggests that First Nations women are a unique subpopulation of offenders. Incarcerated First Nations women are more likely to have been convicted for violent crimes, to be younger, to have higher rates of self-abuse and suicide, and to have higher rates of physical and sexual abuse than non-First Nations female offenders (Comack, 1993; Kendall, 1993b; La Prairie, 1984b; Shaw et al., 1990; Sugar & Fox, 1990).

Until recently, the vast majority of federally sentenced women were housed at P4W (open since 1934) because it was the only federal penitentiary in Canada for female offenders (Blanchette, 1997). Results obtained from psychological assessments were therefore not of much practical utility for security classification purposes. The utility of risk assessments for these purposes, however, has increased in the 1990s because five regional correctional facilities – including a healing lodge – have opened to house women serving sentences of two or more years.

Assessment of Female Offenders

In many respects, the criminogenic needs (i.e., factors that contribute to criminal offending) of incarcerated men and women are similar. Both groups require, for example, programs to address educational and employment concerns and drug and alcohol abuse. There are some important differences, however, between male and female offenders in terms of their criminogenic needs (Axon, 1989), which should be reflected in the assessment and treatment of these populations. Although abuse histories are common among incarcerated samples (Arbour, 1996; Bonta, Pang, & Wallace-Caporetto, 1995; Browne, 1997; Comack, 1996; Kendall, 1993a; Shaw et al., 1990), there is evidence to suggest that female offenders are more likely to report abuse histories than are male offenders (Conly, 1998). (It is not entirely clear, however, the extent to which women's victimization histories are related to their criminal behaviour; see Bonta et al., 1995; Widom, 1989.) Further, female offenders have an even higher incidence of mental disorders than do their male counterparts (Motiuk & Porporino, 1991), and female offenders are more likely than male offenders to engage in self-abusive or suicidal behaviour (Arbour, 1996; Elliot & Morris, 1987; see also Heney, 1990; Liebling, 1994; Loucks & Zamble, 1994). Taken together, these findings suggest that clinicians who work with female offenders should routinely assess abuse histories, mental disorders, and potential for suicide and self-harm. Given the high prevalence of mental illness among female offenders, some investigators (e.g., Ogloff & Nicholls, 1997) recommend that all newly admitted individuals should undergo brief intake assessments to screen for mental illnesses, situational crises, criminogenic needs, and risk of harm to self or others (for further details concerning intake screenings, see the section on MDOs in this chapter and Chapter 8).

Given the lack of agreement concerning the causes of crime committed by women, it is perhaps not surprising that investigators disagree as to whether or not unique assessment measures need to be developed for female offenders (Kendall, 1997). Some researchers argue that assessment measures developed for male offender populations are appropriate for use with female offenders (Blanchette, 1997), whereas others argue that only assessment measures developed and validated specifically for female offender populations should be used with female offenders (Scarth & McLean, 1994). Many commonly used assessment measures are standardized, normed, and validated for use with both men and women and are routinely used with female offenders. In contrast, many risk assessment measures have not been extensively researched among female offenders, particularly First Nations offenders, which means that the reliability and validity of the measures for these groups is, at present, unclear (Scarth & McLean, 1994).

Results from prediction studies have been mixed, and Gendreau and colleagues (Gendreau, Goggin, & Paparozzi, 1996; see also Bonta et al., 1995) contend that prediction research among female offenders is "of the highest priority" (p. 67). Coulson, Ilacqua, Nutbrown, Guilekes, and Cudjoe (1996) found that the Level of Service Inventory (LSI-R, Andrews & Bonta, 1995) had a stronger relationship with recidivism among female offenders than is typically found among male offenders (see Gendreau & Goggin, 1996; Gendreau et al., 1996). Further, there is accumulating evidence to indicate that the PCL-R is a useful measure of psychopathy among female samples (Forth, Brown, Hart, & Hare, 1996; Loucks, 1995; Mailloux, 1999; Neary, 1990; Rutherford, Cacciola, Alterman, & McKay, 1996; Strachan, 1993; Strachan, Williamson, & Hare, 1990; but, also see Salekin, Rogers, & Sewell 1997). For example, Hemphill and Hare (1998) conducted a prospective study and found that female offenders identified as psychopaths on the PCL-R were convicted for violent offences at a faster and higher rate than were female offenders identified as nonpsychopaths on the PCL-R.

In contrast to the research findings with the LSI-R and the PCL-R, Bonta and colleagues (Bonta et al., 1995) found that the Statistical Information on Recidivism (SIR; Nuffield, 1982) scale was not as useful a measure for identifying female recidivists as it was for identifying male recidivists. This is particularly problematic given that the SIR scale is used routinely to assess offenders' levels of general risk for recidivism in the Correctional Service of Canada. Because the SIR has not proved useful at predicting recidivism among female inmates, it is not employed for that purpose. The difficulty though is that there is no equivalent instrument to the SIR for use with women. Research on the SIR with female offenders shows that, although some criminal history variables (e.g., prior criminal history, certain offence types, sentence length) were found to be important predictors of reoffending among both male and female offenders, other variables were not (Bonta et al., 1995). For example, histories of substance abuse, unemployment, and committing offences with associates were found to predict recidivism among male offenders but not among female offenders. These findings affirm the need for further empirical research with female offenders and suggest that variables in some risk assessment instruments may need to be eliminated or modified, or to be added, before they are routinely used with female offenders.

Taken together, these preliminary results indicate that some risk assessment measures developed and normed with men may also be valid for use with women. However, Gendreau and colleagues (1996) hypothesized that "a few factors, possibly of a situational and socially interactive nature, will be found to be unique predictors of female criminality" (p. 67).

Treatment of Female Offenders

Just as assessment approaches need to be tailored to female offenders, so do treatment or intervention approaches (Axon, 1989; Jackson, Hitchen, & Glackman, 1995). To the extent that female offenders have different needs and different psychological concerns than do male offenders, female offenders will also have different intervention requirements. As mentioned in Chapter 8, effective interventions identify criminogenic needs of offenders and implement treatments to address these needs (see also Andrews, 1980, 1983; Bailey, 1966; Gendreau, 1996; Gendreau & Goggin, 1996; Gendreau & Ross, 1979). The goal of this approach is to reduce recidivism by identifying and targeting factors that contribute to offenders' criminal behaviours. Offenders who have high needs for both traditional psychological problems and for criminogenic concerns should be a priority for mental health services (Ogloff & Nicholls, 1997). Interventions that address multiple concerns are needed for female offenders because they, like male offenders, often have multiple and long-standing problems (Correctional Service Canada, 1994a; Rivera, 1996; see also Chapter 8). Moreover, in addition to providing interventions typically provided to male offenders, female offenders may require interventions for mental disorders and for their victimization experiences. Interventions for victimization experiences are particularly important if those experiences contribute to their criminal behaviour, but this point remains controversial (Bonta et al., 1995; Browne, 1997; Kendall, 1997; Lake, 1993; Widom, 1989).

Female offenders require interventions that are delivered in a way that reflects their experiences (Axon, 1989; Jackson et al., 1995). For instance, psychological services should incorporate the unique experiences of women and the spiritual and cultural beliefs of First Nations offenders. Further, sentence lengths should be considered when determining issues to be addressed and treatment strategies to be employed. Psychological services offered in correctional institutions are typically provided in group rather than individual format, presumably because group therapy is more cost effective, more efficient, and allows other offenders with similar experiences to provide support and offer personal coping solutions. Many offenders readily and actively participate in group and peer interventions designed to target life skills, educational upgrading, and vocational needs. Some offenders, however, may be understandably reluctant – at least initially – to discuss highly personal issues such as physical or sexual abuse in a group format. Treatment programs for female offenders might offer individual therapy and/or group therapy, particularly for individuals new to treatment, so that they have an opportunity to become comfortable discussing sensitive topics.

The Report of the Task Force for Federally Sentenced Women (Correctional Service of Canada, 1990) indicates that female offenders require holistic approaches that incorporate interventions for the mind, body, and spirit, and that appreciate the interconnectedness of these components. This approach is consistent with the view that treatment should be approached from a perspective legitimate to that of the treated group. In addition to standard correctional interventions, treatment should involve a variety of creative intervention techniques such as journal writing, art therapy, and role-playing. Treatment providers who work with female offenders are encouraged to use challenging but empathic and nonconfrontational approaches that reduce power differentials between treatment facilitators and offenders (Correctional Service of Canada 1994a). Treatment facilitators play an important role in modelling self-respect, empathy, tolerance, and respect for others.

An important focus of treatment is the successful reintegration of female offenders into society. Bridges among correctional and community services are important and can be provided under the direction of correctional or parole services. Ongoing services may be provided in the community by psychologists, social workers, First Nations liaison workers, and other professionals. The continuity of care at different junctions in the criminal justice system (e.g., remand, prison) has the potential to be excellent among female offenders, because female offenders housed in remand/detention centres, prisons, and penitentiaries are often incarcerated within the same institution in a given region (Ogloff & Nicholls, 1997).

There is currently little published research demonstrating that treatment is associated with a reduction in recidivism among female offenders, but there is also little evidence that it is ineffective or harmful (Blanchette, 1997). Future research should focus on examining the extent to which criminogenic variables – particularly dynamic factors that are potentially amenable to treatment (see Gendreau et al., 1996) – are similar or different between male and female offenders and on the reasons for any similarities and differences (Bonta et al., 1995). An appreciation of the unique needs of female offenders is beginning to emerge but, given their small numbers and high needs, it will require "compromise and ingenuity" to deal effectively with this population (Jackson et al., 1995).

SUMMARY

In this chapter we have examined unique assessment and treatment considerations for five groups of offenders: adolescent offenders, spousal assaulters, sexual offenders, mentally disordered offenders, and female offenders. Several common themes have emerged. First, these diverse offender populations are themselves heterogeneous in terms of their psychological characteristics and treatment needs. It is thus impossible to draw broad generalizations for each offender group concerning patterns of offending and treatment needs. The second theme relates directly to the first; given the heterogeneity in these diverse offender populations, comprehensive assessments and interventions must be tailored to each offender so that individual treatment needs can be addressed. Carefully conducted assessments ideally help clinicians to establish appropriate and efficacious interventions for individual offenders. The third theme concerns the lack of methodologically sound research designs that would allow investigators to establish the utility of interventions designed to reduce criminal behaviour. Program evaluation needs to become firmly integrated into the assessment and treatment process. By working together, researchers and clinicians can develop strong treatment programs, evaluate their efficacy, and improve the delivery of psychological services.

QUESTIONS FOR DISCUSSION

1. Discuss the clinical implications of the heterogeneity and criminal versatility of offender groups for their assessment and treatment.
2. Describe and contrast characteristics of the offender populations discussed in this chapter and indicate how these characteristics might influence the delivery of psychological services.
3. Consider an offender population not described in the current chapter (e.g., mentally disabled offenders, violent offenders), their characteristics, and how these characteristics might influence their assessment and treatment.
4. Treatment evaluation research that is methodologically strong is frequently lacking among offender samples. Describe possible reasons for this, and consider how the evaluation of treatment programs might be integrated into the assessment and treatment process.

RECOMMENDED READING

Boritch, H. (1997). *Fallen women: Female crime and criminal justice in Canada.* Toronto, ON: Nelson.

Dutton, D.G. (1998). *The abusive personality: Violence and control in intimate relationships.* New York: Guilford Press.

Hanson, R.K., & Bussiere, M.T. (1998). Predicting relapse: A meta analysis of sexual offender recidivism studies. *Journal of Consulting and Clinical Psychology, 66*, 348–362.

Hoge, R.D., & Andrews, D.A. (1996). *Assessing the youthful offender: Issues and techniques.* New York: Plenum Press.

Ogloff, J.R.P., Roesch, R., & Hart, S.D. (1994). Mental health services in jails and prisons: Legal, clinical, and policy issues. *Law & Psychology Review, 18*, 109–136.

10. Fitness to Stand Trial and Criminal Responsibility in Canada

James R.P. Ogloff and Karen E. Whittemore

On 18 January 1992 the accused, Mr Wayne Sullivan, his wife, Maureen Sullivan, and a friend of Maureen's (Mrs S.W.) were drinking at a pub in Prince George, British Columbia. Sometime after midnight, Mrs W. drove the Sullivans home due to their state of intoxication. On arrival at the Sullivan's home, Mrs W. joined the Sullivans for a drink. Once inside, Mr Sullivan made several advances towards Mrs W. when his wife was in a different room. He suggested that they have a "threesome," which Mrs W. declined. When Mrs Sullivan rejoined them, Mr Sullivan suggested that the three of them live together. Mrs Sullivan rejected the suggestion and helped her husband to his room. The accused claims that while in the bedroom his wife said "I don't love you. It's S. I love. Now go to bed."

Mrs Sullivan and her friend had talked for 5 or 10 minutes when Mrs W. decided to leave. As she gathered her belongings, she observed the Sullivans at the front door. She reported that she saw a flash, heard a loud noise, and then saw Mrs Sullivan fall to the ground. Mr Sullivan was standing over his wife with a gun in his hand. When she asked if he had shot Maureen, he replied that he had. Mr Sullivan then pointed the gun at Mrs W. and ordered her to go to the bedroom and disrobe. After arguing with Mrs W., Mr. Sullivan called 911.

At trial, Mr Sullivan raised the defence of legal insanity (not criminally responsible on account of mental disorder). The defence called a psychologist and a psychiatrist to provide expert testimony that Mr Sullivan was in a dissociative state at the time of the offence. Further, the experts noted that while in this state, Mr Sullivan would not have had the ability to appreciate the nature and consequences of the acts he committed. By contrast, the psychiatrist called by the Crown stated that Mr Sullivan's drinking, leading up to and at the time of the offence, may have contributed to his behaviour.

However, the psychiatrist doubted that Mr Sullivan had suffered "dissociation."

In the end, the jury found Mr Sullivan not criminally responsible on account of mental disorder. He spent very little time in hospital and is living in the community.

> I may appeal to all who hear me, whether there are any causes more difficult, or, which, indeed, so often confound the learning of the judges themselves, as when insanity, or the effects and consequences of insanity, become the subjects of legal consideration and judgment.
>
> (R. v. Hadfield, 1800)

Several years ago, during the first lecture in a seminar on mental health law and insanity, the first author asked his students why they decided to take the class. One young man, dressed radically with colour-streaked hair, answered, "so I can learn to use the insanity defence." On the last day of the class the same student stayed behind to talk to the professor. He told him that after having taken the class he was embarrassed about the remark he had made on the first day, and said that he realized just how serious the consequences were of being found not guilty by reason of insanity. This student's initial comment reflects the general public's perception of the insanity defence, or what we now call in Canada the not criminally responsible on account of mental disorder defence (NCRMD). Indeed, when someone is found NCRMD, there is often a public outcry that the person has "got off." The *Sullivan* case, presented above, provides a good example. As this chapter will show, the legal system has evolved to a point where, if a person was mentally ill at the time of committing an offence and unable to know what he or she was doing, to know that it was wrong, or to control his or her behaviour, the person can be found NCRMD. Similarly, if a person is so mentally ill that he or she is incapable of participating in his or her defence, or of communicating with a lawyer, courts can find the person unfit to stand trial.

This chapter begins with an introduction to criminal responsibility (legal insanity) and fitness to stand trial. We then turn to a discussion of assessment orders as they relate to both fitness and criminal responsibility and to the role of mental health professionals in fitness and criminal responsibility assessments. Finally, the empirical research pertaining to fitness and criminal responsibility, particularly that which is available in Canada, will be presented.

INTRODUCTION AND OVERVIEW OF THE INSANITY DEFENCE

An immediate question that comes to mind whenever one considers the insanity defence is simple: Why? That is, why do we need an insanity defence? One is hard-pressed to find a more simple answer to this question than that offered by Judge Bazelon in *Durham v. United States* (1954): "The legal and moral traditions of the western world require that those who, of their own free will and with evil intent (sometimes called *mens rea*), commit acts which violate the law, shall be criminally responsible for those acts. Our traditions also require that where such acts stem from and are the product of a mental disease or defect as those terms are used herein, moral blame shall not attach, and hence there will not be criminal responsibility" (p. 876).

As the above excerpt hints, the notion of "madness" can be traced far back in history; however, exculpating mentally ill people for their acts is a relatively recent phenomenon (Perlin, 1989; Walker, 1985). Although ancient Greeks and Romans recognized that some forms of mental illness may affect a person's behaviour, Plato reported in 350 B.C. that the mentally ill and their families were held responsible for the actions of the mentally ill (Walker, 1985). By the time the Justinian Digest, a collection of the doctrines of Roman jurists, was compiled into volumes around A.D. 230, however, it was held that "a madman [who] commit[s] homicide ... is excused by the misfortune of his fate" (cited in Walker, 1985, p. 26). Apparently, it was believed that the mentally ill should be excused because they did not have the capacity to form the requisite mens rea for a criminal act and they were already punished by virtue of their mental condition (Walker, 1985).

Similarly, Weiner (1985) wrote that the Mishna, from the Talmud, a collection of Jewish law written in the second century, contains a provision for exculpating people for their acts. Thus, there appears to have been widespread belief that the mentally ill were not generally to be held responsible for their actions.

The first recorded case of an individual being acquitted by reason of insanity in English law occurred in 1505 (Walker, 1968). Simon and Aaronson (1988) note that by the end of the sixteenth century, "the doctrine of the lack of a guilty mind (or felonious intent) – and hence, lack of criminal responsibility – was well established" (p. 10).

By the eighteenth century, courts were developing "wild beast" standards for acquitting mentally ill offenders. For example, in 1724 an English jury was instructed that an individual acquitted for insanity must be "totally deprived of his understanding and memory, and ... not know what he is doing, no more than an infant, than a brute, or a wild beast" (*R. v. Arnold*, 1724, pp. 764–765; see also, Perlin, 1989; Walker, 1985). In 1736 the well-known English jurist, Lord Hale, was among the first legal commentators in modern times to focus extensively on the subject of the insanity defence (Hale, 1847; Low, Jeffries, & Bonnie, 1986). Because of the difficulty of determining what level or state of insanity is required to cause a "total defect of understanding," Hale wrote that a person with a level of understanding less than that of a normal 14-year-old child is not responsible for his or her actions.

No real progress was made towards developing a uniform standard of insanity, however, until the nineteenth century. The modern approach to the insanity defence was established by the acquittals, by reason of insanity, of James Hadfield in 1800 and Daniel M'Naghten in 1843 (Moran, 1985). In the former case Hadfield, who had tried to shoot King George III, was charged with high treason. At trial, Hadfield pleaded insanity, arguing that he suffered from the delusion that King George III's death would cause the world to end with the Second Advent of Christ (Moran, 1985). The jury's verdict was as follows: "We find the prisoner is not guilty; he being under the influence of insanity at the time the act was committed" (Moran, 1985, p. 35). This phrase became abbreviated into the familiar "not guilty by reason of insanity" verdict, which remained until the revision of our law in 1992.

More important than the insanity standard employed, or the origin of the not guilty by reason of insanity phrase, was the fact that Hadfield's acquittal resulted in the passage of the Criminal Lunatics Act of 1800, which provided for the post-acquittal detention of accused found not guilty by reason of insanity (Moran, 1985). In addition, the Act allowed for the preventive detention of mentally ill people who had either committed criminal acts or were "found in circumstances that suggested criminal activity" (Moran, 1985, p. 35). From this point on, people acquitted of felonies by reason of insanity could be confined in a prison or secure mental hospital for the rest of their lives. As we will see later in this chapter, in Canada it was only in 1991 that the Supreme Court held that automatically confining people acquitted by reason of insanity to secure psychiatric facilities was unconstitutional (*R. v. Swain*, 1991).

The Case of Daniel M'Naghten

Ye people of England; exult and be glad,
For ye're now at the will of the merciless and mad.
Why say ye that but three authorities reign –
Crown, Commons, and Lords! – You omit the insane!
They're a privileg'd class, whom no statute controls,
And their murderous charter exists in their souls,
Do they wish to spill blood – they have only to play
A few pranks – get asylum'd a month and a day
– Then heigh! to escape from the mad-doctor's keys,
And to pistol or stab whomsoever they please.

Thomas Campbell[1]

Perhaps the best-known case regarding the insanity defence, at least until that of John W. Hinckley, Jr in the United States, is the case of Daniel M'Naghten (*R. v. M'Naghten*, 1843). In fact, it has been observed that the Hinckley and M'Naghten cases share some striking similarities (Kamisar, 1982).

Like Hinckley, Daniel M'Naghten's assassination target was the political leader of a nation. Instead of being Ronald Reagan, the president of the United States, however, M'Naghten's target was Sir Robert Peel, the prime minister of Great Britain. Just as Hinckley gravely wounded James Brady, M'Naghten mortally wounded the prime minister's private secretary, Edward Drummond, believing him to be the prime minister (Moran, 1981, 1985). When M'Naghten attempted to fire a second shot, he was arrested and charged with murder.

Daniel M'Naghten's father was able to secure a well-financed defence. The central issue in M'Naghten's case was the proper standard for establishing a legal defence of insanity. M'Naghten was apparently only "partly insane," and purportedly suffered from delusions concerning politics (Moran, 1981, 1985). Needless to say, the jury acquitted Daniel M'Naghten because of his insanity. M'Naghten was committed to Bethlem and, later, Broadmoor Mental Institution where he died approximately 20 years later at age 50 (Moran, 1985; Simon & Aaronson, 1988).

Again like *Hinckley*, as soon as the verdict in the *M'Naghten* case was announced, the public became alarmed that insane people could kill without fear of punishment (Moran, 1985). Queen Victoria[2] and members of the House of Lords also made their disapproval of the verdict known (Simon & Aaronson, 1988).

Just over 2 months after the decision in *M'Naghten* was made public, 15 common law judges in Great Britain were summoned to the House of Lords to help determine the proper standard for criminal responsibility of the criminally insane. Fourteen of the judges agreed that essentially the same standard employed in *M'Naghten* was the correct legal standard (Moran, 1985). The opinion delivered included the *M'Naghten* rules: "A person is presumed sane unless it can be clearly proven that, at the time of the committing of the act, the party accused was labouring under such a defect of reason, from disease of the mind, as not to know the nature and quality of the act he was doing; or, if he did know it, that he did not know he was doing what was wrong. The mode of putting the latter part of the question to the jury ... had generally been, *whether the accused at the time of doing the act knew the difference between right and wrong*" (R. v. M'Naghten (1843), 10 Cl. & Fin. at 203, 8 Eng. Rep. at 720, cited by Moran, 1985, p. 40).

There are three significant substantive elements of the *M'Naghten* standard. First, the decision maker must determine that the accused was suffering from "a defect of reason, from disease of the mind." Today, these words are interpreted to mean that the accused was suffering from a mental disorder. Next, the decision maker must decide whether the evidence shows that the accused did not "know" the "nature and quality of the act he was doing." Thus, the accused must not have *understood* exactly what he or she did. Finally, the *M'Naghten* standard also requires an inquiry to determine whether the accused knew "what he was doing was wrong." An accused who understands his or her act yet does not have the capability of knowing that the act was wrong may also be acquitted under the *M'Naghten* test. Because the final two elements require a subjective exploration of the accused's thinking, the *M'Naghten* test is referred to as a cognitive test of insanity (e.g., Low et al., 1986).

Almost immediately, the *M'Naghten* standard was employed in cases throughout England and the United States (Low et al., 1986). The substantive requirements of the M'Naghten rule are still being used by numerous jurisdictions around the world, including Canada and in many American states (Simon & Aaronson, 1988).

Alternatives to the M'Naghten Standard

The *M'Naghten* standard was by far the most common insanity defence standard employed throughout the latter half of the nineteenth and well into the twentieth century. A number of alternative tests, however, have been proposed in the United States, primarily to deal with the behavioural or "volitional" components of insanity. While it is beyond the scope of this book to discuss these alternative standards in detail, they will be briefly mentioned below.

Irresistible Impulse Test

This test grew out of commentators' discontent with the purely cognitive nature of *M'Naghten*. The idea that individuals should not be held legally responsible for their behaviour when their mental illnesses result in an inability to control it has come to be known as the "irresistible impulse" test (*Parsons v. State*, 1886). Because of its focus on the ability of an individual to control his or her behaviour, the irresistible impulse test, and other forms thereof, are known as "volitional" tests. Although this test did receive some support, it was largely criticized because there is no way to determine whether an accused was actually able to control his or her behaviour (e.g., *King v. Creighton*, 1908; Low et al., 1986).

The Product Test

M'Naghten was also criticized for its strict conceptualization of "mental disease or defect" (Slovenko, 1984). The standard literally requires that the accused must be suffering from a significant mental illness caused by a "disease of the mind." In favouring a broader conceptualization of mental illness, the Supreme Court of New Hampshire and the United States Court of Appeals for the District of Columbia found that people could not be held responsible for any behaviour that was a product of their mental illness (e.g., *Durham v. United States*, 1954; *State v. Jones*, 1871; *State v. Pike*, 1870).

Although the underlying concept of the *Durham* rule – that one is not criminally responsible for one's behaviour if it is a product of mental disease or mental defect – is quite straightforward, practical application of the standard proved to be more cumbersome. For example, it presupposes that a mentally ill person's behaviour is almost exclusively caused by his or her mental illness (Low et al., 1986). It is now generally accepted by many mental health professionals that a great many factors – in addition to mental illness – control human behaviour, even the behaviour of a mentally ill person. Critics also have noted that the *Durham* rule relied too heavily upon expert psychiatric testimony (e.g., Halleck, 1966; Hermann & Sor, 1983).

American Law Institute Standard of Insanity

Working under the auspices of the American Law Institute (ALI), several distinguished legal and medical professionals developed the standard for criminal responsibility that was adopted by the Model Penal Code in the United States (American Law Institute, 1962). The ALI subcommittee recognized that accused individuals could be found not guilty by reason of insanity for both cognitive and volitional reasons. The ALI standard, as set out in section 4.01 of the Model Penal Code, is as follows:

> (1) A person is not responsible for criminal conduct if at the time of such conduct as a result of mental disease or defect he lacks substantial capacity either to appreciate the criminality (wrongfulness) of his conduct or to conform his conduct to the requirements of law.
> (2) As used in this Article, the terms "mental disease of defect" do not include an abnormality manifested only by repeated criminal or otherwise anti-social conduct (ALI, 1962, §4.01).

Several of the U.S. states adopted the ALI test and the ALI standard was the standard in force in the District of Columbia when John Hinckley, Jr was tried.

The Present U.S. Federal Standard of Insanity

After 2 years of hearings following the *Hinckley* case, Congress passed the Insanity Defense Reform Act (IDRA) in 1984. The purpose of the changes was to narrow the grounds by which people could be found to be not guilty by reason of insanity. In essence, the IDRA had the effect of removing the volitional prong of the ALI rule – leaving it substantively like *M'Naghten*, with its focus on the accused's cognitions for purposes of determining whether he or she should be found not guilty by reason of insanity (Perlin, 1989).

The Guilty But Mentally Ill Verdict (GBMI)

The GBMI verdict holds the accused criminally responsible for his or her acts while recognizing that the accused is mentally ill. It is typically employed as an option in addition to the NGRI and guilty verdicts. The rationale for introducing the GBMI option was to reduce the number of insanity acquittals and to prevent the early release of NGRI acquittees (Comment, 1982). The GBMI verdict has been termed an "in-between classification," since accused individuals are neither acquitted nor found guilty in the traditional sense (*People v. Jackson*, 1977). To say the least, the introduction of the GBMI verdict has produced controversy. Some commentators argue that the verdict has been a success because it allows the accused to be held criminally responsible for their actions while enabling them to seek treatment (e.g., Mickenberg, 1987). Critics maintain that the GBMI verdict is "an idea whose time should not have come" (Slobogin, 1985). Slobogin argues that the GBMI verdict is an overreaction to a problem that does not exist – the insanity defence does not allow dangerous accused to simply "get off." Further, those found GBMI are often not given appropriate psychiatric treatment (McGraw, Farthing-Capowich, & Keilitz, 1985; Melton, Petrila, Poythress, & Slobogin, 1997). It is also argued that the verdict only confuses jurors and enables them to find a disproportionate number of accused "guilty" – even innocent ones (Savitsky & Lindblom, 1986).

The Not Criminally Responsible on Account of Mental Disorder Defence in Canada

As a common law country and former colony of Great Britain, Canada's insanity defence standard is an adaptation of the M'Naghten standard, which was adopted in Canada through case law and the Criminal Code in 1894. The insanity standard remained unchanged for almost a century. In 1991, however, in the case of *R. v. Swain*, the insanity defence was challenged on a number of grounds and following the *Swain* case, the Supreme Court of Canada gave Parliament 6 months to change the law. Bill C-30 subsequently altered the legislation governing mentally disordered offenders. In addition to more fundamental changes to the detention of insanity acquittees, the name of the defence was changed from not guilty by reason of insanity (NGRI) to not criminally responsible on account of mental disorder (NCRMD) and the wording of the standard was revised. Despite the change in wording, however, the standard has not changed substantively. Section 16 of the Criminal Code currently outlines the standard as follows: "No person is criminally responsible for an act committed or an omission made while suffering from a mental disorder that rendered the person incapable of appreciating the nature and quality of the act or omission or of knowing that it was wrong." Everyone is presumed not to suffer from a mental disorder so as to be exempt from criminal responsibility until the contrary is proved on the balance of probabilities. Thus, the party who raises the issue has the burden of proving on a balance of probabilities (see Chapter 2) that the accused was suffering from a mental disorder so as to be exempt from criminal responsibility.

In *R. v. Swain* the Supreme Court of Canada ruled that permitting the Crown to raise the issue of criminal responsibility against the wishes of the accused infringes an accused's rights under section 7 (the right to life, liberty, and security of the person) of the Charter. The Crown may only raise the issue under one of two conditions: after the verdict of guilty has been handed down or if the defence raises the issue of the accused's mental state for any purpose. For example, once an accused is found guilty, the Crown could choose to argue that the accused was not criminally responsible at the time of the offence if it believes that the accused requires psychiatric treatment. In practice this rarely, if ever, happens. The second condition under which the Crown can raise the issue of criminal responsibility above the defence's objections is if the defence mentions in their case that the accused was mentally ill. Again, in practice, this happens infrequently.

Although the insanity standard has remained virtually unchanged in its meaning since the M'Naghten standard was introduced, how the defence should be applied has never been clear. Many of the elements contained in the insanity standard are open to more than one interpretation. For example, the meaning of the word "wrong" employed in the standard has been a source of controversy, with courts becoming involved in the debate. In 1977, in the case of *R. v. Schwartz*, the court determined that "wrong" means wrong according to law and not morally wrong. More recently, however, the Supreme Court of Canada decided in *R. v. Chaulk* (1990) that the word "wrong" in section 16 should be interpreted to include morally wrong.

Prior to the Criminal Code changes in 1992, individuals successfully raising the insanity defence were automatically detained in an institution for an indeterminate period of time. In the *Swain* case (1991), the Supreme Court of Canada ruled that indeterminate detention infringed upon the rights of the accused. Currently, under the Criminal Code, where a verdict of not criminally responsible on account of mental disorder is rendered the court may either make a disposition with respect to the accused (s. 672.45) or defer disposition to the review board (s. 672.47). If the court defers to the review board the board must hold a hearing and make a disposition as soon as possible and not later than 45 days after the verdict was rendered (672.47). Under exceptional circumstances, the hearing time may be extended to a maximum of 90 days after the verdict was rendered (s. 672.47).

As with the dispositions for unfit offenders, in making a disposition in respect of an accused found NCRMD, the court or review board must take into consideration the need to protect the public from dangerous individuals, the mental condition of the accused, the reintegration of the accused into society, and other needs of the accused. Several disposition options are available to individuals found NCRMD, including: absolute discharge, which is required by law if the accused is found not to be a "significant threat" to the public; conditional discharge; or detention in hospital (s. 672.54).

INTRODUCTION AND OVERVIEW OF FITNESS TO STAND TRIAL

The doctrine of fitness can be traced back to early English statutes which stipulate that an accused must demonstrate the capacity to defend him- or herself against his or her accusers (Bittman & Convit, 1993). The rationale behind the requirement that an accused be considered fit to stand trial is that "an accused individual must be protected from a conviction that could have resulted from a lack of participation or capacity to make proper judgment" (Roesch, Eaves, Sollner, Normandin, & Glackman, 1981). The degree of capacity required for fitness, however, has been difficult to determine over the years (Whittemore & Ogloff, 1994). It was not until 1992 that the Criminal Code specifically defined the standard to be applied. The absence of guidelines for determining fitness resulted in a reliance on case law to determine the criteria that should be applied. The case of *R. v. Pritchard* (1836) has often been cited as the classic case for the determination of fitness (P.S. Lindsay, 1977). The judge in the *Pritchard* case ruled that three main issues must be determined: "First, whether the prisoner is mute of malice or not; secondly, whether he can plead to the indictment or not; thirdly, whether he is of sufficient intellect to comprehend the course of the proceedings on the trial, so as to make a proper defence – to know that he might challenge any of you to whom he may object – and to comprehend the details of the evidence, which in a case of this nature must constitute a minute investigation" (p. 306). Following from the criteria defined in *Pritchard*, Lindsay (1977) identified three issues that should be determined in a fitness assessment. First, is the accused able to assist in his or her defence? Second, does the accused understand his or her role in the proceedings? Finally, does the accused understand the nature or object of the proceedings?

Mental health professionals are often called upon to conduct fitness and criminal responsibility assessments. While similar issues may arise throughout the evaluation of each, the two concepts are distinct and call for different questions to be answered. An evaluation of fitness to stand trial requires the examiner to assess the accused's current mental condition and determine whether it interferes with his or her ability to perform the legal tasks related to the trial process (outlined in s. 2 of the Criminal Code). Alternatively, assessments of criminal responsibility require the examiner to determine the accused's mental state at the time of the offence and whether the accused's condition interfered with his or her ability to appreciate the offence in question.

The terms under which an individual may be determined fit to stand trial can be found in section 2 of the Criminal Code: "'Unfit to stand trial' means unable on account of mental disorder to conduct a defence at any stage of the proceedings before a verdict is rendered or to instruct counsel to do so, and, in particular, unable on account of mental disorder to: (a) understand the nature or object of the proceedings, (b) understand the possible consequences of the proceedings, or (c) communicate with counsel." An accused is presumed fit to stand trial unless the court is satisfied on a balance of probabilities that he or she is unfit (s. 672.22). The party raising the issue has the burden of proving the issue of unfitness (s. 672.23).

Following the introduction of this standard into the Criminal Code, case law has defined more specifically the elements required for determining the accused's ability to communicate with counsel. In *R. v. Taylor* (1992), the Ontario Court of Appeal held that the test to be applied in determining this issue is one of "limited cognitive capacity" (p. 567). In adopting this standard, the court indicated that the accused need only have the ability to recount to his or her lawyer the facts relating to the offence that would enable the lawyer to properly present the case. The court stipulated that the accused need not have the ability to act in his or her own best interest, as this was found to be too strict a test.

If an accused is found fit to stand trial, the proceedings against him or her will continue. Following the finding of fitness, the accused may be ordered to be detained in custody until the completion of the trial, if there is reason to believe that he or she may become unfit if released from hospital (s. 672.49). If the accused is found unfit to stand trial, the court may make a disposition if it can do so readily, otherwise the review board must make a disposition within 45 days. Taking into account public protection, the reintegration of the accused into society, and the accused's mental condition, the review board has three disposition options: (i) conditional discharge, (ii) detention in hospital, or (iii) a treatment order (s. 673.54).

ROLE OF MENTAL HEALTH PROFESSIONALS IN FITNESS ASSESSMENTS

Assessment Orders

Under the Criminal Code, an accused may be remanded for an assessment of his or her mental condition if the court has reasonable grounds to believe that such an assessment is necessary to determine, among other things, whether the accused is fit to stand trial and/or whether the accused is not criminally responsible on account of mental disorder (s. 672.11). If an accused is remanded for a fitness assessment the duration of the assessment should not exceed 5 days (s. 672.14), but the assessment period may be increased to 30 days where "compelling circumstances exist" or where the accused's consent has been obtained (s. 672.14). Assessment orders for determining criminal responsibility should not exceed 30 days, but again this period may be increased to 60 days where "compelling circumstances exist." The Criminal Code stipulates that the assessment should occur out of custody unless the prosecutor or medical practitioner provides evidence to suggest that custody is necessary (s. 672.16)

Research has examined remands in practice. In British Columbia investigation of remand procedures for the 1992–1993 and 1993–1994 fiscal years revealed that 653 individuals were remanded for assessments of criminal responsibility and/or fitness assessments during the 2-year time periods (Roesch, Ogloff, Hart, Dempster, Zapf, & Whittemore, 1997). Sixty-one per cent were remanded for fitness evaluation only, 15% were remanded for criminal responsibility only, and 24% were remanded for assessments of both fitness and criminal responsibility. Eighty-eight per cent were remanded for inpatient evaluation, while only 12% were remanded for outpatient evaluation. Individuals remanded for fitness were held on average for 16.5 days; those remanded for criminal responsibility were held on average for 22.6 days (Roesch et al., 1997). Thus, although the law stipulates that assessment should occur out of custody, the majority of evaluations continue to be conducted on an inpatient basis and individuals remanded for fitness tend to be held longer in custody than the 5-day period specified in the Criminal Code.

Similar findings have been demonstrated in Alberta (Arboleda-Florez, Crisanti, & Holley, 1995). An examination of individuals remanded during the 1992–1993 fiscal year revealed that 347 individuals were remanded for inpatient assessments during this time period and virtually all of these were for the purpose of assessing fitness to stand trial. These authors stipulate, however, that criminal responsibility may have been assessed during the course of the fitness evaluation, with the result that a formal request for an assessment of criminal responsibility need not have been made. Results further demonstrate that the average duration of the assessment far exceeded 5 days, with a median of 22 days.

Assessment

Mental health professionals are frequently called upon by the courts to evaluate whether an individual is fit to stand trial. While fitness has often been equated with serious mental disorder, mental disorder is necessary but not sufficient for a finding of unfitness (Hess & Thomas, 1963; McGarry, 1965; Roesch, 1979; Roesch & Golding, 1980). Mental disorder is related to fitness only to the extent that it affects the accused's abilities to perform the functions laid down in section 2 of the Criminal Code.

In the past, the criteria for determining fitness have been vague (Lindsay, 1977; Webster, Menzies, & Jackson, 1982). While the Criminal Code lists the necessary elements of fitness it fails to provide the details required to meet each of the three criteria. For example, what specific abilities are required for an individual to understand the nature of the proceedings? Much of the work in the development of assessment instruments has taken place in the United States (see Grisso, 1986 for a review). The standard for incompetent (the American term for fitness to stand trial), in the United States is slightly different from the Canadian counterpart. The current American standard originates from the 1960 U.S. Supreme Court decision in *Dusky v. U.S.*, requiring an examination of whether the accused has "sufficient present ability to consult with his lawyer with a reasonable degree of rational understanding" and a "rational as well as factual understanding of the proceedings against him." It has been argued that the American standard is higher than the Canadian standard since in Canada, as discussed previously, the accused need only demonstrate "limited cognitive capacity" (*R. v. Taylor*, 1992).

In Canada two instruments (see Box 10.1) – the Fitness Interview Test (FIT; Roesch, Webster, & Eaves, 1984) and the Fitness Interview Test-Revised (FIT-R; Roesch, Webster, & Eaves, 1994) – have been developed to assist mental health professionals in assessing the legal issues involved in a fitness assessment in addition to the mental health component.

Box 10.1

Psychological Assessment of Fitness to Stand Trial

The Fitness Interview Test (FIT; Roesch, Webster, & Eaves, 1984) and the Fitness Interview Test-Revised (FIT-R; Roesch, Zapf, Webster, & Eaves, 1999) go a long way towards delineating the specific abilities required for an individual to be found fit to stand trial. Specifically, the FIT-R is composed of three sections. The first section is designed to evaluate an individuals' understanding of the nature and object of the proceedings. As such it assesses an individual's understanding of the following components: the arrest process, the nature and severity of the current charges, the role of key players in the court, issues in the legal process, pleas available and consequences of pleas, and court procedures. The second section evaluates an individual's understanding of the possible consequences of the proceedings, including the range and nature of possible penalties, the available legal defences, and the likely outcome. The third section assesses an individual's ability to communicate with counsel. In particular, this section addresses the accused's capacity to communicate facts to a lawyer, relate to a lawyer, plan a legal strategy, engage in his or her own defence, challenge prosecution witnesses, testify relevantly, and manage courtroom behaviour.

Once each of the three legal sections is evaluated, the interviewer conducts an overall assessment of fitness to stand trial. The first task is to determine whether the accused is currently suffering from a mental disorder as defined in case law. The second task is to assess whether the accused is impaired on any one of the three legal sections of the FIT-R. If the accused has a mental disorder and the mental disorder results in impairment on any one of the three legal components, then the accused would be found unfit to stand trial.

The FIT-R was designed as a screening measure and as such it should overestimate the number of individuals found unfit to stand trial. A comparison of the FIT-R with institution-based decisions of fitness revealed that 100% of individuals found fit by the FIT-R were found fit by psychiatrists. Alternatively, of those individuals found unfit by the FIT-R, 80% were found fit by psychiatrists and 20% were found unfit by psychiatrists (Zapf & Roesch, 1997). Overall, these results suggest that the FIT-R reliably screens out those individuals who are clearly fit to stand trial.

Unlike insanity evaluations, fitness to stand trial does not typically require a retrospective assessment. Exceptions to this general case have been noted by Miller and Germain (1988) where the question of competency is raised after a conviction. Most commonly, however, the evaluation centres on the accused's present capacities to perform specific functions. Focus on the present abilities of the accused make assessment of fitness less onerous than attempts to assess past mental state, as required in insanity evaluations.

Treatment

Individuals found unfit to stand trial are typically held in hospital prior to a determination of their guilt or innocence. The goal of treatment should be to restore the individual to fitness with as little delay as possible. The traditional approach to the treatment of unfit individuals has been medication (Siegel & Elwork, 1990); it is assumed that once the mental disorder is under control, the individual will be restored to competence. To be found fit, however, an individual is required to perform a number of specific tasks. An inability to perform these tasks results in unfitness and treatment planning for unfit accused requires a consideration of the possible reasons an individual may be found unfit. Treatment planning should follow naturally from the assessment of fitness.

As with the assessment of fitness/competence, much of the work in the development of treatment programs has occurred in the United States. While in Canada the use of medication is relied upon almost exclusively to treat unfit individuals, there has been a move in the United States towards offering problem-oriented treatment that focuses on the functional abilities of incompetence. Davis (1985) and Pendleton (1980) described similar approaches for the treatment of individuals found incompetent to stand trial. Davis (1985) recommended an individualized treatment program, suggesting that treatment planning should address the specific reasons the individual was found incompetent. Treatment should focus on functional behaviour that addresses the individual's ability to (1) understand the nature and object of the proceedings, (2) understand the possible consequences of the proceedings, and/or (3) rationally communicate with counsel and participate in his or her own defence. After an understanding of the area of deficiency is noted, individuals may be grouped according to the bases of their deficiency, such as low intellectual functioning, or psychotic-confused behaviour, which is designed to further enhance the focus on the special needs of each group.

For example, the treatment approach taken by Pendleton (1980) focuses on eliminating or reducing those symptoms that interfere with an accused's ability to stand trial. More specifically, treatment is designed to assist an individual's understanding of the court process and proceedings and to develop relationship skills essential for the accused to communicate and cooperate with his or her lawyer. Unique to this treatment approach is the development of a mock trial in which the patient is exposed to a simulated courtroom situation tailored to his or her own case.

Some researchers in the United States have compared a functional, problem-oriented approach with the more traditional practice of medication. Siegel & Elwork (1990) found that treatment focusing on the functional capacities required for competence in addition to medication was more effective in restoring an individual's competence to stand trial than medication alone in psychotic individuals.

Characteristics of Individuals Referred for Fitness Assessments

Individuals referred for fitness assessments are best characterized as single, unemployed men living alone. The majority of these individuals also demonstrate a history of psychiatric problems and previous psychiatric hospitalizations. While many accused referred for fitness evaluations are charged with serious offences such as murder and assault, an equal if not larger number are charged with property offences and other non-violent crimes (Roesch et al., 1981). Indeed, Bittman and Convit (1993) found that individuals found incompetent were more frequently charged with misdemeanours than with felonies, and for non-violent rather than violent crimes. The implication of this finding is that many of these individuals, if convicted, would not be sent to prison, and if they were sent to prison they would be likely to receive relatively short sentences. The concern, as addressed by Roesch and his colleagues (1981) is that individuals found unfit for trial may spend a longer time in an institution than they would if found guilty and sent to prison.

Some researchers have attempted to evaluate the differences between fit and unfit accused. These differences can be categorized into three domains: demographic, criminological and mental health characteristics. In general, in terms of demographics, unfit individuals are more likely to have been living alone, transient, or living in a hotel at the time of arrest than their fit counterparts. Early research has revealed no significant difference between fit and unfit accused in terms of the type of offence committed (Roesch et al., 1981). Additionally, research reveals that there is no relationship between the seriousness of the index offence and the fitness determination (Daniel, Beck, Herath, Schmitz, & Menninger, 1984). With respect to mental health, considerable research suggests that individuals found unfit to stand trial are more likely to receive a diagnosis of psychosis than those found fit for trial (Cooke, 1969; Roesch, 1979; Roesch et al., 1981). Daniel and colleagues (1984) found that a diagnosis involving psychotic disorder was the most important variable distinguishing competent from incompetent accused. It is important to note, however, that not all unfit accused receive such a diagnosis. Thus, psychosis cannot be equated with unfitness. Additionally, while both fit and unfit accused are characterized as having a history of psychiatric hospitalizations, research has indicated that unfit accused are more likely than those found fit to present with such a history (Roesch, 1979). Psychological testing reveals that individuals found unfit are more likely to demonstrate somewhat lower IQs and higher scores on the depression, hysteria, paranoia, psychasthenia, schizophrenia, and anxiety scales of the Minnesota Multiphasic Personality Inventory (MMPI; Cooke, 1969).

As described by observations on the ward of forensic facilities, unfit individuals are more likely than fit individuals to be seen as preoccupied, verbally abusive, hostile, and likely to commit physical assault. These individuals are also more likely to be viewed as restless, socially isolated, talking to themselves, having incoherent or disorganized speech, and engaging in inappropriate laughter and bizarre gestures (Roesch et al., 1981). Additionally, unfit individuals are more likely to be characterized as having delusions, hallucinations, impaired judgment, and incoherent or confused speech (Roesch, 1979; Roesch et al., 1981). Unfit accused are also viewed as restless, evasive, and resentful more frequently than fit accused (Roesch et al., 1981).

Much of the research assessing the characteristics of unfit accused, and the differences between individuals deemed fit and unfit, was conducted a number of years ago. Changes to the fitness evaluation procedure may have occurred with the introduction of the legislation defining unfitness. More current research would help to determine if these differences still exist today.

THE ROLE OF MENTAL HEALTH PROFESSIONALS IN CRIMINAL RESPONSIBILITY ASSESSMENTS

Assessment

The standard for determining criminal responsibility is complex and has been a frequent cause of confusion among both legal and mental health professionals. Against the backdrop of ambiguous criteria lie the problems encountered in attempts to investigate the accused's past mental condition.

As should be clear from the standard set out in section 16 of the Criminal Code, a mental disorder is necessary but not sufficient to render someone not criminally responsible. It must also be determined that the individual was incapable of knowing that the act or omission was wrong, or incapable of appreciating the nature and quality of the act. It is likely to be more difficult to determine the accused's cognitive capacity to know or appreciate than it is to discern whether the individual was suffering from a mental disorder at the time of the offence.

The criminal responsibility standard requires an assessment of the accused's mental state at the time of the offence. This type of retrospective assessment is difficult even under ideal circumstances (Ogloff, Roberts, & Roesch, 1993; Rogers, 1986). An evaluation of criminal responsibility is "an investigative endeavour which attempts to retrospectively reconstruct the cognitive, conative, emotional, motivational, and psychopathological concomitants and determinants of the accused's behaviour at the time of the crime" (Ogloff et al., 1993, p. 169). Ogloff and his colleagues (1993) recommend an enquiry into multiple domains including the psycho-social history of the accused, the present mental status, and the accused's mental state at the time of the offence. Mental health professionals should rely on multiple sources for this information.

There have been few tests developed for the measurement of criminal responsibility and those that do exist have been developed for use in the United States. Realizing the utility of a brief screening instrument, Slobogin and his colleagues developed the Mental State at the Time of the Offense Screening Evaluation (MSE; Slobogin, Melton, & Showalter, 1984). The purpose of the instrument was to "screen out" those individuals whose conduct clearly was not caused by "significant mental abnormality." The MSE is composed of three sections. The first section is designed to elicit information regarding the accused's general psychological history. The questions are designed to identify the presence of any disorder that might form the basis for a legal defence. The second section poses questions about the alleged offence and seeks to determine first, whether significant mental abnormality occurred at the time of the offence, and second, whether such abnormality, if it did exist, influenced the accused's actions. A mental status examination is the focus of the third section; the accused's present mental state may provide important clues about his or her past mental state. Research suggests that the MSE is effective in screening out those individuals who lack the requisite impairment to form the defence of insanity (Slobogin, et al., 1984).

The Rogers Criminal Responsibility Assessment Scales (R-CRAS; Rogers, 1984) have been developed to "systematically quantify critical psychological and situational variables at the time of the crime and to apply a decision model for the determination of sanity" (p. 22). The composition of 30 assessment criteria is designed to standardize the assessment of criminal responsibility, as traditional evaluations are often performed in an idiosyncratic manner, varying in both content and clinical method employed (Rogers & Ewing, 1992).

Treatment

Psychotropic medication is the primary treatment provided in most institutions for individuals found NCRMD. Other treatment programs, such as individual or group counselling, social skills training, occupational and recreational therapy, are often made available to NCRMD acquittees; however, attendance in such programs is frequently undocumented (Golding, Eaves, & Kowaz, 1989). Consequently there is a paucity of research examining the effects of such treatment programs.

Research examining the effectiveness of medication reveals that a significant change in the mental status of the individual occurs between unfitness admission and fitness discharge, and almost no change occurs between other points in time. It appears that the majority of change occurs within the first 6 months of receiving medication, and little change in the level of psychopathology takes place after this time (Golding, Eaves, & Kowaz, 1989).

EMPIRICAL RESEARCH ON THE INSANITY DEFENCE[3]

"Rivers of ink, mountains of printers' lead, and forests of paper have been expended on this issue, which is surely marginal to the chaotic problems of effective, rational and humane prevention of crime" (Morris, 1968, p. 514). It is an understatement to say that there has been a great deal of controversy over the insanity defence. Little research has been conducted in Canada generally, and even less has been conducted on NCRMD acquittees since the legislation was changed in 1992. The research that does exist has been conducted on NGRI acquittees, often in the United States, and is at least somewhat comparable to that which might be obtained with NCRMD acquittees in Canada.

Most of the controversy surrounding the insanity defence has been legal and generally beyond the realm of empirical research. Traditionally, the insanity defence controversy has focused on a legal, moral, or philosophical discussion of what the standard should be. This approach largely overlooks the general impact of insanity defence standards and it overlooks the impact of the language of the insanity standard on the trier of fact (judge or jury). As described by Ogloff, Schweighofer, Turnbull, and Whittemore (1992), however, a substantial amount of empirical research does exist and it falls into five general categories. First, investigators have described the general demographic characteristics of people found NGRI. Second, they have studied detention and release patterns of persons found NGRI. Third, recidivism of NGRI acquittees has been examined. Fourth, empirical research has been conducted on the impact of the insanity defence standards themselves. Finally, researchers have investigated the common perceptions of the insanity defence.

Demographic Characteristics of Persons Found NGRI/NCRMD

The studies that have examined the demographic characteristics of people found NGRI paint a fairly consistent portrait across jurisdictions and despite differing definitions of legal insanity. On the whole, it appears that the popular perception of the NGRI acquittee as a crafty con fooling the system or a mad killer randomly attacking victims bears little resemblance to reality. The NGRI acquittee is usually a seriously disturbed and marginalized member of society. Indeed, the modal NGRI acquittee is a white single male in his late twenties or early thirties with a history of previous hospitalization and/or arrest. He is likely unemployed and lacks a Grade 12 education. He is typically psychotic and tends to have committed a non-violent rather than a violent crime. In addition, it is important to remember that statistics on NGRI crimes reflect original charges; in many cases plea bargaining and other negotiations would likely have reduced the charges against the accused had insanity not been at issue. Thus, charge lists against NGRI acquittees are probably biased towards serious and violent crimes.

A study by Hodgins (1983) provides some information on Canadian NGRI acquittees in Quebec. Unfortunately, Hodgins's sample of 225 includes both NGRI acquittees and those found unfit to stand trial. She notes, however, that "these ... groups of subjects differed little." Her findings are similar to those typically found in American studies. For example, 87% of her sample were male, the average age for the men was 32, their average education level was Grade 8, and 78% were unemployed. Only 10% of the men were married or in common law relationships. Among the women, the average age was 40, average education level was Grade 7, and 93% were unemployed. Thirty-four per cent of the women were living as part of a couple.

The majority (60%) of Hodgins's sample had previously been hospitalized, while a minority (39%) had previously been arrested, with only 19% of these earlier crimes of a violent nature. Fully 45% of the sample were adjudicated incompetent or NGRI for a current crime that was of a violent nature. Given that this figure includes a variety of violent crimes we can only assume that murder represents some fraction of the 45%. Other studies have found that murderers constitute only a minority of those found NGRI. Of the violent crimes, most of the victims (64%) were known by their alleged aggressor. Consistent with most of the American studies, Hodgins found that a majority (76%) of her sample were diagnosed as psychotic. Similar findings were obtained in a study conducted by Rice and Harris (1990) in Ontario.

Detention and Release Patterns of Persons Found NGRI/NCRMD

Steadman (1985) points out three important factors to consider when examining the detention time of NGRI acquittees. First, as mentioned above, NGRI offence charges are arrest charges and not necessarily indicative of the conviction rates that would result from plea bargaining and others factors in the legal process. This is significant since comparison groups of convicted criminals typically will have plea bargained their charges. In New York, for instance, 92% of all criminal felony convictions are plea bargains. It is thus reasonable to expect that many NGRI acquittees may have served less time in a criminal facility than their NGRI offence would indicate. A second issue to keep in mind when comparing NGRI acquittees to other groups is that each group may not be released at the same rate. If only 30% of an NGRI group is released at follow-up, compared to 90% of a felon group, then the majority of NGRI acquittees would still be accumulating detention time. Thus it is often difficult to determine the actual length of detention for an entire sample of NGRI acquittees. Finally, it should also be remembered that hospitalization is ostensibly based on both therapeutic and protective concerns. Depending on the specific jurisdiction being examined, and the criteria for release employed therein, release is contingent upon both the remission of abnormal symptomology and the belief that the person is no longer dangerous.

Research in the United States indicates that NGRI acquittees are detained for variable lengths of time, but generally more serious charges result in longer post-acquittal hospitalizations. While the average length of detention is sometimes less than that of matched felon groups, there is great variability. It seems highly likely that a large number of NGRI acquittees are detained longer than is necessary to satisfy treatment and protection requirements, and indeed that many are hospitalized for longer periods than they would have been detained in correctional facilities had they been found guilty in a trial free of insanity considerations (Ogloff et al., 1992).

The ramifications of the insanity defence in Canada have been detailed by Golding, Eaves, and Kowaz (1989), who obtained outcome information on the 188 persons found NGRI in British Columbia between 1975 and 1983. Noting that the constitutionally permitted purpose of detaining people who have been found NGRI/NCRMD is to treat an accused's mental illness and protect both the accused and society from his or her potential future dangerousness, Golding and his colleagues point out that 60% of their sample were hospitalized and treated as unfit before being found NGRI. Since this initial fitness (competency to stand trial) treatment lasted a median of 172 days, much longer than the probable response time to psychotropic medication, it is likely that in many cases successful treatment had already been achieved *before* an accused was confined as NGRI. Indeed, the authors provide evidence that the most significant improvements across a variety of measures occurred during the initial fitness treatment. Despite this, they report that the average individual spent slightly over $9\frac{1}{2}$ years in confinement or under supervision after being found NGRI. This figure is even more remarkable given the fact that approximately 30% of their sample was found NGRI for minor offences (e.g., nuisance crimes).

Golding and his colleagues also reported finding cases of insanity arising from a variety of offence categories, from minor offences such as nuisance charges and drugs to more serious crimes such as sexual assault and murder. However, they concluded that concern for public safety is an insignificant issue in at least 30% of cases, and detention/supervision times are especially contrary to humane or pragmatic considerations in these cases. Even for violent offenders, it seems unlikely that those successfully treated with medications required such long time periods to be rendered nondangerous. Thus, the legally sanctioned reasons for detainment of those found NGRI – treatment and protection – do not appear to be the only forces operating in release decisions.

Recidivism of NGRI/NCRMD Acquittees

Studies on the recidivism of NGRI acquittees indicate that there are variations across jurisdictions. Nevertheless, when compared to matched felons in the United States, people found NGRI tend to recidivate in roughly equal proportions (Ogloff et al., 1992). The re-arrest rates of NGRI acquittees have been found to range from a low of 9.6% to a high of 65%. These re-offence rates are not significantly different from matched comparison groups. Furthermore, the types of offences tend to be non-violent in nature, although it is probably the case that more non-violent than violent NGRI acquittees are released from hospitals, and are released sooner, so this latter finding is perhaps not surprising.

Hodgins (1983) examined the recidivism rate among Canadian NGRI acquittees and found that 36% of 176 discharged men were arrested on subsequent charges. She also found that more than 80% of the crimes committed during follow-up were non-violent in nature. Unfortunately, no data from a matched sample were provided. In another Canadian study, Golding and his colleagues (1989), in the British Columbia study described in the previous section, also followed NGRI acquittees after their release. They reported that, "62.9% of the individuals experience(d) a 'failure' of community tenure during outpatient supervision, marked by 2.4 hospitalizations" (p. 146). Golding et al. attributed these results to a natural, phasic re-cycling of mental disorder and to the intensive post-release supervision provided in British Columbia. They suggested that expensive criminologically based supervision is probably inappropriate for what is actually a mental health problem.

The Effects of Particular Insanity Defence Standards on the Insanity Acquittal Rate

The question of what effect a particular insanity defence standard has on the insanity acquittal rate is of utmost importance. Indeed, as has been noted elsewhere (Ogloff 1991a), judges, legislators, and commentators have demonstrated some preference for employing one standard in favour of the others. One apparent reason for this differential preference is that judges, legislators, and commentators implicitly believe that the various standards produce different acquittal results. To address this implicit assumption, some researchers have attempted to determine whether the choice of standard results in significantly different NGRI acquittal rates.

There are two general ways to investigate the effect that a particular insanity standard may have on the insanity defence acquittal rate. The first type of research is archival, or naturalistic, ensuring a high level of external validity (see Chapter 1). Researchers could, for instance, compare the insanity acquittal rate across the U.S. states that employ different tests. The other general way of investigating possible effects of the standard for insanity involves experimental analogue research. For example, the researcher could expose actual or simulated triers of fact (i.e., judge and/or jury) to excerpts from insanity defence trials, provide them with different standards of insanity, and have them decide whether they find that the accused is NGRI. These types of research could be considered as complementary rather than independent. Indeed, to the extent that consistency between the methods is achieved, one could be fairly certain that the results obtained were both externally valid and experimentally sound.

Little effort of any sort has been expended to test the impact of employing different insanity defence standards on the insanity acquittal rate. In most studies, it is simply impossible to evaluate all of the extraneous variables in order to determine the extent to which the insanity standard per se produces changes in the insanity acquittal rate. Until longitudinal studies employing time-series analytic procedures are used to compare the trends for insanity acquittal rates across jurisdictions, we will be unable to determine the effect that altering the standards has on the insanity acquittal rate. This type of research is extremely difficult to do, especially since some jurisdictions do not maintain the accurate records necessary to such archival research.

Because of the difficulties that arise when trying to prove causation based on archival work, some researchers have chosen to investigate the effect that different insanity defence instructions have on participants in a controlled laboratory setting, in which a true experimental design may be employed. Ogloff (1991a) investigated the effects of varying insanity defence standards (*M'Naghten* and ALI), the burden of proof (defence and prosecution), and the standard of proof (preponderance of the evidence, clear and convincing evidence, and beyond a reasonable doubt) on mock jurors' verdicts. In a series of two studies, Ogloff presented 403 participants with a videotaped re-enactment of a trial. The jury instructions participants received were complete pattern jury instructions that actual juries would receive in trials in which the insanity defence is at issue. After watching the videotaped trial and reading the insanity defence instructions, participants indicated their verdict for the accused. Consistent with previous studies, Ogloff found that the specific insanity defence standard employed did not have a significant effect on the verdicts of mock jurors. It was somewhat surprising, however, that varying the burden of proof and standard of proof also failed to produce significant differences in the participants' verdicts.

As Ogloff (1991a) and others demonstrate, altering the insanity defence standard has no significant effect on juror verdicts. In contrast, Finkel (1991) showed that changing jurors' verdict schemas by providing them with alternative options to guilty and NGRI does significantly change their verdicts. Finkel's results suggest that jurors do not merely make arbitrary verdicts about accused individuals: the participants in his study were able to make fine, and logical, distinctions regarding the accused's culpability and degree of disability of mind. Finkel's conclusions are supported by further results from the Ogloff (1991a) study. Ogloff (1991a) investigated the factors that mock jurors consider important in making decisions regarding the insanity defence and found that the legal criteria, as set out in the insanity defence standards, were not considered particularly important. Instead, jurors focus on other, perfectly logical, general factors – e.g., the accused's intent to harm, expert testimony, the accused's history of mental illness, the accused's remorse, etc. – when making their decisions.

Some researchers have investigated the extent to which jurors comprehend insanity instructions. Because of the general inaccessibility of actual jurors, these investigations generally employ mock jurors. In the Ogloff (1991a) study, mock jurors' comprehension of the insanity defence standards, burden of proof, and standard of proof were assessed. Ogloff used both a free recall and recognition approach. In the free recall task, participants were asked to write out, in as much detail as they could remember, the insanity defence standard with which they were presented (*M'Naghten* or ALI). Overall, participants were unable to remember the standards very well. The mean per cent of participants who were able to recall the standard correctly was approximately 30%. In the recognition task, where participants were presented with all of the elements from the ALI and *M'Naghten* standards in random order, participants had a great deal of difficulty correctly identifying the elements with which they were presented (highest = 18%, for the accused's acts were a result of mental disease or defect). Although still disconcertingly inaccurate, participants were better at identifying the correct burden of proof (63%) and the correct standard of proof (52%).

If mock jurors are unable to comprehend insanity instructions or burden and standard of proof instructions well, it must be difficult for them to apply the standards to the facts of the cases they are deciding. Nonetheless, jurors do make decisions regarding insanity. The question that arises, then, is what do jurors base their insanity defence decisions on, if not on the insanity instructions provided?

Research on the Public's Attitudes about the Insanity Defence

The public has always seemed troubled by a verdict of NGRI. In 1843, when Daniel M'Naghten was found NGRI for killing the private secretary of the British prime minister, the public rose up in protest (Moran, 1985). More than a century later, the verdict of NGRI in the case of John Hinckley, Jr resulted in a similar public outcry (Slovenko, 1984). The public has long regarded the insanity acquittal as a ticket to freedom (Slovenko, 1984). In fact, far from being a loophole, many have argued that the insanity defence seems better represented by "... a noose that holds the accused person more tightly than any determinate sentence that might have been imposed" (Coles & Grant, 1989).

Recently, public awareness of the NGRI plea has increased (Hans & Slater, 1984), in large part as the result of media coverage of recent NGRI verdicts. However, this increased awareness has not been based on accurate portrayals of the defence. Rarely does the public receive information regarding the criminally insane, but when it does, the focus is usually on those who commit violent crimes. For example, media examinations are most likely to focus on the notorious NGRI acquittees who are released and commit subsequent sensational crimes. Although such cases do exist, they represent but a small minority of all NGRI cases.

In response to questions regarding the disposition of insanity acquittees, many people correctly identify that the acquittee is sent to a psychiatric hospital (Hans & Slater, 1984). However, there is still some misconception regarding the length of time an individual will spend in an institution (Hans & Slater, 1984). Furthermore, there seems to be some distrust in the release procedures. For example, Hans and Slater (1984) found that only one-quarter of their respondents were confident that those found NGRI are released only after it is safe to do so, while the majority (89%), felt that "the insanity defense allows too many people out on the streets" (p. 403).

SUMMARY

As this chapter shows, the law surrounding fitness to stand trial and criminal responsibility has evolved over time and, most recently, in

Canada, there have been a number of changes to the procedures governing the operation of fitness and criminal responsibility. Generally speaking, the available research indicates that neither fitness to stand trial or criminal responsibility are employed more often than is appropriate. Furthermore, the research suggests that many of the public's attitudes toward the criminal responsibility defence are based on misinformation. Continued research is necessary in Canada to continue to gain an understanding of fitness and criminal responsibility and to evaluate the effect of the amendments to the Criminal Code which were enacted by Parliament in 1992.

The empirical findings reviewed in this chapter provide answers to many important questions about the insanity defence. The demographic characteristics of NGRI acquittees are generally inconsistent with public perceptions. Rather than being "brutal killers," many NGRI acquittees have long histories of serious mental illness and commit non-violent crimes. Rather than being an easy way to "get away" with crime, the insanity defence is raised in very few cases, and is successful in even fewer cases. Further, many NGRI acquittees are confined to mental hospitals for long periods of time – sometimes even longer than the time they would have served if they had been found guilty and sentenced for the crime with which they were charged. The re-arrest rates of NGRI acquittees do not appear to differ significantly from matched comparison groups of offenders, and the crimes for which they are re-arrested tend to be non-violent in nature. There is some evidence that the "failures" in the community are due to the nature of mental disorder as opposed to criminogenic factors. Thus, community mental health support and maintenance may be effective in reducing arrest rates.

Historically, the assassination (or attempted assassination) of public figures has often led to a public outcry, followed by revisions to the insanity defence standards. The research that has investigated the impact of varying insanity defence standards on jury verdicts, however, suggests that the legal standard per se does not have a significant effect on the acquittal rate. Varying the standard of proof and burden of proof does not seem to affect the acquittal rate either. Further, there is some evidence that jurors cannot accurately remember the insanity defence standards, the standard of proof, or burden of proof with which they were presented. Nonetheless, jurors appear to use complicated factors in making decisions about the insanity defence; and their decisions seem reasonable.

Even more disturbing than the gaps that remain in the knowledge base about the insanity defence is the fact that the public is confused and overly concerned about it. Contrary to the findings discussed in this chapter, the public believes that the insanity defence is used frequently and that it often serves as a loophole, enabling criminals to escape responsibility for crimes by pleading insanity. Finally, the public sees NGRI acquittees as violent murderers who reoffend if released. Thus, now that a knowledge base about the insanity defence is being developed, it is important that researchers and educators disseminate the research findings to ensure that the public become aware of the myths surrounding the insanity defence.

QUESTIONS FOR DISCUSSION

1. Unlike the United States, Canada has never adopted a volitional test of insanity or criminal responsibility. Reflecting on the criminal responsibility standard in use in Canada, do you believe the standard should be broadened to include an element that would allow for the acquittal of people who, on account of mental disorder, are unable to control their behaviour? Why or why not?
2. Some have argued that the insanity defence is a loophole that allows guilty people to go free. Using the material reviewed in this chapter, discuss whether this position is tenable. In your answer, consider both the legal standard for criminal responsibility and the procedure for dealing with people who have been found NCRMD.
3. The Ontario Court of Appeal and the Supreme Court of Canada have held that the cognitive standard for determining that an accused is unfit to stand trial is that of limited cognitive capacity. Based on your understanding of the doctrine of fitness, does this standard appear appropriate?
4. If, as this chapter shows, people's perceptions of the criminal responsibility defence and the doctrine of fitness to stand trial are largely based on myths, how could the public be persuaded to change their opinions? Based on the material reviewed in the chapter, what information would you use to help change people's minds?

RECOMMENDED READING

Ogloff, J.R.P., Roberts, C.F., & Roesch, R. (1993). The insanity defense: Legal standards and clinical assessment. *Journal of Applied and Preventive Psychology*, 2, 163–178.

Perlin, M.L. (1989). *Mental disability law: Civil and criminal.* Charlottesville, VA: The Mitchie Company.

Roesch, R., Ogloff, J.R.P., Hart, S.D., Dempster, R.J., Zapf, P.A., & Whittemore, K.E. (1997). The impact of Canadian Criminal Code changes on remands and assessments of fitness to stand trial and criminal responsibility in British Columbia. *Canadian Journal of Psychiatry, 42,* 509–514.

Simon, R.J., & Aaronson, D.E. (1988). *The insanity defense: A critical assessment of law and policy in the post-Hinckley era.* New York: Praeger.

Whittemore, K.E., & Ogloff, J.R.P. (1994). Fitness and competency issues in Canadian criminal courts: Elucidating the standards for mental health professionals. *Canadian Journal of Psychiatry, 39,* 198–210.

11. Violence and Risk Assessment

David R. Lyon, Stephen D. Hart, and Christopher D. Webster

On 24 August 1992, Valerie Fabrikant entered the engineering faculty at Concordia University, where he had held a teaching and research position for the previous 13 years. Inside the briefcase he was carrying were three hand-guns and countless rounds of ammunition. Initially, Fabrikant sought out both the chair of the mechanical engineering department as well as the dean who presided over the department, but both men were away. He then walked to his own office where he had arranged to meet Michael Hogben, the president of the Concordia faculty association. At the meeting, Hogben planned to deliver a directive stipulating the conditions by which Fabrikant would be permitted future access to the association's offices. This measure was taken in response to Fabrikant's increasingly aggressive behaviour towards many of the staff and faculty at the university. Hogben never got a chance to deliver the directive. Instead, Fabrikant withdrew a .38 calibre pistol from amongst the arsenal he had brought with him and proceeded to fire three shots into Hogben. In the events that followed, Fabrikant moved through the building, shooting various people as he went, before eventually barricading himself in an office with two hostages. In the office Fabrikant dialed 911, informing the operator he had "made several murders" and needed to speak with a television reporter. A short time later, as he put his gun down to adjust the telephone, Fabrikant was overwhelmed by the hostages and taken into custody by the police. In the final aftermath of the tragedy at Concordia, four people were dead, but the trauma of the events undoubtedly continue to haunt many more. (This summary is based on the 1994 article entitled "Dr. Fabrikant's Solution" by Morris Wolfe in Saturday Night.)

As you read the case of Valerie Fabrikant it may have brought a number of questions to mind. For instance, were there warning signs that could have alerted the administration at Concordia University that Fabrikant was an individual who posed a high risk for violence? If they had known of the situation, could mental health or law enforcement professionals have predicted accurately that Fabrikant would commit the acts he did? If Fabrikant was identified as potentially violent, could anything have been done to reduce the likelihood that he would act violently? All of these questions relate to the concept of risk assessment, a term that has been defined generally as "the process of identifying and studying hazards to reduce the probability of their occurrence" (Hart, 1998b, p. 122). This task is not unique to the psycholegal arena; risk assessment is a central theme in fields as diverse as law, medicine, business, and engineering (Menzies, Webster, & Hart, 1995). Obviously, the specific hazard of interest changes with the field, but the objectives are always the same: to identify and manage potentially damaging outcomes.

In this chapter, we will focus on risk assessment as it relates to violence. We begin with a brief examination of some conceptual issues surrounding the study of violence and its prevalence in Canadian society. Next, we review a few of the junctures within the Canadian legal context where risk assessments occur and some of the methodological difficulties associated with risk assessment research. Finally, we offer a discussion of established "risk markers" and the major approaches currently employed for conducting risk assessments.

DEFINING AND MEASURING VIOLENCE

Efforts to study the prevalence and nature of violence are plagued by a host of troublesome conceptual issues because it is such a complex behavioural phenomenon (Jackson, 1997; Monahan, 1981, 1995). One of the foremost issues researchers must grapple with is a suitable definition of violence. The prospective researcher must have some method for identifying "violent" acts from amongst the entire spectrum of behaviours that might be observed. Frequently, violence is construed as any actual physical act causing harm or injury to another person. By stressing the consequences of the act, however, this definition may be unnecessarily narrow, excluding other important factors like the intent of the perpetrator or the potential for harm. For example, firing a gun at someone is a seemingly violent act regardless of whether or not the intended target is actually hit. More expansive definitions often encompass actual, attempted, or threat-ened acts of harm to another person, but these can be criticized as overly inclusive, capturing behaviours that are not "truly" violent (e.g., verbal threats or property damage). Legal definitions of vio-lence (e.g., sexual assault or stalking) are useful within a specific juris-diction, but generalizations or comparisons to other jurisdictions become problematic where legal definitions are inconsistent with one another. Unfortunately, because there is no "best" definition of vio-lence, it varies from one study to the next.

Researchers must also choose the sources of information they wish to rely upon for their data. The most common of these fall into one of the following three broad categories: official records (e.g., police or hospital files), self-reports (e.g., of perpetrators or victims), or reports from collaterals (e.g., family or friends). Each information source has different strengths and weaknesses that influence the quantity of vio-lence detected and the level of detail available about each violent inci-dent. The limitations associated with individual sources of information have led some researchers to use several methods at once. The advan-tages of this multi-method approach are twofold: first, it may help overcome the potential biases and limitations connected with any sin-gle source of information; and second, it will likely yield relatively high levels of violence because incidents unnoticed by one source may be detected by another (Mulvey & Lidz, 1993). This approach raises its own particular problem for researchers, however, as it is usually the researcher who must decide which information to use when data from different sources conflict.

To facilitate the investigation and understanding of violence, re-searchers frequently conceptualize it along one or more dimensions. As an example, Cornell and colleagues differentiate instrumental vio-lence from reactive violence based on the motivation of the perpetrator and the situational precipitants giving rise to the violence (Cornell et al., 1996). Instrumental violence typically involves premeditated acts carried out to achieve some external gain (e.g., money, power, sex-ual gratification). In other words, instrumental violence is a means to an end. In contrast, reactive violence is an exaggerated emotional response to a provocation, usually in the context of an aggressive act or an insult. It is an end in and of itself. Violence may also be distin-guished according to the relationship that exists between the victim and the offender (e.g., family members versus acquaintances versus strangers) or the severity of harm suffered by the victim (psychological harm versus physical injury versus death). Some studies also discriminate between sexual and nonsexual violence.

Not only have researchers classified violence along a variety of potential dimensions, they have also measured actual violent incidents in different ways. Typically, violence is coded in a dichotomous fashion, as either present or absent, but continuous measures may also be used (e.g., total number of incidents, severity of harm). On other occasions, time-dependent measures are used. These measures might take into account the time to first violence or the number of violent incidents occurring per unit of time at risk.

Ultimately, how an investigator addresses the conceptual issues pertaining to the study of violence depends on a multitude of factors, including the study's purpose, the accessibility of data, and the resources available. Readers need to be aware that the approach taken will have important implications for interpreting a study's results.

VIOLENCE IN THE CANADIAN CONTEXT

Violent crime is a prominent societal concern in Canada. In a 1988 national poll, Canadians indicated they were more fearful of a threatened or actual violent attack than any other type of crime (Canadian Centre for Justice Statistics, 1995). Moreover, the perceptions of crime held by Canadians prompts many to alter their lifestyle and take steps to prevent being victimized (Canadian Centre for Justice Statistics, 1995). How violent is Canadian society? According to 1994 police statistics, most *reported* crimes in Canada are property offences (54.1%); only a relatively small proportion of offences are violent (10%) in nature (Canadian Centre for Justice Statistics, 1996d). The majority of violent crimes during this same year were either common assault (60%) or more serious forms of non-sexual assault (18.1%). Sexual assaults (10.4%) and robberies (9.5%) comprised nearly all the remaining violent crimes. Homicides and other forms of violence accounted for less than 3% of all reported violence.

It is common practice to express the frequency of crimes in terms of rates, that is, the number of crimes per 100,000 people per year. Using 1994 crime rates as the basis for comparison (Canadian Centre for Justice Statistics, 1996d), all forms of assault combined had the highest incidence rate (808 per 100,000 people), followed by sexual assault (108 per 100,000 people), robbery (99 per 100,000 people), and homicide (2 per 100,000 people).

There is a widely held perception among Canadians that crime is escalating. When respondents in a randomized national survey were asked whether crime had increased in frequency, decreased in frequency, or remained about the same, almost half (46%) indicated their belief that crime had risen. A slightly smaller group (43%) felt the level of crime to be about the same, and fewer than 4% thought the crime rate had decreased (Canadian Centre for Justice Statistics, 1995). At first glance, crime statistics seem to bear out these fears. The rate of reported violent crime appears to have undergone a dramatic 49% increase during the 10 years between 1984 and 1994. Most of this rise can be explained by an increase in the number of assaults (Canadian Centre for Justice Statistics, 1996d). Unfortunately, it is difficult to determine if this statistical increase represents an actual expansion in the amount of violent crime or whether it can be attributed merely to changes in the public's tendency to report crime, the introduction of mandatory arrest policies (especially for spousal assault cases), or other factors (Canadian Centre for Justice Statistics, 1996d). Since 1992, violent crime rates actually appear to have declined, although it is too early to tell if this is a short-term fluctuation or the start of a longer-term trend.

Homicide rates traditionally have been viewed as the most stable index of violence because they are relatively insensitive to changes in criminal justice policy or public reporting (Canadian Centre for Justice Statistics, 1996b). According to homicide statistics, the rate of violence has not changed much over the last 20 years or so. As Figure 11.1 illustrates, the homicide rate increased throughout the sixties until the mid-seventies, but it has remained relatively constant or declined since this time. The reason for these fluctuations is unclear, but it may be related to the demographic characteristics of Canadian society. Specifically, the times when homicide rates were highest correspond to the times when "baby boomers" were in their peak ages for acting violently.

Public surveys offer another means of assessing the prevalence of violence in Canadian society. The principal advantage of this method is that it does not depend upon the victim notifying a police agency of the crime, thereby reducing the "dark figure" of unreported crime. In 1993, the federal government carried out a large-scale random telephone survey of Canadians. As expected, the survey found the rate of violence was much higher than official police records indicated. According to the survey, the violent victimization rate was 9,300 per 100,000 people. This is a rate nearly nine times greater than police

Figure 11.1
Canadian homicide rates, 1961–1995

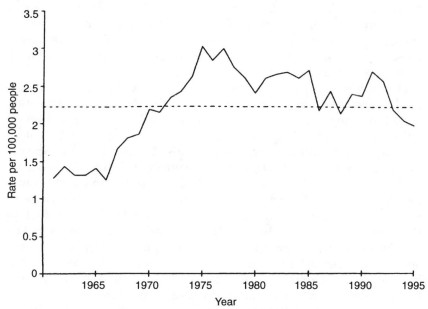

SOURCE: Canadian Centre for Justice Statistics (1996b), p. 14

records reported for the same year (Canadian Centre for Justice Statistics, 1996d, 1996c).

Incidents of violence are not equally distributed throughout the population. The perpetrators of violent crime are overwhelmingly male. Based on 1994 police records, men were responsible for close to 90% of all violent crimes in which a suspect was identified (Canadian Centre for Justice Statistics, 1996d). Conversely, women are more likely to be victimized than are men. The 1993 General Social Survey found women were victimized at a rate of 10,000 per 100,000 people, whereas the comparable rate for men was 8,400 per 100,000 people (Canadian Centre for Justice Statistics, 1996d). In fact, growing awareness regarding the issue of violence against women spurred the federal government to initiate a large-scale survey of Canadian women to assess the problem. Over half the women who were interviewed indicated they had been victims of physical or sexual violence at least once since the age of 16, and 10%

indicated they had been subjected to violence during the 12 months immediately preceding the survey (Johnson and Sacco, 1995; Statistics Canada, 1993). In many cases (20%) the violence was severe enough to cause physical injury (Statistics Canada, 1993). Approximately 40% of the survey participants had been sexually assaulted at one time in their lives (Johnson & Sacco, 1995). The majority of these incidents were never reported to police (Statistics Canada, 1993).

Data also show that young people are disproportionately responsible for violent crime in Canada (Canadian Centre for Justice Statistics, 1996c). Although persons aged 12 to 18 years old comprise only about 10% of the Canadian population, they were responsible for 15% of all violent crime resulting in criminal charges. In particular, the proportion of robbery charges attributed to youths (30%) exceeds their proportion in the population by a factor of three. At the same time, young people account for a much smaller proportion of other violent charges, including homicide (11%), attempted murder (15%), and abduction (6%). The violent crime charge rate for Canada's youth, however, has experienced a steady rise since 1986. More common assaults, robberies, and, to a lesser extent, sexual assaults, accounted for most of the increase, while the rates for homicide, attempted murder, and abduction remained largely unchanged. It is unclear from these latest figures whether the violence rate has begun to peak or whether the upward trend will continue.

In order to gain an appreciation of the relative prevalence of violence in Canadian society it is worth comparing the rates of violence in Canada with those of other countries. Table 11.1 lists the rates of selected violent crimes from various Western countries. With the exception of sexual assaults, Canada appears to have lower rates of lethal and non-lethal violence than the United States; apart from the United States, however, Canada's violent crime rates consistently rank among the highest in the Western world. Of course, in making comparisons of this sort, it is necessary to be mindful of the conceptual and practical methodological issues discussed earlier. Notwithstanding such limitations, however, the general conclusion must be that violence is a serious social problem in Canada.

VIOLENCE AND THE LAW

The notion of "dangerousness," that the actions of particular people must not be allowed to disrupt the peace and order of the state, has a

TABLE 11.1
Violent crime rates (per 100,000 people) for selected countries

Country	Homicide	Assault	Sexual assault	Robbery
United States	9.4	5000	1500	1700
Northern Ireland	5.2	1800	400	500
Italy	3.0	800	1000	1300
Canada	2.4	4400	1800	1100
France	2.4	2000	600	400
Switzerland	1.6	1200	<100	500
Netherlands	1.5	3700	900	900
Sweden	1.4	2700	800	300
England & Wales	1.3	2800	300	900
West Germany	1.2	3100	1700	800
Scotland	1.0	1800	800	500
Norway	1.0	3000	600	500

SOURCE: Canadian Centre for Justice Statistics (1996d), p. 17

long history (Petrunic, 1982). Over the past three decades, there has been increasing movement towards formally integrating assessments of dangerousness and predictions of violence into the law. One of the forces behind this convergence of law and social science was the change that occurred among American civil commitment laws during the sixties. In the United States at that time, "dangerousness to others" became a widely accepted criterion for involuntary hospitalization (Monahan, 1988) and the influence of this legal standard spread to Canada. At present, every province in Canada has "dangerousness to others" among the criteria for civil commitment (see Chapter 12), a standard that necessarily involves some form of risk assessment regarding future violence. Judicial decisions have also created legal responsibilities relating to the prediction of violence in the civil system. Although Canadian case law is not as clearly delineated as its American counterpart, there is little doubt that psychologists and other mental health professionals have a legal duty to take reasonable steps to protect others from potentially dangerous clients in their care (Birch, 1992; Reaves & Ogloff, 1996). Failure to intervene in a timely or effective fashion could result in civil litigation. By implication, this legal duty assumes that mental health experts are capable of recognizing risk markers in individuals and predicting when intervention is required (Douglas & Webster, 1998).

Whereas risk assessments in the civil system have come about through a mixture of case law and statutory changes, within the criminal justice system the expansion of risk assessments has been primarily a function of legislative developments. Historically, the federal government has demonstrated a long-standing interest in chronic and dangerous offenders. During the late 1940s the government introduced two legislative measures specifically designed to deal with this group of offenders (Grant, 1985; Webster, Dickens, & Addario, 1985). The first initiative, habitual criminal legislation, was enacted in 1947; the second initiative, criminal psychopath legislation, was proclaimed 1 year later. Both provided for the possibility of indeterminate detention and together they comprised the forerunner to Canada's dangerous offender legislation (Part XXIV, Criminal Code; Grant, 1985; Webster, Dickens, & Addario, 1985).

The dangerous offender legislation became law in 1977 (Webster et al., 1985). Like its predecessors, the current legislation includes provisions whereby offenders may be incarcerated indefinitely. The Crown may apply to have a person declared a dangerous offender following a conviction for a serious personal injury offence. Once an application is made by the Crown, there must be an assessment performed by an "expert" to determine if the offender poses a threat to the community. This procedural requirement formally embodies the participation of mental health or criminal justice professionals and the process of risk assessment as part of every dangerous offender hearing. The presence of risk assessments within the criminal justice system, however, is not limited to dangerous offender proceedings. Today, assessments of risk are mandated in some form or other at virtually every major junction of the criminal justice system, including the pretrial, sentencing, detention, and release phases (see Box 11.1).

Box 11.1

RISK ASSESSMENTS IN CANADA

CIVIL SETTING

Civil Commitment
The criteria of most provincial mental health provisions provide for the involuntary hospitalization of persons who pose a danger to either themselves or others.
EXAMPLE: under s. 20 of the Ontario *Mental Health Act* (R.S.O.

1990, c. M. 7) a person may be hospitalized if a physician is of the opinion "... the person is suffering from a mental disorder of a nature or quality that likely will result in ... serious bodily harm to the person ... [or] serious bodily harm to another person ..."

Duty to Warn/limitations to confidentiality

Physician-client confidentiality

Mental health professionals could be held liable for failing to take reasonable measures to protect an identifiable third party from a client they knew would try to harm the third party.

EXAMPLE: see the decision of the Alberta Court of Queen's Bench in *Wenden* v. *Trikha* (1991).

Solicitor-client privilege

Solicitor-client privilege can be set aside where there is a compelling public safety interest.

EXAMPLE: see the decision of the Supreme Court of Canada in *Smith* v. *Jones* (1999).

Public Body Records

Some jurisdictions in Canada have information access and privacy laws that require public bodies to release confidential information for public safety reasons. Occasionally these laws have been used to notify the community about the release from prison of a potentially dangerous sex offender.

EXAMPLE: in British Columbia, under s. 25(1) of the *Freedom of Information and Protection of Privacy Act* (R.S.B.C. 1996, c. 165), a public body "must, without delay, disclose to the public ... information (a) about a risk of significant harm ... to the health or safety of the public or a group of people."

Child Protection

General Protections

Provincial laws permit government intervention where children are in need of protection.

EXAMPLE: under s. 11(a) of Saskatchewan's *Child and Family Services Act* (R.S.S. 1978, c-7.2) a child is in need of protection if, among other things, "... the child has suffered or is likely to suffer physical harm ... has been or is likely to be exposed to harmful interaction for a sexual purpose ... [or], has been exposed to domestic violence or severe domestic disharmony that is likely to result in physical or emotional harm to the child."

Custody Disputes

Provincial statutes usually specify the paramount consideration in child custody disputes is the child's "best interests," and therefore any risk a potential guardian poses to the well-being of the child may become an issue in legal proceedings.

EXAMPLE: in Saskatchewan, under s. 17 of the *Children's Law Act* (R.S.S. 1978, c-81.) a court may refuse to enforce a custody order where it is "... satisfied on the balance of probabilities; that the child would suffer serious harm if the child ... remains in the custody of or subject to access by the person entitled to custody or access pursuant to the custody order ..."

Immigration

Federal immigration laws bar admission to people who pose a violence risk to the Canadian public.

EXAMPLE: section 19(1)(g) of the *Immigration Act* (R.S.B.C. 1976–77, c. 52) states that admission to Canada will not be granted to persons for whom "there are reasonable grounds to believe will engage in acts of violence that would or might endanger the lives or safety of persons in Canada."

Employment/Schools

School & Education Acts

School or education acts may include provisions permitting administrative officials to take active steps against employees whose conduct may be harmful to students.

EXAMPLE: under s. 15(5) of the British Columbia *School Act* (R.S.B.C. 1996, c. 412) an employee may be suspended "... if the superintendent of schools is of the opinion that the welfare of the students is threatened by the presence of [the] employee."

Provincial school or education acts also typically have provisions for excluding students who constitute a threat to the health and safety of other students and staff at the school.

EXAMPLE: s. 91(5) of the British Columbia *School Act* (R.S.B.C. 1996, c. 412) allows for the removal of a student who is "... suffering from a communicable disease or other physical, mental or emotional condition that would endanger the health or welfare of the other students, the teacher or the administrative officer."

Labour Regulations

Courts may hold employers liable for occupational violence suffered by their employees and there have been initiatives to enact regulations requiring employers to take steps to prevent violence in the workplace.

EXAMPLE: regulation 4.28 of the British Columbia Workers Compensation Board specifies that "... a risk assessment must be performed in any workplace in which a risk of injury to workers from violence arising out of their employment may be present."

CRIMINAL SETTING

Pretrial

Bail Hearings

Bail may be withheld if it "... is necessary for the protection of the public, having regard to all the circumstances including the substantial likelihood that the accused will, if released from custody, commit a criminal offence ..." *Criminal Code* R.S.C. 1985, s. 515(10)

Young Offender Transfers

Decisions concerning the transfer of young people to adult court "... shall consider the interest of society, which includes the objectives of affording protection to the public and rehabilitation of the young person ..." and where these objectives cannot be reconciled the protection of the public shall be paramount. *Young Offenders Act* R.S.C. 1985, c. Y-1, s. 16(1.1)

Sentencing

Young Offenders

A young person shall only be committed to custody if it is "... necessary for the protection of society having regard to the seriousness of the offence and the circumstances in which it was committed and having regard to the needs and circumstances of the young person." *Young Offenders Act* R.S.C. 1985, c. Y-1, s. 24(1)

Long-term Offenders

The court may impose long-term community supervision where it is satisfied "there is a substantial risk that the offender will reoffend; and there is a reasonable possibility of eventual control of the risk in the community." *Criminal Code* R.S.C. 1985, Part XXIV, s. 753.1(1)

Dangerous Offenders

Indeterminate incarceration may be imposed on dangerous offenders who show either "... a likelihood of causing death or injury to other persons, or inflicting substantial psychological damage on other persons ..." or "... a likelihood of causing injury, pain or other evil to other persons through failure to control his or her sexual impulses." *Criminal Code* R.S.C. 1985, Part XXIV, s. 753(1)

Detention/Release

Institutional Classification

The Correctional Service must "... assign a security classification of maximum, medium, or minimum to each inmate ..." *Corrections and Conditional Release Act* S.C. 1992, c. 20, s. 30

Parole

An inmate may be released on parole if "... there are no reasonable grounds to believe the offender, if released, is likely to commit an offence involving violence before the expiration of the offender's sentence ..." *Corrections and Conditional Release* S.C. 1992, c. 20, s. 102

Statutory Release

The parole board may deny an offender statutory release if it is satisfied "... that the offender is likely, if released, to commit an offence causing the death of or serious harm to another person or a sexual offence involving a child before the expiration of the offender's sentence ..." *Corrections and Conditional Release* S.C. 1992, c. 20, s. 130

Clearly, risk assessments are ubiquitous in Canadian law, and their role is expanding (Douglas, Macfarlane, & Webster, 1996; Menzies et al., 1995). For example, changes to Part XXIV of the Criminal Code created a new category of dangerous person, referred to as the "Long-term Offender." Moreover, legal duties holding employers responsible for protecting their employees from violence at work are beginning to surface in the United States (Levin, 1995a; 1995b) and their influence is being felt in Canada (e.g., Workers Compensation Board of British Columbia regulations).

Similar developments have occurred recently in case law. In *Smith v. Jones* (1999) the issue before the Supreme Court of Canada was whether solicitor-client privilege could ever be set aside in favour of public safety. The Supreme Court ruled the privilege could be displaced, but only where the public safety interest was compelling and outweighed the interest in protecting the confidentiality of solicitor-client communications. In balancing these two competing interests, the Supreme Court announced that the following three factors should be considered: (1) there must be a clear risk to an identifiable group or person; (2) the risk must involve serious physical harm or death; and, (3) the risk must be imminent. In practical terms, the ruling means that before solicitor-client privilege may be lifted, a violence risk assessment should be conducted that addresses each facet of risk (e.g., potential targets, severity, and imminence of the potential violence) specified by the Supreme Court. This decision, together with the creation of new long-term offender laws and workplace violence regulations, signal the expanding role of violence risk assessments in the Canadian legal system.

RISK ASSESSMENT

The Shift away from "Dangerousness"

The predictions mental health professionals offer the courts often play a pivotal role in removing (or securing) an individual's liberty and protecting (or exposing) the public to possible violence. The enormous social ramifications bearing on these assessments eventually attracted queries regarding their accuracy. During the early 1970s, American researchers were presented with several unusual opportunities to follow presumed "dangerous" patients who were released from involuntary hospitalization under court orders and returned to the community (Kozol, Boucher, & Garofalo, 1972; Steadman & Cocozza, 1974; Thornberry & Jacoby, 1979). In each of these studies, the patients' detention in hospital was founded, either explicitly or implicitly, on mental health opinions regarding their perceived dangerousness. Despite fairly lengthy follow-up periods, the studies found that only 15% to 35% of the released patients committed a violent offence after release. The results of these "first generation" studies (Monahan, 1984) suggested that mental health professionals had a tendency to overpredict the extent to which violence actually occurred; that is, they predicted patients would be violent when, in fact, they were not. In an extensive review of this research, Monahan (1981, 1995) reached the often quoted conclusion that "the 'best' clinical research currently in existence indicates that *psychiatrists and psychologists are accurate in no more than one out of three predictions of violent behavior over a several-year period among institutionalized populations that had both committed violence in the past (and thus had high base rates for it) and who were diagnosed as mentally ill"* (emphasis in the original; p. 77).

The pessimistic picture painted by first generation research marked the slow beginnings of the transformation of "violence prediction" into "risk assessment" (Mulvey & Lidz, 1995; Steadman et al., 1993). Although the transition to risk assessment cannot be attributed to any single factor, one major impetus was the legal system's persistent demands for violence predictions (Monahan, 1996; Mulvey & Lidz, 1995). During the aftermath of the first generation studies, there was a flurry of legal cases surrounding violence predictions. Attempts to have such evidence dismissed as wholly unreliable and inaccurate were uniformly rebuffed by the courts in both Canada (*Re Moore and the Queen*, 1984) and the United States (e.g., *Barefoot v. Estelle*, 1983), thereby preserving the legal role of mental health professionals in the prediction of violent behaviour.

Observers have identified two other events of importance in the evolution of formalized risk assessment. Changes to involuntary civil commitment laws and the recent trend towards deinstitutionalizing psychiatric patients have moved more and more people out of hospitals and into the community. These circumstances have forced decision makers to conduct careful assessments to determine those patients for whom continued commitment truly appears warranted and to implement effective programs for managing and supporting those patients who are released (Mulvey & Lidz, 1995). Public and political pressures have also played a role. High-profile media cases involving particularly violent acts perpetrated by persons released from the criminal justice system have made the public acutely aware of the current shortcomings in predictive acumen and have generated pressure for improved policies and procedures (Douglas et al., 1996). These events collectively have created a situation whereby risk assessment has become the "conceptual cornerstone for salvaging the scientific legitimacy of violence assessments in psycholegal settings" (Menzies et al., 1995, p. 93).

The Process of Risk Assessment

Violence risk assessment may be defined as *"the process of evaluating individuals to (1) characterize the likelihood they will commit acts of violence and (2) develop interventions to manage or reduce that likelihood"* (emphasis in the original; Hart, 1998b, p. 122). The two component tasks identified in this definition are analogous to Heilbrun's (1997) "prediction" and "management" models of risk assessment.

The risk assessment process may be distinguished from "assessing dangerousness" or "predicting violence" on a number of conceptual grounds (Steadman et al., 1993). To begin, "dangerousness" implies a dispositional trait such that an individual exhibits an unchanging propensity to all forms of violence, directed towards all types of people, in all types of situations (Borum, Swartz, & Swanson, 1996; Monahan & Steadman, 1994). This conceptualization of dangerousness is incongruent with current notions of risk assessment in three respects. First, risk assessments are founded on empirical knowledge (Menzies et al., 1995), yet there is presently no scientific evidence of a single, global, trait as described above. Second, dangerousness is a vague term that lacks specificity regarding what the danger is, or for whom the danger exists (Webster et al., 1985). In contrast, risk assessments explicitly acknowledge the multifaceted nature of violence by giving consideration to the type of violence, the population at risk, possible contextual inhibitors or disinhibitors, and the type of harm. Third, risk assessment is a continuing process that emphasizes constant reassessment and management modifications to adjust for changes in risk (Steadman et al., 1993; Monahan & Steadman, 1994). Dangerousness, on the other hand, suggests that anything beyond the initial assessment is redundant because it is a relatively static condition, resistant to change.

The task of assessing risk is also not constrained solely to the task of predicting violence (Hart, 1998b). The ability to predict violence accurately is of little utility if no attempt is made to prevent the violence that has been forecasted. In short, "the critical function of risk assessments is violence *prevention*, not violence *prediction*" (emphasis in the original; Hart, 1998b, p. 123).

Identifying and Evaluating Risk Factors

The conceptual transition from dangerousness to risk assessment has been accompanied by a resurgence of social science research on violence. This refocused research has involved a shift away from investigations designed purely to evaluate the abilities of mental health professionals to predict violence towards research concentrating on the identification of risk factors for violence and improving assessment methods and techniques (Monahan, 1996). To find risk factors, researchers attempt to identify characteristics that can be used to distinguish those individuals most likely to act violently from those least likely to act violently.

One of the most common study designs employed in this line of research is the cohort study, wherein a group of participants is evaluated on some risk factor of interest and then followed for a period of time to establish which participants were violent and which were not. At the end of the follow-up period the predictive power of the risk factor is calculated using an appropriate statistical procedure. Although this task may sound relatively straightforward, the interpretation of findings is made difficult by the myriad variations that exist for every aspect of the study design. For example, the risk factors themselves may vary in the way they are defined and measured. The sample could be drawn from a forensic, civil psychiatric, correctional, or community population and may be limited to a particular gender or age group. Follow-up periods differ enormously from one study to the next in terms of their length as well as the extent to which they control or account for intervening variables that might affect individual outcomes (e.g., changes in mental or physical health, treatment initiatives, or supervision by criminal justice system agencies). There is also great diversity in the way the criterion (i.e., violence) is defined and measured. Finally, even the analytical procedures employed vary among studies. Notwithstanding these complexities, there is a growing consensus within the scientific community as to what constitutes the most important correlates and risk factors associated with violence. The purpose of the next section is to highlight and briefly describe some of the more prominent findings in the current literature.

Some Important Risk Factors

Demographic variables

One demographic characteristic exhibiting a relationship to violence is male gender. As Canadian Crime Statistics remind us, for every ten violent crimes reported to police approximately nine are committed by males (Canadian Centre for Justice Statistics, 1996d). Other studies also support an association between male gender and violence (Pearson, Wilmot, & Padi, 1986; Wessely, Castle, Douglas, & Taylor, 1994). These findings, however, must be tempered by other investigations indicating, at least among psychiatric populations, that the rate of violence among women is roughly the same as that among men (Lidz et al., 1993; Swanson, 1994). The value of gender as a risk marker is further attenuated in many settings where risk assessments are performed because males constitute all (or nearly all) the population; in such circumstances, gender, it is of little utility in distinguishing high and low risk groups. An examination of the Canadian correctional population highlights this last point. In 1994–95 approximately 97% of all offenders sentenced to federal correctional institutions were men (Canadian Centre for Justice Statistics, 1996a).

Another demographic characteristic related to violent behaviour is age. Studies consistently find that younger people present a higher risk of engaging in violence than do older people. Youth was one of the few predictors of future violence revealed in first generation studies (Steadman & Cocozza, 1974; Thornberry & Jacoby, 1979). Contemporary studies confirm these earlier findings. For example, a large-scale study undertaken with a sample of 618 inmates in a maximum-security psychiatric facility at Penetanguishene, Ontario, revealed age to be one of the strongest predictors of violent recidivism (Harris, Rice, & Quinsey, 1993). The researchers found age at the time of the offence was inversely related to risk, so that as the offender's age increased the subsequent risk of violent recidivism decreased.

Previous Antisocial and Criminal Behaviour

Several aspects of past antisocial or criminal behaviour have links to violence. It is a well-established principle that past violence is one of the best predictors of future violence (Monahan, 1981, 1995). One way to acquire an overview of the general findings in a given area is through a meta-analysis, which provides a quantified synthesis of independent research investigations. Bonta, Law, and Hanson (1998) performed such a meta-analysis of studies predicting criminal and violent recidivism in mentally disordered offenders. Their review of violent recidivism examined 74 variables in 26 studies. According to their results, a history of violent behaviour, whether it was brought to the attention of criminal justice agencies or not, was one of the strongest predictors of violent recidivism. The findings from numerous other investigations not included in the meta-analysis also demonstrate that previous violence is indeed a strong predictor of subsequent violent conduct (Gardner, Lidz, Mulvey, & Shaw, 1996; Kozol et al., 1972; Menzies & Webster, 1995).

Criminality (i.e., law-breaking behaviour), which may or may not include violent offences, shows a consistent link to violence (Bonta, Law, and Hanson, 1998; Hanson & Bussière, 1998; Harris et al., 1993). The precise reason for this relationship is not clear, but it may be that involvement in the criminal subculture demonstrates a willingness to violate societal expectations and, therefore, these individuals are more likely to act violently as well. Alternatively, it may be that a person engaging in criminal activity is more likely to put him- or herself in a situation where violence is perceived to be the most (or only) workable course of action.

There is also some evidence to suggest that violating the terms of a conditional release is associated with future violence. Conditional release occurs when an individual is permitted back into the community under the proviso that he or she complies with stipulations fixed by a court, a parole board, a review board, or another agency. Harris et al. (1993) found that individuals who did not meet the terms of their probation, parole, or mandatory supervision were at increased risk for violence compared to individuals who complied with their release conditions.

Social Instability and Maladjustment

Social instability and maladjustment in childhood may manifest itself in the community, at school, or in the home (Webster, Douglas, Eaves, & Hart, 1997a). Studies addressing community maladjustment repeatedly show delinquency or offending as a juvenile raises the risk of future violence (Hodgins, 1994; Klassen & O'Connor, 1988b). Similar results exist with respect to functioning at school. For example, one study found that elementary school maladjustment characterized by truancy, verbal or physical altercations with peers, or disciplinary problems (e.g., detentions, suspensions) could predict violence as an adult (Harris et al., 1993). Other studies indicate a disruptive (e.g., parental separation) or dysfunctional family environment is connected to ensuing violence (Bonta et. al., 1998; Harris et al., 1993; Hodgins, 1994; Klassen & O'Connor, 1989). There is also evidence that physical and sexual abuse suffered as a child, be it at home or elsewhere, is a seemingly potent correlate of violence later in life. Widom (1989) followed a large sample of child abuse victims throughout adolescence and into early adulthood. On comparing their arrest records to a nonabused control group, the author found that the abused group had committed significantly more violent offences. This study provides some evidence that social learning mechanisms may be responsible for the relationship between childhood abuse and adulthood violence.

There is now a considerable body of literature indicating that social instability and maladjustment as an adult is associated with an increased probability of violence. It might be expected that people who have trouble interacting with others or conforming to societal expectations will be especially likely to act violently (Douglas & Webster, 1998). Indeed, the inability to secure and retain employment consistently correlates with violence (Bonta et al., 1998; Harris et al., 1993; Menzies & Webster, 1995; Wessely et al., 1994), as does the failure to establish and maintain intimate relationships (Bonta et al., 1998; Harris et al., 1993; Klassen & O'Connor, 1988a).

The presence of strong social networks may decrease the risk for future violence, but it does not necessarily follow that a large network will be always beneficial. One study of mentally ill persons found that larger social networks or social networks composed predominantly of relatives were associated with an increased risk of violence (Estroff, Zimmer, Lachicotte, & Benoit, 1994). The authors' explanation for these counter-intuitive findings is that study participants reacted violently in response to circumstances where they perceived others to be acting aggressively towards them. Since larger social networks represent more opportunity for hostile situations to arise, increased social network size was associated with a greater risk of violence. In this way it seems that the stability and quality of a social network appears to be more important than its sheer size (Estroff & Zimmer, 1994).

Acute Mental Disorder

It was widely accepted in the early 1980s that whatever association existed between mental disorder and violence could largely be explained by demographic and historical artifacts (Monahan, 1981, 1995). Since this time, there has been considerable research on this issue and the results have lead to a re-appraisal of these earlier conclusions. In 1992 Monahan summarized the results of this research, stating "there may be a relationship between mental disorder and violent behavior, one that cannot be fobbed off as chance or explained away by other factors that may cause them both. The relationship, if it exists, probably is not large, but may be important for legal theory and for social policy" (p. 511). It should not be inferred, however, that mental disorder per se causes violence. It is more likely the case that factors associated with mental disorder, such as poor coping skills and altered perceptions of external events, give rise to poor decisions accompanied by violent behaviour (Kropp & Hart, 1997b; Hart, 1998b).

Monahan (1992) was persuaded to re-evaluate the possibility of a relationship between mental disorder and violence by the results from two separate lines of research, one reporting the levels of violence perpetrated by mentally disordered persons and the other reporting the prevalence of mental disorder among people with histories of violence. There is some evidence from the first line of research to indicate that the incidence of violent behaviour is higher among mentally disordered persons than among people without a mental disorder. In one particularly convincing study, interviews were conducted with approximately 10,000 people who resided in one of three large urban centres in the United States (Swanson, Holzer, Ganju, & Jono, 1990). The investigators found that reported violence was five times higher among people who met the criteria for a major mental disorder than among those who did not meet any such criteria. Turning to the second line of research, the results of several studies suggest that the prevalence of mental disorder is much greater among people with violent histories than among people without a history of violence. Monahan (1992) pointed to studies showing that the prevalence of various mental disorders among jail (Teplin, 1990b) and prison (Hodgins & Côté, 1990) inmates far exceeds comparative rates among community residents. When viewed in isolation neither line of research is compelling; however, Monahan (1992) contended that when they were viewed together it was difficult to avoid concluding that a small, but robust relationship exists between mental disorder and violence.

While knowing mental disorder is linked to violence is helpful, it is of limited practical value since 'mental disorder' is a broad label applied to a heterogeneous group of people. It is much more instructive to determine the specific disorders and symptoms that are most predictive of violence. For instance, the literature shows a fairly consistent association between schizophrenia and violence (Binder & McNeil, 1988; Swanson et al., 1990; Wessely et al., 1994) and between mania and violence (Binder & McNeil, 1988; Lowenstein, Binder, & McNeil, 1990; Swanson et al., 1990). Perhaps the most vivid demonstration of these relationships is provided by the findings of Swanson et al. (1990), so it is worth returning to their study once again. According to their data, the percentage of respondents acting violently in the year preceding the survey was 2.1% if no disorder was present, 11.7% among diagnoses of mania, and 12.7% among diagnoses of schizophrenia. Swanson (1994) also calculated estimates of the 1-year probability of violent behaviour occurring by diagnosis using much of the same data. The results are displayed in Figure 11.2. The probability of violent behaviour for males without mental disorder was around 2% and rose steadily across categories of anxiety disorder, affective disorder, and schizophrenia to substance abuse. Figures for women were lower than for men, but reproduced the same pattern. What is of special note is that the probabilities of violence attached to diagnoses for schizophrenia or an affective disorder (which includes mania) were markedly elevated in comparison to the probability of violence associated with the absence of such a diagnosis. Collectively, these results provide some of the clearest evidence to date regarding the relationships of schizophrenia and mania to violence.

Certain psychiatric symptoms are also related to an increased risk of violence. The merit of examining symptomology was underlined in a meta-analysis of the empirical literature pertaining to psychosis and violence (Douglas & Hart, 1998). This analysis revealed that specific psychotic symptoms are associated more strongly with violence than blanket diagnoses of an unspecified mental disorder. The relationship of some psychotic symptoms to violence may be explained by the principle of "rationality-within-irrationality" (Link & Stueve, 1994). This principle postulates that, notwithstanding the basic irrationality of many psychotic symptoms, the events leading up to violence can often be construed as rational within the distorted context. In other words, the symptoms themselves may be irrational in terms of the external

Figure 11.2

Rates of reported violence among people meeting various psychiatric diagnoses

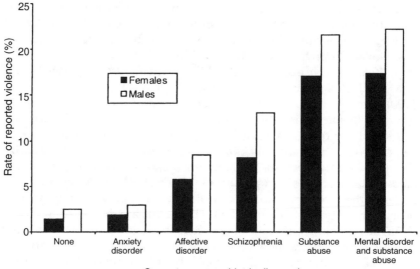

NOTE: From J.W. Swanson, "Mental disorder, substance abuse, and community vio-lence: An epidemiological approach," in J. Monahan & H.J. Steadman (Eds.), *Violence and Mental Disorder*, p. 125. (Chicago: University of Chicago Press, 1994). Reproduced with permission.

reality, but to the actively psychotic individual, the symptoms are experienced as real (e.g., "I know this person is the devil who is intent on destroying us all") and any subsequent violent behaviour may be a rational response to the psychotic experience (e.g., "I must kill the devil before the devil kills us all"). According to the principle of ratio-nality-within-irrationality, violence is most likely to be associated with psychotic symptoms involving either "external factors" that override internal controls (e.g., having one's mind dominated by an outside force) or the threat of harm from others (Link & Stueve, 1994). Link and Stueve (1994) investigated this possibility and their results confirmed their hypothesis: symptoms involving threat or control were more pre-dictive of recent violence than were other psychotic symptoms.

Psychopathy

Psychopathy eclipses all other known risk factors as a predictor of future violence. Hare (1996) has described psychopaths as "intraspecies predators who use charm, manipulation, intimidation, and violence to control others and to satisfy their own selfish needs. Lacking in conscience and in feelings for others, they cold-bloodedly take what they want and do as they please, violating social norms and expectations without the slightest sense of guilt or regret" (p. 26).

The modern concept of psychopathy has existed for many years, but it is only since the development of the Hare Psychopathy Checklist-Revised (PCL-R; Hare, 1991) that valid and reliable assessments of the construct have been possible. Psychopathy, as defined by the PCL-R, comprises two symptom clusters (Harpur, Hakstian, & Hare, 1988; Harpur, Hare, & Hakstian, 1989). The first cluster, known as Factor 1, reflects the interpersonal/affective features of psychopaths including grandiosity, glibness, callousness, and deceitfulness. The second cluster, Factor 2, corresponds to the unstable/antisocial lifestyle of psycho-

---

Box 11.2

Assessing Psychopathy Using the Hare Psychopathy Checklist-Revised

The broad success of the PCL-R as an assessment instrument has reinvigorated interest in the construct of psychopathy. However, conducting a thorough assessment with the PCL-R is time consuming, often requiring upwards of 2 to 3 hours to complete. Unfortunately, this commitment of time is not feasible for many acute institutional settings, where staff and resources are not readily available (Hare, 1996). The demand for a shortened version of the PCL-R that would be suitable for a variety of civil psychiatric and community settings led Dr Robert Hare and his colleagues to develop a screening version of the instrument (PLC:SV; Hart, Cox, & Hare, 1995).

The PCL:SV resembles the PCL-R in most major respects, except that the original 20 items have been condensed into 12 items (Hart et al., 1995). Some modifications were made to the scoring criteria for individual items to ensure the utility of the PCL:SV to populations outside the criminal justice system, where the PCL-R had been developed and employed (Hart, Hare, & Forth, 1994). Structurally, the PCL:SV is divided into two parts, which correspond to Factor 1 (interpersonal/affective) and Factor 2 (unstable/antisocial lifestyle) of the PCL-R. Part 1 consists of the following six characteristics: superficial, grandiose, manipulative, lacks remorse, lacks empathy, and, doesn't accept responsibility. Part 2 includes the following traits: impulsive, poor behaviour controls, lacks goals, irresponsible, adolescent antisocial behaviour, and adult antisocial behaviour.

A recent study by Douglas, Ogloff, Nicholls, and Grant (1999) investigated the predictive ability of the PCL:SV in a sample of 193 civil commitment patients released from a psychiatric institution in western Canada. In conjunction with several other measures, PCL:SV ratings were completed retrospectively from patient files. Follow-up data were obtained from the readmission records of the psychiatric institution, provincial correctional records, and the admission records of numerous hospitals within the province. During the study period, patients were at risk to be violent for an average of more than a year and a half. The data revealed that 73 (38%) of the 193 persons in the sample engaged in some form of violence during the follow-up period. The PCL:SV total score, as well as the individual scores for both component parts, predicted violence at levels greater than chance. Individuals with PCL:SV scores above the median were four times more likely to commit a violent act broadly defined (i.e., including threats and other fear inducing acts) and five times more likely to commit a physically violent act (i.e., a physical attack) than individuals with scores below the median. The PCL:SV also compared favourably to a risk assessment scale specifically constructed for the purpose of predicting violence and managing risk.

These results, together with the existing body of accumulated research on psychopathy, attest to the importance of this construct for the criminal justice system and have assured that the PCL-R and PCL:SV will feature prominently in future investigations in this area. Readers interested in finding out more about psychopathy should refer to Hare (1993).

paths that is characterized by impulsivity, irresponsibility, and a failure to conform to societal expectations (see Box 11.2).

The importance of psychopathy for violence risk assessments arises from three well-grounded findings associated with this disorder (Hart & Hare, 1996). First, the violence of psychopaths tends to be qualitatively different from that of nonpsychopaths. Williamson, Hare, and Wong (1987) found that the violent behaviour of psychopaths was directed predominantly towards male strangers for purposes of retribution or revenge. In contrast, nonpsychopaths were more likely to be violent during the course of an emotional dispute with a female family member or acquaintance. Similar results were reported by a study investigating the relationship of psychopathy to instrumental and reactive violence (Cornell et al., 1996). This study found that although histories of reactive violence were distributed across virtually all violent offenders, instrumental violence was confined to a small subset who exhibited significantly higher PCL-R scores than the others.

Second, psychopaths are "high density" offenders (Hart & Hare, 1997) who are more likely to have histories of community and institutional violence compared to nonpsychopaths (Hart, 1998a). Hare and McPherson (1984) divided 227 federal inmates into high, medium, and low groups on the basis of PCL-R scores. The investigators found that for every year spent free in the community (i.e., potentially able to commit offences), the high psychopathy group received significantly more charges for violent offences, including robbery, assault, possession of a weapon, and kidnapping, than either the low or medium psychopathy groups. These findings are reflected in the percentages of each group with a history of a violent offence. Almost 85% of the high group had at least one violent offence compared to 64% in the medium group and 54% in the low group. Institutional violence exhibited a similar pattern of results. The presence of verbal and physical violence were greatest in the high group (86%) followed by the medium (80%) and low (55%) groups. These results were replicated by Wong (1984) who reported that high psychopathy scores were associated with an increased incidence of institutional infractions; as well, the infractions committed by psychopaths in this study involved more seriously threatening and violent behaviour.

Third, psychopaths recidivate violently with greater frequency than nonpsychopaths. Serin and Amos (1995) followed 300 male offenders released from a federal correctional institution. As in earlier studies, PCL-R scores were used to divide the sample into low, medium, and high groups. The average follow-up period was 5.5 years. During this time, the rate of violent recidivism for the high group exceeded the rate for the low group by a factor of 5. The high group also tended to reoffend violently much more quickly (i.e., over a shorter time period) than either the medium or low groups. For instance, 62% of the high psychopathy group who would eventually reoffend had already done so within 12 months of release compared to 57% and 32% for the medium and low groups, respectively. The same trend has been observed in other studies as well (Harris, Rice, & Cormier, 1991; Serin, 1996). In one study, a sample of 81 federal offenders was followed on average for nearly 30 months (Serin, 1996). As before, high, medium, and low psychopathy groups were differentiated using the PCL-R. Once again the high psychopathy group engaged in violence earlier and at a greater rate relative to the medium and low groups.

Although the findings reviewed here justify the importance of psychopathy for violence risk assessments, they shed little light on why such a link apparently exists. A full understanding of the relationship between psychopathy and violence is still some distance away, but Hart and Hare (1996) have outlined three possible explanations that take account of the existing scientific evidence surrounding psychopathy. One possibility is that the cognitive schemata (i.e., mental framework) of psychopaths makes them more likely to construe the behaviour of others as hostile, prompting violent defensive responses. Alternatively, it may be that biochemical, neurological, or genetic factors gives rise to impulsiveness (Coscina, 1997). Since impulsivity is a key characteristic of psychopathy, it may be implicated in increasing the likelihood of engaging in unplanned, opportunistic acts of violence. Finally, there is some evidence to suggest that psychopaths suffer from a generalized emotional deficit and, consequently, lack many of the emotional restraints (i.e., empathy, fear, guilt, etc.) that normally prevent people from engaging in violence.

Substance Use

The use of alcohol and drugs has long been associated with violence, although the reasons for this connection are not well understood. The role of substance abuse in violence appears to operate in a number of ways. Individuals may engage in violence or place themselves in situations where violence becomes necessary in order to support a drug habit (Klassen & O'Connor, 1994). It has also been suggested that in some circumstances drug or alcohol intoxication disinhibits individuals, thereby raising the likelihood of subsequent violent conduct (Collins, 1990). Other offenders purposefully use drugs or alcohol to calm their nerves prior to carrying out a premeditated offence (Collins, 1990). As these examples demonstrate, the interaction between substance abuse and violence is complex and probably varies as a function of many factors.

Regardless of the exact mechanism(s) involved, there is convincing evidence linking substance use and violence. Swanson (1994) analysed data based on interviews with over 7,000 people drawn from two large American cities. The reported lifetime prevalence of violence was just 9% among the entire sample, but when single-diagnosis substance abusers were analysed separately the prevalence rate was found to be an astonishing 55%. Interestingly, among individuals with a dual diagnosis of substance abuse and another major mental disorder the prevalence rate climbed yet higher, to 64%. The authors emphasize that the additive effect of mental disorder to the risk of violence is relatively minor in comparison to substance abuse alone, which presented a high risk of violence regardless of any other presenting psychopathology. Moreover, 1-year probabilities of violent behaviour calculated for an enlarged sample proved to be relatively high (approximately 22%) irrespective of whether there was only a diagnosis of substance abuse or a second diagnosis was also present (see Figure 11.2).

Sexual Deviance

Deviant sexual fantasies have been implicated as motivational factors behind many sexual offences (Prentky et al., 1989). Sexual deviance may be defined by the presence of a paraphilia. A paraphilia is characterized by a pattern of sexual arousal to objects, situations, or activities considered outside the normative range (Abel & Osborn, 1992). It is important, however, to realize that "not all sex offenders have paraphilias, and not all paraphiles are sex offenders" (Boer, Wilson, Gauthier, & Hart, 1997, p. 334). If sexual deviance is related to sexual offending, it would be expected that sexual offenders should be more sexually deviant than non-sex offenders. Indeed, numerous studies show extrafamilial child molesters can be distinguished from non-sex offenders on the basis of their sexual arousal to children (Lalumière & Quinsey, 1994). Other studies indicate that rapists exhibit higher arousal in response to scenarios of nonconsensual and violent sexual activities than do nonrapists (Lalumière & Quinsey, 1994).

More compelling evidence can be found in a series of studies conducted at Penetanguishene, Ontario, that investigated the best predictors of sexual recidivism among male sex offenders (Quinsey, Rice, & Harris, 1995; Quinsey, Lalumière, Rice, & Harris, 1995). The authors examined the predictive power of a diverse set of variables, which included, among other things, a sexual deviance index based upon phallometric assessments (phallometric assessments measure changes in penile volume or circumference during the presentation of visual or auditory stimuli representing different age groups, gender, nonconsensual sexual, and violent activities). Based on the results of the phallometric assessments, the study found sexual recidivists were significantly more deviant than nonrecidivists.

In a subsequent study (Rice & Harris, 1997) conducted with a larger sample, the authors found an interesting interaction between sexual deviance and psychopathy. Specifically, sexually deviant psychopaths committed sexual offences at a much greater rate than nondeviant or nonpsychopathic offenders. In terms of generally violent reoffences, however, the predictive power of sexual deviance appeared to be negligible.

A meta-analysis of risk factors for sexual recidivism (Hanson & Bussière, 1998) confirms the general findings reported in the Penetanguishene studies. Sexual deviance generally, and a sexual preference for children specifically, showed a strong relationship to future sexual re-offending and little or no association with nonsexual violent reoffending. Collectively, these results indicate sexual deviance is a strong predictor of future sexual violence and may even interact synergistically with psychopathy in a manner that enhances its predictive power; however, the predictive utility of sexual deviance does not appear to extend beyond sexual violence to other violent offences.

Approaches to Risk Assessment

Awareness of risk factors, such as those discussed in the preceding section, may inform evaluators as to what information should be examined, but it does not inform them as to how this information should be considered. Traditionally, evaluators have relied upon one of two different decision-making processes: unstructured clinical judgment or actuarial decision making. In recent years, a third approach, structured clinical guidelines, has emerged. In this section, we will discuss briefly each of these decision-making processes in turn and highlight their strengths and weaknesses.

Unstructured clinical judgment has a long-standing association with the prediction of violence, and much of the first generation research was based on this approach. Few constraints are placed on the decision-making process; evaluators are free to choose which information to review and how to analyse, interpret, and report those data. Accordingly, unstructured clinical judgment has been described as "informal, subjective, [and] impressionistic" (Grove & Meehl, 1996, p. 293). The strength of unstructured clinical judgment lies in its flexibility. It is readily adapted to different information, settings, and populations. As well, it can take account of statistically rare but important information, or emphasize especially critical findings over those that appear less salient to the case.

Detractors of unstructured clinical judgment point to a number of shortcomings. First, unstructured clinical judgment lacks consistency because different evaluators focus on different information and arrive at different conclusions (Dawes, Faust, & Meehl, 1989). Second, these decisions sometimes lack "transparency." Evaluators who fail to specify how or why they reached a decision make it exceedingly difficult for others to challenge their conclusions. Finally, from the broad literature addressing clinical versus actuarial decision making, there is little evidence to suggest that the accuracy of unstructured clinical judgment improves much over chance (Dawes et al., 1989; Grove & Meehl, 1996; Meehl, 1954).

The second traditional approach to risk assessment is actuarial decision making. Actuarial methods of prediction entail the collection of prespecified data that are entered into a mathematical model or set of structured decision rules that combine and weight the data in a predetermined manner to arrive at a final judgment (Dawes et al., 1989; Meehl, 1954; Monahan, 1981, 1995). As this description makes clear, structure is added to each stage of the decision-making process, so it is not surprising to hear the actuarial approach referred to as "mechanical" and "algorithmic" (Grove & Meehl, 1996, p. 293).

Actuarial schemes are frequently associated with statistical or historical data (e.g., sex, criminal history), but this is not a defining characteristic because clinical information (e.g., the presence or absence of specific symptoms or diagnoses) may be utilized as well (Meehl, 1954; Monahan, 1981, 1995). The critical feature distinguishing clinical and actuarial methods is the source of the prediction. In the clinical approach the final prediction is rendered by the clinician, whereas the final prediction of actuarial schemes is a product exclusively of the prescribed operations of the actuarial instrument.

The failings of unstructured clinical judgment are the strength of actuarial methods. The actuarial approach maximizes consistency because the information required, the data coding format, and the data analysis are prespecified and do not vary. By their very nature, actuarial decisions are transparent and easy to review. Discrepancies among evaluators can be located quickly. Perhaps most importantly, actuarial methods improve predictive accuracy. Recent studies tend to show that actuarial risk assessments demonstrate a marked improvement over chance probabilities and they tend to be more accurate than unstructured clinical judgment (Gardner et al., 1996; Harris et al., 1993; Menzies & Webster, 1995; Mossman, 1994).

Although the actuarial approach contributes several tangible benefits to the risk assessment process, there are also a number of drawbacks. First, by confining the evaluation to a finite number of predetermined factors the actuarial method explicitly disregards factors that may be idiosyncratic but crucial to a specific case. Second, because the statistical techniques commonly employed to construct actuarial devices tend to optimize their success in the construction sample (i.e., the sample in which it was developed), their use outside that population is potentially problematic (Gottfredson & Gottfredson, 1986). If the actuarial instrument is used with individuals who do not fit the characteristics of the construction sample (e.g., male vs. female; mentally disordered vs. non-mentally disordered) then it is likely to render inaccurate predictions; the greater the divergence the greater the likelihood of predictive inaccuracies. Third, the tendency to rely on factors shown statistically to have predictive power may lead actuarial instruments to include risk factors that may be objectionable on legal or moral grounds (e.g., sex, race) and to exclude other factors that common sense would deem materially relevant (e.g., homicidal ideation or intent).

Growing unease with both the unstructured clinical judgment and actuarial methods has recently lead to the emergence of structured clinical judgment. This approach involves the establishment of clinical guidelines (Borum, 1996; Douglas, Cox, & Webster, 1999; Hart, 1998b). Clinical guidelines now exist for assessing risk of spousal assault (Kropp, Hart, Webster, & Eaves, 1995), risk of violence among mentally disordered patients and offenders (Webster et al., 1997a) and risk of sexual violence (Boer, Hart, Kropp & Webster, 1997). The idea of using clinical guidelines rests on systematizing the risk assessment process. Such guidelines, properly used, should lead assessors towards sensible, balanced, and practical conclusions. Guidelines and manuals of this kind usually help organize the evaluation process by outlining the qualifications necessary for individuals conducting risk assessments. They also recommend which data should be gathered and the most appropriate methods for collecting them. Ideally, they help identify the core factors associated with the risk of interest according to what the scientific literature and professional consensus indicate are necessary for a comprehensive, reliable, and valid assessment. However, the final decision or recommendation regarding the perceived risk of violence and appropriate case management remain with the evaluator.

Supporters suggest the organization and empirical grounding of clinical guidelines ameliorates problems with consistency and predictive validity while at the same time allowing the evaluator some flexibility in adapting the assessment process appropriately to each specific case (Hart, 1998b). Others strongly oppose any departure from the pure actuarial approach (see Quinsey, Harris, Rice, & Cormier, 1998). Detractors will undoubtedly point to research indicating that any time human judgment is introduced into the decision-making process there is a concomitant decline in predictive accuracy (Dawes et al., 1989; Grove & Meehl, 1996; Quinsey et al., 1998). Certainly, further research is required before a full appraisal of the potential value of clinical guidelines can be properly made, but the early results look promising (Douglas, Ogloff, Nicholls, & Grant, 1999; Kropp, 1998).

The Current Status of Risk Assessment

It is appropriate to conclude this chapter by reviewing the efficacy of our current abilities to assess risk. At the very least, many of the most pessimistic conclusions made in the immediate aftermath of first generation research have begun to fade as the results of subsequent studies, often referred to as second generation research, have become available. The scientific evidence now suggests mental health professionals can predict violence at levels better than chance (Mossman, 1994; Otto, 1992) and it is probably no longer fair to say that the prediction of violence is akin to "flipping coins" (Ennis & Litwack, 1974). A quantified review of selected violence prediction studies from the published literature drew two summary conclusions pertinent to this topic. First, second generation research exhibited greater predictive accuracy than first generation studies (Mossman, 1994). Second, actuarial methods were more accurate than unstructured clinical judgment, but both methods exceeded chance (Mossman, 1994). Although these results are encouraging it is also true that predictive accuracy is far from perfect. The question, therefore, still remains: What is the current status of the risk assessment field?

It is perhaps wise to evaluate the accuracy of violence predictions in the context of other interventions. In 1993, Lipsey and Wilson reviewed over 300 meta-analyses evaluating the efficacy of various psychological, educational, and correctional treatments. For the sake of comparison, the authors also included a number of meta-analyses of medical treatments. Interventions were assessed in terms of effect sizes. One such measure of effect size, which will be familiar to many readers, is the Pearson correlation r. A few of the treatments included in the review, along with their corresponding effect size (Pearson r), are presented in Table 11.2. Psychopathy and psychosis are two risk factors that have been subject to meta-analytic review and constitute useful examples from the risk assessment literature. Psychosis is the weaker of the two predictors, correlating with violence on average about $r = .25$ (Douglas & Hart, 1998). Violence and psychopathy, as assessed using the PCL-R, exhibits a higher correlation, somewhere in the neighbourhood of $r = .27$ (Hemphill, Hare, & Wong, 1998) and $r = .37$ (Salekin, Rogers, & Sewell, 1996). As can be seen in Table 11.2, violence predictions made on the basis of psychosis or psychopathy are more accurate than predictions that relatively smaller classroom sizes will result in correspondingly high academic achievement, that public advertising campaigns will increase the use of seatbelts, that correctional treatment will have a beneficial effect on offenders, or that cardiac bypass surgery will lower mortality.

From a purely statistical standpoint, predictions of violence display at least the same level of effectiveness as correctional treatment programs, cardiac bypass surgery, or low student-teacher ratios. It would, therefore, seem illogical to support the latter without also supporting the former. Moreover, criticisms that comparisons of this nature are inappropriate are not convincing because predictions of violence, which necessarily involve public safety, seem no less serious than other social concerns that relate to public wellness, such as seatbelt use or medical interventions. Although the research suggests the strength of violence predictions is similar, or even superior to, many other well-established interventions, the decision to accept or reject these predictions ultimately remains with administrators, judges, and policy makers.

SUMMARY

Efforts to study violence are hampered by a number of methodological considerations linked to the complex nature of this behaviour. Foremost among these considerations are the difficulties associated with

TABLE 11.2
Average effect sizes for various interventions

Intervention	Effect size (*r*)
Risk Assessment	
Psychopathy, association with violence	.27
(Hemphill, Hare, & Wong, 1998)	
Psychosis, association with violence	.25
(Douglas & Hart, 1998)	
Psychological	
Cognitive behavioural therapy, effects on depression	.44
(Dobson, 1989)	
Psychotherapy, effects on all outcomes	.39
(Smith, Glass, & Miller, 1980)	
Correctional treatment-adults, effects on all outcomes	.12
(Lösel & Koferl, 1989)	
Educational	
Student tutoring, effects on academic achievement	.20
(Cohen, Kulik, & Kulik, 1982)	
Small class size, effects on achievement	.10
(Hedges & Stock, 1983)	
Mass media campaigns, effects on seatbelt use	.07
(Moore, 1990)	
Medical	
Cardiac bypass surgery, effects on angina pain	.37
(Lynn & Donovan, 1980)	
Cyclosporine, effects on organ rejection	.15
(Rosenthal, 1991)	
Cardiac bypass surgery, effects on mortality	.07
(Lynn & Donovan, 1980)	

SOURCE: Lipsey and Wilson (1993)

defining and measuring violence. Studies also vary with respect to the information sources relied upon (e.g. official records, self-reports, collateral reports). A multimethod approach using several different sources simultaneously is probably best because a violent incident undetected by one information source may be detected by another.

Although violence constitutes a minority of all reported crime in Canada, it is a pervasive social problem with serious negative consequences for the wellness of Canadians. Further, the level of violent crime reported in Canada is relatively high compared to other Western nations. There are some indications that the rate of violent crime has experienced a sharp rise over the past decade, but it is difficult to tell whether this reflects a true increase in the actual occurrence of violence or whether it is more properly attributable to changes in reporting, arrest policies, or other factors. Homicide rates, which traditionally have been considered a stable indicator of violence, have not increased over this same period and may even be on the decline. Victims of violence are not evenly distributed throughout Canadian society but tend to be disproportionately concentrated among women and youth.

Over the last few decades, attempts to predict violence have gained an increasingly prominent position within the law. The emergence of violence prediction within the legal system appears to have occurred initially as a result of changes in civil commitment criteria, which began to emphasize "dangerousness to others." Presently, there are many circumstances in both the civil and criminal context that require predictions of violence as a result of statutory provisions or judicial decisions. The accuracy of these predictions was first called seriously into question by research published in the early seventies. The conceptual shift away from dangerousness towards risk assessment is probably the result of "first generation" research combined with pressures to deinstitutionalize psychiatric patients and public sensitivity to predictive failures.

Risk assessment involves two processes: identifying persons likely to commit acts of violence and developing interventions to manage or reduce that likelihood. Despite the difficulty of interpreting the methodologically varied research in this area, there is growing consensus over some of the more important factors that identify persons at risk for violence. Included among these risk factors are age, gender, prior violence, social instability and maladjustment, acute mental illness, substance abuse, psychopathy, and sexual deviation. Psychopathy is probably the single most powerful predictor of future community and institutional violence. Traditionally, the task of predicting violence has been accomplished using unstructured clinical judgment, or, in recent years, actuarial instruments. Unstructured clinical judgment leaves the evaluator free to determine which factors will be the most appropriate for use in the case at hand. In this approach the evaluator is the final source of the prediction. Unstructured clinical judgment embodies the greatest flexibility, but lacks consistency and predictive validity. In contrast, the prediction of an actuarial scheme is produced by the predetermined processes of the instrument itself, removing human judgment from the final prediction phase. Although the structure of the actuarial approach improves consistency and predictive accuracy, it tends to discourage any consideration of case-specific factors. In response to the weaknesses of the traditional approaches some commentators have begun calling for the development of clinical guidelines. The objective of these guidelines is to ensure risk assessments are conducted systematically but leave the evaluator free to modify the assessment appropriately to each specific case. Early research suggests clinical guidelines may hold some promise for improving future risk assessments. Finally, the evidence available indicates that current predictive abilities exceed the level of accuracy that may be achieved by chance alone, but it is also apparent that they are a long way from perfection. Ultimately, the question of whether predictions of violence are sufficiently accurate to warrant their current status within the legal arena is one that remains in the hands of the judiciary and policy makers.

QUESTIONS FOR DISCUSSION

1. Should mental health professionals testify in court regarding risk assessments? What, if any, restrictions should be placed on the testimony they offer?
2. How should the courts deal with cases where different experts present very discrepant assessments of risk (i.e., the so-called battle of the experts)?
3. Accepting that even the most thorough risk assessments will never be completely successful at predicting and managing future violence, are there some junctures in the legal system where they are more or less appropriate (e.g., civil commitment proceedings vs. juvenile transfer decisions *prior* to conviction vs. parole decisions *after* conviction)?
4. Should predictive power (i.e., the ability to predict accurately) be the paramount consideration for selecting and using risk factors, or should legal and even moral considerations play a role? Consider the competing rights of the public versus those of the individual in the situations described below.
   Example 1: Is it appropriate to use static factors (e.g., male gender, or being the victim of child abuse), which are beyond the control of the person being assessed?
   Example 2: In one actuarial risk assessment scheme, violence resulting in death and violence directed towards females were associated with *lower* risk of future violence. Such findings are counter-intuitive. Should items such as these be retained or removed from actuarial schemes?
   Example 3: Drug or alcohol intoxication during the commission of a crime

is sometimes considered by the courts as a mitigating factor, yet substance abuse is often perceived to increase the risk of future violence and may have an adverse effect (from the offender's perspective) on sentencing, parole decisions, and so forth. Should the legal status of a risk factor affect its role in risk assessments?

RECOMMENDED READING

Douglas, K.S., & Webster, C.D. (1998). Predicting violence in mentally and personality disordered individuals. In R. Roesch, S.D. Hart, & J.R.P. Ogloff (Eds.), *Psychology and law: The state of the discipline.* New York: Plenum Press.

Hart, S.D. (1998). The role of psychopathy in assessing risk for violence: Conceptual and methodological issues. *Legal and Criminological Psychology, 3,* 121–137.

Monahan, J., & Steadman, H.J. (Eds.). (1994). *Violence and mental disorder.* Chicago: University of Chicago Press.

Monahan, J. (1996). Violence prediction: The past twenty years and the next twenty years. *Criminal Justice and Behavior, 23(1),* 107–120.

Webster, C.D., & Jackson, M.A. (1997). *Impulsivity: Theory, assessment, and treatment.* New York: Guilford.

PART FOUR

Introduction to Forensic Civil Psychology

12. Civil Commitment and Civil Competence: Psychological Issues

Kevin S. Douglas and William J. Koch

In the early 1980s, George Reid committed a violent robbery, was arrested, and later found not guilty by reason of insanity. He was held in a maximum security psychiatric facility, having been declared under the Ontario Mental Health Act to be an involuntary patient who was incompetent to make treatment decisions for himself. He was diagnosed with schizophreniform psychosis. His psychiatrist, Dr Russell Fleming, proposed to treat him with psychotropic (antipsychotic) medication. Such medication usually has a beneficial effect on symptoms of psychosis, as well restoring cognitive capacity to some extent. However, it also has side effects that many persons find highly undesirable. Under the legislation at the time, a "substitute decision maker" (in this case, a designate of the province) could provide consent to treatment on the behalf of an incompetent person. The psychiatrist applied to this person for consent to treat Mr Reid. The substitute decision maker refused, as Mr Reid had earlier expressed (when he was competent) that he did not want to take psychotropic medication. The psychiatrist appealed this decision to the psychiatric review board in Ontario, which granted consent to treatment. This decision was upheld by the Ontario District Court but later overturned by the Ontario Court of Appeal. The court of appeal held that treatment provided against the consent (even if given earlier) of a person is unconstitutional, violating the right of security of the person under section 7 of the Canadian Charter of Rights and Freedoms. This decision introduced a conundrum into the law: although people could be admitted to hospital involuntarily, the mental illness that gave rise to their involuntary hospitalization could not be treated. Without treatment, patients' illnesses may not ever remit, and patients could then be hospitalized indefinitely. Although Ontario has dealt with this problem through revising its legislation, the Fleming case has dramatic implications for other provinces that may treat patients without their consent, or even against their express wishes. The inherent dilemma is that to provide treatment may be unconstitutional, but to withhold it may give rise to indefinite hospitalization, because the very basis for hospitalization – mental illness – may not remit without treatment.

The case of *Fleming v. Reid* (1991) illustrates and introduces a number of key concepts that will be covered in this chapter on civil commitment and civil competence. For instance, on what legal basis can people be involuntarily detained in a psychiatric institution? Similarly, once a person has been hospitalized, does that person have a right to refuse treatment? How is a person's competence or ability to consent to treatment determined? Competence is important in other areas of life as well. For instance, people can be declared incompetent to manage their own estate, or even to make decisions about their lives. As we will see, psychologists have been very active in terms of conducting research that can assist decision makers in their attempts to come to appropriate decisions in these areas.

In this chapter we deal with several important issues that can arise under Canadian mental health legislation – primarily, provincial Mental Health Acts and Guardianship Acts. The first section of this chapter deals with civil commitment, which involves the process of hospitalizing persons in psychiatric institutions, often involuntarily. The second section deals with civil competence, which is a term used to denote the ability of individuals to make decisions within different legal settings. The focus of this latter section will be on competence to make decisions regarding psychiatric treatment and one's own personal affairs.

OVERVIEW OF CIVIL COMMITMENT LAW

One of the most strongly valued principles in Canadian society is personal freedom and liberty. These rights are so firmly entrenched in our collective value system that they are constitutionally protected in the Charter (section 7; see Chapter 2). Prima facie, civil commitment is a major violation of this right to liberty (Robertson, 1994). The only other process that deprives individuals of liberty is the criminal justice process. That is, if a person is arrested for an offence, he or she may be detained while awaiting trial; if convicted of an offence, he or she may be sentenced to a penal institution. In these circumstances, persons are being punished for having committed criminal offences against society. In the case of civil commitment, however, no such criminal acts are requisite for the involuntary detention of persons within psychiatric or mental health facilities. Further, in comparison to criminal procedures there are fewer safeguards protecting the rights of persons confined under civil commitment legislation.

In its most basic sense, civil commitment is derived from the "parens patriae" model of the state's powers (Robertson, 1994), in which the state is construed as the "parent" of those unable to care for themselves. The state, in this case the provinces, has the statutory right to detain persons if those persons meet certain criteria. It is typically considered to be in the "best interests" of these persons to be detained. Although there is interprovincial discrepancy in terms of precise criteria, most legislation requires that a person be mentally ill, in need of treatment, and pose some sort of danger or threat to the safety of himself/herself or to others. Although each province and territory has legislation that governs civil commitment, one or two physicians or psychiatrists must typically agree that, upon assessment, the person meets the criteria for commitment. Because there are important differences across the provinces, the legislation is summarized in Table 12.1.

Table 12.1 contains several important domains of most civil commitment legislation and outlines how each province's law corresponds to these domains. As can be seen, to be detained under civil commitment legislation, every jurisdiction requires that a person be mentally ill. The definition of mental illness, however, differs across jurisdictions. An important difference lies in the concept of the functional definition of mental illness (Robertson, 1994). An example of this type of definition is found in the legislation of Saskatchewan: "'mental disorder' means a disorder of thought, perceptions, feelings or behaviour that seriously impairs a person's judgment, capacity to recognize reality, ability to associate with others or ability to meet the ordinary demands of life, in respect of which treatment is advisable." Other provinces that use such a functional approach include Alberta, British Columbia, Manitoba, New Brunswick, and Prince Edward Island. Conversely, Ontario and Newfoundland use more traditional definitions of mental illness, which do not specify the effect of the mental illness on the patients' thoughts and behaviour. For example, the focus of this definition is on mental disorder as "a disease or disability of the mind."

The next criterion for admission to a psychiatric facility as an involuntary patient is that the person poses a danger to self or others, or that the person requires hospitalization for his or her safety or protection,

TABLE 12.1
A comparison of civil commitment legislation across Canadian jurisdictions

Specified statutory factors	B.C.	Yukon	Alta.	N.W.T.	Sask.	Man.	Ont.	Que.	N.B.	N.S.	P.E.I.	Nfld.
Requirement of mental disorder	yes	yes	yes	yes	yes	yes	yes	yes	yes	yes	yes	yes
Functional definition of mental illness	yes	yes	yes	yes	yes	yes	no	no	yes	no	yes	no
Requirement of danger to self or others	yes	yes	yes	yes	yes	yes	yes	yes	yes	yes	yes	yes
Strict definition of danger	no	yes	yes	yes	no	yes	yes	no	no	no	no	no
Requirement of need for treatment	yes	no	no	no	yes	yes	no	yes	no	yes	no	no
Right to refuse/consent to treatment	no	no	no	no	no	yes	yes	no	no	yes	no	no
Right to be informed of reasons for detention	yes	yes	yes	yes	yes	yes	yes	yes	yes	no	yes	no
Right to apply for review panel	yes	yes	yes	no	yes	yes	yes	yes*	yes	yes	yes	yes
Specified right to legal counsel	yes	yes	no	yes	no	yes	yes	no	yes	yes	yes	no
Provision for apprehension by peace officer	yes	yes	yes	yes	yes	yes	yes	no	yes	yes	yes	yes
Length of short-term commitment order	48 hrs.	24 hrs.	24 hrs.	48 hrs.	24 hrs.	72 hrs.	72 hrs.	48 hrs.	72 hrs.	48 hrs.	72 hrs.	15 day
Length of initial commitment certificate	1 mo.	21 day	1 mo.	14 day	21 day	3 wks.	2 wks.	21 day	1 mo.	7 day	30 day	1 mo.
Length of second commitment certificate	1 mo.	21 day	1 mo.	1 mo.	21 day	3 mo.	1 mo.	3 mo.	2 mo.	1 mo.	90 day	2 mo.
Length of further commitment certificate	3, 6 mo.	21 day	1, 6 mo.	3, 6 mo.	21 day, 1 yr.	3 mo.	2, 3 mo.	6 mo.	3 mo.	3, 6 mo.	12 mo.	3, 6 mo., 1 yr.
Discharge criteria specified	yes	no	yes	yes	yes	yes	yes	no	yes	no	yes	no
Statutory presence of review panel	yes	yes	yes	no	yes	yes	yes	yes*	yes	yes	yes	yes

TABLE 12.1—(*Concluded*)
A comparison of civil commitment legislation across Canadian jurisdictions

Specified statutory factors	B.C.	Yukon	Alta.	N.W.T.	Sask.	Man.	Ont.	Que.	N.B.	N.S.	P.E.I.	Nfld.
Director may give treatment consent	yes	yes	yes	yes	yes	yes	yes	yes	yes	yes	yes	yes
Specified right to appeal to court	yes	yes	yes	yes	yes	yes	yes	no	no	yes	no	yes
Any person may bring issue before court	yes	yes	yes	yes	yes	yes	yes	yes	yes	yes	yes	yes

Notes: Statutes are as amended by annual provincial amending legislation.
The Manitoba legislature drafted Bill 35 (a new Mental Health Act) in 1998, that was unproclaimed at the time of writing.
"*" under the Quebec column refers to the fact that in the Quebec legislation, the Commission des affaires sociales seems to be the functional equivalent of statutorily created Review Panels in other provinces' schemes. As such, while Quebec does not have a statutory Review Panel per se, it has a body that serves some of the same purposes (e.g., to review the legitimacy of detention).
"??" indicates that the statutes are unclear in this regard.

Statutes: B.C. – Mental Health Act, R.S.B.C. 1996, c. 288; Yukon – Mental Health Act, S.Y.T. 1989–90, c. 28; Alta. – Mental Health Act, S.A. 1988. c. M-13.1; NWT – Mental Health Act, R.S.N.W.T. 1988, c. M-10; Sask. – Mental Health Services Act, S.S. 1984–85–86, c. M-13.1; Man. – Mental Health Act, R.S.M. 1987, c. M110; Ont. – Mental Health Act, R.S.O. 1990, c. M.7; Que. – Mental Patients Protection Act, R.S.Q. 1977, P-41; N.B. – An Act to Amend the Mental Health Act, S.N.B. 1989, c. 23.; N.S. – Hospitals Act, R.S.N.S. 1989, c. 208; P.E.I. – Mental Health Act, S.P.E.I. 1994, c. 39; Nfld. – Mental Health Act, R.S.N. 1990, c. M-9.

or the safety or protection of others. As can be seen in Table 12.1, many provinces have somewhat broadly defined "safety" or "protection" based construals of this criterion. For instance, section 22(2) (c) (ii) of the British Columbia Mental Health Act states that the person must require "care, supervision and control in a Provincial mental health facility for the person's own protection or for the protection of others." Case law in British Columbia has buttressed this broad interpretation of that criterion (*McCorkell v. Riverview Hospital*, 1993). Other provinces have more strict construals. The Ontario Mental Health Act requires, in sections 15(1) (d), (e), and (f), respectively, that the person's mental disorder will likely result in "serious bodily harm to the person," "serious bodily harm to another person," or "imminent and serious physical impairment of the person." Manitoba has similar provisions, with section 16(1.1) (a) (i) of its Act stating that a person must be "likely to cause serious harm to himself or herself or to another person, or to suffer substantial mental or physical deterioration ..." Finally, Alberta may be considered as being somewhat strict in its statutory approach to dangerousness, requiring that the person is "in a condition presenting or likely to present a danger to himself or others ..." (section 2(b)). As Robertson (1994) explains, however, case law has evolved in the separate provinces such that the Ontario legislation has received quite a broad interpretation whereas the Alberta criterion has been interpreted more narrowly.

Another important aspect of civil commitment legislation concerns whether the need for treatment is a specified part of the admission criteria. Again, provinces vary on whether this criterion is explicitly integrated into the legislation. A related issue with potential constitutional implications is whether legislation provides for patients to consent to treatment. Provinces are divided on this issue as well and it is a source of considerable controversy (Robertson, 1994), as we will see.

Although several issues concerning civil commitment have been litigated, the implications of the Charter are perhaps most important and deserve highlighting. As Robertson (1994) points out, the Charter has been influential in recent amendments of mental health law. For example, in *Thwaites v. Health Sciences Centre Psychiatric Facility* (1988) the Manitoba Court of Appeal determined that the relevant legislation violated section 9 of the Charter – the right not to be arbitrarily detained – because, among other things, there were no dangerousness or protection provisions, which, the court held, failed to impair as little as possible a detained person's right not to be arbitrarily detained. However, a similar Prince Edward Island law was upheld in *Re Jenkins* (1986), as was the Ontario law in *Azhar v. Anderson* (1985) and British Columbia's legislation in *McCorkell v. Riverview Hospital* (1993). For additional discussion of constitutional issues surrounding civil commitment, the reader is referred to Robertson (1994).

There are many other important issues surrounding civil commitment, some of which are summarized in Table 12.1. These include whether patients must be informed of the reasons for hospitalization, whether persons have the specified right to apply to review panels (quasi-judicial tribunals that can grant discharge), whether persons have the specified right to legal counsel, whether there is provision in the legislation for peace officers to apprehend apparently mentally disordered persons, the length of the period of detention, and various other matters. The next section will discuss research relevant to civil commitment issues, highlighting, where possible, Canadian efforts.

RESEARCH ON CIVIL COMMITMENT AND PSYCHIATRIC PATIENTS

Description of Civilly Committed Psychiatric Patients

The most basic level of research describes the numbers and characteristics of persons committed to psychiatric facilities. Unfortunately, there are no existing data available in Canada on the number of people involuntarily committed annually. We can, however, gain some insight by looking at the number of people discharged from psychiatric hospitals. For example, in 1992–93 29,991 patients were discharged from psychiatric hospitals (or died while in hospital, a much smaller number) (Statistics Canada, 1995b). The actual number of persons detained in psychiatric hospitals annually would be lower than this figure, due to duplicate admissions and discharges. Regardless, this figure is down substantially from decades ago; in 1957, a period for which data were still collected, 70,300 persons were detained in psychiatric facilities (Dominion Bureau of Statistics, 1955–7). The trend over time towards fewer persons being institutionalized is apparent from 1975 statistics, which show that there were 44,847 inpatients on any given day in that year (Statistics Canada, 1975). The deinstitutionalization movement led to the rapid downsizing of psychiatric facilities.

Who is civilly committed? Of the 29,991 patient separations in 1992–3, 59% (17,652) were men and 41% (12,339) were women (Statistics

Canada, 1995b). The age range of these individuals was clustered in the 25–34 year range. Their mean length of stay, in days, was 274. The majority of patients had schizophrenic diagnoses (8,686; 29%), followed by affective diagnoses (5,429; 18%). Other common diagnoses were alcohol dependence (2,215; 7.4%), adjustment reaction (2,034; 6.8%), personality disorders (1,926; 6.4%), neurotic (anxiety) disorders (1,287; 4.3%), and drug abuse (1,067; 3.6%).

Some recent research findings of persons who had applied for a review panel at a psychiatric hospital in British Columbia provides additional and consistent data. Ogloff and Grant (1997; see also Grant, Ogloff, & Douglas, in press; Douglas, Ogloff, Nicholls, & Grant, 1999; Nicholls, Ogloff, & Douglas, 1997) reported that of their sample of 279 psychiatric patients in British Columbia, 167 (59.9%) were men. The average age at admission was 38.6 and ranged from 17 to 88. The vast majority of patients had previously been admitted to a psychiatric facility (258; 91.2%). Most persons were diagnosed with some sort of psychotic disorder (188; 67.4%) at discharge, with over half of the sample having a schizophrenic diagnosis (140; 50.2%). In general, this sample showed many characteristics of a marginalized group of persons with troubled histories. A mere 12 persons (4.2%) were employed prior to admission. Close to 20% of the sample had been living in skid row hotels or on the streets with no fixed address. Approximately one-quarter of the patients reported having been physically or sexually abused as children. In addition to these experiences, the group, as a whole, engaged in a large amount of criminal and suicidal behaviour.

Because the issue of harm to self and others is legally relevant, the patients' histories of violence and crime were also studied by Ogloff and Grant. As it turns out, a majority of the patients had some history of suicidal or self-injurious behaviour (191; 67.5%); many patients also engaged in self-harm while hospitalized (65; 23.0%). The average number of past offences was 4.65, with the average number of violent offences being approximately 1.0. In all, 65 patients (23.3%) had been previously arrested for violent offences, 137 (49.1%) had been violent to others in the 2 weeks prior to admission, and a surprisingly high number (179, 64.2%) had a documented history of some sort of violent behaviour to others. This profile of the psychiatric patient is consistent with other research on such patients, primarily from American sources (Hiday, 1988).

Other Canadian research adds to our knowledge of psychiatric patients by comparing patients who apply or are discharged by review panels to involuntarily committed patients who do not apply, or who are released by attending physicians. This topic is important because of the significant role played by review panels in mental health law. It is worth understanding their effect on psychiatric patients. Gray, Clark, Higenbottam, Ledwidge, and Paredes (1985) compared 487 involuntary patients who applied for review panels with 2,966 who were eligible to apply but did not. Demographically, in comparison to patients who did not apply for review, patients who did apply were younger, more often male, had fewer years of education, and were more likely unemployed at time of admission. Patients who applied also had a more severe psychiatric history. They were more likely to have had previous hospitalizations, to have had multiple previous hospitalizations, and to have been readmitted after a shorter length of time in the community. Patients who requested review panels were more often schizophrenic and less often mentally retarded. A greater number of patients seeking review had problems at work, with parents, or alcohol abuse. Although the behaviour of these patients was rated as abnormal by psychiatrists more often than was the behaviour of the other patients, patients who sought review, compared to the other patients, were more likely to know who they were, where they were, and what day it was (i.e., referred to as cognitive orientation).

The authors wisely caution that some of the differences between the groups, though highly significant due to the large sample size in the study, may not be of great clinical importance. For instance, the behaviour of the patients was rated as abnormal in 75% of the review patient cases; in the nonreview patient sample, this occurred in 69% of the cases. This difference is statistically significant, although its clinical implications are not clearly demonstrable.

Ledwidge et al. (1987) compared patients released by the review panel with those discharged by the attending physician. By definition, patients who are discharged by the review panel are released against medical advice. The purpose of the study was to examine whether patients released by the review panels were more likely to have troubles in the community and to be readmitted more frequently and quickly than patients released by physicians. The two groups did not differ in terms of rate or time to readmission. Indeed, very few differences between the groups in terms of community adjustment were revealed. Ogloff and Grant (1997), who also compared patients released by review panels to those released by attending physicians, found that those released by panels actually fared better in the community – they were less often violent to others, arrested, or returned to hospital.

Dangerousness to Self and Others and Risk Assessment for Psychiatric Patient Violence

An issue that often arises is whether it is fair to detain persons in part on the basis of forecasts of future dangerous behaviour. This is a reasonable question to ask, because in the past research had shown that psychologists demonstrated a poor ability to predict violence (see Chapter 11; for reviews of this issue, see Borum, 1996; Douglas & Webster, 1999; Monahan, 1981; Webster, Douglas, Eaves, & Hart, 1997a, 1997b). More recent research, however, particularly in the last decade, indicates that accurate predictions are possible (Douglas & Webster, 1999; Mossman, 1994; Rice, 1997; Webster et al., 1997a, 1997b). Much of this research has been conducted by Canadian psychological researchers and is covered in greater detail in other chapters of this book, but its relevance to civil commitment will be summarized here.

All jurisdictions require, in some form or another, that for persons to be involuntarily detained in a mental health facility they must pose some sort of danger or threat to the safety of others or to themselves. Several interrelated issues fall under this topic. Generally, as discussed above, it is important to know the potential levels of harm to self and others that psychiatric patients may cause. More specifically, it is imperative to be able to identify which patients are at greatest risk to harm others or themselves. This task is commonly known as risk assessment for violence, or predicting or assessing dangerousness or violence. Although it is clearly relevant to the legislative issue of dangerousness, safety, or protection, it should be noted that civil commitment legislation provides for patients to be detained not only for risk of harm for physical violence, but also for more general kinds of harm. Put another way, while a violent act (e.g., physically assaulting a person) would satisfy the law, so too may other, more broadly defined, nonviolent acts (e.g., being verbally threatening).

A key component of risk assessment is the relationship between mental disorder and violence. Although opinion is mixed on this issue, a recent meta-analysis by Canadian researchers of over 100 studies suggests that there is a robust association between psychosis and violence (Douglas & Hart, 1996). This relationship held for civil psychiatric patients as well as for other populations (e.g., inmates, forensic patients). The implications of this meta-analysis are that major mental illnesses, such as schizophrenia and mania, elevate the odds of violence in comparison to other mental disorders, and especially in comparison to no mental disorders. Psychotic symptoms, such as hallucinations and delusions, are particularly strongly related to violence.

Knowledge of the relationship between mental disorders and violence can be helpful when deciding whether a person poses a threat to the safety of others (for further discussion of the assessment of violence risk see Chapter 11). Perhaps a more salient issue confronting mental health professionals concerns harm to self, since the potential for harm to self is one of the criterion for involuntary hospitalization. Of course, it is vital to understand the risk of self-injury in order to prevent suicide attempts in civil psychiatric patients, which unfortunately are quite common. For this reason, dozens of suicide assessment inventories have been proposed to guide clinicians' decisions about what factors to consider in these important evaluations (Range & Knott, 1997). Box 12.1 presents the efforts of a Canadian research project, part of which was devoted to the understanding of suicidal and self-injurious behaviour in civilly committed psychiatric patients.

Box 12.1

Suicide and Self-Harm among Psychiatric Patients

There is little doubt that the task of assessing risk for suicide and other self-injurious behaviours is a common and important task for mental health professionals who work with civilly committed psychiatric patients, or mentally ill persons generally. Unfortunately, suicide is quite common among persons with major mental disorders such as schizophrenia or major depression. In order to prevent suicide and other forms of self-injurious behaviour, it is first important to understand the characteristics of those who are suicidal or who have shown self-injurious behaviour. A Canadian research project that was conducted at Riverview psychiatric hospital in the Lower Mainland of British Columbia may help in this regard. This research project carefully studied close to 300 involuntarily committed psychiatric patients (see, generally, Ogloff & Grant, 1997; Douglas, Ogloff, Nicholls, & Grant, 1999).

Some of the findings bear upon the issue of suicide and self-harm. Jack, Nicholls, and Ogloff (1998) found that close to half (*n* = 148) of all patients had engaged in some sort of self-injurious behaviour prior to being hospitalized. More specifically, 40 patients (14% of sample) admitted that they had thoughts of killing themselves (suicidal ideation) just prior to hospitalization, and 28 (10%) actually injured themselves. During the actual hospital stay, 42 patients engaged in self-injurious behaviour.

Jack et al. (1998) used numerous variables in multiple regression analyses in an attempt to predict self-injury that occurred in the hospital. Three related variables were statistically significantly related to self-injury: suicidal ideation while hospitalized; a history of self-injury; and, self-injury in the 2 weeks prior to hospitalization. In addition to these findings, Nicholls, Jack, and Ogloff (1998) found that the presence of verbal and physical aggression *to others* was related to the occurrence of self-injurious behaviour while in the hospital. These results, which are consistent with other research, indicate that there are several important variables that ought to be assessed in evaluating risk for self-injurious behaviour. These relate mainly to other manifestations of violence towards self and others.

Given results such as those described in Box 12.1, what can be said about the prediction of self-harm for the purpose of Mental Health Acts? It is true that suicide risk assessment is still prone to many errors. Persons may be detained on the basis of an imprecise and error-prone practice, but it would be fair to state that some form of guided decision making can lead to predictions that are more accurate than clinicians' global judgments, and far better than chance. Given that the law demands risk assessments, it is clear that clinicians will continue to offer them in the future. It is important that assessment be rooted in state of the discipline practices and knowledge in order to offer ethically and professionally defensible assessments that are as fair as possible to the patients whose liberty may depend on their results.

CIVIL COMPETENCIES

The term competence refers to whether a person has the mental capacity to perform some task. This concept is familiar in the criminal context with respect to competence (fitness) to stand trial, which was covered in Chapter 10. In the civil arena, competence may arise at a number of key legal junctures. And while a person may be incompetent to perform one task, he or she may be competent in other areas. The two main areas discussed below are competence to manage one's affairs under guardianship law and competence to consent to treatment.

Guardianship of the Person and Property

Guardianship refers to the appointment of a person to manage the personal or property affairs of another person who has been deemed incapable or incompetent to manage such affairs (Robertson, 1994). Again, as with civil commitment, important civil rights are at issue, since the right of persons to make decisions about themselves and their estates is effectively taken away and given to another person. The psychologically important and relevant task is making the determination of competence. How do we know if a person is incapable of managing his or her estate?

The Law

As with the other statutory law reviewed in this chapter, legislation concerning property and personal guardianship is the responsibility of the provinces, and not the federal government. In most provinces, personal and property guardianship is governed by the same legislation (Robertson, 1994). Although the legislation varies across provinces, their commonalities will be described here. An in-depth discussion is provided by Robertson (1994).

As with other areas of mental health law, guardianship law is premised on the parens patriae model, the essence of which is that the state may act on behalf of its citizens in certain circumstances, if it is considered to be in their "best interests." The rights that persons have to decide personal affairs (i.e., where to live) or property affairs (i.e., how to manage an estate) may be terminated and put in others' hands. This can happen, in theory, only if the person is deemed incompetent to manage such affairs.

Across jurisdictions, applications for the appointment of guardians may be made to the court. The level of court is the Provincial or Territorial Superior or Supreme Court. These applications typically are supported by affidavits from the applicant setting out in detail the reasons for the application, as well as affidavits from two physicians that state the medical grounds in support of the application. In most jurisdictions, the criteria for incompetence include mental disorder or infirmity and the inability to manage one's affairs (Robertson, 1994).

Medical practitioners must provide evidence regarding the criteria of mental disorder and inability to manage one's estate. One criticism of the existing law is that, with the exception of psychiatrists, most physicians are not trained in matters relating to mental disorder and capacity. As the legislation does not provide detailed descriptions of what constitutes "incapacity," it places the burden on the physician to determine what he or she feels the criteria ought to be. This point is raised by Gordon and Verdun-Jones (1992), who also highlight several other potential limitations of the present guardianship law across Canada: the presence of a mental disorder does not necessitate incapacity, the determination of a single criterion of incapacity is impossible, and incapacity cannot be determined solely through medical assessment. There are no provisions for the involvement of other professionals, such as clinical psychologists, who may be more appropriately trained to assess mental incapacity and to conduct assessments. Finally, there is no requirement that assessments involve the use of objective tests or measures (Gordon & Verdun-Jones, 1992).

Assessment procedures that utilize objective tests have been suggested by some investigators (Anderer, 1990; Grisso, 1986). For instance, Anderer recommended that assessments for personal guardianship cover six functional areas of coping: nutrition, clothing, personal hygiene, health care, residential concerns, and safety. With respect to property guardianship, the management of money, investments, or major expenses and the disposition of assets are considered important. As Gordon and Verdun-Jones (1992) explain, guardianship assessments should include the examination of specific areas of functioning that are relevant to the management of personal and property spheres of living, rather than a global judgment of "incapacity."

Gordon and Verdun-Jones further assert that guardianship law places too great an emphasis on protecting people's estates rather than the people themselves, and they point out that the legislation makes no provision for "partial" guardianship (see also Robertson, 1994). That is, the present law holds that a person is either completely competent in all realms or completely incompetent. It may well be that persons are competent to manage certain areas of their lives but not others.

Robertson (1994) correctly stated that the law of guardianship is highly intrusive, in that it strips a person of essential and core rights. Given the power of the law, it should possess certain features: "It must provide clear and well-reasoned criteria for the appointment of a guardian. There must be effective procedural safeguards. The powers and duties of a guardian must be clearly defined. Above all, the statutory framework must be the product of careful thought, with a view to achieving an acceptable balance between necessary paternalism on the one hand, and individual liberty on the other ... Measured by these standards, the present Canadian law of guardianship fails miserably." (p. 117). Robertson makes this claim on the basis of the criticisms outlined above. He also points out that procedures are cumbersome and the law does not provide enough specificity concerning important issues such as the extent of the guardian's power.

Some of the criticisms of guardianship law, at least in British Columbia, appear to have some verifiable basis. Davies and Taylor (1989) studied 500 applications for guardianship made to the British Columbia Supreme Court between 1966 and 1987. Most applications (62%) were for guardianship of both person and property, with guardianship of the person occurring infrequently by itself. Their results indicated some potentially undesirable practices. Surprisingly, persons who were the subjects of the hearings, and who stood to have many of their rights terminated, were almost never present at the hearings. In fact, over half of the patients were not even aware that the proceedings were taking place. Hearings were attended by lawyers alone, and most lasted fewer than 5 minutes. Medical evidence on affidavits was typically sparse and often amounted to no more than an assertion that the person was incapable of managing his or her affairs and was in need of a guardian. This research seems to indicate that guardianship hearings are given rather superficial treatment by both the courts and legal players.

COMPETENCE TO CONSENT TO TREATMENT

The issue of competence to consent to treatment often arises in the civil commitment context. As previously discussed, mental health acts differ in terms of allowing persons to consent to or deny treatment. Some provinces permit competent patients an absolute right of refusal (Manitoba, Ontario, Quebec, Nova Scotia). One province (Alberta) gives a qualified or conditional right to refuse treatment, in that psychiatrists may apply to review panels to permit the administration of treatment to mentally competent persons who have refused consent. Other jurisdictions, such as British Columbia and Newfoundland, explicitly provide for treatment of competent persons against their will. Prince Edward Island and New Brunswick also provide for involuntary treatment against the wills of nonconsenting people (Robertson, 1994). For those jurisdictions that do allow for patient consent to treatment, the issue of competence to consent to such treatment is of some importance. Some persons may be admitted as involuntary patients, and, if deemed mentally competent to consent to or refuse treatment, may refuse to consent. As a consequence, little can then be done to ameliorate the psychiatric conditions of these patients, which may render it difficult to bring about a mental state that would allow for their eventual release from hospital.

The major legal problem with treating a competent person against his or her will is that it is a flagrant violation of that person's rights, particularly the right of security of the person (section 7 of the Charter). In the case of *Fleming*, which opened this chapter, the Ontario Court of Appeal held that the wishes of a mentally competent person to refuse treatment cannot be ignored, regardless of the beneficial nature of the treatment. The decision in *Fleming*, though not binding in provinces other than Ontario, clearly indicates that some of the legislation that provides for the involuntary treatment of mentally competent and nonconsenting persons may be in violation of section 7 of the Charter and, thus, unconstitutional.

One may wonder how many psychiatric patients are actually competent to consent to treatment. A study carried out in an Ontario provincial psychiatric hospital addressed this question (Hoffman & Srinivasan, 1992). The Ontario Mental Health Act (1990) criteria for competence are that the patient understands the nature of the illness, the treatment, and the consequences of providing or denying consent. Using a semi-structured interview format, the investigators determined that 21 of the 60 patients tested (35%) were deemed to be competent. Of the 39 persons deemed to be incompetent, 10 met some but not all of the criteria. Based on this small sample, it appears that a fair number of persons may actually be competent to consent to treatment, suggesting the importance of performing a thorough assessment of this competence. Based on these findings, the constitutionality of statutes that do not separate commitment and competence to consent to treatment may be in question.

How does the professional called upon to assess competence to consent to treatment go about determining competence in this context? Several provinces provide no clear indication of the criteria used to determine whether an individual is competent or not. In Nova Scotia as well as in Ontario the legislation provides some guidance concerning the factors that ought to be addressed (Robertson, 1994). It is important that a person understands the illness or condition that is to be treated, the nature of the treatment and the potential dangers stemming from both complying with treatment, and foregoing it. In addition, it is vital that consent be valid, or obtained without duress or undue pressure from authorities. Psychological ethics codes dictate that for a person to receive psychological services while hospitalized, such as the assessment or treatment, that person must give informed consent.

As Robertson (1994) reminds us, competence is a construct that is specific to a particular ability or task. As such, the assessment of competence to consent to treatment must involve investigation of factors that bear directly upon the ability to consent. Mental health professionals have discussed several standards of competence that may be used in the determination of competence to consent to treatment (Appelbaum & Grisso, 1995; Appelbaum, Lidz, & Meisel, 1987). These include the ability to choose or to express a preference between receiving treatment and not receiving treatment; the ability to understand information concerning the treatment, and the risks and benefits thereof; the ability to process treatment-related information logically and rationally; and the ability to appreciate the nature and quality of the treatment decision, as well as its implications and consequences. In practice in Canada, however, mental health professionals typically make decisions involving competency in an unsystematic way, relying on their clinical skills.

Mental health and social science professionals, in addition to attempting to elucidate the standards for assessing competence, have developed instruments for competence assessment. Although there have been several such instruments developed, we will describe the "Competency Interview Schedule" (CIS; Bean, Nishisato, Rector, & Glancy, 1994), which was developed in Canada. This group of researchers, which includes psychologists, evaluated the psychometric properties of the CIS in a sample of 96 psychiatric patients admitted to the Clarke Institute of Psychiatry in Toronto and referred for electroconvulsive treatment (ECT). The CIS has 15 questions to rate the patient, using 7–point rating scales. These questions were designed to assess four domains of competence: (1) ability to evidence a choice; (2) ability to understand the issues related to treatment; (3) ability to manipulate information and give a rational decision regarding treatment decisions; and (4) appreciation of the nature of the treatment situation and the consequences of treatment.

Questions designed to assess the ability to evidence a choice require patients to indicate if they are aware of the fact that they have been asked to decide about ECT treatment, whether this decision is difficult, and whether they would prefer to make the decision on their own or have another person make it. To assess patients' abilities to understand issues related to treatment, questions are asked regarding patients' perceptions of the potential harmfulness of treatment, potential benefits of treatment, and whether alternative treatments exist. Concerning the ability to offer a rational reason regarding treatment, patients are asked why they either agreed to or refused treatment, and if they want to get better. Finally, questions that tap appreciation of the nature of the treatment situation have patients indicate their thoughts about the doctor (e.g., whether he or she is acting in their best interests, why he or she has committed them to hospital) as well their thoughts regarding their illness and its prognosis.

Results indicated that the CIS was stable across administrations (good test-retest reliability) and between raters (good interrater reliability). Factor analysis suggested that the CIS was tapping only one factor, which the researchers labelled "general competency." In terms of validity, patients who were deemed competent by attending physicians had lower scores (e.g., indicating fewer problems) on all items than patients who were found incompetent. One particularly useful item on the test in terms of discriminating between competent and incompetent patients concerned the perceived benefits of the treatment. As it turns out, incompetent patients did not have the ability to indicate any benefits to treatment.

FUTURE DIRECTIONS FOR RESEARCH

As is evident in this chapter, some issues relating to commitment and psychiatric patients are better understood than others. For instance, although the risk factors that relate to violence against others and against self are fairly well understood, less is known about effective prevention strategies. What sorts of treatments may reduce the potential for violence against others and against self? This particular issue has relevance both in the institution and in the community once patients are released. Research on effective risk management strategies in hospitals is needed. Some research has identified that lack of community mental health treatment (Swanson et al., 1997), lack of contact with mental health professionals (Estroff & Zimmer, 1994), and difficulty in carrying out daily life tasks (Bartels, Drake, Wallach, & Freeman, 1991) elevate the risk that psychiatric patients will be violent to others. Continued research in this area is important. A useful extension would be to focus on the interaction between these sorts of factors and individual factors such as the nature of mental illness, treatment compliance, and substance abuse.

Another potential area of civil commitment research that is untapped, but important in terms of the effect of law on people, is the extent to which the differing provincial legislation may affect persons subject to civil commitment. There are 12 separate pieces of mental health legislation in Canada. As reviewed in Table 12.1, these vary along dimensions such as the definition of mental illness, the strictness of the dangerousness criterion, the time limitations on initial and subsequent commitment orders, and the specified right to legal counsel. All such factors likely influence who is denied their rights to liberty, the nature of the commitment decision-making task, and the extent to which patients may have their rights recognized. For instance, in jurisdictions requiring a strict definition of "danger," such as Alberta, Manitoba, or Ontario, persons may be less likely to be admitted to hospital than they would be if they were in jurisdictions such as British Columbia, which has a rather liberal danger criterion. This has implications for the well-being (i.e., mental health, physical safety) of persons deemed unsuitable for hospitalization. What happens to these persons? How many end up not receiving treatment, and perhaps homeless and in poor mental health? Do these different statutory regimes have an effect on rates of harm to self or others? Moreover, are estimates of future danger differentially accurate, depending upon the statutory dictates that govern them? These are all issues that warrant exploration because of their potential effects on the Charter rights, mental health, and physical safety of Canadians.

Further, there have been statutory developments in civil commitment that, given their recency, have yet to be the subject of scientific investigation. For instance, Saskatchewan has recently enacted legislation that provides for a form of "outpatient commitment" (Mental

Health Services Amendment Act, 1993; 1996). In essence, this legislation permits psychiatrists to issue "community treatment orders" that mandate certain outpatient treatment regimes which, if not followed, may result in the detention of persons in psychiatric facilities. Among the criteria for this law, generally, is that a psychiatrist has probable cause to believe that a person has a mental disorder for which he or she requires treatment in the community; the person has been involuntarily committed either for a certain period of time or on a certain number of occasions in the previous two years; and that, in the absence of such treatment, the person is likely to harm themselves or others, or to suffer substantial mental or physical deterioration. British Columbia has also recently amended its legislation to include similar provisions.

While some may commend such legislation as actually promoting the rights of patients, in that they may reside in the community rather than the hospital, others may view it as an extension of the social net of control, in that these persons ought not to be and would not otherwise be under any state control in the absence of these legislative criteria. In a way, this legislation can be viewed as a sort of psychiatric probation. Research is sorely needed to evaluate the impact of these laws on patients. Fruitful avenues would include determining whether a greater number of persons actually do fall under the control of the state. Even knowing the defining characteristics of persons subject to community treatment orders is important, although they as yet remain unknown. Further, the legislation requires psychiatrists to make judgments about whether persons actually need treatment in the community in order to prevent harm to self or others. This mandates suicide and violence risk assessment, a topic briefly covered above and thoroughly reviewed elsewhere in this book. However, it does so in a different context than involuntary inpatient commitment, in which the key issue is whether a person must be removed from, rather than merely treated within, society due to risk of harm to self or others. The assessment task attached to community treatment orders, as opposed to involuntary commitment, would seem to call for a greater emphasis on community risk management. To date, there is little direct research on this specific assessment process, or on the applicability of existing risk assessment technology to this task.

A further area of psychological research that is needed concerns issues relating to competence in the guardianship context. Ideas from research on competence to consent to treatment could be borrowed and applied to this issue. It is important to identify key functional areas that should be assessed in making the decision whether a person is competent to manage his or her own personal life and estate. As is evident, there are a great number of areas in the civil law for which psychology can attempt to provide means to understand the law, study the law's assumptions, assist the lawmakers and players, and evaluate legal decisions. While recognizing this, one must be careful not to fail to be critical of the shortcomings of psychology — its theories, its assumptions, and its methods. Nonetheless, psychology can be a valuable lens through which to view the civil law. Many of the subject areas relating to civil commitment and civil competencies lend themselves naturally to psychological inquiry.

SUMMARY

The issues of civil commitment and competence raise crucial ethical, legal, scientific, and clinical issues. Ethically and legally, persons can be deprived of their constitutionally protected liberties and rights under certain conditions. With respect to civil commitment, although there are variations across provincial jurisdictions, persons generally may be detained involuntarily if they are deemed to be mentally ill, in need of treatment, and at some risk to harm themselves or others. Concerning civil competencies, the individual's right to make decisions about him- or herself in terms of basic life domains (i.e., managing one's estate; refusing or consenting to treatment) can be removed if the individual is deemed unable to make such decisions. The scientific and clinical challenges centre on the critical task of identifying those who meet these criteria. In the absence of solid empirical investigation and clinical assessment of such constructs as mental disorder, treatment need, and risk of harm to others and self, unwarranted detainment of persons in civil psychiatric facilities or the removal of the individual's right to make decisions about him- or herself may result. For this reason, it is imperative that research should continue on these complex issues. In fact, it may be asserted that research on these issues stands at the crux of a central dilemma: balancing the rights of persons not to have their rights unduly restricted versus protection of the individual and of society. One function of psychological research on these issues in mental health law is to optimize this balancing task – to ensure that the procedures used, for example, to detain persons in civil psychiatric facilities, are grounded in empirically and clinically defensible bases.

QUESTIONS FOR DISCUSSION

1. What are the main criteria for civil commitment, how do these differ across provinces, and how is psychological research useful in informing decisions regarding whether people meet the criteria for commitment?
2. Describe the key demographic, socio-historical, and psychiatric characteristics of persons who are involuntarily committed to psychiatric institutions. What strategies could be introduced to prevent such persons from requiring hospitalization?
3. In the law of civil commitment and competence, it has been said that the rights of people are pitted against the responsibility of the state (in this context, the provincial government) to care for its citizens. Discuss the rights that potentially may be violated by civil commitment legislation and decisions of incompetence. What is the appropriate balance between individual rights and the state's responsibility to care for its citizens?
4. Research has been conducted on psychiatric patients' abilities to consent to treatment. Discuss potential research strategies that could be used to determine whether a person is competent to manage his or her affairs.

RECOMMENDED READING

Appelbaum, P.S., & Grisso, T. (1995). The MacArthur treatment competence study. I: Mental illness and competence to consent to treatment. *Law and Human Behavior, 19*, 105–126.

Appelbaum, P.S., Lidz, C.W., & Meisel, A. (1987). *Informed consent: Legal theory and clinical practice*. New York: Oxford University Press.

Gordon, M., & Verdun-Jones, S. (1992). *Adult guardianship law in Canada*. Toronto: Butterworths.

Melton, G.B., Petrila, J., Poythress, N.G., & Slobogin, C. (1997). *Psychological evaluations for the courts: A handbook for mental health professionals and lawyers* (2nd ed.). New York: Guilford.

Robertson, G.B. (1994). *Mental disability and the law in Canada* (2nd ed.). Scarborough, ON: Carswell.

13. Psychology's Intersection with Family Law

William J. Koch and Kevin S. Douglas

In the 1970s, adolescent boys with conduct problems were removed from their biological families by the British Columbia ministry responsible for child protection and placed in a remote British Columbia ranch that provided foster care paid for by the ministry. Subsequently, complaints of abusive behaviour at the ranch were made to the same government ministry; these complaints were inadequately investigated. In 1992, after pleading guilty to sexually assaulting 16 adolescent boys in his care, the male owner of the ranch was sentenced to 17 years in prison. In 1997, the Supreme Court of British Columbia found the provincial government liable for damages to four of those boys. The B.C. Supreme Court agreed with the plaintiffs that the offending male was an employee of the government and that the government was responsible for protecting them. The province's lawyers had argued that the offender was merely a provider of services, for whose actions the government could not be held accountable. The four plaintiffs were awarded approximately one million dollars for loss of back and future pay, general and aggravated damages, and money for future counselling. The ruling is currently under appeal. This is believed to be the first time a Canadian superior court has found a government liable for the actions of an employee in a sexual abuse action. The case is of interest for two reasons. First, it illustrates the government's legal duty to protect children and the potential failure of protection even when children are placed under formal protected status. Second, it illustrates the vicarious liability for damages for which an employer can be held responsible with respect to the actions of an employee.

As the case described above suggests, Canadian society espouses a strong interest in protecting children. During the twentieth century, child protection and child and family relations legislation has evolved extensively in an attempt to better protect children but, as we will see in this chapter, the statutory protection of children is easier said than done. Identifying children who are at risk is still very much of a "hit or miss" proposition. Those parental risk factors that have been identified as predictors of child abuse, while widely researched, are confusing and not often easily applicable to individual cases. Moreover, when children are apprehended from dangerous family situations, they seldom receive any rehabilitative care to ameliorate the negative effects of maltreatment. The negative effects of sexual abuse vary among victims. There is also considerable controversy in the scientific literature about the specific long-term effects of sexual abuse.

While child protection law and relevant psychological research have evolved extensively over the past 30 years, professional practice in child protection matters has generally lagged behind. If we are to protect our children, much improvement in this area is still needed. In this chapter we review the history of the child abuse issue; relevant child protection legislation in Canada; and major areas of psychological research related to child abuse, child protection, and sexual abuse. Many children who are not in need of protection can also become the focus of family law through custodial disputes following parental separation and, less frequently, during contested adoptions. Thus in the second half of the chapter we discuss custodial decisions following from divorce, the dilemma posed for law and psychology by contested adoptions, and the current state of forensic psychological practice in the area.

CHILD PROTECTION AND ABUSE ISSUES

Although the first recorded case of prosecution for child abuse occurred in 1874 (*New York Times*, 1874; cited in Peterson & Brown, 1994), child abuse did not become a focus of research attention until the middle of the twentieth century. Kempe, Silverman, Steele, Drogemueler, and Silver first described the effects of child abuse and coined the term "battered child syndrome" in 1962. Since then, research into the nature and causes of child abuse has proliferated.

Pearce and Pezzot-Pearce (1997) define four types of child maltreatment: (1) physical abuse, in which children are injured intentionally through acts of commission or omission; (2) sexual abuse, in which dependent children under the age of legal consent are involved in sexual activities, typically by caregivers; (3) psychological maltreatment, in which children are emotionally neglected, rejected, degraded, or subjected to mental cruelty; and (4) physical neglect, in which children are deprived of the necessities of life, such as food, clothing, and hygiene. Children who experience one form of abuse are likely to suffer from others as well. Physical abuse and neglect, in particular, appear intertwined (Russell & Tranor, 1984).

The following facts underscore the significance of child maltreatment in our society. Abuse-related deaths are a leading cause of child mortality (Daro, 1988; cited in Peterson & Brown, 1994), and "unintentional" injuries kill more children than any of the other leading causes of death (Dershewitz & Williamson, 1977).

Prevalence of Child Abuse

The prevalence of child abuse is difficult to define, due to the value-laden nature of the term and limited epidemiological studies. Statistics Canada data, however, reveal that child victims of violent crimes are typically related to their aggressors. Additional Statistics Canada data from a longitudinal survey of over 22,000 Canadian children indicated that, of 10- and 11-year-olds, 33.4% of those from intact families and 42.8% of those from step-families reported "erratic punishment," comprised of nagging, threatening, or hitting (Cheal, 1996). Straus and Gelles (1986), in two U.S. national probability telephone surveys (1975 and 1985), found that 54 to 58% of parents reported slapping or hitting their children, with more severe violence in 9 to 13% of cases. The data from this study suggest a relatively high rate of violent actions by parents towards their children. Moreover, these estimates are likely to be conservative because the study did not include single parents or families with children all under the age of 3 years, two risk factors for abuse (see below).

It is likely, however, that the official prevalence rates for child abuse underrepresent the actual number of child abuse victims. More recently, we have become aware that documented cases of injuries due to abuse and so-called accidental injuries to children are phenomenologically similar. Ewigman, Kivlahan, and Land (1993) re-examined all the records of fatalities that occurred because of injury to children between birth and 4 years of age in the state of Missouri for the years 1983 through 1986. By reviewing a broad range of records, they concluded that only 11% of these children showed no evidence of having been maltreated. Thus, the majority of "accidental" deaths of young children occur in a context of possible, probable, or definite maltreatment by caregivers. Taken as a whole, physical child maltreatment would appear to be a highly prevalent social problem.

The prevalence of child sexual abuse, on the other hand, is a matter of some controversy, with estimates ranging from 4 to 62% (Salter, 1992). Clearly, even the lower estimate of 4% suggests a substantial problem. The consequences of sexual abuse and controversies related to this unfortunate phenomenon will be discussed later in this chapter.

STATUTORY AND CASE LAW

Society has a vested interest in protecting children. Statutory laws intended to determine when individual children are in need of protection by government agencies have thus been passed. In effect, defining an individual child as "in need of protection" means relieving parents of their legal roles (e.g., guardians), at least temporarily, and perhaps separating the children from their parents. For obvious reasons, the courts do not take this responsibility lightly, and legislatures have been busy fine-tuning related statutes. Most of the provincial statutes related to child protection have been proclaimed within the last decade and continue to evolve. Some of the important facets of these statutes are summarized in Table 13.1.

The age below which an individual is considered a child for the purposes of child protection varies from 16 to 19 years across Canada. All jurisdictions except the Yukon require the reporting of children suspected to be in need of protection. Factors to be considered in determining the child's best interests almost uniformly include family or kinship ties; cultural, racial, linguistic, and religious ties; the child's views; and continuity of care for the child. One notable exception is Newfoundland, where no legal reference is found with respect to sustaining family ties. Approximately half of the provinces give some type of special status to First Nations children. Three of the western provinces have established an Office of Child Advocate. Only British Columbia and Nova Scotia explicitly require that specific services be made available to parents as an alternative to placing their children into protective care. Only British Columbia and Ontario delineate the rights of children held in protective care by the government.

A recent trend in child protection law is the greater specification of objective factors indicating that a child is in need of protection. All jurisdictions now describe such specific factors. As can be seen from Table 13.2, the risk of physical and sexual abuse is considered grounds for protection in all jurisdictions, with the exception of the Northwest Territories (NWT), where statutory wording is vague on this matter. Most jurisdictions consider protection necessary if the parent is unable or unwilling to prevent abuse by a third party. This particular item may require a demonstration that a child has been abused by a third party and/or that a specified third party is at risk for abusing the child. Further, it requires a demonstration that the parent is either unwilling or unable (e.g., because of mental disorder) to protect the child from such abuse. As the reader can appreciate, the determination of need for protection in cases of potential third-party abuse is very complex. Parental denial of necessary health care is also consistently seen as grounds for protection in all provinces. This particular aspect of the law, however, has come into conflict with some religious belief systems (e.g., with respect to blood transfusions).

Child neglect, as opposed to abuse, is a broad term that is best defined as a failure to provide supervision, resources, or other care that can potentially result in physical or emotional harm to the child. Statutory treatment of neglect across Canada is more variable than that for abuse, partly because some jurisdictions do not use the word "neglect" in their legislation. Various combinations of inadequate care and abandonment, however, convey similar meanings. Thus, all jurisdictions can adjudicate child protection in cases where parents have neglected to provide adequate care for their children.

Approximately half of the provinces cite domestic violence or disharmony between spouses as grounds for child protection. Some require a demonstration of damage to the child resulting from the domestic violence. Various characteristics of the children themselves may be grounds for protection, including some conditions (e.g., medical illness) or behaviours (e.g., conduct disorder) that prevent the parents from providing for them adequately. Finally, the concept of emotional harm is well represented in the acts of most provinces. This is important both legally and psychologically. From the legal perspective, inclusion of emotional harm as grounds for protection means that children's emotional well-being is placed on a legal par with their physical well-being. From a psychological perspective, this means that it is important to assess a child's emotional status in making recommendations about protection.

In Quebec, issues relating to child protection are covered in the Civil

TABLE 13.1
Summary of child and family acts across Canadian jurisdictions

Specified statutory factors	B.C.	Yukon	Alta.	N.W.T.	Sask.	Man.	Ont.	N.B.	N.S.	P.E.I.	Nfld.
Age in years used to define children in statutes	<19	<18	<18	<18	<16	*	<18	*	<16	*	<16
Statutory duty to report children in need of protection	yes	no	yes	yes	yes	yes	yes	yes	yes	yes	yes
Specific mention of professionals duty to report children in need of protection	no	no	no	yes	no	yes	yes	yes	yes	no	no
Statute specifies kinship and/or family ties as important in determining best interests of child	yes	no	yes	no	yes	yes	yes	yes	yes	yes	no
Statute specifies child's views as important to consider in determining best interests of child	yes	no	yes	no	yes	yes	yes	yes	yes	yes	option
Statute specifies racial, linguistic, religious, and/or cultural ties as important in determining best interests of child	yes	yes	yes	yes	yes	yes	yes	yes	yes	yes	??
Special treatment of First Nations children in statute	yes	no	yes	no	no	yes	yes	no	yes	no	no
Statute specifies continuity of care as important in determining best interests of child	yes	no	yes	no	yes	yes	??	yes	yes	yes	??
Statute specifies factors showing a child to be in need of protection	yes	yes	yes	yes	yes	yes	yes	yes	yes	yes	yes
Statute defines emotional harm	yes	no	yes	no	no	no	yes	no	yes	yes	no

TABLE 13.1—(*Concluded*)
Summary of child and family acts across Canadian jurisdictions

Specified statutory factors	B.C.	Yukon	Alta.	N.W.T.	Sask.	Man.	Ont.	N.B.	N.S.	P.E.I.	Nfld.
Statute provides for a special Office of Child Advocate	yes	no	yes	no	??	yes	??	??	??	yes	??
Statute requires government to provide support and services to families	yes	no	??	no	??	??	??	??	yes	no	??
Statute specifies rights of children in protective care	yes	no	no	no	no	no	yes	no	no	no	no

Notes: Quebec is excluded from this table because, as described in the text of this chapter, these issues are dealt with generally in the Quebec Civil Code and not in provincial legislation.

An "*" denotes age of majority for the province.

"??" indicates that the statutes are unclear in this regard.

Statutes: B.C. – *Child, Family, & Community Service Act*, R.S.B.C. 1996, c. 46; Yukon – *Children's Act*, S.Y.T. 1986, c. 22; Alta. – *Child Welfare Act*, S.A. 1995, C-8.1; N.W.T. – *Child Welfare Act*, R.S.N.W.T. 1988, c. C-6; Sask. – *Child & Family Services Act*, S.S. 1989–90, c. C-7.2; Man. – *Child & Family Services Act*, S.M. 1985–86, c. 8, S.M. 1993, c. 29; Ont. – *Child & Family Services Act*, R.S.O. 1990, c. C.11; N.B. – *Child & Family Services & Family Relations Act*, R.S.N.B. 1980, c. C-2.1; N.S. – Children & Family Services Act, R.S.N.S. 1990, c. 5; P.E.I. – *Family & Child Services Act*, R.S.P.E.I. 1988, c. F-2; Nfld. – *Child Welfare Act*, R.S.N. 1990, c. C-12.

TABLE 13.2
Factors indicating a child's need for protection by statute across Canadian jurisdictions

Specified statutory factors	B.C.	Yukon	Alta.	N.W.T.	Sask.	Man.	Ont.	N.B.	N.S.	P.E.I.	Nfld.
Child has been, or is likely to be, physically harmed by parent	yes	yes	yes	no	yes	yes	yes	yes	??	yes	yes
Child has been, or is likely to be, sexually abused/exploited by parent	yes	yes	yes	no	yes	yes	yes	yes	yes	yes	yes
Child has been, or is likely to be, physically or sexually abused/exploited by a third party and parent is unwilling or unable to protect child	yes	yes	yes	no	yes	yes	yes	yes	yes	no	yes
Child has been, or is likely to be, harmed by parental neglect	yes	yes	??	yes	yes	??	yes	yes	yes	yes	yes
Child has been exposed to domestic violence likely to result in physical or emotional harm to child	no	no	no	no	yes	no	no	yes	yes	yes	yes
Child has been emotionally harmed by parent's conduct	yes	yes	yes	yes	??	yes	yes	yes	no	yes	yes
Parent has provided inadequately for child	yes	yes	yes	yes	??	yes	yes	yes	??	no	yes
Child has been abandoned by reason of parental neglect, impairment, or death without another designated guardian	yes	yes	yes	yes	yes	??	yes	??	yes	yes	yes
Child has been denied necessary health care	yes	yes	yes	yes	yes	yes	yes	yes	yes	yes	yes
Condition or behaviour of the child prevents the parent from providing adequate care	no	yes	yes	yes	no	yes	no	yes	no	no	yes
Children under the age of 12 years have been charged with violation of some aspect of the Criminal Code or related acts	no	no	no	yes	yes	no	yes	yes	yes	yes	yes

Statutes: B.C. – *Child, Family, & Community Service Act*, R.S.B.C. 1996, c. 46; Yukon – *Children's Act*, S.Y.T. 1986, c. 22; Alta. – *Child Welfare Act*, S.A. 1995, C-8.1; N.W.T. – *Child Welfare Act*, R.S.N.W.T. 1988, c. C-6; Sask. – *Child & Family Services Act*, S.S. 1989–90, c. C-7.2; Man. – *Child & Family Services Act*, S.M. 1985–86, c. 8, S.M. 1993, c. 29; Ont. – *Child & Family Services Act*, R.S.O. 1990, c. C.11; N.B. – *Child & Family Services & Family Relations Act*, R.S.N.B. 1980, c. C-2.1; N.S. – *Children & Family Services Act*, R.S.N.S. 1990, c. 5; P.E.I. – *Family & Child Services Act*, R.S.P.E.I. 1988, c. F-2; Nfld. – *Child Welfare Act*, R.S.N. 1990, c. C-12.

Code (1991). By virtue of the Quebec Civil Code, parents have the duties of custody, education and supervision of their children (art. 599). Article 32 states that "every child has a right to the protection, security and attention" of parents. Relating to the removal of children from the home, article 606 states that courts may, "for a grave reason and in the interest of the child," deprive parents of their parental authority. In making this determination, the court considers the "moral, intellectual, emotional and material needs of the child," as well as the child's "age, health, personality and family environment" (art. 33). The court can then designate who is to be given parental authority (art. 607).

Case Law

The numerous cases in the child protection area are, as one may expect, quite consistent with the legislation. In the interests of brevity, we will highlight the factors considered by the courts in determining whether or not children need protection. Of course, the paramount concern is always what is in the best interests of the child (e.g., *Child & Family Services of Winnipeg v. F. (A. C.)*, 1992, Man. C.A.; *Newfoundland (Director of Child Welfare) v. S. (J.)*, 1994, Nfld. C.A.; *Nova Scotia (Minister of Community Services) v. S. (S. M.)*, 1992; N.S.C.A.; *Prince Edward Island (Director of Child Welfare) v. W. (N.)*, 1994, P.E.I. C.A.; *S. (L. A.) v. British Columbia (Superintendent of Family & Child Service)*, 1995, B.C.C.A.). These provincial appellate level cases illustrate the innumerable circumstances that may arise that could affect whether staying in or being removed from the parents' custody is considered to be in the best interests of the child. The courts have considered parental irresponsibility, neglect, alcohol or drug use, poor coping abilities, and criminal involvement; physical and sexual abuse; suicidal tendencies, unstable and unsafe home environment, psychiatric illness, and poor supervision of children. It is important to emphasize that the courts have made decisions to remove children when the circumstances have had demonstrated negative effects on parenting ability.

Professionals' Knowledge of Reporting Laws

It is commonly said that if persons are unaware of the law, the law cannot be effective in changing behaviour. It is important, then, that professionals who are likely to be in contact with the law are aware of it.

Psychologists by virtue of their work inquire about and observe many of the risk factors for child abuse. Because some jurisdictions hold psychologists and other professionals more accountable for reporting suspected abuse, it is important to know (a) whether those professionals are aware of such legislation, and (b) how likely they are to report cases. For this reason, some researchers have attempted to assess psychologists' knowledge of child protection laws.

The good news is that psychologists are increasingly aware of child abuse reporting laws. Although Swoboda, Elwork, Sales, and Levine found that in 1978 32% of psychologists were unfamiliar with the reporting law in their jurisdiction, a more recent Canadian survey (Beck & Ogloff, 1995) found that fewer than 2% of psychologists were unaware of mandated reporting in their jurisdiction. Nonetheless, actual reporting lags behind professionals' knowledge of reporting laws. Beck and Ogloff (1995) found that 12% of registered psychologists in British Columbia admitted to not having reported suspected child abuse. Reasons for this failure to report were predominantly that psychologists (a) believed that there was insufficient evidence to report and (b) lacked confidence in the child protection services. In responding to hypothetical abusive or neglectful incidents, psychologists were most certain in identifying sexual abuse and child neglect and less certain in identifying physical or emotional abuse. In a similar study by the same researchers, 94% of teachers surveyed were found to be aware of the existence of mandatory child reporting laws in British Columbia (Beck, Ogloff, & Corbishley, 1994), but, only 60% had knowledge of the specifics of this legislation. Sixteen per cent of teachers responded that although they had suspected child abuse in the past, they failed to report their suspicions.

Who Enters Protection and What Happens in Protective Custody?

Child protection authorities apprehend only a small proportion of abused/neglected children. This suggests two questions about the children apprehended. First, what are their behavioural, intellectual, and emotional characteristics? Second, what remedial intervention is available to them? Sadly, these are neglected areas of inquiry. An isolated study offers some insight into the types of children entering protective custody, at least in the United States. Urquiza, Wirtz, Peterson, and Singer (1994) found that 68% of children entering protective care were at least 1.5 standard deviations below the mean on national norms for one or more standardized assessment instruments of cognitive development, academic performance, behaviour problems, emotional well-being, and other adaptive behaviour. Thus, the majority of children who are apprehended by child protection authorities show substantial deficits in some area of cognitive, behavioural, or emotional functioning. Unfortunately, few, if any, jurisdictions routinely screen apprehended children for such deficits. Therefore, most apprehended children with functional deficits likely go undetected and untreated even while in protective care. This is at least partially a function of statutory laws which, in most provinces, neglect to mention any government duty to assess and rehabilitate children who have been apprehended.

We turn now to the psychological research pertaining to child abuse, child protection, and sexual abuse.

CONSEQUENCES OF CHILD MALTREATMENT

Between 1980 and 1989, a Statistics Canada investigation revealed that 542 children under the age of 12 were murdered in Canada. Only 11% of these victims were killed by strangers, while two-thirds were killed by parents. Parents are responsible for approximately one-quarter of assaults, sexual assaults, and other violent crimes perpetrated against children in Canada (Wright & Leroux, 1991). Another Statistics Canada report indicated that 48% of sexual assaults, 30% of non-sexual assault, 57% of other violent offences, and 41% of all violent offences against children under the age of 12 were carried out by family members (La Novara, 1993).

While death and severe physical injury are extreme results of child abuse, there are a number of other problematic short-term consequences that can occur. Abused and neglected children are more likely to show problematic aggression (Dodge, Bates, & Pettit, 1990), as well as other social behaviour deficiencies (Salzinger, Feldman, Hammer, & Rosario, 1993). A related aspect of family violence – the adverse effects on children of witnessing domestic violence between their parents – has been studied by researchers at the London (Ontario) Family Court Clinic. For example, Jaffe, Wolfe, Wilson, and Zak (1986) found that both girls and boys from families characterized by domestic violence (subjects were recruited from transition houses for abused women) showed lower levels of social competence and more internalizing problems. The boys also showed greater externalizing problems than children from nonviolent households.

While there are many problems with the research that has investigated the long-term effects of abuse, including extensive use of retrospective recall and the confounding of other family variables (e.g., intramarital domestic violence; parental psychopathology; alcohol abuse), it appears that reliable long-term consequences of physical child abuse can be identified. These include: adult violent behaviour, adult emotional disturbance, suicidal and self-injurious behaviour, and marital violence on the part of men (reviewed in Malinosky-Rummell and Hansen, 1993). Adults who have been physically abused as children are also more likely to physically abuse their own children; however, this relationship is moderated by multiple historical and proximal factors (Malinosky-Rummell & Hansen 1993). In a large Canadian longitudinal study of over 22,000 children, a strong negative relationship between parenting practices defined as "hostile" and later social relationships of children defined as positive was found (Statistics Canada, 1997a). That is, parents who were often annoyed with their children and told them that they were not as good as other children were substantially more likely to have children with poor relationships with other children, parents, teachers, and siblings. A similar, moderately strong effect was found for "aversive" parenting – a style characterized by physical punishment, removal of privileges, and raising of the voice.

Explanatory Models of Child Maltreatment

Early models of child maltreatment focused primarily on the characteristics of physically abusive parents. For example, Gelles (1973) proposed that physically abusive behaviour on the part of a parent was mediated by that parent's mental health problems. These parental variables were summarized in detail by Wolfe (1985), who stated that physically abusive parents were more likely to be socially isolated; to perceive themselves as under high levels of stress; to be deficient in frustration tolerance, self-esteem, and parenting skills; and to be socially withdrawn. Furthermore, such parents were said to have histories of deprived childhoods and higher ratios of negative to positive interactions with their children.

The problem with parental psychopathology models is that the existence of these characteristics is neither necessary nor sufficient for child maltreatment to occur (Ammerman, 1990; Azar, 1991). As well, it is clear that both child (e.g., disobedience) and ecological (e.g., poverty, psychosocial stress) variables play strong roles in predicting child maltreatment.

More recent models have focused on the explanation of physical abuse (e.g., Milner, 1993) or both physical abuse and neglect (Hillson & Kuiper, 1994). Milner's (1993) social information processing model of physical child abuse draws heavily on the work of Newberger and Newberger and Cook (1983) and Wolfe (1987). This three-stage model states, in brief, that physically abusive parents are characterized by pre-existing cognitive schemas (e.g., belief in the value of physical punishment or the legitimacy of using force in relationships) and perceptual biases with respect to children's behaviour (attending to their child's behaviour less and experiencing more distress secondary to their child's behaviour). Abusive parents are also hypothesized to subsequently interpret or evaluate their child's behaviour more negatively (e.g., as having hostile intent or being more blameworthy), and to use a more restricted set of information in the evaluation of their child's behaviour or to perceive fewer response options with respect to child management. Finally, Milner (1993) hypothesizes that abusive parents have skill deficits or are impeded by factors such as their own distress that limit effective parenting behaviour. Milner's model explicitly notes that psychosocial stress and parental perception thereof interact with the perceptual, evaluative, and response initiation stages described above. Thus, during stressful times, abusive parents may be more prone to perceive their children's behaviour as blameworthy.

Hillson and Kuiper's (1994) model targets both physical abuse and neglect because of the frequent co-occurrence of these problems within the same parents (see, e.g., Russell & Tranor's 1984 finding that 46% of neglect cases also involved physical abuse). Hillson and Kuiper's stress and coping model of maltreatment suggests that parent, child, and ecological risk factors for maltreatment constitute stressors that the parent appraises and with which he or she attempts to cope. Dependent on the parent's appraisal of adequate internal or external resources for coping with these stressors (e.g., child misbehaviour, job demands) and his or her idiosyncratic coping skills, the parent's behaviour will be characterized as facilitative caregiver behaviour (e.g., involving active planning, restraint of negative emotions), neglectful behaviour (e.g., behavioural/mental disengagement), or abusive behaviour (e.g., emotional venting).

While there is evidence to support elements of both the Milner and Hillson and Kuiper models, much work remains to be done in understanding how parent and child characteristics interact with the ecological context to produce physically abusive or neglectful parenting.

Predictors of Child Abuse and Injury

Psychologists are frequently called upon to assess families who are in danger of having a child or children declared to be in need of protection. In these cases, either the government agency of child protection (e.g., British Columbia Ministry of Children and Families) or the court suspects that a child is at risk for maltreatment but lacks sufficient evidence to proceed without expert assistance. A similar scenario applies when a child has been temporarily apprehended by the child protection ministry and the ministry desires expert assistance to determine whether to apply for permanent revocation of parental rights, whether to prolong the apprehension order, or which parental remediation strategies might be appropriate. In effect, the government agencies and courts are asking the psychologist to improve the accuracy and efficacy of their apprehension and remediation decisions in child maltreatment cases.

In order for psychologists to properly assess the risk of child maltreatment, they must be familiar with the correlates of abuse and neglect. Peterson and Brown (1994) articulated the most comprehensive predictive model for child injury; it includes a broad category of outcomes encompassing both neglect and physical abuse. Risk factors for child abuse and accidental child injury can be roughly grouped into classes of sociocultural, caregiver, and child variables.

Within both Canada and the United States, children of low-income families are more likely to die from injury as well as to have more emotional and behavioural difficulties than other children (Nersesian, Petit, Shaper, Lemieux, & Naor, 1985; Statistics Canada, 1997a). Related to low income, households with a high degree of unpredictability and maternal sense of uncontrollability are at elevated risk for child abuse or neglect (Olds, Henderson, Chamberlin, & Tatelbaum, 1986). Household crowding (Gray, Cutler, Dean, & Kempe, 1977) and frequent residence changes (Altemeier, O'Connor, Vietze, Sandler, & Sherrod, 1984) are predictors of subsequent child hospitalization, as well as abuse and neglect. In fact, frequent residence change has been shown to be a stronger predictor of abuse and unintentional injury than other low-income correlates (Beautrais, Fergusson, & Shannon, 1982; Altemeier et al., 1984). More generally, the number of recent negative life events is a predictor of unintentional poisoning of children (Beautrais, Fergusson, & Shannon, 1981), as well as for burns, fractures, and motor vehicle injuries (Beautrais et al., 1982). These, then, are the external stressors with which many parents later labelled as "abusive" or "neglectful" must cope, and which are seen as important in the explanatory models of both Milner (1993) and Hillson and Kuipers (1994).

Caregiver factors that predict child injury can roughly be classified as those reflecting chronic psychopathology and those resulting from external stressors. Thus, early research demonstrated that a parental history of having been abused as a child was correlated with later child abuse (Olson, 1976). While the evidence for this intergeneration transmission of family violence is not entirely consistent (for a review, see Widom 1989), it is currently accepted that a parent's own history of abuse has some predictive potential for that parent's risk of abusing his or her own children. Parents of children who are unintentionally injured are more likely to be risk-takers themselves (Rivara & Mueller, 1987). As well, both maternal depression (Garbarino, 1977) and maternal alcohol abuse (Bijur, Kurzon, Overpeck, & Scheidt, 1992) predict injury in children. Parental variables related to child injury are quite diverse (e.g., risk-taking vs. depression), suggesting that multiple and different parental characteristics may pose risks to children, but likely through different causal pathways.

Factors that indicate inadequate social support and resources for the parenting role consistently predict child abuse, neglect, or child injury. For example, parents of injured children are more likely to be young, single, and socially isolated (McCormick, Shapiro, & Starfield, 1981). The Canadian longitudinal study of children revealed that children from lone-mother families were more likely than those from two-parent families to experience emotional, behavioural, educational, and social difficulties (Statistics Canada, 1997a). It must be emphasized, however, that the majority of children from lone-mother families do not experience difficulties in these areas. Thus, it is likely that differences in parental utilization of social support and coping skills, as discussed by Hillson and Kuipers (1994) are important in mediating the effects of inadequate social support on child abuse.

Parental cognitive and attitudinal factors are also predictive of child injury or abuse. For instance, underestimating infants' motor abilities (Roberts & Wright, 1982) and overestimating older children's self-care abilities (Peterson, 1989) place children at a heightened risk for unintentional injury. Similarly, abusive parents tend to overestimate children's abilities for self-care and self-management (Azar & Rohrbeck, 1986). Supervision and control appear to have bimodal relationships to children's risk of injury. While too lax a supervisory style results in higher rates of injury (Wilson, Baker, Teret, Shock, & Barbarino 1991), a strong need to oversee and control children's behaviour also predicts physical abuse (see, e.g., Monroe & Schellenbach, 1989). Similarly, excessive verbal and physical punishment is associated with abusive parents (Helfer, 1977). These findings are generally consistent with Milner's (1993) model of physical child abuse.

A number of child factors have been found to predict injuries or abuse. Younger children, from birth to four years of age, are at greatest risk for fatal injuries and abuse (Baker, O'Neill, & Karpf, 1984; American Association for Protecting Children, 1986). The next highest risk is for teenagers. Infants with irregular sleeping and eating habits are more likely than others to suffer injury. While the research literature is inconsistent, there is some evidence that a combination of distractibility, hyperactivity, impulsivity, aggressiveness, and non-compliance place children at greater risk for accidental or abusive injury (for a detailed review, see Peterson & Brown, 1994).

Despite the large body of literature on the prediction of child abuse, there are limitations to the utility of the information provided for family court purposes. First, much of the normative research concerning parenting practices is based on samples of Caucasian, upper-middle-class families (Azar, Benjit, Fuhrmann, & Cavallero, 1995), which are unrepresentative of the preponderance of disadvantaged families more commonly subject to child protection investigations. Second, few well-validated measures of empirically demonstrated risk factors have been developed for forensic assessment purposes (Azar, 1992). Third, many of the documented risk factors (e.g., parental depression) may only adversely affect children when mediated through specific pathways. As an important example, Haskett, Myers, Pirrello, and Dombalis (1995) found that parenting style accounted for much of the relationship between parental emotional distress and children's adjustment. This casts doubt in the common belief that parental depression by itself is a risk factor for children's well-being.

It is crucial to remember that both health professionals and family court judges are as prone to societal biases as anyone else. Strong biases exist that label ethnic minority and low socioeconomic status parents as more likely to be abusive even in the context of similar risk factors (Turbett & O'Toole, 1980). A recent flurry of child apprehensions among First Nations communities in British Columbia has drawn public attention to this particular issue.

In short, there are multiple factors that predict negative outcomes for children. Unfortunately, the relationships between these predictor variables (e.g., maternal depression) and adverse child outcomes are not always straightforward.

Sexual Abuse

Research, clinical practice, and legal decisions surrounding sexual abuse (SA) generate great controversy in our society. The first controversy has to do with the consequences of such abuse. It should not be surprising that sexual problems, including an increased risk of adult sexual victimization (Messman & Long, 1996), are found to be common in adults who suffered childhood SA (see, e.g., Browne & Finkelhor, 1986). Sexual abuse victims are also thought to be at an increased long-term risk for substance abuse (Roshenow, Corbett, & Devine, 1988), as well as depression, self-harm, anxiety, lowered self-esteem, and interpersonal distrust (reviewed by Browne & Finkelhor, 1986). In the short term, sexually abused children suffer more anxiety disorders (Green, 1993) and appear to show symptoms consistent with post-traumatic stress disorder (PTSD; Wolfe, Gentile, & Wolfe, 1989). As well, they may show problems with respect to depression, aggression, and inappropriate sexuality (reviewed by Browne & Finkelhor, 1986). A recent review of 45 studies of SA children suggested a high prevalence of fears, PTSD, behaviour problems, lowered self-esteem, and inappropriate sexuality (Kendall-Tackett, Williams, & Finkelhor, 1993). Three important qualifying comments about this review are in order. First, these studies took their child subjects predominantly from sexual abuse evaluation and treatment settings. Given selection biases, they will likely find a relatively higher incidence of negative effects, a criticism that can be applied to much of the early research on this topic. Second, Kendall-Tackett et al. (1993) noted that a number of variables, including occurrence of penetration, duration and frequency of abuse, physical force, perpetrator relationship to the victim, and subsequent maternal support, predicted negative consequences. Third, approximately two-thirds of children in the reviewed studies showed recovery within 12 to 18 months.

Finkelhor (1990) noted two areas of research controversy: how to explain the large number of sexually abused children who show no mental health symptoms, and whether PTSD, as discussed by Wolfe et al. (1989), is a useful framework for describing the impact of SA. According to Finkelhor (1990), somewhere between one-quarter and one-third of childhood victims suffer little or no psychiatric symptomatology. Potential explanations for these findings are measurement insensitivity (e.g., Everson, Hunter, Runyan, Edelsohn, & Coulter, 1989), psychological "denial" by children, or, more plausibly, variability in the severity of the SA stressor and the victim's resiliency. Childhood SA is not a homogeneous variable and can vary widely in frequency, intensity, degree of physical threat or injury, and the extent to which the perpetrator is a trusted family member, acquaintance, or stranger. As well, victims will vary in their pre-existing resiliency as well as in the supportive nature of their family environment. These factors likely account for the wide variability in victims' psychopathological responses to childhood SA.

Finkelhor (1990) has also suggested that the PTSD formulation of SA fails to account for the increased inappropriate sexual behaviour frequently seen in sexually abused children. He also posits that such a conceptualization does not do justice to those victims who fail to meet diagnostic criteria for PTSD, yet suffer disabling depression and sexual difficulties. Such deficits may not easily be captured by mental health diagnoses or common measures of psychological distress, but nonetheless result in significant life impairment. Finkelhor's own model of the effects of SA (Finkelhor & Browne, 1985; Finkelhor, 1990) hypothesizes that sexual abuse may have negative effects in any or all of four developmental areas; sexuality, interpersonal trust, self-esteem, and confidence in the ability to change the world. This model would then predict later deficits in sexual adjustment (e.g., sexual drive deficits); interpersonal relations, as noted perhaps by increased rates of divorce or smaller adult social support networks; and lower than expected academic and vocational achievement.

Another area of controversy involves the extent to which SA is a better predictor of psychological disturbance than more general family relationships or the quality of home environment. Space does not permit a detailed discussion of this debate; however we will discuss two important papers. First, in their National Youth Victimization Prevention Study, Boney-McCoy and Finkelhor (1996) assessed psychological problems, family relationships, and victimization in a representative national sample of children aged 10 to 16 years. Telephone interviews were conducted approximately 15 months apart for 1,400 children.

Child victimization in the intervening 15 months, particularly for sexual abuse, parental assault, and kidnapping, was associated with PTSD and depressive symptoms at the time of the second interview. While a significant portion of the association between victimization and psychological problems was related to pretrauma psychopathology, there was no such connection to the pretrauma parent-child relationship. This finding is strong support for the specific effect of SA on children's psychological functioning, at least in the short term.

With respect to long-term effects, Rind, Tromovitch, and Bauserman (1998) recently published a statistical meta-analysis of the psychological consequences of childhood SA as reported in 59 studies of college students. While this article fuelled a storm of protest in the media and U.S. Congress, its results were clear. College students exposed to childhood SA were on average slightly less well adjusted than appropriate controls, and reports of negative family environments accounted for more variance in self-reported adjustment and appeared confounded with SA. A conservative interpretation of these results might be that in middle to upper socio-economic class university-aged individuals, the negative effects of childhood sexual abuse may be indistinguishable from the more pervasive effects of negative family environment.

CUSTODY AND ACCESS ISSUES

As with the previous major area of child protection, the custody and access area of family law has the "best interests of the child" as an underlying theme. As many as 50% of children in Canada will be affected by parental divorce (Bissett-Johnson & Day, 1986). Recent Statistics Canada data place the divorce rate at approximately 31%, holding steady since the 1980s (Gentleman & Park, 1997). Divorce triggers a practical and legal dilemma concerning the authority and responsibility for, as well as access to, any children of the marriage. While many divorcing parents successfully negotiate a parenting strategy without professional help, a small minority have severe domestic conflict or concerns about the other spouse's ability to parent. The primary custody or access issues mentioned by a sample of Ontario parents were, in order of frequency:

(a) the other parent's poor parenting skills;
(b) problems in providing access visits;

(c)   a parent's perception of the child's wishes;
(d)   domestic violence;
(e)   the parents' own wishes;
(f)   verbal abuse of spouse;
(g)   alcohol or drug use;
(h)   "brainwashing" of the child by the other parent;
(i)   inconsistency in household routine or discipline;
(j)   problems with a new spouse;
(k)   the other parent's emotional stability;
(l)   the child's emotional stability; and
(m)   family of origin interference (Jaffe, Austin, Leschied, & Sas, 1987).

Notable by their absence in this list are concerns with physical or sexual abuse. This is an important difference relative to the child protection literature. By and large, few children who are the subjects of custody and access disputes between divorced parents are seen to be in need of protection by the government, although the best interests of children are paramount in both areas.

Case Law

Many of the issues that arise under the child protection area are relevant to custody and access determinations as well. A major difference from the child protection area, however, is that the court has often to decide between two generally competent and loving parents. Of course, courts can grant joint custody or allow generous access. The best interests of the child are again paramount. In order to determine this, courts in custody and access cases consider the wishes of the children, economic factors, stability of the home environment, parental interest in the children, and attachment of the children to the parent (*Carmichael v. Carmichael*, 1992, N.S.C.A.; *Gunn v. Gunn*, 1994, Man. C.A.; *Lougheed v. Sillett*, 1994, Ont. C.A.; *Medernach v. Medernach*, 1987, Sask. C.A.; *Weaver v. Tate*, 1990, Ont. C.A.; *Williams v. Williams*, 1989, B.C.C.A.). For example, the views of older children or adolescents are much more likely to be considered by the courts because of the pragmatic difficulties in keeping an adolescent in a custodial situation against his or her will. Parents whose housing is unstable are often seen by the courts as being less fit for custody. In other cases, the courts will determine, due to a history of infrequent contact, admission by the affected parties, or a psychological report, that little in the way of an emotional attachment exists between a particular parent and child, and will, on that ground, deny custody to that parent. Courts also assess the conduct of both parents generally, and with respect to discipline, child abuse, drug or alcohol abuse, and similar factors. Many of these factors are routinely considered in psychological research and practice, as the following discussion reveals.

Effects of Parental Characteristics on Children

It is important to note that no single parental characteristic guarantees a bad outcome for children. In general, the greater the number of parental risk factors, the more likely a child will fail to thrive psychologically. Most children undergoing a parental separation will be exposed to some of the risk factors noted below and will still thrive.

The most extensively studied maternal characteristic associated with children's well-being is depression. Up to 10% of Canadian children live with a depressed primary caregiver (Statistics Canada, 1997a). In general, maternal depression has been associated with a number of undesirable parenting practices, including unresponsiveness, inattentiveness, intrusiveness, inept discipline, and negative perceptions of children (reviewed in Gelfand & Teti, 1990). Child problems in response to maternal depression appear to involve disturbances in attachment and compliance to parental requests in very young children and problems in school achievement and interpersonal relationships in older children (Gelfand & Teti, 1990). This particular area is controversial, despite the massive amount of research. For example, the effects of paternal depression are seldom studied and the primary conceptualization of the effects of maternal depression on children's behavioural problems has been that it serves as a non-specific stressor that disrupts the child's adaptation. As mentioned above, parenting style may account for much of the relationship between parental emotional distress and children's adjustment (Haskett, Myers, Pirrello, & Dombalis, 1995), and some authors have noted that socioeconomic disadvantage better predicts maternal parenting dysfunction than does maternal depression (Dumas & Serketich, 1994).

Paternal and maternal substance abuse and antisocial personality disorder (APD) predict conduct problems in boys, with a stronger association with paternal APD (e.g., Frick et al., 1992). Parental anger is a substantial stressor for children of all ages, as is parental conflict (reviewed in Emery, 1994). Parental conflict is particularly important in the context of custody and access assessments because it typically precedes and accompanies divorce and may continue following divorce when parents have to interact with respect to their children. Parental conflict has been linked to increased aggression in children (Porter & O'Leary, 1980), and it has been shown to predict children's adjustment difficulties several years later (Block, Block, & Morrison, 1981). Related to anger and conflict, domestic violence between spouses is associated with higher rates of externalizing problems in boys (Jaffe, Wolfe, Wilson, & Zak, 1986; Wolfe, Jaffe, Wilson, & Zak, 1988), as well as higher rates of internalizing problems in girls and lowered social competence in both genders.

Effects of Divorce on Children

The effects of divorce on children's emotional well-being may be less substantial than is usually assumed. The average effect of divorce on standardized measures of children's psychological distress is relatively small (Amato & Keith, 1991). While divorce is a challenge to most children and has a substantial negative impact on the more vulnerable, most children are resilient and weather the effects of divorce with little measurable harm. Externalizing, rather than internalizing, problems in children are more strongly linked to divorce (Emery, 1988), likely because of disruptions in consistent discipline by parents following divorce. Even those findings of greater disturbance in some areas for children of divorce may not reflect the effects of divorce, per se. Longitudinal data suggest that many of the mental health problems present in children of divorced families existed prior to the divorce (Block, Block, & Gjerde, 1986; Cherlin et al., 1991; Doherty & Needle, 1991). It is also clear that parental conflict in intact families has a more deleterious effect than does divorce per se on children's mental health.

Psychological Practice in Custody Disputes

Custody and access determinations are especially problematic because of the absence of specific guidelines (Mnookin, 1975). While the flexibility given to judges to set custody and access arrangements is intended to work in the best interests of children, some critics have noted that the non-specific "best interests" principle encourages litigation and ill-will. Court judgments are difficult to predict and almost any unflattering attribute of the parents may be considered germane to the court's purpose (Emery, 1994). Further, there has been a long-standing debate as to whether mental health professionals have any relevant expertise for adjudication decisions in child custody litigation (Bolocofsky, 1989; O'Donohue & Bradley, 1999). Recent developments, however, suggest that the future may hold a new model for determining post-divorce custody arrangements. The approximation rule (Scott, 1992) advances the position that custody arrangements following divorce should approximate those arrangements preceding divorce. Adoption of this rule, which has been incorporated in the American Law Institute's model custody statute (Emery, 1999), in legal jurisdictions would bring a more determinate structure to custody adjudication.

Given the absence of clear guidelines for custody determination, the critical reader might reasonably ask on what basis forensic psychologists make custody recommendations. In the United States, the Committee on Professional Practice and Standards (COPPS; 1994) provided 16 recommendations for child custody evaluations that were grouped under 3 classes: (1) Orienting guidelines – purpose of child custody evaluation; (2) General guidelines – preparing for a child custody evaluation; and, (3) Procedural guidelines – conducting a child custody evaluation. Ackerman and Ackerman (1997) surveyed eight hundred practitioners, from whom they were able to obtain only 200 usable completed surveys, about their practices and reasons for making joint versus sole custody recommendations. The 11 most common reasons for psychologists recommending joint custody were:

(a) ability of parents to separate interpersonal conflict from parenting decisions,
(b) quality of relationship of child with each parent,
(c) problems with substance abuse,
(d) psychological stability of parents,
(e) anger and bitterness between parents,
(f) parents' willingness to enter joint custody arrangements,
(g) expressed wishes of the child (age 15),
(h) cooperation with previous court dates,
(i) problems with the law,
(j) current state law, and
(k) each parent's previous involvement in caretaking responsibilities.

It is arguable that psychological assessment procedures as currently developed can, at best, address only 4 of these 11 domains (b, c, d, and e). The other domains are as easily assessed by court officers.

Given psychology's long history in the development and clinical use of psychological tests, it is instructive to know how practising psychologists use psychological tests in custody and access evaluations. In Ackerman and Ackerman's (1997) survey, 92% of psychologists surveyed used the Minnesota Multiphasic Personality Inventory: Second Edition (MMPI-2; Butcher, Dahlstrom, Graham, Tellegen, & Kaemmer, 1989), a well-validated self-report test of psychopathology. Forty-eight per cent used the Rorschach (Exner, 1986), a controversial projective test with tenuous validity for assessing personality. Only 9 and 6%, respectively, used the Parenting Stress Index (PSI; Abidin, 1995) and Child Abuse Potential Inventory (CAPI; Milner, 1986). The PSI is a well-validated self-report instrument that assesses, among other variables, the parent's attachment to the child, acceptance of the parenting role, and perception of the child's behavioural and emotional functioning. The CAPI is another well-validated test that has been used to successfully discriminate groups of abusive and/or neglectful parents from parents in the general population. The differential test usage among practising psychologists identified in Ackerman and Ackerman's survey is disturbing, especially given that the two latter scales were specifically developed for use in evaluating parent-child relations and parenting deficits yet were used by fewer than 10% of all practising psychologists who provided custody and access assessments.

Because of the adversarial nature of custody and access evaluations and the perceived incentives for parents to portray themselves in a positive light (referred to here as "positive impression management"), it is worth knowing the extent to which parents' self-reports on psychological tests are affected by litigation. Bathurst, Gottfried, and Gottfried (1997) described MMPI-2 responses for 508 parents involved in child custody litigation. The litigating parents had mean scores on validity scales measuring positive impression management between 0.5 and 1.0 standard deviations above the normative sample means. This finding was consistent across both genders. Similar MMPI-2 data has recently been published for British Columbia (Posthuma & Harper, 1998) and Ontario (Bagby, Nicholson, Buis, Radovanovic, & Fidler, 1999) for samples of custody litigants. All studies show elevations for these groups on measures of defensiveness. Interestingly, when Baer, Wetter, Nichols, Greene, and Berry (1995) compared students given "fake good" instructions to students taking the MMPI-2 under standard instructions, the fake good sample obtained scores on the positive impression management scales approximately 2.0 standard deviations higher than the control group. These results suggest that any self-report assessment of socially undesirable characteristics within a custody evaluation will be answered in a defensive manner by a large proportion of parents. Psychologists who conduct such assessments will have to take special steps to account for parental defensiveness and to obtain valid portrayals of parents' strengths and weaknesses.

Given the highly emotional and potentially antagonistic nature of custody disputes, it is not surprising to learn that child custody evaluations are a leading cause of ethical complaints against psychologists. Koch (1992) determined that approximately half of all ethics complaints to the College of Psychologists of British Columbia involve child custody evaluations. It is even more disturbing that criticisms of inadequately validated assessment methods have been levelled at practitioners in this field since 1981 (Grisso, 1986; Ziskin, 1981). This suggests that clinical practice in the field of custody evaluation is changing at a snail's pace despite rapid advances in scientific knowledge of related phenomena. While regulatory bodies are attempting to control ethical conduct in this area by developing ethical guidelines (e.g., in British Columbia and Ontario), and texts providing clinical guidelines for practice are proliferating (e.g., Ackerman, 1995, Bricklin, 1995), there is still serious debate about the constructive utility of psychological science in this legal arena. In fact, O'Donohue and Bradley (1999) have recently stated that "mental health professionals have little accurate information or warranted recommendations to offer" in custody evaluations (p. 310).

Box 13.1

Parental Satisfaction with Custody Assessments and Stability of Custody Arrangements

A frequently ignored question concerns the satisfaction of parents with recommendations made by custody and access evaluators. Austin and Jaffe (1990), as part of the large body of research emanating from the Family Court Clinic in London, Ontario, followed up 118 parents who had been involved in custody and access assessments. While obtaining only a 36% return rate on their survey, the parents who completed the survey indicated the greatest satisfaction with receiving third-party information about the children's best interests and avoiding lengthy court proceedings. As could be predicted, custodial parents were most satisfied with the custody arrangement.

These authors also inquired about changes in custody over the follow-up period. One hundred per cent of initial sole custody allocations to the mother remained in place at follow-up, compared with 78% for fathers' sole custody, 50% for the small sample of split custody decisions, and only 25% of the joint custody decisions. This reinforces what has been observed elsewhere – that the more complex or cumbersome custodial arrangements are markedly less stable over time.

This study is a good example of how applied forensic psychologists can answer important questions in the area of family law. Further research of this nature is required. Specifically, it would be worthwhile to know in more detail whether psychological assessments in custody disputes actually reduce legal and court costs, whether there are mental health benefits to the children and adults involved in these assessments, and to what extent these potential benefits outweigh the economic and personal costs of being subjects of such detailed psychological inquiry. As well, the longitudinal stability of different custodial arrangements needs to be studied further as this will have practical implications for court decisions and the recommendations of court-retained experts.

The experience of custody law suits and assessments is generally aversive for all parties concerned. In Box 13.1, we describe research efforts that have attempted to investigate this problem. In other research, a debate has emerged in recent decades as to whether some form of mediation would produce results that are more satisfactory to both children and parents in custody and access disputes. The primary proponent of mediated custody resolution has been Emery (Emery, Matthews, & Wyer, 1991; Emery & Wyer, 1987a, 1987b; Emery, 1994, 1999). In brief, the results of Emery and his colleagues have shown that mediation reduces the frequency of court proceedings and time to settlement and results in improved satisfaction for fathers. Results from other centres, however, have not been so positive. Walker (1993) found that, "while some clients experienced reduced levels of distress immediately following mediation, there was little evidence of this improvement being sustained over time. Income deprivation and trouble with relatives had a major impact on psychological well-being, whereas the mediation experience was rarely able to alleviate such problems directly" (p. 283).

It should be noted that this comparison of Emery's and Walker's studies is somewhat like a comparison of apples and oranges. Emery's studies emanated from his own mediation clinic while Walker surveyed individuals in the community who had used different post-divorce services. It may be safe to conclude that highly structured university-based mediation has benefits for time savings and paternal satisfaction, but the bulk of custody mediation currently performed by practising psychologists and other mental health professionals appears to have few long-term benefits.

CONTESTED ADOPTIONS

Adoption is the act of legally giving up custodial and guardianship rights of one's biological child to another person. Parents who do this are more commonly single women with reduced social support systems and few economic resources. For an adoption to be finalized, consent is required from both biological parents, unless the courts dispense with the parental consent. Two occurrences can result in a legal dispute subsequent to an adoption. First, while not a frequent occurrence, biological mothers sometimes change their minds after the transfer of custody. This may occur in cases in which the mother has suffered undue pressure by extended family or others. Second, the biological father may not have consented to the adoption and may subsequently contest it, seeking custody for himself. This usually occurs in cases where the two parents did not have a continuing relationship after conception. The courts are reluctant to dispense with the consent of such fathers unless they show little or no interest in the parental role.

These situations create a great quandary for law and psychology. All English-speaking provinces in Canada specify that kinship should be considered in determining the best interests of the child (see Table 13.1). Adoption acts have similar provisions. In the case of contested adoptions, adoptive parents typically have numerous social and economic advantages in comparison to the biological parent. While statutory law in Canada favours biological kinship, and adopted children do have significantly more behavioural problems than their non-adopted peers (Wierzbicki, 1993), it is unclear that biological kinship between caregivers and children predicts better psychological outcome. Many commonly held assumptions about the causal role of adoption on the well-being of children appear to have little empirical support. According to Peters, Atkins, and McKay (1999), there are five predominant models that attempt to explain the higher preponderance of mental health problems in adoptees:

(a) genetic predispositions passed on by the biological parents,
(b) the pathological impact of the adoption process per se,
(c) negative effects of pre-adoption parenting,
(d) referral bias among adoptive parents, who allegedly refer adoptive children to mental health facilities at a higher rate than do biological parents, and
(e) impaired relationships between adoptive parents and their adoptive children.

Evidence reviewed by Peters et al. (1999) suggests that evidence for the biological causation of emotional and behavioural problems in adopted children is mixed at best. Importantly for our discussion, there is no substantial evidence that adoptive children suffer a depression in response to their adoptive status, nor is there any significant evidence that adoptees are unduly preoccupied with their adopted status. Neither is there any strong evidence that adopted children and their adoptive parents are less well attached to each other than biologically related families. In fact, more evidence points to mothers of adopted children being more responsive and nurturing than are biological mothers (Rende, Lomkowski, Stocker, Fulker, & Plomin, 1992; Marquis and Detweiler, 1985; cited in Peters et al.,1999). This latter conclusion is particularly important because it suggests that little increased risk of emotional or behavioural dysfunction is associated with the act of adoption.

Some relatively consistent evidence suggests that the emotional and behavioural problems of adopted children are associated with impaired parenting prior to adoption (e.g., Verhulst, Althaus, & Versluis-Den Bieman, 1992). Peters et al. (1999) reviewed a number of studies pointing to a referral bias amongst adoptive parents that results in an increased frequency of referral for mental health interventions for adopted children independent of the children's actual mental health status. Finally, there appears to be very little evidence suggesting that adoptive parents and children have impaired relations that contribute to the increased mental health needs of adoptive children.

In brief, statutory law suggests that the best interests of the child include being placed with biologically related kin and that adoptive children show higher rates of emotional and behavioural problems than do non-adopted children, and popular belief suggests that something about the adoption process or the adoptive parent/child relationship results in these higher rates. Unfortunately, available research suggests that (a) both pre- and post-adoption parenting are substantial influences on the mental health of adopted children, (b) there is little evidence that adoptees react to their adoptive status with increased emotional difficulties, and (c) adoptive parents are, if anything, more attached and nurturing to their adopted children than are biologically related parents to their biological children. Thus, psychological science is in clear conflict with the value accorded by the law to biological paternity.

How then do the courts rule in such cases? A British Columbia case (*In the matter of a female infant, B.C. Birth Registration No. 99–00733, B.C.C.A.*) shows how psychology and the law struggle in this area of litigation. In this case, a baby girl was born to young adult parents who had only a short dating history prior to conception. When the mother determined she was pregnant she broke off her relationship with the father and subsequently, perhaps under some duress from extended family and others, placed her yet-to-be-born child up for adoption. She selected the adoptive parents prior to birth and turned the child over to them 11 days after birth. The biological father did not formally learn of the adoption until the child had been with the adoptive parents for 4 months, at which point he sought custody for himself. Expert evidence was sought with respect to the relative risk factors associated with both the biological father and the adoptive parents, and with respect to the scientific literature relevant to any ill effects that might result from the child's adoptive status or from a change of caregiver at her age. This case was heard in B.C. Supreme Court when the child was 9 months of age and had been in the care of the adoptive parents for all but 11 days of her life.

Briefly, the expert psychological testimony indicated that there was little long-term risk to the child of being of adoptive status and that there were no salient risk factors predicting poor outcome for the child associated with either adoptive parents or with the biological father. In addition, testimony was heard that there was little long-term risk to a child changing caregivers within the first 4 months of life, but that there was an increasing risk of impairment of attachment and associated psychological well-being with a change of caregiver beginning at approximately 1 year of life.

After citing the expert psychological testimony extensively, the British Columbia Supreme Court ruled that the child should be returned to the biological father, because his consent for the adoption had not been properly obtained and because "the various factors here are pretty much in balance except for the biological link' (*In the matter of a female infant, B.C. Birth Registration No. 99–00733*, B.C.S.C.). On appeal one month later, the court of appeal ruled 2 to 1 to overturn the lower court's decision, similarly citing the expert's testimony, but resulting in a differing opinion that more harm to the infant was likely to occur from taking the child from the adoptive parents who had cared for her for 10 months. The reasons given in the appeal ruling were that the trial judge had given predominant weighting to biological kinship little consideration to the uncertainties of adequate caregiving in the biological father's household. The appeal court's decision was appealed to the Supreme Court of Canada. However, the Supreme Court refused to hear the appeal. Previous judgments (e.g., *Catholic Children's Aid Society of Metropolitan Toronto v. CM*) suggest that the Supreme Court considers carefully the concept of "psychological parent" and the potential ill effects of separating a child from caregivers to which she is attached.

As can be seen from the chronology above, two problems are apparent. First, while expert testimony may be sought and subsequently cited in judgment, a strong value in such cases is attached to biological kinship, despite the absence of scientific evidence to support this bias and despite expert testimony to that effect. Further, even when the courts move quickly, the child can spend a year in the care of the adoptive parents before legal resolution. In such cases, the child may develop strong attachments to the adoptive parents prior to the determination of custody through the courts, with unpredictable negative effects subsequent to any disruption of that attachment.

To conclude, while contested adoptions are relatively infrequent, they pose great difficulties for the courts because of discrepancies between legal values and evidence from scientific psychology. Future research could be directed towards evaluating the assumptions underlying the law in this area. In particular, it would seem important to determine when a child would, in fact, be better off with biological parents, and when a child would be better off with adoptive parents. Clearly, this is a complex issue, and one requiring longitudinal, or at least comprehensive cross-sectional, research designs that account for numerous potential confounding variables.

SUMMARY

Two important areas of family law in which psychology plays a significant role are child protection and abuse and custody and access issues. Both of these areas give rise to a large amount of litigation, and, as a consequence, involve psychological input primarily in assessments. Psychology can provide a means of empirically studying many of the important legal issues required by statute and considered by case law, such as the nature and elements of the "best interests" construct, as well as such factors as the predictors and effects of child abuse and divorce and alternative dispute resolution with respect to custody and access. Contested adoptions, while much fewer in number than custody and access cases, present an interesting dilemma in that legal values and psychological science appear to be in conflict.

The decade ahead will witness a number of new research, practice, and legal developments. Comparisons of how practising psychologists address the best interests of the child and subsequent court judgments are certain to be made. Psychologists are also likely to explore the potential parenting factors that may mediate the relationship between social and parental risk factors (e.g., poverty, maternal depression) and children's failures to thrive. Psychological practice in this area will likely show greater conformity to the wealth of scientific findings on children's well-being. We will also learn more about the efficacy of custody mediation as this type of intervention is studied in more detail, and some jurisdictions may adopt the approximation rule in custody determination. Finally, statutory law in this area will likely change, perhaps forcing child protection services to provide more rehabilitative help to those children in need of protection.

QUESTIONS FOR DISCUSSION

1. What are the limitations in generalizing basic research on child abuse to child apprehension decisions made by the courts and practising psychologists?

2. As described in this chapter, the courts use a number of factors to determine child custody between divorcing parents. What parental characteristics appear germane to custody decisions, and what are the limits in their generality?
3. In most jurisdictions in Canada, complaints arising from custody and access evaluations are among the leading cause of complaints against psychologists and psychiatrists. How would you explain this phenomenon?
4. Critically review the fit between criteria used by psychologists to make custody recommendations and the legal standards employed by courts in these matters.

RECOMMENDED READING

Beck, K.A., & Ogloff, J.R.P. (1995). Child abuse reporting in British Columbia: Psychologists' knowledge of and compliance with the reporting law. *Professional Psychology: Research and Practice, 26*, 245–251.

Emery, R.E. (1994). *Renegotiating family relationships: Divorce, child custody, and mediation.* New York: Guilford.

Malinosky-Rummell, R., & Hansen, D.J. (1993). Long-term consequences of childhood physical abuse. *Psychological Bulletin, 114*, 68–79.

Pearce, J.W., & Pezzot-Pearce, T.D. (1997). *Psychotherapy of abused and neglected children.* New York: Guilford.

Wolfe, D.A. (1999). *Child abuse: Implications for children's development and psychopathology.* Thousand Oaks, CA: Sage.

14. Psychological Injuries and Tort Litigation: Sexual Victimization and Motor Vehicle Accidents

Kevin S. Douglas and William J. Koch

A 21-year-old female university student sought biofeedback treatment for headaches from a medical specialist. During treatment, he coerced her into engaging in sexual intercourse on a number of occasions. She became pregnant and later had an abortion. Following an ethics complaint to the College of Physicians and Surgeons, the physician was found guilty of professional misconduct and suspended for one year. Subsequently, this woman sought damages in a tort action, claiming psychological and other stress-related injuries. Prior health records and collateral interviews of the plaintiff revealed no serious emotional or psychological problems, although she had received therapy from a psychiatrist. Prior to the sexual victimization, she had been described as a good student, conscientious, and sociable. After this experience, however, she had to seek treatment with at least six psychiatrists. She was diagnosed with depression, paranoia, and borderline personality disorder. She also experienced headaches, social isolation, interpersonal problems, difficulty in parenting, anxiety, irritability, numerous hypochondriacal concerns, and a variety of physical symptoms. By the time of the personal injury claim, she had been living on social assistance for some years. At the time of her assessment for this claim, she met diagnostic criteria for post-traumatic stress disorder (PTSD) and major depressive episode – recurrent. Although this case has yet to be adjudicated at court, several legal and psychological issues are likely to be central in determining its outcome. First, the plaintiff had some, though not extensive, pre-existing mental health complaints. The plaintiff's lawyer will likely attempt to minimize those pre-existing difficulties, while defence counsel will attempt to make the most of them. References to "borderline personality disorder" may be used in an attempt to show a continuation of a condition that predated the victimization. By this logic, the defendant's action would not be seen as the causal agent behind the complainant's current men-

tal health concerns. Also, the defence lawyer may attempt to show that the plaintiff is exaggerating her mental health symptoms and degree of disability. Data from the forensic psychologist's assessment will be germane to this debate.

The preceding case illustrates numerous issues that will be discussed in the present chapter on psychological issues involved in personal injury litigation. What emotional or psychological "injuries" are likely to stem from victimization? How are these assessed? What legal issues are relevant to emotional injury following victimization? It is considered unjust in our society for one person to be wrongly injured by another without appropriate compensation for losses. Injuries often are financial as well as physical, resulting in medical costs and lost earnings due to work-related disability as well as physical pain and suffering. Psychological injuries (sometimes called mental or emotional injuries) are also increasingly recognized by the courts as having a profound effect on injured parties' lives, including their ability to work, and thus are increasingly compensable. Specific questions then arise. Under what types of law can psychologically injured persons seek redress? What types of psychological injuries occur in what settings? What types of psychological injuries are compensable? Finally, what does psychological research have to say about these injuries, their prevalence, causes, prognosis, and rehabilitation?

Forensic psychologists often assess persons who have been injured in some manner and have brought an action in tort against the person responsible for the injury. Given the particular expertise of psychologists and other mental health professionals, assessment and testimony will typically be of a person's emotional and psychological reactions to some act of wrongdoing. A tort, in its most basic sense, is a civil (i.e., not criminal) wrong or injury (see Chapter 2). The Supreme Court of Canada has maintained that tort litigation is meant to compensate injured parties and restore them to their pre-injury positions (*Ratych v. Bloomer*, 1990). Because tort litigation is a civil proceeding, the burden of proving the injury, that the injury was caused by the defendant, and that the defendant acted intentionally or negligently lies with the plaintiff, or the party alleging the wrong doing. There are literally dozens of possible situations arising from tort law in which psychology may play some role. The examples we present below – a criminal victimization (sexual assault), civil (human) rights violation (sexual harassment), and negligence (vehicular accidents) – while by no means exhaustive, provide some coverage of the range of participation of psychologists in this arena.

SEXUAL VICTIMIZATION

We have chosen to discuss both sexual assault and sexual harassment to demonstrate the role psychologists may play in personal injury litigation. These forms of victimization, though distinct, sometimes share common attributes. In fact, some acts of victimization may be defined both as harassment and assault. Thus issues of concern to the forensic mental health professional who deals with sexual assault or sexual harassment may very well overlap, particularly in terms of the impact on victims' emotional and psychological well-being and assessment issues. We will, of course, draw important distinctions between the constructs, as well as between the effects they may beget.

The prevalence of sexual assault is disturbingly high. In Canada, it is estimated that some 2.5 million Canadian women have been sexually assaulted (Johnson & Sacco, 1995). In 1996, there were 26,762 reported instances of sexual assault in Canada (Statistics Canada, 1996b), although this figure may represent up to a 62% underreporting rate (Statistics Canada, 1994).

Sexual harassment is also common. Canada's largest epidemiological sexual harassment research, conducted by the Canadian Human Rights Commission (CHRC; 1987), surveyed 2,004 women and men and found that roughly 49% of the women and 33% of the men indicated that they had received some form of unwanted sexual attention. The CHRC extrapolated the survey findings to estimate that 1.5 million Canadian workers are subjected to sexual harassment. These estimates are consistent with large-scale surveys in the United States (United States Merit Systems Protection Board [USMSPB], 1981).

In general, research demonstrates that the more severe types of harassment, such as forced sexual touching, sexual bribery, and sexual assault, occur with lower frequency than less serious types such as sexual jokes or comments (Cammaert, 1985; Diaz & McMillin, 1991; Fitzgerald et al., 1988; Loy & Stewart, 1984; Newell, Rosenfeld, & Culbertson, 1995; Samoluk & Pretty, 1994; USMSPB, 1981; see Cammaert, 1985, and Samoluk & Pretty, 1994, for Canadian samples). It also appears that the prevalence of harassment is equally common in academia as in the workplace, although it may be more common in "traditionally" male jobs, and far more likely to be experienced by women than men.

The Law

The general definition of sexual assault is sexual contact with a non-consenting person (see Boer, Hart, Kropp, & Webster, 1997). Various sexual behaviours against children and adults are illegal under several sections of the Criminal Code of Canada. Sexual assault is defined as one type of assault and assault (paragraph 265(1)(a) of the Code) is defined as follows: "A person commits an assault when ... without the consent of the other person, he applies force intentionally to that other person, directly or indirectly." Subsection 265(2) maintains that "[t]his section applies to all forms of assault, including sexual assault ..." There are three "levels" of sexual assault, and these increase in severity: (1) sexual assault (s. 271); (2) sexual assault with a weapon, threats to a third party or causing bodily harm (s. 272); and (3) aggravated sexual assault (s. 273).

When sexual assault is considered in tort law, the criminal definition has only marginal relevance. Sexual assault is a form of the tort of battery, in that it is an intentional, nonconsensual contact of one person by another. Although a person may be criminally charged for sexual assault, a criminal conviction is not required for an action framed in battery to be brought against a person in tort for what would be, in the eyes of the criminal law, a sexual assault.

The legal definition of sexual harassment is typically construed in one of two ways: (1) quid pro quo harassment, which refers to situations in which the employment of persons is made contingent upon their complying with sexual demands, remarks, gestures, or behaviours, and (2) hostile environment harassment, which describes circumstances in which sexual demands, remarks, or behaviours make the work environment intolerable. Sexual harassment is illegal under antidiscrimination legislation, such as the Canadian Human Rights Act (1985) and its provincial counterparts. It is also illegal under the Charter. Specifically, subsection 15(1) of the Charter states: "Every individual is equal before and under the law and has the right to the equal protection and equal benefit of the law without discrimination and, in particular, without discrimination based on race, national or ethnic origin, colour, religion, sex, age or mental or physical disability." It is important to note that the Charter would only apply in cases where the alleged harassment or discrimination occurred between a person and the state or state's representative.

Canadian case law has upheld that sexual harassment is illegal under civil rights legislation on the grounds of gender discrimination. Such was the ruling of the Supreme Court of Canada in *Janzen and Governeau v. Platy Enterprises Ltd.* (1989). Two waitresses successfully argued that their treatment by another employee constituted discrimination. The Supreme Court of Canada ultimately agreed and defined sexual harassment as a subtype of sexual discrimination, and, therefore, illegal. An earlier Supreme Court of Canada case, *Robichaud v. Canada (Treasury Board)* (1987), established that employers are responsible for the actions of their employees in terms of sexual harassment, meaning that an employee may take legal action against a company if a co-worker sexually harasses her or him, as happened in *Janzen.*

Aggarwal (1987) points out that in most sexual harassment cases, the offending behaviour must clearly be of a sexual nature, and it must also be sufficiently egregious, as must any damages suffered by the victim. Typically, the burden of proving harassment – that the behaviour in question was unwanted, offensive, and caused a negative work environment, or that terms of employment were contingent upon sexual acts – and its consequences lies with the plaintiff. Emotional distress and the nervous shock that follow from sexual victimization may be compensated in tort litigation if the defendant could reasonably have foreseen that his or her action would result in such distress or shock.

In cases of sexual harassment or assault, the forensic clinician may be involved in the assessment of victims in various judicial or quasi-judicial settings. For instance, the Canadian Human Rights Commission (CHRC) received 128 complaints of sexual harassment in 1992 (Falardeau-Ramsay, 1994). Some of these cases would have called for the evaluation of the victim. Experts may also assist tribunals of law in explicating the impact of sexual assault on victims as a part of sentencing the offender. Forensic experts may be retained, typically by plaintiffs, to establish that some harm was experienced as a result of the alleged wrongdoing by the respondent. Again, this would involve assessment of victims. To carry out such assessments competently, experts must be cognizant of the relevant law surrounding the case and common psychological, emotional, psychopathological, behavioural, and other effects of sexual assault or harassment.

The Effects of Sexual Victimization

There are obvious overlaps between the effects of sexual harassment and sexual assault. Generally, it may be fair to state that the consequences of sexual assault have the potential to be more acute and severe. This being said, however, psychological research has clearly shown that persons who experience sexual harassment may also experience serious effects. Generally, it may be useful to think of the range of effects as falling into various categories. Doubtless other groups of effects could be proposed; we offer this categorization merely as an heuristic: (1) initial coping responses; (2) work- and school-related effects; (3) physical effects; (4) psychological (subclinical) effects and; (5) psychopathological (clinical) effects. We focus on harassment for the first two categories because many of the effects and much of the research involves coping with and responding to ongoing, persistent experiences in the workplace that often typify harassment.

In the coping response category we are concerned primarily with whether sexual harassment victims' initial responses were internally or externally oriented (Fitzgerald, Swan, & Fischer, 1995). Passive or internally oriented responses include enduring or denying harassment, and are unlikely to bring the harassment to an end (Gutek & Koss, 1993). Externally oriented or assertive reactions include confronting the harasser or pursuing formal channels of recourse. Research would seem to indicate that victims of sexual harassment appear to use fewer external responses compared to internal responses.

Work- and school-related effects of sexual harassment span several concerns. Many victims of harassment either quit work or are fired, or leave school (Coles, 1986; Loy & Stewart, 1984; USMSPB, 1981, 1988). Those who continue to work in the hostile environment may become less productive (Bursten, 1986; Cammaert, 1985; Crull, 1982). Personal relationships in the work or school setting may become strained (Gosselin, 1984; Gutek & Koss, 1993; Morrow, McElroy, & Phillips, 1994). In general, attitudes towards work and work colleagues may become negative (Mansfield et al., 1991; Morrow et al., 1994; Murrell, Olson, & Frieze, 1995; Newell et al., 1995; Reilly, Lott, & Gallogly, 1986). Finally, sexual harassment may lead to impaired motivation and concentration in the work or school setting, which may affect performance (Crull, 1991; Salisbury, Ginorio, Remick, & Stringer, 1986).

Physical effects of sexual harassment include somatic complaints, negative health-related behaviour, and increased health care utilization. Research on sexual harassment victims has demonstrated that they are at increased risk for somatic symptoms such as headaches, appetite and sleep disturbances, weight problems, gastrointestinal disorders, nausea, fatigue, bruxism (nocturnal teeth grinding), and many others (Crull, 1982; Loy & Stewart, 1984; Newell et al., 1995; Salisbury et al., 1986). Similarly, a fair amount of research has shown that sexual assault victims are likely to experience a similar cluster of physical symptoms (Dahl, 1989; Kimerling & Calhoun, 1994; Koss, 1993; Leidig, 1992). Additional physical, or perhaps more accurately here, behavioural, effects common to both sexual harassment and sexual assault victims include increased health care utilization and more frequent negative health-related behaviours such as substance use (Burnam et al., 1988; Gosselin, 1984; Hanson, 1990; Kimerling & Calhoun, 1994; Koss, 1993; Leidig, 1992; Richman, Flaherty, Rospenda, & Christensen, 1992; Robertson, 1990).

The next category of consequences of sexual victimization is best termed psychological, in that these sequela primarily consist of affective and attitudinal responses. As the reader will note, there is a similarity between the reactions of sexual harassment and sexual assault victims. Sexual harassment victims may show symptoms of depression (Cammaert, 1985; Loy & Stewart, 1984), low self-esteem (Gruber & Bjorn, 1986; McCormack, 1985), humiliation and shame (Komaromy, Bindman, Haber, & Sande, 1993; Schneider, 1987), and self-blame (Jensen & Gutek, 1982; Silverman, 1976–77) in response to their experiences. Considerable research has also shown that sexual harassment victims are likely to experience anger, frustration, and disgust (Cammaert, 1985; Frazier & Cohen, 1992; Gosselin, 1984; Jensen & Gutek, 1982; Loy & Stewart, 1984; Silverman, 1976–77). In addition, it is evident that sexual harassment is a fearful experience for many victims (Crull, 1991; Gadlin, 1991; Komaromy et al., 1993; Loy & Stewart, 1984; Schneider, 1987; Silverman, 1976–77). Finally, as a result of the enduring and chronic nature of sexual harassment, and the fact that it gives rise to the various harmful effects described above, it is not surprising that many persons who experience harassment are likely to have problems with stress and anxiety (Cammaert, 1985; Crull, 1991; Gosselin, 1984; Richman et al., 1992; Silverman, 1976–77).

The effects of sexual harassment clearly pose serious health risks to those who must endure them. Sexual assault victims are also forced to deal with such effects, many of which are similar to those associated with harassment. Many sexual assault victims experience depression, threats to self-esteem, humiliation, and shame (Bownes, O'Gorman, & Sayers, 1991; Dahl, 1989; Hanson, 1990; Holgate, 1989; Mackey et al., 1992; Ullman & Siegel, 1993). Many persons who suffer sexual assault understandably react with anger, frustration, disgust (Dahl, 1989), and fear (Burge, 1988; Holgate, 1989). As with sexual harassment, these effects on mental health typically give rise to elevated levels of stress and anxiety (Bownes et al., 1991; Dahl, 1989; Koss, 1993). Finally, research on sexually victimized women shows that many experience diminished trust (Gidycz & Koss, 1991; Leidig, 1992; Reilly et al., 1986; Robertson, 1990) and sexual dysfunction (Bownes et al., 1991; Hanson, 1990; Koss, 1993; Ullman & Seigel, 1993), although the latter has not been researched in sexual harassment victims specifically.

The fifth and final category relates to the most severe effects, and includes psychopathological conditions that would warrant psychiatric diagnoses. It is certainly known that post-traumatic stress disorder (PTSD) is a common effect of sexual assault (Bownes et al., 1991; Burge, 1988; Rothbaum, Foa, Riggs, Murdoch, & Walsh, 1994). As defined by the *Diagnostic and Statistical Manual of Mental Disorders*, fourth edition (DSM-IV; American Psychiatric Association, 1994), PTSD is a reaction to an event that involved threatened or actual death, serious bodily harm, or threat to physical integrity of self or others. It consists of three clusters of symptoms: (1) re-experiencing (intrusive recollections, sense of reliving the trauma; dreams or nightmares, etc.); (2) avoidance and numbing (efforts to avoid thoughts, activities; places, or persons associated with the trauma, decreased interest in significant activities, restricted range of affect; feelings of detachment from others, etc.); and (3) increased arousal (hypervigilance, anger, sleep difficulties, exaggerated startle response, etc.). Although different studies find different incidence rates of PTSD following sexual assault – largely due to methodological differences associated with sampling procedures, definitions of sexual assault, and the measurement of PTSD – it is probably a safe estimate that between 32 and 57% of sexual assault victims develop PTSD (see Acierno, Kilpatrick, & Resnick, 1999, for a review). Other possible disorders that may develop include adjustment disorders, mood disorders (i.e., depression), and substance abuse disorders (Gutek & Koss, 1993; Long, 1994).

Admittedly, the data with respect to sexual harassment are rather sparse, and any conclusions drawn from them must be made with caution. In sexual harassment cases that proceed to litigation, psychiatric diagnoses of PTSD may occur with some frequency (Long, 1994). There is some evidence that sexual harassment is disproportionately prevalent in the histories of women with PTSD (Kilpatrick, 1992, cited in Gutek & Koss). Some research with female Persian Gulf War military personnel has shown that those who experienced more serious physical forms of sexual harassment experienced more severe PTSD symptomatology compared to those who experienced less serious forms or no harassment (Wolfe et al., 1998). Further, women who experienced sexual assault had the most severe PTSD symptomatology.

This study also is important because it is one of the few, if not the only, to evaluate both sexual assault and harassment in the same sample. Consistent with the authors' predictions, there was a dose-response relationship between the severity of the victimization (ranging from less serious forms of verbal harassment to more serious types of sexual assault) and the severity of PTSD symptomatology. We have reviewed harassment and assault together because, in our view, they may be viewed as forms of sexual victimization that fall along a continuum. The data of Wolfe et al. (1998) are consistent with this view.

Sexual assault and harassment often attach to their perpetrators a high degree of moral blameworthiness and frequently involve serious violations of personal security and integrity. The next section of the chapter focuses on an occurrence – the motor vehicle accident – often unaccompanied by any moral stigma, but which may also produce extensive psychological injuries.

MOTOR VEHICLE ACCIDENTS

A Statistics Canada report reveals that there were 1.7 million motor vehicle accidents (MVAs) in 1987 (Millar & Adams, 1991). Approximately 42% of these accidents resulted in injuries. Nearly 4,000 people over the age of 15 died. Motor vehicle accidents are the leading cause of accidental mortality in Canada and account for 50% of all accidental deaths for persons aged 15–24. Each accident, fatality, or injury represents an opportunity for chronic psychological distress. Between 11 and 30% of people injured in an MVA will have some residual psychological distress meriting a diagnosis, with high prevalence rates for conditions of PTSD, accident phobia, major depressive episode, chronic pain complaints, and neuropsychological deficits related to head injuries found in these samples.

If persons have been seriously affected psychologically as a result of an accident, courts may be willing to award damages. More severe injuries, whether physical or psychological, lead to larger awards. In *Correira v. Flamand* (1989), the plaintiff was awarded $10,000 for physical pain and suffering and an additional $15,000 because of a change in lifestyle and deteriorated family relationships. The Supreme Court of Canada upheld an award of $30,000 to a plaintiff who was happy and sociable before an accident but became emotionally unstable, depressed, and withdrawn after it (*Woelk v. Halvorson*, 1981). In another case, the plaintiff developed depression and anorexia nervosa, allegedly as a result of an accident, and was compensated for it (*McCallum v. Waito*, 1983). The fear of travelling by car after an accident has also been compensated by the courts (*Chamberlain v. Robichaud*, 1985), as has the development of paranoid and violent tendencies (*Kovach v. Smith*, 1972). The following discussion focuses on psychological conditions that may occur with some degree of consistency in motor vehicle accident victims.

Post-traumatic Stress Disorder

According to a random survey conducted by Norris (1992), approximately 11% of MVA victims develop PTSD. This study is especially significant because it compared the incidence of PTSD to a variety of traumatic stressors, including sexual assault, MVAs, and natural disasters (i.e., Hurricane Hugo). In this study, the incidence of PTSD following MVAs was only exceeded by that following sexual assault. Other research (e.g., Blanchard, Hickling, Taylor, Loos, & Gerardi, 1994) suggested that up to 48% of those meeting criteria for PTSD also meet criteria for a major depressive episode. In short, a substantial proportion of MVA victims develop severe psychological distress. While many patients improve without treatment, some remain chronically distressed (reviewed in Taylor & Koch, 1995). Post-traumatic stress disorder is a highly prevalent psychological injury resulting from MVAs. Blanchard et al. (1996) found that 70% of their 158 MVA victims could be classified as PTSD with four variables: (1) a prior history of major depression; (2) fear of dying in the MVA; (3) extent of physical injury; and (4) litigation status. The latter factor is difficult to interpret. Litigious individuals may be more likely to claim PTSD, but on the other hand individuals with more severe psychological injuries (i.e., PTSD) may justifiably be more likely to seek compensation for those injuries.

Post-traumatic stress disorder can be debilitating. In addition to its assessment in a litigation context, psychologists have started to conduct research on the treatment of PTSD following MVAs. The goal of this treatment is to ameliorate the distressing symptoms experienced by those with PTSD. As Box 14.1 demonstrates, the treatment of PTSD following MVAs is proving to be a challenging task.

Box 14.1

Patterns and Predictors of Treatment Outcome for MVA-PTSD

One of the first two controlled trials of therapy for MVA-related PTSD is currently ongoing at the University of British Columbia in Vancouver. Controlled treatment trials for psychological injuries resulting from MVAs are especially important given the large economic and social costs associated with this condition and the uncertainty about prognosis or effective rehabilitation for this common condition. In most circumstances, courts are loath to accept the plaintiff's argument that his or her psychological injury does not respond to treatment and that he or she will therefore have an ongoing disability into the indefinite future. To answer the question as to whether there is an effective treatment for MVA-PTSD, Taylor, Fedoroff, and Koch at the University of British Columbia are conducting a controlled trial of cognitive-behavioural treatment. This treatment involves lengthy applied relaxation training, cognitive therapy with respect to patients' increased expectancies of danger, repeated and prolonged imaginal exposure to memories of the MVA, and graduated exposure to driving. Similar in type and structure to treatment successfully used with sexual assault victims and combat veterans with PTSD, this treatment spans 12 2–hour sessions and is conducted in groups of 4 to 6 patients.

Data are available on the first 34 patients to complete treatment. Treated patients showed a moderate-sized reduction on a PTSD Symptom Scale. Although moderate in size, and therefore appreciable in absolute terms, this effect is relatively weak when compared to similar treatments for other classes of PTSD (see Van Etten & Taylor, 1998). A number of people, however, dropped out of the treatment. In comparison to patients remaining in treatment, dropouts tended to have more mental health problems in addition to PTSD, lower incomes, less perceived control over their lives, greater dissatisfaction with previous medical care, more severe PTSD symptoms at intake, and a more stressful experience in dealing with their insurance claims.

It is of some interest that patients completing treatment fell nicely into two clusters – 15 patients showed improvement during treatment, and 13 actually evidenced further deterioration. Individuals who worsened during treatment tended to be younger and had more days of pain-related bedrest. As well, patients who deteriorated attended fewer therapy sessions and had more stressful events, including more MVAs, during the time they were in therapy.

The preliminary data from this study suggests that the best-known treatment for PTSD in general only has a moderate effect for MVA-PTSD. It is unclear at this time just why this class of individuals with PTSD is so difficult to treat. While 67% of the patients were in litigation during treatment, presence of litigation was not a significant predictor of outcome, nor of dropping out. More to the point of the current topic, findings suggest that prognoses are very guarded for individuals who suffer PTSD from vehicular accidents, and should be communicated as such to lawyers and courts. Importantly, however, we now have some greater knowledge as to who will drop out of therapy, and who will deteriorate during therapy.

Further research in this area will attempt to refine our ability to predict which patients will stay in treatment and which will benefit from treatment, as well as develop treatments that effectively address a broader range of the mental health problems faced by MVA victims (Taylor, Fedoroff, & Koch, 1998).

Postconcussion Syndrome

Postconcussion Syndrome (PCS) is a disorder defined by the occurrence of a mild concussion (frequently occurring in MVAs and contact sports such as boxing, hockey, and football), and a cluster of symptoms including attention/concentration deficits, memory problems, headache, vertigo, anxiety, depression, fatigue, irritability, blurred vision, and sensitivity to light (reviewed in Ferguson & Mittenberg, 1996). Postconcussive Syndrome is an interesting disorder because, while it may have an initial neurological basis from a concussive event, symptoms appear to persist primarily because of psychological factors (reviewed in Ferguson & Mittenberg, 1996). Postconcussive symptoms correlate with ratings of daily stress in both mildly head-injured patients complaining of PCS and in normal controls, who may have no fewer PCS symptoms (Gouvier, Cubic, Jones, Brantley, & Cutlip, 1992). This suggests that while PCS may be precipitated by a concussive episode associated with an MVA, it is maintained by factors following the MVA (e.g., interpersonal stress, deficient coping skills).

Other Psychological Conditions

Chronic pain conditions, especially secondary to soft tissue injuries such as whiplash, are highly prevalent in MVAs. While chronic pain may serve to maintain other forms of psychological distress (e.g., PTSD, depression), it is often the focus of litigation itself. Severe head injuries with resultant neuropsychological deficits and disability are also highly prevalent in MVAs. Space limitations prevent us from discussing these particular conditions in further detail.

Legal scholars have also noted that compensation is obtainable for post-physical-injury trauma, which essentially refers to psychological changes and distress subsequent to visible disfigurement (Linden, 1982). Diagnostically, such a condition may be described as an adjustment disorder or, if sufficient distress and preoccupation is present, as traumatically induced body dysmorphic disorder. For example, a young woman who had sustained severe facial injuries in a head-on MVA was returned to what her plastic surgeon, family, and friends felt was her previous appearance. However, for some years afterward she became preoccupied with her appearance, attempting to cover scars that were essentially unobservable to others, making multiple appointments with the plastic surgeon for inquiries about possible further surgeries, with resultant psychological distress.

What Predicts Psychological Distress after MVAs?

Although in litigation a specific vehicular accident may be at issue as the putative cause of a plaintiff's psychological injury, it is becoming clear that many variables play a part in an MVA victim's psychological adjustment. We will briefly discuss the research with respect to PTSD following MVAs, as that is the most extensively researched area. Some of this discussion will be generalizable to predictors of psychological adjustment following sexual assault.

Predictors of PTSD can be roughly categorized by their temporal relationship to the trauma. Victim characteristics preceding the trauma, which we will call predisposing factors, include prior mental health history. Characteristics of the traumatic event (including the victim's immediate subjective response to the trauma, the objective severity of the trauma, and the severity of physical injuries caused by the trauma) may be called event factors. Finally, post-event factors, such as victim coping characteristics and post-injury stresses, may also influence the victim's adjustment.

Predisposing factors that predict psychological disturbance following traumatic injury include pretrauma mental health problems (e.g., Malt & Olafsen, 1992), pretrauma disability status (Malt et al., 1993), and problematic early childhood environment (Breslau, Davis, Andreski, & Peterson, 1991; Malt & Olafsen, 1992). As well, more specific pretrauma histories of either depression (Blanchard et al., 1996; Breslau et al., 1991), or anxiety (Breslau et al., 1991) appear to predict PTSD given a later trauma.

An event factor that appears to have some predictive utility is the subject's perception of threat to his or her life during the trauma (Blanchard et al., 1996; Bryant & Harvey, 1996). The extent of the victim's physical injury has had inconsistent utility in predicting PTSD or psychological distress. While Blanchard et al. (1996, 1997) found that extent of physical injury predicted PTSD 1 to 4 months post-MVA, two separate studies, using a similar injury-rating methodology (Bryant & Harvey, 1995, 1996), found no contributing role of physical injury in the prediction of psychological distress.

With respect to post-event factors, slow recovery from physical injuries appears to predict worse psychological status (Blanchard et al., 1997). Litigation or compensation status has also been shown to predict psychological disturbance by some authors (Blanchard et al., 1996; Bryant & Harvey, 1995). Delahanty et al. (1997) showed that the injured party's perception of other people being responsible for their injury likewise predicts PTSD. It is intuitively plausible that this perception of responsibility will be related to the probability of litigation and to attitudinal changes by the victims concerning their injuries. Avoidant coping style has also been associated with poorer recovery from trauma and post-traumatic psychological distress (Bryant & Harvey, 1995; Malt & Olafsen, 1992; Wolfe, Keane, Kaloupek, Mora, & Wine, 1993) and has substantial merit in predicting psychological distress following accidental injury. Finally, low social support has been found to predict PTSD status 12 months following burn injury (Perry, 1992).

Exacerbation or Maintenance of Symptoms by Litigation

Since Miller's (1961a, 1961b) articles on "accident neurosis," there has been an emotionally laden debate concerning the extent to which psychological and neurological symptoms following MVAs are maintained in part or entirely by prospects of financial compensation. Some data point to the chronicity of psychological distress and other subjective symptoms post-litigation for patients with head trauma (Mersky & Woodforde, 1972), anxiety, depression, and PTSD (Bryant, Mayou, & Lloyd-Bostock, 1997). These studies would suggest that compensation-seeking does not account for a majority of the symptom "picture" of these litigants.

Nonetheless, cross-sectional data comparing similarly injured patients with or without ongoing litigation suggests that litigation itself plays some causal role in symptom complaint and disability. Most persuasive is the statistical meta-analysis by Binder and Rohling (1996) of 17 different studies that compared persons with head-injury with or without financial compensation. Their meta-analysis showed greater abnormality of neuropsychological test performance and greater disability for individuals with prospects of financial compensation. The effect size of .47 was moderate, suggesting a meaningful but not large relationship between compensation and disability. Such findings continue to accumulate with closed-head injuries (e.g., Youngjohn, Davis, & Wolf, 1997), indicating that litigation status predicts greater psychological distress and health concern. The upshot of these diverse studies is that compensation-seeking is a significant predictor but not the sole cause of distress and disability in personal injury litigants.

Missing in these studies of the relationship between litigation and continued psychological distress is a coherent discussion of the mediating factors. What is it about litigation, other than hopes for financial compensation, that leads to greater distress? One concept that has been alluded to is "litigation stress" – the stressful experiences associated with being in litigation and resultant psychological reactions. This phenomenon has been briefly discussed by Weissman (1990). "Involvement in litigation renders plaintiffs susceptible to stressors and to influences that may lead to increased impairment, biased reportage, and retarded recovery. Underlying personality patterns play a critical role in defining and shaping reactions to trauma, to the stress of litigation, and to treatment interventions. Protracted litigation creates conditions that promote mnemonic and attitudinal distortions, as well as conscious and unconscious motivations for secondary gain" (p. 67).

Notably, however, even thoughtful writers like Weissman appear to confound concepts such as secondary gain and personality vulnerability with the stressful nature of litigation and its possible independent role in causing psychological distress. A potential new direction in forensic psychology research will be the empirical quantification of litigation stress and the determination of whether it has any validity in predicting psychological distress in personal injury litigants.

Malingering

The discussion above leads naturally into the concept of malingering – the fabrication of symptoms. This is a topic of concern to the courts in personal injury litigation (see *Del Bello v. Hagel*, 1978). Historically, there have been three different models of malingering: pathogenic, criminological, and adaptational (reviewed in Rogers, 1997). The model seen as most prototypical by forensic psychologists is the so-called adaptational model (Rogers, Sewell, & Goldstein, 1994). Attributes seen by these "experts" to comprise this model include a rational decision based on expected rewards, an attempt to cope with very difficult circumstances, and weighing of alternatives before deciding to feign symptoms. Other perceived important attributes are the subject's consideration of his of her current circumstances and likelihood of success in feigning, trying to make the best of a bad situation, being faced with an unsympathetic system and trying to meet his or her own needs, and involvement in medical-legal evaluations.

Accurate estimates of the base rate of malingering in personal injury litigation are likely impossible to obtain because of the difficulty in defining a "gold standard" for this concept. A gold standard is an agreed-upon criterion against which to validate measurement tools. In the case of malingering, one needs a consensus definition against which researchers can validate different methods of assessment. Unfortunately, psychological consequences of MVAs are sufficiently subjective that no consensus can easily be reached. Malingering research has thus focused primarily on either evaluating measures of motivation or response bias between known groups of litigating and non-litigating persons with the same diagnosis or analogue studies evaluating measures of motivation or response bias in nonclinical subjects, some of whom are instructed to fabricate symptoms and while others are asked to complete the tests truthfully. Three different approaches have been used to construct measures of malingering. The first involves performance measures. For example, within the neuropsychological arena, performance measures of motivation have been developed (e.g., Binder & Willis, 1991). A second approach used for more general psychopathology has involved studies of the tendency to over-endorse mental health symptoms on self-report inventories. The best-performing self-report measures for differentiating instructed "malingerers" from other subjects have been those measures involving the infrequency (F) scale of the MMPI-2 (Berry, Wetter, & Baer, 1995), and its predecessor, the MMPI (Schretlen, 1988). Finally, Rogers, Bagby, and Dickens (1992) recently developed the Structured Interview of Reported Symptoms (SIRS), which attempts to differentiate patients based on such dimensions as the expressed severity of symptoms, breadth of symptoms, bizarreness of symptoms, and consistency of symptom endorsement. While this is a promising strategy, it has not yet been evaluated in detail with personal injury litigants and its item content is less relevant to conditions such as PTSD or depression than to psychotic conditions.

Attributing Causality

Attributing the cause of a current mental health condition to a past event is simpler in law than in psychology. Law uses the concept of "proximate cause," by which is meant an unbroken sequence of events from the trauma to the symptoms without intervening events that could be seen as competing causes. Psychology tends to differentiate three classes of causal variables. Predisposing causes are those social, environmental, or personal vulnerabilities that will make a person more likely to develop a disabling psychological condition subsequent to a trauma. An example of a personal vulnerability for PTSD would be a previous history of depression (cf. Blanchard et al., 1996). Precipitants are those events that are instrumental in starting the course of a particular psychological condition. Fearing for one's life in a frightening MVA or sexual victimization are obvious potential precipitants for PTSD. Maintaining variables for psychological conditions are those environmental, social, personal, or treatment-related events that exacerbate a condition or prevent it from remitting. An example of a maintaining variable for PTSD would be ruminative anger.

Despite these complexities, the forensic question of causality can be reduced to the following distinctions among five alternative conclusions (Erbaugh & Benjamin, 1937, cited in Melton, Petrila, Poythress, & Slobogin, 1997):

1 The trauma was the sole cause of the psychological condition. This finding should logically be infrequent, given the large proportion of individuals who survive frightening MVAs with few psychological symptoms.
2 The trauma was a major precipitating factor. This finding may be more frequent but requires that the litigant had no immediately preceding similar psychological condition.
3 The trauma was an aggravating factor. A potentially frequent finding, this merely requires that some substantive psychological condition was present just prior to the trauma, but that the litigant's condition was substantially worsened by the trauma.
4 The trauma was a minor factor. This requires that the psychological condition was well-established just prior to the trauma, and some minor worsening of the psychological condition occurred subsequent to the trauma.
5 The trauma was unrelated to the psychological condition.

Use of a classification system such as the one above, while of unknown empirical validity, at least focuses psychologists and lawyers on alternative interpretations for the litigant's psychological condition.

SUMMARY

Psychologists may often be involved in the assessment and treatment of persons who have suffered some tortious victimization. A tort is a civil wrong for which the injured party is entitled to compensation. In this chapter, two common types of victimization that often lead to psychological injuries, and hence the involvement of psychologists, were described: sexual victimization and motor vehicle accidents. The role of the psychologist may be to evaluate the psychological injuries that putatively stem from victimization. Psychologists ought to carry out their assessments with cognizance of the legal structure within which they practice. This may entail familiarity with the legal questions that are being addressed (i.e., Did the putative behaviour cause the observed effects? Were there intervening or competing causes? What will the long-term damages to a person's mental health be?).

Sexual victimization (whether through harassment or assault) can lead to serious negative mental health effects. Research has identified common responses to sexual victimization that should be evaluated during a psychological assessment. These fall under broad categories of coping responses, work/school effects, subclinical psychological effects, and clinical psychopathological effects. Motor vehicle victimization can also produce serious mental health effects, such as post-traumatic stress disorder, postconcussion disorder, chronic pain, and depression.

In both contexts, it is important for the clinician to consider causation, intervening causes, pre-existing conditions, the effect of litigation on psychological health, and malingering. The litigation of psychological injuries is complicated, because these multiple pre- and post-event variables may affect psychological adjustment. Due to the courts' scepticism about the legitimacy of these often subjective complaints, much research and professional time has been allocated to the study and diagnosis of malingering. Research in this area suggests that it is common for litigation to exacerbate psychological distress as well as the plaintiff's presentation as being disabled. Nonetheless, courts appear increasingly willing to compensate psychological injuries arising from MVAs and sexual victimization.

Several issues have not received much research attention and little systematic knowledge exists in terms of informing clinical assessments or legal decision makers. Research in this area will likely focus on those pre-disposing and post-injury factors that may maintain, aggravate, or ameliorate psychological distress following either sexual victimization or MVAs. Research on the prediction of psychological maladjustment is important in terms of directing resources for intervention, as well as informing clinical considerations of malingering. It will be important to isolate both protective and vulnerability factors that effect the course of psychological injury after a trauma has been experienced. For instance, certain familial, social, emotional, and psychological factors mitigate, and others aggravate, post-trauma adjustment. More specifically, refinement of psychological treatment strategies for PTSD and other mental health problems arising from traumas has obvious clinical appeal as well as legal benefits. The existence of effective and efficient treatments may facilitate appropriate awards (i.e., neither too high nor too low) from courts for past and future treatment costs. Similarly, the specification of methods to detect symptom exaggeration and malingering would be an asset to both clinicians and legal decision makers.

QUESTIONS FOR DISCUSSION

1. It has been found that litigation itself can sustain or even cause some psychological symptoms in victims of tortious acts. Although the law requires tortfeasors (i.e., the people who commit the tort) to compensate victims for the full amount of their injuries, should they be financially responsible for damages or psychological injuries that stem, perhaps partially, from litigation? Can you think of any strategies to determine which injuries stem directly from the original harm, and which stem from litigation? What strategies might be effective in reducing the stress and other psychological effects of litigation?
2. Many victims of sexual victimization and motor vehicle accidents suffer negative effects. However, not all do. What sorts of factors might distinguish between persons who do and those who do not suffer serious effects from victimization? How could a research study be designed to isolate factors that distinguish between these groups of people?
3. Often, victims of sexual aggression or of motor vehicle accidents are not compensated for many months, if not years, after such victimization. In the meantime, their symptoms may continue untreated. What sort of systemic changes could be made to ameliorate the suffering of victims prior to a judicial determination of fault being made? What sorts of treatments would be effective in reducing the symptoms of victimization?
4. Review the psychological effects of sexual assault and sexual harassment. To what extent are they the same, and how do they differ? Why would we expect to find similarities?

RECOMMENDED READING

Aggarwal, A.P. (1987). *Sexual harassment in the workplace*. Toronto: Butterworths.

Blanchard, E.B., & Hickling, E.J. (1997). *After the crash: Assessment and treatment of motor vehicle accident survivors*. Washington, DC: American Psychological Association.

Hanson, R.K. (1990). The psychological impact of sexual assault on women and children: A review. *Annals of Sex Research, 3*, 187–232.

Koch, W.J., & Taylor, S. (1995). Assessment and treatment of motor vehicle accident victims. *Cognitive & Behavioral Practice, 2*, 327–342.

Taylor, S., & Koch, W.J. (1995). Anxiety disorders due to motor vehicle accidents: Nature and treatment. *Clinical Psychology Review, 15*, 721–738.

PART FIVE

Conclusion

15. Psychology and Law:
Looking towards the Future

James R.P. Ogloff and Regina A. Schuller

The lawyer alone is obdurate. The lawyer and judge and the juryman are sure that they do not need the experimental psychologist. They do not wish to see that in this field preeminently applied experimental psychology has made strong strides ... They go on thinking that their legal instinct and their common sense supplies them with all that is needed and somewhat more ... (Munsterberg, 1909, p. 11)

After reading about the myriad applications of psychology to law described throughout this text, we hope that we have imparted upon you some appreciation for what psychology has to offer the law. The breadth of the law is boundless, as is the extent to which it affects our behaviour. In fact, to the extent that every law is enacted to control human behaviour, each law must make some assumptions concerning human behaviour. As a result, the field of law and psychology is equally broad in scope.

Many potential areas of research and practice, however, have yet to be explored. Indeed, most of the research which has been conducted has been in the area of criminal law – and much of it with jurors (hence the two chapters on juries in this book). Law and psychology is a young field and those who work in the area have really only addressed the tip of the iceberg of potential topics, although researchers are beginning to explore new and unique areas (e.g., white collar crime, income tax evasion, sexual harassment, family law issues).

As you may have (correctly) surmised from reading the chapters in this book, there is as yet no generally agreed upon name for this relatively new and diverse field. As we outlined in the opening chapter, it has been referred to variously as law and psychology, psychology of law, forensic psychology, and legal psychology (Brigham, 1999; Fulero, 1999; Ogloff, 2000). Of these various categorizations, Ogloff (2000) and Small (1993) recommend that the term "legal psychology" might perhaps be most appropriate:

> First, it is sufficiently broad to cover all areas of work at the interface of psychology and law. Second, it signifies the independence – and unique-ness – of the "new" field that interfaces law and psychology. Third, it has not been limited by any recent common usage. Fourth, the term legal psy-chology parallels terms employed to describe other fields of psychology (biological psychology, clinical psychology, cognitive psychology, devel-opmental psychology, etc). Fifth, and conceivably the best reason of all, people working in the area would have a common identity – they would be referred to as "legal psychologists." (Ogloff, 2000, 6).

Although legal psychology is a term we favour, it is a novel title, and therefore we deliberately decided to use the conventional words "law and psychology" in the title of this textbook and throughout.

THE FUTURE OF PSYCHOLOGY AND LAW

The present-day psychology and law movement began late in the 1960s (Grisso, 1991; Ogloff & Finkelman, 1999; Ogloff, Tomkins, & Ber-soff, 1996). A significant milestone occurred along the way in 1976 when, for the first time, "psychology and the law" was reviewed in the *Annual Review of Psychology* (Tapp, 1976). In 1990, Ogloff published an article in *Canadian Psychology* in which he briefly reviewed the field of law and psychology in Canada and argued that there was a need for research and training in the field. It was not until 1994, however, that law and psychology found its way into the *Annual Survey of American Law* (Satin, 1994). In addition to the scholarly/academic movement, clinical psychologists have also become more prominent in providing psychological evaluations and expert testimony in the legal system, typically in the area of criminal law (Melton, Petrila, Poythress, & Slobogin, 1997; Otto, Heilbrun, & Grisso, 1990).

Throughout this text you have been exposed to numerous areas where psychology has been applied to the law (e.g., interviewing chil-dren for legal purposes, investigating the way line-ups are and ought to be conducted, the impact of pretrial publicity on juries, judicial discretion in sentencing, the psychology of offenders, the insanity defence, assessment of risk for violence, and applications of psychology to the law. Despite these applications, the law and psychology movement has not caused any real waves in the law; indeed, it is questionable whether even ripples have appeared. Although written more than 90 years ago – and despite some of the inroads that have been made into the law – the sentiment expressed by Munsterberg in the quotation that opened this chapter resonates to this day.

Almost without a doubt, the greatest obstacle for legal psychology is that lawyers, judges, and policy makers typically have not embraced psychological findings, especially those findings that are critical of legal assumptions. As it stands now, courts sometimes dismiss some of the studies conducted by psychologists as unreliable or invalid. Often, when they do rely upon psychological studies the courts tend to use them more to support a predetermined position than to alter the way the law handles a particular matter. Along these lines, it has been noted that the law uses psychology like a drunk uses a lamp post – more for support than illumination.[1]

Evidence for these rather harsh views of the legal community's receptivity to the field can be found in countless court decisions, statutes, and legal policy decisions. For example, following an extensive review of the judiciary's use – or lack thereof – of child development research in the United States, Hafemeister and Melton (1987) concluded that "the use of social science is still controversial and rather uncommon, especially in state courts. Courts appear unsure of whether and how to use social science to examine the policy questions that they have been asked to decide in recent decades. As a result ... reliance on social science is still largely a "liberal" practice of judges who have an expansive view of the judiciary's role in shaping legal doctrine and protecting disenfranchised groups" (55). This is most unfortunate since, as the many studies and examples of practice presented in this book indicate, psychology has much to offer the law.

There are a variety of reasons why the law does not always make use of relevant psychological research in cases and legislation. As outlined in the opening chapter, some of these stem from the differing, and to some extent conflicting, orientations adopted by the two fields. As well, Ogloff (2000) notes the following two obstacles.

First, lawyers, judges, and other legal policymakers may not be aware of the research that exists. Second, assuming they are aware of the relevant findings, they may choose not to rely upon them. When choosing not to rely on the findings, they may either question their validity, or decide that they will proceed with deliberate indifference to the findings. Thus, for psychology to have a maximum impact on the law, we must ensure that psychological findings relevant to the law find their way into the hands of lawyers, and that the findings we produce are valid and of high quality. Of course, those in the law still may ignore the findings, but the persistent development of valid findings that challenge the validity of laws or legal assumptions will be difficult to ignore over the long term.

In order for the field to continue to establish itself in psychology, not to mention in the law, it must continue to gain recognition and prominence as a topic worthy of mention and discussion.

One of the primary criticisms of the legal community encountered by those in the field is that the work conducted lacks sophistication about the law, thereby limiting its generalizability and acceptability among lawyers and judges. Further compounding the law's sometimes negative view of psychology, psychologists occasionally engage in a "battle of experts" in court, when they disagree strongly about matters for which they are asked to testify. While it is understandable, and quite acceptable, for psychologists to disagree about areas of research or practice that have not yet been well-defined, disagreement with respect to well-established areas is problematic. For example, psychologists testifying about the reliability of eyewitness testimony might easily come to different opinions about how well a particular witness could have identified a perpetrator. However, they could hardly disagree about the general findings of research concerning the reliability of eyewitness testimony. Again, by continuing our work in law and psychology we will increase our knowledge base, thereby decreasing the likelihood that experts will disagree about actual research findings.

While we have clearly made advances in the field's relatively short history, we still have a distance to go. Our discussion is in no way intended to disparage the field or those who practise in it; rather, our intention is instead to highlight areas that can be addressed to further strengthen the application of psychology to the law. Slowly but surely the work of psychologists is being recognized by judges and legislators. As the work in our field becomes stronger and better developed, we can expect more success in convincing those in the law of the important role that psychology can play.

Before closing this chapter, we provide a brief overview of the types of training in law and psychology available for those interested in pursuing legal psychology.

TRAINING IN PSYCHOLOGY AND LAW

There is absolutely no doubt that the future of legal psychology, whatever it holds, belongs to the students in training and those yet to come. Indeed, many current graduate students and some people presently working in the field began just as you have, by taking an undergraduate course in law and psychology. Along with the most recent incarnation of law and psychology has come an awareness of the importance of training and education in the area (see, e.g., Freeman & Roesch, 1992; Grisso, Sales, & Bayless, 1982; Hafemeister, Ogloff, & Small, 1990; Ogloff, 1990; Ogloff et al., 1996; Roesch, Grisso, & Poythress, 1986; Tomkins & Ogloff, 1990; Wexler, 1990). Therefore, it is important to continue to focus on training in law and psychology in a systematic manner. Melton (1987) has urged legal psychologists to "focus on 'thinking like a lawyer' and becoming a comfortable guest, if not an insider, in the legal community" (p. 293). What better way for social scientists and clinical psychologists to become comfortable in the legal community than to be trained in law and psychology – especially if the training provides structured information about the law and the legal system.

As with other aspects of our developing field, until relatively recently, little attention has been given to training needs and opportunities. Indeed, we receive countless e-mail messages, telephone calls, and letters from students throughout North America trying to find out anything they can about training opportunities and careers in legal psychology. The lack of attention to training in legal psychology has been partially rectified by the National Invitational Conference on Education and Training in Law and Psychology, which took place at Villanova Law School in 1995. The Villanova conference as it has come to be known, was attended by approximately 60 invited people from across the field of legal psychology. The overarching purpose of the conference was to develop an agenda for legal psychology training into the twenty-first century. A description of the conference can be found in an article written by Bersoff and colleagues (1997). As well, a number of articles have now been written about training in the field (see Hafemeister, Ogloff, & Small, 1990; Ogloff et al., 1996; Tomkins & Ogloff, 1990).

First and foremost, people who work in the field of law and psychology must be psychologists.[2] This typically requires that they hold a Ph.D. in psychology and obtain special skills, training, and experience in the field. In addition to psychologists, some lawyers and law professors undertake scholarly writing and research in the area of law and psychology. These people may have undergraduate or graduate degrees in psychology; most often, they have worked with psychologists with interests in the law.

Debate over whether legal psychologists need to be formally trained in law (see Grisso, Sales, & Bayless, 1982; Hafemeister, Ogloff, & Small, 1990; Ogloff et al., 1996; Tomkins & Ogloff, 1990) has culminated in consideration of the joint degree programs in which students can obtain both a law degree and a Ph.D. Arguments against dual degree training have emphasized the costs of such training and the fact that most people who work in legal psychology focus on one or two specific areas of law. Those who support dual degree programs, by contrast, argue that while all legal psychologists do not require formal training in law, there are considerable advantages to such training (Hafemeister et al., 1990). Many psychologists with little appreciation of law have "jumped into" legal psychology research only to produce work of questionable validity (see Hafemeister et al., 1990). We want to emphasize here that while it would not be necessary – or even a good idea – for everyone in the field to obtain a law degree, it is nevertheless critical that legal psychologists obtain a clear understanding if not true expertise in the law that relates to their work.

As mentioned previously, there are a number of models and methods by which psychologists are trained to work in law and psychology. First, and still the most common, is what we will call the mentor model. In this model, graduate students learn their skills by working and conducting research with individual faculty members who do research and/or practice in the field of law and psychology. The advantage of this model is that students are offered individual training, typically by a faculty member with experience and prominence in an area of law and psychology. The disadvantages are that students typically receive little formal training in the broad area of the field and they are unlikely to have a "critical mass" of colleagues with whom they can converse and collaborate. An added difficulty for those students wishing to go to graduate school is that it is not easy for them to readily identify mentors with whom they might like to work, and who are willing to take on and supervise students. Students usually rely on

searches of university web pages to locate psychologists studying topics in which the students are interested. In addition, students may
identify possible graduate supervisors by speaking to professors at
their home universities.

The second model is what we call the "limited focus training
model." In this model, students study and conduct research in a
department in which there is more than one person working in the
field of law and psychology. Alternatively, they may study in a department with one person in the field but have access to psychologists in
institutions (e.g., jails or prisons, forensic hospitals) who help enrich
their training experiences. Limited focus training models, while still
being rather narrowly focused, provide students with a wider range of
training experiences than the mentor model allows. Again, though, it is
generally difficult for prospective students to identify psychology
departments that offer some informal training by relying on one or two
people in the field.

The next model includes the actual programs in law and psychology
or forensic psychology. As the appendix to this chapter shows, there
are a number of these programs available, and that number is gradu-
ally growing. Although the programs vary considerably in their detail
and focus, they all provide students with an overview of the field of
law and psychology as well as advanced courses, research experiences,
and practical or applied training in some area of the field. The clear
advantage of these programs is that students have the benefit of being
part of a critical mass of students and faculty with common interests.
Oftentimes the learning and training experiences are enriched by the
expanded opportunities a program can afford them.

The final training model,[3] which has been adopted in a few universities in North America, is a joint or dual degree program in law and
psychology. In these programs, which also are listed in the appendix,
students have the opportunity of pursuing a law degree (a Juris Doctor
or J.D. in the United States and a Bachelor of Laws degree or LL.B. in
Canada) and a Ph.D. in psychology simultaneously. Although these
programs are very demanding, they do allow for students to become
experts in the law. The relative benefit of such training has been discussed in the literature and will not be detailed here (see Hafemeister,
Ogloff, & Small, 1990; Ogloff et al., 1996). Dual degree training is quite
taxing, however, and the cost of the training may not be beneficial in
the end since, in reality, few people will take full advantage of both
degrees. It is our view that while the dual degree option is attractive

and beneficial for some people in our field, a scholar in law and psychology does not need to have a law degree in order to make important and useful contributions to the field.

As a discipline, law and psychology has grown dramatically in Canada. Just 15 years ago there were no formal graduate training programs and few, if any, formal undergraduate courses like the one you have just taken. Today, almost 20 psychology departments offer courses at the undergraduate level in law and psychology, which is one of the primary reasons we were compelled to prepare this book. A number of psychology departments in Canada, albeit only a handful, offer systematic training at the graduate level. As the majority of psychologists who work in the field of law and psychology the only person, or perhaps one of two people, in their departments to do so, much of the graduate training in Canada currently involves primarily the mentor or limited training focus models. To these two models, however, we can now add the first dual LL.B./Ph.D. (in either clinical forensic or experimental psychology and law) graduate program (offered jointly by Simon Fraser University and University of British Columbia) to Canada.

CONCLUSIONS

This is the first textbook of law and psychology to focus on Canadian perspectives. Although the field is not as well developed as it is in the United States, Canadian scholars have developed a large, growing body of psychological research and scholarship relevant to the law. We are grateful to the many authors who have contributed to this book and to you, the readers. It is our hope that this book captures the breadth, enthusiasm, and overall excellence of the work in the field. If we are successful, at the very least, you will have learned a great deal about law and psychology, particularly as it exists in Canada. Perhaps you might even consider pursuing further training.

APPENDIX
TRAINING OPPORTUNITIES IN LAW AND PSYCHOLOGY[4]

The field of psychology and law involves the application of psychological principles to legal concerns, and the interaction of psychology and law for individuals involved in the legal process. Psychologists trained in psychology and law provide psycho-legal research in a variety of areas, develop mental health legal and public policies, and work as both lawyers and psychologists within legal and clinical arenas.

The American Psychology-Law Society, Division 41 of the APA, is actively involved in the training and career development of psychologists within the field of psychology and law. Information on academic training programs is an important component for the continued growth of the field. This section provides a listing and brief description of academic programs that provide psychology and law training. This includes joint Ph.D./J.D. programs, Ph.D. programs with an emphasis on psychology and law, and M.A. programs with psychology and law course work.

As the field of psychology and law has grown in recent decades, a variety of training programs have been developed to meet the needs of students interested in interdisciplinary study and work. In general, there are four models of training in psychology and law. Each model will be described in brief detail below and where relevant, a listing of programs that fit each model follow the description. Detailed information about admission requirements, curricula, internships and practice opportunities, and job opportunities for graduates can be obtained by contacting the individual programs.

Dual Degree Programs

These programs produce scholars and/or practitioners with degrees in both psychology and law. Typically, joint degree students go through two programs as well as a series of courses at the intersection of the two disciplines. The intent is to train students to think psychologically about the law and to think legally about psychologists' knowledge base and research methodologies. Some lawyer-psychologists work as practicing attorneys and some work primarily as psychologists who teach, conduct research, and/or work in applied legal settings. Still others manage to combine the two fields by working to create, implement or analyze policy, or by doing legally sophisticated psychological research and/or practice.

The programs described below have formalized their curricula to allow student interested in two fields to receive integrated training. To be accepted into these programs, student must meet admissions requirements for both the psychology department and the law school, as well as additional requirements for the joint program. On occasion, students have completed dual degrees in institutions without formal joint degree programs.

University of Arizona

The Psychology, Public Policy and Law Program at the University of Arizona is designed to train scholars interested in research and policy careers who will produce theoretically and methodologically sophisticated research in the psychology, policy, and law interface. The Department of Psychology in cooperation with the College of Law offers training in this area leading to the Ph.D. degree, or the J.D.-Ph.D. as concurrent degrees. Students also may apply for a dual major in the Psychology, Policy and Law Program and any other program within the Department of Psychology. The program provides the opportunity for intensive study in three areas: mental health and health policy, mental health-criminal justice interactions, and the analysis of policies and laws for policy planning. Once admitted, training is tailored to match each student's unique academic and research needs. Contact: Dr. Bruce Sales J.D./Ph.D., Director, Psychology, Policy and Law Program, University of Arizona, Tucson AZ 85721, (520) 621–7431.

Allegheny University/Villanova University

Ph.D./JD program through Psychology Department, Allegheny University and Villanova Law School. The program is designed to develop scientist-practitioners within psychology and law to provide research, mental health policy formulation, and clinical application. The joint program's approach is to foster an appreciation of and a facility with both traditions simultaneously. Contact: Dr. Donald N. Bersoff J.D./Ph.D., Director Law-Psychology Program, Allegheny University, Broad and Vine, Mailstop 625, Philadelphia PA, 19102–1192, (215) 762–8084.

University of Nebraska–Lincoln

The Law/Psychology Program at the University of Nebraska offers students a variety of options in psychology and law, including: 1) J.D./Ph.D. degrees; 2) J.D./M.A. degrees; 3) Ph.D./ML.S. degrees; 4) Ph.D. in Forensic Psychology; and 5) Post-Doctoral training. The J.D./M.A. degree is intended for students whose primary interest lies in the area of law, but who wish to obtain some graduate training in psychology. Conversely, the Ph.D./ML.S. (Master of Legal Studies) degree is available to students who have primary interests in psychology and wish to obtain non-professional training in law. Contact: Dr. Steven Penrod, J.D./Ph.D., Psychology and Law Program, University of Nebraska-Lincoln, 318 Burnett Hall, Lincoln NE, 68588–0308, (402) 472–3121.

Pacific Graduate School of Psychology
A joint Ph.D.-J.D. program is offered in conjunction with the Golden Gate University School of Law. The program seeks to develop psychologists who can perform social science research to assist the legal system; to educate clinicians who can contribute to the advancement of forensic psychology; and to produce attorney-psychologists who can develop mental health policy in the legislature and the courts. Contact: Dr. Bruce Bongar Ph.D. ABPP, Director, Program in Psychology and the Law, Pacific Graduate School of Psychology, 940 East Meadow Drive, Palo Alto CA 94303, (650) 843–3419.

Simon Fraser University/University of British Columbia
The SFU/UBC Program in Law and Forensic Psychology provides training leading to either a Ph.D. in psychology or to an LL.B./Ph.D. (Note that in Canada the law degree, an LL.B., is equivalent to the J.D.). The Program is offered jointly by the Simon Fraser University and the University of British Columbia. Regardless of whether they choose to pursue a Ph.D. or a joint LL.B./Ph.D., students may choose to specialize in either clinical-forensic psychology or in experimental psychology and law. Students in the clinical-forensic stream obtain Ph.D.s from either the SFU or UBC program in clinical psychology. Both clinical programs are accredited by the American and Canadian Psychological Associations. Students specializing in experimental psychology and law obtain training in experimental areas of psychology that apply to law, and in policy development and evaluation. Contact: Dr. James R. P. Ogloff, J.D., Ph.D., Director, SFU/UBC Program in Law and Forensic Psychology, Simon Fraser University, Burnaby, British Columbia, Canada, V5A 1S6. (604) 291–3093.

Stanford University
Stanford University offers 4 possible combinations of Psychology/Law training. Students may earn a Ph.D. in psychology with a focus on legal psychology by taking psychology-law seminars and course work. The Ph.D./J.D. degree and program provides training in both psychology and law, and psycho-legal combinations. A J.D. in law with a M.A. in psychology, and a Ph.D. in psychology with a Master of Legal Stud-

ies (M.L.S.) degree can also be obtained. Contact: Dr. David L. Rosenhan Ph.D., Department of Psychology, Stanford University, Stanford CA 94305–2130, (650) 723–3502.

Widener University
This six year program leads to the awarding of the Psy.D. degree by Widener Institute for Graduate Clinical Psychology, and the J.D. degree by Widener School of Law. The program trains lawyer-clinical psychologists to integrate their knowledge of both fields, bring fresh insights to a variety of important psycho-legal problems, and play diverse roles in society, including administration, consultation, forensic practice, policy making, and teaching. Contact: Dr. Amiram Elwork Ph.D./J.D., Director of Law-Psychology Program, One University Place, Widener University, Chester PA 19013–5792. (610) 499–1209.

Ph.D./Psy.D. Programs

The attainment of dual degrees is not necessary to ensure high level psychological research or practice. Many psychologists who work in this field have received advanced degrees in specialized psychology programs that focus on psychology and law. These programs are designed to produce professionals who will function as psychologists and who will work in legal settings or who will conduct research on questions of legal interest. In recent years several stand-alone psychology and law programs have been developed. Typically, these programs have the status equivalent to graduate programs in other sub-specialities of psychology (e.g., clinical, developmental, social) and may have topical content emphases within psychology and law (e.g., clinical psychology and law, community psychology and law, social psychology and law). The bulk of the curriculum involves specially designed courses and seminars in the psychology department and students may also take courses for credit in the law school. The admissions requirements for these programs are comparable to those for other Ph.D. or M.A. programs in the same department. Typically, applicants will be screened by faculty with psychology-law interests. Specific information about individual programs can be obtained by contacting these programs directly.

University of Alabama
Ph.D. in clinical psychology with a concentration in psychology-law

course work. The Psychology-Law concentration provides a focused experience for the individual interested in the study of clinical psychology in forensic (court), correctional, and public safety settings. This program offers training in psychology-law research and in forensic-clinical psychology. Contact: Jill Martin or Dr. Stanley Brodsky Ph.D., Department of Psychology, University of Alabama, Box 870348, Tuscaloosa Alabama, 35487–0348, (205) 348–1919.

Simon Fraser University and the University of British Columbia:
See the information provided above for J.D. Ph.D/Psy.D. programs

California School of Professional Psychology-Fresno
The Psy.D. program in forensic psychology covers general psychology and law concepts, the treatment, assessment, and evaluation of individuals in forensic settings, new and ongoing research in the field of forensic psychology, and training that will help the forensic psychologist work effectively within legal, court, correctional, and public policy systems. The program offers three tracks: criminal justice and administration, applied forensics, and public policy. Contact Dr. Bruce A. Arrigo Ph.D., CSPP-Fresno, 5130 E. Clinton Way, Fresno, CA 93727, (209) 456–2777.

Florida International University
The Department of Psychology at FIU offers a doctoral track in Legal Psychology. The seven faculty associated with this track emphasize the applications of social, cognitive, and industrial/organizational psychology to legal issues. This doctoral program is designed to prepare students for psychological consultation in the legal arena, legal psychology research careers, and university-level teaching Contact: Luz Guadalupe or Dr. Margaret Bull Kovera, Ph.D. Department of Psychology, University Park Campus, Florida International University, 3000 NE 151st Street, North Miami FL, 33181, (305) 348–2881.

University of Illinois at Chicago
Students interested in psychology and law can obtain a Ph.D. in social, cognitive, clinical, or community and prevention psychology. The program provides students with theoretical and methodological training in psychology, and in the application of psychology to the legal field. Training at UIC is designed to prepare students for research positions in academic and non-academic settings. The University of Illinois at

Chicago provides a stimulating, multicultural setting with a variety of research and clinical sites. Contact: Dr. Shari S. Diamond, Ph.D., Department of Psychology (M/C 285), University of Illinois at Chicago, 1007 W. Harrison ST, Chicago IL 60607–7137, (312) 996–3036.

University of Kansas
The Department of Psychology offers a Ph.D. in Social Psychology with speciality training in psychology and law. Course work is a combination of psychology/law and law school courses. There is an emphasis on research and consultation in the legal system. Contact: Dr. Lawrence S. Wrightsman Ph.D., Department of Psychology, 426 Fraser Hall, Lawrence KS 66045, (913) 864–4131.

Long Island University
The Department of Psychology offers a sub-speciality in forensic-clinical psychology. The program emphasizes coursework in forensic assessment, violence/aggression, and domestic violence. Ongoing research is also conducted in these areas. The program offers practicum and internship training at several forensic sites in the New York city area. Contact: Dr. Barry Rosenfield Ph.D., Department of Psychology, Long Island University, Brooklyn NY 11201.

University of Nevada-Reno
Interdisciplinary Ph.D. Program in Social Psychology with speciality training in legal psychology. Emphasis on theoretical and applied research, and psycholegal consultation. Contact: Dr. Ronald C. Dillehay Ph.D., Center for Justice Studies/313, University of Nevada Reno, Reno NV 89557, (702) 492–6636

Queen's University
The Department of Psychology at Queen's University offers a Ph.D. in Forensic Psychology with an emphasis in correctional psychology. Students are trained to conduct research and perform clinical services in correctional settings. Contact: Dr. Vernon Quinsey Ph.D., Department of Psychology, Queen's University, Kingston, Ontario, Canada K7L 3N6, (613) 545–6004.

Sam Houston State University
The Ph.D. program in forensic clinical psychology trains scientists-practitioners in the application of clinical psychology to the criminal justice system. In addition to acquiring basic clinical skills, students

receive training in such areas as forensic assessment and offender therapy. The program is a cooperative venture between the Department of Psychology and the College of Criminal Justice and its six faculty members are drawn from these two departments. Huntsville, the headquarters of the Texas Department of Corrections-one of the largest penal systems in the world – provides a prime location for forensic research and practice. Contact: David K. Marcus Ph.D., Coordinator Forensic Clinical Psychology Program, Department of Psychology, Sam Houston State University, Huntsville, TX 77341, (409) 294–3601.

St. Louis University
St. Louis University offers training in Psychology and Law within the Department of Psychology. This is a Ph.D. program in Social Psychology with an emphasis on legal psychology. Course work is available within an interdepartmental structure. The program provides training for research and consultation within the legal system. Contact: Dr. Richard L. Wiener Ph.D., Department of Psychology, 220 Grand Blvd., Saint Louis University, St. Louis MO. (314) 977–2273.

University of Texas at El Paso
Interested students can study towards a Ph.D. in Applied Psychology with the Psychology and Law Group at UTEP. There are 5 faculty in the group, with interests spanning Psychology and Law. These interests include jury decision making, eyewitness identification and memory, questioning effects in eyewitness reports, forensic psychology, and applied decision making in child abuse cases. Excellent opportunities for collaboration exist with faculty from the allied Criminal Justice Program and the Departments of Political Science and Sociology. The multicultural setting of El Paso provides rich opportunities for research on culturally sensitive aspects of law and behaviour. Contact: Dr. Roy Malpass Ph.D., Department of Psychology, University of Texas at El Paso, El Paso TX 79968–0533, (915) 747–5551.

University of Virginia
The University of Virginia offers a Ph.D. program in clinical and community psychology with a possible focus on research oriented psychology and law curriculum. Primary emphasis on developing research within the psychology-law area, through psychology course work and some law school courses. Psychology faculty have a particularly strong interest in the area of law and children. Contact: Dr. N. Dickon Rep-

pucci Ph.D., Department of Psychology, 102 Gilmer Hall, Charlottesville Virginia, 22901–2477, (804) 979–0671

M.A. Programs

Castleton State College
The Forensic Psychology Program is a research-based Masters of Arts
program designed to prepare students for careers in the various organizations and agencies of the criminal and civil justice systems. There
are three major focus areas: (1) Police Psychology; (2) Psychology and
Law; and (3) Correctional Psychology. Students graduating from the
program will have: (1) comprehensive knowledge of psychology as it
applies to criminal and civil justice systems; (2) research skills to evaluate various issues and programs within these systems; and (3) the communication skills necessary to express their findings effectively to
diverse groups within the systems. Contact: Dr. Curt R. Bartol Ph.D.,
Director of Forensic Psychology, The Office of Graduate Studies, Castleton State College, Castleton VT 05735, (802) 468–1414,

University of Denver
Dual Degree Program through the College of Law and the Department
of Psychology, during which student can earn a J.D. and a M.A. degree.
This is a general program with a primary emphasis on the law degree.
Students can, however, go on to a Ph.D. degree in several different
Department of Psychology programs. Contact: Dr. Norman Watt Ph.D.,
Department of Psychology, 2155 S. Race St., Denver, CO, 80208. (303)
871–3680.

John Jay College of Criminal Justice, City University of New York
MA degree in Forensic Psychology. The program emphasis is the application of psychological insights, concepts, and skills to the understanding and functioning of the criminal justice system. The Department
offers course work in a variety of areas includes corrections, psychol-
ogy/law, public policy, and police work. Contact: Dr. James Wulach
Ph.D., Graduate Coordinator, Forensic Psychology Department, 445
West 59th St., New York NY, 10019, (212) 237–8782.

Informal Specialization Opportunities

Many psychology departments have no formal psychology-law training programs but make informal law-related specialization opportunities available to students enrolled in other psychology graduate programs (e.g., clinical, social, developmental, cognitive, organizational). In fact, some training in psychology and law can probably be obtained at any university with psychology faculty who have research or other scholarly interests in this field. Although the opportunities for integrated coursework and extramural law-related experiences in graduate school will be fewer than in more formalized programs, students trained in this way typically work as researchers or clinicians who use psychology in legal settings or who conduct legally relevant research.

To determine which schools offer informal training opportunities in psychology and law browse through several recent issues of journals in the field (e.g., *Law and Human Behavior; Behavioral Sciences and the Law; Psychology, Public Policy and Law*) and note those individuals whose work is of interest. These people can then be contacted directly and asked about graduate training opportunities.

Postgraduate Training Opportunities

Many psychologists who work in the law obtained their training only after they completed their Ph.D. or Psy.D. (or perhaps after they completed their coursework prior to completing a dissertation). This is especially true for clinical-forensic psychologists. Typically, during the course of graduate training in another subdiscipline of psychology, these students have become interested in some aspect of the law. They then conduct research or seek an internship in a setting that allows them to pursue that interest. Several post-doctoral training opportunities are now available in psychology and law and most do not require previous experience or training in the law. These experiences give the student an opportunity to develop high-level clinical and/or research skills that will assist them in understanding the legal contexts in which they will work. A listing of postgraduate training opportunities in clinical-forensic psychology can be obtained by sending a $10 check, payable to "AAFP," to Randy Otto, Ph.D., Department of Mental Health Law and Policy, University of South Florida, 13301 Bruce B. Downs Blvd., Tampa, FL 33612–3899. Post-graduate training opportunities in other sub-disciplines of psychology and law are arranged informally.

Notes

2: Psychological Applications to Criminal Procedure

1 For example, if someone takes something of yours, many aspects of the law could conceivably be involved. The person may have intended to appropriate your property; at some point in the past, the courts would have created a criminal offence to deal with such conduct. The person may have believed he or she had a right to take the property, according to some agreement you had made; at some point, the courts would have developed a rule in the law of contracts to deal with the situation. The person may have taken your property accidentally; the situation in this case would be governed by some rule of negligence law created by the courts in a previous, similar case. Each of these rules would have been "invented" by the courts in a case that required such a rule to resolve it. The law is the accumulation of many thousands of such rules, developed one at a time, as needed.
2 For instance, "possession" is defined in the Criminal Code, and the possession of many things, such as narcotics, is illegal. In deciding whether someone is illegally in possession of something, however, the courts look to many prior decisions that interpret, expand, or limit the statutory definition.
3 For example, in *R. v. Askov,* (1990) the court essentially imposed time limits for the prosecution of offences of varying severity. Prior to the Charter, the courts would have been unable to do this, but would instead have ruled that such a function was exclusively for Parliament to exercise.

3: Police Investigations

1 At the present time, several civil lawsuits are pending against legal officials and the Saskatchewan government.

5: The Jury: Selecting Twelve Impartial Peers

1 The account of the Homolka and Bernardo trials is developed from various media accounts (see weekly issues of *Macleans* magazine from May 15, 1995 through October 16, 1995; see also the *Globe and Mail* or *Toronto Star* newspapers covering the same time period; see Williams, 1996).
2 Courts Input Statistics System (CISS), statistics provided by the Ministry of the Attorney General.

7: Sentencing, Parole, and Psychology

1 These grids have two dimensions: crime seriousness and criminal history. A sentencing court would establish the level of seriousness of the crime, as well as the number of previous convictions. This calculation would give rise to a fairly narrow range of sentence lengths (in the event that imprisonment was appropriate). Judges would have to choose a sentence length within the range or provide reason for sentencing the offender to a longer or a shorter sentence than that provided by the guidelines system.
2 This is the problem with mandatory minimum penalties; all offenders are treated alike, even though they are not equally culpable.
3 For example, the prison population per 100,000 population was 85 in Austria, 80 in Belgium, 90 in France, 90 in Germany, 90 in Switzerland, 85 in the Netherlands, 85 in Greece, and 60 in Sweden (see Walmsley, 1999).
4 The offenders sentenced to life imprisonment have different parole eligibility dates. Offenders sentenced to life for second degree murder must spend at least 10 years in prison before they can make an application for parole. In some cases of second degree murder the period of parole ineligibility is even longer, depending on the judge's decision. Offenders sentenced to life for other offences (such as manslaughter) are eligible for parole after having served 7 years in prison. The term "life imprisonment," then, is rather imprecise. This is an example of the complexities of the sentencing and parole system in Canada.
5 In January 2000, the Supreme Court of Canada handed down a guideline judgment with respect to the conditional sentence of imprisonment (*R. v. Proulx*). It is still too early to tell whether this judgment will help to promote greater uniformity with regard to the use of this new sanction.

8: The Assessment and Treatment of Offenders and Inmates: General Considerations

1 Unlike adults, adolescents are not automatically eligible via legislation for

parole or statutory releases. Instead, young offenders sentenced to custodial sentences are eligible for ongoing disposition reviews and for changes to their dispositions (see Chapter 9; Bala, 1997; DuWors, 1997, p. 7).

2 The Canadian incarceration rate of 115 per 100,000 people is a distant second to the United States rate of 600 per 100,000 people (Mauer, 1997, cited in Besserer, 1998). There is little evidence to suggest that the high incarceration rate in Canada reflects a high rate of crimes actually experienced by Canadians relative to those experienced by other Western industrialized countries. Results from population surveys indicate that Canadians rank sixth of eleven countries in their rate of reported victimization experiences (Besserer, 1998).

10: Fitness to Stand Trial and Criminal Responsibility in Canada

1 This poem appeared in the *Standard* on March 7, 1843 and was cited by Moran (1981), pp. 19–20.

2 There is evidence to show that Queen Victoria's concern may have arisen from self-interest since she was the target of would-be assassins on three occasions in the 2 years before the *M'Naghten* case. In fact, one of her would-be assassins was acquitted by reason of insanity (Low et al., 1986).

3 Portions of this section of the chapter are excerpted from Ogloff, Schweighofer, Turnbull, and Whittemore (1992) and the reader is referred to that chapter for more comprehensive information concerning the empirical research on the insanity defence.

15: Psychology and Law: Looking towards the Future

1 Attributed to Loh (1981a).

2 Although it is beyond the scope of this chapter, there are many places in the criminal justice system where students with backgrounds in criminology, psychology, and other social sciences might obtain employment (see Ogloff, Tomkins, & Bersoff, 1996).

3 In addition to the graduate training options in law and psychology discussed above, two other methods of training warrant brief mention here: forensic internships and postdoctoral fellowships. Some clinical psychologists obtain training in forensic psychology in formal forensic internships. Both clinical psychologists and experimental psychologists with interests in

law and psychology may pursue formal training in fellowship programs after they have completed their Ph.D.s in psychology.

4 The material in this Appendix is reprinted from the document *Careers and Training in Psychology and Law* written by the Careers and Training Committee of the American Psychology-Law Society/Division 41 American Psychology Association and is reprinted here by permission.

References

Abbey, A., & Harnish, R.J. (1995). Perception of sexual intent: The role of gender, alcohol consumption, and rape supportive attitudes. *Sex Roles, 32*, 297–313.

Abel, G.G., & Osborn, C. (1992). The paraphilias: The extent and nature of sexually deviant and criminal behavior. *Psychiatric Clinics of North America, 15*, 675–687.

Abidin, R.R. (1995). *Parenting stress index professional manual* (3rd ed.) Odessa, FL: Psychological Assessment Resources.

Achenbach, T.M., McConaughy, S.H., & Howell, C.T. (1987). Child/adolescent behavioral and emotional problems: Implications of cross-informant correlations for situational specificity. *Psychological Bulletin, 101*, 213–232.

Acierno, R., Kilpatrick, D.G., & Resnick, H.S. (1999). Posttraumatic stress disorder in adults relative to criminal victimization: Prevalence, risk factors, and comorbidity. In P.A. Saigh & J.D. Bremmer (Eds.), *Posttraumatic stress disorder: A comprehensive text* (pp. 44–68). Boston, MA: Allyn & Bacon, Inc.

Ackerman, M.J. (1995). *Clinician's guide to child custody evaluations.* New York: Wiley.

Ackerman, M.J., & Ackerman, M.C. (1997). Custody evaluation practices: A survey of experienced professionals (revisited). *Professional Psychology: Research and Practice, 28*, 137–145.

Adelberg, E., & Currie, C. (1987). *Too few to count: Women in conflict with the law.* Vancouver: Press Gang.

Aggarwal, A.P. (1987). *Sexual harassment in the workplace.* Toronto: Butterworths.

Agnew, R. (1990). The origins of delinquent events: An examination of offender accounts. *Journal of Research in Crime and Delinquency, 27*, 267–294.

Akehurst, L., Koehnken, G., Vrij, A., & Bull, R. (1996). Lay persons' and police officers' beliefs regarding deceptive behaviour. *Applied Cognitive Psychology, 10*, 461–471.

Alcock, J.E., Carment, D.W., & Sadava, S.W. (1998). *A textbook of social psychology* (3rd ed.). Scarborough, ON: Prentice-Hall Canada.

Allodi, F., Kedward, H., & Robertson, M. (1977). Insane but guilty: Psychiatric patients in jail. *Canada's Mental Health, 25*, 3–7.

Allport, G.W., & Postman, L.J. (1947). *The psychology of rumor.* New York: Holt, Rinehart & Winston.

Altemeier, W., O'Connor, S., Vietze, P., Sandler, H., & Sherrod, K. (1984). Prediction of child abuse: A prospective study of feasibility. *Child Abuse and Neglect, 8*, 393–400.

Amato, P.R., & Keith, B. (1991). Parental divorce and the well-being of children: A meta-analysis. *Psychological Bulletin, 110*, 26–46.

American Association for Protecting Children. (1986). *Highlights of official child neglect and abuse reporting.* Denver, CO: American Humane Society.

American Law Institute. (1962). Model Penal Code. Washington, DC: Author.

American Psychiatric Association. (1994). *Diagnostic and statistical manual of mental disorders* (4th ed.). Washington, DC: Author.

American Psychological Association. (1992). Ethical principles of psychologists and code of conduct. *American Psychologist, 47*, 1597–1611.

American Psychological Association. (1998). Accredited doctoral programs in professional psychology: 1998. *American Psychologist, 53*, 1324–1335.

Ammerman, R.T. (1990). Etiological models of child maltreatment: A behavioral perspective. *Behaviour Modification, 14*, 230–254.

Anderer, S.J. (1990). A model for determining competency in guardianship proceedings. *Mental and Physical Disability Law Reporter, 14*, 107–114.

Anderson, N.H. (1981). *Foundations of information integration theory.* New York: Academic Press.

Andrews, D.A. (1980). Some experimental investigations of the principles of differential association through deliberate manipulation of the structure of service systems. *American Sociological Review, 45*, 448–462.

Andrews, D.A. (1983). The assessment of outcome in correctional samples. In M.L. Lambert, E.R. Christensen, & S.S. DeJulio (Eds.), *The measurement of psychotherapy outcome in research and evaluation.* New York: Wiley.

Andrews, D.A., & Bonta, J. (1995). *LSI-R: The Level of Service Inventory – Revised.* Toronto, ON: Multi-Health Systems.

Andrews, D.A., & Bonta, J. (1998). *The psychology of criminal conduct* (2nd ed.). Cincinnati, OH: Anderson Publishing.

Andrews, D.A., Bonta, J., & Hoge, R.D. (1990). Classification for effective rehabilitation: Rediscovering psychology. *Criminal Justice and Behavior, 17,* 19–52.

Andrews, D.A., & Kiessling, J.J. (1980). Program structure and effective correctional practices: A summary of the CaVIC research. In R.R. Ross & P. Gendreau (Eds.), *Effective correctional treatment* (pp. 441–463). Toronto: Butterworths.

Andrews, D.A., Robblee, M., & Saunders, R. (1984). *The sentencing factors inventory.* Toronto: Ontario Ministry of Correctional Services.

Andrews, D.A., Zinger, I., Hoge, R.D., Bonta, J., Gendreau, P., & Cullen, F.T. (1990). Does correctional treatment work? A clinically relevant and psychologically informed meta-analysis. *Criminology, 28,* 369–404.

Annon, J.S. (1988). Detection of deception and search for truth: A proposed model with particular reference to the witness, the victim, and the defendant. *Forensic Reports, 1,* 303–360.

Apodaca v. Oregon, 406 U.S. 404 (1972).

Appavoo, P.M., & Gwynn, M.I. (1996, August). *Effectiveness of the cognitive interview on delayed eyewitness recall.* Paper presented at the meeting of the American Psychological Association. Toronto.

Appelbaum, P.S., & Grisso, T. (1995). The MacArthur treatment competence study. I: Mental illness and competence to consent to treatment. *Law and Human Behavior, 19,* 105–126.

Appelbaum, P.S., Lidz, C.W., & Meisel, A. (1987). *Informed consent: Legal theory and clinical practice.* New York: Oxford University Press.

Arboleda-Florez, J., Crisanti, A., & Holley, H.L. (1995). The effects of changes in the law concerning mentally disordered offenders: The Alberta experience with Bill C-30. *Canadian Journal of Psychiatry, 40,* 225–233.

Arboleda-Florez, J., & Holley, H.L. (1988). Development of a suicide screening instrument for use in a remand centre setting. *Canadian Journal of Psychiatry, 33,* 595–598.

Arbour, L. (1996). *Commission of inquiry into certain events at: The Prison for Women in Kingston.* Ottawa: Canada Communication Group.

Archer, R.P. (1984). Use of the MMPI with adolescents: A review of salient issues. *Clinical Psychology Review, 4,* 241–251.

Asch, S.E. (1951). Effects of group pressure upon the modification and distortion of judgments. In H. Guetzkow (Ed.), *Groups, leadership and men.* Pittsburgh, PA: Carnegie Press.

Asch, S.E. (1956). Studies of independence and submission to group pressure: I. On minority of one against a unanimous majority. *Psychological Monographs, 70* (9, Whole No. 417).

Attorney General of Canada v. Daniels, [1991] 5 W.W.W. 340 (Sask. C.A.).

Austin, G.W., & Jaffe, P.G. (1990). Follow-up study of parents in custody and access disputes. *Canadian Psychology, 31,* 172–179.

Austin, W., & Williams, T. (1977). A survey of judges' responses to simulated legal cases: Research note on sentencing disparity. *Journal of Criminal Law and Criminology, 68,* 306–310.

Axon, L. (1989). *Model and exemplary programs for female inmates: An international review.* Volume I: Report. Ottawa: Ministry of the Solicitor General of Canada.

Azar, S.T. (1991). Models of child abuse: A metatheoretical analysis. *Criminal Justice and Behavior, 18,* 30–46.

Azar, S.T. (1992). Legal issues in the assessment of family violence involving children. In R.T. Ammerman & M. Hersen (Eds.). *Assessment of family violence: A clinical and legal sourcebook.* New York: Wiley.

Azar, S.T., Benjit, C.L., Fuhrmann, G.S., & Cavallero, L. (1995). Child maltreatment and termination of parental rights: Can behavioral research help Solomon? *Behavior Therapy, 26,* 599–623.

Azar, S.T., & Rohrbeck, C.A. (1986). Child abuse and unrealistic expectations: Further validation of the Parent Opinion Questionnaire. *Journal of Consulting and Clinical Psychology, 54,* 867–868.

Azhar v. Anderson (1985), A.C.W.S. (2d) 121 (Ont. Dist. Ct.).

Baer, R.A., Wetter, M.W., Nichols, D.S., Greene, R., & Berry, D.T.R. (1995). Sensitivity of MMPI-2 validity scales to underreporting of symptoms. *Psychological Assessment, 7,* 419–423.

Bagby, R.M., Nicholson, R.A., Buis, T., Radovanovic, M., Fidler, B.J. (1999). Defensive responding on the MMPI-2 in family custody and access evaluations. *Psychology Assessment, 11,* 24–28.

Bailey, W.C. (1966). Correctional outcome: An evaluation of 100 reports. *Journal of Criminal Law,* Criminology and Police Science, 57, 153–160.

Baker, S.P., O'Neill, B., & Karpf, R.S. (1984). *The injury fact book.* Lexington, MA: Lexington Books.

Bala, N. (1996). False memory "syndrome": Backlash or *bona fide* defense? *Queen's Law Journal, 21,* 423–456.

Bala, N. (1997). *Young offenders law.* Concord, ON: Irwin Law

Bala, N., Hornick, J., & Vogl, R. (1991). *Canadian child welfare law: Children, families and the state.* Toronto: Thompson.

Barefoot v. Estelle, 463 U.S. 880 (1983).

Barland, G.H. (1988). The polygraph test in the USA and elsewhere. In A. Gale (Ed.), *The polygraph test: Lies, truth and science* (pp. 73–95). London: Sage.

Baron, R.A., & Byrne, D. (1991). *Social psychology: Understanding human interaction.* (6th ed.) Toronto: Allyn and Bacon.

Bartels, S.J., Drake, R.E., Wallach, M.A., & Freeman, D. (1991). Characteristic hostility in schizophrenic outpatients. *Schizophrenia Bulletin, 17,* 163–171.

Bartol, C.R., & Bartol, A.M. (1994). *Psychology and law: Research and application* (2nd ed.). Pacific Grove, CA: Brooks/Cole.

Bartusch, D.R.J., Lynam, D.R., Moffitt, T.E., & Silva, P.A. (1997). Is age important? Testing a general versus a developmental theory of antisocial behaviour. *Criminology, 35,* 13–48.

Bathurst, K., Gottfried, A.W., & Gottfried, A.E. (1997). Normative data for the MMPI-2 in child custody litigation. *Psychological Assessment, 9,* 205–211.

Bean, G., Nishisato, S., Rector, N.A., & Glancy, G. (1994). The psychometric properties of the competency interview schedule. *Canadian Journal of Psychiatry, 39,* 368–376.

Beautrais, A.L., Fergusson, D.M., & Shannon, D.T. (1981). Accidental poisoning in the first three years of life. *Australian Paediatric Journal, 17,* 104–109.

Beautrais, A.L., Fergusson, D.M., & Shannon, D.T. (1982). Childhood accidents in a New Zealand birth cohort. *Australian Paediatric Journal, 18,* 238–242.

Beck, K.A., & Ogloff, J.R.P. (1995). Child abuse reporting in British Columbia: Psychologists' knowledge of and compliance with the reporting law. *Professional Psychology: Research and Practice, 26,* 245–251.

Beck, K.A., Ogloff, J.R.P., & Corbishley, A. (1994). Knowledge, compliance, and attitudes of teachers toward mandatory child abuse reporting in British Columbia. *Canadian Journal of Education, 19,* 15–29.

Beitchman, J.H., Zucker, K.J., Hood, J.E., daCosta, G.A., & Akman, D. (1991). A review of the short-term effects of child sexual abuse. *Child Abuse & Neglect, 15,* 537–556.

Bell, J., Browning, J., & Hamilton, A. (1992). *Wife assault intervention: Programs for men. Guiding principles for services in British Columbia.* Vancouver: BC Institute on Family Violence.

Bell, S., & Kuriloff, P., & Lottes, I. (1994). Understanding attributions of blame on stranger and date rape situations: An examination of gender, race, identification, and students' social perceptions of rape victims. *Journal of Applied Social Psychology, 24,* 1719–1734.

Benedek, E.P., & Schetky, D.H. (1987). Problems in validating allegations of sexual abuse: II. Clinical Evaluation. *Journal of the American Academy of Child & Adolescent Psychiatry, 29,* 916–927.

Bennett, W.L., & Feldman, M. (1981). *Reconstructing reality in the courtroom.* New Brunswick, NJ: Rutgers University Press

Ben-Shaker, G., & Furedy, J.J. (1991). *Theories and applications in the detection of deception.* New York: Springer-Verlag.

Berry, D.T.R., Wetter, M.W., & Baer, R.A. (1995). Assessment of malingering. In J.N. Butcher (Ed.), *Clinical personality assessment: Practical approaches.* New York: Oxford.

Berry, J.W., & Kalin, R. (1995). Multicultural and ethnic attitudes in Canada: An overview of the 1991 National Survey. *Canadian Journal of Behavioural Science, 27*, 301–320.

Berry, J.W., & Wells, M. (1994). Attitudes toward Aboriginal peoples and Aboriginal self-government. In J.H. Hylton (Ed.), *Aboriginal self-government in Canada: Current trends and issues*. Saskatoon: Purich Publishing.

Bersoff, D.N., Goodman-Delahunty, J., Grisso, J.T., Hans, V.P., Poythress, N.G., Poythress, N.G., & Roesch, R.G. (1997). Training in law and psychology: Models from the Villanova conference. *American Psychologist, 52*, 1301–1310.

Besserer, S. (1998). Criminal victimization: An international perspective (Catalogue No. 85–002–XPE). *Juristat, 18(6)*. Ottawa: Statistics Canada.

Bibby, R.W. (1987). Bilingualism and multiculturalism: A national reading. In L. Driedger (Ed.), *Ethnic Canada : identities and inequalities* (pp. 158–167). Toronto : Copp Clark Pitman.

Bijur, P.E., Kurzon, M., Overpeck, M.D., & Scheidt, P.C. (1992). Parental alcohol use, problem drinking, and children's injuries. *Journal of the American Medical Association, 267*, 3166–3171.

Binder, L.M., & Rohling, M.L. (1996). Money matters: A meta-analytic review of the effects of financial incentives on recovery after closed-head injury. *American Journal of Psychiatry, 153*, 7–10.

Binder, L.M., & Willis, S.C. (1991). Assessment of motivation after financially compensable minor head trauma. *Psychological Assessment, 3*, 175–181.

Binder, R.L., & McNeil, D.E. (1988). Effects of diagnosis and context on dangerousness. *American Journal of Psychiatry, 145*, 728–732.

Birch, D.E. (1992). Duty to protect: Update and Canadian perspective. *Canadian Psychology, 33*, 94–101.

Birkenmayer, A., & Besserer, S. (1997). *Sentencing in adult provincial courts: A study of nine jurisdictions*. Ottawa: Statistics Canada.

Birkenmayer, A., & Roberts, J.V. (1997). Sentencing in adult provincial courts. *Juristat, 17(1)*, 1–15.

Bissett-Johnson, A., & Day, D.C. (1986). *The new divorce law: A commentary on the Divorce Act, 1985*. Toronto: Carswell.

Bittman, B.J., & Convit, A. (1993). Competency, civil commitment, and the dangerousness of the mentally ill. *Journal of Forensic Sciences, 38*, 1460–1466.

Blanchard, E.B., & Hickling, E.J. (1997). *After the crash: Assessment and treatment of motor vehicle accident survivors*. Washington, DC: American Psychological Association.

Blanchard, E.B., Hickling, E.J., Forneris, C.A., Taylor, A.E., Buckley, T.C., Loos,

W.R., & Jaccard, J. (1997). Prediction of remission of acute posttraumatic stress disorder in motor vehicle accident victims. *Journal of Traumatic Stress, 10,* 215–234.

Blanchard, E.B., Hickling, E.J., Taylor, A.E., Loos, W.R., Forneris, C.A., & Jaccard, J. (1996). Who develops PTSD from motor vehicle accidents? *Behaviour Research and Therapy, 34,* 1–10.

Blanchard, E.B., Hickling, E.J., Taylor, A.E., Loos, W.R., & Gerardi, R.J. (1994). Psychological morbidity associated with motor vehicle accidents. *Behaviour Research and Therapy, 32,* 283–290.

Blanchette, K. (1997, January). Classifying female offenders for correctional interventions. *Forum on Corrections Research, 9,* 36–41.

Bland, R.C., Newman, S.C., Thompson, A.H., & Dyck, R.J. (1998). Psychiatric disorders in the population and in prisoners. *International Journal of Law and Psychiatry, 21,* 273–279.

Block, J.H., Block, J., & Gjerde, P.F. (1986). The personality of children prior to divorce: A prospective study. *Child Development, 57,* 827–840.

Block, J.H., Block, J., & Morrison, A. (1981). Parental agreement-disagreement on child-rearing orientations and gender-related personality correlates in children. *Child Development, 52,* 965–974.

Boer, D.P., Hart, S.D., Kropp, P.R., & Webster, C.D. (1997). *Manual for the Sexual Violence Risk – 20.* Vancouver: British Columbia Institute Against Family Violence.

Boer, D.P., Wilson, R.J., Gauthier, C.M., & Hart, S.D. (1997). Assessing risk of sexual violence: Guidelines for clinical practice. In C.D. Webster & M.A. Jackson (Eds.), *Impulsivity: Theory, assessment, and treatment* (pp. 326–342). New York: Guilford.

Bogart, W.A. (1999). "Guardian of civil rights ... mediaeval relic": The civil jury in Canada. *Law and Contemporary Problems, 61,* 101–115.

Boilard, J.G. (1991), with updates. *Guide to criminal evidence.* Cowansville, PQ: Les Éditions Yvon Blais.

Bolocofsky, D.N. (1989). Use and abuse of mental health experts in child custody determinations. *Behavioral Sciences & the Law, 7,* 197–214.

Boney-McCoy, S., & Finkelhor, D. (1996). Is youth victimization related to trauma symptoms and depression after controlling for prior symptoms and family relationships? A longitudinal, prospective study. *Journal of Consulting and Clinical Psychology, 64,* 1406–1416.

Bonta, J. (1996). Risk-needs assessment and treatment. In A.T. Harland (Ed.), Choosing correctional options that work: Defining the demand and evaluating the supply (pp. 18–32). Thousand Oaks, CA: Sage.

Bonta, J., Law, M., & Hanson, R.K. (1998). The prediction of criminal and violent recidivism among mentally disordered offenders: A meta-analysis. *Psychological Bulletin, 123*, 123–142.

Bonta, J., Pang, B., & Wallace-Capretta, S. (1995). Predictors of recidivism among incarcerated female offenders. *The Prison Journal, 75*, 277–294.

Bonta, J., Zinger, I., Harris, A., & Carriere, D. (1998). The dangerous offender provisions: Are they targeting the right offenders? *Canadian Journal of Criminology, 40*, 377–400.

Boon, J., & Noon, E. (1994). Changing perspectives in cognitive interviewing. *Psychology, Crime & Law, 1*, 59–69.

Borgida, E. (1981). Legal reforms of rape laws. In L. Bickman (Ed.), *Applied Social Psychology Annual* (Vol 2, pp. 63–95). Hillsdale, NJ: Erlbaum.

Boring, E.G. (1950). *A history of experimental psychology* (2nd ed). New York: Appleton-Century-Crofts, Inc.

Boritch, H. (1997). *Fallen women: Female crime and criminal justice in Canada.* Toronto, ON: Nelson.

Borum, R. (1996). Improving the clinical practice of violence risk assessment. *American Psychologist, 51*, 945–956.

Borum, R., Swartz, M., & Swanson, J. (1996). Assessing and managing violence risk in clinical practice. *Journal of Practical Psychiatry and Behavioral Health, 4*, 205–215.

Bottoms, B.L., & Goodman, G.S. (Eds.). (1996). *International perspectives on child abuse and children's testimony: Psychological research and law.* Thousand Oaks, CA: Sage.

Bownes, I.T., O'Gorman, E.C., & Sayers, A. (1991). Assault characteristics and stress disorder in rape victims. *Acta Psychiatrica Scandinavia, 83*, 27–30.

Boyd, N. (1995). *Canadian law: An introduction.* Toronto: Harcourt Brace.

Bradley, M.T., & Rettinger, J. (1992). Awareness of crime-relevant information and the Guilty Knowledge Test. *Journal of Applied Psychology, 77*, 55–59.

Brady, E. (1996). False memory syndrome: "The female malady." *Dalhousie Journal of Legal Studies, 5*, 69–93.

Brandon, R., & Davies, C. (1973). *Wrongful imprisonment.* London: Allen & Unwin.

Brandon, S., Duncanson, I., & Samuel, G. (1979). *English legal history.* London: Sweet & Maxwell.

Brekke, N., & Borgida, E. (1988). Expert psychological testimony in rape trials: A social-cognitive analysis. *Journal of Personality and Social Psychology, 55*, 372–384.

Brekke, N.J., Enko, P.J., Clavet, G., & Seelau, E. (1991). Of juries and court-appointed experts: The impact of nonadversarial versus expert testimony. *Law and Human Behaviour, 15*, 451–475.

Brennan, M., & Brennan, R.E. (1988). *Strange language: Child victims under cross examination* (3rd ed.). Wagga Wagga, NSW, Australia: Riverina Murray Institute of Higher Education.

Breslau, N., Davis, G.C., Andreski, P., Peterson, E. (1991). Traumatic events and posttraumatic stress disorder in an urban population of young adults. *Archives of General Psychiatry, 48*, 216–222.

Brewer, N., & Wilson, C. (Eds.). (1995). *Psychology and policing*. Hillsdale, NJ: Lawrence Erlbaum Associates.

Bricklin, B. (1995). *The custody evaluation handbook: Research-based solutions and applications*. New York: Brunner/Mazel.

Bridges, J.S. (1991). Perceptions of date and stranger rape: A difference in sex role expectations and rape-supportive beliefs. *Sex Roles, 24*, 291–307.

Brigham, J.C. (1999). What is forensic psychology, anyway? *Law and Human Behavior, 23*, 273–298.

Brockman, J., & Rose, V.G. (2001). *Canadian criminal procedure and evidence for the social sciences* (2nd ed.), Scarborough, ON: Nelson Canada.

Bronson, E. (1989). The effectiveness of voir dire in discovering prejudice in high publicity cases, an archival study of the minimization effect. Chico, CA: Dept. of Political Science, California State University.

Brookbank, C., & Kingsley, B. (1998). Adult criminal court statistics, 1997–98 (Catalogue No. 85–002–XIE). *Juristat, 18(14)*. Ottawa: Statistics Canada.

Brooks, N. (1983). *Police guidelines: Pretrial identification procedures*. Ottawa: Law Reform Commission.

Brown v. Board of Education of Topeka, 375 U.S. 483 (1954).

Browne, A. (1997, August). *Prevalence and severity of lifetime physical and sexual victimization among incarcerated women*. Paper presented at the American Psychological Association, Chicago, IL.

Browne, A., & Finkelhor, D. (1986). Impact of child sexual abuse: A review of the literature. *Psychological Bulletin, 99*, 66–77.

Bryant, B., Mayou, R., Lloyd-Bostock, S. (1997). Compensation claims following road accidents: A six year follow-up study. *Medicine Science and the Law, 37*, 326–336.

Bryant, R.A., & Harvey, A.G. (1995). Avoidant coping style and post-traumatic stress following motor vehicle accidents. *Behavior Research and Therapy, 33*, 631–635.

Bryant, R.A., & Harvey, A.G. (1996). Initial posttraumatic stress responses following motor vehicle accidents. *Journal of Traumatic Stress, 9*, 223–234.

Bull, R. (1992). Obtaining evidence expertly: The reliability of interviews with child witnesses. *Expert Evidence, 1*, 5–12.

Bull, R. (1995). Interviewing people with communicative disabilities. In R. Bull

& D. Carson (Eds.), *Handbook of psychology in legal contexts* (pp. 247–260). Toronto: Wiley.

Bull, R. (1998). Obtaining information from child witnesses. In A. Memon, A. Vrij, & R. Bull (Eds.), *Psychology and Law: Truthfulness, accuracy and credibility* (pp. 188–209). London: McGraw-Hill.

Burge, S.K. (1988). Post-traumatic stress disorder in victims of rape. *Journal of Traumatic Stress, 1*, 193–210.

Burnam, M.A., Stein, J.A., Golding, J.M., Siegel, J.M., Sorenson, S.B., Forsythe, A., & Telles, C.A. (1988). Sexual assault and mental disorders in a community population. *Journal of Consulting and Clinical Psychology, 56*, 843–850.

Burns, N., & Meredith, C. (1993). Evaluation of the effectiveness of group treatment for men who batter. In J. Hudson & J. Roberts (Eds.), *Evaluating justice: Canadian policies and programs.* Toronto: Thompson Educational Publishing, Inc.

Bursten, B. (1986). Psychiatric injury in women's workplaces. *Bulletin of the American Academy of Psychiatry and the Law, 14*, 245–251.

Burt, M. (1980). Cultural myths and supports for rape. *Journal of Personality and Social Psychology, 38*, 217–230.

Burt, M., & Albin, R.S. (1981). Rape myths, rape definitions, and probability of conviction. *Journal of Applied Social Psychology, 11*, 212–230.

Burton, A.M. (1997). Recognising familiar and unfamiliar faces. *IEE Colloquium on Image Processing for Security Applications* (1997/074). Available at http://medusa.psy.gla.ac.uk/~mike/videoproj.html

Bussey, K. (1992). Lying and truthfulness: Children's definitions, standards, and evaluative reactions. *Child Development, 63*, 129–137.

Butcher, J.N., Dahlstrom, L., Graham, J.R., Tellgen, A., & Kaemmer, B. (1989). *Minnesota Multiphasic Personality Inventory – 2.* Minneapolis, MN: University of Minnesota Press.

Butcher, J.N., Williams, C.L., Graham, J.R., Archer, R.P., Tellegen, A., Ben-Porath, Y.S., & Kaemmer, B. (1992). *Minnesota Multiphasic Personality Inventory-Adolescent.* Minneapolis, MN: University of Minnesota Press.

Cahill, D., & Mingay, D.J. (1986). Leading questions and the police interview. *Policing, 213*, 212–224.

Cammaert, L.P. (1985). How widespread is sexual harassment on campus? *International Journal of Women's Studies, 8*, 388–397.

Campbell, J.C. (1995). Prediction of homicide of and by battered women. In J.C. Campbell (Ed.), *Assessing dangerousness: Violence by sexual offenders, batterers, and child abusers* (pp. 96–113). Thousand Oaks, CA: Sage.

Campbell, J.C. (1999, November). *Issues in risk assessment in the field of intimate partner violence.* Keynote address presented at the Conference on Risk

Assessment and Risk Management: Implications for the Prevention of Violence. Vancouver, British Columbia.

Canada Evidence Act, R.S.C. (1985), C-5.

Canadian Centre for Justice Statistics. (1993). Common assault in Canada. *Juristat Service Bulletin, 13(6)*, 1–21.

Canadian Centre for Justice Statistics. (1994). Wife assault: The findings of a national survey. *Juristat Service Bulletin, 14(9)*, 1–22.

Canadian Centre for Justice Statistics. (1995). Fear and personal safety. *Juristat Service Bulletin, 15(9)*, 1–21.

Canadian Centre for Justice Statistics. (1996a). Adult correctional services in Canada: Highlights for 1994–95. *Juristat Service Bulletin, 16(7)*, 1–22.

Canadian Centre for Justice Statistics. (1996b). Homicide in Canada. *Juristat Service Bulletin, 16(11)*, 1–14.

Canadian Centre for Justice Statistics. (1996c). The justice data factfinder. *Juristat Service Bulletin, 16(9)*, 1–21.

Canadian Centre for Justice Statistics. (1996d). Violent crime in Canada. *Juristat Service Bulletin, 16(6)*, 1–25.

Canadian Charter of Rights and Freedoms, being Part I of the Constitution Act, 1982, enacted by the Canada Act 1982 (U.K.), c. 11, Sched. B. (R.S.C. (1985), Appendix II, No. 44).

Canadian Human Rights Commission. (1987). *Sexual harassment casebook: 1978–1986*. Ottawa: Minister of Supplies and Services.

Canadian Panel on Violence Against Women (1993). *Changing the landscape: Ending violence – achieving equality*. Ottawa: Minister of Supply and Services, Canada.

Canadian Psychological Association. (1992). *Canadian code of ethics for psychologists*. Old Chelsea, Canada: Author.

Canadian Sentencing Commission. (1987). *Sentencing reform: A Canadian approach*. Ottawa: Supply and Services Canada.

Canadians want laws to be meaner and greener. (1998, June 5). *The Toronto Star*, p. A2.

Carmichael v. Carmichael (1992), 43 R.F.L. (3d) 145, 115 N.S.R. (2d) 45 (C.A.)

Carretta, T.R., & Moreland, R.L. (1983). The direct and indirect effects of inadmissible evidence. *Journal of Law, 2*, 310–334.

Carter, C.A., Bottoms, B.L., & Levine, M. (1996). Linguistic and socioemotional influences on the accuracy of children's reports. *Law and Human Behavior, 20*, 335–358.

Catholic Children's Aid Soc'y of Metropolitan Toronto v. C.M., [1994] 2 S.C.R. 165.

Ceci, S.J., & Bruck, M. (1993). The suggestibility of the child witness: A historical review and synthesis. *Psychological Bulletin, 113*, 403–439.

Ceci, S.J., & Bruck, M. (1995). *Jeopardy in the courtroom: A scientific analysis of children's testimony.* Washington, DC: American Psychological Association.

Ceci, S.J., Crossman, A.M., Gilstrap, L.L., & Scullin, M.H. (1998). Social and cognitive factors in children's testimony. In C.P. Thompson, D.J. Herrmann, et al. (Eds.), *Eyewitness memory: Theoretical and applied perspectives* (pp. 15–30). Mahwah, NJ: Lawrence Erlbaum Associates, Inc.

Ceci, S.J., Ross, D.F., & Toglia, M.P. (1987). Suggestibility of children's memory: Psycholegal implications. *Journal of Experimental Psychology: General, 116*, 38–49.

Chamberlain v. Robichaud (1985), 62 N.B.R. (2d) 73, 161 A.P.R. 73 (Q.B.).

Charrow, R., & Charrow, V. (1979). Making legal language understandable: A psycholinguistic study of jury instructions. *Columbia Law Review, 79*, 1306–1374.

Cheal, D. (1996). Stories about step families. In *Growing up in Canada: National longitudinal survey of children and youth* (pp. 93–191). Ottawa: Minister responsible for Statistics Canada.

Cheffins, R., & Tucker, R. (1976). *The constitutional process in Canada* (2nd ed.). Toronto: McGraw-Hill Ryerson.

Cherlin, A.J., Furstenberg, F.F., Chase-Lansdale, P.L., Kiernan, K.E., Robins, P.K., Morrison, D.R., & Teitler, J.O. (1991). Longitudinal studies of effects of divorce on children in Great Britain and the United States. *Science, 252*, 1386–1389.

Child & Family Services of Winnipeg v. F. (A.C.) (1992), 42 R.F.L. (3d) 337, 81 Man. R. (2d) 149 (C.A.).

Christianson, S.-A. (1992). Emotional stress and eyewitness memory: A critical review. *Psychological Bulletin, 112*, 284–309.

Civil Code of Québec, S.Q. 1991, C. 64.

Clifford, B., & Memon, A. (in press). Obtaining detailed testimony: The Cognitive Interview. In A. Heaton-Armstrong, E. Shepherd, & D. Wolchover (Eds.), *Witness testimony: Psychological investigative and evidential perspectives.* London: Blackstone Press.

Coles, E.M., & Grant, I. (1989). The insanity defence in Canada: A psychologist's point of view. *Health Law in Canada, 10*, 175–182.

Coles, F.S. (1986). Forced to quit: Sexual harassment complaints and agency response. *Sex Roles, 14*, 81–95.

Collins, J.J. (1990). Alcohol and interpersonal violence: Less than meets the eye. In N.Z. Hilton, M.A. Jackson, & C.D. Webster (Eds.), *Clinical Criminology: Theory, research and practice.* Toronto: Canadian Scholars' Press.

Comack, E. (1993). *Women offenders' experiences of physical and sexual abuse: A preliminary report.* Criminology Research Centre, University of Manitoba.

Comack, E. (1996). *Women in trouble: Connecting women's law violations to their histories of abuse.* Halifax: Fernwood.

Comment. (1982). Evaluating Michigan's guilty but mentally ill verdict: An empirical study. *Journal of Law Reform, 16,* 75–112.

Committee on Ethical Guidelines for Forensic Psychologists. (1991). Specialty guidelines for forensic psychologists. *Law and Human Behavior, 15,* 655–665.

Committee on Professional Practice and Standards. (1994). Guidelines for child custody evaluations in divorce proceedings. *American Psychologist, 49,* 677–680.

Conly, C. (1998, November). *The Women's Prison Association: Supporting women offenders and their families.* National Institute of Justice. NY: Women's Prison Association.

Constitution Act, 1867, 30–31 Vict., c. 3 (U.K.).

Cook, S.W. (1984). The 1954 social science statement and school desegregation: A reply to Gerard. *American Psychologist, 39,* 819–832.

Cook, S.W. (1985). Experimenting on social issues: The case of school desegregation. *American Psychologist, 40,* 452–460.

Cooke, G. (1969). The court study unit: Patient characteristics and differences between patients judged competent and incompetent. *Journal of Clinical Psychology, 25,* 140–143.

Cooper, A. (1994). The ABC's of challenge for cause in jury trials: To challenge or not to challenge and what to ask if you get it. *Criminal Law Quarterly, 37,* 62–69.

Cooper, H.H.A., & Redlinger, L.J. (1988). *Catching spies: Principles and practices of counterespionage.* Boulder, CO: Paladin Press.

Cooper, J., Bennett, E.A., & Sukel, H.L. (1996). Complex scientific testimony: How do jurors make decisions? *Law and Human Behavior, 20,* 379–394.

Cooper, M. (1993). *Assessing the risk of repeated violence among men arrested for wife assault: A review of the literature.* Vancouver: British Columbia Institute on Family Violence.

Cooper, M. (1995). *Challenges in programming for wife batterers.* Vancouver: British Columbia Institute on Family Violence.

Corcoran, K.L., & Thomas, L.R. (1991). The influence of observed alcohol consumption on perceptions of initiation of sexual activity in a college dating situation. *Journal of Applied Social Psychology, 21,* 500–507.

Cornell, D., Warren, J., Hawk, G., Stafford, E., Oram, G., & Pine, D. (1996). Psychopathy in instrumental and reactive offenders. *Journal of Consulting and Clinical Psychology, 64,* 783–790.

Corrado, R.R., Bala, N., Linden, R., & LeBlanc, M. (Eds.). (1992). *Juvenile justice in Canada: A theoretical and analytical assessment*. Toronto: Butterworths.

Correctional Service of Canada. (1991). *Mission of the Correctional Service of Canada*. Ottawa: Author.

Correctional Service of Canada. (1994a). *Correctional program strategy for federally sentenced women*. Ottawa: Correctional Service of Canada.

Correctional Service of Canada. (1994b). *Long-term federally sentenced women: Literature review*. Ottawa: Federally Sentenced Women Program.

Correctional Service of Canada. (1996). *Standards and guidelines for the provision of services to sex offenders*. Ottawa: Correctional Service of Canada.

Correctional Service of Canada. (1997). *Basic facts about corrections in Canada, 1997 edition* (Catalogue No. JS 82–17/1997E). Ottawa: Author.

Corrections and Conditional Release Act, S.C. (1992), c. 20.

Correira v. Flamand (1989), 66 Man. R. (2d) 27 (C.A.).

Coscina, D.V. (1997). The biopsychology of impulsivity: Focus on brain serotonin. In C.D. Webster & M.A. Jackson (Eds.), *Impulsivity: Theory, assessment, and treatment* (pp. 95–115). New York: Guilford.

Coulson, G., Ilacqua, G., Nutbrown, V., Guilekes, D., & Cudjoe, F.E. (1996). Predictive utility of the LSI for incarcerated female offenders. *Criminal Justice and Behavior, 23*, 427–439.

Court for mentally ill offers new approach. (1998), June 11. *The Vancouver Sun*, p. A7.

Criminal Code, R.S.C. (1985), c. C-46, as am.

Croft, S. (1995). Helping victims to remember. *Police, November*, 13–14.

Crowne, D.P., & Marlowe, D. (1964). *The approval motive: Studies in evaluative dependence*. New York: Wiley.

Crull, P. (1982). Stress effects of sexual harassment on the job: Implications for counselling. *American Journal of Orthopsychiatry, 52*, 539–544.

Crull, P. (1991). The stress effects of sexual harassment on the job. In M.A. Paludi & R.B. Barickman (Eds.), *Academic and workplace sexual harassment: A resource manual* (pp. 133–144). Albany, NY: SUNY.

Cumberland, J., & Zamble, E. (1992). General and specific measures of public attitudes: release decisions. *Canadian Journal of Behavioral Science, 24*, 442–455.

Cutler, B.L., Berman, G., Penrod, S.D., & Fisher, R.P. (1994). Conceptual, practical, and empirical issues associated with eyewitness identification test media. In D.F. Ross, J.D. Read, & M.P. Toglia (Eds.), *Adult eyewitness testimony: Current trends and development* (pp. 163–181). New York: Cambridge University Press.

Cutler, B.L., Dexter, H.R., & Penrod, S.D. (1990). Nonadversarial methods for sensitizing jurors to eyewitness evidence. *Journal of Applied Social Psychology, 20*, 1197–1207.

Cutler, B.L., & Penrod, S.D. (1995). *Mistaken identification: The eyewitness, psychology, and the law.* New York: Cambridge University Press.

Cutler, B.L., Penrod, S., & Dexter, H. (1989). The eyewitness, the expert psychologist, and the jury. *Law and Human Behavior, 13*, 311–332.

Dahl, S. (1989). Acute response to rape – a PTSD variant. *Acta Psychiatrica Scandinavica, 80*, 56–62.

Daly, M., & Wilson, M. (1988). *Homicide.* Hawthorne, NY: Aldine De Gruyter.

Daniel, A.E., Beck, N.C., Herath, A., Schmitz, M., & Menninger, K. (1984). Factors correlated with psychiatric recommendations of incompetency and insanity. *Journal of Psychiatry & Law, 12*, 527–544.

Daubney, D., & Parry, G. (1999). An overview of Bill C-41 (The Sentencing Reform Act). In J.V. Roberts & D. Cole (Eds.), *Making sense of sentencing.* Toronto: University of Toronto Press.

Davies, G.M. (1986). Capturing likeness in eyewitness composites: The police artist and his rivals. *Medical Science Law, 26*, 283–290.

Davies, G., & Taylor, L. (1989). Private committeeship in British Columbia: A study of due process. *Canadian Journal of Family Law, 8*, 185–205.

Davis, D.L. (1985). Treatment planning for the patient who is incompetent to stand trial. *Hospital and Community Psychiatry, 36*, 268–271.

Davis, J.H. (1980). Group decision and procedural justice. In M.L. Fishbein (Ed.), *Progress in social psychology,* (vol. 1, pp. 157–229). Hillsdale, NJ: Erlbaum.

Davis, J.H., Kameda, T., Parks, C., Stasson, M., & Zimmerman, S. (1989). Some social mechanics of group decision making: The distribution of opinion, polling sequence, and implications of consensus. *Journal of Personality and Social Psychology, 57*, 1000–1012.

Dawes, R.M., Faust, D., & Meehl, P.E. (1989). Clinical versus actuarial judgment. *Science, 243*, 1668–1674.

Deitze, P.M., & Thomson, D.M. (1993). Mental reinstatement of context: A technique for interviewing child witnesses. *Applied Cognitive Psychology, 7*, 97–108.

Delahunty, D.L., Herberman, H.B., Craig, K.J., Hayward, M.C., Fullerton, C.S., Ursano, R.J., & Baum, A. (1997). Acute and chronic distress and posttraumatic stress disorder as a function of responsibility for serious motor vehicle accidents. *Journal of Consulting and Clinical Psychology, 65*, 560–567.

Del Bello v. Hagel (1978), 34 A.R. 242 (C.A.).

Delisle, R.J. (1993). The new rape shield law and the charter. *University of New Brunswick Law Journal, 42*, 335–340.

Delisle, R.J. (1996). *Evidence: Principles and problems* (4th ed.). Scarborough, ON: Carswell.

Delisle, R.J., & Stuart, D. (1996). *Learning Canadian criminal procedure* (4th ed.). Scarborough, ON: Carswell.

Dempster, R.J. (1998). *Prediction of sexually violent recidivism: A comparison of risk assessment instruments*. Unpublished master's thesis, Simon Fraser University.

Dent, H.R., & Newton, S. (1994). The conflict between clinical and evidential interviewing in child sexual abuse. *Psychology, Crime & Law, 1*, 181–186.

Department of Justice Canada. (1996). *Section 745 of the Criminal Code. Fact Sheet*. Ottawa: Department of Justice Canada.

Department of Justice Canada. (1999). *Minister of Justice Introduces New Youth Justice Law*. www document: http://canada.justice.gc.ca/News/Communiques/1999/yoa_en.htm l

DePaulo, B.M., & Pfeifer, R.L. (1986). On-the-job experience and skill at detecting deception. *Journal of Applied Social Psychology, 16*, 249–267.

DePaulo, B.M.., & Kirkendol, S.E. (1989). The motivational impairment effect in the communication of deception. In J.C. Yuille (Ed.), *Credibility assessment* (pp. 51–70). Dordrecht: Kluwer.

Dershewitz, R.A., & Williamson, J.W. (1977). Prevention of childhood household injuries: A controlled clinical trial. *American Journal of Public Health, 67*, 1148–1153.

Deutsch, M., & Gerard, H.G. (1955). A study of normative and informational social influences upon individual judgment. *Journal of Abnormal and Social Psychology, 51*, 629–636.

Devlin, Honourable Lord Patrick (chair). (1976). *Report to the secretary of state for the Home Department of the departmental committee on evidence of identification in criminal cases*. London: Her Majesty's Stationery Office.

Diamond, S. (1994). Reference guide on survey evidence. In Federal Judicial Center, *Reference Manual on Scientific Evidence*. Washington, DC: Federal Judicial Center.

Diamond, S.S. (1997). Illuminations and shadows from jury simulations. *Law and Human Behavior, 21*, 561–571.

Diamond, S.S., & Casper, J.D. (1992). Blindfolding the jury to verdict consequences: Damages, experts, and the civil jury. *Law and Society Review, 26*, 513–563.

Diaz, A.L., & McMillin, J.D. (1991). A definition and description of nurse abuse. *Western Journal of Nursing Research, 13*, 97–109.

Dobson, K.S. (1989). A meta-analysis of the efficacy of cognitive therapy for depression. *Journal of Consulting and Clinical Psychology, 57*, 414–419.

Dodge, K.A., Bates, J.E., & Pettit, G.S. (1990). Mechanisms in the cycle of violence. *Science, 250,* 1678–1683.

Dodge, M., & Greene, E. (1991). Jurors and expert conceptions of battered women. *Violence and Victims, 6,* 271–282.

Doherty, W.J., & Needle, R.H. (1991). Psychological adjustment and substance use among adolescents before and after a parental divorce. *Child Development, 62,* 328–337.

Dominion Bureau of Statistics. (1955–57). *Mental health statistics: Patients in institutions.* Ottawa: Minister of Trade and Commerce.

Donakowski, D.W., & Esses, V.M. (1996). Native Canadians, First Nations, or Aboriginals: The effect of labels of attitudes toward Native peoples. *Canadian Journal of Behavioural Science, 28,* 86–91.

Doob, A.N., and Beaulieu, L. (1992). Variation in the exercise of judicial discretion with young offenders. *Canadian Journal of Criminology, 34,* 35–50.

Doob, A.N., & Kirshenbaum, H.M. (1972). Some empirical evidence and the effect of s. 12 of the Canada Evidence Act upon an accused. *The Criminal Law Quarterly, 15,* 88–96.

Doob, A.N., & Park, N. (1987). Computerized sentencing information for judges: An aid to the sentencing process. *Criminal Law Quarterly, 30,* 54–72.

Doob, A.N., & Roberts, J.V. (1984). Social psychology, social attitudes and attitudes toward sentencing. *Canadian Journal of Behavioural Science, 16,* 269–280.

Doob, A.N., & Roberts, J.V. (1988). Public punitiveness and public knowledge of the facts: Some Canadian surveys. In N. Walker & M. Hough (Eds.), *Public attitudes to sentencing* (pp. 111–133). Aldershot: Gower.

Doris, J. (Ed.). (1991). *The suggestibility of children's recollections: Implications for eyewitness testimony.* Washington, DC: American Psychological Association.

Douglas, J.E., Ressler, R.K., Burgess, A.W., & Hartman, C.R. (1986). Criminal profiling from crime scene analysis. *Behavioral Sciences and the Law, 4,* 401–421.

Douglas, K.S., Cox, D.N., & Webster, C.D. (1999). Violence risk assessment: Science and practice. *Legal and Criminological Psychology, 4,* 149–184.

Douglas, K.S., & Hart, S.D. (1996, March). *Major mental disorder and violent behaviour: A meta-analysis of study characteristics and substantive factors influencing effect size.* Poster presented at the biennial conference of the American Psychology-Law Society's, Hilton Head, South Carolina.

Douglas, K.S., & Hart, S.D. (1998). *Psychosis as a risk factor for violence: A quantitative review of the research.* Manuscript under review.

Douglas, K.S., Lyon, D.R., & Ogloff, J.R.P. (1997). The impact of graphic photographic evidence on mock jurors' decisions in a murder trial: Probative or prejudicial? *Law and Human Behavior, 21,* 485–501.

Douglas, K.S., Macfarlane, E., & Webster, C.D. (1996). Predicting dangerousness in the contemporary Canadian mental health and criminal justice systems. *Canada's Mental Health, 43*, 4–11.

Douglas, K.S., & Ogloff, J. (1997). An investigation of factors influencing public opinion of property bias in Canadian Criminal Code maximum sentences. *Law and Human Behavior, 20*, 395–417.

Douglas, K.S., Ogloff, J.R.P., Nicholls, T.L., & Grant, I. (1999). Assessing risk for violence among psychiatric patients: The HCR-20 violence risk assessment scheme and the Psychopathy Checklist: Screening version. *Journal of Consulting and Clinical Psychology, 67*, 917–930.

Douglas, K.S., & Webster, C.D. (1998). Predicting violence in mentally and personality disordered individuals. In R. Roesch, S.D. Hart, & J.R.P. Ogloff (Eds.), *Psychology and law: The state of the discipline*. New York: Plenum Press.

Douglas, K.S., & Webster, C.D. (1999). Predicting violence in mentally and personality disordered individuals. In R. Roesch, S. Hart, & J.R.P. Ogloff (Eds.), *Psychology and law: The state of the discipline* (pp. 175–239). New York: Plenum Press.

Driedger, E.A. (1983). *The construction of statutes* (2nd ed.). Toronto: Butterworths.

Dull, T.R., & Giacopassi, D.J. (1987). Demographic correlates of sexual and dating attitudes: A study of date rape. *Criminal Justice and Behavior, 14*, 175–193.

Dumas, J.E., & Serketich, W.J. (1994). Maternal depressive symptomatology and child maladjustment: A comparison of three process models. *Behavior Therapy, 25*, 161–181.

Durham v. United States, 214 F.2d 862 (D.C. Cir. (1954).

Dusky v. U.S., 362 U.S. 402 (1960).

Dussault, R., & Borgeat, L. (1986). *Administrative law: A treatise* (2nd ed.). Toronto: Carswell.

Dutton, D.G. (1987). The criminal justice response to wife assault. *Law and Human Behavior, 11*, 189–206.

Dutton, D.G. (1995). *The domestic assault of women: Psychological and criminal justice perspectives*. Vancouver: UBC Press.

Dutton, D.G. (1998). *The abusive personality. Violence and control in intimate relationships*. New York: Guilford Press.

Dutton, D.G., Bodnarchuk, M., Kropp, P.R., Hart, S.D., & Ogloff, J.R.P. (1997). Wife assault treatment and criminal recidivism: An eleven year follow-up. *Journal of Offender Therapy and Comparative Criminology, 41*, 9–23.

Dutton, D.G., & Hart, S.D. (1992a). Evidence for long-term, specific effects of childhood abuse on criminal behaviour in men. *International Journal of Offender Therapy and Comparative Criminology, 36*, 129–137.

Dutton, D.G., & Hart, S.D. (1992b). Risk markers for family violence in a federally incarcerated population. *International Journal of Law and Psychiatry, 15*, 101–112.

DuWors, R. (1997). The justice data factfinder (Catalogue No. 85–002–XPE). *Juristat, 17(13)*. Ottawa: Statistics Canada.

Edelson, J.L., & Syers, M. (1990). Relative effectiveness of group treatments for men who batter. *Social Work Research & Abstracts, 26(2)*, 10–17.

Edgar, A. (1999). Sentencing Options in Canada. In J.V. Roberts and D.P. Cole (Eds.), *Making sense of sentencing*. Toronto: University of Toronto Press.

Editorial Policy. (1996). *Law and Human Behaviour, 20*.

Eich, E., McCauley, D., & Ryan, L. (1994). Mood dependent memory for events of the personal past. *Journal of Experimental Psychology: General, 123*, 201–215.

Ekman, P. (1985). *Telling lies: Clues to deceit in the marketplace, politics, and marriage*. New York: Norton.

Ekman, P., & Friesen, W.V. (1972). Detecting deception from the body or face. *Journal of Personality and Social Psychology, 29*, 288–298.

Ekman, P., & O'Sullivan, M. (1989). Hazards in detecting deceit. In D.C. Raskin (Ed.), *Psychological methods in criminal investigation and evidence* (pp. 297–332). New York: Springer.

Ekman, P., & O'Sullivan, M. (1991). Who can catch a liar? *American Psychologist, 46*, 913–920.

Ekman, P., O'Sullivan, M., & Frank, M.G. (1999). A few can catch a liar. *Psychological Science, 10*, 263–266.

Elliot, L., & Morris, R. (1987). Behind prison doors. In E. Adelberg, & C. Currie (Eds.), *Too few to count: Women in conflict with the law*. Vancouver: Press Gang.

Ellsworth, P. (1989). Are twelve heads better than one? *Law and Contemporary Issues, 52*, 205–224.

Ellsworth, P.C. (1991). To tell what we know or wait for Godot? *Law and Human Behavior, 15*, 77–90.

Ellsworth, P.C., & Mauro, R. (1998). Psychology and law. In D.T. Gilbert, S.T. Fiske, & G. Lindzey (Eds.), *The handbook of social psychology* (pp. 684–732). Boston, MA: McGraw-Hill.

Elwork, A., Alfini, J., & Sales, B. (1982). Toward understandable jury instructions. *Judicature, 65*, 432–443.

Elwork, A., Sales, B.D., & Alfini, J.J. (1977). Juridic decisions: In ignorance of the law or in light of it? *Law and Human Behavior, 1*, 163–189.

Emery, R.E. (1988). *Marriage, divorce, and children's adjustment*. Beverly Hills, CA: Sage.

Emery, R.E. (1994). *Renegotiating family relationships: Divorce, child custody, and mediation*. New York: Guilford Press.

Emery, R.E. (1999). Changing the rules for determining child custody in divorce cases. *Clinical Psychology: Science and Practice, 6,* 323–327.

Emery, R.E., Matthews, S.G., & Wyer, M.M. (1991). Child custody mediation and litigation: Further evidence on the differing views of mothers and fathers. *Journal of Consulting and Clinical Psychology, 59,* 410–418.

Emery, R.E., & Wyer, M.M. (1987a). Child costody mediation and litigation: An experimental evaluation of the experience of parents. *Journal of Consulting and Clinical Psychology, 55,* 179–186.

Emery, R.E., & Wyer, M.M. (1987b). Divorce mediation. *American Psychologist, 42,* 472–480.

English, P., & Sales, B. (1997). A Ceiling or consistency effect for the comprehension of jury instructions. *Psychology, Public Policy, and Law, 3,* 381–401.

Ennis, B.J., & Litwack, T.R. (1974). Psychiatry and the presumption of expertise: Flipping coins in the courtroom. *California Law Review, 62,* 693–752.

Environics Research Group. (1989). *A qualitative investigation of public opinion on sentencing, corrections and parole.* Toronto: Environics Research Group.

Ericson, R. (1982). *Reproducing order: A study of police patrol work.* Toronto: University of Toronto Press.

Estroff, S.E., & Zimmer, C. (1994). Social networks, social support, and violence among persons with severe, persistent mental illness. In J. Monahan & H.J. Steadman (Eds.), *Violence and mental disorder: Developments in risk assessment* (pp. 259–295). Chicago: University of Chicago Press.

Estroff, S.E., Zimmer, C., Lachicotte, W.S., & Benoit, J. (1994). The influence of social networks and social support on violence by persons with serious mental illness. *Hospital and Community Psychiatry, 45,* 669–679.

Everson, M.D., Hunter, W.M., Runyon, D.K., Edelsohn, G.A., Coulter, A. (1989). Maternal support following disclosure of incest. *American Journal of Orthopsychiatry, 59,* 197–207.

Ewigman, B., Kivlahan, C., & Land, C. (1993). The Missouri child fatality study: Underreporting of maltreatment fatalities among children under five years of age, 1983–1986. *Pediatrics, 91,* 330–337.

Exner, J.E. (1986). *The Rorschach: A comprehensive system: Vol 1. Basic foundations* (2nd ed.). New York: Wiley.

Eysenck, H.J. (1964). *Crime and personality.* London: Routledge & Kegan Paul.

Falardeau-Ramsay, M. (1994). When "no" isn't enough: Sexual harassment and the Canadian Human Rights Act. In D. Geller-Schwartz (Ed.), *From awareness to action: Strategies to stop sexual harassment in the workplace* (pp. 45–50). Ottawa: Minister of Supply and Services Canada.

Fancher, R. (1996). *Pioneers of psychology* (3rd ed.) New York: W.W. Norton.

Ferguson, G. (1989). *Canadian criminal jury instructions*. (2nd ed.). Vancouver: Continuing Legal Education Society of British Columbia.

Ferguson, G.A., & Bouck, J.C. (1997). *Canadian Criminal Jury Instructions*. British Columbia: C.L. E.

Ferguson, R.J., & Mittenberg, W. (1996). Cognitive-behavioral treatment of postconcussion syndrome: A therapist's manual. In V.B. Van Hasselt and M. Hersen (Eds.), *Sourcebook of Psychological Treatment Manuals for Adult Disorders* (pp. 615–655). New York: Plenum Press.

Ferris, L.E., Sandercock, J., Hoffman, B., Silverman, M., Barkun, H., Carlisle, J., & Katz, C. (1997). Risk assessments for acute violence to third parties: A review of the literature. *Canadian Journal of Psychiatry, 42*, 1051–1060.

Finkel, N.J. (1991). The insanity defense: A comparison of verdict schemas. *Law and Human Behavior, 15*, 533–555.

Finkelhor, D. (1982). Sexual abuse: A sociological perspective. *Child Abuse and Neglect, 6*, 95–102.

Finkelhor, D. (1984). *Child sexual abuse: New theory and research*. New York: Free Press.

Finkelhor, D. (1990). Early and long-term effects of sexual abuse: An update *Professional Psychology: Research and Practice, 21*, 325–330.

Finkelhor, D. (1994). The international epidemiology of child sexual abuse. *Child Abuse & Neglect, 18*, 409–417.

Finkelhor, D., & Browne, A. (1985). The traumatic impact of child sexual abuse: A conceptualization. *American Journal of Orthopsychiatry, 55*, 530–541.

Finkelhor, D., & Browne, A. (1988). Assessing the long-term impact of child sexual abuse: A review and conceptualization. In G.T. Hotaling & D. Finkelhor (Eds.), *Family abuse and its consequences: New directions in research* (pp. 270–284). Newbury Park, CA: Sage Publications, Inc.

Finkelhor, D., Hotaling, G., Lewis, I., & Smith, C. (1989). Sexual abuse and its relationship to later sexual satisfaction, marital status, religion and attitudes. *Journal of Interpersonal Violence, 4*, 379–399.

Fisher, R.P. (1995). Interviewing victims and witnesses of crime. *Psychology, Public Policy, and Law, 1*, 732–764.

Fisher, R.P., & Geiselman, R.E. (1992). *Memory-enhancing techniques for investigative interviewing*. Springfield: Charles C. Thomas.

Fisher, R.P., Geiselman, R.E., & Raymond, D.S. (1987). Critical analysis of police interviewing techniques. *Journal of Police Science and Administration, 15*, 177–185.

Fisher, R.P., McCauley, M.R., & Geiselman, R.E. (1994). Improving eyewitness testimony with the cognitive interview. In D.F. Ross, J.D. Read, & M.P. Toglia

(Eds.), *Adult eyewitness testimony: Current trends and development* (pp. 245–269). New York: Cambridge University Press.

Fishman, M. (1978). Crime waves as ideology. *Social Problems, 25,* 531–543.

Fiske, S.T., & Taylor, S.E. (1991). *Social Cognition* (2nd ed.). New York: McGraw Hill.

Fitzgerald, L.F., Shullman, S.L., Bailey, N., Richards, M., Swecker, J., Gold, Y., Ormerod, M., & Weitzman, L. (1988). The incidence and dimensions of sexual harassment in academia and the workplace. *Journal of Vocational Behavior, 32,* 152–175.

Fitzgerald, L.F., Swan, S., & Fischer, K. (1995). Why didn't she just report him? The psychological and legal implications of women's responses to sexual harassment. *Journal of Social Issues, 51,* 117–138.

Fitzmaurice, C., & Pease, K. (1987). *The psychology of sentencing.* Manchester: University of Manchester Press.

Fleming v. Reid (1991), 4 O.R. (3d) 74, 82 D.L.R. (4th) 298, 48 O.A.C. 46 (C.A.).

Fontana, J.A. (1992). *The law of search and seizure in Canada* (3rd ed.). Markham, ON: Butterworths.

Ford, D.A., & Regoli, M.J. (1992). The criminal prosecution of wife assaulters: Process, problems, and effects. In N.Z. Hilton (Ed.), *Legal responses to wife assault: Current trends and evaluation.* Newbury Park, CA: Sage.

Forth, A.E., Brown, S.L., Hart, S.D., & Hare, R.D. (1996). The assessment of psychopathy in male and female noncriminals: Reliability and validity. *Personality and Individual Differences, 20,* 531–543.

FosterLee, L., Horowitz, I.A., & Bourgeois, M. (1993). Juror competence in civil trials: The effects of preinstruction and evidence technicality. *Journal of Applied Psychology, 78,* 14–21.

FosterLee, L., Horowitz, I.A., & Bourgeois, M. (1994). Effects of notetaking on verdicts and evidence processing in a civil trial. *Law and Human Behavior, 18,* 567–578.

Frazier, P. (1990). Victim attributions and post-rape trauma. *Journal of Personality and Social Psychology, 59,* 298–304.

Frazier, P.A., & Cohen, B.B. (1992). Research on the sexual victimization of women: Implications for counselor training. *Counseling Psychologist, 20,* 141–158.

Freedman, J.L., & Burke, T.M. (1996). The effect of pretrial publicity: The Bernardo case. *Canadian Journal of Criminology, 38,* 253–270.

Freedman, J.L., Martin, C.K., & Mota, V.L. (1998). Pretrial publicity: Effects of admonition and expressing pretrial opinions. *Legal and Criminal Psychology, 3,* 255–270.

Freeman, R.J., & Roesch, R. (1992). Psycholegal education: Training for forum and function. In D.K. Kagehiro & W.S. Laufer (Eds.), *Handbook of psychology and law* (pp. 567–576). New York: Springer-Verlag.

Frick, P.J., Lahey, B.B., Loeber, R., Stoughamer-Loeber, M., Christ, M.A., & Hanson, K. (1992). Familial risk factors to oppositional defiant disorder and conduct disorder: Parental psychopathology and maternal parenting. *Journal of Consulting and Clinical Psychology, 60,* 49–55.

Friedland, M.L., & Roach, K. (1994). *Criminal law and procedure: Cases and materials* (7th ed.). Toronto: Emond Montgomery.

Fulero, S. (1988). Tarasoff: 10 years later. *Professional Psychology, 19,* 184–194.

Fulero, S. (1999). The American Psychology-Law Society, Division 41 of the American Psychological Association: A Rock and Roll History. In D. Dewsbury (Ed.), *Unification through division: Histories of divisions of the American Psychological Association, Volume 4.* Washington, DC: American Psychological Association Press.

Furby, L., Weinrott, M.R., & Blackshaw, L. (1989). Sex offenders recidivism: A review. *Psychological Bulletin, 105,* 3–30.

Furedy, J.J. (1985). Credulous vs. critical police use of the polygraph in criminal investigations. *Canadian Journal of Criminology, 27,* 491–495.

Furedy, J.J. (1989). The North American CQT polygraph and the legal profession: A case of Canadian credulity and a cause for cultural concern. *The Criminal Law Quarterly, 31,* 431–451.

Furedy, J.J., & Heslegrave, R.J. (1991). The forensic use of the polygraph: A psychophysiological analysis of current trends and future prospects. *Advances in Psychophysiology, 4,* 157–189.

Furedy, J.J., & Liss, J. (1986). Countering confessions induced by the polygraph: Of confessionals and psychological rubber hoses. *Criminal Law Quarterly, 29,* 91–113.

Gabora, N.J., Spanos, N.P., & Joab, A. (1993). The effects of complainant age and expert psychological testimony in a simulated child sexual abuse trial. *Law and Human Behavior, 17,* 103–119.

Gadlin, H. (1991). Careful maneuvers: Mediating sexual harassment. *Negotiation Journal, 7,* 139–153.

Gall, G.L. (1995). *The Canadian legal system* (4th ed.). Scarborough, ON: Carswell.

The Gallup Report (Tue Nov. 14, 1994. Majority oppose homosexuals adopting children. Toronto: Gallup Canada.

Garbarino, J. (1977). The human ecology of child maltreatment: A conceptual model for research. *Journal of Marriage and the Family, 39,* 721–735.

Gardner, W., Lidz, C.W., Mulvey, E.P., & Shaw, E.C. (1996). Clinical versus actuarial predictions of violence in patients with mental illness. *Journal of Consulting and Clinical Psychology, 64,* 602–609.

Gaudet, F., Harris, G., & St John, C. (1932). Individual differences in the sentencing tendencies of judges. *International Journal of Criminal Law, Criminology and Political Science, 23,* 811–818.

Geiselman, R.E., Fisher, R.P., Firstenberg, I., Hutton, L.A., Sullivan, S., Avetissian, I., & Prosk, A. (1984). Enhancement of eyewitness memory: An empirical evaluation of the cognitive interview. *Journal of Police Science and Administration, 12,* 74–80.

Geiselman, R.E., Fisher, R.P., MacKinnon, D.P., & Holland, H.L. (1985). Eyewitness memory enhancement in the police interview: Cognitive retrieval mnemonics versus hypnosis. *Journal of Applied Psychology, 70,* 401–412.

Gelfand, D.M., & Teti, D.M. (1990). The effects of maternal depression on children. *Clinical Psychology Review, 10,* 329–353.

Gelles, R.J. (1973). Child abuse as psychopathology: A sociological critique and reformation. *American Journal of Orthopsychiatry, 43,* 611–621.

Gelles, R.J., & Straus, M.A. (1988). *Intimate violence: The causes and consequences of abuse in the American family.* New York: Simon and Schuster.

Gendreau, P. (1981). Treatment in corrections: Martinson was wrong. *Canadian Psychology, 22,* 332–338.

Gendreau, P. (1996). The principles of effective intervention with offenders. In A.T. Harland (Ed.), *Choosing correctional options that work: Defining the demand and evaluating the supply* (pp. 117–130). Thousand Oaks, CA: Sage.

Gendreau, P., & Goggin, C. (1996). Principles of effective correctional programming. *Forum on Corrections Research, 8,* 38–41.

Gendreau, P., Goggin, G., & Cullen, T. (1999). The effects of prison sentences on recidivism. *User report 1999–3.* Ottawa: Solicitor General Canada.

Gendreau, P., Goggin, C., & Paparozzi, M. (1996). Principles of effective assessment for community corrections. *Federal probation, 60,* 64–70.

Gendreau, P., Little, T., & Goggin, C. (1996). A Meta-analysis of adult offender recidivism: What works! *Criminology, 34,* 575–607.

Gendreau, P., & Ross, R.R. (1979). Effective correctional treatment: Bibliotherapy for cynics. *Crime & Delinquency, 25,* 463–489.

Gendreau, P., & Ross, R. (1987). Effective correctional treatment: Bibliotherapy for cynics. In R. Ross & P. Gendreau (Eds.), *Effective correctional treatment.* Toronto: Butterworths.

Gentleman, J.F., & Park, E. (1997). Divorce in the 1990s. *Health Reports, 9(2),* 53–58.

George, W.H., Cue, K.L., Lopez, P.A., Crowe, L.C., & Norris, J. (1995). Self-reported alcohol expectancies and postdrinking sexual inferences about women. *Journal of Applied Social Psychology, 25,* 164–186.

George, W.H., Gournic, S.J., & McAfee, M.P. (1988). Perceptions of postdrinking female sexuality: Effects of gender, beverage choice, and drink payment. *Journal of Applied Social Psychology, 18,* 1295–1317.

George, W.H., & Marlatt, G.A. (1990). Introduction. In D.R. Laws (Ed.), *Relapse prevention with sex offenders* (pp. 1–31). New York: Guildford Press.

Gerard, H.B. (1983). School desegregation: The social science role. *American Psychologist, 38,* 869–877.

Gidycz, C.A., & Koss, M.P. (1991). Predictors of long-term sexual assault trauma among a national sample of victimized college women. *Violence and Victims, 6,* 175–190.

Gillespie, C. (1989). *Justifiable homicide.* Columbus, OH: Ohio State University Press.

Gilmartin-Zena, P. (1987). Attitudes toward rape: Student characteristics as predictors. *Free Inquiry in Creative Sociology, 15,* 175–182.

Girodo, M. (1983). Undercover operations and law enforcement stress: Getting the pendulum to return. *Royal Canadian Mounted Police Gazette, 45,* 26–28.

Golding, S.L., Eaves, D., & Kowaz, A.M. (1989). The assessment, treatment and community outcome of insanity acquittees: Forensic history and response to treatment. *International Journal of Law and Psychiatry, 12,* 149–179.

Goldman-Eisler, F. (1968). *Psycholinguistics: Experiments in spontaneous speech.* New York: Doubleday.

Gondolf, E.W. (1993). Treating the batterer. In M. Hansen & M. Harway (Eds.), *Battering and Family Therapy: A Feminist Perspective* (pp. 230–257). Newbury Park, CA: Sage Publications.

Goodman, G.S., & Bottoms, B.L. (1993). *Child victims, child witnesses: Understanding and improving testimony.* New York: Guilford Press.

Goodman, G.S., Bottoms, B.L., Schwartz-Kennedy, B.M., & Rudy, L. (1991). Children's testimony about a stressful event: Improving children's reports. *Journal of Narrative and Life History, 1,* 69–99.

Goodman, G.S., & Clark-Stewart, A. (1991). Suggestibility in children's testimony: Implications for sexual abuse investigations. In J. Doris (Ed.), *The suggestibility of children's recollections: Implications for eyewitness testimony* (pp. 92–105). Washington, DC: American Psychological Association.

Goodman, G.S., Taub, E.P., Jones, D.P.H., England, P., Port, L.K., Rudy, L., & Prado, L. (1992). Testifying in criminal court: Emotional effects on child sexual assault victims. *Monographs of the Society for Research in Child Development, 57 (5, Serial No. 229).*

Gordon, M., & Verdun-Jones, S. (1992). *Adult guardianship law in Canada.* Toronto: Butterworths.

Gordon, R.A. (1990). Attributions for blue-collar crime: The effect of subject and defendant race on simulated juror decisions. *Journal of Applied Social Psychology, 20,* 971–983.

Gordon, R.A. (1993). The effect of strong versus weak evidence on the assessment of race stereotypic and race nonstereotypic crimes. *Journal of Applied Social Psychology, 23,* 734–749.

Gordon, R.A., Bindrim, T.A., McNicholas, M.L., & Walden, T.L. (1988). Perceptions of blue-collar and white-collar crimes: The effect of defendant race on simulated juror decisions. *Journal of Social Psychology, 128,* 191–197.

Gordon, R.A., Michels, J.L., & Nelson, C.L. (1996). Majority group perceptions of criminal behavior: The accuracy of race-related crime stereotypes. *Journal of Applied Social Psychology, 26,* 148–159.

Gosselin, H.L. (1984). Sexual harassment on the job: Psychological, social and economic repercussions. *Canada's Mental Health, 34,* 21–24, 32.

Gottfredson, S.D., & Gottfredson, D.M. (1986). Accuracy of prediction models. In A. Blumstein, J. Cohen, J.A. Roth, & C.A. Visher (Eds.), *Criminal careers and "career criminals"* (pp. 212–290). Washington, DC: National Academy Press.

Gouvier, W.D., Cubic, B., Jones, G., Brantley, P., & Cutlip, Q. (1992). Postconcussion symptoms and daily stress in normal and head-injured college populations. *Archives of Clinical Neuropsychology, 7,* 193–211.

Graber, D.A. (1980). *Crime news and the public.* New York: Praeger.

Granger, C. (1996). *The criminal jury trial in Canada.* (2nd ed.). Scarborough, ON: Carswell.

Grant, I. (1985). Dangerous offenders. *Dalhousie Law Journal, 9,* 347–382.

Grant, I., & Douglas, K.D. (in press). The British Columbia Review Panel: Factors influences decision-making. *International Journal of Law and Psychiatry.*

Gray, J., Clark, A., Higenbottam, J., Ledwidge, B., & Paredes, J. (1985). Review panels for involuntary psychiatric patients: Which patients apply? *Canadian Journal of Psychiatry, 30,* 573–576.

Gray, J., Cutler, C., Dean, J., & Kempe, C. (1977). Prediction and prevention of child abuse and neglect. *Child Abuse and Neglect, 1,* 45–58.

Green, A.H. (1993). Child sexual abuse: Immediate and long-term effects and intervention. *Journal of the American Academy of Child and Adolescent Psychiatry, 32,* 890–902.

Greene, E., & Loftus, E.F. (1985). When crimes are joined at trial. *Law and Human Behavior, 9,* 193–207.

Greene, E., Raitz, A., & Linblad, H. (1989). Jurors' knowledge of battered women. *Journal of Family Violence, 4,* 105–125.

Griffiths, C.T., & Verdun-Jones, S.N. (1994). *Canadian criminal justice* (2nd ed.). Toronto: Harcourt Brace.

Grisso, T. (1986). *Evaluating competencies: Forensic assessments and instruments.* New York: Plenum.

Grisso, T. (1991). A developmental history of the American Psychological Law Society. *Law and Human Behavior, 15,* 213–231.

Grisso, T., Sales, B.D., & Bayless, S. (1982). Law-related courses and programs in graduate psychology departments. *American Psychologist, 37,* 267–278.

Grove, W.M., & Meehl, P.E. (1996). Comparative efficiency of informal (subjective, impressionistic) and formal (mechanical, algorithmic) prediction procedures: The clinical-statistical controversy. *Psychology, Public Policy, and Law, 2,* 293–323.

Gruber, J.E., & Bjorn, L. (1986). Women's responses to sexual harassment: An analysis of sociocultural, organizational, and personal resource models. *Social Science Quarterly, 67,* 814–826.

Grubin, D.H., & Kennedy, H.G. (1991). The classification of sexual offenders. *Criminal Behaviour and Mental Health, 1,* 123–129.

Gudjonsson, G.H. (1992). *The psychology of interrogations, confessions and testimony.* Chichester: Wiley.

Gudjonsson, G.H., & MacKeith, J.A.C. (1982). False confessions. Psychological effects of interrogation. In A. Trankell (Ed.), *Reconstructing the past* (pp. 253–269). Deventer, The Netherlands.

Gunn v. Gunn (1994), 10 R.F.L. (4th) 197, 100 Man. R. (2d) 6 (C.A.).

Gutek, B.A., & Koss, M.P. (1993). Changed women and changed organizations: Consequences of and coping with sexual harassment. *Journal of Vocational Behavior, 42,* 28–48.

Haddock, G., Zanna, M.P., & Esses, V. M. (1993). Assessing the structure of prejudicial attitudes: The case of attitudes toward homosexuals. *Journal of Personality and Social Psychology, 65,* 1105–1118.

Haddock, G., Zanna, M.P., & Esses, V.M. (1994). The (limited) role of trait-laden stereotypes in predicting attitudes toward native peoples. *British Journal of Social Psychology, 33,* 83–106.

Hafemeister, T., & Melton, G.B. (1987). The impact of social science research on the judiciary. In G.B. Melton (Ed.), *Reforming the law: Impact of child development research* (pp. 27–59). New York: Guilford.

Hafemeister, T., Ogloff, J.R.P., & Small, M.A. (1990). Training and careers in law and psychology: The perspectives of students and graduates of dual degree programs. *Behavioral Sciences and the Law, 8,* 263–283.

Hak, J.W. (1996). The Young Offenders Act. In J.A. Winterdyk (Ed.), *Issues and perspectives on young offenders in Canada* (pp. 45–77). Toronto: Harcourt Brace.

Hale, M. 1847. *The history of pleas of the Crown.* (1st edition 1736).

Halleck, S. (1966). A critique of current psychiatric roles in the legal process. *Wisconsin Law Review, 1966*, 379–401.

Hamberger, L.K., & Hastings, J.E. (1988). Characteristics of male spouse abusers consistent with personality disorders. *Hospital and Community Psychiatry, 39*, 763–770.

Hamberger, L.K., & Hastings, J.E. (1993). Court-mandated treatment of men who assault their partner: Issues, controversies, and outcomes. In N. Zoe Hilton (Ed.), *Legal responses to wife assault: Current trends and evaluation.* Newbury Park, CA: Sage.

Hamill, R., Wilson, T., & Nisbett, R. (1980). Insensitivity to sample bias: Generalizing from atypical cases. *Journal of Personality and Social Psychology, 39*, 578–589.

Hammersley, R., & Read, J.D. (1985). The effect of participation in a conversation on recognition and identification of the speakers' voices. *Law and Human Behavior, 9*, 71–81.

Hammersley, R.H., & Read, J.D. (1996). Voice identification by humans and computers. In S.L. Sporer, R.S. Malpass, & G. Köhnken (Eds.), *Psychological issues in eyewitness identification* (pp. 117–152). Mahwah, NJ: Lawrence Erlbaum Associates.

Haney, C. (1980). Psychology and legal change: On the limits of a factual jurisprudence. *Law and Human Behavior, 17*, 371–398.

Hans, V.P. (Ed.). (1990). Law and the media [Special issue]. *Law and Human Behavior, 14(5).*

Hans, V.P. (1992). Jury Decision Making. In D.K. Kagehiro & W.S. Laufer (Eds.), *Handbook of Psychology and Law* (pp. 56–76). New York: Springer-Verlag.

Hans, V.P., & Dee, J.L. (1991). Media coverage of law: Its impact on juries and the public. *American Behavioral Scientist, 35*, 136–149.

Hans, V.P., & Doob, A.N. (1976). Section 12 of the Canada Evidence Act and the deliberations of simulated juries. *Criminal Law Quarterly, 18*, 235–253.

Hans, V.P., & Slater, D. (1984). Plain crazy: Lay definitions of legal insanity. *International Journal of Law and Psychiatry, 7*, 105–114.

Hans, V.P., & Vidmar, N. (1986). *Judging the jury.* New York: Plenum Press.

Hansen, K.L., Schaefer, E.G., & Lawless, J.J. (1993). Temporal patterns of normative, informational, and procedural-legal discussion in jury deliberation. *Basic and Applied Social Psychology, 14*, 33–46.

Hanson, R.K. (1990). The psychological impact of sexual assault on women and children: A review. *Annals of Sex Research, 3*, 187–232.

Hanson, R.K. (1997). *The development of a brief actuarial risk scale for sexual offense recidivism.* Ottawa: Department of the Solicitor General of Canada.

Hanson, R.K., & Bussière, M.T. (1996). *Predictors of sexual offender recidivism: A meta-analysis*. User Report No. 1996–04. Ottawa: Department of the Solicitor General of Canada.

Hanson, R.K., & Bussière, M.T. (1998). Predicting relapse: A meta-analysis of sexual offender recidivism studies. *Journal of Consulting and Clinical Psychology, 66*, 348–362.

Hare, R.D. (1991). *Manual for the Hare Psychopathy Checklist – Revised*. Toronto: Multi-Health Systems.

Hare, R.D. (1993). *Without conscience: The disturbing world of the psychopaths among us*. New York: Pocket Books.

Hare, R.D. (1996). Psychopathy: A clinical construct whose time has come. *Criminal Justice and Behavior, 23*, 25–54.

Hare, R.D., & McPherson, L.M. (1984). Violent and aggressive behavior by criminal psychopaths. *International Journal of Law and Psychiatry, 7*, 35–50.

Harney, P., & Muehlenhard, C. (1990). Rape. In E. Graverholz & M. Kurlewski (Eds.), *Sexual coercion*. Lexington, MA: Lexington Books.

Harpur, T.J., Hakstian, A.R., & Hare, R.D. (1988). Factor structure of the Psychopathy Checklist. *Journal of Consulting and Clinical Psychology, 56*, 741–747.

Harpur, T.J., Hare, R.D., & Hakstian, A.R. (1989). A two-factor conceptualization of psychopathy: Construct validity and implications for assessment. *Psychological Assessment: A Journal of Consulting and Clinical Psychology, 1*, 6–17.

Harris, G.T., Rice, M.E., & Cormier, C.A. (1991). Psychopathy and violent recidivism. *Law and Human Behavior, 15*, 625–637.

Harris, G.T., Rice, M.E., & Quinsey, V.L. (1993). Violent recidivism of mentally disordered offenders: The development of a statistical prediction instrument. *Criminal Justice and Behavior, 20*, 315–335.

Hart, S.D. (1998a). Psychopathy and risk for violence. In D.J. Cooke, A.E. Forth, & R.D. Hare (Eds.), *Psychopathy: Theory, research and implications for society* (pp. 355–373). Dordrecht, Netherlands: Kluwer Academic Publishers

Hart, S.D. (1998b). The role of psychopathy in assessing risk for violence: Conceptual and methodological issues. *Legal and Criminological Psychology, 3*, 121–137.

Hart, S.D., Cox, D.N., & Hare, R.D. (1995). *Manual for the Hare Psychopathy Checklist: Screening Version (PCL: SV)*. Toronto: Multi-Health Systems.

Hart, S.D., & Hare, R.D. (1996). Psychopathy and risk assessment. *Current Opinion in Psychiatry, 9*, 380–383.

Hart, S.D., & Hare, R.D. (1997). Psychopathy: Assessment and association with criminal conduct. In D.M. Stroff, J. Breiling & J. Maser (Eds.), *Handbook of Antisocial Behavior* (pp. 22–35). New York: Wiley.

Hart, S.D., Hare, R.D., & Forth, A.E. (1994). Psychopathy as a risk marker for violence: Development and validation of a screening version of the Revised Psychopathy Checklist. In J. Monahan & H.J. Steadman (Eds.), *Violence and mental disorder* (pp. 81–98). Chicago: University of Chicago Press.

Hart, S.D., & Hemphill, J.F. (1989). *Prevalence of and service utilization by mentally disordered offenders at the Vancouver Pretrial Services Centre*. Report submitted to the British Columbia Corrections Branch in fulfilment of contract No. COR-22153.

Hart, S.D., Kropp, P.R., & Hare, R.D. (1988). Performance of male psychopaths following conditional release from prison. *Journal of Consulting and Clinical Psychology, 56*, 227–232.

Hart, S.D., Kropp, P.R., Roesch, R., Ogloff, J.R.P., & Whittemore, K. (1994). Wife assault in community-resident offenders. *Canadian Journal of Criminology, 36*, 435–446.

Hart, S.D., Roesch, R., Corrado, R.R., & Cox, D.N. (1993). The Referral Decision Scale: A validation study. *Law and Human Behavior, 17*, 611–623.

Hartshorne, H., & May, M.A. (1928). *Studies in the nature of character: Book 1. General methods and results*. New York: Macmillan.

Haskett, M.E., Myers, L.W., Pirrello, V.E., & Dombalis, A.O. (1995). Parenting style as a mediating link between parental emotional health and adjustment of maltreated children. *Behavior Therapy, 26*, 625–642.

Hastie, R., Penrod, S.D., & Pennington, N. (1983) *Inside the jury*. Cambridge, MA: Harvard University Press.

Hayes, L.M. (1983). And darkness closes in: National study of jail suicide. *Criminal Justice and Behaviour, 10*, 461–473.

Hayes, L.M. (1994). Prison suicide: An overview and guide to prevention. *Prison Journal, 75*, 431–456.

Healey, K., Smith, C., & O'Sullivan, K. (1998). *Batterer intervention: Program approaches and criminal justice strategies* (JCJ Publication No. 168638). Washington, DC: National Institute of Justice.

Healy, P. (1999). Questions and answers on conditional sentencing in the Supreme Court of Canada. *Criminal Law Quarterly, 42*, 12–37.

Heilbrun, K. (1997). Prediction versus management models relevant to risk assessment: The importance of legal decision-making context. *Law and Human Behavior, 21*, 347–359.

Helfer, R.E. (1977). On the prevention of child abuse and neglect. *Child Abuse and Neglect, 1*, 502–504.

Hemphill, J.F. (1992). *Recidivism of criminal psychopaths after therapeutic community treatment.* Unpublished master's thesis, University of Saskatchewan, Saskatoon, Saskatchewan, Canada.

Hemphill, J.F. (1998). *Psychopathy, criminal history, and recidivism.* Unpublished doctoral dissertation, University of British Columbia, Vancouver, British Columbia, Canada.

Hemphill, J.F., & Hare, R.D. (1998, August). Psychopathy and recidivism among female offenders. In A.E. Forth (Chair), *Female offenders: The forgotten minority.* Symposium conducted at the 106th Annual Convention of the American Psychological Association, San Francisco, California.

Hemphill, J.F., Hare, R.D., & Wong, S. (1998). Psychopathy and recidivism: A review. *Legal and Criminological Psychology, 3,* 139–170.

Hemphill, J.F., & Howell, A.J. (1999). *Adolescent offenders and stages of change.* Unpublished manuscript.

Hemphill, J.F., Templeman, R., Wong, S., & Hare, R.D. (1998). Psychopathy and crime: Recidivism and criminal careers. In D.J. Cooke, A.E. Forth, & R.D. Hare (Eds.), *Psychopathy: Theory, research and implications for society* (pp. 375–399). Dordrecht, The Netherlands: Kluwer.

Heney, J. (1990). *Report of self-injurious behaviour in the Kingston Prison for Women.* Ottawa: Correctional Service of Canada.

Henggeler, S.W., Schoenwald, S.K., & Pickrel, S.G. (1995). Multisystemic therapy: Bridging the gap between university-and community-based treatment. *Journal of Consulting and Clinical Psychology, 63,* 709–717.

Herek, G. (1986). On heterosexual masculinity: Some psychical consequences of the social construction of gender and sexuality. *American Behavioral Scientist, 29,* 563–577.

Herek, G.M. (1988). Heterosexuals' attitudes toward lesbians and gay men: Correlates and gender differences. *Journal of Sex Research, 25,* 451–477.

Herek, G.M. (1989). Hate crimes against lesbians and gay men: Issues for research and policy. *American Psychologist, 44,* 948–955.

Hermann, D.H.J., & Sor, Y.S. (1983). Convicting or confining? Alternative directions in insanity defense reform: Guilty but mentally ill versus new rules for release of insanity acquittees. *Brigham Young University Law Review, 1983,* 499–638.

Hess, J.H., & Thomas, H.E. (1963). Incompetency to stand trial: Procedures, results, and problems. *American Journal of Psychiatry, 119,* 713–720.

Hesson, K., Bakal, D., & Dobson, K.S. (1993). Legal and ethical issues concerning children's rights of consent. *Canadian Psychology, 34,* 317–328.

Heuer, L., & Penrod, S. (1988). Increasing jurors' participation in trials: A field experiment with jury notetaking and question asking. *Law and Human Behavior, 12,* 231–261.

Heuer, L., & Penrod, S. (1989). Increasing jurors' participation in trials. *Law and Human Behavior, 12,* 231–261.

Heuer, L., & Penrod, S. (1994). Juror notetaking and question asking during trials: A national field experiment. *Law and Human Behavior, 18,* 121–150.

Hiday, V.A. (1988). Civil commitment: A review of empirical research. *Behavioral Sciences and the Law, 6,* 15–43.

Hillson, J.M.C., & Kuiper, N.A. (1994). A stress and coping model of child maltreatment. *Clinical Psychology Review, 14,* 261–285.

Hinshaw, S.P., & Zupan, B.A. (1997). Assessment of antisocial behavior in children and adolescents. In D.M. Stoff, J. Breiling, & J.D. Maser (Eds.), *Handbook of antisocial behavior* (pp. 36–50). New York: Wiley.

Hodgins, S. (1983). A follow-up study of persons found incompetent to stand trial and/or not guilty by reason of insanity in Quebec. *International Journal of Law and Psychiatry, 6,* 399–423.

Hodgins, S. (1994). Status at age 30 of children with conduct problems. *Studies on Crime and Crime Prevention, 3,* 41–61.

Hodgins, S. (1995). Assessing mental disorder in the criminal justice system: Feasibility versus clinical accuracy. *International Journal of Law and Psychiatry, 18,* 15–28.

Hodgins, S., & Côté, G. (1990). Prevalence of mental disorders among penitentiary inmates in Quebec. *Canada's Mental Health, 38(1),* 1–4.

Hoffman, B.F. & Srinivasan, J. (1992). A study of competence to consent to treatment in a psychiatric hospital. *Canadian Journal of Psychiatry, 37,* 179–182.

Hogarth, J. (1971). *Sentencing as a human process.* Toronto: University of Toronto Press.

Hoge, R.D., & Andrews, D.A. (1996). *Assessing the youthful offender: Issues and techniques.* New York: Plenum Press.

Hogg, P.W. (1996). *Constitutional law of Canada* (4th ed.). Scarborough, ON.: Carswell.

Holcomb, D.R., Holcomb, L.C., Sondag, K.A., & Williams, N. (1991). Attitudes about date rape: Gender differences among college students. *College Student Journal, 25,* 434–439.

Holgate, A. (1989). Sexual harassment as a determinant of women's fear of rape. *Australian Journal of Sex, Marriage, & Family, 10,* 21–28.

Hollien, H. (1990). *The acoustics of crime.* New York: Plenum Press.

Holmes, R.M. (1989). *Profiling violent crimes: An investigative tool.* Newbury Park, CA: Sage.

Holzworth-Munroe, A., & Stuart, G.L. (1994). Typology of male batterers: Three subtypes and the differences among them. *Psychological Bulletin, 116,* 476–497.

Honts, C.R., Kircher, J.C., & Raskin, D.C. (1995). Polygrapher's dilemma or psychologist's chimaera: A reply to Furedy's logico-ethical considerations for psychophysiological practitioners and researchers. *International Journal of Psychophysiology, 20,* 199–207.

Horowitz, I.A. (1985). The effect of jury nullification instructions on verdicts and jury functioning in criminal trials. *Law and Human Behavior, 9,* 25–36.

Horowitz, I.A. (1988). Jury nullification: The impact of judicial instructions, arguments, and challenges on jury decision making. *Law and Human Behavior, 12,* 439–453.

Horvath, F.S. (1977). The effect of selected variables on interpretation of polygraph records. *Journal of Applied Psychology, 62,* 127–136.

Hotaling, G.T., & Sugarman, D.B. (1986). An analysis of risk markers in husband-to-wife violence: The current state of knowledge. *Violence and Victims, 1,* 101–124.

Hough, M. (1996). People talking about punishment. *Howard Journal, 35,* 191–214.

Hough, M., & Roberts, J.V. (1997). *Attitudes to punishment: Findings from the British crime survey.* London: Home Office.

Hovius, B. (1996). *Family law: Cases, notes, and materials* (4th ed.). Scarborough, ON: Carswell.

Hovius, B., & Youdan, M. (1991). *The law of family property.* Scarborough, ON: Carswell.

Howell, A.J., Enns, R.A. (1995). A high risk recognition program for adolescents in conflict with the law. *Canadian Psychology, 36,* 149–161.

Howell, A.J., Reddon, J.R., & Enns, R.A. (1997). Immediate antecedents to adolescents' offenses. *Journal of Clinical Psychology, 54,* 355–360.

Hudson, S.M., & Ward, T. (1997). Rape: Psychopathology and theory. In D.R. Laws, & W. O'Donohue (Eds.), *Sexual deviance: Theory, assessment, and treatment.* (pp. 332–355). New York: Guilford Press.

Human Rights Act, S.M. 1974, c. 65.

Hylton, J.H. (1994). Get tough or get smart? Options for Canada's youth justice system in the twenty-first century. *Canadian Journal of Criminology, 36,* 229–246.

Hylton, J.H. (1995). Care or control: Health or criminal justice options for the long-term seriously mentally ill in a Canadian Province. *International Journal of Law and Psychiatry, 18,* 45–59.

Hyman, I.E., Jr, Husband, T.H., & Billings, J.F. (1995). False memories of childhood experiences. *Applied Cognitive Psychology, 9*, 181–197.

Iacono, W.G. (1995). Offender testimony: Detection of deception and guilty knowledge. In N. Brewer & C. Wilson (Eds.), *Psychology and policing* (pp. 155–172). Hillsdale, NJ: Lawrence Erlbaum Associates.

Iacono, W.G., & Lykken, D.T. (1997). The validity of the Lie Detector: Two surveys of scientific opinion. *Journal of Applied Psychology, 82*, 426–433.

In the matter of a female infant, B.C. Birth Registration No. 99-00735, Vancouver Registry CA026708 (BCCA, February 8, 2000).

Inbau, F.E., Reid, J.E., & Buckley, J.P. (1986). *Criminal interrogation and confessions* (3rd ed.). Baltimore: Williams & Wilkins.

Insanity Defense Reform Act (IDRA), 18 U.S.C. § 20 (1986 Supp.).

Irving, A. (1943). The psychological analysis of wartime rumour patterns in Canada. *Bulletin of the Canadian Psychological Association, 3*, 40–46.

Island, D., & Letellier, P. (1991). *Men who beat the men who love them: Battered gay men and domestic violence.* Binghampton, NY: Harrington Park Press.

Jack, L.A., Nicholls, T.L., & Ogloff, J.R.P. (1998). *An investigation of inpatient self-injurious behaviour among involuntarily hospitalized patients.* Poster presented at the biennial meeting of the American Psychology-Law Society, Redondo Beach, CA.

Jack, L.A., & Ogloff, J.R.P. (1997). Factors affecting the referral of young offenders for medical and psychological assessment under the Young Offenders Act. *Canadian Journal of Criminology, 39*, 247–273.

Jackson, J. (1997). A conceptual model for the study of violence and aggression. In C.D. Webster & M.A. Jackson (Eds.), *Impulsivity: Theory, assessment, and treatment* (pp. 233–247). New York: Guilford.

Jackson, M.A. (1995). Search for the cause of crime: Biological and psychological perspectives. In M.A. Jackson & C.T. Griffiths (Eds.), *Canadian criminology: Perspectives on crime and criminality* (2nd ed.) (pp. 27–59). Toronto: Harcourt Brace.

Jackson, M.A., & Griffiths, C.T. (Eds.). (1995). *Canadian criminology: Perspectives on crime and criminality* (2nd ed.). Toronto: Harcourt Brace.

Jackson, M., Hitchen, D., & Glackman, W. (1995). *Corrections branch programming for female offenders: Perspectives and visions.* Criminology Research Centre, Simon Fraser University.

Jaffary, S. (1963). *Sentencing of adults in Canada.* Toronto: University of Toronto Press.

Jaffe, P.G., Austin, G., Leschied, A.W., & Sas, L. (1987). Critical issues in the development of custody and access dispute resolution services. *Canadian Journal of Behavioural Sciences, 19*, 405–417.

Jaffe, P.G., Leschied, A.W., Sas, L., & Austin, G.W. (1985). A model for the provision of clinical assessments and service brokerage for young offenders: The London Family Court Clinic. *Canadian Psychology, 26*, 54–61.

Jaffe, P., Wolfe, D., Wilson S.K., & Zak, L. (1986). Family violence and child adjustment: A comparative analysis of girls' and boys' behavioral symptoms. *American Journal of Psychiatry, 143*, 74–77.

James, P.S. (1985). *Introduction to English law* (11th ed.). London: Butterworths.

Janzen and Governeau v. Platy Enterprises Ltd., [1989] 1 S.C.R. 1252.

Jenkins v. United States, 307 F.2d 637 (D.C. Court of Appeals, 1962).

Jensen, I.W., & Gutek, B.A. (1982). Attributions and assignment of responsibility in sexual harassment. *Journal of Social Issues, 38*, 121–136.

Joel, S. (1985). The female offender. In M.H. Ben-Aron, S.J. Hucker, & C.D. Webster (Eds.), *Clinical criminology: The assessment and treatment of criminal behaviour*. Toronto: Clarke Institute of Psychiatry of the University of Toronto.

Johnson v. Louisiana, 406 U.S. 356 (1972).

Johnson, H. (1996). Violent crime in Canada (Catalogue No. 85–002–XPB). *Juristat, 16(6)*. Ottawa: Statistics Canada.

Johnson, H., & Sacco, V.F. (1995). Researching violence against women: Statistics Canada's national survey. *Canadian Journal of Criminology, 37*, 281–304.

Johnson, D., & Russ, I. (1989). Effects on salience of consciousness-raising information on perceptions of acquaintance versus stranger rape. *Journal of Applied Social Psychology, 19*, 1182–1197.

Johnson, J.D. (1994). The effect of rape type and information admissibility on perceptions of rape victims. *Sex Roles, 30*, 781–792.

Johnson, M.K., Hashtroudi, S., & Lindsay, D.S. (1993). Source monitoring. *Psychological Bulletin, 114*, 3–28.

Johnson, M.T. (1993). Memory phenomena in the law. *Applied Cognitive Psychology, 7*, 603–618.

Johnson, S.L. (1985). Black innocence and the white jury. *Michigan Law Review, 83*, 1611.

Jones, D.P., & de Villars, A.S. (1985). *Principles of administrative law*. Toronto: Carswell.

Jones, D.P., & Krugman, R.D. (1986). Can a three-year-old child bear witness to her sexual assault and attempted murder? *Child Abuse & Neglect, 10*, 253–258.

Jones, D.P.H., & McQuiston, M.G. (1988). *Interviewing the sexually abused child*. London: Gaskell.

Jones, S.E. (1987). Judge-versus attorney-conducted voir-dire: An empirical investigation of juror candor. *Law and Human Behavior, 11*, 131–146.

Jurors' racial views can be questioned. (1998), June 5. *The Globe and Mail*, p. A1, A8.

Justice, B. (1994). Making behavioral change the outcome measure in research on violence. *Psychological Reports, 75*, 1202.

Kalbfleisch, P.J. (1994). The language of detecting deceit. *Journal of Language and Social Psychology, 13*, 469–496.

Kalven, H., & Zeisel, H. (1966). *The American jury.* Boston: Little, Brown.

Kamisar, Y. (1982). The assassination attempt. *University of Michigan Law School Law Quadrangle Notes, Fall*, 1.

Kaplan, M.F., & Schersching, C. (1981). Juror deliberation: An information integration analysis. In B. Sales (Ed.), *The trial process* (pp. 235–262). New York: Plenum.

Kassin, S.M. (1997). The psychology of confession evidence. *American Psychologist, 52*, 221–223.

Kassin, S.M. (1998). *Psychology* (2nd ed). Upper Saddle River, NJ: Prentice Hall.

Kassin, S.M., Ellsworth, P.C., & Smith, V.L. (1989). The "general acceptance" of psychological research on eyewitness testimony. *American Psychologist, 44*, 1089–1098.

Kassin, S., Smith, V., & Tulloch, W. (1990). The dynamite charge: Effects on the perceptions and deliberation behavior of mock jurors. *Law and Human Behavior, 14*, 537–550.

Kassin, S.M., & Wrightsman, L.S. (1979). On the requirements of proof: The timing of judicial instruction and mock juror verdicts. *Journal of Personality and Social Psychology, 37*, 1877–1887.

Kassin, S.M., & Wrightsman, L.S. (1985). Confession evidence. In S.M. Kassin & L.S. Wrightsman (Eds.), *The psychology of evidence and trial procedure* (pp. 67–94). Beverly Hills, CA: Sage.

Kassin, S.M., & Wrightsman, L.S. (1988). *The American jury on trial: Psychological perspectives.* New York: Hemisphere Publishing Corporation.

Kebbell, M., Milne, R., & Wagstaff, G. (1999). The cognitive interview: a survey of its forensic effectiveness. *Psychology, Crime and the Law, 5*, 101–115.

Kebbell, M., & Wagstaff, G. (1996). Enhancing the practicality of the cognitive interview in forensic situations. Commentary on Memon & Stevenage on witness-memory. *Pscholoquy, 7(16)*, witness-memory. 3. memon.

Kemp, R., Towell, N., & Pike, G. (1997). When seeing should not be believing: Photographs, credit cards and fraud. *Applied Cognitive Psychology, 11*, 211–222.

Kempe, C., Silverman, F., Steele, B., Drogemueler, W., & Silver, H. (1962). The battered child syndrome. *Journal of the American Medical Association, 181*, 17–24.

Kendall, K. (1993a), August. *Literature review on therapeutic services for women in prison.* Ottawa: Ministry of the Solicitor General, Corrections Branch.

Kendall, K. (1993b), August. *Program evaluation of therapeutic services at the Prison for Women.* Ottawa: Ministry of the Solicitor General, Corrections Branch.

Kendall, K. (1997). Female offenders: Treatment issues. *Proceedings of the sixth Symposium on Violence & Aggression,* June 16–19, 1996, Saskatoon, Saskatchewan: University of Saskatchewan.

Kendall-Tackett, K.A., Williams, L.M., & Finkelhor, D. (1993). Impact of sexual abuse in children: A review and synthesis of recent empirical studies. *Psychological Bulletin, 113,* 164–180.

Kerr, N. (1993). Stochastic models of juror decision making. In R. Hastie (Ed.), *Inside the juror.* New York: Cambridge University Press.

Kerr, N.L., Kramer, G.P., Carroll, J.S., & Alfini, J.J. (1991). On the effectiveness of voir dire in criminal cases with prejudicial publicity: An empirical study. *American University Law Review, 40,* 665–701.

Kerr, N.L., & MacCoun, R.J. (1985). The effects of jury size and polling method on the process and product of jury deliberation. *Journal of Personality and Social Psychology, 48,* 349–363.

Kimerling, R., & Calhoun, K.S. (1994). Somatic symptoms, social support, and treatment seeking among sexual assault victims. *Journal of Consulting and Clinical Psychology, 62,* 333–340.

King v. Creighton (1908), 14 C.C.C. 349.

Klassen, D., & O'Connor, W.A. (1988a). Predicting violence in schizophrenic and non-schizophrenic patients: A prospective study. *Journal of Community Psychiatry, 16,* 217–227.

Klassen, D., & O'Connor, W.A. (1988b). A prospective study of predictors of violence in adult male mental health admissions. *Law and Human Behavior, 12,* 143–158.

Klassen, D., & O'Connor, W.A. (1989). Assessing the risk of violence in released mental patients: A cross-validation study. *Psychological Assessment: A Journal of Consulting and Clinical Psychology, 1,* 75–81.

Klassen, D., & O'Connor, W.A. (1994). Demographics and case history variables in risk assessment. In J. Monahan & H.J. Steadman (Eds.), *Violence and mental disorder* (pp. 229–257). Chicago: University of Chicago Press.

Kluger, R. (1976). *Simple justice: The history of Brown v. Board of Education and Black America's struggle for equality.* New York: Knopf.

Koch, W.J. (1992). *The prevalence and adjudication of ethical complaints about psychologists in British Columbia in 1989–1990.* Unpublished manuscript.

Koch, W.J., & Taylor, S. (1995). Assessment and treatment of motor vehicle accident victims. *Cognitive & Behavioral Practice, 2,* 327–342.

Koehnken, G. (1995). Interviewing adults. In R. Bull and D. Carson (Eds.), *Handbook of psychology in legal contexts* (pp. 215–233). Toronto: Wiley.

Koehnken, G., Thurer, C., & Zorberbier, D. (1994). The cognitive interview: Are interviewers' memories enhanced too? *Applied Cognitive Psychology, 8*, 13–24.

Komaromy, M., Bindman, A.B., Haber, R.J., & Sande, M.A. (1993). Sexual harassment in medical training. *New England Journal of Medicine, 328*, 322–326.

Kong, R. (1998). Canadian crime statistics, 1997 (Catalogue No. 85–002–XPE). *Juristat, 18(11)*. Ottawa: Statistics Canada.

Koss, M.P. (1992). The underdetection of rape: Methodological choices influence incidence estimates. *Journal of Social Issues, 48*, 61–76.

Koss, M.P. (1993). Rape: Scope, impact, interventions, and public policy responses. *American Psychologist, 48*, 1062–1069.

Koss, M.P., Gidycz, C.A., & Wisniewski, N. (1987). The scope of rape: Incidence and prevalence of sexual aggression and victimization in a national sample of higher education students. *Journal of Consulting and Clinical Psychology, 55*, 162–170.

Kovach v. Smith, [1972] 4 W.W.R. 677 (B.C.S.C.).

Kovera, M.B., Gresham, A.W., Borgida, E., Gray, E., & Regan, P.C. (1997). Does expert psychological testimony inform or influence juror decision making? A social cognitive analysis. *Jounal of Applied Psychology, 82*, 178–191.

Kovera, M.B., Levy, R.J., Borgida E., & Penrod, S.D. (1994). Expert testimony in child sexual abuse cases: Effects of expert evidence type and cross examination. *Law and Human Behavior, 18*, 653–674.

Kozol, H., Boucher, R., Garofalo, R. (1972). The diagnosis and treatment of dangerousness. *Crime and Delinquency, 18*, 371–392.

Kramer, G.P., Kerr, N.L., & Carroll, J.S. (1990). Pretrial publicity, judicial remedies, and jury bias. *Law and Human Behavior, 14*, 409–438.

Kropp, P.R. (1998, March). *The Spousal Assault Risk Assessment Guide: Validation and implementation research*. Paper presented at the Biennial Conference of the American Psychology-Law Society, Redondo Beach, California.

Kropp, P.R., & Hart, S.D. (1997a). Assessing risk for violence in wife assaulters: The Spousal Assault Risk Assessment Guide. In C.D. Webster & M.A. Jackson (Eds.), *Impulsivity: Theory, assessment, and treatment*. New York: Guilford.

Kropp, P.R., & Hart, S.D. (1997b). Impulsivity: Theory, assessment, and treatment. In C.D. Webster & M.A. Jackson (Eds.), *Impulsivity: Theory, assessment, and treatment* (pp. 302–325). New York: Guilford.

Kropp, P.R., & Hart, S.D. (in press). The Spousal Assault Risk Assessment Guide (SARA): Reliability and validity in adult male offenders. *Law and Human Behavior*.

Kropp, P.R., Hart, S.D., Webster, C.D., & Eaves, D. (1995). *Manual for the Spousal Assault Risk Assessment Guide* (2nd ed.). Vancouver: British Columbia Institute on Family Violence.

Kropp, P.R., Webster, C.D., Hart, S., & Eaves, D. (1999). *Spousal assault risk assessment: User's guide*. Toronto: Multi-Health Systems, Inc.

Kurz, D. (1993). Physical assaults by husbands: A major social problem. In R.J. Gelles & D.R. Loseke (Eds.), *Current controversies in family violence* (pp. 88–103). Newbury Park, CA: Sage.

Lafree, G., Reskin, B., & Visher, C. (1985). Jurors responses to victims' behavior and legal issues in sexual assault trials. *Social Problems, 32*, 389–407.

Lahey, B.B., & Loeber, R. (1997). Attention-deficit/hyperactivity disorder, oppositional defiant disorder, conduct disorder, and adult antisocial behavior: A life span perspective. In D.M. Stoff, J. Breiling, & J.D. Maser (Eds.), *Handbook of antisocial behavior* (pp. 51–59). New York: Wiley.

Lake, E.S. (1993). An exploration of the violent victim experiences of female offenders. *Violence and Victims, 8*, 41–51.

Lalumière, M.L., & Quinsey, V.L. (1993). The sensitivity of phallometric measures with rapists. *Annals of Sex Research, 6*, 123–138.

Lalumière, M.L., & Quinsey, V.L. (1994). The discriminability of rapists from non-sex offenders using phallometric measures: A meta-analysis. *Criminal Justice and Behavior, 21*, 150–175.

Lamb, M.E., Hershkowitz, I., Sternberg, K.J., Boat, B., & Everson, M.D. (1996). Investigative interviews of alleged sexual abuse victims with and without anatomical dolls. *Child Abuse & Neglect, 20*, 1239–1247.

Lamb, M.E., Sternberg, K.J., Esplin, P.W., Hershkowitz, I., Orbach, Y., & Hovav, M. (1997). Criterion-based content analysis: A field validation study. *Child Abuse & Neglect, 21*, 255–264.

La Novara, P. (1993). A portrait of families in Canada. *Statistics Canada Cat. No. 89–523E*. Ottawa: Minister responsible for Statistics Canada.

La Prairie, C. (1984a). Select socio-economic and criminal justice data on Native women. *Canadian Journal of Criminology, 26*, 161–169.

La Prairie, C. (1984b). Native women and crime. *Perceptions, 7*, 25–27.

La Prairie, C. (1987a). Native women and crime: A theoretical model. *The Canadian Journal of Native Studies, VII*, 121–137.

La Prairie, C. (1987b). Native women and crime in Canada. In E. Adelberg, & C. Currie (Eds.), *Too few to count: Women in conflict with the law*. Vancouver: Press Gang.

Laskin, B. (1986). *Laskin's Canadian constitutional law* (5th ed.). (Revised by N. Finkelstein). Toronto: Carswell.

Latimer v. The Queen (June, 2000). Supreme Court of Canada (No. 26980).

Lavallee v. R. (1990), 55 C.C.C. 3d 97.

Law Reform Commission of Canada (1980). *The jury in criminal trials: (Working paper – Law Reform Commission of Canada; 27)*. Ottawa : The Commission.

Law Society of British Columbia. (1992). *Gender equality in the justice system, Vol. 2.* Vancouver: Law Society.

LeBlanc, M. (1983). Delinquency as an epiphenomenon of adolescence. In R.R. Corrado, M. LeBlanc, & J. Trépanier (Eds.), *Current issues in juvenile justice* (pp. 31–48). Toronto: Butterworths.

LeBlanc, M., & Fréchette, M. (1989). *Male criminal activity from childhood through youth: Multilevel and developmental perspectives.* New York: Springer-Verlag.

Ledwidge, B., Glackman, W., Paredes, J., Chen, R., Dhami, S., Hansen, M., & Higenbottam, J. (1987). Controlled follow-up of patients released by a review panel at one and two years after separation. *Canadian Journal of Psychiatry, 32,* 448–453.

Leichtman, M.D., & Ceci, S.J. (1995). The effects of stereotypes and suggestions on preschoolers' reports. *Developmental Psychology, 31,* 568–578.

Leidig, M.W. (1992). The continuum of violence against women: Psychological and physical consequences. *College Health, 40,* 149–155.

Leippe, M.R. (1994). The appraisal of eyewitness testimony. In D.F. Ross, J.D. Read, & M.P. Toglia (Eds.), *Adult eyewitness testimony: Current trends and development* (pp. 385–418). New York: Cambridge University Press.

Leippe, M.R. (1995). The case for expert testimony about eyewitness memory. *Psychology, Public Policy, and Law, 1,* 909–959.

Leis, T.A., Motiuk, L.L., & Ogloff, J.R.P. (1995). (Eds.). *Forensic psychology: Policy and practice in corrections.* Ottawa: Correctional Service of Canada.

Leo, R.A. (1992). From coercion to deception: The changing nature of police interrogation in America. *Crime, Law, and Social Change, 18,* 35–39.

Leo, R.A. (1996). *Miranda's* revenge: Police interrogation as a confidence game. *Law and Society Review, 30,* 259–288.

Leschied, A.W., Austin, G.W., & Jaffe, P.G. (1988). Impact of the Young Offenders Act on recidivism rates of special needs youth: Clinical and policy implications. *Canadian Journal of Behavioral Science, 20,* 322–331.

Leschied, A.W., & Gendreau, P. (1994). Doing justice in Canada: YOA policies that can promote community safety. *Canadian Journal of Criminology, 36,* 291–303.

Leschied, A.W., & Hyatt, C.W. (1986). Perspective: Section 22(1), consent to treatment order under the Young Offenders Act. *Canadian Journal of Criminology, 28,* 69–78.

Levin, R.L. (1995a). Workplace violence: Navigating through the minefield of legal liability. *Labor Lawyer, 11,* 171–187.

Levin, R.L. (1995b). Workplace violence: Sources of liability, warning signs, and ways to mitigate damages. *Labor Law Journal, 46,* 418–428.

Lidz, C.W., & Mulvey, E.P. (1993). The accuracy of predictions of violence to others. *Journal of the American Medical Association, 269*, 1007–1011.

Liebling, A. (1994). Suicide amongst women prisoners. *Howard Journal of Criminal Justice, 33*, 1–9.

Lind, E.A., & Tyler, T.R. (1988). *The social psychology of procedural justice*. New York: Plenum Press.

Linden, A.M. (1982). *Canadian tort law* (3rd ed). Toronto: Butterworths.

Lindsay, D.S. (1994). Memory source monitoring and eyewitness testimony. In D.F. Ross, J.D. Read, & M.P. Toglia (Eds.), *Adult eyewitness testimony: Current trends and development* (pp. 27–55). New York: Cambridge University Press.

Lindsay, D.S., & Briere, J. (1998). The controversy regarding recovered memories of childhood sexual abuse: Pitfalls, bridges, and future directions. *Journal of Interpersonal Violence, 12*, 631–647.

Lindsay, D.S., Gonzales, V., & Eso, K. (1995). Aware and unaware uses of memories of post event suggestions. In M.S. Zaragoza, J.R. Graham, G.C.N. Hall, R. Hirschman, & Y.S. Ben-Porath (Eds.), *Memory and testimony in the child witness* (pp. 86–108). Thousand Oaks: Sage.

Lindsay, D.S., Johnson, M.K., & Kwon, P. (1991). Developmental changes in memory source monitoring. *Journal of Experimental Child Psychology, 52*, 297–318.

Lindsay, D.S., & Read, J.D. (1994). Psychotherapy and memories of childhood sexual abuse. *Applied Cognitive Psychology, 8*, 281–338.

Lindsay, D.S., & Read, J.D. (1995). "Memory work" and recovered memories of childhood sexual abuse: Scientific evidence and public, professional, and personal issues. *Psychology, Public Policy, and Law, 1*, 846–908.

Lindsay, D.S., Read, J.D., & Sharma, K. (1998). Accuracy and confidence in person identification: The relationship is strong when witnessing conditions vary widely (as they do across real-world witnesses). *Psychological Science, 9*, 215–218.

Lindsay, P.S. (1977). Fitness to stand trial in Canada: An overview in light of the recommendations of the law reform commission of Canada. *Criminal Law Quarterly, 19*, 303–348.

Lindsay, R.C.L. (1994a). Expectations of eyewitness performance: Jurors, verdicts do not follow from their beliefs. In D.F. Ross, J.D. Read, & M.P. Toglia (Eds.), *Adult eyewitness testimony: Current trends and development* (pp. 362–384). New York: Cambridge University Press.

Lindsay, R.C.L. (1994b). Biased lineups: Where do they come from? In D.F. Ross, J.D. Read, & M.P. Toglia (Eds.), *Adult eyewitness testimony: Current trends and development* (pp. 182–200). New York: Cambridge University Press.

Lindsay, R.C.L., Ross, D.F., Lea, J.A., & Carr, C. (1995). What's fair when a child testifies? *Journal of Applied Social Psychology, 25*, 870–888.

Lindsay, R.C.L., Wallbridge, H., & Drennan, D. (1987). Do the clothes make the man? An exploration of the effect of lineup attire on eyewitness identification accuracy. *Canadian Journal of Behavioural Science, 19*, 463–478.

Lindsay, R.C.L., & Wells, G.L. (1985). Improving eyewitness identifications from lineups: Simultaneous versus sequential lineup presentation. *Journal of Applied Psychology, 70*, 556–564.

Link, B.G., & Stueve, A. (1994). Psychotic symptoms and the violent/illegal behavior of mental patients compared to community controls. In J. Monahan & H.J. Steadman (Eds.), *Violence and mental disorder* (pp. 137–159). Chicago: University of Chicago Press.

Lipsey, M.W. (1992). Juvenile delinquency treatment: A meta-analytic inquiry into the variability of effects. In T.D. Cook, H. Cooper, D.S. Cordray, H. Hartmann, L.V. Hedges, R.J. Light, T.A. Louis, & F. Mosteller (Eds.), *Meta-analysis for explanation* (pp. 83–127). New York: Russell Sage Foundation.

Lipsey, M.W., & Wilson, D.B. (1993). The efficacy of psychological, educational, and behavioral treatment: Confirmation from meta-analysis. *American Psychologist, 48*, 1181–1209.

Loftus, E.F. (1979a). *Eyewitness testimony.* Cambridge, MA: Harvard University Press.

Loftus, E.F. (1979b). The malleability of human memory: Information introduced after we view an incident can transform memory. *American Scientist, 67*, 312–320.

Loftus, E.F. (1986). Experimental psychologist as advocate or impartial educator. *Law and Human Behavior, 10*, 63–78.

Loftus, E.F. (1993). The reality of repressed memories. *American Psychologist, 48*, 518–537.

Loftus, E.F., & Doyle, J. (1991). *Eyewitness testimony: Civil and criminal.* (3rd ed.) New York: Kluwer Law Book Publishers.

Loftus, E.F., & Ketcham, K. (1994). *The myth of repressed memory: False memories and allegations of abuse.* New York: St. Martin's Press.

Logan, C. (1918). The psychology of gossip. *Canadian Magazine, 31*, 106–109.

Loh, W.D. (1981a). Perspectives on psychology and law. *Journal of Applied Social Psychology, 11*, 314–355.

Loh, W.D. (1981b). Psycholegal research: Past and Present. *Michigan Law Review, 79*, 659–707.

Long, B.L. (1994). Psychiatric diagnoses in sexual harassment cases. *Bulletin of the American Academy of Psychiatry and the Law, 22*, 195–203.

Longford, G. (1996). *The use of the cognitive interview by police officers trained on the National Investigative Interviewing Course.* Unpublished master's thesis. University of Portsmouth, UK.

Lonsway, K.A., & Fitzgerald, L.F. (1994). Rape myths: In review. *Psychology of Women Quarterly, 18,* 133–164.

Lösel, F. (1998). Treatment and management of psychopaths. In D.J. Cooke, A.E. Forth, & R.D. Hare (Eds.), *Psychopathy: Theory, research and implications for society* (pp. 303–354). Dordrecht, The Netherlands: Kluwer.

Lougheed v. Sillett (1994), 6 R.F.L. (4th) 10 (Ont. C.A.).

Loucks, A.D. (1995). *Criminal behavior, violent behavior, and prison maladjustment in federal female offenders.* Unpublished doctoral dissertation, Queen's University, Kingston, ON, Canada.

Louks, A., & Zamble, E. (1994). Some comparisons of female and male serious offenders. *Forum on Corrections Research, 1,* 22–28.

Lovegrove, A. (1989). *Judicial decision making, sentencing policy and numerical guidance.* New York: Springer-Verlag.

Low, P.W., Jeffries, J.C., & Bonnie, R.J. (1986). *The trial of John W. Hinckley, Jr.: A case study in the insanity defense.* Mineola, NY: Foundation Press.

Lowenstein, M., Binder, R.L., & McNeil, D.E. (1990). The relationship between admission symptoms and hospital assaults. *Hospital and Community Psychiatry, 41,* 311–313.

Loy, P.H., & Stewart, L.P. (1984). The extent and effects of the sexual harassment or working women. *Sociological Focus, 17,* 31–43.

Luus, C.A.E., & Wells, G.L. (1994a). Eyewitness identification confidence. In D.F. Ross, J.D. Read, & M.P. Toglia (Eds.), *Adult eyewitness testimony: Current trends and development* (pp. 348–361). New York: Cambridge University Press.

Luus, C.A.E., & Wells, G.L. (1994b). The malleability of eyewitness confidence: Co-witness and perseverance effects. *Journal of Applied Psychology, 79,* 714–723.

Luus, C.A.E., Wells, G.L., & Turtle, J.W. (1995). Child eyewitnesses: Seeing is believing. *Journal of Applied Psychology, 80,* 317–326.

Lykken, D.T. (1981). *A tremor in the blood.* New York: McGraw-Hill.

M. (K.) v. M. (H.), [1992] 3 S.C.R. 85, 96 D.L.R. (4th) 289, 142 N.R. 321, 57 O.A.C. 321, 14 C.C.L.T. (2d) 1.

MacCoun, R.J., & Kerr, N.L. (1988). Asymmetric influence in mock deliberation: Jurors' bias for leniency. *Journal of Personality and Social Psychology, 54,* 21–33.

Macdonald, J.M., & Michaud, D.L. (1987). *The confession: Interrogation and criminal profiles for police officers.* Denver, CO: Apache.

MacKenzie, D.L., & Goodstein, L. (1985). Long-term incarceration impacts and characteristics of long-term offenders: An empirical analysis. *Criminal Justice and Behavior, 12,* 395–414.

Mackey, T., Sereika, S.M., Weissfeld, L.A., Hacker, S.S., Zender, J.F., & Heard, S. (1992). Factors associated with long-term depressive symptoms of sexual assault victims. *Archives of Psychiatric Nursing, VI,* 10–25.

Mackie, M. (1974). Ethnic stereotypes and prejudice: Alberta Indians, Hutterites, and Ukrainians. *Canadian Ethnic Studies, 6,* 39–52.

MacLeod, M.D., Frowley, J.N., & Shepherd, J.W. (1994). Whole body information: Its relevance to eyewitnesses. In D.F. Ross, J.D. Read, & M.P. Toglia (Eds.), *Adult eyewitness testimony: Current trends and development* (pp. 125–143). New York: Cambridge University Press.

Maier, G.J., & Miller, R.D. (1989). Models of mental health service delivery to correctional institutions. In R. Rosner & R.B. Harmon (Eds.), *Correctional psychiatry: Critical issues in American psychiatry and the law* (pp. 231–241). New York: Plenum.

Mailloux, D.L. (1999). *Victimization, coping, and psychopathy: Associations with violent behavior among female offenders.* Unpublished master's thesis, Carleton University, Ottawa, ON, Canada.

Malinosky-Rummell, R., & Hansen, D.J. (1993). Long-term consequences of childhood physical abuse. *Psychological Bulletin, 114,* 68–79.

Malpass, R.S. (1996). Enhancing eyewitness memory. In S.L. Sporer, R.S. Malpass, & G. Köhnken (Eds.), *Psychological issues in eyewitness identification* (pp. 177–204). Mahwah, NJ: Lawrence Erlbaum Associates.

Malpass, R.S., & Devine, P.G. (1981). Guided memory in eyewitness identification. *Journal of Applied Psychology, 66,* 343–350.

Malt, U.F., Hoivak, B., & Blikra, G. (1993). Psychosocial consequences of road accidents. *European Psychiatry, 8,* 227–228.

Malt, U.F., & Olafsen, O.M. (1992). Psychological appraisal and emotional response to physical injury: A clinical, phenomenological study of 109 adults. *Psychiatric Medicine, 10,* 117–134.

Mansfield, P.K., Koch, P.B., Henderson, J., Vicary, J.R., Cohn, M., & Young, E.W. (1991). The job climate for women in traditionally male blue-collar occupations. *Sex Roles, 25,* 63–79.

Marin, R.J. (1996). *Admissibility of statements* (9th ed.). Aurora, ON: Canada Law Book.

Marlatt, G.A., & Gordon, J. (1980). *Determinants of relapse: Implications for the maintenance of change.* In P.O. Davidson & S.M. Davidson (Eds.), *Behavioral medicine: Changing health lifestyles* (pp. 410–452). New York: Brunner/Mazel.

Marlatt, G.A., & Gordon, J. (1985). *Relapse prevention. New York*: Guilford.

Marques, J.K., Day, D.M., Nelson, C., & West, M.A. (1993). Findings and recommendations from California's experimental treatment program. In G.C.N. Hall, R. Hirschman, J.R. Graham, & M.S. Zaragoza (Eds.), *Sexual aggression: Issues in etiology, assessment and treatment* (pp. 197–214). Washington, DC: Taylor & Francis.

Marquis, K.S., & Detweiler, R.A. (1985). Does adopted mean different? An attributional analysis. *Journal of Personality and Social Psychology, 48,* 1054–1066.

Marshall v. Nova Scotia (A.G.), [1989] 2 S.C.R. 788, 62 D.L.R. (4th) 354, 100 N.R. 73, 93 N.S.R. (2d) 123, 271, 41 Admin. L.R. 121, 50 C.C.C. (3d) 486.

Marshall, L. (1992). The Severity of Violence Against Women Scales. *Journal of Family Violence, 7,* 189–203.

Marshall, L. (1996). Assessment, treatment, and theorizing about sex offenders: Developments during the past twenty years and future directions. *Criminal Justice and Behaviour, 23,* 162–199.

Marshall, W.L., Hudson, S.M., & Ward, T. (1992). Sexual deviance. In P.H. Wilson (Ed.), *Principles and practice of relapse prevention* (pp. 235–254). New York: Guilford Press.

Marshall, W.L., & Pithers, W.D. (1994). A reconsideration of treatment outcome with sex offenders. *Criminal Justice and Behaviour, 21(1),* 10–27.

McCallum v. Waito (1983), 29 C.C.L.T. 1 (Ont. H.C.).

McCann, J.T. (1992). Criminal personality profiling in the investigation of violent crime: Recent advances and future directions. *Behavioral Sciences and the Law, 10,* 475–481.

McCloskey, M., & Egeth, H. (1983). Eyewitness identification: What can a psychologist tell a jury? *American Psychologist, 38,* 550–563.

McCloskey, M., & Zaragoza, M. (1985). Misleading post event information and memory for events: Arguments and evidence against memory impairment hypothesis. *Journal of Experimental Psychology: General, 114,* 1–16.

McCord, J. (1982). The Cambridge-Somerville Youth Study: A sobering lesson on treatment, prevention, and evaluation. In A.J. McSweeny, W.J. Fremouw, & R.P. Hawkins (Eds.), *Practical program evaluation in youth treatment* (pp. 11–23). Springfield, IL: Charles C. Thomas.

McCorkell v. Riverview Hospital, 81 B.C.L.R. (2d) 273, [1993] 8 W.W.R. 169, 104 D.L.R. (4th) 391 (S.C.).

McConville, M., & Baldwin, J. (1982). The role of interrogation in crime discovery and conviction. *British Journal of Criminology, 22,* 165–175.

McCormack, A. (1985). The sexual harassment of students by teachers: The case of students in science. *Sex Roles, 13,* 21–32.

McCormick, C.T. (1972). *Handbook of the law of evidence* (2nd ed.). St Paul, MN: West.

McCormick, M.C., Shapiro, S., & Starfield, B.H. (1981). Injury and its correlates among 1-year-old children. *American Journal of Diseases of Children, 135*, 159–163.

McEvoy, M. (1995–1996). Controversies and courts: The Canadian response to the Disputed Memory debate. *Treating Abuse Today, 5(6)–6(1)*, 13–22.

McGarry, A.L. (1965). Competency for trial and due process via the state hospital. *American Journal of Psychiatry, 122*, 623–631.

McGraw, B.D., Farthing-Capowich, D., & Keilitz, I. (1985). The "guilty but mentally ill" plea and verdict: Current state of the knowledge. *Villanova Law Review, 30*, 117–191.

McLean, M. (1995). Quality investigation? Police interviewing of witnesses. *Medicine, Science and Law, 35*, 116–122.

McMahon, R.J. (1994). Diagnosis, assessment, and treatment of externalizing problems in children: The role of longitudinal data. *Journal of Consulting and Clinical Psychology, 62*, 901–917.

McWilliams, P.K. (1988), with updates. *Canadian criminal evidence*. Aurora, ON: Canada Law Book.

Medernach v. Medernach (1987), 56 Sask. R. 240 (C.A.).

Meehl, P.E. (1954). *Clinical versus statistical prediction: A theoretical analysis and review of the evidence*. Minneapolis, MN: University of Minnesota Press.

Melton, G.B. (1987). Training in psychology and law. In I.D. Weiner & A.K. Hess (Eds.), *Handbook of forensic psychology* (pp. 681–697). New York: Wiley.

Melton, G.B., Petrila, J., Poythress, N.G., & Slobogin, C. (1997). *Psychological evaluations for the courts: A handbook for mental health professionals and lawyers* (2nd ed.). New York: Guilford.

Memon, A. (1998). Telling it all: The Cognitive Interview. In A. Memon, A. Vrij, & R. Bull (Eds.), *Psychology and law: Truthfulness, accuracy and credibility* (pp. 170–187). London: McGraw-Hill.

Memon, A., & Bull, R. (1991). The cognitive interview: Its origins, empirical support, evaluation and practical implications. *Journal of Community & Applied Social Psychology, 1*, 291–307.

Memon, A., & Shuman, D.W. (1998) Juror perception of experts in civil disputes: The role of race and gender. *Law and Psychology Review, 22*, 179–197.

Memon, A., & Stevenage, S.V. (1996a). Interviewing witnesses: What works and what doesn't? *Psycholoquy, 7(6)*, witness-memory. 1. memon.

Memon, A., & Stevenage, S.V. (1996b). A clarification of the importance of comparison groups and accuracy rates with the CI: A reply to Fisher. *Psycholoquy, witness-memory.* 14. memon.

Memon, A., Wark, L., Holley, A., Bull, R., & Koehnken, G. (1996). Interviewer behaviour in investigative interviews. *Psychology, Crime & Law, 3*, 181–201.

Memon, A., Wark, L. Holley, A., Bull, R., & Koehnken, G. (1997). Eyewitness performance in cognitive and structured interviews. *Memory, 5*, 639–656.

Memon, A., & Yarmey, A.D. (1999). Earwitness recall and identification: Comparison of the cognitive interview and the structured interview. *Perceptual and Motor Skills, 88*, 797–807.

Mental Health Act, R.S.O. (1990), c. M-7, s. 20.

Mental Health Services Amendment Act, 1993, S.S. c. 59.

Mental Health Services Amendment Act, 1996, S.S. c. 17.

Menzies, R.J., & Webster, C.D. (1995). Construction and validation of risk assessments in a six-year follow-up of forensic patients: A tridimensional analysis. *Journal of Consulting and Clinical Psychology, 63*, 766–778.

Menzies, R.J., Webster, C.D., & Hart, S.D. (1995). Observations on the rise of risk in psychology and law. In *Proceedings of the Fifth Symposium on Violence and Aggression* (pp. 91–107). Saskatoon: University Extension Press, University of Saskatchewan.

Merskky, H., & Woodforde, J.M. (1972). Psychiatric sequelae of minor head injury. *Brain, 95*, 521–528.

Messman, T.L., & Long, P.J. (1996). Child sexual abuse and its relationship to revictimization in adult women: A review. *Clinical Psychology Review, 16*, 397–420.

Mewett, A.W. (1996). *An introduction to the criminal process in Canada* (3rd ed.). Scarborough, ON: Carswell.

Mewett, A.W., & Manning, M. (1985). *Criminal law* (2nd ed). Toronto: Butterworths.

Mezzo v. The Queen (1986), 30 D.L.R. (4th) 161, 27 C.C.C. (3d) 97.

Mickenberg, I. (1987). A pleasant surprise: The guilty but mentally ill verdict has both succeeded in its own right and successfully preserved the traditional role of the insanity defense. *Cincinnati Law Review, 55*, 943–996.

Milgaard v. Saskatchewan (1994), 118 D.L.R. (4th) 653, 9 W.W.R. 305, 123 Sask. R. 164, 28 C.P.C. (3d) 137.

Milgram, S. (1963). Behavioral study of obedience. *Journal of Abnormal and Social Psychology, 67*, 371–378.

Millar, W., & Adams, O. (1991). *Accidents in Canada: Statistics Canada general social survey analysis series*. Ottawa: Minister of Industry, Science, and Technology.

Miller, G.R., & Stiff, J.B. (1993). *Deceptive communication*. London: Sage.

Miller, H. (1961a). Accident neurosis. *British Medical Journal, 5230*, 919–925.

Miller, H. (1961b). Accident neurosis. *British Medical Journal, 5231*, 992–998.

Miller, R.D., & Germain, E.J. (1988). The retrospective evaluation of competency to stand trial. *International Journal of Law and Psychiatry, 11*, 113–125.

Millon, T. (1987). *Manual for the Millon Clinical Multiaxial Inventory-II*. Minneapolis, MN: National Computing Systems.

Milner, J.S. (1986). *The child abuse potential inventory manual* (2nd ed.). DeKalb, IL: Psytec, Inc.

Milner, J.S. (1993). Social information processing and physical child abuse. *Clinical Psychology Review, 13*, 275–294.

Minister touts community crime plan. (1998), June 5. *The Toronto Star*, p. A27.

Mnookin, R.H. (1975). Child-custody adjudication: Judicial functions in the face of indeterminacy. *Law and Contemporary Problems, 39*, 226–292.

Moffitt, T.E. (1993). Adolescence-limited and life-course-persistent anti-social behaviour: A developmental taxonomy. *Psychological Review, 100*, 674–701.

Monahan, J. (1981). *Predicting violent behavior: An assessment of clinical techniques*. Beverly Hills, CA: Sage.

Monahan, J. (1984). The prediction of violent behavior: Toward a second generation of theory and policy. *American Journal of Psychiatry, 141*, 10–15.

Monahan, J. (1988). Risk assessment of violence among the mentally disordered: Generating useful knowledge. *International Journal of Law and Psychiatry, 11*, 249–257.

Monahan, J. (1992). Mental disorder and violent behavior: Perceptions and evidence. *American Psychologist, 47*, 511–521.

Monahan, J. (1995). *The clinical prediction of violent behavior*. Northvale, NJ: Jason Aronson. (Original work published in 1981).

Monahan, J. (1996). Violence prediction: The past twenty years and the next twenty years. *Criminal Justice and Behavior, 23(1)*, 107–120.

Monahan, J. (1997). Foreword. In C.D. Webster and M.A. Jackson (Eds.), *Impulsivity: Theory, assessment, and treatment* (pp. ix–xi). New York: Guilford.

Monahan, J., & Steadman, H.J. (1994). Toward a rejuvenation of risk assessment research. In J. Monahan & H.J. Steadman (Eds.), *Violence and mental disorder* (pp. 1–17). Chicago: University of Chicago Press.

Monahan, J., & Walker, L. (1988). Social science research in law: A new paradigm. *American Psychologist, 43*, 465–472.

Monahan, J., & Walker, L. (1990). *Social sciences in law: Cases and materials* (2nd ed.). Westbury, NY: Foundation Press.

Monroe, L.D., & Schellenbach, C.J. (1989). Relationship of Child Abuse Potential Inventory scores to parental responses: A construct validity study. *Child and Family Behavior Therapy, 11*, 39–58.

Moran, G., & Cutler, B.L. (1991). The prejudicial impact of pretrial publicity. *Journal of Applied Social Psychology, 21*, 345–367.

Moran, G., & Cutler, B.L. (1997). Bogus publicity items and the contingency between awareness and media-induced pretrial prejudice. *Law and Human Behavior, 21*, 339–344.

Moran, R. (1981). *Knowing right from wrong: The insanity defense of Daniel McNaughton.* New York: Macmillan, Free Press.

Moran, R. (1985). The modern foundation for the insanity defense: The cases of James Hadfield (1800) and Daniel McNaughtan (1843). *Annals of the American Academy of Political and Social Science, 477*, 31–42.

Morris, A. (1990). Women, crime and criminal justice: Gender differences in crime. In N.A. Hilton, M.J. Jackson, and C.D. Webster (Eds.), *Clinical criminology: Theory, research and practice.* Toronto: Canadian Scholars' Press.

Morris, N. (1968). Psychiatry and the dangerous criminal. *Southern California Law Review, 41*, 514–586.

Morrow, P.C., McElroy, J.C., & Phillips, C.M. (1994). Sexual harassment behaviors and work related perceptions and attitudes. *Journal of Vocational Behavior, 45*, 295–309.

Mossman, D. (1994). Assessing predictions of violence: Being accurate about accuracy. *Journal of Consulting and Clinical Psychology, 62*, 783–792.

Motiuk, L.L., & Porporino, F.J. (1991). *The prevalence, nature and severity of mental health problems among federal male inmates in Canadian penitentiaries* (Research Report No. 24). Ottawa: Correctional Service of Canada.

Muehlenhard, C.L., & Linton, M.A. (1987). Date rape and sexual aggression in dating situations: Incidence and risk factors. *Journal of Counselling Psychology, 34*, 186–196.

Muir, G., Lonsway, K., & Payne, D. (1996). Rape myth acceptance among Scottish and American students. *Journal of Social Psychology, 136*, 261–162.

Mulvey, E.P., & Lidz, C.W. (1993). Measuring patient violence in dangerousness research. *Law and Human Behavior, 17*, 277–288.

Mulvey, E.P., & Lidz, C.W. (1995). Conditional prediction: A model for research on dangerousness to others in a new era. *International Journal of Law and Psychiatry, 18*, 129–143.

Munsterberg, H. (1908). *On the witness stand.* Garden City, NY: Doubleday.

Munsterberg, H. (1909). *On the witness stand: Essays on psychology and crime.* New York: Doubleday.

Murray, K., & Gough, D.A. (Eds.). (1991). *Interviewing in child sexual abuse.* Edinburgh: Scottish Academic Press.

Murrell, A.J., Olson, J.E., & Frieze, I.H. (1995). Sexual harassment and gender discrimination: A longitudinal study of women managers. *Journal of Social Issues, 51*, 139–149.

Myers, D.G. (1999). *Social Psychology* (6th ed.). New York: McGraw Hill.

Myers, J.E.B. (1993). Expert testimony regarding child sexual abuse. *Child Abuse and Neglect, 17*, 175–185.

Myers, M. (1979). Rule departures and making law: Juries and their verdicts. *Law and Society, 13*, 781–797.

National Institute of Justice. (1996). *Convicted by juries, exonerated by science: Case studies in the use of DNA evidence to establish innocence after trial*. Washington, DC: NCJ 161258.

National Institute of Justice. (1999). *Eyewitness evidence: A guide for law enforcement*. Washington, DC: NCJ 178240.

National Parole Board. (1986). *Mission statement of the national parole board* (Catalogue No. JS92–31/1986).Ottawa: Minister of Supply and Services Canada.

National Parole Board. (1999a). *National Parole Board policy manual* [On-line]. Available Internet: http://www.npb-cnlc.gc.ca/mantoce.htm.

National Parole Board. (1999b). *Public perceptions vs. reality* [On-line]. Available Internet: http://www.npb-cnlc.gc.ca/quize.htm.

Neary, A. (1990). *DSM-III and Psychopathy Checklist assessment of antisocial personality disorder in Black and White female felons*. Unpublished doctoral dissertation, University of Missouri, St. Louis.

Neil v. Biggers, 409 U.S. 188 (1972).

Neisser, U., & Harsch, N. (1992). Phantom flashbulbs: False recollections of hearing the story about Challenger. In U. Neisser and E. Winograd (Eds.), *Affect and accuracy in recall: Studies of flashbulb memories*. New York: Cambridge University Press.

Nemeth, C. (1981). Jury trials: Psychology and the law. *Advances in Experimental Social Psychology, 14*, 309–367.

Nersesian, W.S., Petit, M.R., Shaper, R., Lemieux, D., & Naor, E. (1985). Childhood death and poverty: A study of all childhood deaths in Maine, 1976 to 1980. *Pediatrics, 75*, 41–50.

Newberger, C.M., & Cook, S.J.U. (1983). Parental awareness and child abuse: A cognitive-developmental analysis of urban and rural samples. *American Journal of Orthopsychiatry, 53*, 512–524.

Newell, C.E., Rosenfeld, P., & Culbertson, A.L. (1995). Sexual harassment experiences and equal opportunity perceptions of navy women. *Sex Roles, 32*, 159–168.

Newfoundland (Director of Child Welfare) v. S. (J.) (1994), 115 Nfld., & P.E.I.R. 14, 360 A.P.R. 14 (Nfld. C.A.).

Nicholls, T.L., Jack, L.A., & Ogloff, J.R.P. (1998). *Comorbidity of violence against self and violence against others in a civil psychiatric population*. Poster presented at the biennial meeting of the American Psychology-Law Society, Redondo Beach, CA.

Nicholls, T.L., Ogloff, J.R.P., & Douglas, K.S. (1997). *Comparing risk assessments with female and male psychiatric outpatients: Utility of the HCR-20 and Psychopathy Checklist: Screening Version.* Paper presented at the annual convention of the American Psychological Association, Chicago.

Nickerson, S., Mayo, C., & Smith, A. (1986). Racism in the courtroom. In J.F. Dovidio & S.L. Gaertner (Eds.), *Prejudice, discrimination, and racism* (pp. 255–278). Orlando, FL: Academic.

Niedermeier, K.E., Horowitz, I.A., & Kerr, N.L. (1999). Informing jurors of their nullification power: A route to a just verdict or judicial chaos? *Law and Human Behavior, 23,* 331–351.

Nietzel, M.T., & Dillehay, R. (1982). Psychologists as consultants for changes of venue: The use of public opinion surveys. Paper presented at the Annual meeting of the Academy of Criminal Justice Sciences, Louisville, KY.

Nietzel, M.T., McCarthy, D.M., & Kern, M.J. (1999). Juries: The current state of the empirical literature. In R. Roesch, S.D. Hart, & J.R.P. Ogloff (Eds.), *Psychology and the law: The state of the discipline* (pp. 23–52). New York: Kluwer Academic/Plenum Publishers.

Nisbett, R.E., & Wilson, T.D. (1977). Telling more than we can know: Verbal reports on mental processes. *Psychological Review, 84,* 231–259.

Norris, F.H. (1992). Epidemiology of trauma: Frequency and impact of different potentially traumatic events on different demographic groups. *Journal of Consulting and Clinical Psychology, 60,* 409–418.

Norris, J. (1998). R. v. McIntoch: "Soft sciences" in the Ontario Court of Appeal. *Sexual Offences Law Reporter, 4,* 6–8.

Norris, J., & Cubbins, L.A. (1992). Dating, drinking, and rape effects of victim's and assailant's alcohol consumption on judgements of their behavior and traits. *Psychology of Women Quarterly, 16,* 179–191.

Norris, J., & Edward, M. (1995). Myths, hidden facts and common sense: Expert opinion evidence and the assessment of credibility. *Criminal Law Quarterly, 38,* 73–103.

Notification of sex offenders' release debated. (1998, June 11). *Winnipeg Free Press,* p. A12.

Nova Scotia (Minister of Community Services) v. S. (S.M.) (1992), 112 N.S.R. (2d) 258, 307 A.P.R. 258, 41 R.F.L. (3d) 321 (C.A.).

Nuffield, N. (1982). *Parole decision-making in Canada: Research towards decision guidelines.* Ottawa: Ministry of Supply and Services Canada.

O'Donohue, W., & Bradley, A.R. (1999). Conceptual and empirical issues in child custody evaluations. *Clinical Psychology: Science and Practice, 6*, 310–322.

Ofshe, R.J. (1992). Inadvertent hypnosis during interrogation: False confession due to dissociative state; mis-identified multiple personality and the Satanic cult hypnosis. *International Journal of Clinical and Experimental Hypnosis, XL*, 125–156.

Ofshe, R.J., & Watters, E. (1994). *Making monsters: False memories, psychotherapy, and sexual hysteria.* New York: Scribner.

Ogloff, J.R.P. (1990). Law and psychology in Canada: The need for training and research. *Canadian Psychology, 31*, 61–73.

Ogloff, J.R.P. (1991a). A comparison of insanity defence standards on juror decision making. *Law and Human Behavior, 15*, 509–531.

Ogloff, J.R.P. (1991b). *The use of the insanity defence in British Columbia: A qualitative analysis.* Ottawa: Department of Justice Canada.

Ogloff, J.R.P. (1995a). Information sharing and related ethical and legal issues for psychologists working in corrections. In T.A. Leis, L.L. Motiuk, & J.R.P. Ogloff (Eds.), *Forensic psychology: Policy and practice in corrections* (pp. 15–23). Ottawa: Correctional Service of Canada.

Ogloff, J.R.P. (1995b). Navigating the quagmire: Legal and ethical guidelines. In D. Martin & A. Moore (Eds.), *First steps in the art of intervention* (pp. 347–376). Pacific Grove, CA: Brooks/Cole.

Ogloff, J.R.P. (1996, July). *The Surrey Pretrial Mental Health Program: Community component evaluation.* British Columbia Forensic Psychiatric Services Commission.

Ogloff, J.R.P. (1998). *A review of mental health services in the British Columbia Corrections Branch: Planning for essential services.* Corrections Branch for British Columbia.

Ogloff, J.R.P. (1999). Ethical and legal contours of forensic psychology. In R. Roesch, S.D. Hart, & J.R.P. Ogloff (Eds.), *Psychology and law: The state of the discipline* (pp. 405–422). New York, NY: Kluwer Academic/Plenum Publishers.

Ogloff, J.R.P. (2000). Two steps forward and one step backward: The law and psychology movement(s) in the 20th century. *Law and Human Behavior, 24*, 457–483.

Ogloff, J.R.P. (in press). Jingoism, dogmatism and other evils in legal psychology: Lessons learned in the 20th century. In R. Roesch, R. Corrado, & R. Dempster (Eds.), *Psychology in the courts: International advances in knowledge.* Amsterdam: Harwood Academic.

Ogloff, J.R.P., & Finkelman, D. (1999). Law and psychology: An overview. In R. Roesch, S.D. Hart, & J.R.P. Ogloff (Eds.), *Psychology and law: The state of the discipline* (pp. 1–20). New York, NY: Kluwer Academic/Plenum Publishers.

Ogloff, J.R.P., Finkelman, D., Otto, R.K., & Bulling, D.J. (1990). Preventing the detention of non-criminal mentally ill people in jails: The need for emergency protective custody units. *Nebraska Law Review, 69*, 434–471.

Ogloff, J.R.P., & Grant, I. (1997, August). *Involuntary commitment, review panel decision making, and risk assessment*. Symposium presented at the annual meeting of the American Psychological Association, Chicago.

Ogloff, J.R.P., & Nicholls, T.L. (1997, June). *A review of the delivery of services at the Burnaby Correctional Centre for Women*. Correctional Service of Canada.

Ogloff, J.R.P., & Otto, R.K. (1989). Mental health interventions in jails. In P.A. Keller & S.R. Heyman (Eds.), *Innovations in clinical practice: A source book* (Volume 8, pp. 357–369). Sarasota, FL: Professional Resource Exchange.

Ogloff, J.R.P., & Otto, R.K. (1991). Are research participants truly informed? Readability of informed consent forms used in research. *Ethics and Behavior, 1*, 239–252.

Ogloff, J.R.P., & Polvi, N.H. (1998). Legal evidence and expert testimony. In D. Turner & M. Uhlemann (Eds.), *A legal handbook for the helping professional* (2nd ed.) (pp. 379–401). Victoria, BC: The Sedgewick Society for Consumer and Public Education.

Ogloff, J.R.P., Roberts, C.F., & Roesch, R. (1993). The insanity defense: Legal standards and clinical assessment. *Applied and Preventative Psychology, 2*, 163–178.

Ogloff, J.R.P., Roesch, R., & Hart, S.D. (1994). Mental health services in jails and prisons: Legal, clinical, and policy issues. *Law and Psychology Review, 18*, 109–136.

Ogloff, J.R.P., & Rose, V.G. (in press). Challenge for cause in Canadian criminal jury trials: Legal and psychological perspectives. *Alberta Law Review*.

Ogloff, J.R.P., Schweighofer, A., Turnbull, S., & Whittemore, K. (1992). Empirical research and the insanity defense: How much do we really know? In J.R.P. Ogloff (Ed.), *Psychology and law: The broadening of the discipline* (pp. 171–210). Durham, NC: Carolina Academic Press.

Ogloff, J.R.P., Tien, G., Roesch, R., & Eaves, D. (1991). A model for the provision of jail mental health services: An integrative, community-based approach. *Journal of Mental Health Administration, 18*, 209–222.

Ogloff, J.R.P., Tomkins, A.J., & Bersoff, D.N. (1996). Education and training in psychology and law/criminal justice: Historical foundations, present structures, and future developments. *Criminal Justice and Behavior, 23*, 200–235.

Ogloff, J.R.P., & Vidmar, N. (1994). The impact of pretrial publicity on jurors: A study to compare the relative effects of television and print media in a child sex abuse case. *Law and Human Behavior, 18*, 507–525.

Olds, D.L., Henderson, C.R., Chamberlin, R., & Tatelbaum, R. (1986). Preventing child abuse and neglect: A randomized trial of nurse home visitation. *Pediatrics, 78,* 65–78.

Olson, R. (1976). Index of suspicion: Screening of child abusers. *American Journal of Nursing, 76,* 108–110.

O'Mahony, P. (1992). The Kerry Babies case: Towards a social psychological analysis. *Irish Journal of Psychology, 13,* 223–238.

Ontario Law Reform Commission. (1994). *Consultation paper on the use of jury trials in civil cases.* Toronto: Ontario Law Reform Commission.

Ornstein, P.A., Gordon, B.N., & Larus, D.M. (1992). Children's memory for a personally experienced event: Implications for testimony. *Applied Cognitive Psychology, 6,* 49–60.

Ortiz, D. (1984). *Gambling scams.* New York: Dodd, Mead & Co.

Osborne, J.A. (1995). The Canadian criminal law. In M.A. Jackson & C.T. Griffiths (Eds.), *Canadian criminology: Perspectives on crime and criminality* (2nd ed.) (pp. 273–306). Toronto: Harcourt Brace.

O'Shea, K.A., & Fletcher, B.R. (1997). *Female offenders: An annotated bibliography.* Westport, CT: Greenwood.

Ottawa, churches seek common front on suits. (1998), June 9. *The Vancouver Sun,* p. A5.

Otto, A.L., Penrod, S.D., & Dexter, H.R. (1994). The biasing impact of pretrial publicity on juror judgments. *Law and Human Behavior, 18,* 453–469.

Otto, R. (1992). The prediction of dangerous behavior: A review and analysis of "second generation" research. *Forensic Reports, 5,* 103–133.

Otto, R.K., Heilbrun, K., & Grisso, T. (1990). Training and credentialing in forensic psychology. *Behavioral Sciences and the Law, 8,* 217–232.

Otto, R.K., Ogloff, J.R.P., & Small, M.A. (1991). Confidentiality and informed consent in psychotherapy: Clinicians' knowledge and practices in Florida and Nebraska. *Forensic Reports, 4,* 379–389.

Paciocco, D.M. (1996). The evidence of children: Testing the rules against what we know. *Queen's Law Journal, 21,* 345–393.

Paciocco, D., & Steusser, L. (1996). *Essentials of Canadian law: The law of evidence.* Concord, ON: Irwin Law.

Paglia, A., & Schuller, R.A. (1998). Jurors' use of hearsay evidence: The effects of type and timing of instructions. *Law and Human Behavior, 22,* 501–518.

Palmer, T. (1996). Programmatic and nonprogrammatic aspects of successful intervention. In A.T. Harland (Ed.), *Choosing correctional options that work: Defining the demand and evaluating the supply* (pp. 131–182). Thousand Oaks, CA: Sage.

Palys, T., & Divorski, S. (1986). Explaining sentence disparity. *Canadian Journal of Criminology, 28*, 347–362.

Parsons v. State, 81 Ala. 577, 2 So. 854 (1886).

Pearce, J.W., & Pezzot-Pearce, T.D. (1997). *Psychotherapy of abused and neglected children*. New York: Guilford.

Pearson, M., Wilmot, E., & Padi, M. (1986). A study of violent behaviour among in-patients in a psychiatric hospital. *British Journal of Psychiatry, 149*, 232–235.

Pendergrast, M. (1995). *Victims of memory: Incest accusations and shattered lives*. Hinesburg, VT: Upper Access, Inc.

Pendleton, L. (1980). Treatment of persons found incompetent to stand trial. *American Journal of Psychiatry, 137*, 1098–1100.

Pennington, N., & Hastie, R. (1986). Evidence evaluation in complex decision making. *Journal of Personality and Social Psychology, 51*, 242–258.

Pennington, N., & Hastie, R. (1988). Explanation-based decision making: Effects of memory structure on judgement. *Journal of Experimental Psychology: Learning, Memory, and Cognition, 14*, 521–533.

Pennington, N., & Hastie, R. (1993). Reasoning in explanation-based decision making. *Cognition, 49*, 123–163.

Penrod, S., & Cutler, B. (1995). Witness confidence and witness accuracy: Assessing their forensic relation. *Psychology, Public Policy, and Law, 1*, 817–845.

People v. Jackson, 80 Mich. App. 244, (1977).

Perlin, M.L. (1989). *Mental disability law: Civil and criminal*. Charlottesville, VA: Mitchie Company.

Perlman, N.B., Ericson, K.I., Esses, V.M., & Isaacs, B.J. (1994). The developmentally handicapped witness. *Law and Human Behaviour, 18*, 171–187.

Perry, S., Difede, J., Musngi, G., Frances, A.J., & Jacobsberg, L. (1992). Predictors of posttraumatic stress disorder after burn injury. *American Journal of Psychiatry, 149*, 931–935.

Peters, B.R., Atkins, M.S., & McKay, M.M. (1999). Adopted children's behavior problems: A review of five explanatory models. *Clinical Psychology Review, 19*, 297–328.

Peterson, C. (1993) Institutionalized racism: The need for reform of the criminal justice system. *McGill Law Journal, 38*, 147–179.

Peterson, L. (1989). Latchkey children's preparation for self-care: Overestimated, underrehearsed, and unsafe. *Journal of Clinical Child Psychology, 18*, 36–43.

Peterson, L., & Brown, D. (1994). Integrating child injury and abuse-neglect research: Common histories, etiologies, and solutions. *Psychological Bulletin, 116*, 293–315.

Petrunic, M. (1982). The politics of dangerousness. *International Journal of Law and Psychiatry, 5*, 225–253.

Pfeifer, J.E. (1990). Reviewing the empirical evidence of jury racism: Findings of discrimination or discriminatory findings? *Michigan Law Review, 69*, 230–250.

Pfeifer, J.E., & Brigham, J.D. (1993). Psychologists and the law: Experiences on non-clinical forensic witnesses and consultants. *Ethics and Behavior, 3*, 329–343.

Pinizzotto, A.J. (1984). Forensic psychology: Criminal personality profiling. *Journal of Police Science and Administration, 12*, 32–40.

Pinizzotto, A.J., & Finkel, N.J. (1990). Criminal personality profiling: An outcome and process study. *Law and Human Behavior, 14*, 215–234.

Pipe, M.-E. (1996). Children's eyewitness memory. *New Zealand Journal of Psychology, 25*, 36–43.

Pipe, M.-E., Goodman, G.S., Quas, J., Bidrose, S., Ablin, D., & Craw, S. (1997). Remembering early experiences during childhood: Are traumatic events special? In J.D. Read & D.S. Lindsay (Eds.), *Recollections of trauma: Scientific evidence and clinical practice* (pp. 417–424). New York: Plenum.

Pithers, W.D., Marques, J.K., Gibat, C.C., & Marlatt, G.A. (1983). Relapse Prevention with sexual aggressives: A self-control model of treatment and maintenance of change. In J.G. Greer & I.R. Stuart (Eds.), *The sexual aggressor: Current perspectives on treatment* (pp. 214–239). New York: Van Nostrand Reinhold.

Pogrebin, M.R., & Poole, E.D. (1987). Deinstitutionalization and increased arrest rates among the mentally disordered. *Journal of Psychiatry and Law, 15*, 117–127.

Polvi, N. (1997). Assessing risk of suicide in correctional settings. In C.D. Webster & M.A. Jackson (Eds.), *Impulsivity: Theory, assessment and treatment*. New York: Guilford Press.

Poole, D.A., & Lindsay, D.S. (1995). Interviewing preschoolers: Effects of non-suggestive techniques, parental coaching, and leading questions on reports of nonexperienced events. *Journal of Experimental Child Psychology, 60*, 129–154.

Poole, D.A., Lindsay, D.S., Memon. A., & Bull, R. (1995). Psychotherapy and the recovery of childhood sexual abuse: U.S. and British practitioners' opinions, practices, and experiences. *Journal of Consulting and Clinical Psychology, 63*, 426–437.

Poole, D.A., & White, L.T. (1995). Tell me again and again: Stability and change in the repeated testimonies of children and adults. In Maria S. Zargoza & John R. Grahm (Eds.), *Memory and testimony in the child witness. Applied psy-*

chology: Individual, social, and community issues, Vol. 1. (pp. 24–43). Thousand Oaks, CA: Sage Publications.

Pope, K.S., Butcher, J.N., & Seelen, J. (1993).*The MMPI, MMPI-2, and MMPI-A in court: A practical guide for expert witnesses and attorneys.* Washington, DC: American Psychological Association.

Porter, B., & O'Leary, K.D. (1980). Marital discord and child behavior problems. *Journal of Abnormal Child Psychology, 80,* 287–295.

Porter, S., & Yuille, J.C. (1996). The language of deceit: An investigation of the verbal clues to deception in the interrogation context. *Law and Human Behavior, 20,* 443–458.

Porter, S., Yuille, J.C., & Lehman, D.R. (1999). The nature of real, implanted, and fabricated memories for emotional childhood events: Implications for the recovered memory debate. *Law and Human Behavior, 23,* 517–537.

Posthuma, A.B., & Harper, J.F. (1998). Comparison of MMPI-2 responses of child custody and personal injury litigants. *Professional Psychology: Research and Practice, 29,* 437–443.

Prentky, R.A., Burgess, A.W., Rokous, F., Lee, A., Hartman, C., Ressler, R., & Douglas, J. (1989). The presumptive role of fantasy in serial sexual homicide. *American Journal of Psychiatry, 146,* 887–891.

Price, D. (1991). *Fraudbusting.* London: Mercury Books.

Prince Edward Island (Director of Child Welfare) v. W. (N.) (1994), 10 R.F.L. (4th) 203, 124 Nfld., and P.E.I.R 180 (P.E.I.C.A.).

Prochaska, J.O., DiClemente, C.C., & Norcross, J.C. (1992). In search of how people change: Applications to addictive behaviors. *American Psychologist, 47,* 1102–1114.

Quinsey, V.L., Harris, G.T., Rice, M.E., & Cormier, C.A. (1998). *Violent offenders: Appraising and managing risk.* Washington, DC: American Psychological Association.

Quinsey, V.L., Harris, G.T., Rice, M.E., & Lalumière, M.L. (1993). Assessing treatment efficacy in outcome studies of sex offenders. *Journal of Interpersonal Violence, 8,* 512–523.

Quinsey, V.L., Lalumière, M.L., Rice, M.E., & Harris, G.T. (1995). Predicting sexual offenses. In J.C. Campbell (Ed.), *Assessing dangerousness: Violence by sexual offenders, batterers, and child abusers* (pp. 114–137). Thousand Oaks, CA: Sage Publications.

Quinsey, V.L., Rice, M.E., & Harris, G.T. (1995). Actuarial prediction of sexual recidivism. *Journal of Interpersonal Violence, 10,* 85–105.

R. v. Alkerton (1992), 72 C.C.C. 3d 184 (Ont. C.A.).

R. v. Alli (1996), 110 C.C.C. (3d) 283 at 285 (Ont. C.A.).

R. v. Andrade (1985), 18 C.C.C. 3d 41 (Ont. CA).

R. v. Arnold (1724), 16 How. St. Tr. 694 (K.B.).

R. v. Askov, [1990] 2 S.C.R. 1199.

R. v. Atfield (1983), 25 Alta. L.R. (2d) 97, 42 A.R. 294 (Alta. CA).

R. v. B. (G.), [1990] 2 S.C.R. 3, 111 N.R. 1, 77 C.R. (3d) 327, 56 C.C.C. (3d) 161.

R. v. Betker (1997), 115 C.C.C. (3d) 421, 33 O.R. (3d) 321 (C.A.).

R. v. Born with a Tooth (1993), 22 C.R. (4th) 232, 81 C.C.C. (3d) 393 (Alta. Q.B.).

R. v. Carter, [1994] B.C.J. No. 920 (B.C.S.C.) (Q.L.).

R. v. Chaulk, [1990] 3 S.C.R. 1303.

R. v. D. (R. R.) (1989), 69 C.R. (3d) 267, 47 C.C.C. (3d) 97, 72 Sask. R. 142 (C.A.).

R. v. Daviault (1994), 93 C.C.C. 3d 21.

R. v. Duhamel (1981), 1 W.W.R. 22, 56 C.C.C. (2d) 46, 133 D.L.R. (3d) 546, 40 N.R. 225 (Alta. C.A.).

R. v. Edwards (unreported), Ont. C.A., February 13, 1996.

R. v. Emile, [1988] 5 W.W.R. 481 (N.W.T. C.A.)

R. v. English (1993), 111 Nfld., and P.E.I.R. 323, 84 C.C.C. (3d) 544 (Que. C.A.).

R. v. Gayme (1991), 7 C.R.D. 725.

R. v. Gauld, [1994] O.J. No. 1477 (Gen. Div.) (Q.L.)

R. v. Hadfield (1800), 27 St. Tr. 1281, 1312.

R. v. Halliday (1992), 77 C.C.C. 3d 184.

R. v. Hubbert (1975), 29 C.C.C. (2d) 279, 31 C.R.N.S. 27, 11 O.R. (2d) 464 (C.A.).

R. v. Keegstra, [1992] A.J. No. 294 (Q.B.) (Q.L.).

R. v. Kenny (1996), 108 C.C.C. (3d) 349, 142 Nfld., and P.E.I.R. 250 (C.A.).

R v. Kliman (1996), 71 B.C.A.C. 241, 47 C.R. (4th) 137, 107 C.C.C. (3d) 549; *acquit* [1998] B.C.J. No. 49 (S.C.) (Q.L.).

R. v. Koh et al. (1998), O.J. No. 5425, Ontario Court of Appeal, Lexis 859.

R. v. L. (D. O.), [1993] 4 S.C.R. 419, 161 N.R. 1, 25 C.R. (4th) 285, 85 C.C.C. (3d) 289, 18 C.R.R. (2d) 257.

R. v. Lavallee (1988), 65 C.R. 3d 387.

R. v. Levogiannis, [1993] 4 S.C.R. 475, 160 N.R. 1, 25 C.R. (4th) 325, 85 C.C.C. (3d) 327, 18 C.R.R. (2d) 242.

R. v. Marinelli, [1988] O.J. No. 836 (Distr. Crt.) (Q.L.).

R. v. Marquard, [1993] 4 S.C.R. 223, 108 D.L.R. (4th) 47, 159 N.R. 81, 25 C.R. (4th) 1, 85 C.C.C. (3d) 193.

R. v. MacGregor (December, 1993), Ontario Court of Justice (General Division), unreported.

R. v. McGuiness, Ballantyne & Ballantyne, [1997] B.J. No.1695 (B.C.S.C.) (Q.L.).

R. v. McIntosh (1997), 117 C.C.C. (3d) 385 (Ont. C.A.)

R. v. Miloszewski, Synderek, Nikkel, Leblanc and Kluch. Reasons for judgment, Provincial Court of B.C. File Number 96687–03–D2.

R. v. M'Naghten (1843), 10 Cl. and F. 200, 8 Eng. Rep. 718.

R. v. Mohan, [1994] 2 S.C.R. 9, 114 D.L.R. (4th) 419, 166 N.R. 245, 29 C.R. (4th) 243, 89 C.C.C. (3d) 402.

R. v. Morgentaler, [1988] 1 S.C.R. 30.

R. v. Musson (1996), 3 C.R. (5th) 61 (Ont. Ct. (Gen. Div.)).

R. v. Nadhee (1993), 26 C.R. (4th) 109 (Ont. Ct. (Gen. Div.).

R. v. Nepoose (1991), 85 Alta. L.R. (2d) 8 (Q.B.).

R. v. Nikolovski, [1996] 3 S.C.R. 1197, 31 D.R. (3d) 280, 141 D.L.R. (4th) 647, 214 N.R. 333, 3 C.R. (5th) 362, 111 C.C.C. (3d) 403.

R v. Norman (1993), 26 C.R. (4th) 256, 87 C.C.C. (3d) 153, 16 O.R. (3d) 134 (C.A.).

R. v. O. (H. W.), [1997] O.R. No. 2287 (Gen. Div.).

R. v. Oakes, [1986] 1 S.C.R. 103.

R. v. O'Connor, [1995] 4 S.C.R. 411, 130 D.L.R. (4th) 235, 191 N.R. 1, 44 C.R. (4th) 1, 103 C.C.C. (4th) 1.

R. v. Parks (1993), 24 C.R. (4th) 81, 84 C.C.C. (3d) 353, 15 O.R. (3d) 324, 65 O.A.C. 122.

R. v. Peter To Kan Tsang (1987), 1 W.C.B. (2d) 200.

R. v. Pritchard (1836), 7 Car., and P. 304

R. v. Proulx, 2000, SCC 5.

R. v. Savoy (1997), 6 C.R. (5th) 61.

R. v. Schwartz (1977), 34 C.R.N.S. 138, 29 C.C.C. (2d) 1 (S.C.C.)

R. v. Seaboyer, [1991] 2 S.C.R. 577.

R. v. Sherratt (1991), 1 S.C.R. 509, 3 C.R. (4th) 129, 63 C.C.C. (3d) 193.

R. v. Sophonow (No. 2) (1986), 25 C.C.C (3d) 415.

R. v. Sterling (1995), 102 C.C.C. (3d) 481, 137 Sask. R. 1 (C.A.).

R. v. Swain (1991), 63 C.C.C. (3d) 481 (S.C.C.).

R. v. Taylor (1992), 77 C.C.C. (3d) 551 (Ont. C.A.).

R. v. Theberge (1995), No. 2666–90 Ont. C.J. (Ont. Gen. Div. Mar. 16, 1995).

R. v. Turnbull et al. (1976), 63 Cr. App. R. 132.

R. v. Welch (1996), (Ont. Gen. Div.) [unreported].

R. v. Williams (1994), 90 C.C.C. (3d) 194.

R. v. Williams (1996), 106 C.C.C. (3d) 215 (B.C.C.A.)

R. v. Williams (1998), 124 C.C.C. (3d) 481.

Range, L.M., & Knott, E.C. (1997). Twenty suicide assessment instruments: Evaluation and recommendations. *Death Studies, 21*, 25–58.

Raskin, D.C. (1989). Polygraph techniques for the detection of deception. In D.C. Raskin (Ed.), *Psychological methods in criminal investigation and evidence* (pp. 247–296). New York: Springer.

Raskin, D.C., & Esplin, P.W. (1991). Statement Validity Assessment: Interview procedures and content analysis of children's statements of sexual abuse. *Behavioral Assessment, 13,* 265–291.

Rattner, A. (1988). Convicted but innocent: Wrongful conviction and the criminal justice system. *Law and Human Behavior, 12,* 283–293.

Ratych v. Bloomer, [1990] 1 S.C.R. 940.

Re Moore and the Queen (1984), 10 C.C.C. (3d) 306 (Ont. H.C.J.).

Re Jenkins (1986), 59 Nfld., and P.E.I.R 62, 178 A.P.R. 62 (P.E.I.S.C.)

Re Ontario (Commission on Proceedings Involving Guy Paul Morin), [1998] O.J. No. 337 (Q.L.).

Read, J.D. (1994). Understanding bystander misidentifications: The role of familiarity and contextual knowledge. In D.F. Ross, J.D. Read, & M.P. Toglia (Eds.), *Adult eyewitness testimony: Current trends and development* (pp. 56–79). New York: Cambridge University Press.

Read, J.D. (1996). From a passing thought to a false memory in 2 minutes: Confusing real and illusory events. *Psychonomic Bulletin & Review, 3,* 105–111.

Read, J.D. (in press). The recovered/false memory debate: Three steps forward, two steps back? *Expert Evidence.*

Read, J.D., & Bruce, D. (1984). On the external validity of questioning effects in eyewitness testimony. *International Review of Applied Psychology, 33,* 33–49.

Read, J.D., & Connolly, D. (1999, July). *The response of Canadian criminal courts to delayed allegations of childhood sexual abuse: The roles of memory and memory impairment.* Presented at the International Conference on Psychology and Law, Dublin.

Read, J.D., & Lindsay, D.S. (Eds.). (1997). *Recollections of trauma: Scientific evidence and clinical practice.* New York: Plenum.

Read, J.D., & Lindsay, D.S. (in press). "Amnesia" for summer camps and high school graduation: Memory work increases reports of prior periods of remembering. *Journal of Traumatic Stress.*

Read, J.D., Lindsay, D.S., & Nicholls, T. (1998). The relationship between confidence and accuracy in eyewitness identification studies: Is the conclusion changing? In C.P. Thompson, D.J. Herrmann, J.D. Read, D. Bruce, D.G. Payne, & M.P. Toglia (Eds.), *Eyewitness memory: Theoretical and applied perspectives* (pp. 107–130). Mahwah, NJ: Lawrence Erlbaum Associates.

Read, J.D., Yuille, J.C., & Tollestrup, P. (1992). Recollections of a robbery: Effects of arousal and alcohol upon recall and person identification. *Law and Human Behavior, 16,* 425–446.

Reaves, R.P., & Ogloff, J.R.P. (1996). Liability for professional misconduct. In L.J. Bass (Ed.), *Professional conduct and discipline in psychology* (pp. 117–142). Washington, DC: American Psychological Association.

Reid Report, Issue No. 9 (October 1994). Toronto.

Reilly, M.E., Lott, B., & Gallogly, S.M. (1986). Sexual harassment of university students. *Sex Roles, 15,* 333–358.

Rende, R.D., Lomkowski, C.L., Stocker, C., Fulker, D.W., & Plomin, R. (1992). Genetic and environmental influences on maternal and sibling interaction in middle childhood: A sibling adoption study. *Developmental Psychology, 28,* 484–490.

Renzetti, C.M. (1992). *Violent betrayal: Partner abuse in lesbian relationships.* Newbury Park, CA: Sage.

Rice, M.E. (1997). Violent offender research and implications for the criminal justice system. *American Psychologist, 52,* 414–423.

Rice, M.E., & Harris, G.T. (1990). The predictors of insanity acquittal. *International Journal of Law and Psychiatry, 13,* 217–224.

Rice, M.E., & Harris, G.T. (1997). Cross-validation and extension of the Violence Risk Appraisal Guide for child molesters and rapists. *Law and Human Behavior, 21,* 231–241.

Rice, M.E., Harris, G.T., & Quinsey, V.L. (1990). A follow-up of rapists assessed in a maximum-security psychiatric facility. *Journal of Interpersonal Violence, 5,* 435–448.

Rice, M.E., Quinsey, V.L., & Harris, G.T. (1991). Sexual recidivism among child molesters released from a maximum security psychiatric institution. *Journal of Consulting and Clinical Psychology, 59,* 381–386.

Richardson, D., & Campbell, J.L. (1982). Alcohol and rape: The effect of alcohol on attributions of blame for rape. *Personality and Social Psychology Bulletin, 8,* 468–476.

Richman, J.A., Flaherty, J.A., Rospenda, K.M., & Christensen, M.L. (1992). Mental health consequences and correlates of reported medical student abuse. *Journal of the American Medical Association, 267,* 692–694.

Rind, B., Tromovitch, P., & Bauserman, R. (1998). A meta-analytic examination of assumed properties of child sexual abuse using college samples. *Psychological Bulletin, 124,* 22–53.

Rivara, F.P., & Mueller, B.A. (1987). The epidemiology and causes of childhood injuries. *Journal of Social Issues, 43,* 13–31.

Rivera, M. (1996, March). *Needs assessment: Mental health resources for federally sentenced women in the regional facilities.* Ottawa: Correctional Service of Canada.

Roberts, J.V. (1995). New data on sentencing trends in provincial courts. *Criminal Reports, 34,* 181–196.

Roberts, J.V. (1999). Sentencing trends and sentencing disparity. In J.V. Roberts & D. Cole (Eds.), *Making sense of sentencing.* Toronto: University of Toronto Press.

Roberts, J.V., & Birkenmayer, A. (1997). Sentencing in adult provincial courts. *Juristat, 17(1)*.

Roberts, J.V., & Cole, D.P. (Eds.). (1999a). *Making sense of sentencing*. Toronto: University of Toronto Press.

Roberts, J.V., & Cole, D.P. (1999b). Sentencing and early release arrangements for offenders convicted of murder. In J.V. Roberts and D.P. Cole (Eds.), *Making sense of sentencing*. Toronto: University of Toronto Press.

Roberts, J.V., & Doob, A.N. (1990). News media influences on public views of sentencing. *Law and Human Behavior, 14*, 451–468.

Roberts, J.V., Nuffield, J. and Hann, R. (1999). *Parole and the Canadian public: Attitudinal and behavioral responses*. Unpublished manuscript, Department of Criminology, University of Ottawa.

Roberts, J.V., & Stalans, L. (2000). *Public opinion, crime and criminal justice*. Boulder, CO: Westview Press.

Roberts, J.V., and von Hirsch, A. (1999). Legislating the purposes and principles of sentencing. In J.V. Roberts and D.P. Cole (Eds.), *Making sense of sentencing*. Toronto: University of Toronto Press.

Roberts, M.C., & Wright, L. (1982). Role of the pediatric psychologist as consultant to pediatricians. In J. Tuma (Ed.), *Handbook for the practice of pediatric psychology* (pp. 251–289). New York: Wiley-Interscience.

Robertson, D. (1990). Counselling women who have been sexually assaulted. *British Psychological Society, 16*, 46–53.

Robertson, G.B. (1994). *Mental disability and the law in Canada* (2nd ed.). Scarborough, ON: Carswell.

Robichaud v. Canada (Treasury Board), [1987] 2 S.C.R. 84.

Robinson, D., Porporino, F.J., Millson, W.A., Trevethan, S., & MacKillop, B. (1998). A one-day snapshot of inmates in Canada's adult correctional facilities (Catalogue No. 85–002–XPE). *Juristat, 18(8)*. Ottawa: Statistics Canada.

Roe, C.M., & Schwartz, M.F. (1996). Characteristics of previously forgotten memories of sexual abuse: A descriptive study. *Journal of Psychiatry and Law, 24*, 189–206.

Roehl, J., & Guertin, K. (1998). *Current use of dangerousness assessments in sentencing domestic violence offenders*. (Grant No. SJI-97-181-078). State Justice Institute, California.

Roesch, R. (1979). Determining competency to stand trial: An examination of evaluation procedures in an institutional setting. *Journal of Consulting and Clinical Psychology, 47*, 542–550.

Roesch, R. (1995). Mental health interventions in pretrial jails. In G. Davies, S. Lloyd-Bostock, M. McMurran, & C. Wilson (Eds.), *Psychology, law, and criminal justice: International developments in research and practice* (pp. 520–531). Berlin, Germany: De Gruyter.

Roesch, R., Eaves, D., Sollner, R., Normandin, M., & Glackman, W. (1981). Evaluating fitness to stand trial: A comparative analysis of fit and unfit defendants. *International Journal of Law and Psychiatry, 4*, 145–157.

Roesch, R., & Golding, S.L. (1980). *Competency to stand trial.* Champaign, IL: University of Illinois Press.

Roesch, R., Grisso, T., & Poythress, N.G. (1986). Training programs, courses, and workshops in psychology and law. In M.F. Kaplan (Ed.), *The impact of social psychology on procedural justice* (pp. 83–108). Springfield, IL: C.C. Thomas.

Roesch, R., Ogloff, J.R.P., Hart, S.D., Dempster, R.J., Zapf, P.A., & Whittemore, K.E. (1997). The impact of Canadian Criminal Code changes on remands and assessments of fitness to stand trial and criminal responsibility in British Columbia. *Canadian Journal of Psychiatry, 42*, 509–514.

Roesch, R., Ogloff, J.R.P., Zapf, P.A., Hart, S.D., & Otto, R. (1998). Jail and prison inmates. In A.S. Bellack & M. Hersen (Series Eds.) & N.N. Singh (Vol. Ed.), *Comprehensive clinical psychology: Volume 9. Applications in diverse populations* (pp. 85–104). New York: Pergamon.

Roesch, R., Webster, C.D., & Eaves, D. (1984). *The Fitness Interview Test: A method for examining fitness to stand trial.* Toronto: Centre of Criminology, University of Toronto.

Roesch, R., Webster, C.D., & Eaves, D. (1994). *The Fitness Interview Test – Revised: A method for examining fitness to stand trial.* Unpublished manuscript, Simon Fraser University. (Available from Ronald Roesch, Department of Psychology, Simon Fraser University, Burnaby, B.C. V5A 1S6).

Roesch, R., Zapf, P., Webster, C.D., & Eaves, D. (1999). *The Fitness Interview Test.* Simon Fraser University: Mental Health Law & Policy Institute.

Rogers, R. (1984). *Rogers Criminal Responsibility Assessment Scales.* Odessa, FL: Psychological Assessment Resources.

Rogers, R. (1986). *Conducting insanity evaluations.* New York: Van Nostrand Reinhold Company.

Rogers, R. (Ed.). (1988). *Clinical assessment of malingering and deception.* New York: Guilford.

Rogers, R. (1997). *Clinical assessment of malingering and deception* (2nd ed.). New York: Guilford.

Rogers, R., Bagby, R.M., & Dickens, S.E. (1992). *Structured interview of reported symptoms: Professional manual.* Odessa, FL: Psychological Assessment Resources.

Rogers, R., & Ewing, C.P. (1992). The measurement of insanity: Debating the merits of the R-CRAS and its alternatives. *International Journal of Law and Psychiatry, 15,* 113–123.

Rogers, R., Salekin, R.T., Sewell, K.W., Goldstein, A., & Leonard, K. (1998). A comparison of forensic and nonforensic malingerers: A prototypical analysis of explanatory models. *Law and Human Behavior, 22,* 353–367.

Rogers, R., Sewell, K.W., & Goldstein, A.M. (1994). Explanatory models of malingering: A prototypical analysis. *Law and Human Behavior, 18,* 543–552.

Rose, V.G. (1982). *Parties to an offence.* Toronto: Carswell.

Rosenbaum, R.L., & Horowitz, M.J. (1983). Motivation for psychotherapy: A factorial and conceptual analysis. *Psychotherapy: Theory, Research, and Practice, 20,* 346–354.

Rosenfeld, B.D. (1992). Court-ordered treatment of spouse abuse. *Clinical Psychology Review, 12,* 205–226.

Rosenhan, D., Eisner, S., & Robinson, R. (1994). Notetaking can aid recall. *Law and Human Behavior, 18,* 53–61.

Roshenow, D.J., Corbett, R., & Devine, D. (1988). Molested as children: A hidden contribution to substance abuse? *Journal of Substance Abuse Treatment, 5,* 13–18.

Rosine, L. (1995). Critical incident stress and its management in corrections. In T.A. Leis, L.L. Motiuk, & J.R.P. Ogloff (Eds.), *Forensic psychology: Policy and practice in corrections* (pp. 213–226). Ottawa: Correctional Service of Canada.

Rosnow, R.L., & Fine, G.A. (1976). *Rumor and gossip: The social psychology of hearsay.* New York: Elsevier.

Ross, D.F., Ceci, S.J., Dunning, D., & Toglia, M.P. (1994). Unconscious transference and lineup identification: Toward a memory blending approach. In D.F. Ross, J.D. Read, & M.P. Toglia (Eds.), *Adult eyewitness testimony: Current trends and development* (pp. 80–100). New York: Cambridge University Press.

Ross, D.F., Read, J.D., & Toglia, M.P. (Eds.). (1994). *Adult eyewitness testimony: Current trends and developments.* New York: Cambridge University Press.

Rossmo, D.K. (1995). Geographic profiling: Target patterns of serial murderers. Unpublished doctoral dissertation. Simon Fraser University, Burnaby, BC.

Rossmo, D.K. (1996). Targeting victims: Serial killers and the urban environment. In T. O'Reilly-Fleming (Ed.), *Serial and mass murder: Theory, research and policy* (pp. 133–153). Toronto: Canadian Scholars' Press.

Rothbaum, B.O., Foa, E.B., Riggs, D.S., Murdock, T., & Walsh, W. (1992). A prospective examination of post-traumatic stress disorder in rape victims. *Journal of Traumatic Stress, 5,* 455–475.

Roy, A. (1985). Suicide and psychiatric patients. *Psychiatric Clinics of North America, 8,* 227–241.

Ruby, C.C. (1994). *Sentencing* (4th ed.). Markham, ON: Butterworths.

Russell, A.B., & Tranor, C.M. (1984). *Trends in child abuse and neglect: A national perspective.* Denver, CO: American Humane Association.

Rutherford, M.J., Cacciola, J.S., Alterman, A.I., & McKay, J.R. (1996). Reliability and validity of the Revised Psychopathy Checklist in women methadone patients. *Assessment, 3,* 145–156.

S. (L.A.) v. British Columbia (Superintendent of Family & Child Service) (31 March 1995), Doc. V01858 (B.C.C.A.).

Sacco, V.F. (1995). Fear and personal safety (Catalogue No. 85–002). *Juristat, 15(9).* Ottawa: Statistics Canada.

Saks, M.J. (1977). *Jury verdicts.* Lexington, MA: Lexington.

Saks, M.J., & Hastie, R. (1978). *Social psychology in court.* New York: Van Nostrand Reinhold.

Saks, M.J., & Marti, M.W. (1997). A meta-analysis of the effects of jury size. *Law and Human Behavior, 21,* 451–467.

Salekin, R.T., Rogers, R., & Sewell, K.W. (1996). A review and meta-analysis of the Psychopathy Checklist and Psychopathy Checklist-Revised: Predictive validity of dangerousness. *Clinical Psychology: Science and Practice, 3,* 203–215.

Salekin, R.T., Rogers, R., & Sewell, K.W. (1997). Construct validity of psychopathy in a female offender sample: A multitrait-multimethod evaluation. *Journal of Abnormal Psychology, 106,* 576–585.

Salekin, R.T., Rogers, R., Ustad, K.L., & Sewell, K.W. (1998). Psychopathy and recidivism among female inmates. *Law and Human Behavior, 22,* 109–128.

Salhany, R.E. (1991). *The police manual of arrest, seizure & interrogation* (5th ed.). Scarborough, ON: Carswell.

Salhany, R.E. (1994). *A basic guide to evidence in criminal cases* (3rd ed.). Toronto: Thomson Professional Publishing.

Salhany, R.E. (1994) with updates. *Canadian criminal procedure* (6th ed.). Aurora, ON: Canada Law Book.

Salisbury, J., Ginorio, A.B., Remick, H., & Stringer, D.M. (1986). Counseling victims of sexual harassment. *Psychotherapy, 23,* 316–324.

Salter, A.C. (1992). Epidemiology of child sexual abuse. In W. O'Donohue & J.H. Geer (Eds.), *The sexual abuse of children: Clinical issues* (vol. I) (pp. 108–138). Hillsdale, NJ: Lawrence Erlbaum Associates, Inc.

Salzinger, S., Feldman, R.S., Hammer, M., & Rosario, M. (1993). The effects of physical abuse on children's relationships. *Child Development, 64,* 169–187.

Samoluk, S.B., & Pretty, G.M.H. (1994). The impact of sexual harassment simulations on women's thoughts and feelings. *Sex Roles, 30,* 679–699.

Sandys, M., & Dillehay, R.C. (1995). First-ballot votes, predeliberation dispositions, and final verdicts in jury trials. *Law and Human Behavior, 19,* 175–195.

Satin, M.I. (1994). Law and psychology: A movement whose time has come. *Annual Survey of American Law, 1994,* 581–630.

Sattler, J.M. (1988). *Assessment of children* (3rd ed.). San Diego, CA: Author.

Saunders, D.G. (1992). A typology of men who batter women: Three types derived from cluster analysis. *American Journal of Orthopsychiatry, 62,* 264–275.

Saunders, D.M., Vidmar, N., & Hewitt, E. (1982). Eyewitness testimony and the discrediting effect. In S.M.A. Lloyd-Bostock & B.R. Clifford (Eds.), *Evaluating witness evidence.* Toronto: John Wiley & Sons.

Savitsky, J.C., & Lindblom, W.D. (1986). The impact of the guilty but mentally ill verdict on juror decisions: An empirical analysis. *Journal of Applied Social Psychology, 16,* 686–701.

Saywitz, K.J. (1995). Improving children's testimony: The question, the answer, and the environment. In M. Zaragoza, J.R. Graham, et al. (Eds), *Memory and testimony in the child witness. Applied psychology: Individual, social, and community issues, Vol. 1.* (pp. 113–140). Thousand Oaks, CA: Sage Publications.

Scarth, K., & McLean, H. (1994). The psychological assessment of women in prison. *Forum on Corrections Research, 6,* 32–35.

Schichor, D., & Sechrest, D. (Eds.). (1996). *Three strikes and you're out. Vengeance as public policy.* Thousand Oaks, CA: Sage.

Schiff, S. (1993) with supplements. *Evidence in the litigation process* (4th ed.). Toronto: Thomson Professional Publishing.

Schneider, B.E. (1987). Graduate women, sexual harassment, and university policy. *Journal of Higher Education, 58,* 46–65.

School Act, R.S.B.C. (1996), c. 412.

Schretlen, D.J. (1988). The use of psychological tests to identify malingered symptoms of mental disorder. *Clinical Psychology Review, 8,* 451–476.

Schuller, R.A. (1990). The impact of battered woman syndrome testimony on juror decision making: *Lavallee v. R.* considered. *Windsor Yearbook of Access to Justice, 10,* 105–126.

Schuller, R.A. (1992). The impact of battered woman syndrome evidence on jury decision processes. *Law and Human Behavior, 16,* 597–619.

Schuller, R.A., & Cripps, J. (1998). Expert evidence pertaining to battered women: The impact of gender of expert and timing of testimony. *Law and Human Behavior, 22,* 17–31.

Schuller, R.A., & Hastings, P.A. (1996). Trials of battered women who kill: The impact of alternative forms of expert evidence. *Law and Human Behavior, 20,* 167–187, 555–573.

Schuller, R.A., & Hastings, P.A. (2000). Jurors' decisions in sexual assault trials: The impact of complainant sexual history. Annual Meeting of the Canadian Psychological Association, Ottawa, 28 June–2 July.

Schuller, R.A., Smith, V.L., & Olson, J.M. (1994). Jurors' decisions in trials of battered women who kill: The role of prior beliefs and expert testimony. *Journal of Applied Social Psychology, 24,* 316–337.

Schuller, R.A., & Wall, A.M. (1998). The effects of defendant and complainant intoxication on mock jurors' judgements of sexual assault. *Psychology of Women Quarterly, 22,* 555–573.

Scott, E.S. (1992). Pluralism, parental preference, and child custody. *California Law Review, 80,* 615–672.

Seagrave, J. (1997). *Introduction to policing in Canada.* Scarborough, ON: Prentice Hall.

Selzer, M. (1971). The Michigan Alcoholism Screening Test: The quest for a new diagnostic instrument. *American Journal of Psychiatry, 127,* 1653–1658.

Serin, R.C. (1996). Violent recidivism in criminal psychopaths. *Law and Human Behavior, 20,* 207–217.

Serin, R.C., & Amos, N. (1995). The role of psychopathy in the assessment of dangerousness. *International Journal of Law and Psychiatry, 18,* 231–238.

Serin, R.C., Malcolm, P.B., Khanna, A., & Barbaree, H.E. (1994). Psychopathy and deviant sexual arousal in incarcerated sexual offenders. *Journal of Interpersonal Violence, 9,* 3–11.

Severance, L., & Loftus, E. (1982). Improving the ability of jurors to comprehend and apply criminal jury instructions. *Law and Society Review, 17,* 153–197.

Sharpe, R.J. (Ed.). (1987). *Charter litigation.* Toronto: Butterworths.

Shaw, M. (1994). Women in prison: A literature review. *Forum on Corrections Research, 6,* 13–18.

Shaw, M., Rodgers, K., Blanchette, J., Hattem, T., Thomas, L.S., & Tamarack, L. (1990). *Survey of federally sentenced women: Report to the Task Force on the prison survey.* Ottawa: Ministry of the Solicitor General of Canada. User Report No. (1991)–94.

Shepherd, E. (1995). Representing and analysing the interviewee's account. *Medical Science and Law, 35,* 122–135.

Shepherd, J.W., Ellis, H.D., & Davies, G.D. (1982). *Identification evidence: A psychological evaluation.* Aberdeen: Aberdeen University Press.

Sherman, L.W. (1992). *Policing domestic violence: Experiments and dilemmas.* New York: Free Press.

Shoukatallie v. Regina (1962), A.C. 81.

Siegel, A.M., & Elwork, A. (1990). Treating incompetence to stand trial. *Law and Human Behavior, 14,* 57–65.

Silverman, D. (1976–77). Sexual harassment: Working women's dilemma. *Quest: A Feminist Quarterly, 3*, 15–24.

Simon, R.J., & Aaronson, D.E. (1988). *The insanity defense: A critical assessment of law and policy in the post-Hinckley era.* New York: Praeger.

Simon, R.J., & Eimermann, T. (1971). The jury finds not guilty: Another look at media influence on the jury. *Journalism Quarterly, 48*, 343–344.

Simourd, L., & Andrews, A. (1994). Correlates of delinquency: A look at gender differences. *Forum on Corrections Research, 6*, 26–31.

Skinner, H.A. (1982). The Drug Abuse Screening Test. *Addictive Behaviour, 7*, 363–371.

Slobogin, C. (1985). The guilty but mentally ill verdict: An idea whose time should not have come. *George Washington Law Review, 53*, 494–527.

Slobogin, C., Melton, G.B., & Showalter, C.R. (1984). The feasibility of a brief evaluation of mental state at the time of the offense. *Law and Human Behavior, 8*, 305–320.

Slovenko, R. (1984). The meaning of mental illness in criminal responsibility. *Journal of Legal Medicine, 5*, 1–61.

Small, M.A. (1993). Legal psychology and therapeutic jurisprudence. *Saint Louis University Law Journal, 37*, 675–700.

Smith v. Jones, [1999] 1 S.C.R. 455.

Smith, V.L. (1991). Impact of pretrial instruction on jurors' information processing and decision making. *Journal of Applied Psychology, 76*, 220–228.

Smith, V.L., & Kassin, S. (1993). Effects of the dynamite charge on the deliberations of deadlocked mock juries. *Law and Human Behavior, 17*, 625–643.

Solicitor General Canada. (1998). *Corrections and Conditional Release: Statistical Overview.* Ottawa: Solicitor General Canada.

Solomon, R., Feldthusen, B., & Mills, S. (1991). *Cases and materials on the law of torts* (3rd ed.). Scarborough, ON: Carswell.

Some resist humanizing "the accused." (1998), June 10. *The Toronto Star*, p. B5.

Somers, J.M., & Marlatt, G.A. (1992). Alcohol problems. In P.H. Wilson (Ed.), *Principles and practice of relapse prevention* (pp. 23–42). New York: Guilford Press.

Sopinka, J., Lederman, S.N., & Bryant, A.W. (1992). *The law of evidence in Canada.* Markham, ON: Butterworths.

Spence, D.P. (1994). Narrative truth and putative child abuse. *International Journal of Clinical and Experimental Hypnosis, 42*, 289–303.

Sporer, S.L. (1994). Decision times and eyewitness identification accuracy in simultaneous and sequential lineups. In D.F. Ross, J.D. Read, & M.P. Toglia (Eds.), *Adult eyewitness testimony: Current trends and development* (pp. 300–327). New York: Cambridge University Press.

Sporer, S.L., Köhnken, G., & Malpass, R.S. (1996). Introduction: 200 years of mistaken identification. In S.L. Sporer, R.S. Malpass, & G. Köhnken (Eds.), *Psychological issues in eyewitness identification* (pp. 1–6). Mahwah, NJ: Lawrence Erlbaum Associates.

Sporer, S.L., Malpass, R.S., & Koehnken, G. (Eds.). (1996). *Psychological issues in eyewitness identification*. Mahwah, NJ: Lawrence Erlbaum Associates.

Sporer, S.L., Penrod, S.D., Read, J.D., & Cutler, B.L. (1995). Choosing, confidence, and accuracy: A meta-analysis of the confidence-accuracy relation in eyewitness identification studies. *Psychological Bulletin, 118*, 315–327.

Standing Committee on Justice and the Solicitor General. (1993). Four-year review of the act to amend the criminal code and the Canada Evidence Act (Sexual Offenses). House of Commons. Issue No. 101

Stasser, G., & Davis, J.H. (1981). Group decision making and social influence: A social interaction sequence model. *Psychological Review, 88*, 523–551.

Stasser, G., Kerr, N.L., & Bray, R.M. (1982). The social psychology of jury deliberations: Structure, process, and product. In N.L. Kerr & R. Bray (Eds.), *The psychology of the courtroom* (pp. 221–256). New York: Academic Press.

State v. Jones, 50 N.H. 369 (1871).

State v. Pike, 49 N.H. 399 (1870).

Statistics Canada. (1975). Mental health statistics, volume III: Institutional facilities, services and finances, 1975. Ottawa: Minister of Industry, Trade and Commerce.

Statistics Canada. (1990). Women and crime. *Juristat, 10*. Ottawa, Canada: Statistics Canada, Canadian Centre for Justice Statistics.

Statistics Canada. (1993), November 18. The Violence Against Women Survey: Highlights. *The Daily.*

Statistics Canada. (1994). *Criminal justice processing of sexual assault cases.* Ottawa: Minister responsible for Statistics Canada.

Statistics Canada. (1995a). Canadian Crime Statistics, 1994. *Juristat, 15*, pp. 1–22.

Statistics Canada. (1995b). *Mental health statistics, 1992–93.* Ottawa: Minister responsible for Statistics Canada.

Statistics Canada. (1995c). *Youth court statistics 1993–1994.* Ottawa, Canada: Statistics Canada, Canadian Centre for Justice Statistics.

Statistics Canada. (1996a). *Adult correctional services in Canada 1994–95* (Catalogue No. 85–211). Ottawa: Statistics Canada, Canadian Centre for Justice Statistics.

Statistics Canada. (1996b). Canadian crime statistics. *Juristat Service Bulletin: Canadian Centre for Justice Statistics, 17(8)*, 1–13.

Statistics Canada. (1996c). *The justice data factfinder Juristat, 16(9)*. Ottawa: Statistics Canada, Canadian Centre for Justice Statistics.

Statistics Canada. (1996d). *Youth court statistics 1994–1995*. Ottawa: Statistics Canada, Canadian Centre for Justice Statistics.

Statistics Canada. (1997a). Canadian children in the 1990s: Selected findings of the national longitudinal survey of children and youth. *Canadian Social Trends, 44*, 2–9.

Statistics Canada. (1997b). Canadian crime statistics, 1996. *Juristat, 17*. Ottawa: Statistics Canada, Canadian Centre for Justice Statistics.

Statistics Canada. (1997c). The justice data factfinder. *Juristat, 17*. Ottawa: Statistics Canada, Canadian Centre for Justice Statistics.

Statistics Canada. (1998a). *Adult correctional services in Canada 1996–97* (Catalogue No. 85-211-XIE). Ottawa: Statistics Canada, Canadian Centre for Justice Statistics.

Statistics Canada. (1998b). A one-day snapshot of inmates in Canada's adult correctional facilities. *Juristat, 18(8)*, 1–10.

Statistics Canada. (1999). *Youths and adults charged in criminal incidents, Criminal Code and federal statutes, by sex*. Ottawa: Statistics Canada, Canadian Centre for Justice Statistics.

Steadman, H.J. (1985). Empirical research on the insanity defense. *Annals of the American Academy of Political and Social Science, 477*, 58–81.

Steadman, H.J., & Cocozza, J. (1974). *Careers of the criminally insane*. Lexington, MA: Lexington Books.

Steadman, H.J., Monahan, J., Robbins, P.C., Appelbaum, P., Grisso, T., Klassen, D., Mulvey, E.P., & Roth, L. (1993). From dangerousness to risk assessment: Implications for appropriate research strategies. In S. Hodgins (Ed.), *Mental disorder and crime* (pp. 39–62). London: Sage.

Steblay, N.M., Besirevic, J., Fulero, S.M., & Jimenez-Lorente, B. (1999). The effects of pretrial publicity on juror verdicts: A meta-analytic review. *Law and Human Behavior, 23*, 219–235.

Steele, C.M., & Josephs, R.A. (1990). Alcohol myopia: Its prized and dangerous effects. *American Psychologist, 45*, 921–933.

Steller, M., & Boychuk, T. (1992). Children as witnesses in sexual abuse cases: Investigative interview and assessment techniques. In H. Dent and R. Flin (Eds.), *Children as witnesses* (pp. 47–71). New York: Wiley.

Stern, W. (1904). Realistic experiments. *Wirklichkeitsversuche Beitrage zur Psychologie der Aussage, 2*, 1–31.

Steward, M.S., Bussey, K., Goodman, G.S., & Saywitz, K.J. (1993). Implications of developmental research for interviewing children. *Child Abuse & Neglect, 17*, 25–37.

Stoff, D.M., Breiling, J., & Masser, J.D. (Eds.). (1997). *Handbook of antisocial behaviour*. New York: Wiley.

Strachan, C.E. (1993). *The assessment of psychopathy in female offenders.* Unpublished doctoral dissertation, Department of Psychology, University of British Columbia.

Strachan, C.E., Williamson, S., & Hare, R.D. (1990). *Psychopathy and female offenders.* Unpublished manuscript, Department of Psychology, University of British Columbia.

Strasburger, L.H., Gutheil, T.G., & Brodsky, A. (1997). On wearing two hats: Role conflict in serving as both psychotherapist and expert witness. *American Journal of Psychiatry, 154,* 448–456.

Straus, M.A. (1993). Physical assaults by wives: A major social problem. In R.J. Gelles & D.R. Loseke (Eds.), *Current controversies in family violence* (pp. 67–87). Newbury Park, CA: Sage.

Straus, M.A., & Gelles, R.J. (1986). Societal change and change in family violence from 1975–1985. *Journal of Marriage and the Family, 48,* 465–479.

Straus, M.A., Gelles, J.R., & Steinmetz, S. (1980). *Behind closed doors: Violence in the American family.* New York: Doubleday Anchor Press.

Sue, S., Smith, R.E., & Caldwell, C. (1973). Effects of inadmissible evidence on the decisions of simulated jurors: A moral dilemma. *Journal of Applied Social Psychology, 3,* 345–353.

Sugar, F., & Fox, L. (1990). *Survey of federally sentenced Aboriginal women in the community.* Native Women's Association of Canada.

Suggs, D., & Sales, B.D. (1978). The art and science of conducting the voir dire. *Professional Psychology, 9,* 367–388.

Sunnafrank, M., & Fontes, N.E. (1983). General and crime related racial stereotypes and influence of juridic decisions. *Cornell Journal of Social Relations, 17,* 1–15.

Surette, R. (1998). *Media, crime, and criminal justice: Images and realities* (2nd ed.). Belmont, CA: Wadsworth.

Swanson, J.W. (1994). Mental disorder, substance abuse, and community violence: An epidemiological approach. In J. Monahan & H.J. Steadman (Eds.), *Violence and mental disorder* (pp. 101–136). Chicago: University of Chicago Press.

Swanson, J., Estroff, S., Swartz, M., Borum, R., Lachicotte, W., Zimmer, C., & Wagner, R. (1997). Violence and severe mental disorder in clinical and community populations: The effects of psychotic symptoms, comorbidity, and lack of treatment. *Psychiatry: Interpersonal and Biological Processes, 60,* 1–22.

Swanson, J.W., Holzer, C., Ganju, V., & Jono, R. (1990). Violence and psychiatric disorder in the community: Evidence from the Epidemiological Catchment Area surveys. *Hospital and Community Psychiatry, 42,* 79–80.

Swoboda, J.S., Elwork, A., Sales, B.D., & Levine, D. (1978). Knowledge of and compliance with privileged communication and child abuse-reporting laws. *Professional Psychology, 9*, 448–457.

Szymanski, L.I., Devlin, A.S., Chrisler, J.C., & Vyse, S. (1993). Gender role and attitudes toward rape in male and female college students. *Sex Roles, 29*, 37–57.

Tanford, J.A., & Cox, M. (1987). Decision processes in civil cases: The impact of impeachment evidence on liability and credibility judgments. *Social Behavior, 2*, 165–182.

Tanford, S., & Cox, M. (1988). The effects of impeachment evidence and limiting instructions on individual and group decision making. *Law and Human Behavior, 12*, 477–497.

Tanford, S., & Penrod, S. (1986). Jury deliberations: Discussion content and influence processes in jury decision-making. *Journal of Applied Social Psychology, 16*, 322–347.

Tanovich, D.M., Paciocco, D.M., & Skurka, S. (1997). *Jury selection in criminal trials: Skills, science, and the law.* Concord, ON: Irwin Law.

Tapp, J.L. (1976). Psychology and the law: An overview. *Annual Review of Psychology, 27*, 359–404.

Tarasoff v. Regents of the University of California, 17 Cal. 3d 425, 131 Cal. Rptr. 14, 551 P.2d 334 (1976).

Taylor, S., Fedoroff, I.C., & Koch, W.J. (1998, September). *Posttraumatic stress disorder due to motor vehicle accidents: Patterns and predictors of response to cognitive-behaviour therapy.* Paper presented at the conference "Road Accidents and the Mind: An In-depth Study of Psychological Symptoms after Road Accidents." Bristol, England.

Taylor, S., & Koch, W.J. (1995) Anxiety disorders due to motor vehicle accidents: Nature and treatment. *Clinical Psychology Review, 15*, 721–738.

Teplin, L.A. (1983). The criminalization of the mentally ill: Speculation in search of data. *Psychological Bulletin, 94*, 54–67.

Teplin, L.A. (1984). Criminalizing mental disorder: The comparative arrest rate of the mentally ill. *American Psychologist, 39*, 794–803.

Teplin, L.A. (1990a). Detecting disorder: The treatment of mental illness among jail detainees. *Journal of Consulting and Clinical Psychology, 58*, 233–236.

Teplin, L.A. (1990b). The prevalence of severe mental disorder among male urban jail detainees: Comparison with the Epidemiologic Catchment Area program. *American Journal of Public Health, 80*, 663–669.

Teplin, L.A., & Swartz, J. (1989). Screening for severe mental disorder in jails: The development of the Referral Decision Scale. *Law and Human Behavior, 13*, 1–18.

Testa, M., & Parks, K.A. (1996). The role of women's alcohol consumption in sexual victimization. *Aggression and Violent Behavior, 1*, 217–234.

Thompson, C.P., Herrmann, D., Read, J.D., Bruce, D., Payne, D., & Toglia, M.P. (1998). *Eyewitness testimony: Theoretical and applied perspectives.* Mahwah, NJ: Lawrence Erlbaum Associates.

Thompson, W.C., Fong, G.T., & Rosenhan, D.L. (1981). Inadmissible evidence and juror verdicts. *Journal of Personality and Social Psychology, 40,* 453–463.

Thornberry, T., & Jacoby, J. (1979). *The criminally insane: A community follow-up of mentally ill offenders.* Chicago: University of Chicago Press.

Thwaites v. Health Sciences Centre Psychiatric Facility, [1988] 3 W.W.R. 217, 40 C.R.R. 326, 48 D.L.R. (4th) 338 (C.A.)

Tien, G., Ogloff, J.R.P., Roesch, R., Wilson, D., Grant, F., & Mah, B. (1993, October). *Surrey pretrial mental health project: Evaluation report of the management committee.* British Columbia Forensic Psychiatric Services Commission.

Tollestrup, P.A., Turtle, J.W., & Yuille, J.C. (1994). Actual victims and witnesses to robbery and fraud: An archival analysis. In D.F. Ross, J.D. Read, & M.P. Toglia (Eds.), *Adult eyewitness testimony: Current trends and development* (pp. 144–160). New York: Cambridge University Press.

Tolman, R.M. (1989). The development of a measure of psychological maltreatment of women by their male partners. *Violence and Victims, 4,* 159–178.

Tomkins, A.J., & Ogloff, J.R.P. (1990). Training and career options in psychology and law. *Behavioral Sciences and the Law, 8,* 205–216.

Trankell, A. (1972). *Reliability of evidence.* Stockholm: Beckmans.

Tremblay, P. (1989). Les fondements de la metrique penale. *Canadian Journal of Criminology, 31,* 117–144.

Tremblay, P., Gravel, S., and Cusson, M. (1987). Equivalences penales et solutions de rechange a l'emprisonnment: la metrique implicite des tribunaux criminels. *Criminologie, 20,* 69–89.

Tulving, E., & Thomson, D.M. (1973). Encoding specificity and retrieval processes in memory. *Psychological Review, 80,* 352–373.

Turbett, J.P., & O'Toole, R. (1980). *Physician's recognition of child abuse.* Paper presented at the annual meeting of the American Sociological Association, New York.

Turtle, J. (1995). *Officers: What do they want? What have they got?* Paper presented at the first biennial meeting of the Society for Applied Research in Memory and Cognition, Vancouver, BC.

Tyler, T.R. (1990). *Why people obey the law.* New Haven, CT: Yale University Press.

U.K. Criminal Justice Act 1967, c. 80, s. 13.

Ullman, S.E., & Siegel, J.M. (1993). Victim-offender relationship and sexual assault. *Violence and Victims, 8,* 121–134.

Undeutsch, U. (1982). Statement reality analysis. In A. Trankell (Ed.), *Reconstructing the past: The role of psychologists in criminal trials*. Stockholm: P.A. Norstedt & Soeners foerlag.

Undeutsch, U. (1989). The development of Statement Reality Analysis. In J.C. Yuille (Ed.), *Credibility assessment: A unified theoretical and research perspective* (pp. 101–119). Dordrecht, The Netherlands: Kluwer.

United States Merit Systems Protection Board. (1981). *Sexual harassment in the federal government: Is it a problem?* Washington, DC: U.S. Government Printing Office.

United States Merit Systems Protection Board. (1988). *Sexual harassment in the federal government: An update*. Washington, DC: U.S. Government Printing Office.

United States v. Sokolow, 109 S.Ct. 1581 (1989).

Urquiza, A.J., Wirtz, S.J., Peterson, M.S., Singer, V.A. (1994). Screening and evaluating abused and neglected children entering protective custody. *Child Welfare, 73*, 115–171.

van der Kolk, B., & Fisler, R. (1995). Dissociation and the fragmentary nature of traumatic memories: Overview and exploratory study. *Journal of Traumatic Stress, 8*, 505–525.

Varendonck, J. (1911). Les temoignages d'enfants dans un proces retentissant (The testimony of children in a famous trial). *Archives de Psychologie, 11*, 129–171.

Vachon, M.M. (1994). It's about time: The legal context of policy changes for female offenders. *Forum on Corrections Research, 6*, 3–6.

Van Etten, M., & Taylor, S. (1998). Comparative efficacy of treatments for post-traumatic stress disorder: A meta-analysis. *Clinical Psychology and Psychotherapy, 5*, 126–144.

Verdun-Jones, S. (1993). *Criminal law in Canada*. (2nd ed.). Toronto: Harcourt Brace.

Verhulst, F.C., Althaus, M., & Versluis-Den-Bieman, H.-J. (1992). Damaging backgrounds: Later adjustment of international adoptees. *Journal of the American Academy of Child and Adolescent Psychiatry, 29*, 94–103.

Vermont Network of Sex Offender Therapists. (1995). *Practice guidelines for the assessment and treatment of sex offenders*. Waterbury, VT: Vermont Department of Corrections.

Vidmar, N. (1979). The other issues in jury simulation research. *Law and Human Behavior, 3*, 95–106.

Vidmar, N. (1995). *Medical malpractice and the American jury: Confronting myths about jury incompetence, deep pocket, and outrageous damage awards*. Ann Arbour, MI: University of Michigan Press.

Vidmar, N. (1997). Pre-trial prejudice and the presumption of guilt in sex abuse trials. *Law and Human Behavior, 21*, 5–25.

Vidmar, N., Beale, S.S., Rose, M., & Donnelly, L.F. (1997). Should we rush to reform the criminal jury? Consider conviction rate data. *Judicature, 80(6)*, 286–290.

Vidmar, N., & Dittenhoffer, T. (1981). Informed public opinion and death penalty attitudes. *Canadian Journal of Criminology, 23*, 43–55.

Vidmar, N., & Judson, J. (1981). The use of social science in a change of venue application. *Canadian Bar Review, 59*, 76–102.

Vidmar, N., & Melnitzer, J. (1984). Juror prejudice: An empirical study of a challenge for cause. *Osgoode Hall Law Journal, 22*, 487–501.

Visher, C.A., Lattimore, P.K., & Linster, R.L. (1991). Predicting the recidivism of serious youthful offenders using survival models. *Criminology, 29*, 329–366.

Vrij, A. (1998a). Interviewing suspects. In A. Memon, A. Vrij, & R. Bull (Eds.), *Psychology and law: Truthfulness, accuracy and credibility* (pp. 124–146). London: McGraw-Hill.

Vrij, A. (1998b). Nonverbal communication and credibility. In A. Memon, A. Vrij, & R. Bull (Eds.), *Psychology and law: Truthfulness, accuracy and credibility* (pp. 32–58). London: McGraw-Hill.

Vrij, A., & Akehurst, L. (1998). Verbal communication and credibility: Statement validity assessment. In A. Memon, A. Vrij, & R. Bull (Eds.), *Psychology and law: Truthfulness, accuracy and credibility* (pp. 3–31). London: McGraw-Hill.

Vrij, A., & Graham, S. (1997). Individual differences between liars and the ability to detect lies. *Expert Evidence, 5*, 144–148.

Wagenaar, W.A., & Loftus, E.F. (1990). Ten cases of eyewitness identification: Logical and procedural problems. *Journal of Criminal Justice, 18*, 291–319.

Walker, J. (1993). Co-operative parenting post-divorce: Possibility or pipedream? *Journal of Family Therapy, 15*, 273–293.

Walker, N. (1968). *Crime and insanity in England, Vol. 1: The historical perspective.* Edinburgh: Edinburgh University Press.

Walker, N. (1985). The insanity defense before 1800. *Annals of the American Academy of Political and Social Science, 477*, 25–30.

Walker, N.E. (1997). Should we question how we question children? In J.D. Read & D.S. Lindsay (Eds.), *Recollections of trauma: Scientific evidence and clinical practice* (pp. 517–522). New York: Plenum.

Walker, N.E., & Hunt, J.S. (1998). Interviewing child victim-witnesses: How you ask is what you get. In C.P. Thompson, D.J. Herrmann, et al. (Eds.), *Eye-*

witness memory: Theoretical and applied perspectives (pp. 55–87). Mahwah, NJ: Lawrence Erlbaum Associates, Inc.

Wall, A.M., & Schuller, R.A. (2000). Sexual assault and defendant/victim intoxication: Jurors' perceptions of guilt. *Journal of Applied Social Psychology, 30,* 253–274.

Walmsley, R. (1999). World Prison Population List. *Research Findings Number 88.* London: Home Office, Research Development and Statistics Directorate.

Ward, T., McCormack, J., Hudson, S.M., & Polaschek, D. (1997). Rape: Assessment and treatment. In D.R. Laws & W. O'Donohue (Eds.), *Sexual deviance: Theory, assessment, and treatment* (pp. 356–393). New York: Guilford.

Wardhaugh, B. (1989). Socratic civil disobedience: Some reflections on Morgentaler (Morgentaler, Smoling et al. v. The Queen, 44 D.L.R. 4th 385). *Canadian Journal of Law and Jurisprudence, 2,* 91–110.

Watson, S.M., Henggeler, S.W., & Borduin, C.M. (1985). Interrelations among Multidimensional Family Therapy outcome measures. *Family Therapy, 12,* 185–196.

Weaver v. Tate (1990), 28 R.F.L. (3d) 188 (Ont. C.A.).

Webster, C.D., Dickens, B.M., & Addario, S.M. (1985). *Constructing dangerousness: Scientific, legal and policy implications.* Toronto: University of Toronto Centre of Criminology.

Webster, C.D., Douglas, K.S., Eaves, D., & Hart, S.D. (1997a). *HCR-20: Assessing risk for violence (version 2).* Vancouver: Simon Fraser University.

Webster, C.D., Douglas, K.S., Eaves, D., & Hart, S.D. (1997b). Assessing risk of violence to others. In C.D. Webster & M.A. Jackson (Eds.), *Impulsivity: Theory, assesment, and treatment* (pp. 251–277). New York: Guilford.

Webster, C.D., Hucker, S.J., & Grossman, M.G. (1993). Treatment programmes for mentally ill offenders. In K. Howells & C.R. Hollin (Eds.), *Clinical approaches to the mentally disordered offender* (pp. 87–109). Chichester: Wiley.

Webster, C.D., & Jackson, M.A. (1997). *Impulsivity: Theory, assessment, and treatment.* New York: Guilford.

Webster, C.D., Menzies, R.J., & Jackson, M.A. (1982). *Clinical assessment before trial.* Toronto: Butterworths.

Wechsler, D. (1996). *Wechsler Intelligence Scale for Children–Third Edition Manual Canadian Supplement.* Toronto: Psychological Corporation.

Weiner, B. (1985). Mental disability and criminal law. In S. Brakel, J. Parry, & B. Weiner (Eds.), *The mentally disabled and the law* (3rd ed.) (pp. 763–773). Washington, DC: American Bar foundation.

Weiner, R.L., Habert, K., Shkodriani, G., & Staebler, C. (1991). The social psychology of jury nullification: Predicting when jurors disobey the law. *Journal of Applied Social Psychology, 21,* 1379–1401.

Weingardt, K.R., Toland, H.K., & Loftus, E.F. (1994). Reports of suggested memories: Do people truly believe them? In D.F. Ross, J.D. Read, & M.P. Toglia (Eds.), *Adult eyewitness testimony: Current trends and development* (pp. 3–26). New York: Cambridge University Press.

Weissman, H.N. (1990). Distortions and deceptions in self presentation: Effects of protracted litigation in personal injury cases. *Behavioral Sciences and the Law, 8,* 67–74.

Weiten, W., & Diamond, S.S. (1979). A critical review of the jury simulation paradigm: The case of defendant characteristics. *Law and Human Behavior, 3,* 71–93.

Wells, G.L. (1978). Applied eyewitness-testimony research: System variables and estimator variables. *Journal of Personality and Social Psychology, 12,* 1546–1557.

Wells, G.L. (1984). How adequate is human intuition for judging eyewitness testimony? In G.L. Wells & E.F. Loftus (Eds.), *Eyewitness testimony: Psychological perspectives.* New York: Cambridge University Press.

Wells, G.L. (1993). What do we know about eyewitness identification? *American Psychologist, 48,* 553–571.

Wells, G.L. (1995). Scientific study of witness memory: Implications for public policy and law. *Psychology, Public Policy, and Law, 1,* 726–731.

Wells, G.L., & Bradfield, A.L. (1998). "Good, you identified the suspect": Feedback to eyewitnesses distorts their reports of the witnessing experience. *Journal of Applied Psychology, 83,* 360–376.

Wells, G.L., & Cutler, B.L. (1990). The right to counsel at videotaped lineups: An emerging dilemma. *Connecticut Law Review, 22,* 373–395.

Wells, G.L., & Loftus, E.F. (1991). Commentary: Is this child fabricating? Reactions to a new assessment technique. In J. Doris (Ed.), *The suggestibility of children's recollections: Implications for eyewitness testimony* (pp. 168–171). Washington, DC: American Psychological Association.

Wells, G.L., & Murray, D.M. (1983). What can psychology say about the *Neil v. Biggers* criteria for judging eyewitness accuracy? *Journal of Applied Psychology, 68,* 347–362.

Wells, G.L., & Seelau, E.P. (1995). Eyewitness identification: Psychological research and legal policy on lineups. *Psychology, Public Policy, and Law, 1,* 765–791.

Wells, G.L., Seelau, E.P., Rydell, S.M., & Luus, C.A.E. (1994). Recommendations on properly conducted lineup identification tasks. In D.F. Ross, J.D. Read, & M.P. Toglia (Eds.), *Adult eyewitness testimony: Current trends and development* (pp. 223–244). New York: Cambridge University Press.

Wells, G.L., Small, M., Penrod, S., Malpass, R.S., Fulero, S.M., & Brimacombe,

C.A.E. (1998). Eyewitness identification procedures: Recommendations for lineups and photospreads. *Law and Human Behavior, 23,* 603–647.

Wells, G.L., & Turtle, J.W. (1987). Eyewitness testimony research: Current knowledge and emergent controversies. *Canadian Journal of Behavioural Science, 19,* 363–387.

Wenden v. Trikha (1991), 116 A.R. 81 (Q.B.).

Wessely, S.C., Castle, D., Douglas, A.J., & Taylor, P.R. (1994). The criminal careers of incident cases of schizophrenia. *Psychological Medicine, 24,* 483–502.

Wexler, D.B. (1990). Training in law and behavioral sciences: Issues from a legal educator's perspective. *Behavioral Sciences and the Law, 8,* 197–204.

Whipple, G.M. (1911). Psychology of testimony and report. *Psychological Bulletin, 8,* 307–310.

White, S., & Quinn, K.M. (1988). Investigatory independence in child sexual abuse evaluations: Conceptual considerations. *Bulletin of the American Academy of Psychiatry and the Law, 16,* 269–278.

Whitely, S. (1985). *Jurisdiction in criminal law.* Toronto: Carswell.

Whittemore, K.E., & Ogloff, J.R.P. (1994). Fitness and competency issues in Canadian criminal courts: Elucidating the standards for mental health professionals. *Canadian Journal of Psychiatry, 39,* 198–210.

Widom, C. (1989). Does violence beget violence? A critical examination of the literature. *Psychological Bulletin, 106,* 13–28.

Wierzbicki, M. (1993). Psychological adjustment of adoptees: A meta-analysis. *Journal of Clinical Child Psychology, 22,* 447–454.

Wigmore, J.H. (1909). Professor Musterberg and the psychology of testimony. *Illinois Law Review, 3,* 399–434.

Wigmore, J.H. (1970). *Evidence (Vol. 3).* (Revised by J.H. Chadbourn.) Boston: Little, Brown.

Williams v. Florida, 399 U.S. 78 (1970).

Williams v. Williams (1989), 24 R.F.L. (3d) 86 (B.C.C.A.).

Williams, S. (1996). *Invisible darkness: The strange case of Paul Bernardo and Karla Homolka.* Toronto: Little, Brown.

Williams, S.M. (1995). Sex offender assessment guidelines. In T.A. Leis, L.L. Motiuk, & J.R.P. Ogloff (Eds.), *Forensic psychology: Policy and practice in corrections* (pp. 122–131). Ottawa: Correctional Service of Canada.

Williamson, S.E., Hare, R.D., & Wong, S. (1987). Violence: Criminal psychopaths and their victims. *Canadian Journal of Behavioural Science, 19,* 454–462.

Wilson, J.R., & Bornstein, B.H. (1998). Methodological considerations in pretrial publicity research: Is the medium the message? *Law and Human Behavior, 22,* 585–597.

Wilson, M., Baker, S., Teret, S., Shock, S., & Barbarino, J. (1991). *Saving children: A guide to injury prevention*. New York: Oxford University.

Wimer, H., Gruber, S., & Perner, J. (1984). Young children's conception of lying: Lexical realism – moral subjectivism. *Journal of Experimental Child Psychology, 37*, 1–30.

Winslow, L. (1962). The instructions ritual. *Hastings Law Journal, 13*, 456– 470.

Wissler, R., & Saks, M. (1985). On the inefficacy of limiting instructions. *Law and Human Behavior, 9*, 37–48.

Woelk v. Halvorson, [1981] 1 W.W.R. 289, [1980] 2 S.C.R. 430, 114 D.L.R. (3d) 385.

Wolf, S., & Montgomery, D.A. (1977). Effects of inadmissible evidence and level of judicial admonishment to disregard on the judgments of mock jurors. *Journal of Applied Social Psychology, 7*, 205–219.

Wolfe, D.A. (1985). Child-abusive parents: An empirical review and analysis. *Psychological Bulletin, 97*, 462–482.

Wolfe, D.A. (1987). *Child abuse: Implications for child development and psychopathology.* Sage Publications: Newbury Park, CA.

Wolfe, D.A., Jaffe, P., Wilson, S.K., & Lydia, Zak. (1988). A multivariate investigation of children's adjustment to family violence. In G.T. Hotaling & D. Finkelhor, J.T. Kirkpatrick, & M.A. Straus (Eds), *Family abuse and its consequences: New directions in research* (pp. 228–241). Newbury Park, CA: Sage.

Wolfe, J., Keane, T.M., Kaloupek, D.G., Mora, C.A., & Wine, P. (1993). Patterns of positive readjustment in Vietnam combat veterans. *Journal of Traumatic Stress, 6*, 179–193.

Wolfe, J., Sharkansky, E.J., Read, J.P., Dawson, R., Martin, J.A., & Ouimette, P. (1997). Sexual harassment and assault as predictors of PTSD symptomatology among U.S. female Persian Gulf war military personnel. *Journal of Inter-Personal Violence, 13*, 40–57.

Wolfe, M. (1994, July/August). Dr. Fabrikant's solution. *Saturday Night, 109(6)*, 11–59.

Wolfe, V.V., Gentile, C., & Wolfe, D.A. (1989). The impact of sexual abuse on children: A PTSD formulation. *Behavior Therapy, 20*, 215–228.

Wong, S. (1984). *The criminal and institutional behaviours of psychopaths*. Ottawa: Ministry of the Solicitor General.

Wright, C., & Linden, A. (1970). *The law of torts* (5th ed.). Toronto: Butterworths.

Wright, C., & Leroux, J.P. (1991). Children as victims of violent crime. *Juristat Service Bulletin: Canadian Centre for Justice Statistics, 11(8)*, 1–13.

Wrightsman, L.S., Nietzel, M.T., & Fortune, W.H. (1998). *Psychology & the legal system* (4th ed.). Pacific Grove, CA: Brooks/Cole Publishing Co.

Yapko, M.D. (1994). *Suggestions of abuse: True and false memories of childhood sexual trauma*. Toronto: Simon & Schuster.

Yarmey, A.D. (1986). Perceived expertness and credibility of police officers as eyewitnesses. *Canadian Police College Journal, 10,* 31–51.

Yarmey, A.D. (1990). *Understanding police and police work: Psychosocial issues.* New York: New York University Press.

Yarmey, A.D. (1993). Stereotypes and recognition memory for faces and voices of good guys and bad guys. *Applied Cognitive Psychology, 7,* 419–431.

Yarmey, A.D. (1995). Earwitness speaker identification. *Psychology, Public Policy, and Law, 1,* 792–816.

Yarmey, A.D. (1998). Person identification in showups and lineups. In C.P. Thompson, D.J. Herrmann, J.D. Read, D. Bruce, D.G. Payne, & M.P. Toglia (Eds.), *Eyewitness memory: Theoretical and applied perspectives* (pp. 131–154). Mahwah, NJ: Lawrence Erlbaum Associates.

Young Offenders Act, R.S.C. (1985), c. Y-1.

Youngjohn, J.R., Davis, D., & Wolf, I. (1997). Head injury and the MMPI-2: Paradoxical severity effects and the influence of litigation. *Psychological Assessment, 9,* 177–184.

Yuille, J.C. (1988). The systematic assessment of children's testimony. *Canadian Psychology, 19,* 247–261.

Yuille, J.C., & Cutshall, J.L. (1986). A case study of eyewitness memory of a crime. *Journal of Applied Psychology, 75,* 268–273.

Yuille, J.C., & Daylen, J. (1998). The impact of traumatic events on eyewitness memory. In C.P. Thompson, D.J. Herrmann, J.D. Read, D. Bruce, D.G. Payne, & M.P. Toglia (Eds.), *Eyewitness memory: Theoretical and applied perspectives* (pp. 155–178). Mahwah, NJ: Lawrence Erlbaum Associates.

Yuille, J., Hunter, R., Joffe, R., & Zaparniuk, J. (1993). Interviewing children in sexual abuse cases. In G. Goodman and B. Bottoms (Eds.), *Child victims, child witnesses: Understanding and improving testimony* (pp. 95–116). New York: Guilford Press.

Yuille, J.C., & McEwan, N.H. (1985). Use of hypnosis as an aid to eyewitness memory. *Journal of Applied Psychology, 70,* 389–400.

Yuille, J.C., & Wells, G.L. (1991). Concerns about the application of research findings: The issue of ecological validity. In J.L. Doris (Ed.), *The suggestibility of children's recollections* (pp. 118–128). Washington, DC: American Psychological Association.

Zamble, E. (1992). Behavior and adaptation in long-term prison inmates: Descriptive longitudinal results. *Criminal Justice and Behavior, 19,* 409–425.

Zamble, E., & Kalm, K. (1990). General and specific measures of public attitudes toward sentencing. *Canadian Journal of Behavioural Science, 22,* 327–337.

Zamble, E., & Porporino, F. (1988). *Coping, behaviour and adaptation in prison inmates.* New York: Springer Verlag.

Zamble, E., & Porporino, F. (1990). Coping, imprisonment, and rehabilitation: Some data and their implications. *Criminal Justice and Behavior, 17*, 53–70.

Zamble, E., & Quinsey, V.L. (1997). *The criminal recidivism process*. Cambridge: Cambridge University Press.

Zapf, P.A., & Roesch, R. (1997). Assessing fitness to stand trial: A comparison of institution-based evaluations and a brief screening interview. *Canadian Journal of Community Mental Health, 16*, 53–66.

Zaragoza, M.S., Graham, J.R., Hall, G.C.N., Hirschman, R., & Ben-Porath, Y.S. (Eds.). (1995). *Memory and testimony in the child witness*. Thousand Oaks, CA: Sage Publications.

Zeisel, H. (1971). And then there were none: The diminution of the federal jury. *University of Chicago Law Review, 38*, 710–724.

Zeisel, H., & Diamond, S.S. (1978). The effect of peremptory challenges on jury verdict: An experiment in a federal district court. *Stanford Law Review, 30*, 491–531.

Zimbardo, P.G. (1967). The psychology of police confessions. *Psychology Today,* June, 17–20, 25–27.

Ziskin, J. (1981). *Coping with psychiatric and psychological testimony*. Venice, CA: Law & Psychology Press.

Zuckerman, M., DePaulo, B.M., & Rosenthal, R. (1981). Verbal and nonverbal communication of deception. *Advances in Experimental Social Psychology, 14*, 1–59.

Zuckerman, M., & Driver, R.E. (1985). Telling lies: Verbal and nonverbal correlates of deception. In W.A. Siegman and S. Feldstein (Eds.), *Multichannel integration of nonverbal behavior* (pp. 129–147). Hillsdale, NJ: Erlbaum.

Subject Index

Note: Page numbers ending in 't' indicate a table.
Page numbers ending in 'f' indicate a figure.

acquaintance rape, 168–70
actuarial decision making, 343–4
actus reus concept, 40–1
adjournment, pretrial prejudicial information, 139
administrative law, 53
admission, 52–3. *See also* confessions
adolescent offenders: assessment and treatment of, 250–5; characteristics of, 251–3; High Risk Recognition Group, 243–5; relevant law, 250–1
adoption, contested, 401–5
Alberta, mental health law, 358
alcohol intoxication, and date rape, 168–71
American Law Institute (ALI), insanity standard, 290
antisocial behaviour, 242; of adolescent offenders, 252–4
archival records, 163–4
assessment: of adolescent offenders, 250-5; criminal responsibility, 301–3; of female offenders, 277–9; fitness to stand trial, 296–8; of inmates, 219; mentally disordered offenders, 270–2; of offenders, 238–41; orders, 295–6; process, 239–41; of sexually violent behaviour, 263, 264; spousal assaulters, 255–61. *See also* treatment
Attention-Deficit/Hyperactivity Disorder (ADHD), 254
automatism, 41
Average effect sizes for interventions, 347t

bail hearings, risk assessment, 325
battered child syndrome, 376
battered women syndrome: expert testimony, 171–2; simulated trials, 172; stereotypes, 171
behaviourial deep freeze, 231
boomerang effect, 176
British Columbia Mental Health Act, 358

Canada Evidence Act (CEA), 49, 116–17

Case Index

Author Index